STUDY GUIDE

to accompany

MICROECONOMICS

SECOND EDITION

Krugman | Wells

Elizabeth Sawyer Kelly
University of Wisconsin-Madison

WORTH PUBLISHERS

Study Guide
by Elizabeth Sawyer Kelly
to accompany
Krugman/Wells: Microeconomics, Second Edition

ISBN 13: 978-1-4292-1756-9
ISBN 10: 1-4292-1756-1

First Printing

Printed in the United States of America

Worth Publishers
41 Madison Avenue
New York, NY 10010
www.worthpublishers.com

STUDY GUIDE

Contents

Key to Corresponding Chapter Numbers

	Microeconomics	*Economics*	*Macroeconomics*
First Principles	Chapter 1	Chapter 1	Chapter 1
Economic Models: Trade-offs and Trade	Chapter 2	Chapter 2	Chapter 2
Supply and Demand	Chapter 3	Chapter 3	Chapter 3
Consumer and Producer Surplus	Chapter 4	Chapter 4	
The Market Strikes Back	Chapter 5	Chapter 5	Chapter 4
Elasticity	Chapter 6	Chapter 6	
Taxes	Chapter 7	Chapter 7	
International Trade	Chapter 8	Chapter 8	Chapter 5
Making Decisions	Chapter 9	Chapter 9	
The Rational Consumer	Chapter 10	Chapter 10	
Consumer Preferences and Consumer Choice	Chapter 11	Chapter 11	
Behind the Supply Curve: Inputs and Costs	Chapter 12	Chapter 12	
Perfect Competition and the Supply Curve	Chapter 13	Chapter 13	
Monopoly	Chapter 14	Chapter 14	
Oligopoly	Chapter 15	Chapter 15	
Monopolistic Competition and Product Differentiation	Chapter 16	Chapter 16	
Externalities	Chapter 17	Chapter 17	
Public Goods and Common Resources	Chapter 18	Chapter 18	
The Economics of the Welfare State	Chapter 19	Chapter 19	
Factor Markets and the Distribution of Income	Chapter 20	Chapter 20	
Uncertainty, Risk, and Private Information	Chapter 21	Chapter 21	

Preface

This Study Guide is designed for use with **Microeconomics, *Second Edition*** by Paul Krugman and Robin Wells. It is intended to help you evaluate your understanding of the material covered in the textbook and thereby reinforce the key concepts you need to learn.

For each chapter, the Study Guide is organized as follows:

Before You Read the Chapter
- Summary: an opening paragraph that provides a brief overview of the chapter.
- Objectives: a numbered list outlining and describing the material that you should have learned in the chapter. These objectives can be easily used as a study tool.
- Key Terms: a list of bold key terms with their definitions. This section includes room for note-taking.

After You Read the Chapter
- Tips: a numbered list of learning tips with graphical analysis.
- Problems and Exercises: a set of 10-15 comprehensive problems.

Before You Take the Test
- Chapter Review Questions: a set of approximately 30 multiple-choice questions that focus on the key concepts from the text that you should grasp after reading the chapter. These questions are designed for quick exam preparation.

Answer Key
- Answers to Problems and Exercises: detailed solutions to the Problems and Exercises in the Study Guide.
- Answers to Chapter Review Questions: solutions to the multiple-choice questions in the Study Guide—along with thorough explanations.

Answers as well as explanatory solutions can be found at the end of each chapter. Students often use an answer section to simply check if they have gotten the "right" answer. I caution you to use the answer section accompanying each chapter with an eye to getting the highest possible value from the exercises provided. In economics, the reasoning used in coming to conclusions and correctly modeling the problems are as important as coming to an accurate answer. Explanations for each problem have been provided in order for you to check that your understanding of the concepts has been appropriately applied.

The study of economics has the potential of altering the way you evaluate and understand the world. I hope that your use of this guide will help you in your study of basic microeconomics principles and will provide a jumping-off point for further study in the economics field.

Elizabeth Sawyer Kelly

First Principles

▶ BEFORE YOU READ THE CHAPTER

Summary

This chapter provides a brief overview of twelve general principles underlying the study of economics. These principles are explored and discussed at greater length as you work your way through the text. This first chapter indicates the breadth and depth of economics as a course of study by delineating these twelve principles, which describe how individuals make choices and how individual choices interact.

Chapter Objectives

This chapter introduces a set of principles that will guide your study of economics.

Objective #1. Resources—land, labor, capital, and human capital—are scarce, so individuals as well as societies must make choices about how to use these resources.

Objective #2. The opportunity cost, or the real cost of something, is what you must give up to get it.

Objective #3. Decisions about how much to produce and how much to consume are made at the margin. These decisions invariably involve a trade-off, or a comparison of the costs and benefits of producing more or consuming more.

Objective #4. People usually exploit opportunities to make themselves better off—in other words, people respond to incentives.

Objective #5. There are gains from trade.

Objective #6. Markets move toward equilibrium, a situation in which no individual would be better off doing something different.

Objective #7. Resources should be used as efficiently as possible to achieve society's goals. However, there is a trade-off between efficiency and equity: decisions based solely on efficiency may be highly inequitable.

Objective #8. Markets usually lead to efficiency.

Objective #9. When markets fail to achieve efficiency, government intervention can improve society's welfare. Markets may fail due to (1) the existence of side effects from individual actions that are not accounted for in the market; (2) the prevention of mutually beneficial trades by an individual or individuals so they can capture a greater share of resources; or (3) the inability to produce some goods, due to the nature of these goods, efficiently by the market.

Objective #10. One person's spending is another person's income.

Objective #11. Spending sometimes gets out of line with the economy's capacity to produce goods and services. It is possible for the economy's spending to be less than, or greater than, the current level of production.

Objective #12. Government policies can change the level of spending in an economy.

Key Terms

Notes

individual choice the decision by an individual of what to do, which necessarily involves a decision of what not to do.

resource anything, such as land, labor, and capital, that can be used to produce something else; includes natural resources (from the physical environment) and human resources (labor, skill, intelligence).

scarce in short supply; a *resource* is scarce when there is not enough of the resources available to satisfy all the various ways a society wants to use them.

opportunity cost the real cost of an item: what you must give up in order to get it.

trade-off a comparison of costs and benefits of doing something.

marginal decision a decision made at the "margin" of an activity to do a bit more or a bit less of an activity.

marginal analysis the study of *marginal decisions*.

incentive anything that offers rewards to people who change their behavior.

interaction (of choices) my choices affect your choices, and vice versa; a feature of most economic situations. The results of this interaction are often quite different from what the individuals intend.

trade in a market *economy*, individuals provide goods and services to others and receive goods and services in return.

Key Terms *(continued)*

gains from trade by dividing tasks and trading, people can get more of what they want through *trade* than they could if they tried to be self-sufficient.

specialization each person specializes in the task that he or she is good at performing.

equilibrium an economic situation in which no individual would be better off doing something different.

efficient description of a market or *economy* that takes all opportunities to make some people better off without making other people worse off.

equity fairness; everyone gets his or her fair share. Since people can disagree about what is "fair," equity is not as well defined a concept as efficiency.

Notes

■ AFTER YOU READ THE CHAPTER

Tips

Tip #1. The study of economics is cumulative. You should master each topic as it is presented since later topics build on earlier topics.

Tip #2. Pay attention to new vocabulary and make sure you know, understand, and can apply these terms. Your instructor will expect you to do more than just define the terms: you must also be able to indicate through your work an ability to apply these terms in a meaningful manner.

Tip #3. Plan to spend time every day studying economics. Review your lecture notes, review the vocabulary, work on the practice questions, and identify what questions you have about the material. Once you formulate your questions, seek out answers by returning to your text, your lecture notes, your classmates, or your professor.

Tip #4. Think about the topics that might be on an exam and the kinds of questions that might be asked about these topics—questions that are strictly definitional, questions that apply the definitions in a problem-solving setting, and questions that force you to really think about the material and apply your knowledge. Most college-level exams include questions designed to make you think about the material.

Tip #5. You might find it helpful to create a set of flash cards to help you study. For this chapter the set of flash cards would include a card for each principle and a card for each new vocabulary word. On the vocabulary cards, put the word on one side of the card and its definition on the other. In the upper corner of each card, note the chapter the card comes from— for example, you might write "Ch. 1" on the cards for this chapter to remind you where this material was first presented. Then, make a point of reviewing these flash cards throughout the day until you feel confident you have absorbed this material.

Problems and Exercises

1. For each of the following situations describe the opportunity costs of each decision.

   a. Sarah considers two options for Saturday night: she can attend a concert that costs $10 per ticket or she can go to the free movie offered at the student union. She decides to attend the concert.

   b. A new business in town debates paying $20,000 for a prime location versus $10,000 for a less perfect location. The business estimates that it will eventually serve the same number of customers in either location, but that it will take 6 months before the suboptimal location provides the same outcome as the prime location. The business decides to purchase the $10,000 property.

   c. Jamie is given a choice for his next holiday from school: he can be an unpaid intern at a company or he can earn $2,000 working as a camp counselor. He decides to take the internship.

   d. Roberto is studying for two midterms this week. He figures he has 20 available hours to study for both midterms. If he studies all 20 hours for the economics exam he will undoubtedly get an A on the exam, but he will at best make a C on his organic chemistry test. If he studies all 20 hours for the organic chemistry test he will get an A on the organic chemistry exam, but he will likely earn a D on his economics test. Roberto decides to devote all of his available time to economics since he has determined that he does not wish to pursue a premed major.

2. The following table presents the possible combinations of study time available to Roberto this week as he prepares for his two midterms (one in economics and the other in organic chemistry). Assume Roberto has 20 hours available to study and that he will use all 20 hours studying economics and chemistry.

Hours of study time spent on economics	Hours of study time spent on organic chemistry	Grade in economics	Grade in organic chemistry
0	20	60	90
5	15	70	85
10	10	80	75
15	5	86	73
20	0	90	70

Roberto currently plans to study 10 hours for economics and 10 hours for organic chemistry.

a. If he alters his plan and studies 15 hours for economics, what is the opportunity cost of that decision?

b. If he alters his plan and studies 15 hours for organic chemistry, what is the opportunity cost of that decision?

c. If he alters his plan and studies 20 hours for economics, what is the opportunity cost of that decision?

d. If he alters his plan and studies 20 hours for organic chemistry, what is the opportunity cost of that decision?

3. **a.** Joe is trying to decide whether or not to have another piece of cake at dinner tonight. Describe how Joe can use the principle of marginal analysis to decide whether or not to eat this piece of cake.

b. A local government is debating whether or not to institute a stricter recycling ordinance for their community. Suppose the cost of the additional recycling restrictions is $500,000 a year due to the need to have additional labor and capital available to meet the demands of the new ordinance. This community uses marginal analysis to make their decisions and decides to adopt this stricter recycling ordinance. What do you know about the benefits this community will receive from implementing this ordinance?

c. Susy is recovering from knee surgery and has a number of exercises she needs to do each day to enhance that recovery. These exercises are tedious and at times painful. If Susy uses the principle of marginal analysis to make her decisions, what must be true about the costs and benefits of doing these exercises if Susy is to do them on a daily basis?

4. The two health insurance organizations in a community are trying to encourage their members to embrace healthier lifestyles. Healthlines is willing to pay 25 percent of the class fee for exercise classes offered at the local gym. Longhealth is willing to refund 50 percent of the class fee at the end of the class, provided that the instructor signs a form verifying that the member has attended at least 80 percent of the classes. Which fee structure is likely to result in the larger improvement in lifestyle choices? Explain the reasoning that underlies your answer.

5. Matt and Sarah are teenagers in Everycity, USA. Both of their families are concerned about their teenagers staying out late. Matt's family has a rule that if he returns home after midnight (even one minute late!) he loses his driving privileges for two weeks and cannot go out during that time. Sarah's family does not have a rule. Instead, before she goes out for the evening, Sarah and her family negotiate an expected time of return and Sarah then strives to honor this agreement. When she is running later than expected she calls her family so they will not be unduly worried. Compare and contrast these two approaches, paying particular attention to the set of incentives that the two approaches offer Matt and Sarah.

6. Suppose that Bill and Mary are the only individuals living in a community and that this community has no contact with the rest of the world. Bill grows tomatoes and corn while Mary grows wheat and onions. How does trade between Bill and Mary benefit both of them?

7. Wisconsin produces cheese and corn while Georgia produces peaches and peanuts. How does trade between these two states benefit the individuals who live in these two states?

8. **a.** Pedro enjoys getting a cup of coffee on his way to campus each morning. He can get a cup at Joe's for $1.50 or he can get a cup at Mary's for $2.00. The coffee is equivalent at both places and the waiting time in line is equivalent as well. Is this an equilibrium situation? Explain your answer.

   b. Suzanne eats a hamburger for lunch every Wednesday. She can purchase her hamburger at the Big Bun for $5.50 or she can purchase a similar hamburger at The Real McCoy for $7.00. Is this an equilibrium situation? Explain your answer.

9. **a.** The cafeteria at your college offers two desserts each night: soft-serve ice cream and some kind of cake or pie. Each night the cafeteria runs out of the soft-serve ice cream and finds that it has a surplus of the cake or pie. Is this situation efficient? Explain your answer.

   b. A community provides bus service to its residents and charges $2.00 per ride. At this price, 98% of residents refuse to ride the buses and instead drive their cars. The community has serious air pollution problems from automobile emissions. Is this an efficient situation? Explain your answer.

   c. A community ponders implementing a no-smoking ordinance that would eliminate smoking in all businesses, government offices, and public places. Smokers are upset and argue that their rights are being violated by this proposed ordinance. An independent analyst estimates that the benefits of the ordinance will be $100,000 a year while the cost of implementing the ordinance will be $40,000. Would it be efficient to implement the ordinance? Explain your answer.

10. France is debating a change in their unemployment insurance policy. Historically the country has been willing to provide generous benefits to the unemployed for a substantial period. The country is now debating whether to reduce the length of time that unemployed people can collect these benefits. Comment on the efficiency and equity aspects of this proposed change in policy.

11. The government of a country decides to mandate that all people younger than twenty-five years old must be in school and must pursue a college education. The government also passes the necessary legislation to fund this education for all of its citizens. Comment on the efficiency and equity aspects of this proposed policy.

12. Government sometimes intervenes to alter people's decisions. For each of the following situations comment on how the government intervention provides an incentive to change behavior and what the desired change in behavior is.

    a. The government offers a free bus pass to all citizens living in metropolitan areas.

    b. The government offers individuals an income tax refund of $2,000 a year if they reduce the number of cars they own in their household by one car.

    c. The government requires all children younger than sixteen years old to be in school; and failure to comply results in the child's guardian being sent to jail.

    d. The college you attend requires you to have an up-to-date immunization record before you can move into your dormitory.

13. A community sits on a rocky seacoast and each year several large ships run up against the rocks and sink. The community would benefit from installing a lighthouse, but the lighthouse has not been built because no individuals are willing to pay for the construction of this lighthouse, knowing that once the lighthouse is built they can enjoy the lighthouse even if they did not contribute to its construction. Is there a solution to this problem? Explain your answer.

14. An economy experiences a recession in which the level of production of goods and services is lower than the level the economy is capable of producing. As the level of production falls, people decrease their level of spending. What can you conclude in general about the level of people's income in this economy?

15. An economy has a fixed amount of resources available to it during any given period. If there is too much spending in the economy during this time, how will the economy respond?

16. What can the government do to alter the level of spending during a recession? What can the government do to alter the level of spending during a period of inflation?

BEFORE YOU TAKE THE TEST

Chapter Review Questions

1. Camillo is offered two jobs: one pays a salary of $30,000 per year and offers four weeks of vacation, and the other job pays a salary of $32,000 per year and offers two weeks of vacation. What is the opportunity cost for Camillo of taking the job offering $32,000 per year?

a. $2,000 plus two weeks of vacation per year

b. $2,000 per year

c. two weeks of vacation per year

d. $30,000 plus two weeks of vacation per year

2. Ning decides to attend a special speaker presentation tonight at her college instead of staying in her dorm and listening to her music collection. Which of the following statements is true?

a. Ning faces no opportunity cost with regard to her decision since listening to music or attending the speaker are both free events.

b. The opportunity cost of Ning's decision is so small that it is not worth calculating.

c. The opportunity cost of Ning's decision is the loss of her evening of music listening.

d. The opportunity cost of Ning's decision includes the cost associated with hearing the speaker.

3. A firm is debating the purchase of an additional piece of machinery. The firm estimates that the machine will enable them to increase their revenue by $1,000 a month, but it will increase their monthly costs by $750. This firm applies the principle of marginal analysis and decides that

a. it should purchase the machine since the benefits from this additional equipment exceed the costs.

b. it should not purchase the machine since the benefits from this additional equipment are less than the costs.

4. Marie is training for a triathlon. She will need to be able to swim, bike, and run to compete successfully. On Tuesdays, Thursdays, and Saturdays she always swims, while on Mondays and Fridays she runs. On Wednesdays she bikes. On Sundays she can choose to rest, bike, swim, or run. When Marie chooses to rest on Sundays it must be the case that
   a. Marie is lazy and not pushing herself to her fullest potential.
   b. Marie perceives that the benefit of a day of rest exceeds the cost of a day of rest.
   c. Marie has lost sight of her goal to compete successfully in the triathlon.
   d. Marie is not able to compare the benefits and costs associated with biking, swimming, and running.

5. Scarcity of resources implies that
   a. people can do whatever they want and do not need to worry about making choices.
   b. life involves making choices about how to best use these scarce resources.
   c. societies need to invest time and money to discover more resources.
   d. only very wealthy individuals are not constrained by their resources.

6. Each day people make decisions about what to wear, what to eat, or where to work,
   a. since they all face constraints that mean they cannot do everything they would like to do.
   b. without regard to the level of resources that are available to them.

7. The university in Smart, USA, has a parking problem and is looking into programs to alleviate the parking shortage. Which of the following ideas is likely to decrease by the greatest amount the number of cars parking on campus each day?
   a. Faculty and staff at the university all receive free parking permits.
   b. Faculty and staff at the university all pay a set fee per year for parking permits.
   c. Faculty and staff at the university must pay an hourly fee for each hour that they park on campus.
   d. Faculty and staff are exempt from any parking policies at the university since they need to be able to come to campus to do their jobs.

8. Salespeople working at Department Store of Suburbia are offered two compensation plans. Plan A pays the worker $4.00 per hour plus a 5% sales commission on the total dollar value of sales that this worker makes. Plan B pays the worker $6.00 per hour and does not include a sales commission. Total sales per hour per salesperson averages $100. Which of the following statements is true?
   a. Plan A will result in the salespeople being less helpful to customers than does plan B.
   b. Plan A will result in the salespeople being more helpful to customers than does plan B.

9. Trade between two individuals
   a. rarely is beneficial.
   b. usually benefits only one of the trading partners.
   c. usually requires some form of coercion.
   d. is beneficial to both of the individuals.

10. Trade between two countries
   a. always benefits the economically wealthier country more than the economically weaker country.
   b. usually benefits only one of the trading partners.
   c. usually is the result of some form of coercion.
   d. is beneficial to both of the countries.

11. An equilibrium
   a. is a situation where people have exploited all opportunities to make themselves better off.
   b. is a situation in which no individual would be better off doing something different.
   c. usually is reached through changes in prices, which increase or decrease until there are no longer opportunities for individuals to make themselves better off.
   d. Answers (a), (b), and (c) are all true.

12. A situation is efficient when
   a. it is producing the maximum gains from trade that are possible given the resources available.
   b. the price of the good under consideration is as low as possible.
   c. one person is made better off even if some other person is made worse off.
   d. one group of people are made better off even if it harms some other group of people.

13. A college keeps its library open all night throughout the semester even though students study in the library after midnight only in the weeks immediately before midterms and final exams. This situation is
   a. efficient, since no one can be made better off with the available resources.
   b. inefficient, since the college could close the library after midnight for those weeks that are not right before the midterms or final exams and use the freed-up resources to provide other, more highly valued, services.
   c. too much of an administrative headache to solve.
   d. equitable, since it does not discriminate between different weeks in the semester.

14. A government policy gives everyone under thirty a subsidy no matter what their level of income. From the perspective of the people under thirty, this policy
   a. may be equitable, since it guarantees everyone under thirty the same level of subsidy, but it is probably not efficient.
   b. is efficient, since the government simply writes a check for the same amount to everyone under thirty.

15. A government policy gives everyone under thirty a subsidy no matter what their level of income. But, if you are a member of the ethnic group that runs the government you receive a subsidy that is twice the size of the subsidy paid to people who do not belong to this ethnic group. From the perspective of the people under thirty, this policy
   a. is inequitable, since the individual's ethnic identity alters the level of the subsidy available to the individual.
   b. is equitable, since each person under thirty is treated the same as every other person under thirty in their ethnic group.

16. Government intervention in a market
   a. is never a good idea.
   b. can improve an outcome if the market fails to provide the good or the right amount of the good.
   c. should not occur if there are side payments from the provision of the good that the market does not include.
   d. always reduces the level of efficiency.

17. When one group of people in an economy decreases their spending, this will
   a. have no effect on the level of income of other people in the economy.
   b. increase the level of income of other people in the economy.
   c. decrease the level of income of other people in the economy.
   d. lead to inflationary pressures in this economy.

18. When one group of people in an economy increases their spending, this will
   a. have no effect on the level of income of other people in the economy.
   b. increase the level of income of other people in the economy.
   c. decrease the level of income of other people in the economy.
   d. lead to inflationary pressures in this economy.

19. When there is too much spending in an economy, this leads to
   a. a recession in that economy.
   b. inflation in that economy.

20. In a recession, the government can increase the level of spending in the economy by
   a. decreasing taxes.
   b. decreasing government spending.

■ ANSWER KEY

Answers to Problems and Exercises

1. **a.** Sarah's decision to attend the concert has two opportunity costs: attending the concert means that she will be unable to attend the movie, and in addition, to attend the concert she must pay $10 for a ticket. Her decision to attend the concert means that she is giving up whatever she could have purchased with the $10.

   b. The business gives up $10,000 to get the property, but this is not an opportunity cost since the business must have a business location to exist. However, there is an opportunity cost to this decision: the business gives up the additional business it would have gotten at the prime location during the first six months.

   c. When he decides to take the internship, Jamie incurs an opportunity cost of $2,000, since he is giving up this income to work in the intern position.

   d. Roberto's opportunity cost with regard to his studying is his diminished grade in organic chemistry. (Obviously Roberto might want to consider some combination of studying that allows him to prepare for both exams, but this question did not offer that possibility.)

2. Remember that opportunity cost measures what is given up, so when Roberto studies more for his economics exam, he is giving up time he could devote to his organic chemistry exam. This decision will therefore affect his organic chemistry grade. Similarly, if Roberto devotes more time to studying for his organic chemistry exam, then he will be giving up points on his economics exam.

   a. The opportunity cost of studying 15 hours for the economics exam instead of 10 hours is two points on the organic chemistry exam.

   b. The opportunity cost of studying 15 hours for the organic chemistry exam instead of 10 hours is ten points on the economics exam.

   c. The opportunity cost of studying 20 hours for the economics exam instead of 10 hours is five points on the organic chemistry exam.

   d. The opportunity cost of studying 20 hours for the organic chemistry exam instead of 10 hours is twenty points on the economics exam.

3. **a.** Joe will want to think about the benefits of eating another slice of cake (tastes good, delays the start of his studying, prolongs the amount of time he can spend with his friends) to the costs of eating another slice of cake (an additional hour of exercise to maintain a steady weight, a feeling of guilt, an unhealthy balance in his diet). If Joe decides that the costs associated with the additional slice of cake outweigh the benefits, he will decide not to eat the cake. But if he decides that the benefits outweigh the costs, he will eat the cake.

   b. Since the community enacts the ordinance, it must be the case that the benefits from the new ordinance outweigh the costs; in other words, the community must anticipate that this ordinance will generate more than $500,000 worth of benefits to their community.

   c. Susy must perceive that the benefits of doing the exercises each day are greater than the costs of doing them every day.

4. Longhealth's policy rewards people who not only sign up for the class but also participate in the class. If the goal is to alter people's lifestyle choices toward more exercise, then Longhealth's policy offers the better set of incentives. Although Healthlines subsidizes the exercise class, it does not provide any incentive to ensure that members actually attend and participate in the class.

5. The incentives Matt faces are quite clear: being late carries a major penalty, so Matt will try hard to make sure he gets home on time. This may lead Matt to drive faster than is optimal in order to avoid his family's wrath. Unfortunately, the set of incentives offered to Matt may get him home early on most nights, but it may also result in a tragic outcome if he is running late. Sarah, on the other hand, faces a set of incentives that encourages her growth by forecasting what she is going to do, taking responsibility for what she is doing, and recognizing that even a well-planned evening may run late. Sarah knows that she is responsible for getting in at the time she agreed to, but she also knows that if she is running late she need not speed to get home.

6. Without trade, Bill would have only tomatoes and corn to eat; by trading, Bill gets more variety in his diet. This argument is also true for Mary, who would have only wheat and onions to eat if she did not trade with Bill.

7. Without trade, both states would have less variety in the goods available to their residents. With trade, Wisconsin residents can enjoy Georgia peaches and peanuts and Georgia residents can enjoy Wisconsin cheese and corn.

8. **a.** This is not an equilibrium situation. If the coffee is equivalent and the waiting times the same, then people should go to Joe's for the less expensive cup of coffee. One would anticipate that over time the price at Mary's will fall and that the price of Joe's will rise until the two prices converge.

    b. This is not an equilibrium situation. If the hamburgers are equivalent, then people should go to the Big Bun for the less expensive hamburger. One would anticipate that over time the price of hamburgers at the two restaurants will converge at a single price.

9. **a.** This is not an efficient situation since clearly the cafeteria is failing to provide the type of dessert that is preferred by the students. The cafeteria could make students better off by providing a larger amount of soft-serve ice cream and a smaller amount of cake or pie.

    b. If we assume that the air pollution seriously impacts the quality of life in this community, then this is not an efficient situation. If the community drove less and rode the bus more, then the quality of life would be enhanced in the community and people would be better off. The community might be able to move toward this outcome by reducing the price of bus transportation dramatically and by instituting other types of charges for those who opt to travel by car.

    c. Yes, it would be efficient to implement this ordinance. It would even be possible to compensate the smokers for their loss of rights and still have the benefits from the ordinance exceed the costs of the ordinance.

10. The proposed policy moves the country toward a more efficient outcome, since a reduction in the length of time that unemployed people can collect benefits will encourage the unemployed to resume work and therefore result in fewer wasted resources. People may feel that this policy change is unfair, however, since historically the country has been willing to provide more generous support to the unemployed.

11. Because this policy covers all individuals within the designated group, it is equitable, but it is highly inefficient since it requires everyone to do the same thing regardless of their interests and abilities. The policy also requires a large amount of resources to implement that the government could use in alternative ways. For example, the government might want to provide job training in fields that would be beneficial to the economy but are not taught in a college curriculum (for example, carpentry, mechanical repair, drafting).

12. **a.** The government subsidizes bus ridership by providing free bus passes, which reduces the cost of riding the bus while increasing the cost of using a car. The government wishes to encourage people to use the bus system more and the private transportation system less.

b. The government provides a financial reward for altering your household's car usage. By reducing the number of cars in each household, the government hopes to reduce the number of miles driven and the emissions from automobiles.

c. The government's incentive here is a negative incentive. Guardians do not wish to serve time in jail, and their wish to avoid this outcome will result in their children going to school.

d. The college wants to reduce the risk of transmission of highly communicable diseases in the dormitories. They limit your ability to engage in student activities until you can provide proof that you are immunized.

13. In this case, the lighthouse will not be built through the contributions of individuals in the community. The market will fail to provide the lighthouse, but the government can intervene by imposing a tax for the construction of the lighthouse and then providing these funds to the community for the construction.

14. When people reduce their spending and purchase fewer goods and services, the level of income that other people in the economy earn is reduced since the purchases by one group of people represent income for another group of people. In a recession, the level of spending and the level of income fall in an economy.

15. With a fixed amount of resources in an economy during a given period, there is a limit to the amount of goods and services the economy can produce. If spending is greater than this economic capacity, then this puts pressure on the prices of goods and services to rise, leading to inflationary pressures. Too much spending in an economy results in inflation.

16. A recession implies that the level of spending in the economy is too low. The government can stimulate spending by decreasing the level of taxes, by increasing the level of government spending, or by having the central bank increase the money supply. When there is inflation in an economy, the government can slow down spending by increasing the level of taxes, by decreasing the level of government spending, or by having the central bank decrease the money supply. The textbook will discuss these issues in much greater detail in subsequent chapters.

Answers to Chapter Review Questions

1. **Answer c.** The opportunity cost of taking the job includes what must be given up. In this case, Camillo is giving up two weeks of vacation since the other job offers four weeks of vacation instead of two weeks. He is not giving up any salary when he selects the job paying $32,000.

2. **Answer c.** Ning's opportunity cost is measured by what she must give up when she chooses to do something else. In this case, when Ning decides to attend the lecture she is giving up a night of listening to music in her dorm room.

3. **Answer a.** The firm should purchase this equipment since the addition to revenue ($1,000 a month) is greater than the addition to cost ($750 a month).

4. **Answer b.** In making a decision about whether to run, swim, bike, or rest, Marie should compare the benefits she gets from additional exercise to the costs she incurs from this additional exercise. When she elects to rest, she perceives that the additional costs of the exercise exceed the additional benefits of the exercise.

5. **Answer b.** When resources are scarce, this implies that people and societies must make decisions about how to use those scarce resources since the scarcity of resources is a constraint on production and consumption.

6. **Answer a.** People must make decisions every day because they do not have an infinite amount of time, income, or resources that would allow them to do everything they might want to do.

7. **Answer c.** To get the university community to curtail their parking on campus by the greatest amount, the university should adopt a program that makes drivers aware of the cost of bringing a car on campus every time they drive on campus. Thus, charging an hourly parking fee is the best choice offered, since this fee will serve to remind drivers that bringing a car to campus will cost them something each time they drive on campus and park. In contrast, a single annual fee does not reward the purchaser for reducing the number of times they park on campus during the year; free parking indicates that parking on campus does not cost anything and will result in people parking on campus more often; and exempting the staff from parking fees eliminates incentives to get staff to think about alternatives to driving on campus and parking.

8. **Answer b.** When salespeople are awarded the base salary plus a commission, they are encouraged to be helpful to shoppers in the hope of boosting their sales figures. When offered a flat hourly rate, they have no incentive to provide helpful service beyond the minimum required by the store, since their compensation will not be impacted by their extra effort.

9. **Answer d.** Individuals who elect to trade with one another do so because the trade is beneficial to them. As long as trade is a choice, then the decision to trade with one another must indicate that the trade is beneficial to both parties.

10. **Answer d.** Countries that elect to trade with one another do so because the trade is beneficial to them. As long as trade is a choice, then the decision to trade with one another must indicate that the trade is beneficial to both parties.

11. **Answer d.** All three of these responses describe equilibrium. They are true either by definition or by implication.

12. **Answer a.** Answers (c) and (d) are essentially the same answer, with answer (c) focusing on the individual while answer (d) focuses on the group: both are incorrect. That leaves answers (a) and (b): a situation is efficient when no one can be made better off through a different outcome. This implies that the maximum gains from trade are achieved when a situation is efficient, and this does not necessarily occur when price is as low as possible.

13. **Answer b.** Since college students do not use the library throughout the semester in the early morning hours, the college is not utilizing its scarce resources efficiently when it elects to keep the library open all night. It would be more efficient to open the library all night only during those weeks when students would actually avail themselves of these hours.

14. **Answer a.** This policy treats everyone under thirty equally and so it is an equitable policy from that perspective. However, the policy is not efficient since it does not consider whether this is an efficient use of the resources involved.

15. **Answer a.** This policy is not equitable since it does not treat everyone under thirty equally: instead it discriminates on the basis of ethnicity.

16. **Answer b.** This is a definitional statement. Answer (a) is incorrect since there are times when government intervention is helpful (for example, regulation of certain industries or laws restricting pollution); answer (c) is incorrect since government intervention may be called for when there are side payments that the market does not account for; and answer (d) is incorrect since there are occasions when government intervention can improve the efficiency of the market.

17. **Answer c.** This is true by definition. If spending is reduced by one group in an economy, then some other individuals in the economy will not receive as much income as they initially did due to this reduction in spending.

18. **Answer b.** This is true by definition. An increase in spending in an economy indicates that some people in that economy will receive that additional spending and, hence, their incomes will rise.

19. **Answer b.** When spending increases at a faster pace than the production of goods and services, then this leads to upward pressure on the prices of those goods and services. Hence, this spending will lead to inflation.

20. **Answer a.** If the government decreases taxes, this tax decrease results in people having higher net incomes and, therefore, more income available to spend. This leads to greater spending. In contrast, if the government decreases government spending, there is less spending in the economy.

chapter 2

Economic Models:
Trade-offs and Trade

▮ BEFORE YOU READ THE CHAPTER

Summary

This chapter introduces the concept of model building and then discusses two different economic models, the model of production possibility frontiers and the model of comparative advantage. Models are a simplified representation of reality, and the study of economic models will be a crucial aspect of your study of economics. The two models presented in this chapter provide a simplified framework for discussing the concept of opportunity cost, trade-offs, scarcity, efficiency, and gains from trade. The chapter also discusses the distinction between positive and normative economics.

Chapter Objectives

Objective #1.   A model is a simplified representation of reality that is used to better understand real-life situations. Underlying every model is a set of assumptions.

Objective #2.   The production possibility frontier is a model that represents the production possibilities available to an individual or to an economy. The production possibility frontier model assumes that the individual (or country) has a set amount of resources, a set level of technology, and a set amount of time, and then the production possibility frontier delineates a set of points that indicate the maximum amount of two goods that can be produced by this individual (or country) given their resources, technology, and available time. For simplicity, this study guide refers to production possibility frontiers in terms of production by countries rather than individuals, but the arguments made from the perspective of countries also hold for individuals. Figure 2.1 illustrates a linear production possibility frontier for a country, where the frontier indicates the maximum amount of goods X and Y that can be produced from the available resources and technology. Points A and B are points that lie on the production possibility frontier and are feasible production points for this country. Points C and D are points that lie inside the production possibility frontier: this country can produce these points—they are feasible—but the country is not using their available resources fully. Points C and D are therefore feasible points, but not efficient points. Points E and F lie outside the production possibility frontier and are therefore not feasible points of production for this country.

Figure 2.1

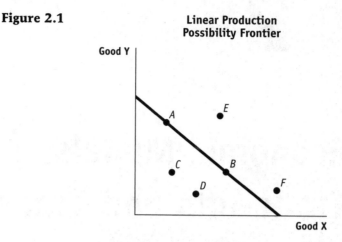

Linear Production
Possibility Frontier

Objective #3. The simplest version of this production possibility frontier model assumes that the frontier is linear and thus has a constant slope. This implies that the opportunity cost of producing another unit of the good measured on the x-axis stays the same as you move along the production possibility frontier. In Figure 2.2 the opportunity cost of moving from point A to point B, and the opportunity cost of moving from point C to point D are illustrated. Remember that opportunity cost measures what you give up to get something: thus, when moving from point A to point B, opportunity cost is measured in terms of good Y, the good you give up to get more of good X; whereas, when moving from point C to point D, opportunity cost is measured in terms of good X, the good you give up to get more of good Y. The lines that are bold in Figure 2.2 indicate the opportunity cost of moving from point A to point B or from point C to point D.

Figure 2.2

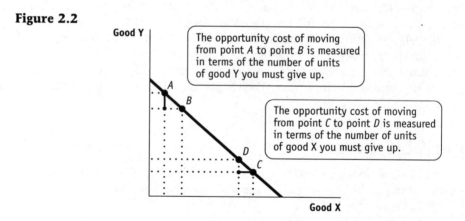

Objective #4. A more realistic production possibility frontier is one that is bowed out from the origin: this implies that as the country produces more and more of one of the goods, the opportunity cost of producing this good increases. The production possibility frontier has this shape due to specialization of resources: some of the resources available to the country are more suited to produce good X than they are good Y. When the country decides to increase the production of one type of good, the first few units can be produced at relatively low opportunity cost since resources can be shifted from the production of one good to the production of the other good that are not particularly well suited to the production of the first good. However, the opportunity cost eventually will rise since the increased production of this good eventually will require the use of resources that are ill-suited to produce this good. Figure 2.3 illustrates a bowed-out production possibility frontier and the opportunity cost of getting one more unit of the good measured on the x-axis. Notice that as we get more and more units of good X, the opportunity cost of each additional unit of X is larger than the opportunity cost of the preceding unit.

Figure 2.3

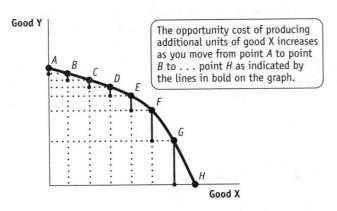

The opportunity cost of producing additional units of good X increases as you move from point *A* to point *B* to . . . point *H* as indicated by the lines in bold on the graph.

Objective #5. There are two types of efficiency to discuss with respect to production possibility frontiers: productive efficiency and allocative efficiency. Productive efficiency refers to producing at a point that lies on the production possibility frontier. Points that lie inside the frontier are inefficient, since it is possible to increase the level of production from the given set of resources. Allocative efficiency refers to producing the right mix of goods from the available resources. For an economy to be allocatively efficient it must allocate its resources in such a way as to make consumers as well off as possible. Another way of saying this is that an allocatively efficient economy produces the mix of goods that people want.

Objective #6. For an economy to be efficient it must achieve productive and allocative efficiency: it must not waste resources and it must produce the right mix of goods.

Objective #7. The production possibility frontier illustrates scarcity in that there are points of production that cannot be produced because the level of resources and/or technology constrain production. The production possibility frontier illustrates trade-offs: getting more of good X requires giving up some of good Y.

Objective #8. Economic growth can be illustrated with the production possibility frontier model. When the frontier shifts away from the origin, this means that the represented economy can now produce more of good X and good Y. The production possibility frontier shifts out when there are increases in resources or increases in the available level of technology.

Objective #9. The model of production possibility frontiers can also be used to illustrate the gains from trade, which is referred to as the model of comparative advantage. This model assumes that there are two countries, that there are two goods that the countries produce, and that each country has a set amount of resources, technology, and time available to them. Furthermore, this model assumes that the two countries have different opportunity costs of production. In this model, countries benefit from specializing in the production of that good for which they have the comparative advantage, or lower opportunity cost of production, and then trade with each other. Countries do not have to have absolute advantage in production to benefit from trade: the benefits from trade only require that countries have different opportunity costs of production for the two goods and that each country specialize in producing the good that they can produce at lower opportunity cost relative to the other country.

Objective #10. Positive economics is factual and descriptive, whereas normative economics is about what ought to be or what should be. Positive economics is objective and can be tested for accuracy, and it often involves forecasting. Normative economics is subjective and prescriptive, and it is value based. However, it is possible to rank normative policies designed to achieve a certain prescription on the basis of the efficiency of each policy.

Objective #11. Economists may come to different conclusions because they have different values or because they use different economic models.

Key Terms

model a simplified representation of a real situation that is used to better understand real-life situations.

other things equal assumption in the development of a model, the assumption that all relevant factors except the one under study remain unchanged.

production possibility frontier illustrates the trade-offs facing an economy that produces only two goods. It shows the maximum quantity of one good that can be produced for any given quantity produced of the other.

factors of production the *resources* used to produce goods and services. Labor and capital are examples of factors.

technology the technical means for producing goods and services.

comparative advantage the advantage conferred on an individual or nation in producing a good or service if the *opportunity cost* of producing the good or service is lower for that individual or nation than for other producers.

absolute advantage the advantage conferred on an individual in an activity if he or she can do it better than other people.

barter people directly exchange goods or services that they have for goods or services that they want.

circular-flow diagram represents the transactions in an *economy* by two kinds of flows around a circle: flows of physical things such as goods or labor in one direction and flows of money to pay for these physical things in the opposite direction.

household a person or a group of people that share their income.

firm an organization that produces goods and services for sale.

markets for goods and services markets in which *firms* sell goods and services that they produce to *households*.

factor markets markets in which *firms* buy the *resources* they need to produce goods and services.

income distribution the way in which total income is divided among the owners of the various factors of production.

positive economics the branch of economic analysis that describes the way the *economy* actually works.

normative economics the branch of economic analysis that makes prescriptions about the way the *economy* should work.

forecast a simple prediction of the future.

Key Terms *(continued)*

variable a quantity that can take on more than one value.

horizontal axis the horizontal number line of a graph along which values of the *x*-variable are measured; also referred to as the *x-axis*.

x-axis the horizontal number line of a graph along which values of the *x*-variable are measured; also referred to as the *horizontal axis*.

vertical axis the vertical number line of a graph along which values of the *y*-variable are measured; also referred to as the *y-axis*.

y-axis the vertical number line of a graph along which values of the *y*-variable are measured; also referred to as the *vertical axis*.

origin the point where the axes of a two-variable graph meet.

causal relationship the relationship between two variables in which the value taken by one variable directly influences or determines the value taken by the other variable.

independent variable the determining variable in a causal relationship.

dependent variable the determined variable in a causal relationship.

curve a line on a graph, which may be curved or straight, that depicts a relationship between two variables.

linear relationship the relationship between two variables in which the *slope* is constant and therefore is depicted on a graph by a *curve* that is a straight line.

nonlinear relationship the relationship between two variables in which the *slope* is not constant and therefore is depicted on a graph by a *curve* that is not a straight line.

positive relationship a relationship between two variables in which an increase in the value of one variable is associated with an increase in the value of the other variable. It is illustrated by a *curve* that slopes upward from left to right.

negative relationship a relationship between two variables in which an increase in the value of one variable is associated with a decrease in the value of the other variable. It is illustrated by a *curve* that slopes downward from left to right.

horizontal intercept the point at which a *curve* hits the *horizontal axis*; it indicates the value of the *x*-variable when the value of the *y*-variable is zero.

vertical intercept the point at which a *curve* hits the *vertical axis*; it shows the value of the *y*-variable when the value of the *x*-variable is zero.

slope a measure of how steep a line or curve is. The slope of a line is measured by "rise over run"—the change in the *y*-variable between two points on the line divided by the change in the *x*-variable between those same two points.

nonlinear curve a curve in which the *slope* is not the same between every pair of points.

absolute value the value of a number without regard to a plus or minus sign.

Key Terms *(continued)*

tangent line a straight line that just touches a *nonlinear curve* at a particular point; the *slope* of the tangent line is equal to the slope of the nonlinear curve at that point.

maximum the highest point on a *nonlinear curve*, where the *slope* changes from positive to negative.

minimum the lowest point on a *nonlinear curve*, where the *slope* changes from negative to positive.

time-series graph a two-variable graph that has dates on the *horizontal axis* and values of a variable that occurred on those dates on the *vertical axis*.

scatter diagram a graph that shows points that correspond to actual observations of the *x*- and *y*-variables; a *curve* is usually fitted to the scatter of points to indicate the trend in the data.

pie chart a circular graph that shows how some total is divided among its components, usually expressed in percentages.

bar graph a graph that uses bars of varying height or length to show the comparative sizes of different observations of a variable.

truncated cut; in a truncated axis, some of the range of values are omitted, usually to save space.

omitted variable an unobserved *variable* that, through its influence on other variables, creates the erroneous appearance of a direct *causal relationship* among those variables.

reverse causality the error committed when the true direction of causality between two *variables* is reversed, and the *independent variable* and the *dependent variable* are incorrectly identified.

AFTER YOU READ THE CHAPTER

Tips

Tip #1. This chapter introduces the concept of models. This is a crucial concept that forms the basis of the majority of material you study in the rest of the course. In working with models it is important to understand the simplifying assumptions underlying whatever model you are using.

Tip #2. Many of the models you will encounter in this course make the other-things-equal assumption, which means that the model considers only one change at a time while holding everything else constant. Make sure you understand this basic assumption before working with the models introduced in the chapter.

Tip #3. Economic models can be described verbally, but they can also be represented by graphs or equations. You will want to be comfortable working with all three types of representations. The appendix to Chapter 2 provides an introduction to graphs in economics.

Tip #4. Throughout the course you will find it helpful to be able to sketch graphs to illustrate the ideas you are analyzing. You should practice making precise, numerically significant graphs, but you also should practice less formal graphs that sketch the nature of the relationship rather than the precise mathematical relationship.

Tip #5. Opportunity cost can be measured using the production possibility frontier model. To do this calculation pick a point on the production possibility frontier and identify how much of each good is being produced. Then pick a second point on the production possibility frontier and identify the new levels of production. The opportunity cost is measured as the number of units of the good you must give up to get more of the other good. Note that both points must be on the production possibility frontier. Figure 2.4 illustrates the measurement of opportunity cost when moving from point A to point B. In this example, the opportunity cost is measured as the amount of good Y, $Y_1 - Y_2$, that must be given up to increase the production of good X from its initial value of X_1 to the new level X_2. The bold line indicates the amount of good Y that is given up to increase the production of good X from X_1 to X_2.

Figure 2.4

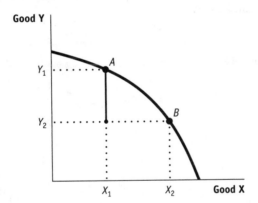

Tip #6. You should practice working with the models and with specific techniques introduced with each model. For instance, you should be comfortable calculating opportunity cost using the production possibility frontier model. You also should be comfortable comparing the opportunity cost of production for two countries and deciding which good each country should specialize in producing.

Tip #7. If you are using flashcards, make sure you include the following cards: (a) a linear production possibility frontier indicating feasible and infeasible points as well as efficient and inefficient points, (b) a production possibility frontier bowed out from the origin showing these same concepts, and (c) an example of comparative advantage that illustrates two countries and then calculates each country's comparative advantage. Also, don't forget to include a card for each new vocabulary word as well as the chapter heading on each card.

Tip #8. Calculating opportunity cost in a problem is often challenging for students initially. Let's explore a fail-safe method for this calculation based on a linear production possibility frontier (this is the type of production possibility frontier that we will use in the comparative advantage model). First, construct the production possibility frontier and, since it is linear, calculate the slope of the frontier. Then use this slope measure to generate the opportunity costs you want: the opportunity cost of producing one more unit of the good measured on the x-axis is given by the slope, since the slope tells us the change in the y-variable divided by the change in the x-variable. Thus, if the slope of the production possibility frontier is –2, then the opportunity cost of producing an additional unit of good X is 2 units of good Y. To find the opportunity cost of the good produced on the y-axis, we simply need to use the reciprocal of the slope. Thus, if the slope of the linear production possibility frontier is –2, then the opportunity cost of producing one more unit of good Y is ½ unit of good X, since this is the amount of good X we must give up to get one more unit of good Y. The problems in this chapter will give you a chance to practice this reasoning and this technique.

Tip #9. Once you can calculate the opportunity cost of producing good X or good Y then you can compare the opportunity costs faced by two countries. The model of comparative advantage illustrates that countries will benefit from trade when they specialize and produce the good that has the lowest opportunity cost of production relative to the other country.

Problems and Exercises

1. Suppose that you wish to travel from your college campus to a nearby community. You go online to download a map to guide you on your trip. How is this map an example of a model? How does it simplify reality? How do you evaluate whether or not your map helps you better understand the world?

2. The production possibilities frontier model holds resources, technology, and the time period constant in order to construct a path of points that represents the maximum amount of two goods an economy can produce given the constraints of their resources and technology during the given time period. This model allows us to consider the effect of an increase in resources while holding everything else constant. In this example, what is it that we are holding constant? Describe the effect of this change in resources on this economy's production possibility frontier.

3. Suppose you are stranded on an island by yourself and must therefore produce all the goods you consume. You consume clams and mangos exclusively. If you devote all your available time to harvesting clams, you can harvest 100 clams in a week. If you devote all your available time to collecting mangos, you can find 200 mangos in a week.

a. Imagine it is possible for you to divide your time between harvesting clams and collecting mangos and that you can even find fractional amounts of both goods. Draw a sketch of your production possibility frontier for a week, placing mangos on the x-axis and clams on the y-axis.

Clams per week

Mangos per week

b. Now, sketch your production possibility frontier for a two-week period. Describe what happens to your production possibility frontier when you increase the amount of time available for production.

Clams per two week period

Mangos per two week period

c. Now, imagine you invent a clam rake that enhances your ability to harvest clams. With this invention you are able to increase your clam harvest to a maximum of 200 clams a week if you spend all your time on clams. Your invention has no effect on your ability to collect mangos. Sketch your new production possibility frontier. Describe in words the effect of a change in technology that affects the ability to produce one of the goods, but not both of the goods.

Clams per
week

Mangos per week

d. Suppose you have your clam rake and, in addition, you procure knowledge over time that enhances your ability to collect mangos. Your ability to gather mangoes increases to 300 mangos a week due to this knowledge. Sketch your new production possibility frontier based on this knowledge and your use of the clam rake. In effect you have experienced a change in technology that has a positive effect on the production of both goods. Describe in words the effect of this change on the production possibility frontier.

Clams per
week

Mangos per week

4. Let's return to the example given in Problem 3.

   a. What is the opportunity cost of harvesting a clam given the original information in Problem 3?

   b. What is the opportunity cost of collecting a mango given the original information in Problem 3?

   c. What is the slope of the production possibility frontier that you sketched in your answer to Problem 3a? How does this slope measure relate to the answers you provide in parts (a) and (b) of this question?

   d. What happened to the slope of the production possibility frontier once you invent the clam rake (Question 3c)? What happens to the opportunity cost of harvesting clams once you invent the clam rake? What happens to the opportunity cost of collecting mangos once you invent the clam rake?

5. The country of Orange manufactures sofas and lamps. With its available resources and technology, Orange can manufacture in a year 1,000 sofas and 0 lamps or 0 sofas and 250 lamps. It can also manufacture any combination of sofas and lamps that lie on the straight line connecting these two points.

   a. Sketch Orange's production possibility frontier, placing sofas on the y-axis and lamps on the x-axis.

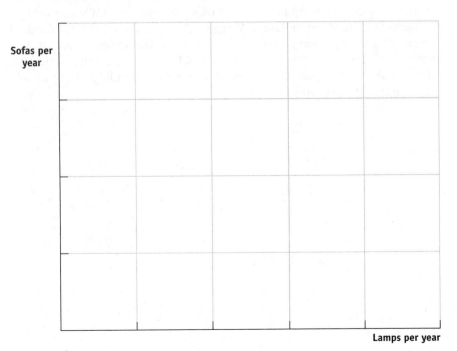

b. Fill in the following table by listing some of the feasible and efficient combinations of production available to Orange each year given its resources and technology.

Combination	Number of lamps possible	Number of sofas possible
A	0	
B	50	
C		500
D		200
E	225	
F	250	

c. What is the slope of the production possibility frontier for Orange?

d. What is the opportunity cost of producing one additional sofa for Orange?

e. What is the opportunity cost of producing one additional lamp for Orange?

f. What is the value of the y-intercept for Orange? (Hint: in this example the y-intercept is the number of sofas Orange can produce if it does not produce anything else.)

g. Write an equation for the production possibility frontier for Orange using S to stand for sofas and L to stand for lamps. Write this equation in y-intercept form. (Hint: this means that the equation will be written with S on the left-hand side of the equation, where the S stands for the value of the variable measured on the vertical axis of your sketch.) Verify that each of the combinations you found in part (b) of this problem are true in the equation you wrote.

6. The country of Utopia produces two goods from its available resources and technology. The only resource that Utopia has is labor. It takes 3 hours of labor to produce 2 widgets and 4 hours of labor to produce 1 gadget. For this question assume that the production possibility frontier for Utopia is a straight line.

    a. Sketch the production possibility frontier for the country of Utopia. (Hint: to do this you must first decide on a relevant time period. You might pick 20 hours, or 2,000 hours, or 2 million hours as your labor constraint, for example, and then you would sketch your production possibility frontier based on this amount of available time and labor.) Draw your production possibility frontier with widgets on the y-axis and gadgets on the x-axis.

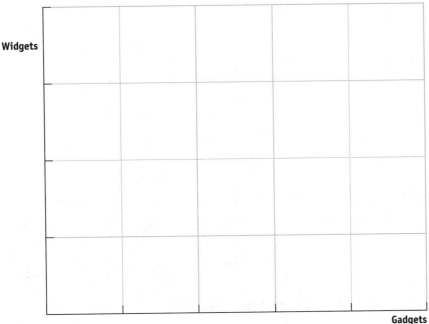

    b. What is the slope of your production possibility frontier?

    c. What is the opportunity cost of producing an additional widget in Utopia?

    d. What is the opportunity cost of producing an additional gadget in Utopia?

7. The country of Jonesville produces two goods from its available resources and technology. The only resource that Jonesville has is labor. The following table gives the amount of labor necessary to produce a widget or a gadget. For this question assume that the production possibility frontier for Jonesville is a straight line.

	Number of hours of labor needed to produce a gadget	Number of hours of labor needed to produce a widget
Jonesville	2	5

a. Suppose that you want to draw a production possibility frontier for Jonesville. What must you do first to draw your sketch?

b. Sketch the production possibility frontier for Jonesville assuming that Jonesville has 120 hours of labor available. Place gadgets on the x-axis and widgets on the y-axis.

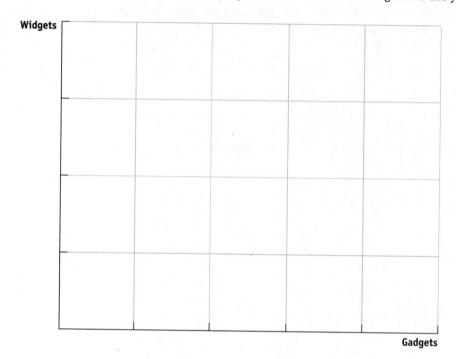

c. What is the slope of the production possibility frontier?

d. What is the opportunity cost of producing an additional gadget?

e. What is the opportunity cost of producing an additional widget?

f. Suppose that Jonesville has 240 hours of labor instead of 120 hours of labor. Does this affect the opportunity cost of producing widgets or gadgets? Explain your answer.

8. The following table provides six possible production combinations that Smithtown can produce from their available resources and technology during this year. Assume that Smithtown only produces bicycles and tents from their available resources.

Combination	Bicycles	Tents
A	100	0
B	90	10
C	70	25
D	40	36
E	10	42
F	0	44

a. Sketch Smithtown's production possibility frontier. Measure bicycles along the x-axis and tents along the y-axis.

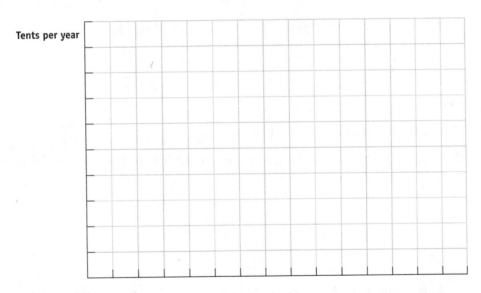

Tents per year

Bicycles per year

b. Suppose Smithtown is currently producing at combination C. If Smithtown chooses to produce at combination B, what is the opportunity cost of moving from combination C to combination B?

c. Suppose Smithtown is currently producing at combination C. If Smithtown chooses to produce at combination D, what is the opportunity cost of moving from combination C to combination D?

d. Smithtown's production possibility frontier is not linear. Provide an explanation for why the production possibility frontier is not linear.

9. Suppose an economy produces two goods in a year using its available resources and technology. This economy's resources are specialized.

   a. Describe the general shape of this economy's production possibility frontier.

   b. If this economy currently produces only one of these two goods, what do you know must be true about the opportunity cost of producing more and more units of the good that is not being currently produced?

   c. If this economy is to be productively efficient, what must be true about its production of these two goods?

   d. If this economy is to be allocatively efficient, what must be true about its production of these two goods?

   e. Suppose this economy is deemed to be efficient. What must occur for this statement to be true?

10. Economists believe that specialization and trade is beneficial when it is based on comparative advantage. Briefly explain why economists believe this to be true.

11. There are two islands in the middle of the ocean and these two islands produce fish and baskets. Big Island can produce either 100 fish per day and 0 baskets per day or 0 fish per day and 200 baskets per day. Big Island can also produce any combination of fish and baskets that lies on their linear production possibility frontier. Small Island can produce either 80 fish per day and 0 baskets per day or 0 fish per day and 80 baskets. Like Big Island, Small Island has a linear production possibility frontier.

a. Sketch two graphs. Sketch Big Island's production possibility frontier on the first graph and sketch Small Island's production possibility frontier on the second graph. Place fish/day on the y-axis and baskets/day on the x-axis.

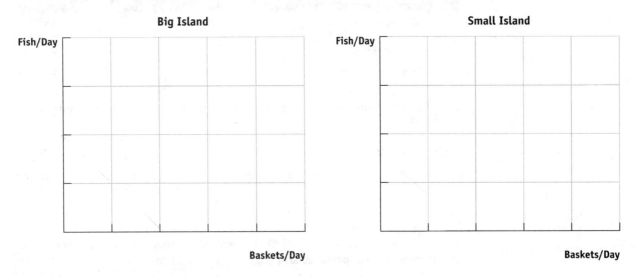

b. What is the slope of Big Island's production possibility frontier?

c. What is the slope of Small Island's production possibility frontier?

d. What is the opportunity cost of producing an additional basket on Big Island? What is the opportunity cost of producing an additional basket on Small Island? Which island can produce baskets at lower opportunity cost?

e. What is the opportunity cost of producing an additional fish on Big Island? What is the opportunity cost of producing an additional fish on Small Island? Which island can produce fish at lower opportunity cost?

f. What good should Big Island specialize in producing?

g. What good should Small Island specialize in producing?

12. There are two islands in the middle of the ocean, and these two islands produce fish and baskets. Big Island can produce either 100 fish per day and 0 baskets per day or 0 fish per day and 200 baskets per day. Big Island can also produce any combination of fish and baskets that includes these two combinations and lies on their linear production possibility frontier. Small Island can produce either 80 fish per day and 0 baskets per day or 0 fish per day and 80 baskets. Like Big Island, Small Island has a linear production possibility frontier. Currently there is no trade between the two islands. The current production for both islands is given in the table below.

Initial production	Fish	Baskets
Big Island	80	40
Small Island	30	50
Total production	110	90

a. Is Big Island producing at a productively efficient point? Explain your answer.

b. Is Small Island producing at a productively efficient point? Explain your answer.

Referring back to question 11, let's analyze what happens to total production if these countries decide to specialize and trade according to their comparative advantage.

c. Suppose that Big Island decides to produce 50 baskets instead of 40 baskets. How many fish will Big Island be able to produce if its basket production is increased to 50 baskets?

d. Suppose that Small Island decides to produce 40 fish instead of 30 fish. How many baskets will Small Island be able to produce if its fish production is increased to 40 fish?

e. Fill in the table below showing the new levels of production given the information in parts (c) and (d).

New production	Fish	Baskets
Big Island		50
Small Island	40	
Total production		

f. Does specialization and trade benefit both islands in this example? Explain your answer.

Referring back to question 11, let's analyze what happens to total production if these countries decide to specialize and trade without regard to their comparative advantage.

g. Suppose that Big Island decides to produce 30 baskets instead of 40 baskets. How many fish will Big Island be able to produce if its basket production is increased to 30 baskets?

h. Suppose that Small Island decides to produce 20 fish instead of 30 fish. How many baskets will Small Island be able to produce if its fish production is increased to 20 fish?

i. Fill in the table below showing the new levels of production given the information in parts (c) and (d).

New production	Fish	Baskets
Big Island		30
Small Island	20	
Total production		

j. Does specialization and trade benefit both islands in this example? Explain your answer.

k. What must be true for specialization and trade to be beneficial? (Hint: think about the two examples in this problem and how they differ before you write your answer.)

13. Suppose that Jane and Bob live on an island far away from any other countries. Jane and Bob both produce widgets and gadgets from their available resources, but they do not currently trade with one another. The table below gives the number of hours of labor needed to produce one widget or one gadget for Bob and Jane. For this example let's assume that Jane and Bob each have 120 hours of labor time.

	Hours of labor needed to produce a widget	Hours of labor needed to produce a gadget
Bob	2	4
Jane	3	1.5

a. Sketch two graphs: on the first graph draw Bob's production possibility frontier and on the second graph draw Jane's production possibility frontier. Place widgets on the y-axis and gadgets on the x-axis. Label both graphs carefully.

Bob's Production Possibility Frontier

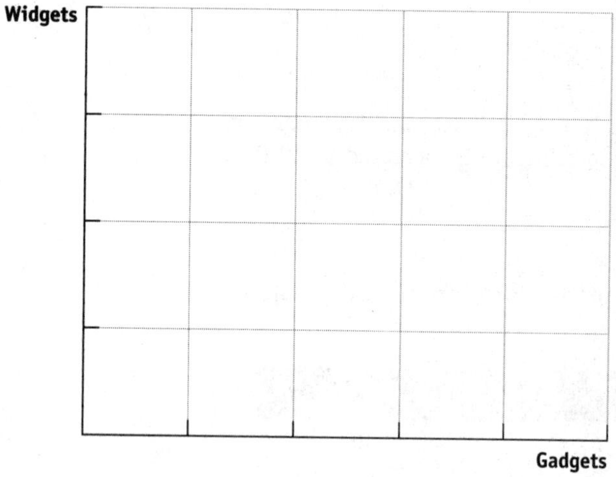

Widgets

Gadgets

Jane's Production Possibility Frontier

Widgets

Gadgets

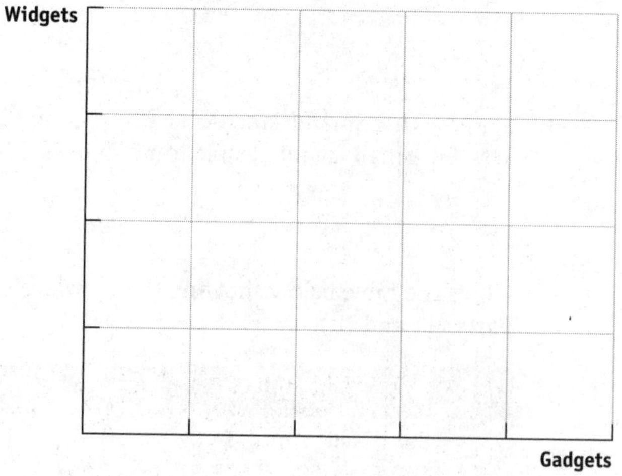

b. Suppose that Bob and Jane devote half of their labor time to producing gadgets and half to producing widgets. Fill in the following table based on this allocation of labor.

Initial production	Widgets	Gadgets
Bob		
Jane		
Total production		

c. What is Bob's opportunity cost of producing an additional gadget? What is Jane's opportunity cost of producing an additional gadget? Who can produce gadgets at lower opportunity cost?

d. What is Bob's opportunity cost of producing an additional widget? What is Jane's opportunity cost of producing an additional widget? Who can produce widgets at lower opportunity cost?

e. Bob and Jane decide to specialize and trade. What good should Bob specialize in producing?

f. Bob and Jane decide to specialize and trade. What good should Jane specialize in producing?

g. Bob and Jane specialize according to their comparative advantage and give us this partially filled in table that provides some information about their production. Fill in the missing information on the table assuming that Bob and Jane are both productively efficient.

New production	Widgets	Gadgets
Bob	46	
Jane		60
Total production		

14. Decide whether each of the following statements is a normative statement or a positive statement, then explain your answer.

   a. The gasoline tax is projected to yield $10 million in tax revenue next year.

   b. If the gasoline tax was raised by 10 cents per gallon, the tax revenue from this tax would increase by 4%.

   c. The state should raise the gasoline tax for the coming year. An increase in the tax will reduce congestion and smog, which is more important than the cost to commuters if they shift from private car transportation to public transportation.

   d. Mandatory school enhances the work skills of students.

   e. The age of mandatory school attendance should be extended, since this will provide greater benefits to our economy.

   f. An extension of mandatory school attendance will increase government education costs by $2 million for the state.

15. Economists sometimes disagree about positive economics, but more often they disagree about normative economics. Briefly define both of these terms and then explain why economists do not always agree.

▮ BEFORE YOU TAKE THE TEST

Chapter Review Questions

1. Models
  a. are an exact replica of reality.
  b. bear no resemblance to real life.
  c. are a simplification of the real world.
  d. are made more complicated by the assumptions that underlie the model.

2. There are a limited number of possible economic models.
  a. True b. False

3. The other-things-equal assumption means that
  a. all economic models hold the same variables constant.
  b. all economic models vary only one variable at a time, and that variable is always the same for all economic models.
  c. only one variable is allowed to change in a model at a time so that the analyst using the model can focus on the effect of that change on the model.
  d. lots of variables are allowed to change in a model at one time so that the analyst using the model can focus on the effect of all these changes on a single variable of interest.

4. Suppose Mike has a linear production possibility frontier in the production of potatoes and tomatoes. If Mike devotes all his time to the production of potatoes, he can produce 1,000 pounds of potatoes a year; if he devotes all his time to the production of tomatoes, he can produce 2,000 pounds of tomatoes a year. Which of the following combinations of potatoes and tomatoes are not feasible for Mike?
  a. 1,000 pounds of potatoes and 2,000 pounds of tomatoes per year
  b. 1,000 pounds of potatoes and 0 pounds of tomatoes per year
  c. 0 pounds of potatoes and 2,000 pounds of tomatoes per year
  d. 500 pounds of potatoes and 1,000 pounds of tomatoes per year

5. Suppose Mike has a linear production possibility frontier in the production of potatoes and tomatoes. If Mike devotes all his time to the production of potatoes, he can produce 1,000 pounds of potatoes a year; if he devotes all his time to the production of tomatoes, he can produce 2,000 pounds of tomatoes a year. Which of the following combinations of potatoes and tomatoes are not efficient for Mike?
  a. 500 pounds of potatoes and 500 pounds of tomatoes per year
  b. 500 pounds of potatoes and 1,000 pounds of tomatoes per year
  c. 750 pounds of potatoes and 500 pounds of tomatoes per year
  d. 250 pounds of potatoes and 1,500 pounds of tomatoes per year

6. Utopia has a linear production possibility frontier in the production of widgets and gadgets. It can produce three gadgets per hour of labor time or four widgets per hour of labor time. What is the opportunity cost of producing one widget in Utopia?

a. 3 gadgets

b. 4 widgets

c. 0.75 gadget

d. 1.33 gadgets

7. Jonesville produces widgets and gadgets and its production possibility frontier is linear. The following table provides the number of units of labor necessary to produce 1 gadget or 1 widget in Jonesville.

	Number of hours of labor needed to produce a gadget	Number of hours of labor needed to produce a widget
Jonesville	5	10

Suppose that Jonesville has 100 hours of labor. What is the maximum number of widgets it can produce?

a. 10 widgets

b. 20 widgets

c. 1 widget

d. 100 widgets

8. Jonesville produces widgets and gadgets and its production possibility frontier is linear. The following table provides the number of units of labor necessary to produce 1 gadget or 1 widget in Jonesville.

	Number of hours of labor needed to produce a gadget	Number of hours of labor needed to produce a widget
Jonesville	5	10

Suppose that Jonesville has 100 hours of labor. What is the maximum number of widgets and gadgets it can produce if it devotes half of its labor time to the production of widgets and half of its labor time to the production of gadgets?

a. 20 gadgets and 5 widgets

b. 10 gadgets and 5 widgets

c. 5 gadgets and 20 widgets

d. 5 gadgets and 10 widgets

9. Jonesville produces widgets and gadgets and its production possibility frontier is linear. The following table provides the number of units of labor necessary to produce 1 gadget or 1 widget in Jonesville.

	Number of hours of labor needed to produce a gadget	Number of hours of labor needed to produce a widget
Jonesville	5	10

Suppose that Jonesville initially has 100 hours of labor. What happens to the opportunity cost of producing a widget if Jonesville's labor resource increases to 200 hours of labor?

a. The opportunity cost of producing a widget decreases.

b. The opportunity cost of producing a widget increases.

c. The opportunity cost of producing a widget does not change.

d. The opportunity cost of producing a widget may increase, decrease, or remain unchanged depending on the number of gadgets that are produced in Jonesville.

10. Jonesville produces widgets and gadgets and its production possibility frontier is linear. The following table provides the number of units of labor necessary to produce 1 gadget or 1 widget in Jonesville.

	Number of hours of labor needed to produce a gadget	Number of hours of labor needed to produce a widget
Jonesville	5	10

Suppose that Jonesville has 100 hours of labor. Which of the following combinations of widgets and gadgets is not feasible for Jonesville to produce?

a. 4 gadgets and 8 widgets

b. 7 gadgets and 7 widgets

c. 8 gadgets and 6 widgets

d. 0 gadgets and 10 widgets

11. Utopia has a linear production possibility frontier in the production of widgets and gadgets. It can produce 3 gadgets per hour of labor time or 4 widgets per hour of labor time. Suppose that Utopia has 120 hours of labor time and that it chooses to divide its labor time equally between the production of widgets and gadgets. What is the maximum number of widgets Utopia can produce given this decision?

a. 480 widgets

b. 240 widgets

c. 60 widgets

d. 15 widgets

12. Suburbia has a production possibility frontier bowed out from the origin for the two goods, guns and butter, that Suburbia produces from its available resources and technology. The following table describes six points that lie on Suburbia's production possibility frontier.

Combination	Number of guns	Pounds of butter
A	0	80
B	10	75
C	20	65
D	30	50
E	40	30
F	50	0

Suppose Suburbia is initially producing at point D. What is the opportunity cost of moving to point E?

a. 10 guns

b. 40 guns

c. 20 pounds of butter

d. 30 pounds of butter

13. Suburbia has a production possibility frontier bowed out from the origin for the two goods, guns and butter, that Suburbia produces from its available resources and technology. The following table describes six points that lie on Suburbia's production possibility frontier.

Combination	Number of guns	Pounds of butter
A	0	80
B	10	75
C	20	65
D	30	50
E	40	30
F	50	0

Suppose Suburbia is initially producing at point D. What is the opportunity cost of moving to point B?

a. 25 pounds of butter

b. 20 guns

c. 10 guns

d. 75 pounds of butter

14. Suburbia has a production possibility frontier bowed out from the origin for the two goods, guns and butter, that Suburbia produces from its available resources and technology. The following table describes six points that lie on Suburbia's production possibility frontier.

Combination	Number of guns	Pounds of butter
A	0	80
B	10	75
C	20	65
D	30	50
E	40	30
F	50	0

Suburbia is currently producing 50 pounds of butter and 20 guns. This combination is

a. allocatively efficient, since butter is tastier than guns.

b. productively efficient, since it is a feasible point for Suburbia to produce.

c. infeasible, because Suburbia cannot produce this combination given its resources and technology.

d. feasible but inefficient, since it is a combination that lies inside the production possibility frontier.

15. Which of the following statements is true?

    I. Points that lie on the production possibility frontier are allocatively efficient.

    II. Points that lie on the production possibility frontier are productively efficient.

  a. Statement I is true.

  b. Statement II is true.

  c. Statements I and II are true.

  d. Statements I and II are false.

16. An economy is allocatively efficient provided that

  a. it produces at any point along its production possibility frontier.

  b. it produces the right mix of goods from its available resources.

  c. no resources are wasted.

  d. all of the above statements are true about allocative efficiency.

17. Suppose there are two countries, Texia and Urbania, that produce food and clothing and currently do not trade. Both countries have linear production possibility frontiers. Texia, if it devotes all of its resources to food production, can produce 1,000 units of food this year and 0 units of clothing. If Texia devotes of all of its resources to clothing production this year, it can produce 500 units of clothing and 0 units of food. Urbania can either produce 500 units of food this year and 0 units of clothing, or it can produce 200 units of clothing this year and 0 units of food. _____ has the absolute advantage in the production of clothing and _____ has the absolute advantage in the production of food.

  a. Texia; Texia   c. Urbania; Texia

  b. Texia; Urbania   d. Urbania; Urbania

18. Suppose there are two countries, Texia and Urbania, that produce food and clothing and currently do not trade. Both countries have linear production possibility frontiers. Texia, if it devotes all of its resources to food production can produce 1,000 units of food this year and 0 units of clothing. If Texia devotes of all of its resources to clothing production this year, it can produce 500 units of clothing and 0 units of food. Urbania can either produce 500 units of food this year and 0 units of clothing, or it can produce 200 units of clothing this year and 0 units of food. _____ has the comparative advantage in the production of clothing and _____ has the comparative advantage in the production of food.

  a. Texia; Texia   c. Urbania; Texia

  b. Texia; Urbania   d. Urbania; Urbania

19. Suppose there are two countries, Texia and Urbania, that produce food and clothing and currently do not trade. Both countries have linear production possibility frontiers. Texia, if it devotes all of its resources to food production can produce 1,000 units of food this year and 0 units of clothing. If Texia devotes of all of its resources to clothing production this year, it can produce 500 units of clothing and 0 units of food. Urbania can either produce 500 units of food this year and 0 units of clothing, or it can produce 200 units of clothing this year and 0 units of food. Each country devotes half of its resources to the production of food and half of its resources to the production of clothing. Total clothing production is equal to _____ and total food production is equal to _____ .

  a. 600; 500   c. 100; 250

  b. 250; 500   d. 350; 750

20. Suppose there are two countries, Texia and Urbania, that produce food and clothing and initially do not trade. Both countries have linear production possibility frontiers. Texia, if it devotes all of its resources to food production can produce 1,000 units of food this year, and 0 units of clothing. If Texia devotes of all of its resources to clothing production this year, it can produce 500 units of clothing and 0 units of food. Urbania can either produce 500 units of food this year and 0 units of clothing or it can produce 200 units of clothing this year and 0 units of food. Suppose that Texia and Urbania decide to specialize and trade. If Texia increases its clothing production to a total of 400 units, how many units of food will Texia be able to produce if it is productively efficient?
a. 100 units c. 300 units
b. 200 units d. 400 units

21. Specialization and trade benefits
a. usually only one of the trading partners.
b. the wealthier country more than the poorer country.
c. the poorer country more than the wealthier country.
d. both countries if they specialize according to their comparative advantage.

22. Which of the following statements is true about positive economics?
I. Positive economics is about how the world should work.
II. Positive economics is about how the world works.
III. Positive economics is descriptive.
a. Statements I, II, and III are all true.
b. Statements I and III are true.
c. Statements II and III are true.
d. Statement II is true.

23. Which of the following statements is an example of normative economics?
I. The United States should pass a value-added tax, since this is a tax that will work best for the country.
II. A value-added tax will add $10 billion to the administrative costs of the U.S. tax system.
III. A value-added tax will increase the economic burden of taxes on poor people by 15%.
a. Statements I, II, and III are all examples of normative economics.
b. Statements I and III are examples of normative economics.
c. Statements I and II are examples of normative economics.
d. Statement I is an example of normative economics.

ANSWER KEY

Answers to Problems and Exercises

1. The map is an example of a model because it simplifies the real world while trying to enable the user to better understand that world. It simplifies the real world by leaving out many things—for example, your map may only show the main roads in your community, or it might leave out major landmarks that you might find helpful, such as park and school names. The map is helpful to you provided it enables you to get from your starting point to your destination. Although it simplifies the real-world, it should still provide key insights into that world.

2. Technology and the time period are being held constant so that we can focus on the effect of a change in the level of resources on this economy's production possibility frontier. If resources increase, we would expect the production possibility frontier to shift out because the economy should be able to produce more of both goods now that there are more resources to work with.

3. **a.**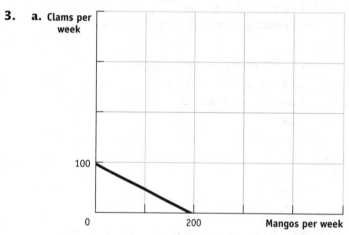

    b. An increase in the time period, holding everything else constant, increases the level of production.

    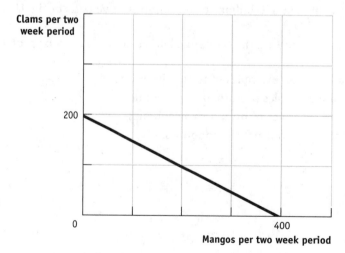

c. The invention of the clam rake shifts the production possibilities frontier out along the clam axis since it is now possible to produce more clams in the same time period.

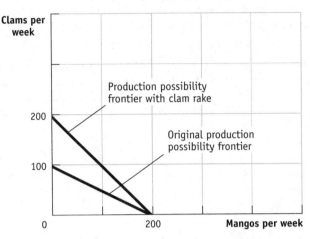

d. Technological change shifts the production possibility frontier away from the origin and therefore results in the possibility of greater production of both goods.

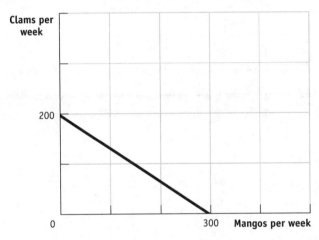

4. a. The opportunity cost of harvesting a clam is measured in terms of the number of mangoes you must give up when you harvest a clam. In the original example, you must give up 2 mangoes for every clam you harvest.

b. The opportunity cost of collecting a mango is measured in terms of the number of clams you must give up when you collect a mango. In the original example, you must give up ½ clam for every mango you collect.

c. The slope of the production possibility frontier is –2 (remember, you calculate this as the rise/run, or the change in the y-variable divided by the change in the x-variable). The slope tells us what the change in the y-variable is for a 1-unit change in the x-variable. In this case, the slope tells us what the change in the number of clams is for a 1-unit change in mangoes: when mango collection increases by 1 unit, then clam harvesting decreases by 2 units; when mango collection decreases by 1 unit, then clam harvesting increases by 2 units. The negative sign of the slope tells us that these two variables move in opposite directions: an increase in mangoes requires a decrease in clams, or a decrease in mangoes requires an increase in clams. The slope measure tells us what the opportunity cost of one more mango is, since mangoes are measured on the horizontal axis in this example. If we take the reciprocal of the slope (in this case, $-\frac{1}{2}$) it would give us the opportunity cost of producing one more unit of the good on the y-axis. In this case harvesting one more clam has an opportunity cost of $\frac{1}{2}$ mango since that is the amount of mangoes we must give up to get one more clam.

d. The invention of the clam rake changed the slope of the production possibility frontier from -2 to -1 and therefore changed the opportunity cost of producing both goods. The opportunity cost of collecting a mango is now 1 clam and the opportunity cost of harvesting one clam is 1 mango.

5. a.

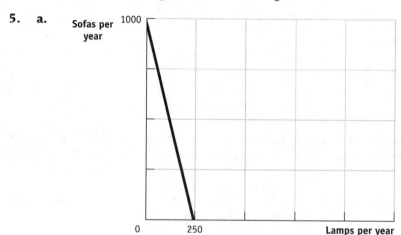

b.

Combination	Number of lamps possible	Number of sofas possible
A	0	1,000
B	50	800
C	125	500
D	200	200
E	225	100
F	250	0

c. The slope of the production possibility frontier is -4 (you can find this by looking at the rise/run, or in this case, $-1000/250$).

d. The opportunity cost of producing one more sofa is $\frac{1}{4}$ lamp. (Hint: remember that because sofas are measured on the y-axis, you can find the opportunity cost by taking the reciprocal of the slope measure.)

e. The opportunity cost of producing one more lamp is 4 sofas. (Hint: remember that because lamps are measured on the x-axis, you can find the opportunity cost by using the slope measure.)

f. The y-intercept is 1,000, since if Orange uses all of its resources and technology to produce sofas, this is the maximum number of sofas it can produce in a year.

g. The equation for Orange's production possibility frontier is $S = 1,000 - 4L$. You can verify that all the combinations work in this equation by substituting the value of the number of lamps in one of the combinations and verifying that the equation generates the number of sofas you found in the table. For example, if L equals 225, then $S = 1,000 - 4(225)$ or $S = 100$ (the value you found in the table).

6.   a. To draw the production possibility frontier, you first need to identify the number of hours of labor that Utopia has available. Since it takes 3 hours of labor to produce 2 widgets (or 1.5 hours of labor to produce 1 widget) and 4 hours of labor to produce 1 gadget, you will find it helpful to select an amount of time that is divisible by both three and four. So, for instance, 12 hours would work, as would 120 hours, or 240 hours, or an infinite number of other numbers that are divisible by both three and four. For our sketch let's suppose that there are 120 hours of labor available to Utopia and that its citizens can produce either widgets or gadgets or some combination of the two goods. If they devote all of their labor time to widget production, they can produce 80 widgets since (120 hours of labor/3 hours of labor) × (2 widgets) = 80 widgets. If they devote all of their labor time to gadget production, they can produce 30 gadgets since (120 hours of labor/4 hours of labor) × (1 gadget) = 30 gadgets. The graph below illustrates Utopia's production possibility frontier.

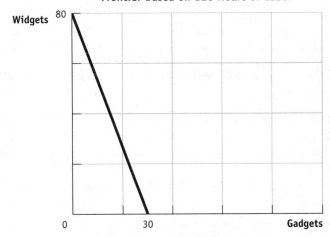

Utopia's Production Possibility Frontier Based on 120 Hours of Labor

The values of your intercepts will be different depending on the number of hours of labor you assume Utopia has, but the slope of the production possibility frontier should be the same as the one drawn above.

b. The slope of the production possibility frontier is –8/3.

c. The opportunity cost of producing an additional widget in Utopia is 3/8 gadget.

d. The opportunity cost of producing an additional gadget in Utopia is 8/3 widget.

7.   a. You must first decide how much labor Jonesville has so that you can calculate the maximum amount of widgets and gadgets Jonesville can produce. Since you know gadgets take 2 hours of labor and widgets take 5 hours of labor, you will want to pick a number of hours that is divisible by both two and five. For example, 10 hours would work, or 100 hours, or 20 hours, or 2,000 hours—there is an infinite number of labor quantities that would work in constructing this production possibility frontier.

b.

Production Possibility Frontier for Jonesville Based on 120 Hours of Labor

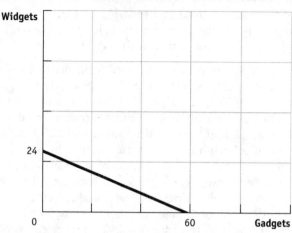

c. The slope of the production possibility frontier is −24/60, or −4/10, or −0.4.

d. Recall that you can use the slope measure to quickly find the opportunity cost of producing one more unit of the good measured on the x-axis. To produce one more gadget, you must give up 0.6 widget, therefore the opportunity cost of an additional gadget is 0.6 widget.

e. Recall that you can use the reciprocal of the slope measure to quickly find the opportunity cost of producing one more unit of the good measured on the y-axis. To produce one more widget, you must give up 1/0.4 gadgets, therefore the opportunity cost of an additional widget is 2.5 gadgets.

f. If Jonesville has an increase in the amount of labor available to use in producing gadgets and widgets, it can produce more gadgets and more widgets. That is, Jonesville's production possibility frontier will shift out from the origin. But the slope of the new production possibility frontier will be the same as the one drawn based upon 120 hours of labor, thus the opportunity cost of producing widgets or gadgets will not change for Jonesville.

8. a.

Production Possibility Frontier for Smithtown

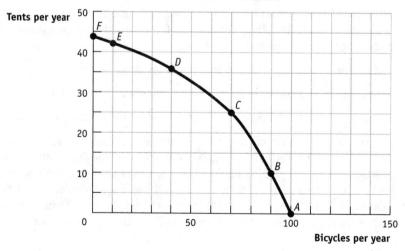

b. The opportunity cost of moving from point *C* to point *B* is measured in terms of the number of units of production you give up. In this case you give up 15 tents, so this is the opportunity cost.

c. The opportunity cost of moving from point *C* to point *D* is 30 bicycles.

d. Smithtown's resources are not equally well suited to produce bicycles and tents. If Smithtown initially devotes all of its resources to producing bicycles, then some of its resources that are currently going into the production of bicycles are not particularly productive at producing bicycles. Smithtown can move some of these resources away from bicycle production and into tent production without decreasing its bicycle production significantly. However, as Smithtown decides to produce more and more tents, this will eventually require moving resources that are well suited to bicycle production into tent production where they are less productive. This specialization of resources results in a production possibility frontier that is bowed out from the origin.

9. a. This economy's production possibility frontier must be bowed out from the origin if the economy's resources are specialized: this implies that the opportunity cost of producing more and more units of one of the goods increases because increased production of this good requires the economy to use resources that would be more productive producing the other good.

b. The opportunity cost of producing more and more units of the good will increase due to the shape of the production possibility frontier, which is bowed out from the origin.

c. To be productively efficient, this economy must be producing at a point that is located on the production possibility frontier.

d. To be allocatively efficient, this economy must be producing at a point that represents the optimal mix of these two goods for the economy.

e. To be efficient, the economy must be both productively and allocatively efficient—that is, it must produce not only on the production possibility frontier, but it must also produce the right mix of goods.

10. Economists believe that specialization and trade based on comparative advantage results in a greater level of production than is possible without specialization and trade. Economists argue that, so long as opportunity costs differ, specialization in the production of the good that has a lower opportunity cost will enhance the overall level of production available and will therefore be beneficial.

11. a.

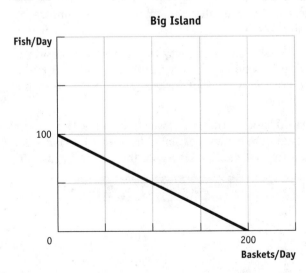

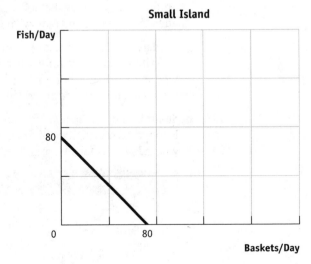

b. The slope of Big Island's production possibility frontier is –1/2.

c. The slope of Small Island's production possibility frontier is –1.

d. The opportunity cost of producing an additional basket for Big Island is ½ fish. The opportunity cost of producing an additional basket for Small Island is 1 fish. Big Island can produce an additional basket at a lower opportunity cost than can Small Island.

e. The opportunity cost of producing an additional fish for Big Island is 2 baskets. The opportunity cost of producing an additional fish for Small Island is 1 basket. Small Island can produce an additional fish at a lower opportunity cost than can Big Island.

f. Big Island should specialize in producing baskets, since it can produce baskets at a lower opportunity cost than can Small Island.

g. Small Island should specialize in producing fish, since it can produce fish at a lower opportunity cost than can Big Island.

12. a. Big Island is producing at a productively efficient point because 80 fish and 40 baskets lies on its linear production possibility frontier.

b. Small Island is producing at a productively efficient point because 30 fish and 50 baskets lies on its linear production possibility frontier.

c. Big Island will be able to produce 75 fish. The easiest way to calculate this answer is to write an equation for Big Island's production possibility frontier: $F = (-1/2)B + 100$, where F is the symbol for fish and B is the symbol for baskets. Thus, if $B = 50$ then F must equal 75 according to this equation.

d. Small Island will be able to produce 40 baskets. The easiest way to calculate this answer is to write an equation for Small Island's production possibility frontier: $F = (-1)B + 80$, where F stands for fish and B stands for baskets. Thus, if $F = 40$ then B must equal 40.

e.

New production	Fish	Baskets
Big Island	75	50
Small Island	40	40
Total production	115	90

f. Specialization and trade is beneficial to both islands since the total production of fish is increased to 115 fish instead of the original 110. This change in fish production does not change the level of basket production. Thus, the two islands can increase the amount of goods available to them if they specialize according to their comparative advantage and then trade with one another.

g. Big Island will be able to produce 85 fish. The easiest way to calculate this answer is to write an equation for Big Island's production possibility frontier: $F = (-1/2)B + 100$, where F is the symbol for fish and B is the symbol for baskets. Thus, if $B = 30$ then F must equal 85 according to this equation.

h. Small Island will be able to produce 60 baskets. The easiest way to calculate this answer is to write an equation for Small Island's production possibility frontier: $F = (-1)B + 80$, where F stands for fish and B stands for baskets. Thus, if $F = 20$ then B must equal 60.

i.

New production	Fish	Baskets
Big Island	85	30
Small Island	20	60
Total production	105	90

j. Specialization and trade is not beneficial to both islands in this example since the total production of fish decreased to 105 fish instead of the original 110. This change in fish production does not change the level of basket production. Thus, the two islands decrease the amount of goods available to them when they specialize and trade with one another without paying attention to their comparative advantage.

k. For specialization and trade to be beneficial for two countries they must have different opportunity costs of production and they must also specialize according to their comparative advantage.

13. a.

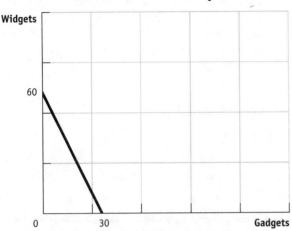

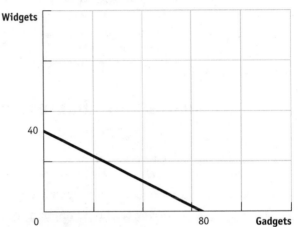

b.

Initial production	Widgets	Gadgets
Bob	30	15
Jane	20	40
Total production	50	55

c. Bob's opportunity cost of producing an additional gadget is 2 widgets, whereas Jane's opportunity cost of producing an additional gadget is ½ widget. Jane can produce gadgets at a lower opportunity cost than can Bob.

d. Bob's opportunity cost of producing an additional widget is ½ gadget, whereas Jane's opportunity cost of producing an additional widget is 2 gadgets. Bob can produce widgets at a lower opportunity cost than can Jane.

e. Bob should specialize in producing widgets.

f. Jane should specialize in producing gadgets.

g.

Initial production	Widgets	Gadgets
Bob	46	7
Jane	10	60
Total production	56	67

14. a. Positive: this statement is a forecast of the tax revenue from the gasoline tax. It is verifiable and hence, positive.

b. Positive: this is also a forecast, and although it may be wrong, it can be verified through the data once the data is available.

c. Normative: this is a value statement that reflects one person's viewpoint of the way the world should work. It is not refutable since it reflects a person's opinion and not a set of facts.

d. Positive: this statement can be tested for its accuracy.

e. Normative: this statement reflects the opinions of the speaker.

f. Positive: this is a forecast.

15. Positive economics is descriptive, whereas normative economics is prescriptive—that is, positive economics is objective and expresses how the world works, while normative economics is subjective and expresses how the world should work. Economists may differ because of positive economics: they may use different models with different assumptions that lead to different conclusions. Economists may also disagree over normative economics: economists may not share the same values and will therefore reach different conclusions about how the world should work. Economists can evaluate alternative policies in terms of their efficiency at reaching stated goals.

Answers to Chapter Review Questions

1. **Answer c.** This is a simple definition of "model."

2. **Answer b.** This is not a true statement since there are an infinite number of possible models. Models can vary, for example, due to their focus of attention, their underlying assumptions, and their degree of complexity.

3. **Answer c.** The assumption "other things equal" implies that everything else is being held equal or constant while considering the effect of changing one variable. Answer (a) is incorrect since different economic models have different economic variables. Answer (b) is incorrect since different variables may be varied in different models or even within a particular model. Answer (d) is incorrect with regard to the other-things-equal assumption, which is used to isolate the effect of a single change on the rest of the model.

4. **Answer a.** Mike can produce 1,000 pounds of potatoes and 0 pounds of tomatoes a year or he can produce 2,000 pounds of tomatoes and 0 pounds of potatoes a year. His resources do not allow him to produce a combination of 1,000 pounds of potatoes and 2,000 pounds of tomatoes in a year. Thus, answer (a) is not feasible, while answers (b) and (c) are feasible. Answer (d) is also feasible since if Mike devotes half of his resources this year to producing potatoes and half of his resources this year to producing tomatoes, he will be able to produce 500 pounds of potatoes and 1,000 pounds of tomatoes this year.

5. **Answer a.** Any combination of production of potatoes and tomatoes that lies on Mike's linear production possibility frontier is an efficient combination. An inefficient combination must lie inside his production possibility frontier. His linear production possibility frontier includes the two points (1,000 pounds of potatoes, 0 pounds of tomatoes) and (0 pounds of potatoes, 2,000 pounds of tomatoes), and we can use these two points to write an equation for his production possibility frontier. If potatoes are measured on the y-axis and are denoted by P, and tomatoes are measured on the x-axis and denoted by T, then Mike's production possibility frontier is $P = 1,000 - \frac{1}{2} T$. Substitute the number of tomatoes provided in each answer into this equation to calculate the number of potatoes Mike can produce when he produces that level of tomatoes. Thus, for answer (b), when Mike produces 1,000 pounds of tomatoes, the equation states that he will be able to produce 500 pounds of potatoes, which is the number of potatoes given in answer (b). Answers (c) and (d) also fit the equation. Thus, answers (b), (c), and (d) all identify production combinations that are on the production possibility frontier. But answer (a) does not fit the equation: when Mike produces 500 pounds of tomatoes, the equation says that he will be able to produce 750 pounds of potatoes, while answer (a) says that he will produce 500 pounds of potatoes. The combination in answer (a) is a combination that lies inside Mike's production possibility frontier.

6. **Answer c.** Since in Utopia 4 widgets can be produced in the same amount of labor time as 3 gadgets, then 1 widget can be produced in the same amount of labor time as ¾ gadget. Thus, the opportunity cost of producing 1 widget is measured by the number of gadgets that must be given up, in this case ¾ of a gadget.

7. **Answer a.** Jonesville uses all of its labor to produce widgets. With 100 hours of labor, it can produce 10 widgets since the production of each widget takes 10 hours of labor.

8. **Answer b.** When Jonesville devotes 50 hours of labor to widget production, it can produce 5 widgets. When Jonesville devotes 50 hours of labor to gadget production, it can produce 10 gadgets. Thus, when Jonesville divides its labor evenly between widget and gadget production, the maximum amount of gadgets it can produce is 10 while the maximum amount of widgets it can produce is 5.

9. **Answer c.** Since the number of hours needed to produce each widget and each gadget has not changed in Jonesville, the opportunity cost of producing these goods does not change. Jonesville does see its linear production possibility frontier shift out due to the increase in the amount of available labor, but the new production possibility frontier has the same slope as the original production possibility frontier.

10. **Answer b.** A combination of gadgets and widgets is not feasible for Jonesville if that combination lies outside of its production possibility frontier. If gadgets are measured on the vertical axis and widgets are measured on the horizontal axis, then the production possibility frontier can be written as $G = 20 - 2W$, where G is the symbol for gadgets and W is the symbol for widgets. Answer (a) lies on the production possibility frontier since $G = 20 - 2(8) = 4$. Answer (c) lies on the production possibility frontier since $G = 20 - 2(6) = 8$. Answer (d) lies on the production possibility frontier since $G = 20 - 2(10) = 0$. Answer (b) does not lie on the production possibility frontier nor does it lie inside the production possibility frontier: $G = 20 - 2(7) = 6$, but the answer in (b) has gadgets equal to 7 and not 6. The combination of 7 widgets and 7 gadgets lies beyond the production possibility frontier for Jonestown.

11. **Answer b.** Utopia plans to devote 60 hours of labor to the production of widgets. If the production of 4 widgets takes one hour of labor time, then 60 hours of labor is enough labor to produce 240 widgets.

12. **Answer c.** The opportunity cost of moving from point D to point E is measured by what Suburbia must give up when it makes this move. At point D, Suburbia has 50 pounds of butter, while at point E, Suburbia has only 30 pounds of butter; thus, when moving from point D to point E, Suburbia must give up 20 pounds of butter. Notice that when measuring the opportunity cost of moving from one point of a production possibility frontier to another point on the production possibility frontier, it is important to provide the unit of measurement as well as the numerical value.

13. **Answer b.** The opportunity cost of moving from point D to point B is measured by what Suburbia must give up when it makes this move. In this case, Suburbia is giving up guns to get more butter. Moving from point D to point B, Suburbia gives up 20 guns.

14. **Answer d.** From the table, we know that Suburbia can produce 50 pounds of butter and 30 guns (point D on the production possibility frontier). When Suburbia produces 50 pounds of butter and 20 guns, it is producing at a point that is inside its production possibility frontier and hence it is producing at a feasible but inefficient point, since the point does not lie on the production possibility frontier. Alternatively, Suburbia could produce 20 guns and 65 pounds of butter (point C) according to the table. Its choice of 20 guns and 50 pounds of butter is also not efficient from this perspective.

15. **Answer b.** Allocative efficiency focuses on producing the right mix of goods and services. Without additional information, we cannot identify which point is the allocatively efficient point on the production possibility frontier. Productively efficient refers to the

maximum production feasible from the available resources. All points on the production possibility frontier are productively efficient.

16. **Answer b.** This is true by definition.

17. **Answer a.** Given the resources that Texia and Urbania have this year, Texia is able to produce more food and more clothing than Urbania this year.

18. **Answer b.** For every unit of clothing that Texia produces it must give up 2 units of food, while for Urbania the opportunity cost of producing 1 unit of clothing is 2.5 units of food. Thus, the opportunity cost of producing clothing is lower for Texia than it is for Urbania. Texia therefore has the comparative advantage in producing clothing while Urbania has the comparative advantage in producing food.

19. **Answer d.** When Texia devotes half of its resources to food production and half of its resources to clothing production, it can produce 500 units of food and 250 units of clothing. When Urbania devotes half of its resources to food production and half of its resources to clothing production, it can produce 250 units of food and 100 units of clothing. Thus, under this arrangement, total food production is 750 units and total clothing production is 350 units.

20. **Answer b.** Texia's production possibility frontier can be written as $F = 1,000 - 2C$, where F is the number of units of food and C is the number of units of clothing. When Texia produces 400 units of clothing, the maximum amount of food it can produce is 200 units: $F = 1,000 - 2(400) = 200$.

21. **Answer d.** The logic of comparative advantage is that both trading parties benefit through specialization and trade based on their comparative advantage.

22. **Answer c.** Positive economics is objective, factual, and can be subject to proof. In contrast, normative economics is subjective and expresses what ought to happen or what should happen. Statements II and III are both statements that describe positive economics, since positive economics describes and analyzes how the world works.

23. **Answer d.** Normative economics is subjective and value oriented. Both statements II and III are positive statements that can be evaluated as to their factual accuracy. Statement I is a normative statement since it expresses someone's subjective opinion and therefore cannot be proven true or false.

chapter **3**

Supply and Demand

■ BEFORE YOU READ THE CHAPTER

Summary

Chapter 3 describes a competitive market and then develops the model of supply and demand for this type of market. The chapter describes the demand and supply curves, explains the distinction between movements along a curve versus a shift of the curve, discusses the primary determinants of supply and demand, and defines the meaning of equilibrium in this model. The chapter also discusses how a market eliminates shortages and surpluses through changes in price and quantity so that the market returns to its equilibrium.

Chapter Objectives

Objective #1. A competitive market is a market that has many buyers and many sellers of the same good or service. No buyer or seller can affect the price of the good or service in a competitive market.

Objective #2. A demand schedule shows the relationship between possible prices of the good or service and the quantity of that good or service demanded at those different prices. As the price increases, the quantity demanded decreases: price and quantity demanded are inversely related to one another. A demand curve is the graphical representation of the demand schedule. The demand curve is drawn with the price of the good on the vertical axis and the quantity demanded on the horizontal axis. Demand curves usually slope downward: this is referred to as the "law of demand." Demand refers to the entire demand curve, while quantity demanded refers to a specific quantity demanded at a specific price.

Objective #3. The quantity demanded depends on many factors, but the primary determinants of the quantity demanded are the price of the good, the changes in the price of related goods, and changes in income, tastes, expectations, and the number of consumers. A change in the price of the good, holding everything else constant, will cause a movement along the curve and a change in the quantity demanded. A change in any other determinant of demand, holding everything else constant, will cause a shift in the demand curve. At any given price, the quantity demanded will increase when demand shifts to the right and decrease when demand shifts to the left.

Objective #4. The chapter discusses several kinds of specific types of goods.

- Two goods are substitutes if a decrease in the price of one of the goods causes a decrease in the demand for the other good. As the price of the first good decreases, people increase the quantity of this good they demand, which results in a reduction in the overall demand for the other, substitute good. Two goods are complements if a decrease in the price of one of the goods causes an increase in the demand for the other good. As the price of the first good decreases, people increase the quantity of this good they demand, which results in an increase in the overall demand for the other, complementary, good.

- A good is a normal good if a decrease in income causes a decrease in the demand for the good. A good is an inferior good if a decrease in income causes an increase in the demand for the good.

Objective #5. A market demand curve illustrates the combined quantity demanded by all consumers in the market. The market demand curve is found by horizontally adding together the individual demand curves. At each price the quantity demanded by each individual is added together to give the total quantity demanded at that price.

Objective #6. The quantity of a good or service supplied by a producer depends on the price producers are offered for their product. The supply schedule illustrates the relationship between various prices and the quantity of the good supplied at each of these prices. Generally speaking, the quantity supplied increases as the price increases, holding everything else constant. A supply curve is the graphical representation of a supply schedule. Usually a supply curve is upward sloping: the quantity supplied increases as the price increases.

Objective #7. The quantity supplied depends on many factors, but the primary determinants of the quantity supplied are the price of the good, the price of its inputs, the price of related goods, and changes in technology, expectations, and the number of producers. A change in the price of the good causes a movement along the supply curve; a change in one of the other supply determinants, other than price, causes a shift in the supply curve. A rightward shift in the supply curve is an increase in supply; a leftward shift in the supply curve is a decrease in supply. An increase in the price of inputs, holding everything else constant, will cause a decrease in supply. This means that the supply curve shifts to the left, and at every price the quantity supplied is now less than it was initially.

Objective #8. Two goods are substitutes in production when an increase in the price of one of these goods results in greater production of this good and reduced production of the other good. Two goods are complements in production when an increase in the price of one of these goods results in greater production of both goods.

Objective #9. The market supply curve is found by horizontally adding together the individual supply curves. At each price, the quantity supplied by each firm is added together to create the market supply curve. As the number of individual producers increases there is an increase in supply.

Objective #10. A competitive market is in equilibrium at the price at which the quantity demanded equals the quantity supplied. This price is called the equilibrium price. The quantity associated with this equilibrium price is called the equilibrium quantity. The equilibrium price is the market-clearing price, since at this price the quantity demanded equals the quantity supplied. The equilibrium in a market occurs at the point of intersection between the demand and supply curves.

Objective #11. At a given price, if the quantity supplied of the good is greater than the quantity demanded of the good, there is a surplus, or excess supply, in the market. If there is excess supply, prices will fall until the quantity supplied equals the quantity demanded. At a given price, if the quantity supplied of the good is less than the quantity demanded of the good, there is a shortage, or excess demand, in the market. If there is excess demand, prices will rise until the quantity supplied equals the quantity demanded.

Objective #12. A shift in the demand curve, holding everything else constant, causes a change in the equilibrium price and quantity. The shift in the demand curve causes a movement along the supply curve. An increase in demand leads to a rise in both the equilibrium price and equilibrium quantity. A decrease in demand leads to a fall in both the equilibrium price and equilibrium quantity. A shift in the supply curve, holding everything else constant, causes a change in the equilibrium price and quantity. The shift in the supply curve causes a movement along the demand curve. An increase in supply leads to a fall in the equilibrium price and a rise in the equilibrium quantity. A decrease in supply leads to a rise in the equilibrium price and a fall in the equilibrium quantity.

Objective #13. If demand and supply both change simultaneously but without specific information about the relative magnitude of these changes, there will be ambiguity about the value of either the new equilibrium price or the new equilibrium quantity. The four possible outcomes of these changes are summarized in Table 3.1.

Table 3.1

Shift in demand	Shift in supply	Effect on equilibrium price	Effect on equilibrium quantity
Right	Left	Increase	Ambiguous
Right	Right	Ambiguous	Increase
Left	Left	Ambiguous	Decrease
Left	Right	Decrease	Ambiguous

Key Terms

Notes

competitive market a market in which there are many buyers and sellers of the same good or service, none of whom can influence the price at which the good or service is sold.

supply and demand model a model of how a *competitive market* works.

demand schedule a list or table showing how much of a good or service consumers will want to buy at different prices.

quantity demanded the actual amount of a good or service consumers are willing to buy at some specific price.

demand curve a graphical representation of the *demand schedule*, showing the relationship between quantity demanded and price.

law of demand a higher price for a good or service, other things equal, leads people to demand a smaller quantity of that good or service.

shift of the demand curve a change in the *quantity demanded* at any given price, represented graphically by the change of the original *demand curve* to a new position, denoted by a new demand curve.

Key Terms *(continued)*

movement along the demand curve a change in the *quantity demanded* of a good that results from a change in the price of that good.

substitutes pairs of goods for which a rise in the price of one of the goods leads to an increase in the demand for the other good.

complements pairs of goods for which a rise in the price of one good leads to a decrease in the demand for the other good.

normal good a good for which a rise in income increases the demand for that good—the "normal" case.

inferior good a good for which a rise in income decreases the demand for the good.

individual demand curve a graphical representation of the relationship between *quantity demanded* and price for an individual consumer.

quantity supplied the actual amount of a good or service producers are willing to sell at some specific price.

supply schedule a list or table showing how much of a good or service producers will supply at different prices.

supply curve a graphical representation of the *supply schedule*, showing the relationship between *quantity supplied* and price.

shift of the supply curve a change in the *quantity supplied* of a good or service at any given price, represented graphically by the change of the original *supply curve* to a new position, denoted by a new supply curve.

movement along the supply curve a change in the *quantity supplied* of a good that results from a change in the price of that good.

input a good or service used to produce another good or service.

individual supply curve a graphical representation of the relationship between *quantity supplied* and price for an individual producer.

equilibrium price the price at which the market is in *equilibrium*, that is, the quantity of a good or service demanded equals the quantity of that good or service supplied; also referred to as the *market-clearing price*.

equilibrium quantity the quantity of a good or service bought and sold at the *equilibrium* (or *market-clearing*) *price*.

market-clearing price the price at which the market is in *equilibrium*, that is, the quantity of a good or service demanded equals the quantity of that good or service supplied; also referred to as the *equilibrium price*.

surplus the excess of a good or service that occurs when the quantity supplied exceeds the quantity demanded; surpluses occur when the price is above the *equilibrium price*.

shortage the insufficiency of a good or service that occurs when the quantity demanded exceeds the quantity supplied; shortages occur when the price is below the *equilibrium price*.

AFTER YOU READ THE CHAPTER

Tips

Tip #1. A full understanding of this chapter is critical for your study of economics. The model of supply and demand is used repeatedly in a variety of settings throughout the remainder of this course. You should work with the material in this chapter until you are confident that you know it well and that you understand the techniques, vocabulary, and information in the chapter. Pay particular attention to the distinction between supply and the quantity supplied, demand and the quantity demanded, and shifts of a curve versus movements along a curve. You also should know the determinants of demand and the determinants of supply, and fully understand the meaning of equilibrium in a market and how to find the equilibrium price and equilibrium quantity.

Tip #2. A demand curve is usually downward sloping. The negative slope of a demand curve implies that the quantity demanded of a good or service is inversely related to its price. Another way to express this idea is that as the price of the good decreases, holding everything else constant, consumers will want to buy more units of the good. Figure 3.1 illustrates this law of demand: at P_1, Q_1 units of the good are demanded; as the price of the good falls from P_1 to P_2, the quantity demanded of the good increases from Q_1 to Q_2.

Figure 3.1

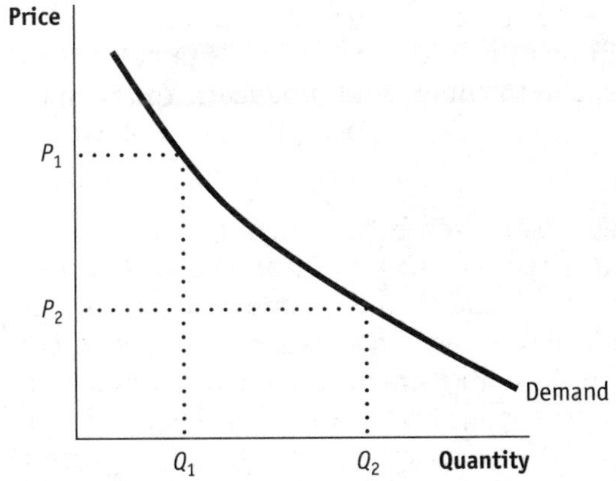

[Figure: Demand curve. Vertical axis labeled "Price" with P_1 above P_2; horizontal axis labeled "Quantity" with Q_1 to the left of Q_2. A downward-sloping curve labeled "Demand" passes through the points (Q_1, P_1) and (Q_2, P_2).]

Tip #3. A supply curve is usually upward sloping. The positive slope of a supply curve implies that the quantity supplied of a good or service is directly related to its price. Another way to express this idea is that as the price of the good decreases, holding everything else constant, producers will want to supply fewer units of the good. Figure 3.2 illustrates this idea: at P_1, Q_1 units of the good are supplied; as the price of the good falls from P_1 to P_2, the quantity supplied of the good decreases from Q_1 to Q_2.

Figure 3.2

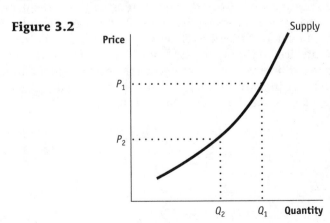

[Figure: Supply curve. Vertical axis labeled "Price" with P_1 above P_2; horizontal axis labeled "Quantity" with Q_2 to the left of Q_1. An upward-sloping curve labeled "Supply" passes through the points (Q_2, P_2) and (Q_1, P_1).]

Tip #4. A demand curve illustrates the relationship between the price of the good and the quantity demanded at each specific price. In drawing the demand curve, the other determinants of demand are held constant; this constancy is referred to as the other-things-equal assumption. This assumption allows economists to consider a change in a single variable while holding all other potentially important variables constant. In the examples throughout the remainder of the course, we typically consider a single change in a situation while holding the other variables constant. Students often struggle with this concept and have trouble working with the model of supply and demand because they do not limit themselves to considering a single change at a time.

Tip #5. Besides the price of the good, the quantity demanded of a good is affected by the following variables: changes in the price of related goods, changes in income, changes in tastes and preferences, changes in expectations, and changes in the number of consumers. You will need to know this list of variables as well as how each of these variables affects the demand curve.

Tip #6. A supply curve illustrates the relationship between the price of the good and the quantity supplied at each specific price. In drawing the supply curve, the other determinants of supply are held constant; this constancy is another example of the other-things-equal assumption.

Tip #7. Besides the price of the good, the quantity supplied of a good is affected by the following variables: changes in input prices, changes in the price of related goods, and changes in technology, expectations, and the number of producers. You need to know this list of variables as well as how each of these variables affects the supply curve.

Tip #8. Economists make a distinction between demand and the quantity demanded. The quantity demanded refers to a specific quantity associated with a specific price (as in Figure 3.1, where Q_1 is associated with P_1 and Q_2 is associated with P_2). Demand refers to the entire demand curve. Although this may sound like a matter of semantics, economists view this distinction as highly important. Economists make the same distinction between supply and the quantity supplied. The quantity supplied refers to a specific quantity associated with a specific price (as in Figure 3.2, where Q_1 is associated with P_1 and Q_2 is associated with P_2). Supply refers to the entire supply curve.

Tip #9. Economists also make a distinction between a movement along a curve and a shift of the curve. A movement along a curve is caused by a change in the good's price, while a shift in a curve is caused by a change in some variable other than the price of the good.

- Figure 3.3 illustrates this distinction for a demand curve. There is a movement from point A to point B when the price decreases from P_1 to P_2, and there is a shift in the demand curve from D_1 to D_2 due to a change in some other determinant of demand. A shift causes the quantity demanded of the good to change at every price—for example, at P_1 in Figure 3.3, the shift causes the quantity demanded to increase from Q_1 to Q_3 (compare point A to point C). Figure 3.3 illustrates an increase in demand when the demand curve shifts to the right from D_1 to D_2. A decrease in demand would be illustrated by the demand curve shifting to the left (in Figure 3.3 this would be a shift from D_2 to D_1).

Figure 3.3

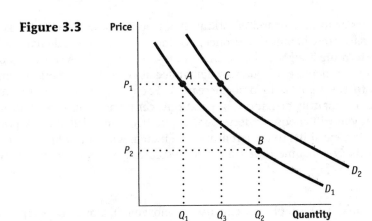

- Figure 3.4 illustrates this distinction for a supply curve. There is a movement from point A to point B when the price decreases from P_1 to P_2, and there is a shift in the supply curve from S_1 to S_2 due to a change in some other determinant of supply. A shift causes the quantity supplied of the good to change at every price—for example, at P_1 in Figure 3.4, the shift causes the quantity supplied to increase from Q_1 to Q_3 (compare point A to point C). Figure 3.4 illustrates an increase in supply when the supply curve shifts to the right from S_1 to S_2. A decrease in supply would be illustrated by the supply curve shifting to the left (in Figure 3.4 this would be a shift from S_2 to S_1).

Figure 3.4

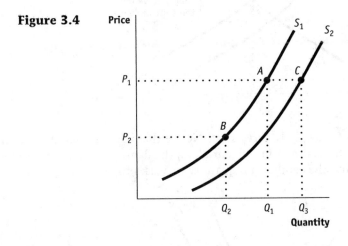

Tip #10. Students initially find it easier to understand the concepts of substitutes and complements if they think about concrete examples. (In Chapter 6 the concept of cross-price elasticity of demand will provide a formal way to determine if two goods are substitutes or complements.) For example, consider soft drinks and popcorn. Two different brands of soft drinks are substitutes: holding all other demand determinants constant, if the price of one brand increases, then the demand for the other soft drink will increase since it is now relatively cheaper and the two goods can easily serve as substitutes for one another. In contrast, if the price of soft drinks increases, holding everything else constant, then the demand for popcorn will decrease. Popcorn and soft drinks are consumed together: they are complements to one another, which implies that if one of these goods gets more expensive (and therefore, you move upward along that good's demand curve), the quantity demanded of that good decreases. This in turn leads to a decrease in the demand for the complementary good. Questions about substitutes and complements are far easier to interpret if you take the time to think of two specific goods.

Tip #11. You will find it easier to understand questions about normal and inferior goods if you think of specific examples. (In Chapter 6 the concept of income elasticity of demand will provide a formal way to determine if a good is a normal or an inferior good.) A normal good is a good that you will choose to increase the quantity demanded at every price as your income increases (demand shifts to the right as income increases). For example, as your income increases you will increase the quantity demanded of vacations, car travel, and recreation. An inferior good is a good that you will choose to decrease the quantity demanded at every price as your income increases (demand shifts to the left as income increases). For example, as your income increases you will likely consume fewer fast-food restaurant meals or generic pasta dinners.

Tip #12. A shift in the demand or supply curve causes a movement along the supply or demand curve. Figure 3.5 illustrates this idea for a demand curve shift. Notice that when demand shifts to the left (a decrease in demand) this causes a movement along the supply curve: the equilibrium price falls from P_1 to P_2 and the equilibrium quantity falls from Q_1 to Q_2.

Figure 3.5

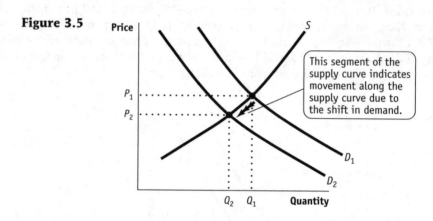

Figure 3.6 illustrates this idea for a supply curve shift. Notice that when supply shifts to the right (an increase in supply) this causes a movement along the demand curve: the equilibrium price falls from P_1 to P_2 and the equilibrium quantity increases from Q_1 to Q_2.

Figure 3.6

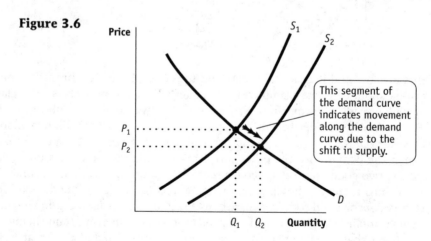

Tip #13. The market equilibrium occurs at the point of intersection of the demand and supply curves. Figure 3.7 indicates that equilibrium at point E, where the equilibrium price is P_1 and the equilibrium quantity is Q_1. If the price is greater than the equilibrium price, there is excess supply, or a surplus, in the market. Figure 3.7 illustrates a situation of excess supply at the price P_2. Note that at price P_2 the quantity supplied is Q_3, while the quantity demanded is Q_2. If the price is less than the equilibrium price, there is excess demand, or a shortage, in the market. Figure 3.7 illustrates a situation of excess demand at the price P_3. Note that at price P_3 the quantity supplied is Q_5, while the quantity demanded is Q_4.

Figure 3.7

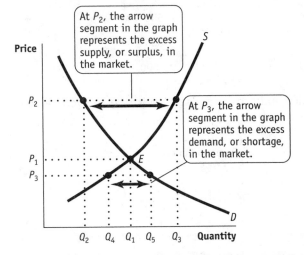

At P_2, the arrow segment in the graph represents the excess supply, or surplus, in the market.

At P_3, the arrow segment in the graph represents the excess demand, or shortage, in the market.

Tip #14. If you are given an equation for the demand curve and an equation for the supply curve, you can solve these two equations for the equilibrium price and equilibrium quantity. For example, suppose demand is given by the equation $P = 10 - Q$ and supply is given by the equation $P = Q$. To find the equilibrium, recall that in equilibrium the quantity demanded equals the quantity supplied; thus, $10 - Q = Q$, or the equilibrium quantity equals 5. Replace Q in either equation with 5 and you will find that the equilibrium price is 5.

Tip #15. Often a quick sketch of a demand and supply curve is all that you need to answer questions about the effect of a change in the market on the equilibrium price or equilibrium quantity. Practice drawing a quick representation of the demand and supply curves as you do this chapter's problems, recognizing that you do not always need a precisely plotted graph to find a solution or to guide your solution of a problem.

Tip #16. As always, if you are making a set of flash cards, make one for each new definition or concept and then review these cards (as well as the cards from the earlier chapters).

Problems and Exercises

1. Why is the assumption that there are many buyers and many sellers in a competitive market important?

2. You are given the following information about demand in the competitive market for bicycles.

Price per bicycle	Quantity of bicycles demanded per week
$100	0
80	100
60	200
40	500
20	800
0	1,000

a. Graph this demand schedule placing price on the vertical axis and quantity on the horizontal axis.

Demand Curve

Price

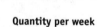

Quantity per week

b. Suppose the price is initially $40. If the price rises by $20, what happens to the quantity demanded?

c. Suppose the price is initially $40. If the price falls by $40, what happens to the quantity demanded?

3. For each of the following situations in the table below, fill in the missing information. First, determine whether the situation causes a shift or a movement along the demand curve; then, if it causes a shift, determine whether the demand curve shifts to the right or to the left.

Situation	Specified market	Movement or shift	Rightward or leftward shift in demand
People's income increases	Market for exotic vacations		
People's income decreases	Market for goods sold in secondhand shops		
Price of bicycles increases	Market for bicycles		
Price of tennis balls increases	Market for tennis racquets		
Price of movie tickets decreases	Popcorn at movie theaters		
Popularity of music-playing device increases	Market for music-playing device		
Popularity of branded clothing items decreases	Market for brand-name designer clothing		
Winter clothing to go on sale next month	Market for winter clothing		
Increase in urban residents	Market for apartments in urban areas		

4. Suppose a market has three consumers (this will simplify the work you need to do!): Joe, Maria, and Chao. Their demand schedules are given in the table below.

Price	Quantity demanded by Joe	Quantity demanded by Maria	Quantity demanded by Chao
$0	10	20	5
1	8	16	4
2	6	12	3
3	4	8	2
4	2	4	1

a. On the graphs below, sketch a graph of Joe's demand curve, Maria's demand curve, and Chao's demand curve. Then sketch the market demand curve based on the demand of these three individuals.

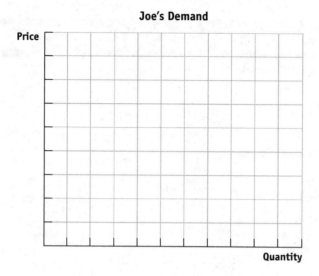

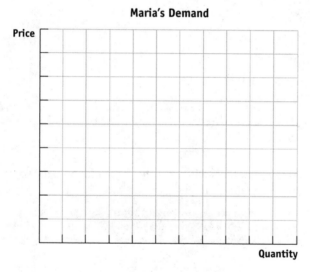

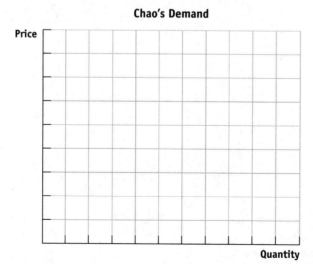

Market Demand

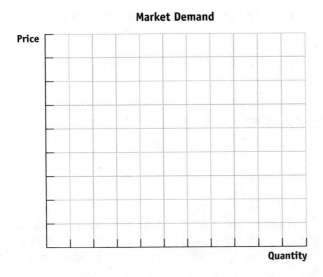

b. Summarize the market demand curve you found by filling in the following table.

Price	Quantity demanded in market
$0	
1	
2	
3	
4	

5. The following graph represents the supply curve for the production of widgets in Town Center.

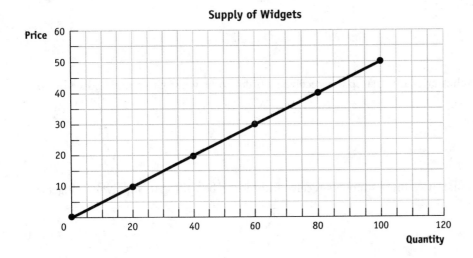

Supply of Widgets

a. At a price of $20, how many widgets are producers willing to supply?

b. At a price of $40, how many widgets are producers willing to supply?

c. Suppose there are ten widget producers in Town Center and that the price of widgets is $50. If each widget producer produces exactly the same amount of widgets as every other widget producer, how many widgets will each producer produce at this price?

d. Suppose the price is initially $30 but then falls to $20. What is the change in the quantity supplied?

e. Suppose the price is initially $30 but then increases to $50. What is the change in the quantity supplied?

f. What price must suppliers receive in order to be willing to supply 80 widgets?

g. What price must suppliers receive in order to be willing to supply 40 widgets?

h. What does the slope of a typical supply curve imply about the relationship between price and the quantity supplied?

6. For each of the following situations in the table below, fill in the missing information: first, determine whether the situation causes a shift or a movement along the supply curve; then, if it causes a shift, determine whether the supply curve shifts to the right or to the left.

Situation	Specified market	Movement or shift	Rightward or leftward shift in supply
Labor costs for air travel and cruise ships increase	Market for exotic vacations		
Prices of office equipment and phone service rise by 40%	Market for call center services		
Price of bicycles increases	Market for bicycles		
Price of leather boots increases	Market for beef products		
Price of leather boots increases	Market for leather belts		
New technology for music-playing device revealed	Market for music-playing devices		
Price of brand-name designer clothing increases	Market for brand-name designer clothing		
Stock market prices expected to fall next quarter	Stock market today		
Increase in number of coffee shop owners in the metro area	Market for coffee shops in the metro area		

7. The demand and supply schedules for Healthy Snacks, Inc., is provided in the table below.

Price	Quantity demanded	Quantity supplied
$ 0	1,000	0
10	800	125
20	600	275
30	400	400
40	200	550
50	0	675

a. Draw a sketch of the demand and supply curves for Healthy Snacks, Inc. Don't worry about drawing a precise graph but instead focus on drawing a simple rendering of the underlying relationships captured in the above table. This drawing should be accurate with regard to *x*-intercepts and *y*-intercepts and it should also indicate the point of equilibrium.

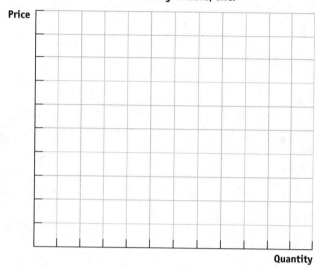

Demand and Supply Curves for Healthy Snacks, Inc.

b. From the table, what is the equilibrium price and the equilibrium quantity in this market? Indicate these on your graph.

c. Fill in the following table based on the data given to you. Assume that for each row in the table, the price is as given and that you are calculating the number of units of excess demand or excess supply. (Hint: some of the cells in your table will be left empty—for example, if there is excess supply, then there isn't excess demand.)

Price	Excess Demand	Excess Supply
$ 0		
10		
20		
30		
40		
50		

d. Why is a situation of excess demand referred to as a shortage? Explain using a simple graph to illustrate your answer.

e. Why is a situation of excess supply referred to as a surplus? Explain using a simple graph to illustrate your answer.

8. Use the following graph to answer this next set of questions. The graph illustrates the competitive market for garbage cans in Cleantopia.

Market for Garbage Cans in Cleantopia

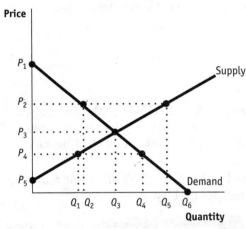

a. What is the equilibrium price in this market?

b. What is the equilibrium quantity in this market?

c. Suppose the current price of garbage cans in Cleantopia is P_2. Describe this market in detail and explain what you think will happen in this market.

d. Suppose the current price of garbage cans in Cleantopia is P_4. Describe this market in detail and explain what you think will happen in this market.

e. Suppose at the current market price the quantity demanded equals Q_4. Describe this market and identify the quantity supplied given this information. What do you expect will happen in this market?

f. Suppose at the current market price the quantity supplied equals Q_5. Describe this market and identify the quantity demanded given this information. What do you expect will happen in this market?

g. At what price is the quantity demanded equal to zero? What does it mean to have the quantity demanded equal to zero?

h. At what price is the quantity supplied equal to zero? What does it mean to have the quantity supplied equal to zero?

9. The competitive market for bicycles in Pedal City is described by the demand curve $P = 2,000 - 2Q$ and the supply curve $P = 6Q$. There are twenty bicycle manufacturers in Pedal City and each of these manufacturers produces the same number of bicycles as every other manufacturer.

a. Using the two equations for the demand and supply curves, fill in the following table describing the demand and supply schedules for bicycles in Pedal City.

Price	Quantity demanded	Quantity supplied
$ 0		
240		
480		
720		
960		
1,200		
1,440		
1,680		
1,920		

b. Examine the table you created in (a) and provide a range of prices that you expect the equilibrium price to fall between. Why do you expect the equilibrium price to fall within this range?

c. Sketch a graph of the demand and supply curves for bicycles in Pedal City.

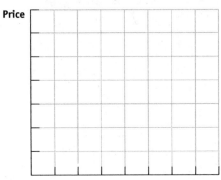

Market for Bicycles in Pedal City

Price

Quantity

d. If the current price for bicycles is $240, how many bicycles will be supplied in Pedal City and how many bicycles will a single manufacturer produce? At a price of $240, how many bicycles will be demanded? At a price of $240, is the market in equilibrium? Explain your answer.

e. If the current price for bicycles is $480, how many bicycles will be supplied in Pedal City and how many bicycles will a single manufacturer produce? At a price of $480, how many bicycles will be demanded? At a price of $480, is the market in equilibrium? Explain your answer.

f. If the current price for bicycles is $1,680, how many bicycles will be supplied in Pedal City and how many bicycles will a single manufacturer produce? At a price of $1,680, how many bicycles will be demanded? At a price of $1,680, is the market in equilibrium? Explain your answer.

g. Calculate the equilibrium price and the equilibrium quantity in the market for bicycles in Pedal City.

10. For each of the following situations, sketch a graph of the initial market demand (D_1) and supply (S_1) curves and indicate the initial equilibrium price (P_1) and equilibrium quantity (Q_1), and then sketch any changes in the market demand (D_2) and supply (S_2) curves and indicate the new equilibrium price (P_2) and equilibrium quantity (Q_2). For each situation, identify which curve(s) shift and whether or not there is a movement along the demand or supply curves.

a. The price of gasoline increases by 40 percent. What happens in the market for bicycles?

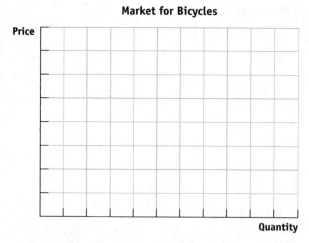

Market for Bicycles

b. The price of gasoline increases by 40 percent. What happens in the market for fuel-inefficient SUVs?

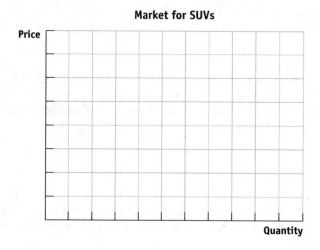

Market for SUVs

c. New technology for music-playing devices is developed. What happens in the market for music-playing devices?

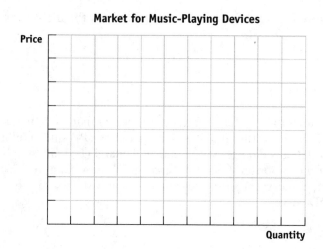

Market for Music-Playing Devices

d. The price of labor decreases. What happens in the market for fast-food restaurants?

Market for Fast-Food Restaurants

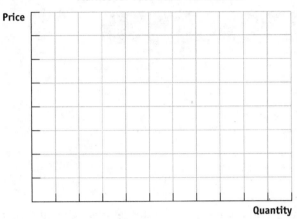

e. Income increases and good X is a normal good. What happens in the market for good X?

Market for Good X

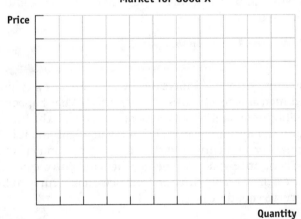

f. Income increases and good X is an inferior good. What happens in the market for good X?

Market for Good X

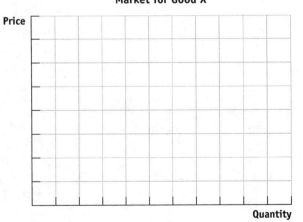

11. You are given the following information about the demand and supply schedules for gadgets in Micro Town. Assume that gadgets in Micro Town are produced in a competitive market.

Price	Quantity demanded	Quantity supplied
$ 0	100	0
2	80	20
4	60	40
6	40	60
8	20	80
10	0	100

a. From the above data, write an equation expressing the demand schedule and an equation expressing the supply schedule.

b. Using the equations you wrote in part (a), find the equilibrium price and the equilibrium quantity in this market.

c. Now suppose that the quantity demanded increases by 20 units at every price and that the quantity supplied increases by 40 units at every price. What happens to the equilibrium price and equilibrium quantity in this market relative to the initial levels of the equilibrium price and equilibrium quantity? (Hint: you might find it helpful to draw a sketch of the original demand curve and then the new demand curve to help guide you in your work. Then, once you have the new demand curve equation, you could draw a sketch of the original supply curve and the new supply curve to help you calculate the new supply curve equation.)

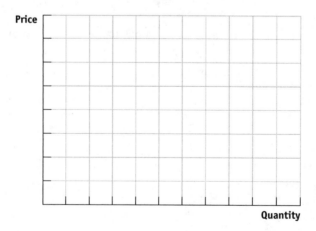

d. Now suppose that the quantity demanded increases by the same amount as in part (c), but that the quantity supplied increases by only 10 units at every price. What happens to the equilibrium price and the equilibrium quantity in this market relative to the initial levels of the equilibrium price and equilibrium quantity?

e. In parts (c) and (d), the demand and supply curves shifted to the right. If you knew the direction of these shifts, but did not know the size or magnitude of the shift, what would you know about the new equilibrium price and quantity?

12. Let's generalize the findings of question 11 for four different situations in which both the demand and supply curves shift at the same time. In each of these situations we assume that we know the direction of the shift but not the size of the shift. Fill in the table below for each of the possible situations. The first situation (the one in question 11) has already been done for you.

Situation	Effect on equilibrium price	Effect on equilibrium quantity
Demand shifts to the right and supply shifts to the right	May increase, decrease, or remain the same	Increases
Demand shifts to the left and supply shifts to the left		
Demand shifts to the right and supply shifts to the left		
Demand shifts to the left and supply shifts to the right		

BEFORE YOU TAKE THE TEST

Chapter Review Questions

1. Competitive markets are characterized as having
   a. many buyers and a single seller.
   b. many buyers and a few sellers.
   c. many buyers and many sellers.
   d. a few buyers and many sellers.

2. Sue goes to the store to purchase a bottle of shampoo. When she gets to the store she discovers that her brand of shampoo is on sale for $4 a bottle instead of the usual $5.99 per bottle. According to the law of demand, we can expect that
   a. Sue will purchase one bottle of shampoo.
   b. Sue will not purchase the shampoo.
   c. Sue will likely purchase more than one bottle of shampoo.
   d. Sue will substitute away from her usual brand of shampoo and instead purchase an alternative brand.

3. The law of demand states that the quantity demanded is an inverse function of its price. This means that
   a. as price increases, the quantity demanded decreases.
   b. as price increases, the quantity demanded increases.
   c. the demand curve shifts to the left with increases in price.
   d. the demand curve shifts to the right with increases in price.

4. Consider the market for mangos. Suppose researchers discover that eating mangos generates large health benefits. Which of the following statements is true?
   a. This discovery will not affect the market for mangos.
   b. This discovery will cause the demand for mangos to shift to the right.
   c. This discovery will cause the price of mangos to decrease due to a movement along the demand curve for mangos.
   d. This discovery will cause a movement along the demand curve for mangos.

5. Consider the demand curve for automobiles. An increase in the price of automobiles due to a shift in the supply curve will
   a. cause a movement along the demand curve for automobiles.
   b. result in an increase in the quantity of automobiles demanded.
   c. have no effect on the quantity of automobiles demanded since the change occurred on the supply side of the model.
   d. Answers (a) and (b) are both true statements.

6. The prices of flat-screen TVs are expected to fall next year. Which of the following statements about the market for flat-screen TVs this year are true?
   I. Consumers will decrease their demand for flat-screen TVs at all prices this year in anticipation of the decrease in flat-screen TV prices next year.
   II. Flat-screen TV prices today are likely to decrease due to these expectations.
   III. Flat-screen TV prices today are likely to increase due to these expectations.
   a. Statement I is true.
   b. Statement II is true.
   c. Statement III is true.
   d. Statements I and II are true.
   e. Statements I and III are true.

7. Peanut butter and jelly are considered to be complements in the diet of many people. Holding everything else constant, if the price of peanut butter increases, then the demand for
    a. peanut butter will shift to the left.
    b. peanut butter will shift to the right.
    c. jelly will shift to the left.
    d. jelly will shift to the right.

8. Ham and turkey are considered to be substitutes in the diet of many people. Holding everything else constant, if the price of ham decreases, then the demand for
    a. turkey will shift to the left.
    b. turkey will shift to the right.
    c. ham will shift to the left.
    d. ham will shift to the right.

9. Consider two goods: good X and good Y. Holding everything else constant, the price of good Y increases and the demand for good X decreases. Good X and good Y are
    a. complements.
    b. substitutes.
    c. not related to one another.

10. Consider two goods: good X and good Y. Holding everything else constant, the price of good Y decreases and the demand for good X decreases. Good X and good Y are
    a. complements.
    b. substitutes.
    c. not related to one another.

11. Holding everything else constant, Jon's income increases. If Jon's demand for good X decreases, then it must be the case that good X is a(n)
    a. inferior good.
    b. normal good.
    c. complement.
    d. substitute.

12. Jon's income increases by 10% this year while his purchases of steak increase by 4% this year over last year's purchases of steak. Holding everything else constant, Jon considers steak to be a(n)
    a. inferior good.
    b. normal good.
    c. complement.
    d. substitute.

13. Smalltown experiences an increase in its population due to the economic opportunities available in Smalltown. This event is likely to
    a. cause the demand curve for many products in Smalltown to shift to the right.
    b. cause the demand curve for many products in Smalltown to shift to the left.
    c. have little effect on the demand for products in Smalltown.
    d. cause the supply curve for many products in Smalltown to shift to the left.

14. A market is initially composed of 100 buyers. Holding everything else constant, if an additional 100 buyers join this market, then this will

   a. have no effect on the market demand curve since there is a limit to how many units of the good can be demanded at any price.

   b. cause the market demand curve to shift to the left since the good's price will necessarily increase when there are more buyers.

   c. cause the market demand curve to shift to the right as the additional demand of these new consumers is added to the initial demand curve.

   d. cause a movement along the demand curve as the price of the good rises due to the increase in the number of buyers.

15. Consider a market composed of three consumers: Peter, Anya, and Pablo. The market demand schedule is given in the table below. Which of the possible individual demand schedules provided in the answer selection is most likely to correspond to this market demand schedule?

Price	Market quantity demanded
$10	100
20	75
30	50
40	25

a.

Price	Quantity demanded by Peter	Quantity demanded by Anya	Quantity demanded by Pablo
$10	25	25	40
20	20	20	35
30	15	14	16
40	10	10	5

b.

Price	Quantity demanded by Peter	Quantity demanded by Anya	Quantity demanded by Pablo
$10	25	25	50
20	20	15	35
30	15	10	25
40	10	10	5

c.

Price	Quantity demanded by Peter	Quantity demanded by Anya	Quantity demanded by Pablo
$10	25	25	55
20	15	20	35
30	10	15	20
40	5	10	5

d.

Price	Quantity demanded by Peter	Quantity demanded by Anya	Quantity demanded by Pablo
$10	25	25	50
20	20	20	35
30	15	15	20
40	10	10	5

16. Consider a supply curve. When the price of the good increases, then this results in a movement along the supply curve resulting in a greater
   a. supply of the good.
   b. quantity supplied.

17. The cost of ground beef used to produce Fast Wally's hamburgers increases. Holding everything else constant, this will result
   a. in the supply curve shifting to the left.
   b. in the supply curve shifting to the right.
   c. in a movement along the supply curve to a smaller quantity supplied.
   d. in a movement along the supply curve to a greater quantity supplied.

18. The cost of raw materials used to produce Ever Strong Batteries decreases. Holding everything else constant, this will result
   a. in the supply curve shifting to the left.
   b. in the supply curve shifting to the right.
   c. in a movement along the supply curve to a smaller quantity supplied.
   d. in a movement along the supply curve to a greater quantity supplied.

19. Input prices decrease for a manufacturer. Holding everything else constant, this implies that at any given price the manufacturer will supply
   a. more of the good.
   b. less of the good.

20. A manufacturer produces two different products from its fixed set of resources. When the manufacturer increases the production of the first good, it must necessarily reduce the level of production of the second good due to these fixed resources. These two goods are
   a. complements in production.
   b. substitutes in production.

21. A sawmill operator produces lumber used in the construction industry as well as sawdust used for pet bedding. An increase in the supply of lumber is likely to
   a. increase the supply of sawdust, since lumber and sawdust are complements in production.
   b. decrease the supply of sawdust, since lumber and sawdust are complements in production.
   c. increase the supply of sawdust, since lumber and sawdust are substitutes in production.
   d. decrease the supply of sawdust, since lumber and sawdust are substitutes in production.

22. Research and development results in the discovery of a new technology for electricity generation. Holding everything else constant, this discovery will
    a. increase the supply of electricity.
    b. increase the quantity supplied of electricity.
    c. decrease the supply of electricity.
    d. decrease the quantity supplied of electricity.

23. The sawmill industry expects lumber prices to rise next year due to growing demand for the construction of new homes. Holding everything else constant, this expectation will shift
    a. the supply curve for lumber this year to the left.
    b. the supply curve for lumber this year to the right.

24. The graph below illustrates the supply curve for the competitive market for widgets. Currently there are sixteen producers in this market and each producer produces exactly the same amount of widgets as every other producer. Suppose the price of widgets is $40. If all the producers continue to produce the same amount as every other producer, what will be the level of production for each producer?

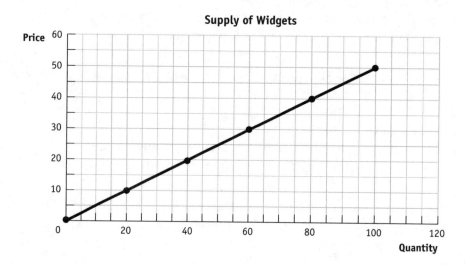

Supply of Widgets

    a. 8 widgets
    b. 10 widgets
    c. 5 widgets
    d. 20 widgets

25. The market demand curve for a product is the horizontal summation of the individual demand curves for the product, holding the
    a. quantity demanded constant.
    b. price constant.

26. Which of the following statements is true about equilibrium in a competitive market for a good?

    I. In equilibrium, the quantity demanded equals the quantity supplied.

    II. The equilibrium price and the equilibrium quantity correspond to the price and quantity at which the demand curve intersects the supply curve.

    III. In equilibrium, every consumer who wishes to consume the product is satisfied.

  a. Statement I is true.

  b. Statement II is true.

  c. Statement III is true.

  d. Statements I and II are true.

  e. Statements I, II, and III are true.

27. The competitive market for widgets is described by the following table.

Price	Quantity demanded	Quantity supplied
$ 0	400	0
20	300	100
40	200	200
60	100	300
80	0	400

If the current price is $20, then there is a(n)

  a. excess supply of 200 widgets.

  b. shortage of 200 widgets.

  c. excess demand of 100 widgets.

  d. surplus of 100 widgets.

28. The competitive market for widgets is described by the following table.

Price	Quantity demanded	Quantity supplied
$ 0	400	0
20	300	100
40	200	200
60	100	300
80	0	400

If the current price is $60, then there is a(n)

  a. excess supply of 200 widgets.

  b. excess demand of 200 widgets.

  c. shortage of 100 widgets.

  d. surplus of 100 widgets.

29. The competitive market for widgets is described by the following table.

Price	Quantity demanded	Quantity supplied
$ 0	400	0
20	300	100
40	200	200
60	100	300
80	0	400

The equilibrium quantity in this market is _____ and the equilibrium price is _____ .

a. 300 widgets; $20
b. 200 widgets; $20
c. 200 widgets; $40
d. 200 widgets; $60

30. The competitive market for widgets is described by the following table. Furthermore, you are told that both the demand curve and the supply curve are linear.

Price	Quantity demanded	Quantity supplied
$ 0	400	0
20	300	100
40	200	200
60	100	300
80	0	400

Which of the following equations is the demand equation for widgets?

a. $Q = 80 - 5P$
b. $P = 80 - 5Q$
c. $Q = 400 - 5P$
d. $Q = 1/5P$

31. The competitive market for widgets is described by the following table. Furthermore, you are told that both the demand curve and the supply curve are linear.

Price	Quantity demanded	Quantity supplied
$ 0	400	0
20	300	100
40	200	200
60	100	300
80	0	400

Which of the following equations is the supply equation for widgets?

a. $P = 5Q$

b. $P = 1/5Q$

c. $Q = 1/5P$

d. $Q = 100 + 1/5Q$

32. Use the following graph of a competitive market for candles to answer this question.

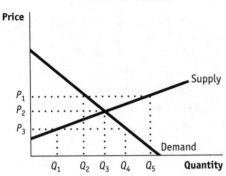

Market for Candles

At a price of P_1, there is an

a. excess supply of the good equal to $Q_2 - Q_5$.

b. excess supply of the good equal to $Q_5 - Q_2$.

c. excess supply of the good equal to $Q_3 - Q_2$.

d. excess demand for the good equal to $Q_3 - Q_2$.

33. Use the following graph of a competitive market for candles to answer this question.

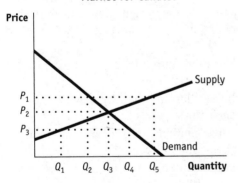

Market for Candles

At a price of P_3, there is an

a. excess demand for the good of $Q_4 - Q_1$.

b. excess demand for the good of $Q_1 - Q_4$.

c. excess demand for the good of $Q_3 - Q_2$.

d. excess supply of the good of $Q_3 - Q_2$.

34. In the competitive market for candles, there is an increase in the number of people purchasing candles and a decrease in the cost of beeswax, a major ingredient in the production of candles. Which of the following statements is true?
    a. The equilibrium price and the equilibrium quantity of candles will increase.
    b. The equilibrium price and the equilibrium quantity of candles will decrease.
    c. The equilibrium price may increase, decrease, or remain the same, but the equilibrium quantity will increase.
    d. The equilibrium quantity may increase, decrease, or remain the same, but the equilibrium price will increase.

35. Consumers in Mayville consider houses and apartments to be substitutes. There is an increase in the price of houses in Mayville at the same time three new apartment buildings are opened in Mayville. In the market for apartments in Mayville
    a. the equilibrium price will rise relative to its level before these two events.
    b. the equilibrium price will fall relative to its level before these two events.
    c. the equilibrium quantity will rise relative to its level before these two events.
    d. the equilibrium quantity will fall relative to its level before these two events.

36. The production of good X requires labor inputs and therefore the price of good X is directly affected by labor costs. Suppose that the price of labor increases while simultaneously people's income rises. If good X is a normal good, then we know in the market for good X
    a. the equilibrium price will increase and the equilibrium quantity may increase, decrease, or remain the same relative to their initial levels.
    b. the equilibrium price will decrease and the equilibrium quantity may increase, decrease, or remain the same relative to their initial levels.
    c. the equilibrium quantity will increase and the equilibrium price may increase, decrease, or remain the same relative to their initial levels.
    d. the equilibrium quantity will decrease and the equilibrium price may increase, decrease, or remain the same relative to their initial levels.

37. People's income rises, while simultaneously there is a technological advance in the production of good X. Good X is an inferior good. Given this information we know in the market for good X
    a. the equilibrium price will increase and the equilibrium quantity may increase, decrease, or remain the same relative to their initial levels.
    b. the equilibrium price will decrease and the equilibrium quantity may increase, decrease, or remain the same relative to their initial levels.
    c. the equilibrium quantity will increase and the equilibrium price may increase, decrease, or remain the same relative to their initial levels.
    d. the equilibrium quantity will decrease and the equilibrium price may increase, decrease, or remain the same relative to their initial levels.

38. The price of bubble gum increases at the same time that sugar, a major ingredient in candy, gets more expensive. If candy and bubble gum are substitutes, what happens to the equilibrium price and the equilibrium quantity in the market for candy?
    a. The equilibrium price will increase and the equilibrium quantity may increase, decrease, or remain the same relative to their initial levels.
    b. The equilibrium price will decrease and the equilibrium quantity may increase, decrease, or remain the same relative to their initial levels.
    c. The equilibrium quantity will increase and the equilibrium price may increase, decrease, or remain the same relative to their initial levels.
    d. The equilibrium quantity will decrease and the equilibrium price may increase, decrease, or remain the same relative to their initial levels.

ANSWER KEY

Answers to Problems and Exercises

1. This assumption results in a market situation in which no buyer (or group of buyers) and no seller (or group of sellers) can affect the market price. In a competitive market the interaction of demand and supply determines the equilibrium price and the equilibrium quantity rather than the behavior of a particular buyer and/or seller.

2. **a.**

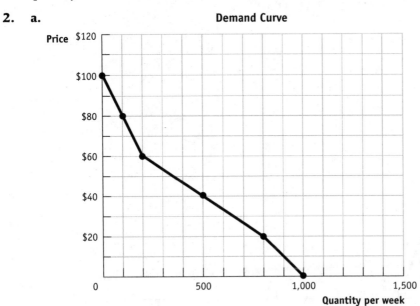

Demand Curve

b. If the price rises to $60, the quantity demanded will fall by 300 units, from 500 bicycles to 200 bicycles.

c. If the price falls to $0, the quantity demanded will increase by 500 units, from 500 bicycles to 1,000 bicycles.

3.

Situation	Specified market	Movement or shift	Rightward or leftward shift in demand
People's income increases	Market for exotic vacations	Shift	Rightward
People's income decreases	Market for goods sold in secondhand shops	Shift	Rightward
Price of bicycles increases	Market for bicycles	Movement	
Price of tennis balls increases	Market for tennis racquets	Shift	Leftward
Price of movie tickets decreases	Popcorn at movie theaters	Shift	Rightward
Popularity of music-playing device increases	Market for music-playing device	Shift	Rightward
Popularity of branded clothing items decreases	Market for brand-name designer clothing	Shift	Leftward
Winter clothing to go on sale next month	Market for winter clothing	Shift	Leftward
Increase in urban residents	Market for apartments in urban areas	Shift	Rightward

4. a. Note: these sketches are not drawn to scale since they are meant to be a guide rather than a perfect mathematical rendering of the data in the table. To find the market demand curve, hold price constant and ask how many units are demanded by all the consumers at this price. For example, at a price of $3, Joe demands 4 units, Maria demands 8 units, and Chao demands 2 units for a total market demand of 14 units at a price of $3. Repeat this for another price (e.g., for a price of $4, Joe demands 2 units, Maria demands 4 units, and Chao demands 1 unit for a total market demand of 7 units).

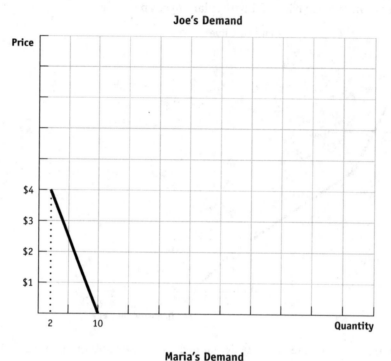

Joe's Demand

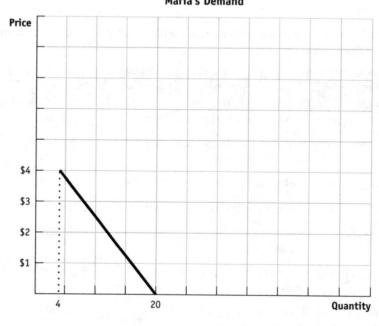

Maria's Demand

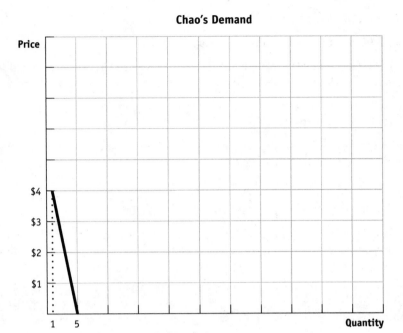

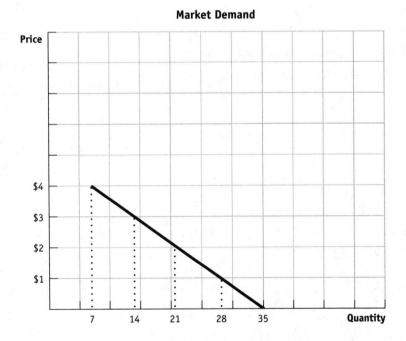

b. Summarize the market demand curve you found by filling in the following table.

Price	Quantity demanded in market
$0	35
1	28
2	21
3	14
4	7

5. **a.** At a price of $20, producers are willing to supply 40 units.

    b. At a price of $40, producers are willing to supply 80 units.

    c. At a price of $50, 100 widgets are supplied. Thus, if there are ten producers producing exactly the same number of widgets, then each producer must produce 10 widgets.

    d. When price falls from $30 to $20, the number of widgets supplied decreases by 20 widgets (from 60 widgets to 40 widgets).

    e. When price rises from $30 to $50, the number of widgets supplied increases by 40 widgets (from 60 widgets to 100 widgets).

    f. Suppliers are willing to supply 80 widgets if the price is $40.

    g. Suppliers are willing to supply 40 widgets if the price is $20.

    h. The typical supply curve is upward sloping: its slope is positive. This implies that the quantity supplied increases when price increases and that the quantity supplied decreases when price decreases.

6.

Situation	Specified market	Movement or shift	Rightward or leftward shift in supply
Labor costs for air travel and cruise ships increase	Market for exotic vacations	Shift	Leftward
Prices of office equipment and phone service rise by 40%	Market for call center services	Shift	Leftward
Price of bicycles increases	Market for bicycles	Movement	
Price of leather boots increases	Market for beef products	Shift	Rightward
Price of leather boots increases	Market for leather belts	Shift	Leftward
New technology for music-playing device revealed	Market for music-playing devices	Shift	Rightward
Price of brand-name designer clothing increases	Market for brand-name designer clothing	Movement	
Stock market prices expected to fall next quarter	Stock market today	Movement	
Increase in number of coffee shop owners in the metro area	Market for coffee shops in the metro area	Shift	Rightward

7. a.,b. Equilibrium occurs at the price at which the quantity demanded equals the quantity supplied. From the table we can see that the quantity demanded equals the quantity supplied at a price of $30. The equilibrium price is thus $30 and the equilibrium quantity is 400 units. This point is illustrated in the graph in part (d).

c.

Price	Excess demand	Excess supply
$ 0	1,000 units	
10	675 units	
20	325 units	
30	Equilibrium	Equilibrium
40		350 units
50		675 units

d. When there is excess demand this means that the quantity demanded by consumers is greater than the quantity supplied by producers. The market for some reason does not provide an adequate amount of the good, and thus there is a shortage of the good. The figure below illustrates a shortage at a price of P_1. Note that at P_1, the quantity demanded is Q_1, the quantity supplied is Q_2, and the excess demand is equal to $Q_1 - Q_2$. When a market has excess demand, this implies that the current price of the good is less than the market-clearing price.

Illustration of a Situation of Excess Demand, or a Shortage

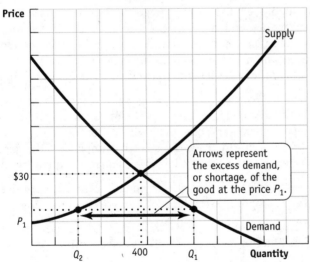

Arrows represent the excess demand, or shortage, of the good at the price P_1.

e. When there is excess supply this means that the quantity demanded by consumers is less than the quantity supplied by producers. The market for some reason provides too much of the good, and thus there is a surplus of the good. The figure below illustrates a surplus at a price of P_1. Note that at P_1, the quantity demanded is Q_1, the quantity supplied is Q_2, and the excess supply is equal to $Q_2 - Q_1$. When a market has excess supply of a good, this implies that the current price in the market is greater than the market-clearing price.

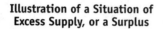

Illustration of a Situation of Excess Supply, or a Surplus

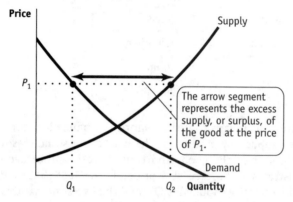

The arrow segment represents the excess supply, or surplus, of the good at the price of P_1.

8. a. The equilibrium price in this market is P_3 since the quantity demanded (Q_3) equals the quantity supplied (Q_3) at this price.

b. Q_3.

c. At P_2 there is an excess supply, or surplus, of the good, since the quantity supplied equals Q_5 while the quantity demanded equals Q_2. The price should fall toward the equilibrium price. As the price falls, consumers will increase the quantity demanded of the good while producers will decrease the quantity supplied of the good until the price reaches the point where the quantity demanded equals the quantity supplied.

d. At P_4 there is an excess demand, or shortage, for the good, since the quantity supplied equals Q_1 while the quantity demanded equals Q_4. The price should rise toward the equilibrium price. As the price increases, consumers will reduce the quantity demanded of the good while producers will increase the quantity supplied of the good until the price reaches the point where the quantity demanded equals the quantity supplied.

e. When the quantity demanded is equal to Q_4, this implies that the current price in the market is P_4, which is the situation of excess demand described in part (d).

f. When the quantity supplied is equal to Q_5, this implies that the current price in the market is P_2, which is the situation of excess supply described in part (c).

g. At P_1 the quantity demanded is equal to zero. This implies that at a price of P_1 the price is too high for consumers to be willing to demand the product.

h. At P_5 the quantity supplied is equal to zero. This implies that at a price of P_5 the price is too low for producers to be willing to supply the good.

9. **a.**

Price	Quantity demanded	Quantity supplied
$ 0	1,000	0
240	880	40
480	760	80
720	640	120
960	520	160
1,200	400	200
1,440	280	240
1,680	160	280
1,920	40	320

b. Examination of the table reveals that prices less than or equal to $1,440 result in a situation of excess demand, while prices greater than or equal to $1,680 result in a situation of excess supply. Thus, the equilibrium price will fall somewhere in the range of $1,440 to $1,680 in this market.

c.

Market for Bicycles in Pedal City

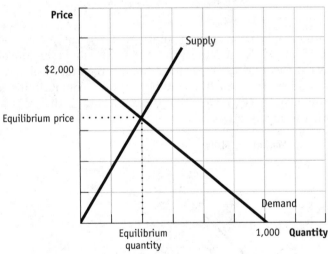

d. At a price of $240, 40 bicycles will be supplied and each manufacturer will produce 2 bicycles. At a price of $240, 880 bicycles will be demanded. The market is not in equilibrium since there is an excess demand for bicycles.

e. At a price of $480, 80 bicycles will be supplied and each manufacturer will produce 4 bicycles. At a price of $480, 760 bicycles will be demanded. The market is not in equilibrium since there is an excess demand for bicycles.

f. At a price of $1,680, 280 bicycles will be supplied and each manufacturer will produce 14 bicycles. At a price of $1,680, 160 bicycles will be demanded. The market is not in equilibrium since there is an excess supply of bicycles.

g. Since $P = 2,000 - 2Q$ and $P = 6Q$, we can use this information to write $2,000 - 2Q = 6Q$. Solving this equation gives us the equilibrium quantity of 250 bicycles. Substituting this quantity into either the demand equation or the supply equation yields the equilibrium price: $P = 2,000 - 2(250) = \$1,500$, or $P = 6(250) = \$1,500$.

10. a. Gasoline and bicycles are substitutes for one another. When the price of gasoline rises, people substitute away from gasoline toward bicycle transportation. This is illustrated in the graph below with the demand curve for bicycles shifting to the right, resulting in a higher equilibrium price (P_2) and a higher equilibrium quantity (Q_2). Note that there is a shift in the demand curve and a movement along the supply curve.

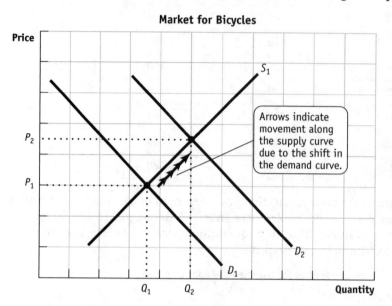

b. Gasoline and SUVs are complements for one another. When the price of gasoline rises, people find that driving SUVs is relatively more expensive and therefore decrease their demand for SUVs at every price. This is illustrated in the graph below with the demand curve for SUVs shifting to the left, resulting in a lower equilibrium price (P_2) and a lower equilibrium quantity (Q_2). Note that there is a shift in the demand curve and a movement along the supply curve.

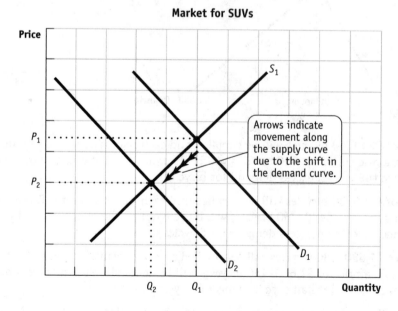

c. New technology shifts the supply curve to the right from S_1 to S_2. This causes a movement along the demand curve and results in a decrease in the equilibrium price and an increase in the equilibrium quantity. This is illustrated in the figure below.

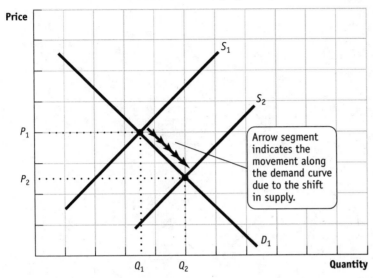

Market for Music-Playing Devices

d. When the price of labor decreases, this causes the supply of the good to shift to the right since labor is an input in the production of fast-food meals. This results in a movement along the demand curve and a decrease in the equilibrium price and an increase in the equilibrium quantity.

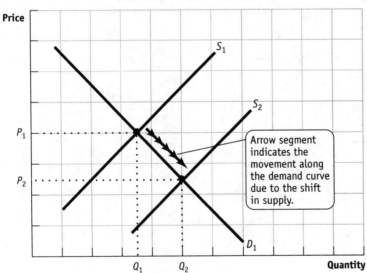

Market for Fast-Food Restaurants

e. An increase in income shifts the demand curve to the right if the good is a normal good. This shift in demand causes a movement along the supply curve and an increase in both the equilibrium price and the equilibrium quantity.

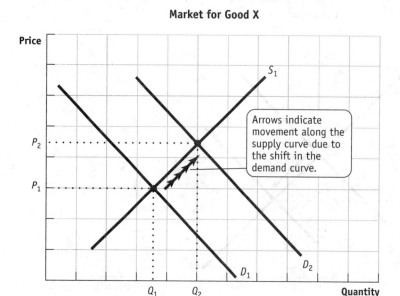

Market for Good X

f. An increase in income shifts the demand curve to the left if the good is an inferior good. This shift in demand causes a movement along the supply curve and a decrease in both the equilibrium price and the equilibrium quantity. The graph below illustrates this situation.

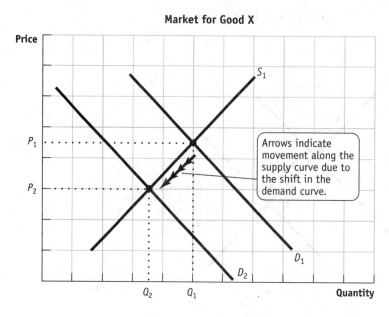

Market for Good X

11. a. The demand equation is $P = 10 - (1/10)Q$ and the supply equation is $P = (1/10)Q$.

b. Solving the two equations from part (a), we find that the equilibrium price equals \$5 and the equilibrium quantity equals 50.

c. To find the new equilibrium price and quantity, we need to know the new demand and supply curves. Draw a sketch of the original demand curve and the new demand curve (shifted to the right at every price by 20 units) to guide you in your calculations. The figure below illustrates this sketch.

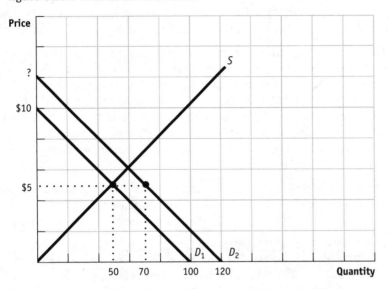

We know from part (b) that the initial equilibrium is at price $5 and the equilibrium quantity is 50, which gives us two points on the new demand curve: (70, 5) and (120, 0). We also know that the new demand curve is parallel to the original demand curve and thus has the same slope as the original demand curve. But we do not know the y-intercept for the new demand curve. To find the equation, let's write the new equation as $P = b - (1/10)Q$. This equation has the same slope as the original demand curve, but has not yet identified the y-intercept. To find the value of b, let's substitute the coordinates of one of the points we know is on D_2: thus, using (70, 5) yields $5 = b - (1/10)70$, or $b = 12$. So our new demand curve equation is $P = 12 - (1/10)Q$. Use the same technique to find the new supply curve equation. The graph below sketches the original demand and supply curve and also the new supply curve, which illustrates an increase of 40 units in the quantity supplied at every price. We know the coordinates of two points on this new supply curve—(40, 0) and (90, 5)—and we also know that the new supply curve has the same slope as the original supply curve. So we can rewrite the new supply curve as $P = b + (1/10)Q$ and then use one of our known points to solve for b, the y-intercept. Thus, using (90, 5) we get $5 = b + (1/10)90$, or $b = -4$, and the new supply curve is $P = (1/10)Q - 4$.

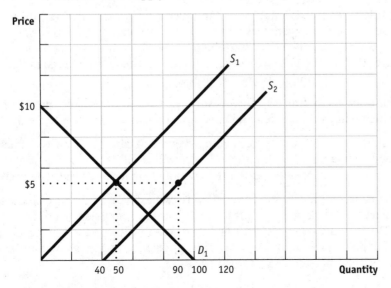

Using the new demand curve and new supply curve, we can easily solve for the equilibrium price and the equilibrium quantity in this market. Since $P = 12 - (1/10)Q$ and $P = (1/10)Q - 4$, we have $12 - (1/10)Q = (1/10)Q - 4$, or the equilibrium quantity (Q) equals 80. Then replacing Q with 80 in either the demand or supply equation, we find that the equilibrium price (P) equals 4. In this case, the equilibrium price decreases relative to its initial level, while the equilibrium quantity increases relative to its initial level.

d. Since the change in the quantity demanded at each price is the same as in part (c), we know that the new demand curve can be written as $P = 12 - (1/10)Q$. But we need to use the same technique as we employed in part (c) to find the new supply curve. When you do this, you will find that the new supply curve equation is $P = (1/10)Q - 1$. Solving these two equations for the equilibrium price and the equilibrium quantity, we find that the new equilibrium price is 5.5 while the new equilibrium quantity is 65 units. In this case, the equilibrium price and the equilibrium quantity increase relative to their initial quantities.

e. You would know with certainty that the equilibrium quantity increased, but you would not know if the equilibrium price increased, decreased, or remained the same, since you do not know the magnitude of the shifts in the demand and supply curves.

12.

Situation	Effect on equilibrium price	Effect on equilibrium quantity
Demand shifts to the right and supply shifts to the right	May increase, decrease, or remain the same	Increases
Demand shifts to the left and supply shifts to the left	May increase, decrease, or remain the same	Decreases
Demand shifts to the right and supply shifts to the left	Increases	May increase, decrease, or remain the same
Demand shifts to the left and supply shifts to the right	Decreases	May increase, decrease, or remain the same

Answers to Chapter Review Questions

1. **Answer c.** This is a definitional statement.

2. **Answer c.** The law of demand states that as the price of the good decreases, the quantity demanded of the good increases. Since the shampoo is on sale, its price has fallen and the law of demand suggests that the quantity demanded should therefore increase.

3. **Answer a.** This is a definitional statement. An inverse function of two variables means that an increase in one of the variables will result in a decrease in the other variable, or a decrease in one of the variables will result in an increase in the other variable. The law of demand states that as the price of the good increases, the quantity demanded of the good decreases; thus, price and quantity are inversely related.

4. **Answer b.** This research finding is likely to result in an increase in tastes and preferences for mangos, which will cause the demand curve for mangos to shift to the right.

5. **Answer a.** A shift in the supply curve holding everything else constant will cause the price of the good to increase. This increase in price will result in a movement along the demand curve, since as the price increases, the quantity demanded of the good decreases.

6. **Answer d.** The expected fall in flat-screen TV prices next year will cause the demand curve for flat-screen TVs this year to shift to the left as consumers decrease the quantity of flat-screen TVs they demand at every price. This will result in a movement along the supply curve for flat-screen TVs this year. This price expectation should result in a decrease in the price of flat-screen TVs this year.

7. **Answer c.** Since peanut butter and jelly are considered complements in this example, an increase in the price of peanut butter will cause the demand curve for jelly to shift to the left, since as fewer units of peanut butter are demanded due to the higher price of peanut butter, fewer units of jelly will also be demanded at any given price for jelly.

8. **Answer a.** Since ham and turkey are substitutes, when the price of ham decreases, this causes the quantity of ham demanded to increase. As more units of ham are demanded, fewer units of turkey are demanded at every price. The demand for turkey therefore shifts to the left.

9. **Answer a.** As the price of good Y increases, this results in a decrease in the quantity demanded of good Y. Since the demand for good X decreases, this implies that good Y and good X are consumed together; thus good X and good Y are complements.

10. **Answer b.** As the price of good Y decreases, this results in an increase in the quantity demanded of good Y. Since the demand for good X increases when the quantity demanded of good Y decreases, this implies that good X is a substitute for good Y.

11. **Answer a.** When Jon's income increases, the quantity of good X he demands at any given price falls, which implies that good X is an inferior good.

12. **Answer b.** Both Jon's income and the quantity of steak he demands increases; therefore steak is a normal good.

13. **Answer a.** An increase in population shifts the demand curve to the right, as the increase in population implies a larger number of consumers of the product.

14. **Answer c.** An increase in the number of buyers causes the quantity demanded of the good to increase at every price, and the demand curve shifts to the right.

15. **Answer d.** To find the market demand curve, hold price constant and then add the quantity of the good demanded by each of the consumers. Thus, if the price of the good is $10, then the total of Peter's, Anya's, and Pablo's demand must add up to 100 units according to the table provided in the question.

16. **Answer b.** This question is asking you to recall that a change in the price of the good, holding everything else constant, results in a movement along the curve. This movement along the curve causes a change in the quantity supplied and not a change in the supply curve.

17. **Answer a.** Ground beef is an input in the production of Fast Wally's hamburgers. When ground beef gets more expensive, this increases the cost of producing hamburgers, which causes the supply curve to shift to the left.

18. **Answer b.** When the cost of raw materials decreases, more batteries can be produced at any given price. This decrease in the cost of raw materials causes the supply curve for batteries to shift to the right.

19. **Answer a.** When input prices decrease, producers are willing to supply more units of the good at every price.

20. **Answer b.** Since an increase in the production of one of the goods results in a decrease in the production of the other good, these two goods must be substitutes in production.

21. **Answer a.** Sawdust and lumber are complements in production. As the producer increases its production of lumber, the production of sawdust is also increased since sawdust is a by-product of lumber production.

22. **Answer a.** New technology causes the supply curve to shift to the right, resulting in an increase in the quantity supplied of the good at every price.

23. **Answer a.** The sawmill industry will want to decrease the supply of lumber they provide to the market this year due to their expectation that next year's lumber prices will be higher. At every price the quantity of lumber supplied this year will be decreased, and the supply curve for lumber this year shifts to the left.

24. **Answer c.** When the price is $40, 80 widgets are produced. Since there are sixteen producers in this market and each of these producers produce the same amount of widgets, this implies that each producer must be producing 5 widgets.

25. **Answer b.** This is a definitional statement. The market demand curve is found by holding price constant and then adding together the quantities demanded by each consumer in the market. This process is repeated for other prices.

26. **Answer d.** The first two statements are fairly straightforward, but statement III may be somewhat appealing at first glance. At equilibrium, however, even though the quantity demanded equals the quantity supplied, this does not imply that every potential consumer of the good is consuming the good. Those consumers who would like to consume the good, but who are unwilling to pay the equilibrium price, will not consume the good.

27. **Answer b.** At a price of $20, 300 widgets are demanded while 100 widgets are supplied. Thus, at a price of $20 there is an excess demand, or shortage, of 200 widgets.

28. **Answer a.** At a price of $60, 100 widgets are demanded while 300 widgets are supplied. Thus, at a price of $60 there is an excess supply, or surplus, of 200 widgets.

29. **Answer c.** The equilibrium quantity is the quantity at which demand equals the quantity supplied. The equilibrium quantity is 200 widgets, and the equilibrium price is $40.

30. **Answer c.** To find the demand curve, you can either plot the demand curve (although this is time consuming) or you can calculate the slope (rise/run = $-20/100 = -1/5$) and then use the slope-intercept form, $y = mx + b$, to write the equation. Thus, $P = (-1/5)Q + 80$, or solving for Q, $Q = 400 - 5P$.

31. **Answer b.** To find the supply curve, you can either plot the supply curve (although this is time consuming) or you can calculate the slope (rise/run = $20/100 = 1/5$) and then use the slope-intercept form, $y = mx + b$, to write the equation. Thus, $P = (1/5)Q + 0$.

32. **Answer b.** At P_1 the quantity demanded is Q_2 units while the quantity supplied is Q_5 units. The quantity supplied is greater than the quantity demanded at P_1: this excess supply is equal to $Q_5 - Q_2$.

33. **Answer a.** At P_3 the quantity demanded is Q_4 units while the quantity supplied is Q_1 units. The quantity demanded is greater than the quantity supplied at P_3: this excess demand is equal to $Q_4 - Q_1$.

34. **Answer c.** Since we do not know the relative magnitude of the shifts in the demand and supply curves, we cannot know for certain what happens to both the equilibrium price and the equilibrium quantity. The demand curve shifts to the right with the increase in the number of people purchasing candles, while the supply curve shifts to the left with the increase in the price of one of the inputs to candle production. The equilibrium price will increase, but the equilibrium quantity may increase, decrease, or remain the same depending on the relative magnitude of the shifts in the two curves.

35. **Answer c.** The demand curve for apartments shifts to the right with the increase in the price of houses (houses and apartments are substitute goods for consumers in Mayville), while the supply curve for apartments also shifts to the right with the opening of the new apartment buildings. Since we do not know the magnitude of the shifts in the demand and supply curves, we know that the equilibrium quantity is now larger, but the equilibrium price may increase, decrease, or remain the same with these shifts in the demand and supply curves.

36. **Answer a.** The demand curve for good X shifts to the right since good X is a normal good and income has increased. At the same time, the supply curve for good X shifts to the left since the price of labor has increased. These two shifts result in the equilibrium price increasing while the equilibrium quantity may have increased, decreased, or remained the same depending on the magnitude of the shifts in the demand and supply curves.

37. **Answer b.** Since good X is an inferior good, the increase in income results in the demand curve for good X shifting to the left. At the same time, the technological advance causes the supply curve for good X to shift to the right. The equilibrium price will decrease, but the equilibrium quantity may increase, decrease, or remain the same depending on the magnitude of the shifts in the demand and supply curves.

38. **Answer a.** The supply curve for candy shifts to the left with the increase in the price of sugar, while the demand curve for candy shifts to the right with the increase in the price of bubble gum. The equilibrium price will increase, but the equilibrium quantity may increase, decrease, or remain the same depending on the magnitude of the shifts in the demand and supply curves.

Consumer and Producer Surplus

BEFORE YOU READ THE CHAPTER

Summary

Chapter 4 develops the concepts of producer surplus, consumer surplus, and total surplus and then illustrates the connection between these concepts and the demand and supply model. The chapter also explains how total surplus can be used to show the gains from trade and to evaluate the efficiency of a market.

Chapter Objectives

Objective #1. The demand and supply model illustrates how much consumers and producers gain from participating in a market. A consumer's willingness to pay refers to the maximum price the consumer would pay to purchase an item. The demand curve is defined by the willingness of consumers to pay.

Objective #2. An individual's consumer surplus is the difference between the individual's willingness to pay and the price he/she pays for the good: consumer surplus measures the net gain the consumer receives when he/she purchases the good. Total consumer surplus is the sum of the individual consumer surpluses achieved by all the buyers of the good. Total consumer surplus is equal to the area under the demand curve but above the price.

- The area of consumer surplus is a triangle for a smooth demand curve or a series of rectangles for a step-shaped demand curve.

- Holding everything else constant, a decrease in price increases consumer surplus while an increase in price decreases consumer surplus.

Objective #3. The seller's price is the lowest price the seller is willing to sell the good for. Individual producer surplus is the difference between the price the good sells for and the lowest price the seller is willing to accept for the good: individual producer surplus measures the net gain the seller receives from selling the good. Total producer surplus is the sum of the individual producer surplus achieved by all the sellers of the good. Total producer surplus is equal to the area above the supply curve but beneath the price.

- The area of producer surplus is a triangle for a smooth supply curve or a series of rectangles for a step-shaped supply curve.

- Holding everything else constant, a decrease in price decreases producer surplus and an increase in price increases producer surplus.

Objective #4.   Total surplus is the sum of consumer and producer surplus. At the market equilibrium, total surplus is maximized: the market equilibrium allocates the consumption of the good among potential consumers and the sales of the good among potential sellers in order to achieve the maximum possible gains to society. In a well-functioning market, total surplus cannot be increased by reallocating consumption among consumers, reallocating sales among sellers, or by changing the quantity traded. In fact, each of these actions diminishes the level of total surplus in the market.

- Preventing a sale in a market that would have taken place in equilibrium reduces both consumer and producer surplus, resulting in a loss of total surplus. Increasing sales beyond the equilibrium quantity similarly reduces consumer surplus, producer surplus, and total surplus, since such a sale would represent a situation where the buyer's willingness to buy must be less than the seller's cost.

Objective #5.   Total surplus is maximized at the market equilibrium: (a) the market allocates consumption of the good to those potential consumers who place the highest value on the good; (b) the market allocates sales of the good to those sellers who have the lowest cost of producing the good; (c) the market ensures that any purchase represents a situation where the buyer values the good more than the seller values the good; and (d) the market ensures that no sales are made in which the seller values the good more than the purchaser does. Markets are efficient when total surplus is maximized.

- Even though the market equilibrium maximizes total surplus, this does not imply that it maximizes the outcome for any individual buyer or seller. Subsequent chapters consider situations of market intervention where individual buyers or sellers are made better off than they would be at the market equilibrium.

Objective #6.   Well-defined property rights are required for a market to function effectively. Well-defined property rights identify the owner of valuable resources and goods, and this ownership makes it possible for mutually beneficial transactions to occur. Economic signals are also necessary for markets to function. The best economic signal is price because the price of a good conveys the consumer's willingness to pay and the producer's cost.

Objective #7.   Markets can fail to be efficient: this is called market failure. Markets fail when someone prevents mutually beneficial trades from occurring, when there are side effects that the market does not take into account, or because some goods are unsuited for efficient management by markets. Subsequent chapters consider these situations.

Key Terms

willingness to pay the maximum price a consumer is prepared to pay for a good.

individual consumer surplus the net gain to an individual buyer from the purchase of a good; equal to the difference between the buyer's *willingness to pay* and the price paid.

total consumer surplus the sum of the *individual consumer surpluses* of all the buyers of a good in a market.

consumer surplus a term often used to refer both to *individual consumer surplus* and to *total consumer surplus*.

cost (of seller) the lowest price at which a seller is willing to sell a good.

individual producer surplus the net gain to an individual seller from selling a good; equal to the difference between the price received and the seller's *cost*.

total producer surplus the sum of the *individual producer surpluses* of all the sellers of a good in a market.

producer surplus a term often used to refer both to *individual producer surplus* and to *total producer surplus*.

total surplus the total net gain to consumers and producers from trading in a market; the sum of the *producer surplus* and the *consumer surplus*.

property rights the rights of owners of valuable items, whether *resources* or goods, to dispose of those items as they choose.

economic signal any piece of information that helps people make better economic decisions.

inefficient describes a market or *economy* in which there are missed opportunities: some people could be made better off without making other people worse off.

market failure occurs when a market fails to be efficient.

Notes

■ AFTER YOU READ THE CHAPTER

Tips

Tip #1. To master the key concept in this chapter, you must be able to locate the areas of surplus in the graphs of the supply and demand model. You will want to work with the concepts of consumer surplus, producer surplus, and total surplus until you feel confident that you can find these areas in your graphs.

Tip #2. Figure 4.1 illustrates the concept of consumer surplus for a step-shaped demand curve. The area of consumer surplus consists of a series of rectangles that lie under the demand curve but above the market price. Each of these rectangles has been shaded separately in Figure 4.1, but the area of consumer surplus is the entire shaded area. Those consumers whose willingness to pay is equal to or greater than the market price will purchase the good for the market price, and their consumer surplus represents the net gain they receive from purchasing the good.

Figure 4.1

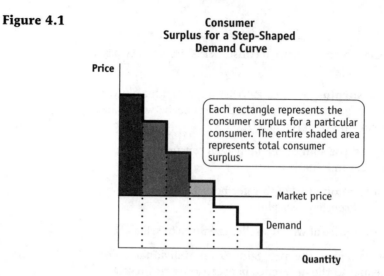

Tip #3. Figure 4.2 illustrates the concept of consumer surplus for a smooth demand curve. The area of consumer surplus consists of the area under the demand curve but above the market price. In Figure 4.2, the area of consumer surplus is shaded. The value of consumer surplus can be found by calculating the area of this shaded triangle. The consumer surplus represents the net gain consumers receive from purchasing the good.

Figure 4.2

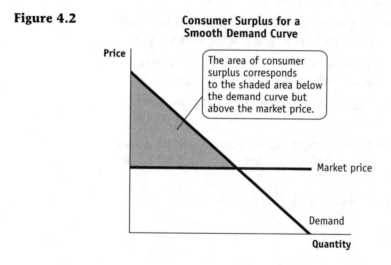

Tip #4. Figure 4.3 illustrates the concept of producer surplus for a step-shaped supply curve. The area of producer surplus consists of a series of rectangles that lie above the supply curve but below the market price. Each of these rectangles has been shaded as separate rectangles in Figure 4.3, but the area of producer surplus is the entire shaded area. Those producers whose willingness to sell is equal to or less than the market price, will sell the good for the market price, and their producer surplus represents the net gain they receive from selling the good.

Figure 4.3

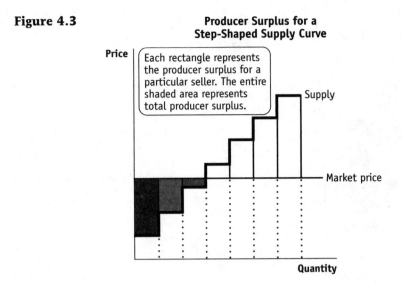

Producer Surplus for a Step-Shaped Supply Curve

Tip #5. Figure 4.4 illustrates the concept of producer surplus for a smooth supply curve. The area of producer surplus is the shaded region above the supply curve but beneath the market price. The value of producer surplus can be found by calculating the area of this shaded triangle. The producer surplus represents the net gain producers receive from selling the good.

Figure 4.4

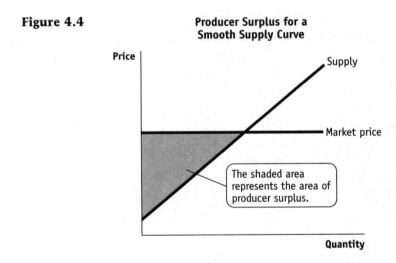

Producer Surplus for a Smooth Supply Curve

Tip #6. Figures 4.5 and 4.6 illustrate total surplus, which is the sum of consumer surplus and producer surplus. Figure 4.5 illustrates this concept for step-shaped demand and supply curves, and Figure 4.6 illustrates this concept for smooth demand and supply curves.

Figure 4.5

**Total Surplus for Step-Shaped
Demand and Supply Curves**

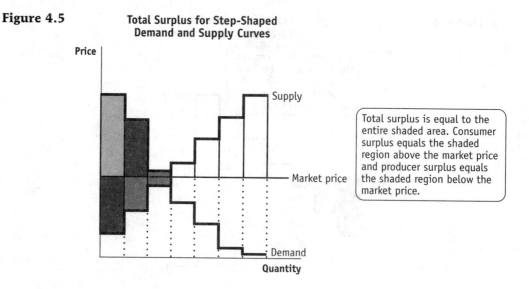

Total surplus is equal to the entire shaded area. Consumer surplus equals the shaded region above the market price and producer surplus equals the shaded region below the market price.

Figure 4.6

**Total Surplus for Smooth
Demand and Supply Curves**

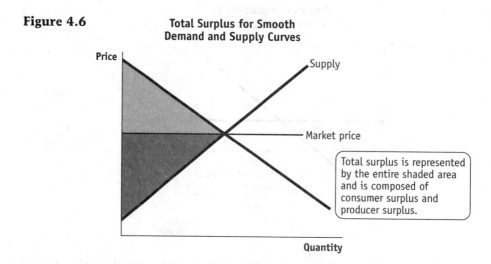

Total surplus is represented by the entire shaded area and is composed of consumer surplus and producer surplus.

Tip #7. If you are using flash cards, make sure you make up a set with this chapter's new vocabulary and concepts. Review all of your flash cards on a regular basis to make sure you are not forgetting any terms or concepts.

Problems and Exercises

1. The following table expresses the amount people are willing to pay to buy a new music-playing device. Use this information to answer this series of questions.

Name of person	Price willing to pay
Joe	$100
Mary	200
Lucinda	150
Pete	50
Mario	300

   a. Who places the highest value on this good? Explain your answer.

   b. Who places the lowest value on this good? Explain your answer.

   c. If the good is offered at a price of $100, who would buy it?

   d. If the good is offered at a price of $50, who would buy it?

   e. Construct a step-shaped demand curve illustrating the demand for a music-playing device for these five consumers.

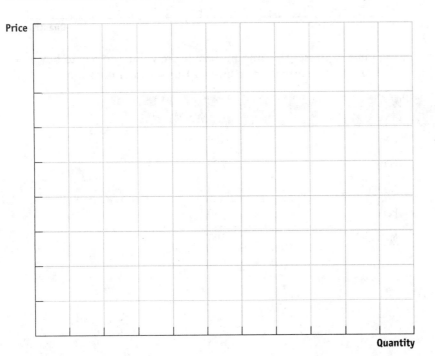

f. On the graph, shade in the area that represents Mary's consumer surplus if the good sells for $100. Label this area clearly. Calculate the value of Mary's consumer surplus.

g. On the graph, shade in the area that represents Mario's consumer surplus if the good sells for $100. Label this area clearly. Calculate the value of Mario's consumer surplus.

h. Create a new graph that is a duplicate of the one you drew for part (e) and shade in the entire area of consumer surplus if the good sells for a price of $100. Calculate the value of consumer surplus at this price.

2. The following table expresses the amount people are willing to pay to buy a new music-playing device. Use this information to answer this series of questions.

Name of person	Price willing to pay
Joe	$100
Mary	200
Lucinda	150
Pete	50
Mario	300

a. If the market price is $175, who will buy the good and what is the value of total consumer surplus?

b. Suppose the market price is $175, but a decision is made to allocate the two units of the good that are demanded at that price to Mario and Lucinda. What is the value of total consumer surplus in this case?

c. Why does the reallocation of the good in part (b) reduce the value of consumer surplus? What are the implications of the reduction in consumer surplus that occurs when the good is not allocated to those buyers who place the highest value on the good?

3. Demand for widgets in Marksville is given by the equation $P = 100 - Q$.

a. If the market price of widgets in Marksville is $50, what is the value of consumer surplus in this market?

b. If the market price of widgets in Marksville is $40, what is the value of consumer surplus in this market?

c. For a linear downward sloping demand curve, what happens to consumer surplus when the market price rises?

d. Suppose the market price of widgets is $30 in Marksville. Will at least 80 widgets be demanded at this price? Explain your answer.

e. Suppose the market price of widgets is $30 in Marksville. Will at least 60 widgets be demanded at this price? Explain your answer.

4. The following table provides a list of sellers of organic apples and the lowest price each seller is willing to accept for a bushel of apples. Assume that each seller will only offer a single bushel of apples for sale. Use this information to answer this series of questions.

Seller	Lowest price seller is willing to accept for a bushel of apples
Ski Top Orchards	$6.00
J. Appleseed's Finest	7.25
Red's Organic	5.80
Pure Apples	8.25
Nature's Medicine	8.00

a. Draw a diagram of this step-shaped supply curve.

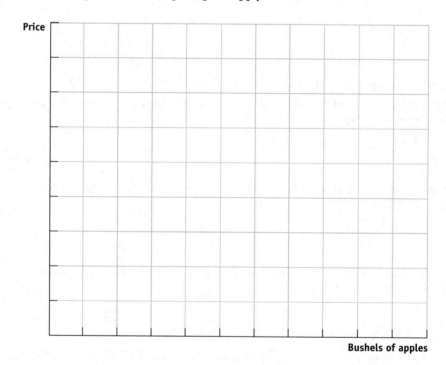

b. If only one bushel of apples is sold, which seller is most likely to make this sale? Explain your answer.

c. If the market price is $7.50, what is the value of the producer surplus received by J. Appleseed's Finest?

d. If the market price is $7.50, what is the value of the producer surplus received by Ski Top Orchards?

e. Redraw your sketch from part (a) and indicate the area of total producer surplus in this market if the market price is $7.50. What is the value of this producer surplus?

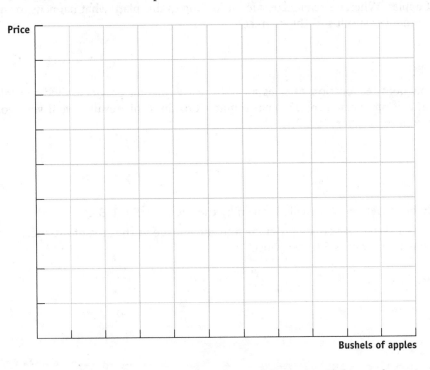

f. Which sellers will sell a bushel of apples in this market if the market price is $7.50?

5. The following table provides a list of sellers of organic apples and the lowest price each seller is willing to accept for a bushel of apples. Assume that each seller will only offer a single bushel of apples for sale. Use this information to answer this series of questions.

Seller	Lowest price seller is willing to accept for a bushel of apples
Ski Top Orchards	$6.00
J. Appleseed's Finest	7.25
Red's Organic	5.80
Pure Apples	8.25
Nature's Medicine	8.00

a. Suppose the market price of apples is $7.00 a bushel. At this price, which of the above potential sellers will agree to sell a bushel of apples? What is the value of producer surplus when the market price of apples is $7.00 a bushel?

b. Suppose the market price of apples is $7.00 a bushel and that J. Appleseed's Finest is forced to sell a bushel of apples while Ski Top Orchards is forced to not sell a bushel of apples. When we reallocate sales according to this plan, what happens to the value of producer surplus in this market?

c. How does reallocation of sales away from the market-provided allocation alter the value of producer surplus? What implications does this result have if your goal is to maximize producer surplus?

6. Supply of widgets in Marksville is given by the equation $P = 1/3\ Q$.

a. Draw a sketch of this supply curve and then shade in the area of producer surplus if the market price is $10 per widget.

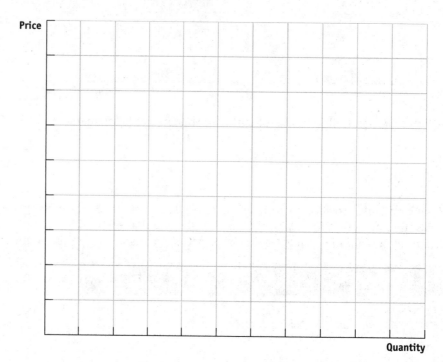

b. If the market price of widgets is $10, what is the value of producer surplus in this market?

c. If the market price of widgets is $20, what is the value of producer surplus in this market?

   d. For a linear upward-sloping supply curve, what happens to producer surplus when the market price rises due to an increase in demand?

   e. Suppose the market price is $30 per widget in Marksville. Will at least 80 widgets be supplied at this price? Explain your answer.

   f. Suppose the market price is $30 per widget in Marksville. Will at least 60 widgets be supplied at this price? Explain your answer.

7. Demand for widgets in Marksville is given by the equation $P = 100 - Q$, while the supply of widgets is given by the equation $P = 1/3\ Q$.

   a. Draw a sketch of the demand and supply curves and mark the equilibrium price and the equilibrium quantity. Solve the two equations for the specific equilibrium price and equilibrium quantity.

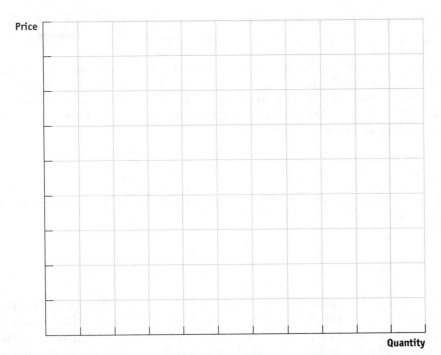

   b. On the graph identify the areas of producer surplus and consumer surplus. Calculate a numeric value for each of these areas.

   c. What is the value of total surplus in the market for widgets?

d. Suppose that the price of an input in the production of widgets increases so that supply is affected and changes by 60 units. Draw a new graph indicating the changes in the market for widgets due to this input price change. Label the new equilibrium price and equilibrium quantity as well as the initial equilibrium price and quantity.

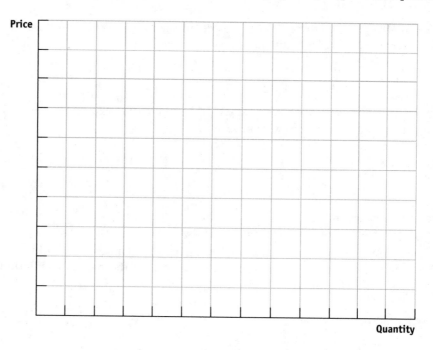

e. On the graph you drew for part (d), label the areas that correspond to producer and consumer surplus. Calculate a numeric value for consumer surplus and producer surplus. (Hint: when you calculate these values, use the graph you have drawn to guide the math steps you need to take to compute these areas.) Compare your answers in part (e) to your answers in part (b).

f. What happened to total surplus in the market for widgets when input prices increased?

8. George is considering the purchase of some new shirts for work. He is willing to pay $35 for the first shirt, $25 for the second shirt, and $15 for the third. Oxford Clothiers, his favorite shirt manufacturer, currently is selling shirts for $28 a shirt. What is the efficient number of shirts for George to buy? What is George's consumer surplus in this situation? Explain your answers.

BEFORE YOU TAKE THE TEST

Chapter Review Questions

1. To answer this question, use the following table that expresses the amount people are willing to pay for a dinner tonight at Fast Eddy's Grill.

Name of consumer	Price willing to pay
Matt	$20
Donovan	15
Savannah	8
Gertrude	12
Anna	7

If a dinner at Fast Eddy's tonight sells for $10, what is the value of Donovan's consumer surplus?
a. $20
b. $15
c. $10
d. $5

2. To answer this question, use the following table that expresses the amount people are willing to pay for a dinner tonight at Fast Eddy's Grill.

Name of consumer	Price willing to pay
Matt	$20
Donovan	15
Savannah	8
Gertrude	12
Anna	7

If a dinner at Fast Eddy's tonight sells for $9, what is the value of the total consumer surplus?
a. $20
b. $15
c. $10
d. $5

3. To answer this question, use the following table that expresses the amount people are willing to pay for a dinner tonight at Fast Eddy's Grill.

Name of consumer	Price willing to pay
Matt	$20
Donovan	15
Savannah	8
Gertrude	12
Anna	7

If a dinner at Fast Eddy's tonight sells for $11, who will not purchase a dinner at this restaurant?

a. Matt

b. Donovan

c. Savannah

d. Gertrude

4. To answer this question, use the following table that expresses the amount people are willing to pay for a dinner tonight at Fast Eddy's Grill.

Name of consumer	Price willing to pay
Matt	$20
Donovan	15
Savannah	8
Gertrude	12
Anna	7

If a dinner at Fast Eddy's tonight costs $4, what is the value of the consumer surplus tonight?

a. $80

b. $42

c. $32

d. $12

5. To answer this question, use the following table that expresses the amount people are willing to pay for a dinner tonight at Fast Eddy's Grill.

Name of consumer	Price willing to pay
Matt	$20
Donovan	15
Savannah	8
Gertrude	12
Anna	7

All five of these consumers want to go out to dinner together at Fast Eddy's tonight. Assuming each consumer pays for his or her own dinner, what is the maximum price that Fast Eddy can charge for each dinner if they all go out?

a. $5

b. $6

c. $7

d. $8

6. The market demand curve for peanuts in Carterville is given by the equation $P = 1 - 0.001Q$, where price is measured in dollars and peanuts are sold by the bag. If the market price is $0.50 per bag, the quantity demanded will equal _____ and the value of consumer surplus will be _____.

a. 5 bags; $125

b. 50 bags; $125

c. 500 bags; $125

d. 5,000 bags; $125

7. The market demand curve for peanuts in Carterville is given by the equation $P = 1 - 0.001Q$, where price is measured in dollars and peanuts are sold by the bag. If the market price is $0.20 per bag, the quantity demanded will equal _____ and the value of consumer surplus will be _____.
   a. 80 bags; $640
   b. 80 bags; $320
   c. 800 bags; $640
   d. 800 bags; $320

8. For a given linear demand curve, the value of consumer surplus
   a. decreases as the market price decreases.
   b. decreases as the market price increases.
   c. increases as the market price increases.
   d. Answers (a) or (c) are possible.

9. For a given linear demand curve, an increase in consumer surplus must be due to a(n)
   a. decrease in the market price.
   b. increase in the market price.

10. To answer this question, use the following table that expresses the number of dinners Fast Eddy's Grill is willing to prepare tonight at different prices.

Total number of dinners prepared	Price per dinner
1	$ 3
2	6
3	10
4	12
5	15

If a dinner at Fast Eddy's tonight sells for $10, what is the value of Fast Eddy's producer surplus?
   a. $11
   b. $9
   c. $16
   d. $19

11. To answer this question, use the following table that expresses the relationship between each dinner and the lowest price Fast Eddy's Grill is willing to accept to prepare that dinner.

	Lowest price Fast Eddy is willing to accept
First dinner	$ 3
Second dinner	6
Third dinner	10
Fourth dinner	12
Fifth dinner	15

If a dinner at Fast Eddy's tonight sells for $13, what is the value of Fast Eddy's producer surplus?
   a. $10
   b. $17
   c. $20
   d. $21

12. To answer this question, use the following table that expresses the relationship between each dinner and the lowest price Fast Eddy's Grill is willing to accept to prepare that dinner.

	Lowest price Fast Eddy is willing to accept
First dinner	$ 3
Second dinner	6
Third dinner	10
Fourth dinner	12
Fifth dinner	15

If the price of a dinner at Fast Eddy's tonight is $9, how many dinners will Fast Eddy sell?

a. 1 dinner
b. 2 dinners
c. 3 dinners
d. 4 dinners

13. To answer this question, use the following table that expresses the relationship between each dinner and the lowest price Fast Eddy's Grill is willing to accept to prepare that dinner.

	Lowest price Fast Eddy is willing to accept
First dinner	$ 3
Second dinner	6
Third dinner	10
Fourth dinner	12
Fifth dinner	15

If the price of a dinner at Fast Eddy's tonight is $13, how many dinners will Fast Eddy sell?

a. 1 dinner
b. 2 dinners
c. 3 dinners
d. 4 dinners

14. To answer this question, use the following table that expresses the relationship between each dinner and the lowest price Fast Eddy's Grill is willing to accept to prepare that dinner.

	Lowest price Fast Eddy is willing to accept
First dinner	$ 3
Second dinner	6
Third dinner	10
Fourth dinner	12
Fifth dinner	15

Which of the following dinner prices will lead to Fast Eddy's highest value of producer surplus?

a. $9
b. $10
c. $11
d. $12

15. Use the following graph to answer this question.

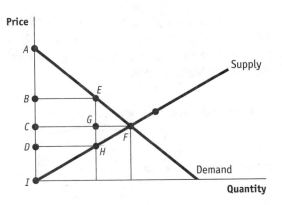

When this market is in equilibrium, consumer surplus is equal to area

a. *AEB.*

b. *EFG.*

c. *ACF.*

d. *CFI.*

16. Use the graph in question 15 to answer this question. When this market is in equilibrium, producer surplus is equal to area

a. *BEGC.*

b. *GFH.*

c. *DHI.*

d. *CFI.*

17. Use the graph in question 15 to answer this question. When this market is in equilibrium, total surplus is equal to area

a. *AFI.*

b. *BEFHD.*

c. *BEHD.*

d. *EFH.*

18. Which of the following statements is true?

   I. In a well-functioning market, each transaction that occurs represents a situation in which the value the buyer places on the good is greater than or equal to the value that the seller of the good places on the good.

   II. In a well-functioning market, all trades are mutually beneficial.

   III. In any well-functioning market situation, it is possible to reallocate sales so as to increase total surplus.

a. Statement I is true.

b. Statement II is true.

c. Statements I and II are true.

d. Statements I, II, and III are true.

19. In a well-functioning market

a. any reallocation of the good or service away from the market equilibrium necessarily increases total surplus.

b. any purchase that does not occur must be because the value the potential consumer places on the good exceeds the value the potential seller places on the good.

c. any purchase that does not occur must be because the value the potential seller places on the good exceeds the value the potential consumer places on the good.

d. consumers who place the lowest value on the good are the first ones able to consume the good.

20. The concept of producer surplus illustrates the idea that the market works to allocate sales to
    a. potential sellers who most value the right to sell the good, as indicated by their ability to produce the good at lowest cost.
    b. potential consumers who most value the right to consume the good, as indicated by their willingness to purchase the good at the highest price.

21. To make mutually beneficial trades in the marketplace, it is necessary to have
    a. well-defined property rights.
    b. government regulation of all transactions.
    c. some type of centralized decision making in the economy.
    d. many buyers and many sellers.

22. Which of the following statements is true about economic signals?
    I. Economic signals provide the vital information needed if markets are to function well.
    II. Economic signals refer only to the market price of the good.
    III. Economic signals help guide decision makers in their transactions in the marketplace.
    a. Statement I is true.
    b. Statement II is true.
    c. Statement III is true.
    d. Statements I and III are true.

23. Which of the following situations describes a situation of market failure?
    I. A seller has market power and is able to prevent a mutually beneficial transaction from occurring.
    II. A producer generates significant pollution when it produces its product but does not consider the cost of that pollution when pricing the product for the market.
    III. Important information about a good is not equally shared by all people.
    a. Statements I and II describe situations of market failure.
    b. Statements I and III describe situations of market failure.
    c. Statements I, II, and III describe situations of market failure.
    d. Statements II and III describe situations of market failure.

▌ANSWER KEY

Answers to Problems and Exercises

1. **a.** Mario places the highest value on this good since the price he is willing to pay ($300) is higher than the price any other consumer in this market is willing to pay.

b. Pete places the lowest value on this good since the price he is willing to pay ($50) is lower than the price any other consumer in this market is willing to pay.

c. If the good sells for $100, it will be purchased only by those consumers willing to pay $100 or more for the good. At this price Joe, Mary, Lucinda, and Mario will buy the good.

d. All five consumers would buy the good at this price since their willingness to buy is equal to or greater than $50.

e.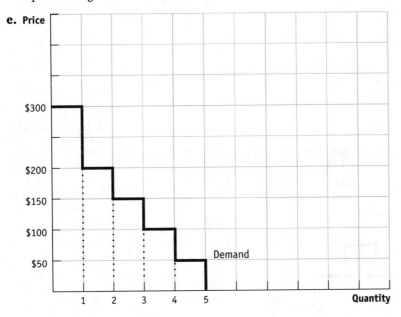

f. Mary's consumer surplus equals $200 − $100 = $100.

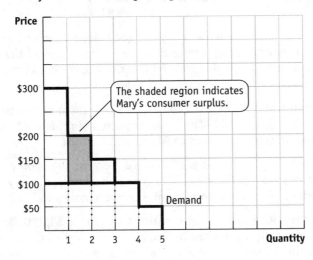

The shaded region indicates Mary's consumer surplus.

g. Mario's consumer surplus equals $300 − $100 = $200.

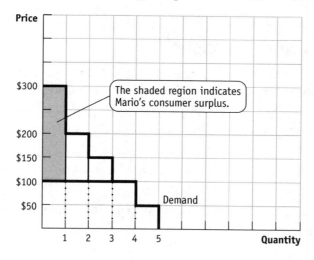

h. Total consumer surplus equals $350.

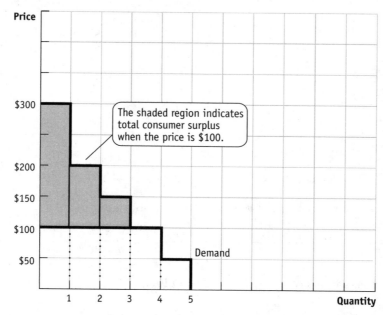

2. **a.** At a market price of $175, Mario and Mary will buy the good since they are the only potential consumers who are willing to pay a price that is equal to or greater than the market price. The value of consumer surplus is $150 (Mario receives consumer surplus of $125 while Mary receives consumer surplus of $25).

b. Mario has a consumer surplus of $300 − $175, or $125, while Lucinda's consumer surplus is equal to $150 − $175, or −$25. The total consumer surplus is therefore equal to $100 when the two units are allocated to Mario and Lucinda.

c. Consumer surplus is reduced when the good is reallocated, because the good goes to consumers who place a lower value on the good. This type of reallocation, away from the market's allocation, results in a failure to maximize consumer surplus.

3. **a.** When the price of widgets is $50, the value of consumer surplus is $1,250. To calculate the value of consumer surplus, you need to find the y-intercept of the demand curve ($100) and the quantity demanded (50 units) when the price is $50. Since the demand curve is smooth and linear, the value of consumer surplus is equal to the area under the demand curve and above the price: CS = (1/2)($100/widget − $50/widget)(50 widgets) = $1,250.

b. Use the process outlined in part (a) but with a price of $40 per widget instead of $50 per widget: CS = (1/2)($100/widget − $40/widget)(60 widgets) = $1,800.

c. When the market price rises, the consumer surplus decreases.

d. When the market price of widgets is $30, only 70 widgets will be demanded. At this price 80 widgets will not be sold.

e. Yes, when the market price is $30, the demand curve tells us 70 widgets will be demanded.

4.   **a.**

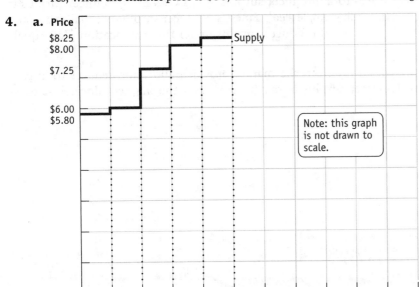

b. Red's Organic is the most likely seller at this quantity since they are willing to accept the lowest price for a bushel of apples.

c. At a price of $7.50 per bushel, the producer surplus for J. Appleseed's Finest is $0.25, or the difference between the market price and the seller's cost.

d. At a price of $7.50 per bushel, the producer surplus for Ski Top Orchards is $1.50, or the difference between the market price and the seller's cost.

e. The value of the producer surplus is $3.45 when the market price is $7.50.

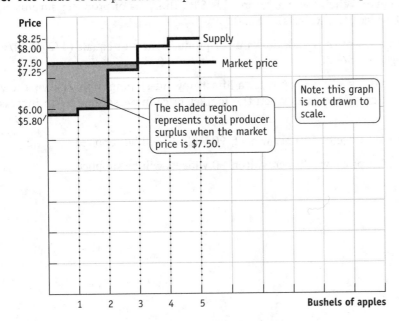

    f. Ski Top Orchards, J. Appleseed's Finest, and Red's Organic will each sell a bushel of apples when the market price is $7.50.

5. **a.** At a price of $7.00 a bushel, Ski Top Orchards and Red's Organic will be willing to sell apples. The value of producer surplus is equal to $1.00 for Ski Top Orchards and $1.20 for Red's Organic, for a total producer surplus of $2.20.

    b. When the sales in this market are reallocated away from the market-determined allocation, this reduces total producer surplus. Red's Organic's producer surplus is still equal to $1.20, while J. Appleseed's Finest's producer surplus is equal to $7.00 − $7.25, or −$0.25. Thus, total producer surplus under this reallocation plan equals $0.95.

    c. Reallocation of sales away from the market-provided allocation reduces total producer surplus. Producer surplus is maximized when the market allocates sales of the good.

6. **a.**

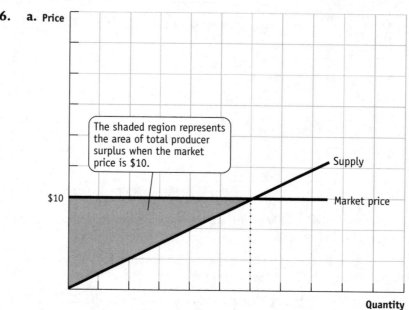

    b. The value of producer surplus is equal to the area under the market price and above the supply curve. When the market price is $10, this area of producer surplus equals $(1/2)(\$10/\text{widget})(30\ \text{widgets}) = \$150$.

    c. When the market price is $20, the value of producer surplus equals $(1/2)(\$20/\text{widget})(60\ \text{widgets}) = \$600$.

    d. Holding everything else constant, for a linear upward-sloping supply curve, the value of producer surplus increases when the market price increases due to an increase in demand.

    e. Yes, at a market price of $30 per widget, 90 widgets will be supplied.

    f. Yes, at a market price of $30 per widget, 90 widgets will be supplied.

7. **a.** Price

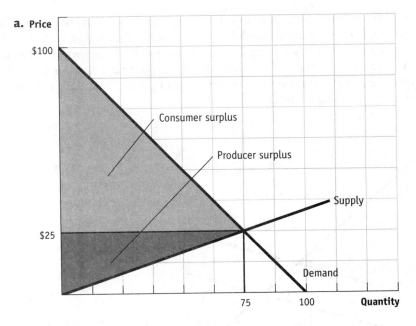

Since demand equals supply in equilibrium, we know $100 - Q = (1/3)Q$. Solving for Q, we find that the equilibrium quantity equals 75 widgets and the equilibrium price is $25.

b. Consumer surplus equals $(1/2)(\$100/\text{widget} - \$25/\text{widget})(75 \text{ widgets}) = \$2{,}812.50$. Producer surplus equals $(1/2)(\$25/\text{widget} - \$0/\text{widget})(75 \text{ widgets}) = \$937.50$.

c. The value of total surplus in this market equals the sum of producer and consumer surplus, or $3,750.00. Alternatively, you can calculate this area as follows: TS = $(1/2)(\$100/\text{widget} - \$0/\text{widget})(75 \text{ widgets}) = \$3{,}750.00$.

d. Price

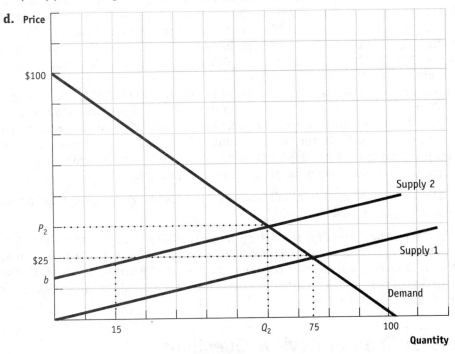

An increase in the price of an input causes the supply curve to shift to the left. In this example, the supply curve shifts to the left by a horizontal distance of 60 units. This tells us that if suppliers initially offered 75 units at a price of $25 per widget, they will now offer 15 widgets at a price of $25 per widget. This leftward shift in the supply curve causes the equilibrium price to rise from $25 to P_2 and the equilibrium quantity to decrease from 75 widgets to Q_2.

e.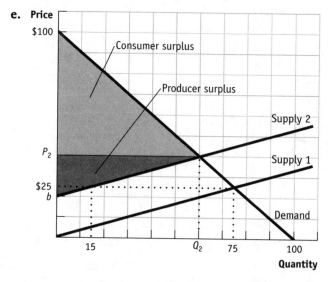

The calculation of consumer surplus and producer surplus is challenging in this problem. You need to write an equation for the new supply curve and then use this new equation with the original demand curve to calculate the numeric values of Q_2 and P_2. The new supply curve has the same slope as the original supply curve, but it has a different y-intercept. We can rewrite the new supply curve as $P = (1/3)Q + b$ and then substitute the coordinates (15, 25) into this equation to find the value of b. When you do this, you find that b, the y-intercept, has a value of 20. Thus, the new supply curve is $P = (1/3)Q + 20$. Using the new supply curve and the original demand curve, we can find Q_2 and P_2: $100 - Q = (1/3)Q + 20$, or $Q_2 = 60$ widgets and $P_2 = $50. To find consumer surplus, we calculate the area of the shaded region marked "consumer surplus" in the above figure: CS = $(1/2)($100/widget − $40/widget)(60 widgets) = $1,800. To find producer surplus, we calculate the area of the shaded region marked "producer surplus" in the above figure: PS = $(1/2)(P_2 − b)(Q_2$ widgets) = $(1/2)($40/widget − $20/widget)(60 widgets) = $600. Both consumer and producer surplus are decreased when the price of an input increases.

f. Total surplus in the market initially was equal to $3,750. When input prices increased, total surplus decreased to $2,400.

8. George will purchase one shirt since the price he is willing to pay for that shirt ($35) is greater than or equal to the price Oxford Clothiers must receive ($28) to be willing to sell the shirt. George will receive a consumer surplus of $7 when he purchases this shirt. George will not purchase two shirts since the value of the second shirt from George's perspective ($25) is less than the seller's price ($28).

Answers to Chapter Review Questions

1. **Answer d.** The value of Donovan's consumer surplus is the difference between the price Donovan is willing to pay ($15) and the market price ($10) of the good.

2. **Answer a.** When the price of a dinner is $9, Matt, Donovan, and Gertrude are willing to purchase a dinner, since the price they are willing to pay is greater than the $9 price. Matt's consumer surplus is equal to $20 − $9, or $11; Donovan's consumer surplus is

equal to $15 – $9, or $6; and Gertrude's consumer surplus is equal to $12 – $9, or $3. Adding these three numbers together gives a total consumer surplus of $20.

3. **Answer c.** At a price of $11 per dinner, we know that Savannah and Anna are both unwilling to purchase a dinner since the prices they are willing to pay are less than the $11 price.

4. **Answer b.** The value of consumer surplus is the difference between the price each consumer is willing to pay and the market price for all those consumers who are willing to purchase a dinner at the current dinner price. Thus, the total value of consumer surplus is equal to $42.

5. **Answer c.** The maximum price Fast Eddy can charge per dinner is $7, since this is the highest price that Anna is willing to pay for a dinner. Any price greater than $7 would eliminate Anna from purchasing a dinner.

6. **Answer c.** To find the quantity demanded at a price of $0.50 a bag, simply plug $0.50 into the given demand equation for the price and then solve for the quantity. To find the consumer surplus, you need to calculate the area under the demand curve and above the price of $0.50. This area is equal to (1/2)($1 – $0.50)(500 – 0), or $125.

7. **Answer d.** To find the quantity demanded at a price of $0.20 a bag, simply plug $0.20 into the given demand equation for the price and then solve for the quantity. To find the consumer surplus, you need to calculate the area under the demand curve and above the price of $0.20. This area is equal to (1/2)($1 – $0.20)(800 – 0), or $320.

8. **Answer b.** Since the value of consumer surplus is equal to the area under the demand curve and above the given price, this implies that for any given demand curve an increase in the price will decrease the value of consumer surplus.

9. **Answer a.** This follows from the same reasoning as that given in the answer to question 8.

10. **Answer a.** When a dinner sells for $10, Fast Eddy will provide 3 dinners. Eddy would have been willing to sell the first dinner for $3, and thus his producer surplus is equal to $10 – $3, or $7. Fast Eddy would be willing to sell the second dinner for $6, and thus his producer surplus for this dinner is equal to $10 – $6, or $4. Fast Eddy is willing to sell the third dinner for $10, and thus his producer surplus on the third dinner is equal to $0. His total producer surplus is equal to $11.

11. **Answer d.** To answer this question, use the same reasoning as in question 10. The total producer surplus is equal to $21.

12. **Answer b.** Fast Eddy is only willing to sell 2 dinners at a price of $9 per dinner since the third, fourth, and fifth dinners must sell for more than this $9 price.

13. **Answer d.** Fast Eddy is willing to sell 4 dinners at a price of $13. He is unwilling to sell the fifth dinner since he must receive at least $15 to be willing to provide this dinner.

14. **Answer d.** Fast Eddy will have the greatest producer surplus at a dinner price of $12. When the price is $11, his producer surplus is equal to $14, and when the price is $12, his producer surplus is equal to $17.

15. **Answer c.** Consumer surplus is equal to the area under the demand curve and above the equilibrium price. Since the equilibrium price is equal to C in the graph, this implies that the area of consumer surplus is equal to area ACF.

16. **Answer d.** Producer surplus is equal to the area above the supply curve and below the equilibrium price, which is area CFI in the graph.

17. **Answer a.** Total surplus is the sum of consumer and producer surplus, which is equal to area AFI.

18. **Answer c.** In a well-functioning market the equilibrium provides the maximum total surplus, and it is impossible in a well-functioning market to reallocate sales so as to

increase total surplus. Statements I and II are fairly transparent, straightforward, and true while statement III is false.

19. **Answer c.** In a well-functioning market, the equilibrium provides the maximum total surplus. Hence, answer (a) is not true. Purchases of a good in a well-functioning market imply that the value the consumer places on the good is greater than or equal to the value that the producer places on the good; hence, answer (b) is not true. Answer (d) is untrue: consumers who place the lowest value on the good are not the first consumers to get the good, and the consumers willing to pay the highest price for the good are the first consumers of the good. Answer (c) is true: producers will not sell the good if the value they place on the good is greater than the value consumers have for the good.

20. **Answer a.** Producer surplus measures the difference between the price producers are willing to accept for the good and the market price. Answer (b) is not true because it is focused on consumers.

21. **Answer a.** For the marketplace to function well, property rights must be well defined. Mutually beneficial trades do not require government regulation of all transactions, nor do they require centralized decision making or many buyers and many sellers.

22. **Answer d.** Statement I is true since economic signals provide important information to help individuals recognize which trades are mutually beneficial. Statement II is not true since price is only one of many potential economic signals. Statement III is true since economic signals help guide decision makers with regard to making transactions.

23. **Answer c.** Each of these statements describes a situation of market failure. Statement I focuses on market failure that occurs when one party—the monopolist—prevents mutually beneficial trades from occurring; Statement II focuses on market failure that is the result of an external cost that the market fails to include when determining the equilibrium quantity of the good to produce; and Statement III focuses on market failure that results from information problems.

chapter 5

The Market Strikes Back

Summary

This chapter develops the ideas of price controls and quantity controls in competitive markets and then illustrates how the implementation of these types of controls reduces the efficiency of a market. In particular, the chapter discusses effective price ceilings, whereby the government sets the price of the good below the equilibrium price; effective price floors, whereby the government sets the price of the good above the equilibrium price; and quantity controls, whereby the government limits the amount of the good available to a level lower than the equilibrium level of output. The chapter also discusses the distributional impact of market interventions.

Chapter Objectives

Objective #1. Price controls refer to the government's intervention in a market to set the price of the good or service at some level other than the equilibrium price. A price ceiling is the maximum price for a good or service allowed by the government, and a price floor is the minimum price for a good or service allowed by the government.

Objective #2. An effective price ceiling in a competitive market creates a situation of excess quantity demanded. If the price ceiling is set above the equilibrium price in the market, the price ceiling will not be effective and therefore will have no effect on the equilibrium price and the equilibrium quantity in the market.

Objective #3. An effective price ceiling prevents a market from being efficient because the price ceiling prevents transactions from occurring that would make some people better off without making other people worse off. In particular, an effective price ceiling prevents demanders who are willing to pay more for the good from consuming the good since the good's supply is artificially limited by the imposed price ceiling. Inefficiency arises because the price ceiling:

- reduces the quantity of the good available;

- reduces the value of total surplus;

- misallocates the good or service among consumers;

- wastes resources, as consumers spend resources searching for the good that is artificially scarce due to the price ceiling; and

- reduces the quality of the available units that would have been supplied in the absence of the price ceiling.

Objective #4.   Price ceilings provide incentives for illegal activities. Price ceilings are primarily instituted because they benefit some particular group of demanders.

Objective #5.   An effective price floor in a competitive market creates a situation of excess quantity supplied. If the price floor is set below the equilibrium price in the market, the price floor will have no effect on the equilibrium price and the equilibrium quantity in the market.

Objective #6.   An effective price floor results in market inefficiency because it prevents transactions from occurring that would make some people better off without making other people worse off. In particular, an effective price floor prevents suppliers who are willing to supply the good from selling the good since the good's demand is artificially limited by the imposed price floor. Inefficiency arises because the price floor:

- reduces the quantity of the good demanded;

- reduces the value of total surplus;

- misallocates the provision of the good or service by sellers;

- wastes resources, as suppliers search the market for a potential demander of the good; and

- increases the quality of the available units above the level that would have been demanded in the absence of the price floor.

Objective #7.   Price floors provide an incentive for illegal or black market activities, including the bribery and corruption of government officials. Price floors are primarily instituted because they benefit a particular group of sellers.

Objective #8.   The government may also implement quantity controls or a quota in a market. In this case the government sets a limit on the total quantity of the good that can be bought and sold in the market. This quantity is usually limited through the selling of licenses that legally grant the holder of the license the right to supply the good. Quantity controls always set a maximum amount allowed. To be binding in the market, the quota must be set below the equilibrium quantity.

Objective #9.   A quota or quantity control creates a wedge between the price consumers are willing to pay for the good and the price at which producers are willing to supply the good. The difference between these two prices is the quota rent, or the income that the license holder receives from their ownership of a valuable commodity (the license).

Objective #10. Quantity controls are inefficient because they prevent some mutually beneficial transactions from occurring, since the demand price for a given quantity (the quota amount) is greater than the supply price for that quantity. These missed transactions create an incentive to evade the quota limit, often through illegal activity.

Key Terms

price controls legal restrictions on how high or low a market price may go.

price ceiling a maximum price sellers are allowed to charge for a good or service; a form of *price control.*

price floor a minimum price buyers are required to pay for a good or service; a form of *price control.*

deadweight loss the loss in total surplus that occurs whenever an action or a policy reduces the quantity transacted below the efficient market *equilibrium quantity.*

inefficient allocation to consumers a form of inefficiency in which people who want the good badly and are willing to pay a high price don't get it, and those who care relatively little about the good and are only willing to pay a low price do get it; often a result of a *price ceiling.*

wasted resources a form of inefficiency in which people expend money, effort, and time to cope with the shortages caused by a *price ceiling.*

inefficiently low quality a form of inefficiency in which sellers offer low-quality goods at a low price even though buyers would prefer a higher quality at a higher price; often a result of a *price ceiling.*

black market a market in which goods or services are bought and sold illegally, either because it is illegal to sell them at all or because the prices charged are legally prohibited by a *price ceiling.*

minimum wage a legal floor on the wage rate. The wage rate is the market price of labor.

inefficient allocation of sales among sellers a form of inefficiency in which sellers who would be willing to sell a good at the lowest price are not always those who actually manage to sell it; often the result of a *price floor.*

inefficiently high quality a form of inefficiency in which sellers offer high-quality goods at a high price even though buyers would prefer a lower quality at a lower price; often the result of a *price floor.*

quantity control an upper limit, set by the government, on the quantity of some good that can be bought or sold; also referred to as a *quota.*

quota an upper limit, set by the government, on the quantity of some good that can be bought or sold; also referred to as a *quantity control.*

quota limit the total amount of a good under a *quota* or *quantity control* that can be legally transacted.

license the right, conferred by the government, to supply a good.

demand price the price of a given quantity at which consumers will demand that quantity.

Key Terms *(continued)*

supply price the price of a given quantity at which producers will supply that quantity.

wedge the difference between the *demand price* of the quantity transacted and the *supply price* of the quantity transacted for a good when the supply of the good is legally restricted. Often created by a *quantity control*, or *quota*.

quota rent the difference between the *demand price* and the *supply price* at the *quota limit*; this difference, the earnings that accrue to the license-holder, is equal to the market price of the *license* when the license is traded.

■ AFTER YOU READ THE CHAPTER

Tips

Tip #1. Students often find it confusing to remember the difference between a price floor and a price ceiling.

- A floor is a surface that you stand on and that is solid. A price floor is the *lowest* price that can be charged for a good. Figure 5.1 illustrates a price floor. To be effective, a price floor must be set at a price that is greater than the equilibrium price. At P_F, Q_1 units will be supplied and Q_2 units will be demanded. An effective price floor always results in a surplus of the good.

Figure 5.1

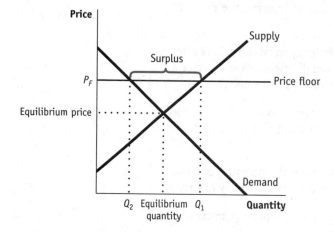

- A ceiling is a surface that you hope is solid and stays above your head. A price ceiling is the *highest* price that can be charged for a good. Figure 5.2 illustrates a price ceiling. To be effective, a price ceiling must be set at a price that is less than the equilibrium price. At P_C, Q_1 units will be supplied and Q_2 units will be demanded. An effective price ceiling always results in a shortage of the good.

Figure 5.2

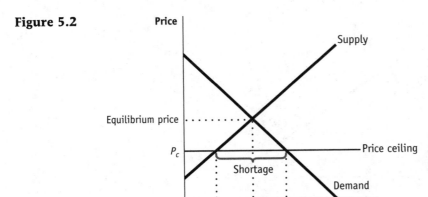

Tip #2.   A quota, or quantity control, is a policy implemented by the government to set a maximum amount of the good or service that can be sold in a market. A quota has no effect if it is set at a level greater than the equilibrium quantity; to be effective a quota must be set at a level smaller than the equilibrium quantity. Figure 5.3 illustrates an effective quantity control, or quota, where the maximum allowed quantity is set by the government at Q_1. At Q_1 demanders are willing to pay P_1 for each unit of the good they consume, while suppliers are willing to supply the good at price P_2. This difference, $P_1 - P_2$, is referred to as a wedge. This wedge corresponds to the quota rent the license holder of the good receives when the quantity control is imposed in a market. This quota rent represents the additional compensation the license holder receives from selling the good in a market where the quantity of the good has been artificially restricted.

Figure 5.3

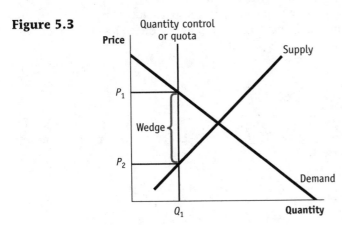

Problems and Exercises

1.   Use the graph below to answer the following questions.

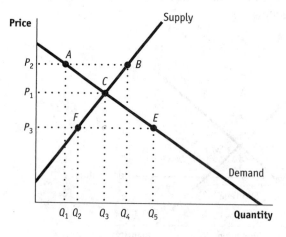

a.   Identify the equilibrium price and the equilibrium quantity.

b.   Suppose a price floor of P_3 is implemented by the government in this market. Describe what will happen to the price and quantity once this price floor is implemented.

c.   Suppose a price floor of P_2 is implemented by the government in this market. Describe what will happen to the price and quantity once this price floor is implemented.

d.   What must be true about a price floor in a market for a good or service in order for that price floor to be effective?

e.   You are told that an effective price floor has been implemented in this market and that the resultant surplus is greater than $Q_4 - Q_1$. What do you know about the level of this price floor?

2. Use the graph below to answer the following questions.

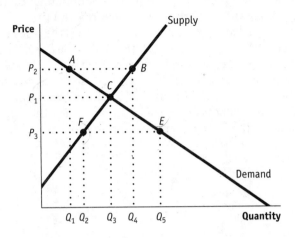

a. Identify the equilibrium price and the equilibrium quantity.

b. Suppose a price ceiling of P_2 is implemented by the government in this market. Describe what will happen to the price and quantity once this price ceiling is implemented.

c. Suppose a price ceiling of P_3 is implemented by the government in this market. Describe what will happen to the price and quantity once this price ceiling is implemented.

d. What must be true about a price ceiling in a market for a good or service in order for that price ceiling to be effective?

e. You are told that an effective price ceiling has been implemented in this market and that the resultant shortage is smaller than $Q_5 - Q_2$. What do you know about the level of this price ceiling?

3. Consider the market for housing in Metropolitan City, where all housing units are exactly the same. Currently the equilibrium price of housing is $2,000 a month and local residents consume 1,500 units of housing. The local residents argue that housing is too expensive and that an effective price ceiling should be implemented. Once the price ceiling is implemented by the local government council, only 1,200 units of housing are supplied in this market. Is this an efficient level of housing for Metropolitan City? Explain your answer. To support your answer, provide two sketches: in the first sketch indicate the equilibrium quantity, the equilibrium price, and the area of total surplus; in the second sketch indicate the price ceiling, the area of total surplus, and the area that represents the efficiency loss due to the reduction in the quantity of housing units.

4. A price ceiling is implemented in the market for housing in Metropolitan City, where all housing units are identical. You know that before the price ceiling is implemented, the demand for housing in Metropolitan City is given by the equation $P = 1,000 - 0.1Q_D$ and the supply of housing is given by the equation $P = 200 + 0.3Q_S$.

    a. Prior to the implementation of the price ceiling, what is the equilibrium price for housing in Metropolitan City and what is the equilibrium quantity of housing?

    b. Fill in the following demand and supply schedules for this market given the above equations.

Price	Quantity demanded	Quantity supplied
$ 200		
400		
600		
800		
1,000		

c. When the price ceiling is implemented, a housing shortage develops. This shortage is equal to 4,000 housing units. Calculate the price ceiling in this market for housing. (Hint: you may find the table from part (b) helpful in thinking about this problem.)

d. Who benefits from the imposition of the price ceiling in the market for housing in Metropolitan City?

e. Who is hurt by the imposition of a price ceiling in the market for housing in Metropolitan City?

f. Why is this price ceiling apt to result in black market activities in the market for housing? Provide at least two examples of potential black market activities.

g. Does an effective price ceiling in this market result in too many or too few resources being allocated to the market for housing in Metropolitan City? Explain your answer.

5. Farmers in Corntopia successfully lobby their government to enact a price floor for their agricultural commodity. The price floor is set at $10 above the equilibrium price. The initial demand and supply curves for agricultural production in Corntopia are as follows: $P = 100 - Q$ and $P = Q$, where price is per bushel and quantity is measured in bushels.

a. What is the level of the price floor in this market?

b. How many units of the agricultural product will be demanded and supplied at this price floor level?

c. Suppose the government purchases the surplus in this market once the price floor is implemented. What will be the cost to the government of buying this surplus?

d. Given the price floor, what is the expenditure consumers make when purchasing this commodity? Do not include in your calculation the cost to the government of buying the surplus.

e. What is total farm revenue equal to in this market once the price floor is implemented? What is the relationship between total farm revenue, consumer expenditure, and government expenditure on the good, given the price floor? Does total farm revenue increase when the government enacts a price floor? Explain your answer.

f. Who benefits from the enactment of a price floor in this market?

6. a. Draw a graph of the demand and supply curves given to you in problem 5. Label the equilibrium price and the equilibrium quantity on this graph. Shade in the area that corresponds to total farm revenue in this market and label this area clearly.

Price

Quantity

b. Redraw the graph of the demand and supply curves given to you in problem 5, and draw in a line indicating the price floor. On the graph, indicate the quantity demanded and the quantity supplied using the values you found in problem 5. Shade in and clearly label the areas that correspond to consumer expenditure on the good and government expenditure on the good, given the price floor.

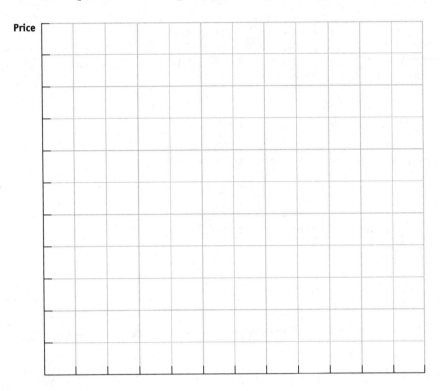

Price

Quantity

7. Consider the following graph.

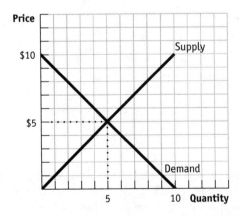

Price

$10

$5

Supply

Demand

5   10 **Quantity**

a. What price are consumers willing to pay for this good if 1 unit of the good is produced? What price must sellers receive to be willing to sell 1 unit of the good? Given that resources are scarce, should this first unit of the good be produced? Explain your answer.

b. What price are consumers willing to pay for the second unit of the good if 2 units are produced? What price must sellers receive to be willing to sell this second unit of the good? Given that resources are scarce, should the second unit of this good be produced? Explain your answer.

c. Generalize your findings from parts (a) and (b) of this question. What is the optimal amount of the good to be produced expressed in terms of the consumers' willingness to pay and the sellers' costs?

d. If this market produces a total of 4 units of this good, are resources being underallocated or overallocated to this market? Explain your answer.

e. What is the inefficiency cost that occurs if this market produces and sells only 4 units of the good?

8. Consider the following graph.

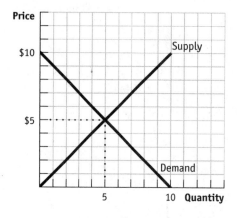

a. What price are consumers willing to pay for this good if 8 units of the good are produced? What price must sellers receive to be willing to provide 8 units of the good? Given that resources are scarce, should this market produce 8 units of the good? Explain your answer.

b. What price are consumers willing to pay if 7 units are produced? What price must sellers receive to be willing to produce 7 units of the good? Given that resources are scarce, should this market produce 7 units of the good? Explain your answer.

c. Given your findings in parts (a) and (b), make a general statement about the optimal amount of the good to produce expressed in terms of the consumers' willingness to pay and the sellers' costs.

d. If this market produces a total of 9 units of the good, are resources being underallocated or overallocated to this market? Explain your answer.

e. What is the inefficiency cost that occurs if this market produces and sells 9 units of the good?

9. Consider the labor market in Utopia. You are told that the equilibrium wage in this market is $10 per hour and that the equilibrium amount of labor in this market is 1,000 hours of labor. Furthermore, you know that at a wage of $14 per hour, 600 hours of labor are demanded and 1,400 hours of labor are supplied. The workers in Utopia successfully lobby Utopia's government for the implementation of a price floor. This price floor results in 1,200 hours of labor being supplied and 800 hours of labor being demanded.

a. Use the above information to derive the labor demand curve for Utopia. Assume this labor demand curve is linear. In your equation, abbreviate the price of labor, or its hourly wage rate, as W, and the quantity of labor demanded, measured as hours of labor, as L. Hint: you may find sketching a graph of the above information helpful.

Wage rate per hour of labor

Quantity of hours of labor

b. Use the above information to derive the labor supply curve for Utopia. Assume this labor supply curve is linear. In your equation, abbreviate the hourly wage rate as *W* and the hours of labor supplied as *L*.

c. What wage rate did the government set when it implemented the price floor?

d. Describe the effects of this price floor on the labor market in Utopia. Who benefits from the price floor? Who is hurt by the price floor?

10. The market for taxi rides in Metropolia this week is described in the following table. Assume that all taxi rides are the same in Metropolia.

Price of taxi rides	Quantity of taxi rides demanded per week	Quantity of taxi rides supplied per week
$ 1	200	40
2	180	60
3	160	80
4	140	100
5	120	120
6	100	140
7	80	160
8	60	180
9	40	200
10	20	220

a. What is the equilibrium price and the equilibrium quantity of taxi rides in Metropolia per week?

Suppose the government of Metropolia institutes a medallion system that limits the number of taxi rides available in Metropolia per week to 80 taxi rides.

b. At what price will consumers want to purchase 80 taxi rides per week?

c. At what price will suppliers be willing to supply 80 taxi rides per week?

d. What price will a taxi medallion rent for in this market? Explain your answer.

e. Draw a graph of the taxi ride market in Metropolia. On this graph, indicate the quota limit, the demand price, the supply price, and the medallion's rental price.

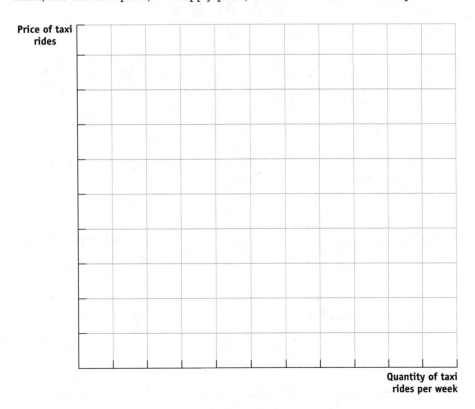

f. What is the total value of the taxi medallions per week in Metropolia?

BEFORE YOU TAKE THE TEST

Chapter Review Questions

1. The implementation of an effective price ceiling
   a. decreases the area of producer surplus.
   b. increases the area of producer surplus.

2. The implementation of an effective price floor
   a. decreases the area of consumer surplus.
   b. increases the area of consumer surplus.

3. When demanders can make a strong moral or political case for lower prices in a market, the government may decide to enact an effective
   a. price floor.   b. price ceiling.

4. When suppliers can make a strong moral or political case for higher prices in a market, the government may decide to enact an effective
   a. price floor.   b. price ceiling.

5. Consider minimum-wage legislation requiring that all workers receive a wage payment greater than the equilibrium market wage. Which of the following two groups is more likely to have advocated for this legislation?
   a. demanders of labor   b. suppliers of labor

6. When the government intervenes in a market to regulate prices, this is an example of a
   a. quantity control.   c. price ceiling.
   b. price floor.   d. price control.

7. When the government institutes an upper limit on prices, this is referred to as a
   a. quantity control.   c. price ceiling.
   b. price floor.   d. price control.

8. When the government institutes a lower limit on prices, this is referred to as a
   a. quantity control.   c. price ceiling.
   b. price floor.   d. price control.

9. Use the information in the table below to answer the following question.

Price	Quantity demanded	Quantity supplied
$ 20	200	0
40	150	50
60	100	100
80	50	150
100	0	200

If the government mandates that prices in this market can fall no lower than $50, this results in

a. a situation of excess quantity demanded.

b. a situation of excess quantity supplied.

c. fewer than 100 units being supplied in this market.

d. no effect in this market, since the equilibrium price is greater than $50.

10. Use the information in the table below to answer the following question.

Price	Quantity demanded	Quantity supplied
$ 20	200	0
40	150	50
60	100	100
80	50	150
100	0	200

Suppose a price floor of $40 is implemented in this market. This results in
a. an excess demand of 100 units.
b. an excess supply of 100 units.
c. no effect in this market, since the price floor is set below the equilibrium price.
d. no effect in this market, since the price floor is set above the equilibrium price.

11. Use the information in the table below to answer the following question.

Price	Quantity demanded	Quantity supplied
$ 20	200	0
40	150	50
60	100	100
80	50	150
100	0	200

Suppose a price ceiling of $40 is implemented in this market. This results in
a. an excess demand of 100 units.
b. an excess supply of 100 units.
c. no effect in this market, since the price ceiling is set below the equilibrium price.
d. a temporary shortage of the good while prices rise, and the quantity demanded and the quantity supplied adjust until they are equal.

12. Use the information in the table below to answer the following question.

Price	Quantity demanded	Quantity supplied
$ 20	200	0
40	150	50
60	100	100
80	50	150
100	0	200

If the price ceiling is set at $40 in this market, then
a. too few resources are being allocated to the production of this good.
b. too many resources are being allocated to the production of this good.

13. Which of the following statements are true?

    I. Price ceilings are inefficient because they result in too much of the good being produced in the market.

    II. Price ceilings are inefficient because they result in the production of goods with too low a level of quality.

    III. Price ceilings are inefficient because they lead to wasted resources since they increase the amount of time consumers must search for the price-controlled good.

    a. Statement I is true.

    b. Statement II is true.

    c. Statements I and II are true.

    d. Statements II and III are true.

14. Use the information in the table below to answer the following question.

Price	Quantity demanded	Quantity supplied
$ 20	200	0
40	150	50
60	100	100
80	50	150
100	0	200

If the price ceiling is set at $40 in this market, the loss in total surplus in this market equals

    a. $2,000.

    b. $1,000.

    c. $500.

    d. $200.

15. An effective price ceiling typically causes an inefficient allocation of the good to

    a. consumers of the good.

    b. producers of the good.

16. Black market or illegal activities increase with the imposition of price controls in markets. Black markets result in

    a. improving the situation of all participants in the price-controlled market.

    b. worsening the situation for those people who attempt to obey the rules and restrictions imposed by the government in a price-controlled market.

    c. have little or no real impact in price-controlled markets.

    d. the creation of greater respect in society for the need to obey all laws.

17. Use the following graph to answer this question.

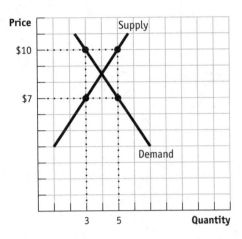

An effective price floor is implemented in the market depicted in the graph. This price floor generates an excess quantity supplied of 2 units in this market. This price floor must be equal to

a. $10.

b. $7.

18. Use the following graph to answer this question.

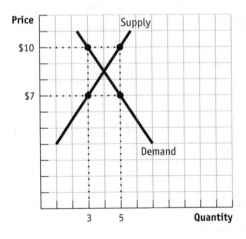

An effective price floor is enacted in this market, and with this price floor the government promises to purchase any unwanted units produced. If the price floor is set at $10, then the government will spend _____ purchasing the unwanted units of the good.

a. $50

b. $30

c. $21

d. $20

19. Use the following graph to answer this question.

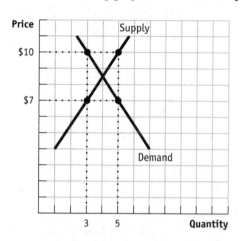

An effective price floor is enacted in this market at a price of $10. With this price floor, consumers' expenditure on this good will equal

a. $50.

b. $30.

c. $21.

d. $20.

20. Which of the following statements is true?

a. An effective price ceiling reduces the quantity of the good available to consumers, while an effective price floor increases the quantity of the good available to consumers.

b. An effective price floor reduces the quantity of the good available to consumers, while an effective price ceiling increases the quantity of the good available to consumers.

c. Government intervention in markets in the form of effective price ceilings or price floors increases the quantity of the good available to consumers.

d. Government intervention in markets in the form of effective price ceilings or price floors decreases the quantity of the good available to consumers.

21. Use the graph below to answer this question. Different areas in the graph are labeled with letters.

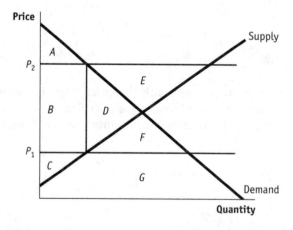

An effective price floor set at P_2 results in a loss of total surplus equal to

a. area D.

b. areas A and C.

c. area E.

d. area G.

22. When a price is artificially set above the equilibrium price in a market, who determines the quantity of the good bought and sold in the market?

a. demanders

b. suppliers

23. When suppliers determine the quantity of the good bought and sold in a market, this must be due to the imposition of an effective
    a. price floor.   b. price ceiling.

24. An effective price floor prevents suppliers from competing for customers through lower prices, so suppliers compete for customers by offering goods with
    a. greater quality than consumers desire.
    b. lower quality than consumers desire.

25. Which of the following statements is true?
    I. An effective price floor benefits some suppliers.
    II. An effective price floor benefits all demanders.
    III. An effective price floor results in a persistent surplus.
    IV. An effective price floor results in an inefficiently high level of quality in the good offered by suppliers.
    a. Statements I and III are true.
    b. Statements I, III, and IV are true.
    c. Statements III and IV are true.
    d. Statements II, III, and IV are true.

26. A quantity control or quota
    a. limits the price that suppliers can charge for the good or service in the regulated market.
    b. limits the price that demanders must pay for the good or service in the regulated market.
    c. limits the amount of the good or service available in the regulated market.
    d. increases the amount of the good or service available in the regulated market to an amount that exceeds the equilibrium quantity.

27. A quota limit imposed on a market
    a. restricts the amount of the good available in that market.
    b. results in a payment being made by the government to the license holder.
    c. places a lower limit on the amount of the good provided in the regulated market.
    d. places an upper limit on the price of the good provided in the regulated market.

28. Which of the following statements is true?
    I. Quantity controls are inefficient since they prevent mutually beneficial transactions from occurring.
    II. Quantity controls in a market result in too many resources being allocated to that market.
    III. Quantity controls result in a wedge: the price demanders are willing to pay for the last unit is less than the price suppliers must receive to produce this last unit.
    a. Statement I is true.
    b. Statement II is true.
    c. Statements I and III are true.
    d. Statements I, II, and III are true.

29. Quantity controls
    a. provide an incentive to engage in illegal activities.
    b. result in underproduction of the good or service in the market where the quota limit has been imposed.
    c. result in a less efficient outcome than the market outcome.
    d. Answers (a), (b), and (c) are all true statements.

◼ ANSWER KEY

Answers to Problems and Exercises

1. **a.** The equilibrium price is P_1 and the equilibrium quantity is Q_3.

   b. This is not an effective price floor since the price floor of P_3 is less than the equilibrium price P_1. Since it is a nonbinding/ineffective price floor, the equilibrium price and quantity will not change.

   c. This is an effective price floor since the price floor of P_2 is greater than the equilibrium price P_1. At P_2, Q_1 units of the good will be demanded and Q_4 units of the good will be supplied. This excess supply of $Q_4 - Q_1$ will not be eliminated by price decreases since the price is artificially set at P_2 by the government and is not allowed to decrease. An effective price floor creates a situation of excess supply, or a surplus, that is not eliminated by changes in the price of the good because the price has been set at a level that is greater than the market-clearing price.

   d. For a price floor to have an effect in a market, the price floor must be set at a price that is greater than the equilibrium price.

   e. The price floor must be set at a price that is greater than P_2 since we know from part (c) that the surplus in the market at P_2 equals $Q_4 - Q_1$.

2. **a.** The equilibrium price is P_1 and the equilibrium quantity is Q_3.

   b. This is not an effective price ceiling since the price ceiling of P_2 is greater than the equilibrium price P_1. Since it is a nonbinding/ineffective price ceiling, the equilibrium price and quantity will not change.

   c. This is an effective price ceiling since the price ceiling of P_3 is less than the equilibrium price P_1. At P_3, Q_5 units of the good will be demanded and Q_2 units of the good will be supplied. This excess demand of $Q_5 - Q_2$ will not be eliminated by price increases since the price is artificially set at P_3 by the government and is not allowed to increase. An effective price ceiling creates a situation of excess demand, or a shortage, that is not eliminated by changes in the price of the good because the price has been set at a level that is less than the market-clearing price.

   d. For a price ceiling to have an effect in a market, the price ceiling must be set at a price that is less than the equilibrium price.

   e. The price ceiling must be set at a price that is greater than P_3 but still less than the equilibrium price of P_1. We know this because when the price ceiling is set at P_3, the shortage is equal to $Q_5 - Q_2$, and the new price ceiling results in a smaller shortage than the shortage at price P_3.

3. The market is in equilibrium when there are 1,500 units of housing offered at the price of $2,000 per month, so 1,200 is not an efficient level of housing. The price ceiling forces consumers to reduce their consumption of the good from the efficient level. In the sketch below, the shaded area represents the total surplus received when 1,500 units of housing are supplied at a price of $2,000 per unit.

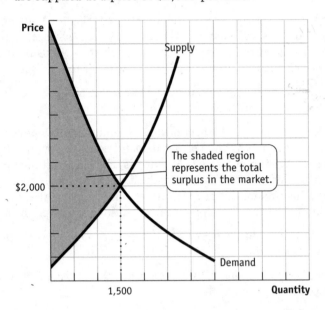
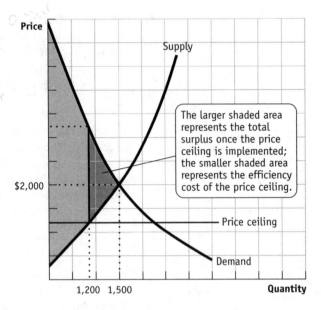

The second sketch illustrates the area of total surplus once the effective price ceiling is implemented. Notice that the area of total surplus is reduced relative to its initial level: the amount of this loss in total surplus is the measure of the efficiency cost of the reduction in quantity provided in the market due to the imposition of the price ceiling.

4.   a. The equilibrium price is $800 per unit of housing and the equilibrium quantity of housing is 2,000 units.

b.

Price	Quantity demanded	Quantity supplied
$ 200	8,000	0
400	6,000	666.67
600	4,000	1,333.33
800	2,000	2,000
1,000	0	2,666.67

c. From the table in part (b), you know that a price ceiling of $400 is too low (the shortage is greater than 4,000 units of housing at this price) while a price ceiling of $600 is too high (the shortage at this price is less than 4,000 units of housing). You could try some prices between $400 and $600 or you could solve this problem algebraically. The shortage of 4,000 units is the difference between the quantity demanded and the quantity supplied at the price ceiling, or in other words, $Q_S + 4,000 = Q_D$. Thus, the demand equation can be rewritten as $P_C = 1,000 - 0.1(Q_S + 4,000)$ and the supply equation is equal to $P_C = 200 + 0.3Q_S$, where P_C is the price ceiling level. Solving this set of equations, we find that the quantity supplied is equal to 1,000 units. Thus, the quantity demanded is equal to 5,000 units while the price ceiling level is $500.

d. The people lucky enough to get one of the housing units supplied at the price ceiling price benefit from this government intervention. These individuals pay less than the market-clearing price for their housing unit.

e. Consumers who want housing but who cannot find housing due to the price ceiling are hurt by the decision to implement the price ceiling. Additionally, as landlords fail to maintain the housing units in Metropolitan City, the whole community is affected as the general condition of the housing stock deteriorates. And if a black market develops in the housing market, this will erode the general level of lawful behavior in the community.

f. Since the quantity demanded of housing exceeds the quantity supplied of housing at the price ceiling, persistent shortages will exist in this market. Consumers eager to find housing will resort to activities that are illegal—for example, subletting housing units at rates higher than the price ceiling rate or making illegal payments to landlords.

g. Too few resources are devoted to the housing market. We know this because the effective price ceiling creates a persistent shortage in the market for housing.

5. **a.** The level of the price floor in this market is $60 per bushel. To find the price floor level, first solve for the equilibrium price in the market: set demand equal to supply. Thus, $100 - Q = Q$, and thus the equilibrium quantity is 50 bushels of the agricultural commodity. We can then substitute this quantity into either the demand or supply equation to find the equilibrium price. The equilibrium price is $50 per bushel. If the price floor is set $10 above the equilibrium price, we know the price floor must be at $60 per bushel.

b. At $60 per bushel, demanders demand 40 bushels and suppliers supply 60 bushels. There is an excess supply of 20 bushels.

c. If the government buys the surplus 20 bushels at the price floor level of $60 per bushel, it will spend $1,200.

d. Consumers demand 40 bushels at the price of $60 per bushel. The expenditure by consumers on the product will equal $2,400.

e. Total farm revenue equals the total number of bushels supplied times the price floor, or (60 bushels)($60 per bushel), or $3,600. Total farm revenue equals the sum of consumer expenditure on the good plus government expenditure on the good. Total farm revenue without the price floor is equal to the equilibrium price times the equilibrium quantity, or (50 bushels) ($50 per bushel), or $2,500. Total farm revenue increases with the imposition of an effective price floor.

f. The farmers benefit from the imposition of the price floor since it increases total farm revenue.

6. **a.**

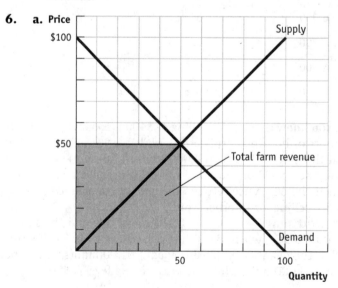

b.

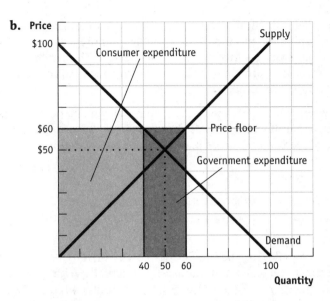

7. **a.** To answer this set of questions, you need the demand and supply equations that correspond to the graph. Using the graph as a reference, we can write the demand equation as $P = 10 - Q$ and the supply equation as $P = Q$. Plugging a quantity value of 1 into both of these equations reveals that demanders are willing to pay $9 for the first unit and suppliers need to receive $1 to produce this first unit. Clearly this first unit should be produced since the value to the consumer ($9) exceeds the seller's cost of producing it ($1).

b. Using the equations found in part (a), we can substitute a value of 2 for the quantity in both equations to find that demanders are willing to pay $8 for the second unit and suppliers need to receive $2 to produce the second unit. The second unit of the good should be produced since its value to consumers ($8) exceeds the seller's cost of producing it ($2).

c. The optimal amount of the good to produce is the amount at which the consumers' willingness to pay for the last unit exactly equals the producers' cost of producing the last unit. So long as the value the consumer places on the good (the price they are willing to pay) exceeds the cost the seller must receive to produce the good, not enough of the good is being produced.

d. Resources are being underallocated to this market since consumers are willing to pay $6 for the last unit produced (the fourth unit) while suppliers are willing to sell this last unit so long as the price is at least equal to $4. When the value the consumers place on the last unit produced is greater than the cost of producing this last unit, not enough of the good is being produced.

e. The inefficiency cost would equal $1. The inefficiency cost is (1/2)(the price consumers are willing to pay − the price sellers must receive)(the equilibrium market quantity of the good − the actual level of production), or (1/2)($6/unit − $4/unit) (5 units − 4 units), or $1.

8. **a.** To answer this set of questions, you need the demand and supply equations. Using the graph as a reference, we can write the demand equation as $P = 10 - Q$ and the supply equation as $P = Q$. Plugging a quantity of 8 into both of these equations, we find that consumers are willing to pay a price of $2 for the good and suppliers need to receive a price of $8 for the good to produce 8 units. Since the value the consumer places on the eighth unit ($2) is less than the cost of producing the eighth unit ($8), the eighth unit should not be produced.

b. Using the same reasoning as outlined in answer (a), we find that consumers are willing to pay $3 per unit if 7 units are produced and suppliers require a price of $7 per unit to be willing to produce 7 units. Since the value of the seventh unit to the consumer ($3) is less than the cost of producing the seventh unit for the producer ($7), the seventh unit should not be produced.

c. The optimal amount of the good to produce is the amount at which the consumers' willingness to pay for the last unit exactly equals the producers' cost of producing the last unit. So long as the value the consumer places on the good (the price they are willing to pay) is less than the cost the seller must receive to produce the good, too much of the good is being produced.

d. Resources are being overallocated to this market: too much of this good is being produced since the value consumers place on the last unit produced is less than the cost to sellers of producing the last unit.

e. The inefficiency cost would equal $16. The inefficiency cost is (1/2)(the price sellers must receive – the price consumers are willing to pay)(the actual level of production – the equilibrium market quantity of the good), or (1/2)($9/unit – $1/unit)(9 units – 5 units), or $16.

9. a. The information you are given in this problem can be represented as follows:

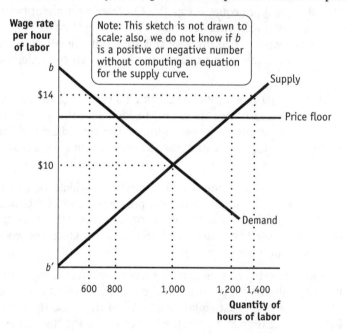

Thus, we know two points of the labor demand curve: (1,000, $10) and (600, $14). Use these two points to compute the slope of the demand curve: slope = rise/run = $(y_1 - y_2)/(x_1 - x_2) = (10 - 14)/(1{,}000 - 600) = -0.01$. The demand equation can be written as $W = b - 0.01L$. Then, use one of the points that you know is on the demand curve—either (1,000, $10) or (600, $14)—with this equation to solve for b. Thus, $W = b - 0.01L$ can be written as $10 = b - 0.01(1{,}000)$, or $b = 20$. The labor demand curve is therefore $W = 20 - 0.01L$.

b. Use a similar procedure to write the supply equation: $W = 0.01L + b'$, where b' is the y-intercept of the labor supply curve. Then use one of the points that you know is on the supply curve—either (1,000, $10) or (1,400, $14)—with this equation to identify the value of b'. Thus, $W = 0.01L + b'$ can be rewritten as $10 = 0.01(1{,}000) + b'$ and b' therefore equals 0. The labor supply equation is thus $W = 0.01L$.

c. At the price floor, we know that the quantity of labor demanded is 800 units. Substitute this number for L in the labor demand equation: W = 20 − 0.01(800), or W = $12 per hour of labor. To verify that the price floor has been set at a wage of $12 per hour of labor, check your answer with the labor supply equation. At the price floor, we know the quantity of labor supplied is equal to 1,200 units. Using this number for L in the labor supply equation, we find W = 0.01(1,200), or W = $12 per hour of labor.

d. This price floor creates a surplus of labor when the price floor is set at a wage rate of $12 per hour of labor. In a labor market, a surplus of labor implies that there is unemployment: workers who want to work (i.e., they are willing to supply their labor at the prevailing wage rate) cannot find work (i.e., there is insufficient demand for their services at the prevailing wage rate). Workers lucky enough to get a job paying $12 per hour benefit from the price floor while workers who are unable to find work at that wage rate are harmed by the price floor.

10. a. Equilibrium occurs when the quantity demanded equals the quantity supplied. From the table, we can see that the equilibrium price is $5 and the equilibrium quantity is 120 taxi rides per week.

b. Consumers will demand 80 taxi rides per week at a price of $7.

c. Suppliers are willing to supply 80 taxi rides per week for a price of $3.

d. The medallion will rent for $4 per taxi ride, or the difference between the demand price and the supply price when the quantity of taxi rides is limited to 80 rides per week.

e.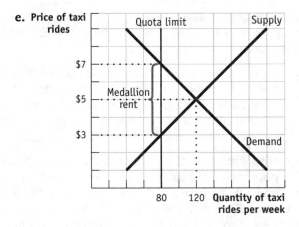

f. The taxi medallions are worth the product of the medallion rent per ride times the number of taxi rides per week. Thus, the taxi medallions' worth per week equals ($4 per taxi ride)(80 taxi rides), or $320.

Answers to Chapter Review Questions

1. Answer a. Since an effective price ceiling reduces the price that producers receive and consumers pay, this results in a decrease in producer surplus.

2. Answer a. Since an effective price floor increases the price that producers receive and consumers pay, this results in a decrease in consumer surplus.

3. Answer b. Demanders desire lower prices for the good and this can be achieved through the enactment of an effective price ceiling, since it reduces the price below the equilibrium price.

4. **Answer a.** Producers desire higher prices for the good and this can be achieved through the enactment of an effective price floor, since it raises the price above the equilibrium price.

5. **Answer b.** Suppliers of labor will receive this higher wage and therefore benefit from it. Demanders of labor will find that this higher wage increases the cost of hiring labor, and they will not benefit from it.

6. **Answer d.** The government can intervene in a market to regulate prices so that they are lower than the equilibrium level (an effective price ceiling) or higher than the equilibrium level (an effective price floor). Both are examples of price controls.

7. **Answer c.** An upper limit on prices establishes a price level for a product that is less than the equilibrium price and cannot be exceeded. This is an example of an effective price ceiling.

8. **Answer b.** A lower limit on prices establishes a minimum price level for a product that is in excess of the equilibrium price for that product. This is an example of an effective price floor.

9. **Answer d.** Setting a lower limit on prices of $50 in this market is an example of an ineffective price floor since a price floor of $50 is less than the equilibrium price of $60. This price floor would have no effect on the market.

10. **Answer c.** Setting a price floor of $40 in this market is an example of an ineffective price floor since a price floor of $40 is less than the equilibrium price of $60. This price floor would have no effect on the market.

11. **Answer a.** A price ceiling of $40 results in 150 units being demanded and 50 units being supplied. This is therefore a situation of excess demand of 100 units.

12. **Answer a.** At a price ceiling of $40, consumers wish to consume 150 units of the good while suppliers are only willing to supply 50 units of the good. This indicates that too few resources are being allocated to this market.

13. **Answer d.** Statement I is incorrect because price ceilings result in too little of the good being produced in the market. Statement II is correct because when price is limited to a level below the equilibrium price, producers have an incentive to reduce the quality of the product they provide to the market. Statement III is correct because an effective price ceiling results in greater costs as demanders seek out the artificially scarce good.

14. **Answer b.** The total surplus in the market when there is no price ceiling is equal to $4,000. With the imposition of the effective price ceiling the total surplus equals $3,000. To find these areas of total surplus, sketch a graph and then calculate the relevant areas. The initial total surplus is equal to (1/2)($100/unit – $20/unit)(100 units) or $4,000. The total surplus with the effective price ceiling is equal to (1/2)($100/unit –$80/unit)(50 units) + (1/2)($40/unit – $20/unit)(50 units) + ($80/unit – $40/unit)(50 units), or $3,000. The graph below illustrates this.

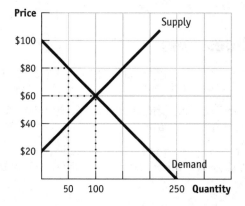

The change in total surplus is $4,000 – $3,000, or $1,000.

15. **Answer a.** An effective price ceiling limits the amount of the good available to consumers in the market by limiting the price to a level that is less than the equilibrium price. Producers produce the amount they are willing to produce at that price, and they do not expand production even though consumers are willing to consume more units of the good.

16. **Answer b.** Answers (a) and (b) are mutually exclusive: if one of these answers is correct, then the other must by necessity be incorrect. Reading answer (b) helps to identify a group that is hurt by black market activities: those individuals who decide not to engage in black market activities are left worse off because of their obedience to the rules imposed by the price-controlled market. Answer (c) is incorrect since price controls do affect markets and do have impacts when they are effective. Answer (d) is also incorrect since price-controlled markets generate black market activities, which are against the law.

17. **Answer a.** An effective price floor is the minimum price that can be charged for a good, and this price must be set above the equilibrium price. At a price of $10, the quantity demanded is 3 units while the quantity supplied is 5 units. At a price floor of $10, there will be excess supply of 2 units. The price floor must equal $10.

18. **Answer d.** At a price floor of $10, the excess supply is 2 units. If the government purchases these 2 units at $10 each, the cost to the government of this purchase is $20.

19. **Answer b.** With a $10 price floor, consumers in this market will demand 3 units of the good. Their expenditure on the good will equal ($10/unit)(3 units), or $30.

20. **Answer d.** Effective price ceilings and price floors both reduce the quantity of the good available to consumers, so answers (a), (b), and (c) are not true.

21. **Answer a.** When the price floor is set at P_2, the area of total surplus is equal to areas $A + B + C$. Without the price floor, the area of total surplus is equal to areas $A + B + C + D$. The loss in total surplus due to the imposition of the effective price floor is equal to area D.

22. **Answer a.** When the price is artificially set above the equilibrium price, demanders determine the quantity demanded in the market since they select the quantity they are willing to demand based on the price of the good.

23. **Answer b.** A price ceiling is set below the equilibrium price. This limits the price that can be charged for a good in the market. Producers take this price and then determine the number of units of the good they are willing to provide in the market at this price.

24. **Answer a.** When producers cannot compete for customers through prices, they must look for other ways to compete. One way is to offer goods of higher quality, and with an effective price floor producers will compete by offering higher-quality goods.

25. **Answer b.** Statement I is correct because those suppliers who are lucky enough to sell their good at the higher price are benefited. Statement III is also correct since an effective price floor results in excess supply of the good. Statement IV is correct as well because suppliers will compete for customers by offering higher-quality goods since they cannot compete for customers by offering lower prices. Statement II is incorrect: demanders of this good now have to pay a higher price than they would have in a freely functioning market.

26. **Answer c.** A quota control by definition is a limit on the number of units of the good that can be offered in the market. Answers (a) and (b) are both incorrect since they discuss price controls rather than quantity controls. Answer (d) is also incorrect since a quota limit reduces the amount of the good available rather than increasing the amount of the good available.

27. **Answer a.** Answer (a) is the basic definition of a quota limit. Answer (b) is incorrect since there is no assumption of the government making a payment to the license holder when there is a quota limit. Answer (c) is incorrect since a quota limit represents the maximum amount of the good allowed in a market rather than the minimum amount. Answer (d) is incorrect since it focuses on price controls rather than quantity controls.

28. **Answer a.** Statement I is correct because quantity controls restrict the amount of output to a level that is less than the equilibrium amount of output, and thus are inefficient since they prevent mutually beneficial trades from occurring. Because quantity controls restrict output, this implies that too few resources are devoted to the production of the good, so statement II is incorrect. Quantity controls do result in a wedge being created, but that wedge is the difference between the price consumers are willing to pay and the price producers must receive to provide the good, thus statement III is incorrect.

29. **Answer d.** Quantity controls restrict output, result in too few resources being devoted to the production of the good, and create an incentive for black market activities as consumers seek out alternative methods for getting the scarce good.

chapter 6

Elasticity

Summary

This chapter develops the concept of elasticity, which provides a numerical measure of the responsiveness of quantity to changes in prices or income. The price elasticity of demand measures the responsiveness of the quantity demanded to changes in the price of the good, while the price elasticity of supply measures the responsiveness of the quantity supplied to changes in the price of the good. Income elasticity of demand measures the responsiveness of the quantity demanded to changes in income. Cross-price elasticity of demand measures the responsiveness of the quantity demanded to changes in the price of another good. This chapter also discusses the factors that influence these elasticities.

Chapter Objectives

Objective #1. The price elasticity of demand measures the responsiveness of the percentage change in the quantity demanded to the percentage change in the price of the good. Thus, the price elasticity of demand can be written as

$$\text{Price elasticity of demand} = \frac{\%\text{ change in the quantity demanded of good X}}{\%\text{ change in the price of good X}}$$

Since demand curves typically slope downward, a positive change in price (i.e., a price increase) results in a negative change in the quantity demanded (i.e., a decrease in quantity demanded). Thus, the price elasticity of demand is usually a negative number. By convention, economists measure the price elasticity of demand in absolute value terms so that the negative sign is eliminated.

$$\text{Price elasticity of demand} = \left| \frac{\%\text{ change in the quantity demanded of the good}}{\%\text{ change in the price of the good}} \right|$$

a. The calculation of the percentage change in the quantity demanded of good X can be found using the formula

$$\%\text{ change in quantity demanded} = \frac{\text{change in quantity demanded}}{\text{initial quantity demanded}} \times 100$$

b. The calculation of the percentage change in the price of good X can be found by using the formula

$$\% \text{ change in the price of good X} = \frac{\text{change in price of good X}}{\text{initial price of good X}} \times 100$$

c. To generate consistent measures for price elasticities, regardless of an increase or decrease in price, economists calculate the percentage changes using the midpoint method. For example, consider two points on a demand curve: (Q_1, P_1) and (Q_2, P_2). The percentage change in quantity demanded using the midpoint method can be expressed as

$$\% \text{ change in quantity demanded} = (Q_2 - Q_1)/[(Q_2 + Q_1)/2]$$

while the percentage change in price is expressed as

$$\% \text{ change in price} = [(P_2 - P_1)/(P_2 + P_1)/2]$$

Using these two formulas, the price elasticity of demand formula using the midpoint method can be written as

$$\text{Price elasticity of demand} = \left| \frac{\dfrac{Q_2 - Q_1}{Q_2 + Q_1}}{\dfrac{P_2 - P_1}{P_2 + P_1}} \right| = \left| \frac{\dfrac{Q_2 - Q_1}{Q_2 + Q_1}}{\dfrac{P_2 - P_1}{P_2 + P_1}} \right|$$

Objective #2. Consider a numerical example illustrating the mathematical relationships described in Objective 1. Suppose the demand curve for good X is given by the equation $P = 100 - Q$ and you are asked to compute the price elasticity of demand when quantity increases from 80 units to 90 units on this demand curve. First you need to calculate the price demanders are willing to pay when the quantity demanded is equal to 90 units: this price is $10. Then, you need to calculate the price demanders are willing to pay when the quantity demanded is equal to 80 units: this price is $20. Figure 6.1 below provides a graph of this demand curve with point A on the demand curve corresponding to a price of $10 and a quantity demanded of 90 units and point B on the demand curve corresponding to a price of $20 and a quantity demanded of 80 units.

Figure 6.1

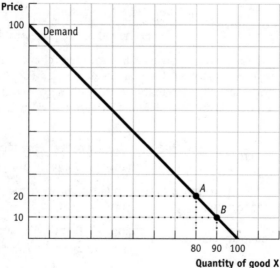

Using this information, you can then calculate the percentage change in the quantity demanded of good X and the percentage change in the price of good X using the midpoint method. Thus,

The percentage change in the quantity demanded of good X =
$[(80 - 90)/2]/[(80 + 90)/2] \times 100 = -5.9$

The percentage change in the price of good X =
$[(20 - 10)/2]/[(20 + 10)/2] \times 100 = 33.3$

To find the price elasticity of demand, take the absolute value of the percentage change in the quantity demanded of good X divided by the percentage change in the price of good X. Thus,

The price elasticity of demand = 5.9/33.3 = 0.18

Suppose that the price had originally been $10 and that the price had increased to $20. Does the price elasticity of demand change if you move from along the demand curve from the point (90, 10) to the point (80, 20)? The midpoint method of calculating the price elasticity of demand insures that the calculation of elasticity does not depend upon the direction of movement along the demand curve from one point to another. To see this recalculate the price elasticity of demand moving from point B to point A.

The percentage change in the quantity demanded of good X =
$[(90 - 80)/2]/[(90 + 80)/2] \times 100 = 5.9$

The percentage change in the price of good X =
$[(10 - 20)/2]/[(10 + 20)/2] \times 100 = -33.3$

To find the price elasticity of demand, take the absolute value of the percentage change in the quantity demanded of good X divided by the percentage change in the price of good X. Thus,

The price elasticity of demand = 5.9/33.3 = 0.18

The midpoint method of calculating the price elasticity of demand results in the price elasticity of demand being the same whether we move from point A to point B or from point B to point A.

Objective #3. A vertical demand curve indicates that the quantity demanded is completely unresponsive to price changes. A vertical demand curve is perfectly inelastic and its measure of price elasticity of demand equals zero.

Objective #4. A horizontal demand curve indicates that the quantity demanded is extremely responsive to price changes: even a small increase in price results in demand dropping to zero units, while a small decrease in price results in an extremely large increase in the quantity demanded. A horizontal demand curve is perfectly elastic and its measure of price elasticity of demand equals infinity.

Objective #5. A large value for the price elasticity of demand indicates that consumers are highly responsive to changes in the price of the good. Referring to the formula for the price elasticity of demand (the general formula given in Objective 1), a price elasticity of demand value that is greater than one implies that the percentage change in the quantity demanded in absolute value terms is greater than the percentage change in the price of the good in absolute value terms. When the price elasticity of demand is greater than one, demand is elastic.

Objective #6. A small value for the price elasticity of demand indicates that consumers are less responsive to changes in the price of the good. A price elasticity of demand value that is less than one implies that the percentage change in the quantity demanded in absolute value terms is less than the percentage change in the price of the good in absolute value terms. Thus, when price changes, consumers respond with a relatively small change in the quantity of the good they demand. When the price elasticity of demand is less than one, demand is inelastic.

Objective #7. When the price elasticity of demand equals one, the demand is unit elastic. A price elasticity of demand value of one implies that the percentage change in the quantity demanded of good X is exactly equal to the percentage change in the price of good X in absolute value terms.

Objective #8. For a straight line demand curve that intersects both the vertical and horizontal axes, the midpoint of that demand curve is the unit elastic point. Above the midpoint, demand is elastic, while below the midpoint, demand is inelastic. Figure 6.2 illustrates this idea.

Figure 6.2

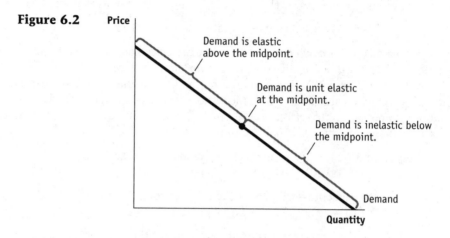

Objective #9. Total revenue is affected by the price elasticity of demand. If demand is inelastic, then an increase in price causes total revenue to increase. If demand is elastic, then an increase in price causes total revenue to decrease. An increase in price that moves symmetrically around the unit elastic point has no effect on total revenue.

Objective #10. A change in price affects total revenue in two ways: first, the price effect is the change in total revenue due to the change in the price of the good, and second, the quantity effect is the change in total revenue due to the change in the number of units of the good sold. The price effect is stronger than the quantity effect when demand is inelastic; the quantity effect is stronger than the price effect when demand is elastic; and the price effect and the quantity effect exactly offset each other when demand is unit elastic.

  a. Figure 6.3 illustrates the effect on total revenue of an increase in price when demand is relatively inelastic. Starting at point E, total revenue is initially P_1Q_1 or the sum of areas B and A. When price increases to P_2 (point F), total revenue changes to P_2Q_2, or the sum of areas C and B. In this example, area A represents the quantity effect, while area C represents the price effect. When price increases, the quantity effect on total revenue is negative while the price effect on total revenue is positive, with the price effect dominating the quantity effect and leading to an increase in total revenue.

Figure 6.3

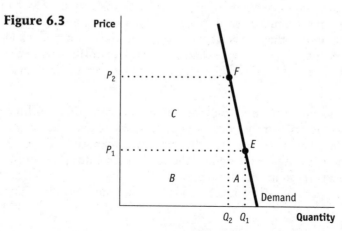

b. Figure 6.4 illustrates the effect on total revenue of an increase in price when demand is relatively elastic. When demand is elastic, the effect on total revenue of the quantity effect (area A) is larger than the price effect (area C).

Figure 6.4

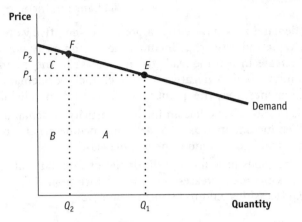

c. The table below summarizes the relationship between the price elasticity of demand and the effect of changes in price on total revenue, the price effect, and the quantity effect.

Demand	Price	Total revenue	Price effect	Quantity effect
Elastic	Increases	Decreases		Dominates
Elastic	Decreases	Increases		Dominates
Inelastic	Increases	Increases	Dominates	
Inelastic	Decreases	Decreases	Dominates	
Unit elastic	Increases	No effect	Exactly offsets quantity effect	Exactly offsets price effect
Unit elastic	Decreases	No effect	Exactly offsets quantity effect	Exactly offsets price effect

Objective #11. Price elasticity of demand is affected by the number of available substitutes, whether the good is a necessity or a luxury, and the time period for adjustment to the price change. Demand is more elastic when there are close substitutes, when the good is a luxury, and/or when there is more time to adjust to the price change. Demand is less elastic when there are no close substitutes, when the good is a necessity, and/or when there is little time to adjust to the price changes.

Objective #12. The cross-price elasticity of demand between goods A and B is equal to the percentage change in the quantity demanded of good A divided by the percentage change in the price of good B. That is,

$$\text{Cross-price elasticity of demand} = \frac{\%\ \text{change in the quantity demanded of good A}}{\%\ \text{change in the price of good B}}$$

Cross-price elasticity of demand may be a positive or negative number, and the sign of the cross-price elasticity of demand is critical to the interpretation of the meaning of a particular cross-price elasticity value. A positive cross-price elasticity of demand indicates that good A and good B are substitutes: if the price of good B increases, this leads to an increase in the quantity of good A demanded. A negative cross-price elasticity of demand indicates that good A and good B are complements: if the price of good B increases, this leads to a decrease in the quantity of good A demanded.

Objective #13. The income elasticity of demand is equal to the percentage change in the quantity demanded of the good divided by the percentage change in income. That is,

$$\text{Income elasticity of demand} = \frac{\% \text{ change in the quantity demanded of the good}}{\% \text{ change in income}}$$

Income elasticity of demand may have either a positive or negative value. A positive income elasticity of income value indicates that income and the quantity demanded move in the same direction: an increase in income leads to an increase in the quantity demanded, and thus the good is a normal good. A negative income elasticity of demand value indicates an inferior good: as income increases, the quantity of the good demanded decreases.

    a. A good that is income elastic has an income elasticity of demand that is greater than one. When income increases, demand for income-elastic goods rises faster than income. Luxury goods tend to be income elastic.

    b. Income-inelastic goods have income elasticities of demand that are positive but less than one. When income increases, demand for income-inelastic goods rises slower than income. Necessities tend to be income inelastic.

Objective #14. The price elasticity of supply is defined as the percentage change in the quantity supplied of good A divided by the percentage change in the price of good A. To get consistent measures of the price elasticity of supply, the percentage changes in quantity supplied and price are both calculated using the midpoint method. Thus, the price elasticity of supply can be expressed as

$$\text{Price elasticity of supply} = \frac{\% \text{ change in the quantity supplied of good A}}{\% \text{ change in the price of good A}}$$

or, for two points (Q_1, P_1) and (Q_2, P_2) on a supply curve

$$\text{Price elasticity of supply} = \left| \frac{\dfrac{Q_2 - Q_1}{Q_2 + Q_1}}{\dfrac{2}{\dfrac{P_2 - P_1}{P_2 + P_1}}} \right| = \left| \frac{\dfrac{Q_2 - Q_1}{Q_2 + Q_1}}{\dfrac{P_2 - P_1}{P_2 + P_1}} \right|$$

    a. A vertical supply curve has a price elasticity of supply equal to zero and is an example of a perfectly inelastic supply curve.

    b. A horizontal supply curve has a price elasticity of supply equal to infinity and is an example of a perfectly elastic supply curve.

Objective #15. The price elasticity of supply is affected by the availability of inputs and the time period for adjustment. Supply is more price elastic the greater the availability of inputs and/or in the long run when full adjustment to price changes has occurred.

Key Terms

price elasticity of demand the ratio of the percent change in the *quantity demanded* to the percent change in the price as we move along the *demand curve* (dropping the minus sign).

Notes

Key Terms *(continued)*

midpoint method a technique for calculating the percent change in which changes in a variable are compared with the average, or midpoint, of the starting and final values.

perfectly inelastic demand the case in which the *quantity demanded* does not respond at all to changes in the price; the *demand curve* is a vertical line.

perfectly elastic demand the case in which any price increase will cause the *quantity demanded* to drop to zero; the *demand curve* is a horizontal line.

elastic demand when the *price elasticity of demand* is greater than 1.

inelastic demand when the *price elasticity of demand* is less than 1.

unit-elastic demand the case in which the *price elasticity of demand* is exactly 1.

total revenue the total value of sales of a good or service (the price of the good or service multiplied by the quantity sold).

cross-price elasticity of demand a measure of the effect of the change in the price of one good on the *quantity demanded* of the other; it is equal to the percent change in the quantity demanded of one good divided by the percent change in the price of another good.

income elasticity of demand the percent change in the quantity of a good demanded when a consumer's income changes divided by the percent change in the consumer's income.

income-elastic demand when the *income elasticity of demand* for a good is greater than 1.

income-inelastic demand when the *income elasticity of demand* for a good is positive but less than 1.

price elasticity of supply a measure of the responsiveness of the quantity of a good supplied to the price of that good; the ratio of the percent change in the *quantity supplied* to the percent change in the price as we move along the *supply curve*.

perfectly inelastic supply the case in which the *price elasticity of supply* is zero, so that changes in the price of the good have no effect on the *quantity supplied*; the perfectly inelastic *supply curve* is a vertical line.

perfectly elastic supply the case in which even a tiny increase or reduction in the price will lead to very large changes in the *quantity supplied*, so that the *price elasticity of supply* is infinite; the perfectly elastic *supply curve* is a horizontal line.

▮ AFTER YOU READ THE CHAPTER

Tips

Tip #1. Economists calculate a variety of elasticities because these measures provide important insights into the relationship between two different variables. All elasticities are calculated as the ratio between the percentage changes in quantity (either the quantity demanded or the quantity supplied) to the percentage change in some other related variable. Elasticities are unit-free, making them an ideal measure of sensitivity of one variable to changes in another variable. In general, we can think of elasticity as being defined as

$$\text{Elasticity} = \frac{\%\ \text{change in quantity (either quantity demanded or quantity supplied)}}{\%\ \text{change in a related variable}}$$

a. The price elasticity of demand is thus

$$\text{Price elasticity of demand} = \left| \frac{\%\ \text{change in the quantity demanded of good A}}{\%\ \text{change in the price of good A}} \right|$$

b. The price elasticity of supply is thus

$$\text{Price elasticity of supply} = \frac{\%\ \text{change in the quantity supplied of good A}}{\%\ \text{change in the price of good A}}$$

c. The cross-price elasticity of demand is thus

$$\text{Cross-price elasticity of demand} = \frac{\%\ \text{change in the quantity demanded of good A}}{\%\ \text{change in the price of good B}}$$

d. The income elasticity of demand is thus

$$\text{Income elasticity of demand} = \frac{\%\ \text{change in the quantity demanded of good A}}{\%\ \text{change in income}}$$

Tip #2. In general, to find the percentage change in a variable requires dividing the change in the variable by its initial value and then multiplying this value by 100. That is,

$$\%\ \text{change in a variable} = \frac{\text{the change in the variable}}{\text{the initial value of the variable}} \times 100$$

Tip #3. The midpoint method is used in calculating the price elasticity of demand and the price elasticity of supply. This method modifies the formula given in Tip 2 so that the results of the elasticity calculation provide a measure that is not dependent on which point on the demand or supply curve is designated the initial point. Objective 1c provides the formula for the midpoint method of calculating the price elasticity of demand, and Objective 13 provides the formula for the price elasticity of supply.

Tip #4. Total revenue is equal to the price per unit times the quantity. Total revenue at any given price is equal to the area of a rectangle whose height is the price and whose width is the quantity demanded at this price. Figure 6.5 illustrates this concept of total revenue for the given demand curve.

Figure 6.5

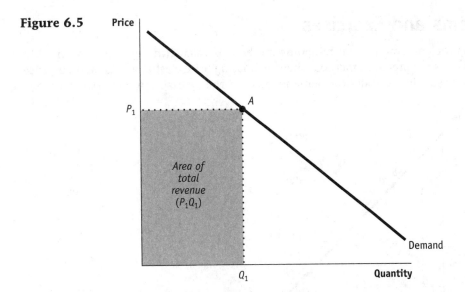

At point A, the price is P_1 and the quantity demanded is Q_1. The total revenue for the firm when the price equals P_1 is $P_1 \times Q_1$ (the shaded area in the graph).

Tip #5. For a given demand curve, a change in price causes total revenue to change because of two effects—the price effect and the quantity effect. Figure 6.6 illustrates these effects.

Figure 6.6

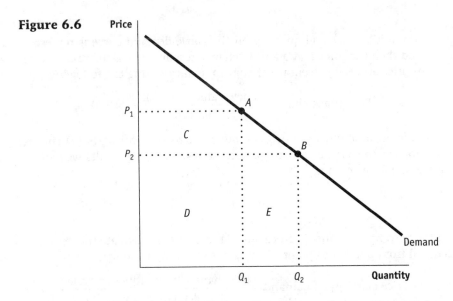

Suppose we are initially at point A with price P_1 and quantity Q_1. Then total revenue equals P_1Q_1, or the sum of areas C and D. If price decreases to P_2, then this causes a movement along the demand curve to point B with price P_2 and quantity Q_2. Total revenue is now equal to P_2Q_2, or the sum of the areas D and E. The price effect on total revenue is measured by area C: it reflects the change in revenue (in this case a loss in revenue) that arises from selling the original quantity Q_1 for the new price of P_2 instead of the initial price of P_1. The quantity effect on total revenue is measured by area E: it reflects the change in total revenue (in this case a gain in revenue) that arises from selling an additional $Q_2 - Q_1$ units of the good at the new price P_2. A similar argument holds for increases in price: you will find it helpful to redo this example starting at point B and moving to point A and thinking about the price and quantity effects.

Problems and Exercises

1. This problem explores the midpoint method of calculating percentages and why this method is the preferred method when calculating price elasticity of demand or price elasticity of supply. Consider the demand curve in the figure below to answer this question.

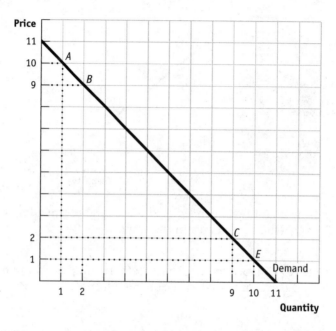

a. Suppose the initial price and quantity on the above demand curve is represented by point A and then the price and quantity change to point B. Calculate the percentage change in price and the percentage change in quantity using the following formula:

$$\text{Percentage change} = \frac{\text{new value} - \text{old value}}{\text{old value}} \times 100$$

Note: we are purposefully *not* using the midpoint method for parts (a) through (e) of this problem so that we can compare these results to the results we would get if using the midpoint method.

b. Using the percentage changes you calculated in part (a), calculate the price elasticity of demand from point A to point B, using the following formula:

$$\text{Price elasticity of demand} = \left| \frac{\% \text{ change in quantity demanded}}{\% \text{ change in price}} \right|$$

c. Redo part (a) starting at point B and moving to point A. Use the same formula as that given in part (a).

d. Calculate the price elasticity of demand from point B to point A using the formula given in part (b).

e. Are your values for the price elasticity of demand the same in parts (a) and (d)?

Now, let's recalculate the price elasticity of demand using the midpoint method.

f. Suppose you are initially at point *A* and that you move to point *B*. Calculate the percentage change in price and the percentage change in quantity using the following (midpoint method) formula:

$$\% \text{ change} = \frac{\text{new value} - \text{old value}}{\dfrac{\text{old value} + \text{new value}}{2}} \times 100$$

g. Using the percentage changes you calculated in part (f), calculate the elasticity of demand from point *A* to point *B* using the following formula:

$$\text{Price elasticity of demand} = \left| \frac{\% \text{ change in quantity demanded}}{\% \text{ change in price}} \right|$$

where both percentage changes have been calculated using the midpoint method.

h. Suppose you now start at point *B* and move to point *A*. Calculate the percentage change in price and the percentage change in quantity using the formula given in part (f).

i. Calculate the price elasticity of demand from point *B* to point *A* using the formula given in part (g).

j. Are the values you calculated for the price elasticity of demand using the midpoint method the same in parts (g) and (i)? Summarize the significance of the midpoint method when calculating the price elasticity of demand or the price elasticity of supply.

2. Use the figure from problem 1 to answer this question.

a. Calculate a value for the price elasticity of demand between points *C* and *E* using the midpoint method. Does it matter which point you select as your initial point?

b. Compare the value you calculated in part (a) of this problem with the price elasticity of demand value between points *A* and *B* that you calculated in part (g) of problem 1. Are these two price elasticities of demand the same?

c. Demand is elastic when the absolute value of the percentage change in the quantity demanded exceeds the absolute value of the percentage change in the price. Given the values you compared in part (b), is demand elastic between points *A* and *B* or between points *C* and *E*?

d. Demand is inelastic when the absolute value of the percentage change in the quantity demanded is less than the absolute value of the percentage change in the price. Given the values you compared in part (b), is demand inelastic between points *A* and *B* or between points *C* and *E*?

3. Use the figure below of a linear demand curve to answer this set of questions.

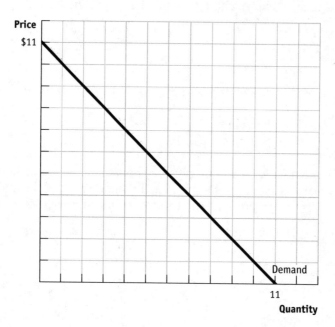

a. Based on the above figure, fill in the following table:

Price	Quantity demanded	Total revenue
$ 0		
1		
2		
3		
4		
5		
6		
7		
8		
9		
10		
11		

b. At what price is total revenue maximized? (Hint: this may be a price that is *not* included in your table.)

c. Suppose the price is initially $6, but it then decreases to $5. Calculate the elasticity of demand between these two points on the demand curve using the midpoint method.

d. Based on your calculations in part (c), describe the relationship between the absolute value of the percentage change in the quantity demanded and the absolute value of the percentage change in price when moving from a price of $6 to a price of $5.

4. For each of the following pairs of goods, identify which good is likely to have the more elastic price elasticity of demand, and then provide an explanation for your choice.

a. Golden delicious apples and all fruit

b. Gasoline and ice cream

   c. Leisure travel and business travel

5. Suppose there are two goods, good A and good B. When the price of good A increases from $10 to $12, the quantity of good B demanded changes from 4 units to 6 units.

   a. Calculate the cross-price elasticity of demand (use the simple formula for percentage changes rather than the midpoint method).

   b. What is the relationship between good A and good B? Explain your answer and provide an example of two goods that have this relationship.

6. Suppose there are two goods, good C and good D. The cross-price elasticity of demand for these two goods is equal to –0.2.

   a. What is the relationship between good C and good D? Explain your answer.

   b. Suppose the price of good C increases from $1 to $2. What do you estimate will be the percentage change in the quantity demanded of good D? (Use the simple formula for percentage changes rather than the midpoint method.)

   c. Suppose when the price of good C is $1 that 10 units of good D are demanded. What will be the quantity demanded of good D when the price of good C increases to $2?

   d. Suppose the cross-price elasticity of demand between two goods is negative and you would like to sell more units of one of these goods. What do you hope will happen to the price of the other good? Explain your answer.

7. Summer Ice, a company that specializes in ice cream treats, wishes to raise its total revenue. It can identify two different groups of buyers: children and adults. Currently its ice cream treats are uniformly priced at $2.00 per serving. Summer Ice is considering reducing the price of its treats to $1 (a 67% decrease in price using the midpoint method). From its market research, it knows that the two groups of buyers are likely to respond according to the data in the table below:

Price	Quantity demanded by children	Quantity demanded by adults
$2	100	100
1	300	120

a. What is the price elasticity of demand for each of these groups? Use the midpoint method to calculate these price elasticities.

b. What is Summer Ice's current total revenue if they sell their ice cream treats at a price of $2?

c. What is Summer Ice's total revenue if they sell their ice cream treats at a price of $1?

d. What is Summer Ice's total revenue if they price their treats differently to the two groups and charge the higher price ($2) to adults and the lower price ($1) to children?

e. What is Summer Ice's total revenue if they price their treats differently to the two groups and charge the lower price ($1) to adults and the higher price ($2) to children?

f. What pricing scheme in parts (b) through (e) results in the greatest total revenue for Summer Ice? Using your knowledge of price elasticity of demand, explain why this is the best pricing scheme with regard to maximizing Summer Ice's total revenue in this market.

8. When Mario's income increases by 10%, his consumption of noodles decreases from 100 units a year to 70 units a year, while his consumption of salmon increases from 20 units a year to 60 units a year.

a. What is Mario's income elasticity of demand for noodles?

   b. What is Mario's income elasticity of demand for salmon?

   c. Is either of these goods income elastic for Mario?

   d. Is either of these goods income inelastic for Mario?

   e. From Mario's perspective, is either of these goods a luxury good? Explain your answer.

   f. From Mario's perspective, is either of these goods an inferior good? Explain your answer.

9. Government officials in Wonderland are concerned that the economy is entering a recession. They anticipate that this recession will lead to lower levels of production and higher levels of unemployment, thus resulting in many people experiencing a decrease in their income. Suppose there are two producers in Wonderland: producer A knows that the income elasticity of demand for his product equals −0.6 while producer B knows that the income elasticity of demand for his product equals 0.5. Which producer is likely to view this recession as a more significant problem for his company? Explain your answer.

10. The following table describes a linear supply curve for bicycles in Microland.

Price	Quantity supplied of bicycles
$ 0	0
100	200
200	400
300	600
400	800
500	1,000

a. Graph this supply curve and then write an equation for this supply curve in slope-intercept form.

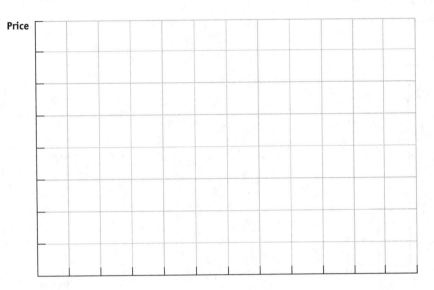

Price

Quantity

b. Suppose suppliers initially sell bicycles for $200 but then decrease their price to $100. Using the midpoint method, what is the value of the price elasticity of supply between these two points on the supply curve?

c. Suppose suppliers initially sell bicycles for $400 and then the price increases to $500. Using the midpoint method, what is the value of the price elasticity of supply between these two points on the supply curve?

d. Did your values in part (b) and part (c) of this question differ or were they the same? You might redo this problem with another set of values for a different linear demand curve that goes through the origin. Do you get the same result? Generalize your findings in a simple statement.

11. Let's redo the last example, but for a linear supply curve that does not pass through the origin. The table below describes a supply curve that has these characteristics.

Price	Quantity supplied of bicycles
$100	0
200	200
300	400
400	600
500	800

a. Graph this supply curve and then write an equation for this supply curve in slope-intercept form.

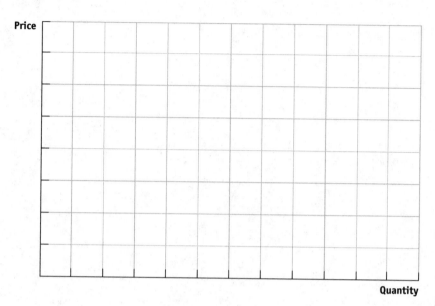

b. Suppose suppliers initially sell bicycles for $200 but then decrease their price to $100. Using the midpoint method, what is the value of the price elasticity of supply between these two points on the supply curve?

c. Suppose suppliers initially sell bicycles for $400 and then the price increases to $500. Using the midpoint method, what is the value of the price elasticity of supply between these two points on the supply curve?

d. Did your values in parts (b) and (c) of this question differ?

12. Briefly describe the factors that influence price elasticity of demand, and then describe the factors that influence price elasticity of supply.

BEFORE YOU TAKE THE TEST

Chapter Review Questions

1. When the absolute value of the percentage change in quantity demanded is greater than the absolute value of the percentage change in price, demand is
   a. inelastic.
   b. elastic.

2. If the price is initially $10 and then increases to $15, the absolute value of the percentage change in price using the midpoint method is
   a. 50%.
   b. 40%.
   c. 5%.
   d. 4%.

3. The midpoint method for calculating price elasticities provides a means of
   a. ensuring that all price elasticities have positive values.
   b. ensuring that all price elasticities have negative values.
   c. generating consistent measures of price elasticities between two points on a demand or supply curve without regard to which point is the initial point.
   d. simplifying the calculation of price elasticities so that all elasticity values are whole numbers.

4. A horizontal demand curve is perfectly
   a. elastic.
   b. inelastic.

5. If the price elasticity of demand between two points on a demand curve is equal to 1.5, then demand between those two points is
   a. price elastic.
   b. price inelastic.

6. If the price elasticity of demand equals infinity, then the demand curve is
   a. horizontal.
   b. vertical.

7. A small value (less than one) for the price elasticity of demand indicates that consumers are very price
   a. sensitive and that a small percentage change in price will lead to a large percentage change in the quantity demanded when both changes are measured in absolute value terms.
   b. insensitive and that a small percentage change in price will lead to an even smaller percentage change in the quantity demanded when both changes are measured in absolute value terms.

Use the diagram below of a linear demand curve to answer the next three questions.

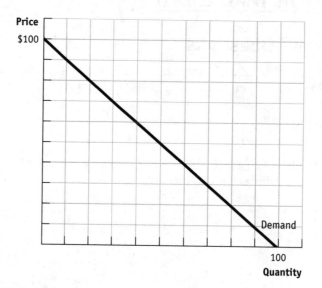

8. Suppose price is initially $60. If price increases to $70, this will cause the quantity demanded to decrease while
  a. total revenue increases.
  b. total revenue decreases.
  c. total revenue does not change.
  d. the effect on total revenue depends on consumers' reactions to the price increase.

9. Suppose you are a producer and the demand curve in the graph represents the demand for your product. Furthermore, suppose you are currently selling this product at a price of $30. If you raise the price to $40 and demand remains unchanged, total revenue will _____ because the price effect is _____ than the quantity effect.
  a. increase; larger
  b. increase; smaller
  c. decrease; larger
  d. decrease; smaller

10. Suppose you are a producer and the demand curve in the graph represents the demand for your product. To maximize total revenue you should sell the good for _____, resulting in total revenue of _____.
  a. $100; $100,000
  b. $60; $2,400
  c. $40; $2,400
  d. $50; $2,500

Use the figure below to answer the next two questions, where point A is the midpoint of the depicted linear demand curve.

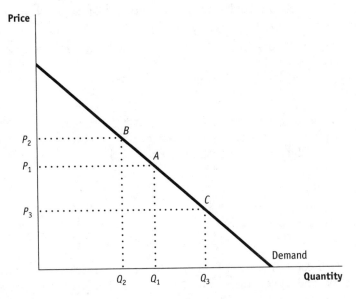

11. At prices greater than P_1 demand is _____, while at prices less than P_1 demand is _____, and at price P_1 demand is _____.
   a. elastic; elastic; unit elastic
   b. inelastic; inelastic; unit elastic
   c. elastic; inelastic; unit elastic
   d. inelastic; elastic; unit elastic

12. Suppose price is initially at P_1. Which of the following statements is true?
   a. If price rises to P_2, then the quantity effect will dominate over the price effect and total revenue will increase.
   b. If price falls to P_3, then the quantity effect will dominate over the price effect and total revenue will increase.
   c. If price rises to P_2, then the price effect will dominate over the quantity effect and total revenue will increase.
   d. If price falls to P_3, then the price effect will dominate over the quantity effect and total revenue will decrease.

13. Which of the following statements is true?
   a. The longer the time period of adjustment to a change in the price of the good, the more elastic the demand for that good.
   b. Goods that have many close substitutes typically have price elastic demand.
   c. The demand for nonessential goods is more elastic than the demand for goods that are necessities.
   d. All of the above statements are true.

14. Tea and coffee are often viewed as substitutes for one another. Which of the following cross-price elasticity values is most likely for tea and coffee?
   a. −0.5
   b. 1.5

15. The price of movie tickets increased 10% this year. Which of the following statements is most likely to be true?

    a. The quantity of popcorn sold at movie theaters decreased this year.

    b. Video movie rentals increased this year.

    c. If the price elasticity of demand for movie tickets is greater than one, total revenue at the movie theaters decreased.

    d. All of the above statements are true.

16. The cross-price elasticity of demand between movie tickets and movie theater popcorn is estimated to equal −0.6. Suppose movie ticket prices increased by 20% this year. The percentage change in the quantity demanded of movie theater popcorn will be a(n)

    a. increase of 1.2%

    b. increase of 12%.

    c. decrease of 1.2%.

    d. decrease of 12%.

17. This year Joe's income increased by 15% while the quantity of bananas he demanded increased by 8% and the quantity of orange juice he demanded increased by 6%. Which of the following statements is true for Joe?

    a. Bananas are a normal good and orange juice is an inferior good.

    b. Bananas are an inferior good and orange juice is a normal good.

    c. Bananas and orange juice are both normal goods.

    d. Bananas and orange juice are both inferior goods.

18. Use the data in the table below to answer this question. The table provides information about prices, quantity demanded, and income for Sue for two different years.

Year	Good	Price	Quantity demanded	Income
2004	Pizza	$ 6	10	
2004	Books	9	4	
2004				$200
2005	Pizza	6	7.5	
2005	Books	9	5	
2005				250

    Calculate Sue's income elasticity of demand for pizza for this time period. Sue's income elasticity of demand for pizza equals _____ and pizza is a(n) _____ good.

    a. 1; normal

    b. 1; inferior

    c. 1.65; inferior

    d. 1.65; normal

19. Use the information in the table below to answer this question.

Good	Quantity demanded initially	Price initially	Quantity demanded after price change	New price
Pizza	10	$ 6	8	$6
Books	4	12	5	9

Calculate the cross-price elasticity of demand between the quantity demanded of pizza and the price of books. What is the relationship between pizza and books given this cross-price elasticity of demand value?

a. Pizza and books are complements.

b. Pizza and books are substitutes.

c. Pizza is an inferior good and books are a normal good.

d. Pizza is a normal good and books are an inferior good.

20. Suppose the income elasticity of demand for a good is greater than one. Which of the following statements is true?

a. The percentage change in the quantity demanded of this good is larger than the percentage change in income.

b. This good is a necessity, since as income increases the quantity demanded of the good increases.

c. This good is an inferior good, since as income increases the quantity demanded of the good increases at a much greater rate than the rate of increase in income.

d. This good could not be a luxury good, since income and the quantity demanded have a positive relationship.

21. Suppose there is an influx of new workers in a community. This will likely result in

a. an increase in the price elasticity of demand for all normal goods.

b. an increase in the price elasticity of supply for goods produced in this community.

c. a decrease in the price elasticity of demand for most goods.

d. little change in any elasticity measure for this community.

22. Acme Manufacturing produces 1,000 widgets when the price of widgets is $20 per widget, and 1,200 widgets when the price of widgets is $22 per widget. Using the midpoint method, what is the value of the price elasticity of supply?

a. 1.9   c. 0.5

b. 0.6   d. 2

23. Acme Manufacturing originally was able to produce 1,000 widgets at a price of $20 per widget, and 1,200 widgets at a price of $22 per widget. Suppose that there is an influx of new workers into the community and Acme now finds it can produce 1,200 widgets at a price of $20 per widget, and 1,600 widgets at a price of $22 per widget. Which statement best describes Acme's situation?

a. Acme's supply curve is now more price-inelastic which implies that as the price increases Acme can now supply a greater quantity of the good than it could initially.

b. Acme's supply curve is unaffected by this change in labor: a price increase for widgets simply causes a movement along the supply curve for widgets.

c. Acme's supply curve is now more price-elastic which implies that as the price increases Acme can now supply a greater quantity of the good than it could initially.

d. The availability of labor has an unpredictable effect on Acme Manufacturing.

ANSWER KEY

Answers to Problems and Exercises

1. **a.** % change in price = $[(9 - 10)/10] \times 100 = -10\%$
% change in quantity = $[(2 - 1)/1] \times 100 = 100\%$

b. Price elasticity of demand = $|100\%/ - 10\%| = 10$

c. % change in price = $[(10 - 9)/9] \times 100 = 11\%$
% change in quantity = $[(1 - 2)/2] \times 100 = -50\%$

d. Price elasticity of demand = $|-50\%/11\%| = 4.5$

e. No, the measures calculated for the price elasticity of demand using the simple percentage formula yield different price elasticities of demand measures when moving from point A to point B or from point B to point A.

f. % change in price = $\dfrac{(9 - 10)}{\dfrac{(10 + 9)}{2}} = -10.5\%$

% change in quantity = $\dfrac{(2 - 1)}{\dfrac{(1 + 2)}{2}} = 66.7\%$

g. Price elasticity of demand = $|66.7\%/-10.6\%| = 6.3$

h. % change in price = $\dfrac{(10 - 9)}{\dfrac{(9 + 10)}{2}} = 11\%$

% change in quantity = $\dfrac{(1 - 2)}{\dfrac{(2 + 1)}{2}} = -66.7\%$

i. Price elasticity of demand = $|-66.7\%/10.6\%| = 6.3$

j. Yes, the midpoint method yields the same measure for price elasticity of demand whether you start at point A and move to point B, or move from point B to point A. This consistent measure of price elasticity, whether for the price elasticity of demand or the price elasticity of supply, simplifies the use of elasticity by providing a value that is not dependent on the initial starting point.

2. **a.** Price elasticity of demand = $\left|\dfrac{\% \text{ change in quantity demanded}}{\% \text{ change in price}}\right|$

Price elasticity of demand = $\left|\dfrac{\dfrac{(10 - 9)}{\dfrac{(9 + 10)}{2}}}{\dfrac{(1 - 2)}{\dfrac{(2 + 1)}{2}}}\right| = \left|\dfrac{11\%}{-66.7\%}\right| = 0.16$

With the midpoint method for calculating price elasticities, it does not matter which point is the initial point.

b. No, the price elasticity of demand between points A and B equals 6.1, while the price elasticity of demand between points C and E equals 0.16.

c. Demand is elastic between points *A* and *B:* we know the absolute value of the percentage change in the quantity demanded exceeds the absolute value of the percentage change in price since the ratio has a value greater than one.

d. Demand is inelastic between points *C* and *E:* we know the absolute value of the percentage change in the quantity demanded is less than the absolute value of the percentage change in price since the ratio has a value less than one.

3. a.

Price	Quantity demanded	Total revenue
$ 0	11	$ 0
1	10	10
2	9	18
3	8	24
4	7	28
5	6	30
6	5	30
7	4	28
8	3	24
9	2	18
10	1	10
11	0	0

b. From the table, we can see that total revenue equals $30 when the price is $5 or when the price is $6. At a price of $5.50—the midpoint of the demand curve—we find that total revenue equals $30.25. For a linear demand curve, total revenue is maximized at the midpoint of the demand curve.

c. Price elasticity of demand $= \left| \dfrac{\dfrac{(5-6)}{(6+5)}}{\dfrac{2}{\dfrac{(5-6)}{(6+5)}{2}}} \right| = 1$

d. When the price elasticity of demand equals one, the absolute value of the percentage change in the quantity demanded equals the absolute value of the percentage change in the price.

4. a. The price elasticity of demand for golden delicious apples should be far more elastic than the price elasticity of demand for all fruit since there are many possible substitutions for golden delicious apples and far fewer substitute goods for all fruit. Hence, a price increase is likely to result in a significant change in the percentage change in the quantity demanded of golden delicious apples and a far smaller percentage change in the quantity demanded of all fruit.

b. The price elasticity of demand for ice cream should be greater than the price elasticity of demand for gasoline since there are far more available substitutes for ice cream than there are for gasoline.

c. The price elasticity of demand for leisure travel should be greater than the price elasticity of demand for business travel since business travelers must get to their destination within a relatively small window of time, and hence are less sensitive to price than are leisure travelers.

5. a. Cross-price elasticity of demand = $\dfrac{\text{\% change in the quantity demanded of good B}}{\text{\% change in the price of good A}}$

% change in the quantity demanded of good B = $(6 - 4)/4 = 0.5$

% change in the price of good A = $(12 - 10)/10 = 0.2$

Cross-price elasticity of demand = $0.5/0.2 = 2.5$

b. Good A and good B are substitutes because as the price of good A increases the quantity demanded of good B increases. There are many examples of two goods that are substitutes: coffee and tea, butter and margarine, olive oil and safflower oil, taxi rides and bus rides, tennis and golf.

6. a. A negative cross-price elasticity of demand implies that the percentage change in the quantity demanded of one good moves in the opposite direction to the percentage change in the price of a related good. Thus, if the price of good Y increases, then the quantity demanded of good X decreases. We know that two related goods are either substitutes or complements. In this case, a negative cross-price elasticity of demand indicates that the two goods are complements. (In contrast, a positive cross-price elasticity of demand tells us the two goods are substitutes.)

b. Cross-price elasticity of demand = -0.2

$-0.2 = \dfrac{\text{\% change in the quantity demanded of good D}}{\text{\% change in the price of good C}}$

$-0.2 = \dfrac{\text{\% change in the quantity demanded of good D}}{100\%}$

% change in the quantity demanded of good D = -20%

c. With a cross-price elasticity of -0.2, a 100% increase in the price of good C will cause the quantity demanded of good D to fall by 20% (using the simple formula for percentage changes rather than the midpoint method). Thus, if the quantity demanded of good D was initially 10 units, then the quantity demanded of good D will be 8 units after the increase in the price of good C.

d. When the cross-price elasticity of demand is negative, a decrease in the price of one good will lead to an increase in the quantity demanded of the other good.

7. a. The price elasticity of demand for children is equal to 1.5 and the price elasticity of demand for adults is equal to 0.27. Therefore, for the quantities and prices given in this example, the demand for Summer Ice is elastic for children and inelastic for adults.

b. Total revenue = ($2/treat)(200) = $400

c. Total revenue = ($1/treat)(420) = $420

d. Total revenue = ($2/treat)(100) + ($1/treat)(300) = $500

e. Total revenue = ($1/treat)(120) + ($2/treat)(100) = $320

f. Summer Ice will earn the greatest total revenue by charging children $1 per treat and adults $2 per treat: charging a higher price to the group of consumers with inelastic demand and a lower price to those consumers with elastic demand. In effect, this pricing scheme recognizes that the absolute value of the percentage change in the quantity demanded by adults is less than the absolute value of the percentage change in the price of the good, while the absolute value of the percentage change in the quantity demanded by children is greater than the absolute value of the percentage change in the price of the good. Thus, decreasing price to the adult group of buyers reduces total revenue, while reducing price to the child group of buyers increases total revenue.

8.   **a.** Income elasticity of demand for noodles $= \dfrac{-30\%}{10\%} = -3$

b. Income elasticity of demand for salmon $= \dfrac{200\%}{10\%} = 20$

c. Salmon

d. Neither good is income inelastic since neither good has an income elasticity of demand value that is positive but is less than one.

e. Salmon is a luxury good since the value of the income elasticity of demand for salmon is greater than one. As Mario's income increases, his demand for salmon increases at an even faster rate.

f. Noodles are an inferior good, since as Mario's income increases his demand for noodles decreases. A negative value for the income elasticity of demand indicates that the good is an inferior good.

9.   Producer B will feel the impact more than producer A since demand for producer B's product will fall as income falls. In contrast, the negative income elasticity of demand value for producer A indicates that as income falls, the quantity demanded of producer A's product will increase.

10.   **a.** $P = (1/2)Q$

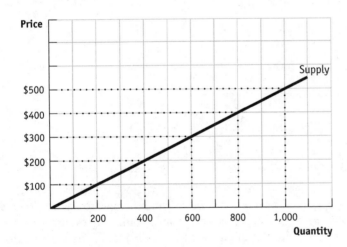

b. Price elasticity of supply $= \left| \dfrac{\dfrac{200 - 400}{\dfrac{400 + 200}{2}}}{\dfrac{100 - 200}{\dfrac{200 + 100}{2}}} \right| = 1$

c. Price elasticity of supply $= \left| \dfrac{\dfrac{1{,}000 - 800}{\dfrac{800 + 1{,}000}{2}}}{\dfrac{500 - 400}{\dfrac{400 + 500}{2}}} \right| = 1$

d. The values are the same in parts (b) and (c). Redoing the exercise for a different linear demand curve that passes through the origin yields the same value. Thus, as long as the supply curve is linear and passes through the origin, the price elasticity of supply equals one for all points on the supply curve.

11. a. $P = (1/2)Q + 100$

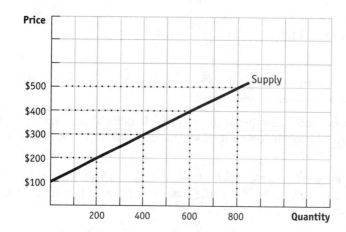

b. Price elasticity of supply = $\left| \dfrac{\dfrac{0 - 200}{\dfrac{200 + 0}{2}}}{\dfrac{100 - 200}{\dfrac{200 + 100}{2}}} \right| = 3$

c. Price elasticity of supply = $\left| \dfrac{\dfrac{800 - 600}{\dfrac{600 + 800}{2}}}{\dfrac{500 - 400}{\dfrac{400 + 500}{2}}} \right| = 1.28$

d. The values in parts (b) and (c) differ.

12. The price elasticity of demand depends on the availability of close substitutes, whether the good is a necessity or a luxury, and how much time consumers have to adjust to the price change. The price elasticity of supply depends on the availability of resources to expand production and the amount of time that producers have to adjust to the price change.

Answers to Chapter Review Questions

1. **Answer b.** Demand is price elastic when the absolute value of the percentage change in the quantity demanded is greater than the absolute value of the percentage change in price. This is definitional.

2. **Answer b.** To find this value, you take the absolute value of the following:

    $$\left| \dfrac{15 - 10}{\dfrac{10 + 15}{2}} \right| \times 100$$

    This gives you the absolute value of the percentage change in price, which is equal to 40%.

3. **Answer c.** Price elasticities may have negative values or positive values. For example, for both cross-price elasticity of demand and income elasticity of demand, the values may be

positive, negative, or equal to zero. The midpoint method for calculating price elasticities provides a method for getting identical values no matter which point is your initial point when making the calculation. Price elasticities are not always whole numbers.

4. **Answer a.** This is definitional: it is an extreme case of elasticity in which demanders are extremely price sensitive.

5. **Answer a.** Since the value of price elasticity of demand is greater than one, this implies that the absolute value of the percentage change in the quantity demanded is greater than the absolute value of the percentage change in price, which means that demand is elastic between these two points.

6. **Answer a.** This is definitional: when the demand curve is horizontal, it tells us that consumers are very price sensitive, and at the current price there is infinite demand for the good. When the demand curve is perfectly vertical, it tells us that consumers are not price sensitive, since no matter what the price they will continue to demand the same amount of the good.

7. **Answer b.** When the price elasticity of demand has a value less than one, this implies that the absolute value of the percentage change in the quantity demanded is less than the absolute value of the percentage change in the price of the good. Consumers are not price sensitive: they will continue to demand a similar amount of the good even though the price has increased.

8. **Answer b.** When price rises from $60 to $70, total revenue changes from $2,400 to $2,100. The price of $60 is above the midpoint on the given demand curve, so an increase in price above $60 implies that price is increasing in the elastic region of the demand curve. As price rises in the elastic portion of the demand curve, this results in a decrease in total revenue.

9. **Answer a.** When price rises from $30 to $40, you are moving along the demand curve in the inelastic region. An increase in price in the inelastic region of the demand curve results in an increase in total revenue. In this case, total revenue was initially $2,100, and with the price increase total revenue is now equal to $2,400.

10. **Answer d.** Total revenue is maximized at the unit elastic point on the demand curve. For a linear demand curve, this occurs at the midpoint. In this example, the midpoint is at a price of $50 and a quantity of 50 units.

11. **Answer c.** This is definitional: above the midpoint on a linear demand curve, demand is elastic; below the midpoint on a linear demand curve, demand is inelastic; and at the midpoint on a linear demand curve, demand is unit elastic.

12. **Answer d.** When price rises above P_1, the quantity effect is dominant over the price effect and this dominance results in total revenue decreasing. When price falls below P_1, the price effect is dominant over the quantity effect and this dominance results in total revenue decreasing.

13. **Answer d.** All of these statements are true. When there are many substitutes available for a good, demand is more elastic. Demand is also more elastic the longer the time period for adjustment. Goods that are not necessities and therefore do not have to be consumed have more elastic demand than do goods that are necessities.

14. **Answer b.** Two goods are substitutes for one another when the cross-price elasticity of demand between the two goods is positive. This elasticity is positive, since as the price of one of the goods increases this leads to an increase in the quantity demanded of the other good.

15. **Answer d.** Each of these statements is likely to be true. Popcorn sold at movie theaters is likely to be a complementary good with respect to movie tickets. When movie tickets increase in price, fewer movie tickets are demanded, and this decrease in the quantity demanded results in fewer units of popcorn being sold. Similarly, movie tickets and video rentals are likely to be substitutes with respect to each other: an increase in the price of movie tickets will likely result in increased demand for video rentals. If the price elasticity of demand for movie tickets is greater than one, this implies that demand is elastic, and an increase in price in the elastic segment of the demand curve causes total revenue to decrease.

16. **Answer d.** To compute this answer, first recall that the cross-price elasticity is the ratio of the percentage change in the quantity demanded of good A divided by the percentage change in the price of good B. The question provides the value for the cross-price elasticity of demand as well as the percentage change in the price of movie tickets. Plugging these values into our equation for cross-price elasticity of demand, we have $-0.6 = x/20\%$ where x is the percentage change in the quantity demanded of movie theater popcorn. Solving this equation, the percentage change in the quantity demanded of movie theater popcorn is a decrease of 12%.

17. **Answer c.** Joe's income increased and so did his consumption of both bananas and orange juice. Therefore they both must be normal goods.

18. **Answer b.** To find the income elasticity of demand, recall that this is the ratio of the percentage change in the quantity demanded of the good divided by the percentage change in income. The percentage change in the quantity demanded of pizza is -25% (using the simple formula for percentage changes given in the Chapter Objectives section of the Study Guide), while the percentage change in income is also 25%. Thus, the income elasticity of demand is equal to -1. Pizza is an inferior good, since as income increases, the quantity demanded decreases.

19. **Answer b.** As the price of books decreases we see from the table that the quantity of pizzas demanded decreases. This tells us that these two goods are substitutes for one another since as the price of one of the goods decreases this leads consumers to substitute away from the other good and decrease the quantity they demand of the other good at every price.

20. **Answer a.** When income elasticity of demand is greater than one, this tells us that the good is not an inferior good, since as income increases this leads to an increase in the quantity demanded of the good. From the definition of income elasticity of demand, a value greater than one implies that the percentage change in the quantity demanded of the good is greater than the percentage change in income. When the income elasticity of demand is greater than one, this implies that the good is a luxury, since the percentage increase in the quantity demanded is increasing at a faster rate than the percentage increase in income.

21. **Answer b.** When there is an influx of new workers into a community, labor becomes more plentiful. Since labor is an input in the production of goods, this likely makes the supply of goods more elastic.

22. **Answer a.** To find the price elasticity of supply, use the midpoint method and calculate the percentage change in the quantity supplied divided by the percentage change in the price of the good. Thus, the price elasticity of supply equals

$$\frac{\dfrac{1{,}200 - 1{,}000}{\dfrac{1{,}000 + 1{,}200}{2}}}{\dfrac{22 - 20}{\dfrac{20 + 22}{2}}} = 1.9$$

23. **Answer c.** If you sketch out the relationships between price and the quantity supplied, you will notice that the influx of workers results in Acme Manufacturing supply's curve shifting out to the right. This causes the price elasticity of supply to increase, resulting in more price-elastic supply. Calculation of the new value of the price elasticity of supply would be equal to

$$\frac{\dfrac{1{,}600 - 1{,}200}{\dfrac{1{,}200 + 1{,}600}{2}}}{\dfrac{22 - 20}{\dfrac{20 + 22}{2}}} = 3$$

Supply is now more price elastic.

chapter 7

Taxes

BEFORE YOU READ THE CHAPTER

Summary

This chapter considers the topic of taxes and the effect of taxes on supply and demand. In addition, the chapter considers the issues of tax efficiency and equity; tax incidence, which analyzes who actually bears the economic burden of a particular tax; the deadweight loss associated with taxation; and the difference between progressive and regressive taxes. The chapter also provides a description of the U.S. tax system.

Chapter Objectives

Objective #1. Taxes are necessary to provide governments with funds to provide services that the public wants. However, taxes usually have a cost that exceeds the money the government actually receives from the tax, because the imposition of a tax distorts the incentives to engage in mutually beneficial transactions. An efficient tax is one that distorts incentives as little as possible. An equitable tax is a tax that is considered fair. With regard to tax policy, there is a tradeoff between efficiency and equity: a tax may be highly efficient, but then it is apt to be quite inequitable, and vice versa.

Objective #2. A simple tax to consider when analyzing the effects of taxes on consumers and producers is an excise tax, which is a tax that is charged on each unit of a good or service that is sold. An excise tax imposed on producers has the effect of shifting the supply curve to the left by a vertical amount equal to the excise tax. In effect, producers recognize that the excise tax effectively increases their cost of production, since now they must remit to the government an amount equal to the excise tax for every unit of the good they sell. Figure 7.1 illustrates a market in which an excise tax has been levied on producers of the good. Note that the initial supply curve and the supply curve with the excise tax are parallel to one another and that the vertical distance between these two supply curves is equal to the amount of the excise tax. Study Figure 7.1 as you read the bullet points summarizing the effects of this excise tax on this market.

Figure 7.1

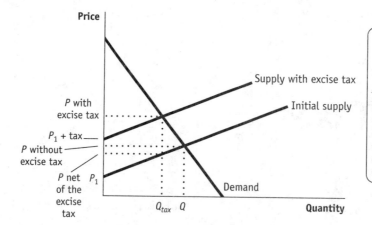

Notice that the initial supply curve y-intercept is at P_1 and when the excise tax is imposed, this y-intercept increases by the amount of the excise tax so that the y-intercept is now P_1 + tax. Also, when the excise tax is imposed, the equilibrium quantity in the market decreases from Q to Q_{tax}.

- The imposition of the tax reduces the quantity of the good sold in the market. The tax, because it effectively raises the price of the good, distorts incentives, and this distortion results in missed opportunities for mutually beneficial transactions. In the graph, the reduction in consumption from Q units to Q_{tax} units is a measure of the missed opportunities for mutually beneficial transactions that arise with the imposition of the tax.

- When the excise tax is imposed, producers sell the good for the price marked "P with excise tax." But producers do not get to keep all of this money since they must pay the government the excise tax, which can be measured as the vertical distance between the two supply curves. Thus, after producers pay the tax, they get to keep the price marked "P net of the excise tax." From the producers' point of view the effect of the excise tax is that they are now selling fewer units of the good, Q_{tax} instead of Q, and they are receiving the price "P net of the excise tax" for each unit of the good they sell rather than the original price before the imposition of the tax. The cost of the tax to producers is therefore equal to (P without excise tax – P net of the excise tax)(Q_{tax}). Figure 7.2 illustrates the area of producer tax incidence (PTI). The area of PTI is smaller than the consumer tax incidence (CTI), but it is possible for the areas to be the same size or for PTI to be greater than the CTI, depending on the elasticities of the demand and supply curves.

- From the consumers' point of view, the excise tax raises the price of the good from "P without excise tax" to "P with excise tax" while simultaneously reducing the amount of the good transacted in the market from Q to Q_{tax}. Thus, the cost of the excise tax to the consumer is equal to (P with excise tax – P without excise tax)(Q_{tax}). Figure 7.2 illustrates the area of CTI. The area of PTI is smaller than the area of CTI, but it is possible for the areas to be the same size or for PTI to be greater than the CTI, depending on the elasticities of the demand and supply curves.

Figure 7.2

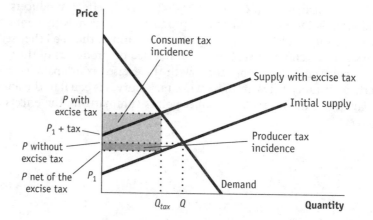

- The incidence of the tax on consumers and producers is dependent on the price elasticity of the demand and supply curves. When demand is relatively price inelastic and supply is relatively price elastic, the economic incidence of the tax falls primarily on consumers. When demand is relatively price elastic and supply is relatively price inelastic, the economic incidence of the tax falls primarily on producers. Figure 7.3 illustrates how these price elasticities can affect the CTI and PTI.

Figure 7.3

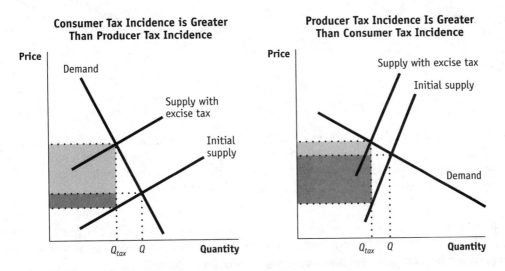

- The tax revenue from an excise tax can be calculated as the product of the tax per unit times the number of units of the good sold. The tax revenue is also equal to the sum of PTI plus CTI. In Figure 7.3, the tax revenue in each graph is equal to the sum of the two shaded rectangles. The tax revenue is equal to the area of the rectangle whose height is the tax wedge between the supply and demand curves and whose width is the quantity of the good bought and sold when the tax is imposed. The amount of tax revenue raised by an excise tax depends on the tax rate and the price elasticities of supply and demand. For a given tax rate, tax revenue is greater if the price elasticities of supply and demand are both low, since the quantity demanded of the good isn't reduced very much when the tax increases the price of the good. Theoretically it is possible to raise a tax rate to a high enough level that tax revenue falls, or to reduce the tax rate to a level at which tax revenue rises, but in practice politicians take this possibility into account when setting tax rates.

- The excise tax entails the cost that producers and consumers pay to the government, but it also imposes costs over and above the tax revenue collected in the form of inefficiency that arises when the market provides only the Q_{tax} amount of the good instead of the original Q. This reduction in output due to the tax reflects the mutually beneficial exchanges that the tax prevents. The value to society of these lost exchanges can be measured as the deadweight loss (DWL) associated with the tax.

- All real-world taxes impose some DWL, but a badly designed tax results in a larger DWL than a well-designed tax. Figure 7.4 identifies the area of DWL and tax revenue when an excise tax is imposed. The graphs contrast two different markets and the level of DWL that occurs with the imposition of an excise tax of $x per unit. Taxes imposed on a good whose price elasticity of demand and/or supply is elastic results in a relatively larger DWL than the same size tax imposed on a good whose price elasticity of demand and/or supply is inelastic. This occurs because the change in the quantity demanded is greater when demand and/or supply is price elastic than when demand and/or supply is price inelastic. Thus, to minimize the inefficiency of a tax, policymakers want to tax goods whose demand and/or supply are relatively inelastic. Conversely, if policymakers wish to discourage a particular activity by taxing it, they will decrease consumption relatively more if demand and/or supply are relatively elastic.

Figure 7.4

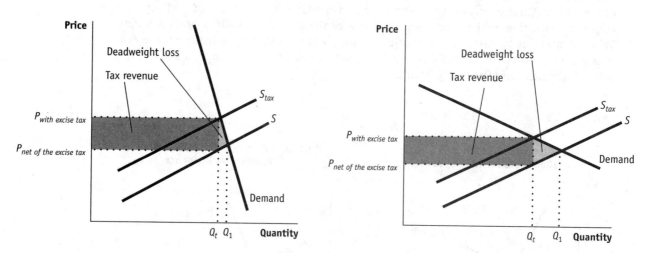

- The area of DWL is the sum of the consumer surplus and the producer surplus that is lost when the excise tax is imposed. The DWL does not include the administrative costs incurred by the government and by taxpayers to pay the tax. The total inefficiency caused by a tax is the sum of the DWL and its administrative costs.

Objective #3. The efficiency of a tax is not the only consideration in designing a tax system. Equity, or fairness, is also a key consideration. There are two primary principles of tax fairness: the benefits principle and the ability-to-pay principle.

- The benefits principle of tax fairness is that those who benefit from the public spending should bear the burden of the tax that pays for the spending.

- The ability-to-pay principle of tax fairness is that those who have greater ability to pay should bear a greater burden of the tax than those who have less ability to pay. This principle typically is interpreted to mean that those who have higher income should pay higher taxes than those with lower income. In addition, this principle is also sometimes used to justify the idea that those taxpayers with higher income should pay a higher percentage of their income in taxes.

Objective #4. A lump-sum tax is a tax that is the same for all people regardless of any actions people take. This is an efficient tax since the tax does not distort incentives. However, a lump-sum tax is perceived as a highly unfair tax since it does not distinguish among taxpayers according to their ability to pay. The example of a lump-sum tax illustrates the trade-off between efficiency and equity: taxes that are highly efficient are apt to be highly inequitable, and taxes that are equitable tend to be inefficient.

Objective #5. In the U.S. federal tax system, both the ability-to-pay and the benefits principles guide the tax system. The federal income tax reflects the ability-to-pay principle: families with low incomes pay little or no income tax while families with high incomes pay a larger share of their income in income taxes than does the average family. The FICA, or payroll tax, in contrast, is based on the benefits principle. This tax funds the Social Security system, and since the benefits of the Social Security system are primarily designed to assist low- and middle-income people, the FICA tax is levied only on incomes up to a maximum level.

Objective #6. Every tax consists of two pieces: the tax base and the tax structure.

- The tax base refers to the measure or value that determines how much tax an individual pays. For example, the tax base might be income or property value. Other types of taxes are based on payroll, sales, profits, or wealth.

- The tax structure specifies how the tax depends on the tax base. The tax structure is often expressed as a percentage. There are three types of tax structure: proportional, regressive, and progressive.

  a. The simplest tax structure is a proportional tax, in which the tax is the same percentage of the base regardless of the taxpayer's income or wealth. A proportional tax is applied uniformly without regard to the benefits or ability-to-pay principles.

  b. A regressive tax structure is a tax in which the tax rises less than in proportion to income: this tax structure results in high-income taxpayers paying a smaller percentage of their income than low-income taxpayers.

  c. A progressive tax structure is a tax in which the tax rises more than in proportion to income: this tax structure results in high-income taxpayers paying a larger percentage of their income than low-income taxpayers. A progressive tax structure has an adverse effect on incentives, since the tax takes away a larger share of income as the level of income increases.

- The marginal tax rate is the percentage of an increase in income that is taxed away. As the marginal tax rate increases, this creates an incentive for taxpayers to take action to avoid the tax. There is an adverse incentive effect when the tax system leans too heavily toward the ability-to-pay principle. Concerns about efficiency push the tax system to balance equity against efficiency, and this efficiency concern results in a moderating influence on progressive tax systems.

Objective #7.   The U.S. tax system reflects a mix of progressive and regressive taxes. This mix primarily is due to the difference between levels of government and the fact that different taxes are based on different principles.

- State and local governments do not apply the ability-to-pay principle, since they are subject to tax competition. These governments recognize that people may move to other locations to avoid high levels of taxation.

- At the federal level of government, the government employs a variety of taxes, with some of these taxes based on the ability-to-pay principle and some based on the benefits principle.

Key Terms

Notes

excise tax a tax on sales of a good or service.

incidence (of a tax) a measure of who really pays a tax.

tax rate the amount of tax people are required to pay per unit of whatever is being taxed.

administrative costs (of a tax) the *resources* used (which is a cost) by government to collect the tax, and by taxpayers to pay it, over and above the amount of the tax, as well as to evade it.

benefits principle the principle of tax fairness by which those who benefit from public spending should bear the burden of the tax that pays for that spending.

ability-to-pay principle the principle of tax fairness by which those with greater ability to pay a tax should pay more tax.

lump-sum tax a tax that is the same for everyone, regardless of any actions people take.

Key Terms *(continued)*

trade-off between equity and efficiency the dynamic whereby a well-designed tax system can be made more efficient only by making it less fair, and vice versa.

tax base the measure or value, such as income or property value, that determines how much tax an individual pays.

tax structure specifies how a tax depends on the *tax base;* usually expressed in percentage terms.

income tax a tax on the income of an individual or family.

payroll tax a tax on the earnings an employer pays to an employee.

sales tax a tax on the value of goods sold.

profits tax a tax on the profits of a firm.

property tax a tax on the value of property, such as the value of a home.

wealth tax a tax on the wealth of an individual.

proportional tax a tax that is the same percentage of the *tax base* regardless of the taxpayer's income or wealth.

progressive tax a tax that takes a larger share of the income of high-income taxpayers than of low-income taxpayers.

regressive tax a tax that takes a smaller share of the income of high-income taxpayers than of low-income taxpayers.

marginal tax rate the percentage of an increase in income that is taxed anyway.

AFTER YOU READ THE CHAPTER

Tips

Tip #1. Students often struggle with finding the new supply curve once an excise tax has been imposed. This is not difficult if you start by recognizing that the new supply curve should be parallel to the old supply curve and have a y-intercept that is equal to the initial y-intercept plus the amount of the excise tax per unit. If you are working with equations, you should write the supply equation in slope-intercept form and then simply increase the constant in this term by the amount of the excise tax.

Tip #2. The imposition of an excise tax in a market in general reduces both consumer and producer surplus. Let's consider a market where there is no excise tax and then look at the same market with an excise tax. Figure 7.5 illustrates a market in which there is no excise tax: *CS* is the area of consumer surplus and *PS* is the area of producer surplus.

Figure 7.5

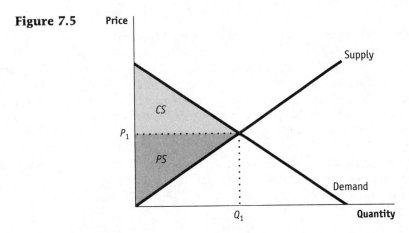

In Figure 7.6, an excise tax is imposed on this market. This excise tax shifts the supply curve to the left by a vertical distance equal to the excise tax. Once the market adjusts to this excise tax, notice that the areas of CS and PS are both decreased. Part of the original area of CS is now CTI and represents the economic incidence of the tax on consumers. Part of the original area of PS is now PTI and represents the economic incidence of the tax on producers. Part of the original area of CS is now DWL captured from CS, and part of the original area of PS is now DWL captured from PS. It is important to see that the excise tax redistributes CS and PS in two ways: some of this surplus goes to the government when it collects tax revenue from the excise tax (the tax revenue is equal to the sum of the areas of producer and consumer tax incidence), and some of this surplus is simply lost because the tax imposes an efficiency cost on this market (the area of DWL). Study this graph carefully.

Figure 7.6

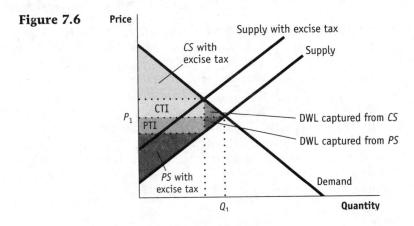

Tip #3. Students often have trouble with the analysis of the excise tax. The most common error is to think that when an excise tax is imposed on a good that this results in the price of the good increasing by the full amount of the tax. Let's go through several examples to work on this issue. Each of the examples use the following labels: P_1 is the original price of the good, Q_1 is the original equilibrium quantity of the good, Q_t is the equilibrium quantity of the good once the excise tax is imposed, P_t is the gross price of the good once the excise tax is imposed, and P_n is the net price that the producer receives after the producer pays the excise tax to the government. In addition, each example also indicates the area that corresponds to CTI, PTI, and DWL. Remember that tax revenue is always equal to the sum of the CTI and the PTI.

- In our first example, consider a market in which demand is perfectly inelastic. What happens in this market if an excise tax is imposed on producers of this good? Figure 7.7 illustrates this situation. Notice that the excise tax causes the price of the good to increase from P_1 to P_t, where the increase in the price is exactly equal to the amount of the excise tax. In this example the excise tax does cause the price of the good to increase by the full amount of the tax: this occurs because demand is perfectly inelastic, which means that the quantity demanded does not change as the price of the good changes. Figure 7.7 also illustrates that when the demand curve is perfectly inelastic, the demanders of the good pay the entire economic burden of the tax: there is no PTI, and tax revenue in this case is exactly equal to CTI. In Figure 7.7, you can see that the original equilibrium price, P_1, is equal to the net price (P_n) that the producer receives after the producer pays the excise tax. Note that an excise tax placed on a good with perfectly inelastic demand does not create a DWL, since there is no change in the quantity demanded of the good with the increase in price due to the tax. This tells us that this is an efficient tax because it does not cause consumers to distort their behavior: they continue to buy the same amount of the good as they did prior to the imposition of the tax. Study Figure 7.7 carefully until you can easily see these points.

Figure 7.7

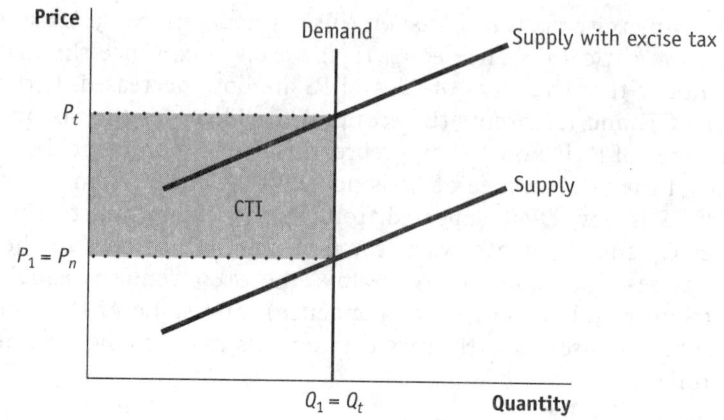

- Let's consider a second example in which the demand curve is perfectly elastic. Figure 7.8 illustrates this situation. Notice that when the demand curve is perfectly elastic, the excise tax does not cause the price of the good to increase at all. Instead, producers find that the excise tax simply results in their selling less of the good at the prevailing market price (thus, $P_1 = P_t$). In this example, there is no CTI because consumers do not end up paying more for the good with the tax. There is PTI, though, because producers find that the net price they receive when they sell the good has fallen by the full amount of the excise tax. In this example, the tax revenue is equal to PTI. The excise tax also distorts consumption decisions: notice that there is a DWL associated with the tax. The DWL can be calculated as $1/2(P_t - P_n)(Q_1 - Q_t)$. This is not an efficient tax because it results in a DWL. Again, study Figure 7.8 until these points are clear to you.

Figure 7.8

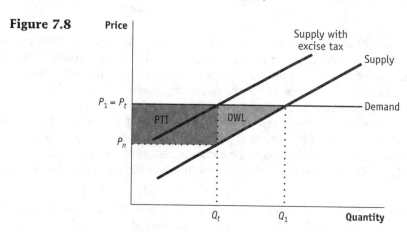

- Now for a third and more representative example, since the demand curve is neither perfectly inelastic nor perfectly elastic. Figure 7.9 illustrates this situation. Notice that when the excise tax is imposed, this causes the supply curve to shift to the left, which results in a movement along the demand curve. Because the demand curve is downward sloping, but not vertical, this movement causes the price of the good to increase relative to its initial level. But notice that P_t is not equal to P_1 plus the tax: P_t is higher than the original price before the tax, but the increase in price is not equal to the excise tax. In this example, there is both CTI and PTI. Consumers find that with the tax they purchase fewer units of the good and each unit of the good they purchase now costs P_t instead of the original P_1. From the consumer perspective, the excise tax results in the price of the good rising by $P_t - P_1$. CTI is therefore equal to $(P_t - P_1)(Q_t)$. The producer finds that the tax results in their selling fewer units of the good, and each unit of the good they sell now sells for P_n instead of the original P_1 once they pay the government the excise tax. From the producer perspective, the excise tax results in the price of the good falling by $P_1 - P_n$. PTI is therefore equal to $(P_1 - P_n)(Q_t)$. In this example, the excise tax results in fewer units of the good being sold, which indicates that the excise tax distorts choices in this market and therefore there is a DWL associated with this tax. The DWL can be calculated as the area $1/2(P_t - P_n)(Q_1 - Q_t)$. Review this graph thoroughly until you are very comfortable with it. In particular, pay close attention to the fact that the price with the excise tax does not rise by the full amount of the tax.

Figure 7.9

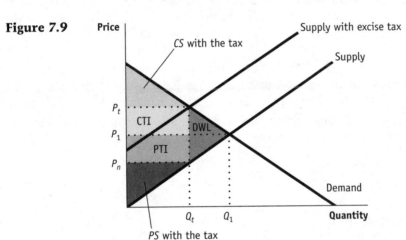

Tip #4. There is one final issue about excise taxes that requires some practice and thought: the effect of price elasticity on the effects of the excise tax on CTI, PTI, and DWL. Practice drawing some graphs with different price elasticities of demand and the same supply curve to see how the price elasticity of demand affects these three measures. Then practice drawing some graphs with different price elasticities of supply and the same demand curve to see how the price elasticity of supply affects these three measures. For each graph you draw, label the area that corresponds to CTI, PTI, and DWL.

Tip #5. When evaluating the tax structure of a tax, you should compare the tax revenue collected from a taxpayer relative to income with the tax revenue collected from another taxpayer relative to that taxpayer's income. A tax is regressive if the percentage of the tax revenue relative to income falls as income rises. A tax is progressive if the percentage of the tax revenue relative to income rises as income rises.

Problems and Exercises

1. Describe two different approaches to equity when designing a tax structure. How do these two approaches differ? What are the advantages of each approach? What are the disadvantages of each approach?

2. The government wishes to limit the quantity of alcoholic beverages sold and therefore is considering the imposition of an excise tax on the market for alcoholic drinks. Suppose the market for alcoholic drinks can be described by the following demand and supply equations:

    $$\text{Demand: } Q = 10{,}000 - 2{,}000P$$
    $$\text{Supply: } Q = 2{,}000P$$

    where P is the price of an alcoholic drink and Q is the quantity of alcoholic drinks sold and consumed during the time period. The proposed excise tax is $2 per alcoholic drink.

    a. Draw a graph representing the initial market for alcoholic drinks. Label the equilibrium price P_1, and the equilibrium quantity Q_1.

    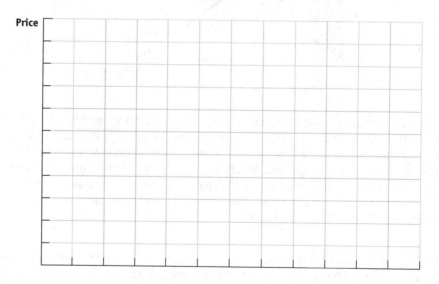

    b. Compute the numeric value of P_1 and Q_1 in this market.

c. What is the value of consumer and producer surplus (*CS* and *PS*) in this market prior to the imposition of the tax? Shade in these two areas on your graph in part (a) and label these areas clearly. What is the value of total surplus before the tax?

d. Suppose the excise tax is implemented and producers are legally responsible for paying the tax. Draw a new graph representing this market now that the excise tax has been implemented. Label the new equilibrium price with the tax (P_t), the new equilibrium quantity with the tax (Q_t), and the net price received by producers after they pay the tax to the government (P_n).

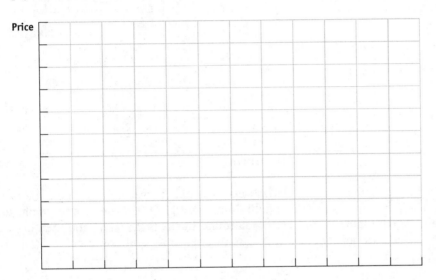

Quantity of alcoholic drinks

e. Calculate the numeric values of P_t, Q_t, and P_n that you marked on your graph in part (d).

f. On your graph from part (d), label the areas that correspond to consumer surplus with the tax (CS_t), producer surplus with the tax (PS_t), CTI, PTI, and DWL.

g. Calculate the value of CS_t, PS_t, CTI, PTI, tax revenue, and DWL once the tax is implemented. Is the sum of (CS_t) + (PS_t) + (tax revenue) + DWL equal to the original value of total surplus before the tax was implemented?

h. Suppose the excise tax is raised to $3 per alcoholic drink. What is the effect of this price increase on tax revenue? Provide a qualitative answer as well as a quantitative answer.

3. The textbook emphasizes that the effect of an excise tax depends on the price elasticities of demand and supply. This question and question 4 explore the relationship between elasticity and the excise tax.

   a. Draw two graphs side by side, and draw a demand curve that is the same in both graphs. (Hint: this means that the y-intercept and the x-intercept for these two demand curves are the same in the two graphs.) Label this curve D in both graphs.

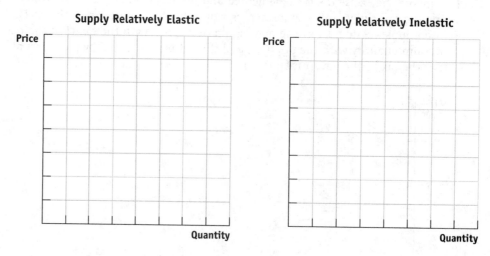

   b. In the first graph, draw a relatively elastic supply curve and label the initial equilibrium price P_1 and the initial equilibrium quantity Q_1. In the second graph, mark P_1 and Q_1 (the same P_1 and Q_1 as you found in the first graph) and then draw a relatively inelastic supply curve that goes through this equilibrium point. Label the supply curve in both graphs S_1.

   c. In the first graph, draw a second supply curve that shows the effect of an excise tax. This second supply curve should be drawn parallel to the first supply curve. Label the equilibrium price with the tax P_t, the equilibrium quantity with the tax Q_t, and the net price firms receive after they pay the tax P_n. In addition, on this graph, label consumer surplus with the tax (CS_t), producer surplus with the tax (PS_t), CTI, PTI, and DWL.

   d. In the second graph, draw a second supply curve that shows the effect of an excise tax which is exactly the same excise tax as in the first graph. (Hint: the y-intercept of the new supply curve for each graph is equal to the y-intercept of the original supply curve plus the excise tax.) Label all the same items for this graph that you labeled in the first graph.

   e. Compare the two graphs and comment on the effect of price elasticity of supply on your results.

4. a. Draw two graphs side by side. In both graphs, draw a supply curve that is identical. Label this curve S_1.

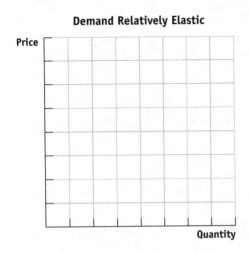

Demand Relatively Elastic

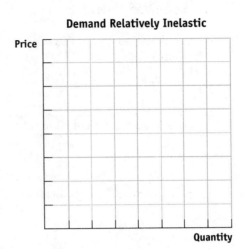

Demand Relatively Inelastic

b. In the first graph, draw a demand curve (D) that is relatively elastic. Label the initial equilibrium price P_1 and the initial equilibrium quantity Q_1. In the second graph, mark P_1 and Q_1 (the same P_1 and Q_1 as in the first graph) and then draw a relatively inelastic demand curve through this equilibrium point. Label this curve D.

c. In both graphs, draw a second supply curve that illustrates an excise tax. The two supply curves should be identical and should be labeled S_t. On both graphs, label the equilibrium price with the tax P_t; the equilibrium quantity with the tax Q_t; and the net price firms receive after they pay the tax P_n. In addition, on both graphs, label consumer surplus with the tax (CS_t), producer surplus with the tax (PS_t), CTI, PTI, and DWL.

d. In which graph is the DWL greater?

e. In which graph is the CTI greater?

f. In which graph is the PTI greater?

5. For each of the following, identify whether you think the tax is based on the ability-to-pay principle or the benefits principle.

   a. Inherited wealth is taxed according to the following schedule: for individuals inheriting less than $50,000 a year, there is no tax; for individuals inheriting $50,000 to $150,000 a year, the tax is 10% of the inherited amount; and for individuals inheriting more than $150,000 a year, the tax is 25% of the inherited amount.

   b. A sales tax is applied to all consumer goods bought during the year.

   c. A tax of $25 per individual is charged for the use of the state park system.

   d. A progressive income tax is adopted that requires low-income taxpayers pay a negative tax and high-income taxpayers pay a greater proportion of their income than do middle-income taxpayers.

6. For each of the taxes in problem 5, identify whether the tax is proportional, regressive, or progressive. Explain your answer.

BEFORE YOU TAKE THE TEST

Chapter Review Questions

1. The cost of a tax is equal to
   a. the tax revenue raised by the tax.
   b. the tax revenue raised by the tax, plus the deadweight loss associated with the tax, plus whatever administrative costs that compliance with the tax incurs.
   c. the tax revenue raised by the tax plus the deadweight loss associated with the tax.
   d. the deadweight loss associated with the tax and the administrative costs that compliance with the tax entails.

Answer the next seven questions based on the following information. The graph below represents the market for cigarettes in Tinseltown. D is the demand curve, S_1 is the supply curve, and S_t is the supply curve after an excise tax has been imposed on cigarettes. Letters A through K represent areas in the graph. Prices are denoted as P_1, P_2, P_3, P_4, and P_5. Quantities are denoted as Q_1, Q_2, Q_3, and Q_4.

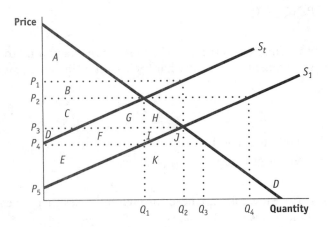

2. The excise tax in the graph is equal to
    a. $P_1 - P_4$.
    b. $P_2 - P_4$.
    c. $P_4 - P_5$.
    d. Answers (a) and (c) both measure the excise tax.
    e. Answers (b) and (c) both measure the excise tax.

3. The consumer surplus before the tax is equal to the sum of areas
    a. A, B, C, G, and H.
    b. A and B.
    c. A, B, C, D, E, F, G, H, and I.
    d. D, E, F, and I.

4. The producer surplus before the tax is equal to the areas
    a. A, B, C, G, and H.
    b. A and B.
    c. A, B, C, D, E, F, G, H, and I.
    d. D, E, F, and I.

5. The tax revenue collected by the government when this excise tax is imposed is equal to
    a. $(P_1 - P_3)(Q_2)$.   c. $(P_2 - P_4)(Q_2)$.
    b. $(P_2 - P_4)(Q_1)$.   d. $(P_2 - P_3)(Q_1)$.

6. The deadweight loss from a consumer's perspective is equal to area(s)
    a. H.   c. H and I.
    b. I.   d. C, G, and H.

7. The efficiency cost of this excise tax can be measured as area(s)
    a. G and H.   c. I and J.
    b. H and I.   d. H, I, and J.

8. A mathematical expression for the deadweight loss caused by this excise tax is
   a. $(P_2 - P_4)(Q_2)$.
   b. $(P_2 - P_4)(Q_2 - Q_1)$.
   c. $(1/2)(P_2 - P_4)(Q_2 - Q_1)$.
   d. $(1/2)(P_2 - P_3)(Q_2 - Q_1)$.

9. The income tax in Tinseltown is a flat tax that requires everyone to pay 10% of their income to the government no matter what their level of income. This tax is
   a. efficient.
   b. proportional.
   c. regressive.
   d. based on the ability-to-pay principle.
   e. based on the benefit principle.

10. The highways in Tinseltown are financed through toll taxes that are collected from people driving on these highways. This tax is
   a. efficient.
   b. proportional.
   c. based on the ability-to-pay principle.
   d. based on the benefit principle.

11. In this year's presidential election in Tinseltown, one of the candidates is running on a platform that advocates a change in the income tax. This candidate proposes that individuals in the bottom half of the income distribution should pay 50% of their income to the government, while individuals in the top half of the income distribution should pay 30% of their income. This candidate reasons that the higher-income individuals will still end up paying a lot of money to the government. The tax structure advocated by this candidate is
   a. regressive.   c. proportional.
   b. progressive.   d. efficient.

Answer the next six questions based on the following information. The market for soft drinks in Tinseltown is given by the following demand and supply equations:

$$\text{Demand: } P = 100 - 2Q$$
$$\text{Supply: } P = 2Q$$

Where P is the market price measured in cents and Q is the market quantity measured in bottles of soft drink. Tinseltown is considering imposing an excise tax on soft drink producers of 20 cents a bottle.

12. If this excise tax is imposed, the new supply curve with the excise tax will be
   a. $P = 2Q + 20$.   c. $P = 2(Q + 20)$.
   b. $P = 2Q - 20$.   d. $P = 2(Q - 20)$.

13. If this excise tax is imposed, the price of soft drinks in Tinseltown will increase by _____ cents.
   a. 20   c. 10
   b. 30   d. 0

14. If this excise tax is imposed, the tax revenue collected by the government will equal

a. $1.

b. $2.

c. $3.

d. $4.

15. If this excise tax is imposed, the deadweight loss associated with the tax will equal

a. $5.

b. $4.

c. $1.

d. $0.50.

16. The loss in consumer surplus due to the imposition of this excise tax equals

a. $6.25.

b. $4.

c. $2.25.

d. $0.25.

17. If this excise tax is imposed, the producer tax incidence is equal to

a. $1.

b. $2.

c. $2.25.

d. $4.

18. An excise tax is imposed on producers of a good. For a given supply curve, the more price elastic the demand for the product, the greater the tax incidence on

a. consumers.

b. producers.

19. An excise tax is imposed on producers of a good. For a given demand curve, the more inelastic the supply of the product, the greater the tax incidence on

a. consumers.

b. producers.

20. When the price elasticity of demand is low and the price elasticity of supply is high, the burden of an excise tax falls primarily on

a. sellers of the product.

b. buyers of the product.

21. When the price elasticity of demand is high and the price elasticity of supply is low, the burden of an excise tax falls primarily on

a. sellers of the product.

b. buyers of the product.

22. You are told that the initial supply curve in a market is $P = Q$ and the initial demand curve in the market is $P = 100 - Q$. An excise tax is imposed in this market and it results in the government collecting $1,250 in tax revenue. The excise tax in this market is equal to

a. $10.

b. $20.

c. $25.

d. $50.

23. Excise taxes cause deadweight loss when the excise tax

a. raises the price of the good being taxed.

b. decreases the quantity of the good supplied and demanded in the market.

c. creates an incentive for mutually beneficial exchanges to take place.

d. Answers (a), (b), and (c) are all true.

24. The deadweight loss due to the imposition of an excise tax is lowest when
   a. demand is relatively inelastic and supply is relatively elastic.
   b. demand is relatively inelastic and supply is relatively inelastic.
   c. demand is relatively elastic and supply is relatively elastic.
   d. demand is relatively elastic and supply is relatively inelastic.

25. Policymakers wishing to dramatically decrease the consumption of a good by using an excise tax will find that the success of this policy depends on
   a. the price elasticity of demand.
   b. the price elasticity of supply.
   c. the price elasticities of either demand or supply.
   d. the size of the excise tax. The price elasticities of supply and demand have no impact on how successful the policy is with regard to decreasing the consumption of the good.

26. Which of the following statements is true?
   I. The ability-to-pay principle of taxation says that all individuals have the ability to pay tax and should therefore not be exempt from paying taxes.
   II. The ability-to-pay principle of taxation when applied in the design of a tax system results in all individuals paying their fair share of taxes.
   III. The ability-to-pay principle of taxation and the benefits principle of taxation result in the same outcome with regard to designing tax systems.
   a. Statement I is true.
   b. Statement II is true.
   c. Statement III is true.
   d. Statements I and III are true.
   e. Statements II and III are true.
   f. None of the above statements are true.

Use the following table to answer the next three questions. The table provides information about pre-tax income and then gives after-tax income for three different tax structure proposals.

Pre-tax income	Proposal 1: After-tax income	Proposal 2: After-tax income	Proposal 3: After-tax income
$ 20,000	$ 15,000	$ 15,000	$ 15,000
32,000	24,000	27,000	22,400
40,000	30,000	35,000	27,200
80,000	60,000	75,000	52,000
200,000	150,000	195,000	120,000

27. Policymakers wish to impose a proportional, or flat, tax based on income. Which proposed tax structure represents this choice?
   a. Proposal 1
   b. Proposal 2
   c. Proposal 3

28. Policymakers wish to impose a regressive tax based on income. Which proposed tax structure represents this choice?

    a. Proposal 1

    b. Proposal 2

    c. Proposal 3

29. What percentage of income does an individual pay in taxes under proposal 2 if that individual's pre-tax income is $40,000?

    a. 0.125%

    b. 1.25%

    c. 12.5%

    d. 125%

30. The marginal tax rate is

    a. the total number of dollars paid as a tax divided by the taxpayer's income.

    b. the total amount of tax revenue collected by the government divided by the economy's total income.

    c. the percentage of an increase in income that is taxed away.

    d. the percentage of income paid as taxes by the lowest quintile of income in the economy.

31. In contrast to taxes at the federal level, taxes at the state and local level of government in the United States

    a. apply the ability-to-pay principle more frequently.

    b. tend to be more proportional.

    c. tend to be more regressive.

    d. tend to be more progressive.

ANSWER KEY

Answers to Problems and Exercises

1. There are two basic principles underlying the equity of a tax system: the ability-to-pay principle and the benefits principle.

    -   With the ability-to-pay principle, individuals with greater ability to pay have a larger tax burden. The advantage of this principle in guiding the design of a tax structure is that it focuses on people's economic ability to pay the tax. Its disadvantage is the failure to link tax payments with government services. For example, an individual with a high income generally has greater ability to pay taxes than an individual with low income (one can think of some exceptions to this: someone with high medical expenses that more than offset their high income or a low-income person with great wealth), but the high-income individual may not benefit from government services to the same extent as the low-income taxpayer. The well-to-do may not use the public park system (they may belong to clubs or have their own expansive yards) or the public school system (their children go to private school). From an equity standpoint, the ability-to-pay principle misses this connection between the level of tax payment and the benefits received from the government.

    -   The benefits principle argues that tax systems are fair when the taxpayer's payment aligns with the level of benefits the taxpayer receives from the government. This principle argues for higher taxes for those who receive higher benefits. This seems theoretically fair, but the practical realities of applying this principle are difficult: low-income individuals may receive a disproportionate amount of benefits from the government. The benefits principle misses the connection between the level of tax payment and the ability of the taxpayer to make this payment.

2. **a.**

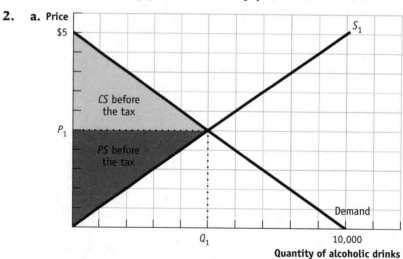

    b. To find P_1 and Q_1, use the demand and supply equations: $10{,}000 - 2{,}000P = 2{,}000P$. Solving for P yields an equilibrium price of $2.50. Plug this price into either the demand or the supply equation to find the equilibrium quantity: $Q_1 = 10{,}000 - (2{,}000)(2.50) = 5{,}000$ alcoholic drinks.

c. Consumer surplus (CS) before the imposition of the tax equals the area of a triangle, and can be computed as $(1/2)(\$5/\text{drink} - \$2.50/\text{drink})(5{,}000 \text{ drinks}) = \$6{,}250$. Producer surplus (PS) before the imposition of the tax equals the area of a triangle, and can be computed as $(1/2)(\$2.50/\text{drink})(5{,}000 \text{ drinks}) = \$6{,}250$. Total surplus is the sum of CS and PS, or $\$12{,}500$.

d.

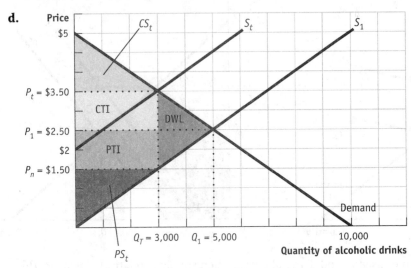

e. The new supply curve with this excise tax is $Q = 2{,}000P - 4{,}000$. (To find this new supply curve, it is easiest to rewrite the initial supply curve, in slope intercept form: $P = (1/2{,}000)Q$. Then add the amount of the excise tax to the y-intercept of this equation since the excise tax shifts the supply curve vertically upward by an amount equal to the tax. Thus, $P = (1/2{,}000)Q + 2$, or $Q = 2{,}000P - 4{,}000$. Combine this new supply equation with the demand equation to find P_t and Q_t. $P_t = \$3.50$ and $Q_t = 3{,}000$ drinks. To find P_n, remember that the price producers receive after they pay the tax is equal to the price with the tax minus the excise tax, or $P_t -$ excise tax. P_n is equal to $\$1.50$.

f. See graph in part (d).

g. CS with the tax $= CS_t = (1/2)(\$5/\text{drink} - \$3.50/\text{drink})(3{,}000 \text{ drinks}) = \$2{,}250$

PS with the tax $= PS_t = (1/2)(\$1.50/\text{drink})(3{,}000 \text{ drinks}) = \$2{,}250$

CTI $= (\$1/\text{drink})(3{,}000 \text{ drinks}) = \$3{,}000$

PTI $= (\$1/\text{drink})(3{,}000 \text{ drinks}) = \$3{,}000$

DWL $= (1/2)(\$2/\text{drink})(5{,}000 \text{ drinks} - 3{,}000 \text{ drinks}) = \$2{,}000$

Tax revenue $= $ CTI $+$ PTI $= $ (excise tax per drink)(number of drinks sold) $= (\$2/\text{drink})(3{,}000 \text{ drinks}) = \$6{,}000$

The sum of $CS_t + PS_t +$ tax revenue $+$ DWL $= \$12{,}500$ and is therefore equal to the original total surplus prior to the imposition of the tax.

h. When the excise tax is raised to $\$3$, we know this causes price to increase and quantity to decrease in this market. Quantity falls to 2,000, which would result in tax revenues of $2{,}000 \times \$3$. Thus, tax revenue remains unchanged at $\$6{,}000$.

3. a–d.

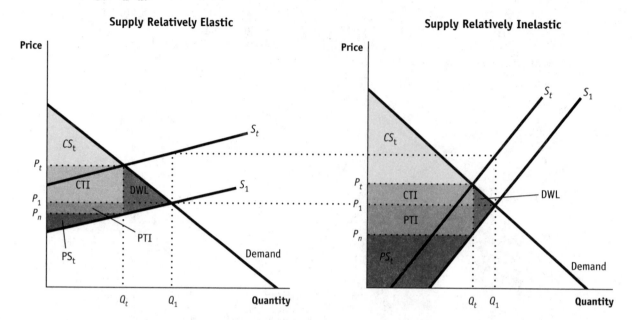

e. For a given excise tax and demand curve, when supply is relatively inelastic, the excise tax results in a smaller DWL than when supply is relatively elastic. For a given excise tax and demand curve, quantity changes by a larger amount when supply is relatively elastic. Tax revenue depends on the relative elasticities of both the demand and the supply curve.

4. a–c.

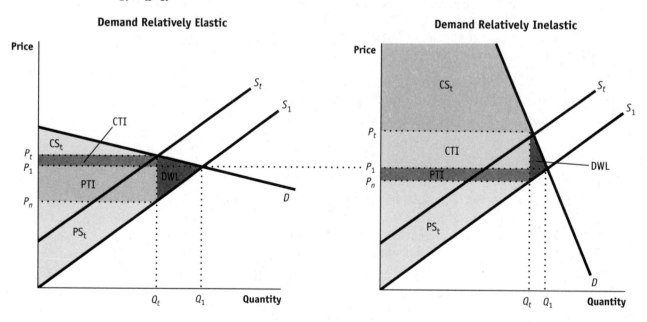

d. The DWL is greater in the graph in which demand is relatively elastic.

e. The CTI is greater in the graph in which demand is relatively inelastic.

f. The PTI is greater in the graph in which demand is relatively elastic.

5. a. Ability-to-pay principle, since as inherited wealth increases, this should reflect an increased ability to pay an inheritance tax.

b. Benefits principle, since the purchaser of the product receives the consumption benefits of that product.

    c. Benefits principle, since the individual paying the tax is the individual enjoying the use of the park.

    d. Ability-to-pay principle, since the tax increases with income.

6. **a.** This is a progressive tax, since as inherited wealth increases, the percentage of the tax to that wealth increases.

    b. This is a regressive tax, since the tax rises less than in proportion to income: because low-income individuals spend a greater proportion of their income on consumer goods, low-income individuals pay a higher percentage of their income than high-income individuals.

    c. This is a regressive tax, since it is a flat amount charged to each taxpayer without regard to income or wealth. This tax is a larger proportion of a low-income person's income and a smaller proportion of a high-income person's income.

    d. This one is given to you: it's a progressive tax!

Answers to Chapter Review Questions

1. **Answer b.** When the government imposes a tax, this clearly results in the government receiving tax revenue which is a cost to the taxpayer, but the imposition of a tax imposes greater costs than just the tax revenue collected. The tax also imposes an efficiency cost (the DWL) as the tax causes a distortion in consumer behavior. The tax also imposes an administrative cost associated with complying with the tax.

2. **Answer e.** The excise tax is equal to the vertical distance between the original supply curve and the supply curve with the tax. At quantity Q_2, the vertical distance is equal to $P_1 - P_3$: this is the same distance as $P_2 - P_4$ or $P_4 - P_5$.

3. **Answer a.** The area of consumer surplus is the area above the equilibrium price and below the demand curve. Before the tax is implemented, the equilibrium price is P_3 and thus the area of consumer surplus is equal to the areas A, B, C, G, and H.

4. **Answer d.** The area of producer surplus is the area that lies beneath the equilibrium price and above the supply curve. Before the imposition of the tax, the equilibrium price is P_3 and the area of producer surplus is the sum of areas D, E, F, and I.

5. **Answer b.** The tax revenue collected by the government is equal to the product of the tax per unit and the number of units of the good sold when the tax is implemented. In this example, the tax per unit is $(P_2 - P_4)$ and the number of units sold is Q_1, so the tax revenue is equal to $(P_2 - P_4)(Q_1)$.

6. **Answer a.** When the excise tax is imposed, the consumer reduces consumption of the good. Some of the consumer's original consumer surplus is captured by the government: the consumer's tax incidence measures the economic burden of the tax borne by consumers. The consumer also loses a part of the original consumer surplus due to the efficiency cost of the tax: in this graph, this is represented as area H.

7. **Answer b.** The excise tax imposes an efficiency cost equal to the deadweight loss. This deadweight loss is represented by the areas H and I in the graph. Prior to the imposition of the excise tax, total surplus is equal to the sum of consumer and producer surplus. When the tax is imposed on this market, part of this total surplus is captured by the government as tax revenue, but part of the total surplus is lost to consumers and producers due to the distortion the tax causes with respect to the level of consumption of the good. This distortion is measured by areas H and I.

8. **Answer c.** The area of deadweight loss can be calculated as an area of a triangle: thus, this area is equal to one-half times the product of the excise tax per unit and the change in quantity due to the imposition of the tax. In this example, the excise tax per unit is equal to $(P_2 - P_4)$ and the change in quantity is $(Q_2 - Q_1)$.

9. **Answer b.** This is an example of a proportional tax, since the tax is the same proportion of everyone's income. High-income people pay 10% of their income as do low-income people. This tax is not based on the benefits principle, since the amount of tax you pay is not tied to the level of government services you receive, nor is the tax based on the ability-to-pay principle, since the government does not take into account the individual's ability to pay when collecting the tax.

10. **Answer d.** Those individuals who make use of the highways in Tinseltown pay the tax that provides these highways. These individuals benefit from the highways and they pay the tax to support the construction of these highways. No distinction is made with regard to the individual taxpayer's ability to pay: if the individual uses the highway then they pay the toll.

11. **Answer a.** Since lower-income individuals will pay a larger percentage of their income to the government with this tax structure, this tax structure is regressive.

12. **Answer a.** The new supply curve will be parallel to the original supply curve but will have a y-intercept that is 20 cents greater than the original supply curve's y-intercept. Since the original supply curve intercepts the y-axis at zero, this means that the new supply curve with the excise tax will intercept the y-axis at 20.

13. **Answer c.** To answer this question, you must know the original price of soft drinks in Tinseltown before the excise tax and the price of soft drinks in Tinseltown after the imposition of the excise tax. The original price of soft drinks is 50 cents, and when the tax is implemented the price will rise to 60 cents. The increase in the price equals 10 cents.

14. **Answer d.** The tax revenue is equal to the tax per unit times the number of units sold. When the excise tax is implemented, 20 bottles of soft drinks will be sold at a price of 60 cents each. But 20 cents of that price represents the excise tax, so the government will collect 20 cents per bottle sold, or a total of $4.

15. **Answer d.** The deadweight loss can be calculated as the area of a triangle. The deadweight loss is equal to (1/2)(excise tax per unit)(the original equilibrium quantity − the equilibrium quantity with the excise tax), or (1/2)(20 cents per unit)(25 units − 20 units), which equals $0.50.

16. **Answer c.** The original consumer surplus is equal to $6.25 and the new consumer surplus after the imposition of the excise tax is equal to $4.00, which means the loss in consumer surplus due to the tax is equal to $2.25.

17. **Answer b.** The producer tax incidence is a measure of the economic burden of the excise tax on producers. Producers prior to the excise tax sold their good for 50 cents a bottle. With the excise tax the price of soft drinks increases to 60 cents a bottle, but the government receives 20 cents of that price. The producer therefore keeps only 40 cents for every soft drink the producer sells. From the producer's perspective, the excise tax results in a decrease in the price of soft drinks from 50 cents a bottle to 40 cents a bottle. The producer sells 20 bottles of soft drinks once the excise tax is imposed, and the producer tax incidence is therefore equal to 10 cents a bottle times the 20 bottles, or $2.

18. **Answer b.** When demand is more elastic, this implies that consumers are price sensitive and that a small change in price will result in a large change in the quantity demanded. Hence, an excise tax places a greater economic burden on suppliers in this case.

19. **Answer b.** When supply is inelastic, this implies that a small increase in price will cause a relatively large change in the quantity demanded; when supply is elastic, a small increase in price will cause a relatively small change in the quantity demanded. For a given demand curve, an excise tax results in greater tax incidence on producers when supply is inelastic.

20. **Answer b.** When price elasticity of demand is low (implying a relatively steep demand curve) while price elasticity of supply is high (implying a relatively flat supply curve), the economic burden of an excise tax falls primarily on consumers since the excise tax causes a relatively large increase in price and a relatively small decrease in the quantity demanded.

21. **Answer a.** When price elasticity of demand is high (implying a relatively flat demand curve) while price elasticity of supply is low (implying a relatively steep supply curve), the economic burden of an excise tax falls primarily on producers since the excise tax causes a relatively small increase in price and a relatively large decrease in the quantity demanded.

22. **Answer d.** One way to solve this problem is to draw a graph with the initial supply and demand curves and then calculate what the tax revenue would equal for each of the excise tax rates. For each level of the excise tax, the supply curve with the tax could be written as $P_s = Q_s +$ (the amount of the excise tax), where P_s is the supply price and Q_s is the quantity supplied at that price. Then, use this equation plus the demand equation and each level of the excise tax to calculate the equilibrium quantity, the equilibrium price with the tax, and then the tax revenue generated by the tax. Thus, if the excise tax is equal to $50 per unit, then the equilibrium quantity in the market once the tax is imposed is 25 units, the equilibrium price with the tax is $75, and the tax revenue is equal to ($50/unit)(25 units) = $1,250.

23. **Answer b.** An excise tax creates a deadweight loss because it discourages mutually beneficial exchanges from taking place. The excise tax creates a deadweight loss by altering the amount of the good supplied and demanded in the market. An increase in price due to the excise tax is not sufficient to create a deadweight loss, because if the demand curve is perfectly inelastic, there is no deadweight loss due to the tax.

24. **Answer b.** The deadweight loss from an excise tax is smallest when both the demand and supply curves are relatively inelastic, since this implies that the percentage increase in the price is relatively greater than the percentage decrease in the quantity supplied and demanded in the market.

25. **Answer c.** A policy to reduce consumption of a good through the imposition of an excise tax is more successful when the activity being discouraged is elastically demanded or supplied.

26. **Answer f.** The ability-to-pay principle is based on the principle that those with greater ability to pay a tax should pay more than those with less ability to pay the tax. The benefits principle is based on the principle that those who benefit from public spending should bear the burden of the tax that pays for that spending. In the first statement, it is possible to think of individuals who lack the ability to pay a tax (the unemployed, the disabled, the retired, children, etc.). In the second statement, the ability-to-pay principle results in those with higher incomes paying higher taxes: some of these individuals may not feel that the resultant tax system and its economic distribution are fair. In the third statement, the two principles distribute tax burden quite differently: the benefits principle considers the connection between the recipients of the government's spending programs and the level of taxes these individuals pay, while the ability-to-pay principle does not consider who receives the benefits of government spending programs, but instead focuses on sheer ability to pay the tax.

27. **Answer a.** A flat tax collects the same percentage of the base regardless of the taxpayer's income or wealth. Proposal 1 represents a flat tax, since this tax is 25% of the pre-tax income regardless of the level of pretax income.

28. **Answer b.** A regressive tax structure is one in which the tax rises less than in proportion to income so that high-income taxpayers pay a smaller percentage of their income than do low-income taxpayers. Proposal 2 taxes individuals with income of $20,000 at a rate of 25% of their income, while individuals with income of $200,000 are taxed at a rate of 2.5% of their income.

29. **Answer c.** An individual earning a pre-tax income of $40,000 pays $5,000 in taxes under proposal 2. To convert this to a percentage, divide (5,000/40,000) and then multiply this value by 100.

30. **Answer c.** The marginal tax rate is a measure of the change in tax divided by the change in income. Answer (a) measures the average tax rate for a taxpayer, since it computes the value of (taxes paid/income). Answer (b) measures the ratio of total taxes paid to total income. Answer (d) measures the average tax rate paid by taxpayers in the lowest quintile in a society.

31. **Answer c.** State and local taxes are more regressive than federal taxes, which are overall quite progressive. State and local governments recognize that a decision to tax high-income individuals more heavily than low-income individuals may result in the high-income individuals moving to other localities where taxes are lower.

chapter 8

International Trade

BEFORE YOU READ THE CHAPTER

Summary

This chapter discusses international trade and the gains from trade that are possible through specialization according to comparative advantage. The chapter explores the sources of comparative advantage, and also provides a model to illustrate the distributional consequences of trade. This model provides a method for considering who benefits and who loses from international trade and why the benefits from trade outweigh the losses from trade. The chapter also considers the impact of tariffs and quotas and how tariffs and quotas create market inefficiencies and reduce the area of total surplus. Finally, the chapter discusses why governments engage in trade protection and the effect of international trade agreements on the international flow of goods and services.

Chapter Objectives

Objective #1. Trade is beneficial to both parties that engage in the trade, whether they are individuals or countries. Countries that specialize in producing different goods and then trade these goods with other countries benefit from this trade. Goods and services purchased from abroad are called imports, and goods and services sold abroad are called exports. Countries trade goods and services with one another, but they also invest funds: this linking of the markets for goods and services as well as financial assets between different countries is referred to as globalization.

Objective #2. A country has the comparative advantage in producing a good or service when that country can produce the good or service at a lower opportunity cost than can other countries. A simple way to model international trade is to use linear production possibility frontiers to analyze trade between two countries. The straight line production possibility frontiers implies that the opportunity cost of producing the two goods does not change as the level of production of these two goods changes. This model is known as the Ricardian model of international trade.

Objective #3. Autarky refers to the situation in which a country does not engage in trade with any other countries. The Ricardian model of international trade allows a comparison to be made between a situation in which two countries trade with one another versus a situation in which the two countries act as autarkies and do not trade with one another. The Ricardian model of international trade results in the following conclusions:

- When countries specialize according to comparative advantage and then trade with one another, the total amount of goods and services produced is greater than when the countries do not engage in specialization and trade.

- No country will engage in trade unless the relative price of the good traded is less than its opportunity cost of producing the good in autarky.

Objective #4.   For example, consider two countries, country A and country B, that have linear production possibility frontiers for the production of two goods: good X and good Y. These two countries and their production possibility frontiers are illustrated in Figure 8.1.

Figure 8.1

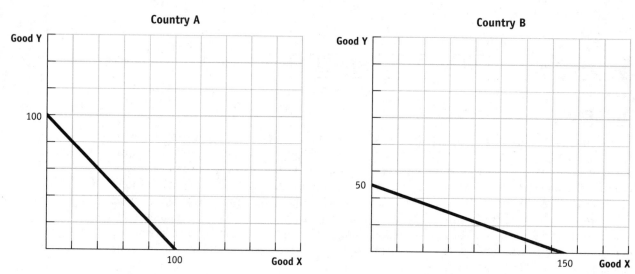

The opportunity cost of country A producing one more unit of good X is equal to 1 unit of good Y, since country A must give up 1 unit of good Y to produce an additional unit of good X according to their production possibility frontier illustrated in Figure 8.1. The opportunity cost of country B producing one more unit of good X is equal to 1/3 unit of good Y since country B must give up 1/3 unit of good Y to produce an additional unit of good X according to their production possibility frontier illustrated in Figure 8.1. Comparison of these two opportunity costs reveals that country B can produce good X at lower opportunity cost than can country A, since country B gives up fewer units of good Y to get one more unit of good X. Country B has the comparative advantage in producing good X. Country A has the comparative advantage in producing good Y, since the opportunity cost of producing 1 unit of good Y for country A is 1 unit of good X, while for country B the opportunity cost of producing 1 unit of good Y is 3 units of good X. Both countries can benefit by specializing in the production of the good they can produce at lower opportunity cost and then trading.

- As an example, suppose the two countries initially do not trade and that country A produces 50 units of good X and 50 units of good Y while country B produces 75 units of good X and 25 units of good Y. Total production without trade is summarized in the table below.

	Production of good X	Production of good Y
Country A	50	50
Country B	75	25
Total production	125	75

- Now, suppose the two countries specialize according to their comparative advantage: country A produces 0 units of good X and 100 units of good Y while country B produces 150 units of good X and 0 units of good Y. The table below summarizes the result of this specialization. Notice that the total production of both goods increases when the two countries specialize.

	Production of good X	Production of good Y
Country A	0	100
Country B	150	0
Total production	150	100

- Let's digress a moment and consider what would happen if the two countries specialized, but produced those goods for which they did not have the comparative advantage: this implies that country A produces good X while country B produces good Y. The table below summarizes what happens when countries do not specialize according to their comparative advantage: total production decreases! Specialization is beneficial only when countries produce those goods for which they have lower opportunity cost of production.

	Production of good X	Production of good Y
Country A	100	0
Country B	0	50
Total production	100	50

- Once countries decide to specialize according to comparative advantage and to trade, they then need to decide on the price of these traded goods. In our example, country A will be willing to trade good Y for any price between 1 unit of good X (country A's opportunity cost of producing good Y) and 3 units of good X (country B's opportunity cost of producing good Y). Within this range of relative prices, country A benefits from trading with country B rather than producing the good themselves. Using similar reasoning, country A will be willing to trade good X for any price between 1/3 a unit of good Y and 1 unit of good Y.

Objective #5. Gains from trade depend on comparative advantage and not absolute advantage. Comparative advantage is based on the opportunity cost of producing the good and not the absolute amount of resources used to produce the good. A country with low wage rates generally reflects low labor productivity, while a country with high wage rates reflects high labor productivity.

- One fallacy with regard to trade is the pauper labor fallacy, which is the belief that a high-wage country importing goods produced by workers in a low-wage country is an action that results in harming workers in the high-wage country.

- A second fallacy with regard to trade is the sweatshop labor fallacy, which is the belief that trade must be bad for workers in low-wage countries since the wages paid to workers in these countries is so much lower than the wages paid to workers in high-wage countries.

- Both the pauper labor fallacy and the sweatshop labor fallacy fail to recognize that trade is to the advantage of both the high-wage and the low-wage country, because both are able to achieve a higher standard of living through trade with one another.

Objective #6. Comparative advantage arises because of differences in climate, differences in factor endowments, and differences in technology.

- Climate and seasonal differences (northern hemisphere versus southern hemisphere) play a significant role in comparative advantage, since some goods can only be produced in certain climates or during certain seasons.

- The Heckscher-Ohlin model finds that a country has a comparative advantage in producing those goods whose production is intensive in the factors that are abundant in that country compared to other countries. This finding arises because the opportunity cost of a given factor is low when that factor is relatively abundant. This argument also helps to explain incomplete specialization, which is the situation when a country continues to produce a good that it also imports. A country will engage in incomplete specialization whenever that country has factor endowments that make it economically feasible for them to produce the good. A country can still gain from trade even if it does not completely specialize.

- Technological differences can also drive comparative advantage. Technological differences may arise due to accumulated experience or because of innovations that one country has made that other countries have not adopted.

Objective #7.   The model of demand and supply can be used to analyze the benefits of international trade. Figure 8.2 illustrates a market for a country that does not trade. In this figure, domestic demand represents the total demand for this good from individuals who live in this country, while domestic supply represents the total supply of this good from firms producing this good in this country. In autarky, the equilibrium in this market would be determined by the intersection of the domestic demand curve with the domestic supply curve: P_A is the equilibrium price and Q_A is the equilibrium quantity under autarky. Consumer and producer surplus are indicated in the figure, and total surplus in this market equals the sum of consumer and producer surplus.

Figure 8.2

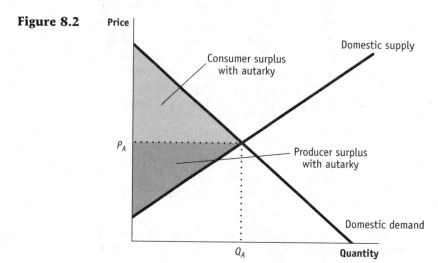

Consider what happens in this market if this country opens to trade. Suppose the world price for this good is lower than the autarky price (P_A) for this good. In Figure 8.3, this world price (P_W) is drawn on the graph. Notice that if the country opens to trade, the quantity of the good demanded domestically in this country at the world price (Q_D) will be greater than the amount of the good supplied domestically at this price (Q_S). This excess demand will be satisfied by the country importing ($Q_D - Q_S$) units of the good. Trade will also change the areas of consumer and producer surplus in this country: consumer surplus will increase as consumers get more units of the good at a lower price, while producer surplus decreases as domestic producers sell fewer units of the good at the lower price. Study Figure 8.3 carefully and recall that consumer surplus is the area that is beneath the demand curve but above the equilibrium price, while producer surplus is the area that is above the supply curve but below the equilibrium price. With trade, total surplus increases, but domestic producers of this good see a reduction in their producer surplus while domestic consumers see an increase in their consumer surplus. In the case of an imported good, domestic consumers benefit while domestic producers lose. Trade is beneficial since total surplus increases, but trade has distributional consequences as you can see from what happens to the areas of consumer and producer surplus.

Figure 8.3

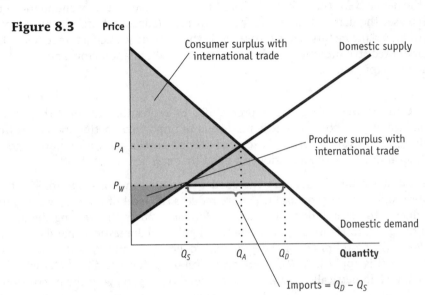

We can use the same analysis to consider the situation when the world price is greater than the autarky price. Starting from Figure 8.2, a market under autarky, let's consider a situation in which the world price exceeds the autarky price. Figure 8.4 illustrates this example: P_W is the world price and, in this case, when this country opens to trade, it finds that the quantity demanded domestically at the world price (Q_D) is less than the amount supplied domestically at this price (Q_S). This excess supply of ($Q_S - Q_D$) will be exported to other countries. Figure 8.4 also identifies the areas of consumer surplus and producer surplus once trade is allowed. As in Figure 8.3, we find that the area of total surplus is larger than in autarky. However, the distribution of the surplus has changed: in Figure 8.3, domestic consumers benefited from trade while domestic suppliers were hurt; in Figure 8.4, domestic suppliers benefit from trade while domestic consumers are hurt. In both of these examples we find that trade is beneficial since it increases total surplus, but that trade has distributional consequences.

Figure 8.4

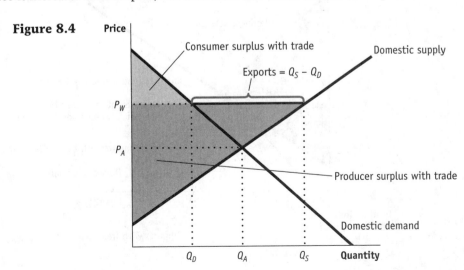

Objective #8.   A country's industries can be broken down into two broad categories: exporting industries that produce goods and services to be sold abroad, and import-competing industries that produce goods and services also imported from abroad. When a country opens to trade, this leads to higher production in the exporting industries and lower production in the import-competing industries, and these changes affect the demand for factors of production in these two types of industries. The Heckscher-Ohlin model posits that international trade increases the demand for those factors of production that are relatively abundant in the country and decreases the demand for those factors of production that are relatively scarce. Thus, the price of abundant factors tends to rise while the price of scarce factors tends to fall. This price movement redistributes income toward a country's abundant factors and away from a country's less abundant factors.

Objective #9.   Countries engage in trade protection, or protection, to limit the level of imports with the idea of protecting domestic producers in import-competing industries from foreign competition. Tariffs are a form of excise tax levied on the sales of imported goods, while quotas are legal limits on the quantity of a good that can be imported.

- Figure 8.5 illustrates a tariff placed on the good represented in this diagram. The tariff raises the world price of the good and therefore reduces the level of imports while simultaneously reducing the overall domestic demand for the good and increasing the domestic supply of the good. In Figure 8.5, the domestic supply and domestic demand curves are illustrated. P_W is the world price for the good with open trade, and P_T is the price of the good once the tariff is applied. At P_T, the quantity supplied domestically is Q_{ST} while the quantity demanded domestically is Q_{DT}. Thus, the level of imports with the imposition of the tariff is ($Q_{DT} - Q_{ST}$). The tariff results in a decrease in consumer surplus, an increase in producer surplus, and the capture of some of the consumer surplus as tariff revenue that the government earns. These areas are marked on the graph. In addition, the tariff results in deadweight loss: some mutually beneficial trades fail to occur and the economy wastes some resources on inefficient production since some producers produce the good even though their costs are greater than the world price of P_W. These two areas of deadweight loss are also identified on the graph. Study Figure 8.5 carefully and then compare it to Figure 8.3 to see how a tariff changes the outcome in this market. Notice that the tariff redistributes part of the consumer surplus to domestic producers and to the government as well as creating the areas of deadweight loss.

Figure 8.5

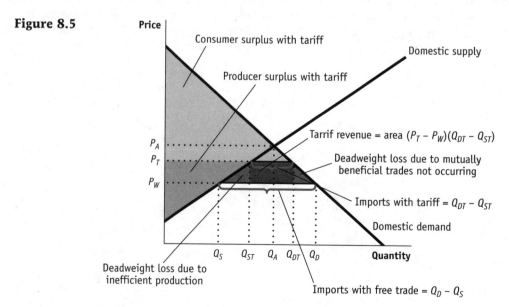

- Imposition of a quota in a market with free trade creates a limit on the number of units of the good that can be imported into the domestic market. This legal limit is typically administered through a license whereby the license holder purchases the legal right to import a certain number of units of the good into the domestic market. A quota results in a similar outcome as the tariff, but with one crucial difference. With a quota, the area labeled tariff revenue is now license-holder revenue. Instead of the government earning tax revenue from the imposition of the tariff, the quota results in the license holder earning quota rents equal to the area $(P_Q - P_W)(Q_{D\ QUOTA} - Q_{S\ QUOTA})$. The quota results in an increase in the domestic producer surplus and a decrease in the domestic consumer surplus. In addition, the quota results in the same two areas of deadweight loss that occurred with the tariff. Figure 8.6 illustrates the impact of a quota of $(Q_{D\ QUOTA} - Q_{S\ QUOTA})$ units on the market.

Figure 8.6

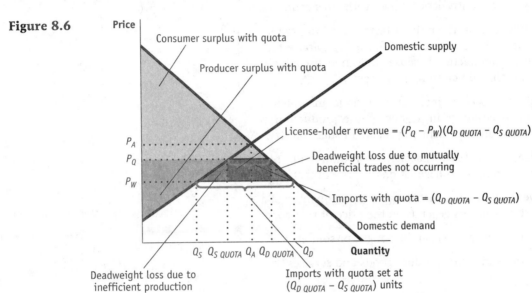

Objective #10. Advocates of tariffs and quotas offer three common arguments for trade protection: national security, job creation, and the infant industry argument. The national security argument focuses on the need to protect domestic suppliers of crucial goods from foreign competition. The job creation argument focuses on the additional jobs that are created in the import-competing industries when these industries are protected by a tariff or quota. The infant industry argument claims that newly emerging industries (those in their infancy) may need trade protection to get established. Despite these arguments, most trade protection reflects the political influence of the import-competing producers.

Objective #11. Trade protection hurts domestic consumers as well as foreign export industries. Because countries care about each other's trade policies, they engage in international trade agreements. These agreements involve treaties that pledge countries will engage in less trade protection in return for a promise from other countries that they will also engage in less trade protection. The North American Free Trade Agreement (NAFTA) and the European Union (EU) are examples of trade agreements between groups of countries. Global trade agreements that cover most of the world also are in place, and the World Trade Organization WTO oversees these global trade agreements. The WTO provides the framework for the extensive and complex negotiations that are involved in major international agreements; in addition, the WTO resolves disputes among its members.

Objective #12. Globalization or growing world trade has generally been seen as a positive outcome. However, concerns have arisen over the growing wage gap between more educated and less educated workers. In addition, the growth of offshore outsourcing has generated concerns about increasing economic insecurity.

Key Terms

imports goods and services purchased from other countries.

exports goods and services sold to other countries.

globalization the phenomenon of growing economic linkages among countries.

Ricardian model of international trade a model that analyzes international *trade* under the assumption that *opportunity costs* are constant.

autarky a situation in which a country does not trade with other countries.

factor intensity the difference in the ratio of factors used to produce a good in various industries. For example, oil refining is capital-intensive compared to clothing manufacture because oil refiners use a higher ratio of capital to labor than do clothing producers.

Hecksher–Olin model a *model* of international trade in which a country has a *comparative advantage* in a good whose production is intensive in the factors that are abundantly available in that country.

domestic demand curve a *demand curve* that shows how the quantity of a good demanded by domestic consumers depends on the price of that good.

domestic supply curve a *supply curve* that shows how the quantity of a good supplied by domestic producers depends on the price of that good.

world price the price at which a good can be bought or sold abroad.

exporting industries industries that produce goods and services that are sold abroad.

import-competing industries industries that produce goods and services that are also imported.

free trade *trade* that is unregulated by government *tariffs* or other artificial barriers; the levels of *exports* and *imports* occur naturally, as a result of supply and demand.

trade protection policies that limit *imports*.

protection an alternative term for *trade protection;* policies that limit *imports*.

tariff a tax levied on *imports*.

import quota a legal limit on the quantity of a good that can be imported.

international trade agreements treaties by which countries agree to lower *trade protections* against one another.

North American Free Trade Agreement (NAFTA) a *trade* agreement among the United States, Canada, and Mexico.

European Union (EU) a customs union among 27 European nations.

World Trade Organization (WTO) an international organization of member countries that oversees *international trade agreements* and rules on disputes between countries over those agreements.

offshore outsourcing businesses hiring people in another country to perform various tasks.

AFTER YOU READ THE CHAPTER

Tips

Tip #1.   Students often struggle with the concept of comparative advantage and how it relates to the opportunity cost of producing the good. One fail-safe method for analyzing this type of problem is to follow these steps. (1) Identify the two individuals or the two countries (for the rest of this tip we assume that we are analyzing the comparative advantage with regard to two countries) that are involved in the problem. (2) Identify the two goods that are being produced. (3) For each country, draw a graph that illustrates the production possibility frontier for that country. Make sure you label the graph with the country's name and the two axes with the good being produced. This labeling is very important since it helps ensure that you do not confuse the two countries or the two goods. (4) Find the slope of the production possibility frontier and then use this slope to calculate the opportunity cost of producing one more unit of the good measured along the x-axis. You can use the slope in this manner since the slope equals the "rise/run"—that is, the slope tells you the change in the y-variable divided by the change in the x-variable. So, for example, if one more unit of the x-variable was produced, the slope of the production possibility frontier would tell you how many units of the y-variable must be given up to produce this additional unit of the x-variable. (5) Under each country's graph, write a statement using this slope measure that says "OC of producing 1 good X is equal to [slope value] good Y." This statement just reminds you of what the opportunity cost of producing that additional unit of good X is. Below this statement write another statement that says "OC of producing 1 good Y is equal to [1/slope] good X." (6) Compare the opportunity cost of producing good X between the two countries, and decide which country can produce good X at the lowest opportunity cost. Circle the label on the x-axis for this country to identify the country that has the comparative advantage in producing good X. Then, on the other country's graph, circle the label on the y-axis to identify the country that has the comparative advantage in producing good Y. Figure 8.7 provides an example of this method. Note the labels, the OC statements, and the circling of the relevant labels as a means of identifying the country's comparative advantage. Faithful adherence to this method will certainly assure you of getting this concept right.

Figure 8.7

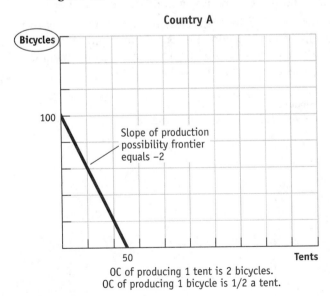

OC of producing 1 tent is 2 bicycles.
OC of producing 1 bicycle is 1/2 a tent.

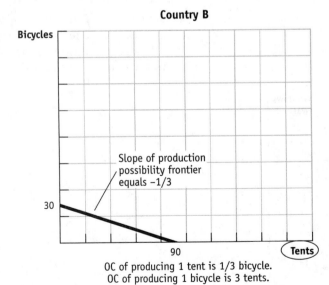

OC of producing 1 tent is 1/3 bicycle.
OC of producing 1 bicycle is 3 tents.

Tip #2. Students struggle with deciding what the relevant range of relative prices is for a good when countries specialize and then trade. Let's use the information in Figure 8.7 to work through a method for calculating this range of relative prices. Start with the good measured on the x-axis: tents. From the OC statements below the two graphs, we can see that the OC of producing 1 tent is between 1/3 bicycle (country B's OC) and 2 bicycles (country A's OC). You can think about placing these two limits on a number line and noting that the relative price of 1 tent must fall somewhere between the lowest possible relative price of 1/3 bicycle and the highest possible relative price of 2 bicycles. Figure 8.8 illustrates this number-line approach.

Figure 8.8

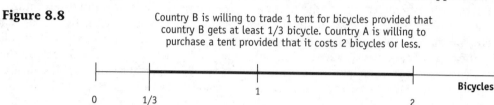

Country B is willing to trade 1 tent for bicycles provided that country B gets at least 1/3 bicycle. Country A is willing to purchase a tent provided that it costs 2 bicycles or less.

Tip #3. Working with quotas is often difficult for students: a quota is a legally established limit to the amount of imports a country allows during a given period. An alternative way of thinking about this legal limit is to recognize that the quota is the amount of imports that leads to the sum of the quantity supplied domestically plus the quota amount equaling the quantity demanded domestically. Thus, if you are told the quantity demanded domestically and the quantity supplied domestically at a given price, you can then calculate what the necessary quota would be in order for the total quantity supplied of the good (both the domestic production plus the world production) to equal the quantity demanded domestically. With this thought in mind, go back and revisit Figure 8.6 to see if you can apply this concept to the graph.

Problems and Exercises

1. Paula and Harry both produce lawn care and window washing services, and they both have an equal number of hours available to them each week to engage in providing these services. Paula is able to clean 1/2 windows or care for 1 yard per hour, and Harry can clean 1 window or 2 yards per hour. Currently Paula and Harry divide their work time evenly between cleaning windows and doing yard work. Both Paula and Harry work forty hours a week.

    a. Suppose that Paula and Harry initially work independently of each other. Draw two graphs, with one graph illustrating Paula's production possibility frontier and the other graph illustrating Harry's production possibility frontier. Measure windows washed on the vertical axis and yards cared for on the horizontal axis.

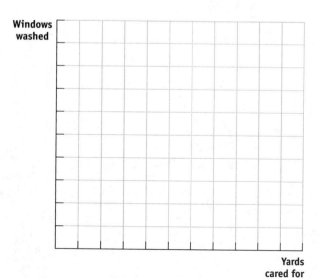

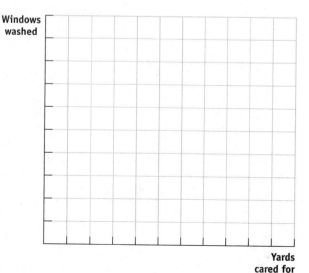

b. Who has the absolute advantage in performing yard care? Who has the absolute advantage in window washing?

c. Suppose both Paula and Harry divide their available time evenly between washing windows and doing yard care. Fill in the following table based on this assumption.

	Number of windows washed	Number of yards cared for
Paula		
Harry		
Total		

d. What is Paula's opportunity cost of washing a window? What is Paula's opportunity cost of caring for a yard?

e. What is Harry's opportunity cost of washing a window? What is Harry's opportunity cost of caring for a yard?

f. Who has the comparative advantage in washing windows? Who has the comparative advantage in caring for a yard? Explain your answers.

g. Assume that both Paula and Harry specialize according to comparative advantage and that both Paula and Harry produce only one type of good. Fill in the table below based on this specialization. What happens to total production of lawn care and window washing when Paula and Harry specialize according to their comparative advantage?

	Number of windows washed	Number of yards cared for
Paula		
Harry		
Total		

h. If both Harry and Paula specialize according to their comparative advantage and then trade with one another, what is the range of prices they will both accept for 1 washed window?

2. Titania and Phoenix are two countries that both produce steel and oats from their available resources. The production possibility frontiers for both countries are linear, and the table below provides information about the number of labor hours (the only resource either country uses in producing these two goods) it takes for each country to produce 1 unit of steel or 1 unit of oats. Assume that Titania and Phoenix both have 60 hours of labor available to produce either steel or oats or some combination of steel and oats.

	Number of labor hours needed to produce 1 unit of steel	Number of labor hours needed to produce 1 unit of oats
Titania	5	2
Phoenix	4	3

a. On two separate graphs, draw the production possibility frontiers for Titania and Phoenix. Place steel on the vertical axis and oats on the horizontal axis.

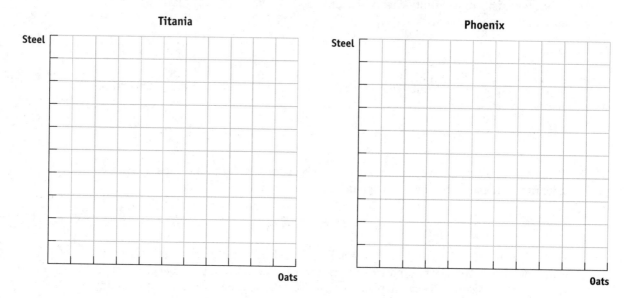

b. Which country has the absolute advantage in producing steel? Which country has the absolute advantage in producing oats?

c. What is the opportunity cost of producing 3 units of steel for Titania? What is the opportunity cost of producing 3 units of steel for Phoenix?

d. What is the opportunity cost of producing 5 units of oats for Titania? What is the opportunity cost of producing 5 units of oats for Phoenix?

e. Which country has the comparative advantage in producing steel? Which country has the comparative advantage in producing oats? Explain your answers.

f. Suppose that Titania and Phoenix both specialize according to their comparative advantage and then trade with one another. Furthermore, suppose that when they specialize these two countries only produce one type of good. What is the range of prices that steel will trade for once this specialization takes place? What is the range of prices that oats will trade for once this specialization takes place?

g. Titania proposes that Phoenix accept 1 unit of oats for 1 unit of steel. Will Phoenix agree to this trading price? Explain your answer.

3. Finlandia and Sweetland are two autarkies possessing equal resources. Both Finlandia and Sweetland produce two goods: food (F) and clothing (C). The table below provides information about the maximum amount of these two goods that these two countries can produce if they devote all of their resources to the production of just one good. Assume that the production possibility frontiers for both Finlandia and Sweetland are linear.

	Food	Clothing
Finlandia	1,000 units	2,000 units
Sweetland	600 units	1,800 units

a. On two separate graphs, draw Finlandia and Sweetland's production possibility frontiers. Place units of food on the vertical axis and units of clothing on the horizontal axis.

Finlandia

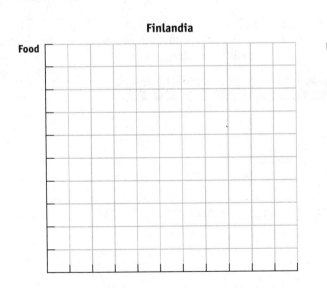

Food

Clothing

Sweetland

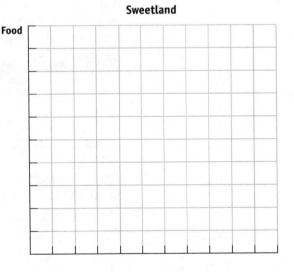

Food

Clothing

b. Both Finlandia and Sweetland currently produce at points that are located on their production possibility frontiers. Based on this information, fill in the table below. (Hint: you may find it helpful to write an equation for each country's production possibility frontier.)

	Food	Clothing
Finlandia	500 units	
Sweetland		900 units
Total production		

c. Suppose Finlandia and Sweetland open their economies to trade, but neither country fully understands the concept of comparative advantage. Suppose Finlandia and Sweetland adjust their production as given in the table below. Fill in the rest of the table assuming that both countries produce at points that are on their production possibility frontiers. Are Finlandia and Sweetland specializing according to their comparative advantage? Explain your answer.

	Food	Clothing
Finlandia	250 units	
Sweetland		390 units
Total production		

d. Finlandia and Sweetland alter their production once again in hopes of reaping the benefits of specialization and trade. Fill in the table below based on both countries producing on their production possibility frontiers.

	Food	Clothing
Finlandia		400 units
Sweetland		
Total production	892 units	

e. Given the production possibility choices Finlandia and Sweetland make in part (d), do these countries reap the advantages of specialization and trade?

4. Do you agree or disagree with the following statement: "Comparative advantage depends on the amount of resources used to produce a good." Explain your answer.

5. Do you agree or disagree with the following statement: "If two workers have different labor productivity, then their wage rates will usually differ from one another, with the worker with greater labor productivity earning a higher wage rate." Explain your answer.

6. What are the major sources of comparative advantage?

7. The Heckscher-Ohlin model predicts that countries have a comparative advantage in producing those goods whose production is intensive in the factors that are abundantly available in that country compared to other countries. What does the Heckscher-Ohlin model predict about factor prices for abundant resources versus less abundant resources? Explain your answer.

8. Use the graph below to answer this next set of questions. The graph depicts the domestic demand and domestic supply of bicycles in a small closed economy.

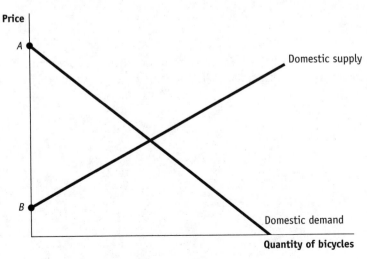

a. In the preceding graph, label the equilibrium price (P_e) and the equilibrium quantity (Q_e) for this autarky. Label the areas that correspond to producer surplus and consumer surplus.

b. Provide a mathematical expression for the areas of producer and consumer surplus based on the symbols and labels in the graph.

c. The same graph is replicated below, but this time the world price is also drawn on the graph. Suppose this autarky opens to trade. On the graph, indicate the quantity supplied domestically ($Q_{S_{dom}}$) and the quantity demanded domestically ($Q_{D_{dom}}$) when this country opens to trade. Identify how many bicycles this country will import or export when it opens its economy to trade.

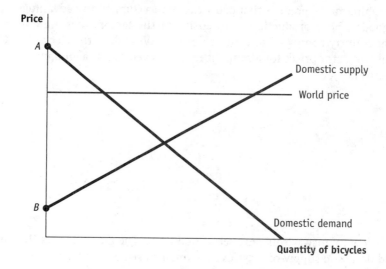

d. On the graph in part (c), label the areas that correspond to producer surplus with trade and consumer surplus with trade. Who benefits in this example from trade? Explain your answer.

e. The initial graph is replicated below, but this time the world price is also drawn on the graph. Suppose this autarky opens to trade. On the graph, indicate the quantity supplied domestically ($Q_{S_{dom}}$) and the quantity demanded domestically ($Q_{D_{dom}}$) when this country opens to trade. Identify how many bicycles this country will import or export when it opens its economy to trade.

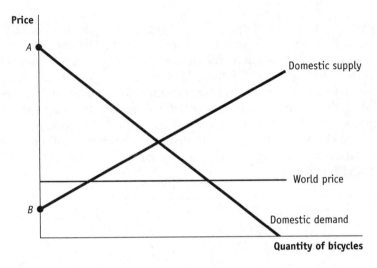

f. On the graph in part (e), label the areas that correspond to producer surplus with trade and consumer surplus with trade. Who benefits in this example from trade? Explain your answer.

9. Suppose the market for TVs in the small closed economy of Kennet can be described by the following domestic demand curve and domestic supply curve:

Domestic demand: $Q = 1,000 - (1/2)P$

Domestic supply: $Q = (1/2)P$

(Hint: for this question you will find it helpful to sketch graphs of the market.)

a. What is the equilibrium price and quantity in the market for TVs in Kennet? What is the value of consumer surplus, producer surplus, and total surplus?

b. Suppose Kennet opens to trade and the world price for TVs is $1,200. What is the quantity supplied domestically, the quantity demanded domestically, and the number of TVs imported into or exported out of Kennet given this world price? What happens to the value of consumer surplus, producer surplus, and total surplus when Kennet opens to trade?

c. Given the information and the analysis you did in part (b), who benefits from trade in the television market when Kennet opens its economy? Explain your answer.

d. Suppose Kennet's economy is still open to trade, but domestic demand in Kennet has significantly increased so that at every price domestic demand is now 500 units higher than it was initially. Although domestic demand in Kennet has increased, this has not impacted the world price for TVs since Kennet is a small economy. Given this change in demand, how many TVs will be domestically supplied and domestically demanded? Will Kennet import or export TVs? Calculate the numeric value of Kennet's imports or exports. What is the value of consumer surplus, producer surplus, and total surplus given this change in demand? (Hint: you will find it helpful to draw a sketch of these changes in the market for TVs and to calculate the new domestic demand equation.)

10. Pepperville is a small economy that currently operates as an autarky. In the market for green peppers, domestic demand and domestic supply can be represented as $P = 5,000 - 0.5Q$ and $P = 1.5Q$, respectively, where P is the price per ton of green peppers and Q is the quantity of green peppers measured in tons.

a. Identify the equilibrium price and quantity of green peppers in Pepperville. What is the value of consumer surplus and producer surplus?

b. The current world price of green peppers is $3,000 per ton, and domestic producers of green peppers are lobbying the government of Pepperville to remain an autarky. Explain why domestic producers of green peppers are not in favor of open trade in the green pepper market.

c. Domestic consumers of green peppers in Pepperville successfully lobby the Pepperville government to open trade in the green pepper market. How many tons of green peppers will be imported into or exported out of Pepperville, given the world price of $3,000 per ton when this market opens to trade? What is the value of consumer surplus and producer surplus with trade?

Domestic producers wage a successful campaign to enact a tariff in the market for green peppers. The tariff effectively raises the price of green peppers to $3,450 per ton. Answer questions (d) through (g) based on this tariff. Assume the world price for green peppers is unchanged and equal to $3,000 per ton.

d. How many tons of green peppers will be imported into Pepperville once this tariff is enacted?

e. What is the value of consumer surplus and producer surplus once this tariff is implemented?

f. What is the tariff revenue the government earns with this tariff?

g. What is the deadweight loss associated with this tariff?

h. Pepperville is considering replacing the tariff on green peppers with a quota. If consumer surplus and producer surplus are to remain the same under the quota as they are with the tariff, what must the amount of the quota equal?

i. From the domestic consumers' perspective, which trade policy—closed economy, open economy, or open economy with a tariff or quota—would they prefer? Explain your answer.

j. From the domestic producers' perspective, which trade policy—closed economy, open economy, or open economy with a tariff or quota—would they prefer? Explain your answer.

k. Given your answers in (i) and (j), why do governments frequently adopt tariffs or quotas in particular markets?

11. Evansville is a small closed economy. The domestic demand curve for shoes is given by the equation $P = 200 - Q$, where P is the price for a pair of shoes and Q is the quantity of pairs of shoes demanded. The domestic supply curve for shoes is given by the equation $P = 10 + Q$. Currently the world price of shoes is $40 a pair. Evansville is considering opening their economy to trade, and the government is debating three possible trade positions. Option I is to open the economy to trade with no trade protection intervention in the market. Option II is to open the economy to trade but limit the amount of pairs of shoes imported to a quota of 50 pairs of shoes. Option III is to open the economy to trade but impose a tariff on the shoe market that would increase the price of shoes to $80 a pair.

a. Analyze these three policies and enter your findings in the table below.

	Option I	Option II	Option III
Pairs of shoes imported			
Consumer surplus			
Producer surplus			
Tariff revenue or quota rent			
Deadweight loss			

b. From the perspective of domestic consumers, which is the best option?

c. From the perspective of domestic producers, which is the best option?

d. Which option results in the greatest efficiency cost? Explain your answer.

12. For each of the statements below, decide whether the statement reflects a desire for trade protection on the basis of national security, job creation, or the infant industry argument.

a. Even though clothing can be produced more cheaply in other countries, clothing is a necessity, and if imports of clothing are disrupted by civil unrest in these foreign countries, our country will be ill prepared to provide for our citizens. The domestic clothing industry should therefore receive some form of trade protection.

b. Since our economy is oil dependent and much of our oil comes from foreign economies, our economic well-being may be jeopardized by war or international disturbance. The domestic oil industry should therefore receive some form of trade protection from foreign oil producers.

c. As call centers are opened in foreign countries, our country is losing many entry-level positions. The industries moving these call centers overseas should be discouraged from doing this via trade measures.

d. The new product developed by corporation Z is a product that needs to be protected until corporation Z has had time to fully develop and market the idea.

e. The country of Fantasia, until recently a provider of raw materials to the rest of the world, has begun to develop a manufacturing sector in its economy. People in Fantasia argue that these industries need to have trade protection during this early period of development.

BEFORE YOU TAKE THE TEST

Chapter Review Questions

1. International trade based on comparative advantage is
   a. beneficial to some of the countries involved in the trade, but not beneficial to other countries.
   b. beneficial to all of the countries involved in the trade.
   c. rarely benefits any of the countries involved in the trade.
   d. only beneficial to relatively rich countries.

2. Sarah purchases wine from France, cheese from Italy, wheat crackers from Minnesota, potatoes from Idaho, and lamb from Australia. Sarah lives in New York.
   a. Sarah purchases imports of wine, cheese, and lamb.
   b. Sarah purchases only domestically produced goods, since she can purchase all of these goods at her local grocery store.
   c. The wine, cheese, and lamb represent exports from the perspective of the United States.
   d. Answers (a) and (c) are both true.

Use the following information to answer the next six questions. The table below gives information about the production possibility frontiers for two countries, Smallville and Gooseville, that each produce two types of goods, bicycles and cheese. Two possible production points on each country's production possibility frontier are given in the table. Both countries have linear production possibility frontiers.

	Bicycles	Tons of cheese
Smallville	1,000	0
Smallville	0	2,000
Gooseville	1,500	0
Gooseville	0	1,500

3. Suppose that Smallville and Gooseville have the same amount of resources and technology. Which of the following statements is true?
   a. Smallville has the absolute advantage in producing bicycles and Gooseville has the absolute advantage in producing cheese.
   b. Smallville has the absolute advantage in producing bicycles and cheese.
   c. Gooseville has the absolute advantage in producing bicycles and cheese.
   d. Smallville has the absolute advantage in producing cheese and Gooseville has the absolute advantage in producing bicycles.

4. The opportunity cost of producing one more bicycle in Smallville is
   a. greater than the opportunity cost of producing one more bicycle in Gooseville.
   b. less than the opportunity cost of producing one more bicycle in Gooseville.
   c. equal to 2 tons of cheese.
   d. answers (a) and (c) are correct.
   e. answers (b) and (c) are correct.

5. Suppose that both countries are in autarky and do not engage in trade. In autarky, both countries choose to produce at the midpoint of their production possibility frontiers. Total cheese production is equal to _____ and total bicycle production is equal to
   _____ .
   a. 1,750 tons of cheese; 1,750 bicycles
   b. 1,750 tons of cheese; 1,250 bicycles
   c. 1,250 tons of cheese; 1,750 bicycles
   d. 1,250 tons of cheese; 1,250 bicycles

6. Suppose that both countries decide to specialize according to their comparative advantage and trade with one another. Then
   a. Smallville will produce cheese and Gooseville will produce bicycles.
   b. Smallville will produce bicycles and Goosevillle will produce cheese.

7. When the two countries specialize according to their comparative advantage and then trade with one another, the price of a bicycle measured in terms of cheese will be
   a. less than ½ ton of cheese.
   b. greater than 1 ton of cheese.
   c. between 1 ton of cheese and 2 tons of cheese.
   d. between ½ ton of cheese and 1 ton of cheese.

8. Suppose both countries specialize according to their comparative advantage and then trade. Which of the following represents the maximum possible amount of total production given this specialization?

    a. 3,500 tons of cheese and 2,500 bicycles

    b. 2,500 tons of cheese and 2,500 bicycles

    c. 2,000 tons of cheese and 1,500 bicycles

    d. 1,750 tons of cheese and 1,250 bicycles

9. When a production possibility frontier is linear, this implies that

    a. the opportunity cost of producing either of the two goods represented is constant and does not change.

    b. the country will have both a comparative and absolute advantage in producing both of the goods depicted relative to its trading partner.

    c. trade of either good to other countries will always be beneficial for this country.

    d. this country can not have a comparative advantage in the production of either good.

10. When a country does not engage in trade with other countries, this is referred to as

    a. independence.   c. Ricardian economics.

    b. autarky.   d. Heckscher-Ohlin economics.

11. Which of the following statements is true?

    I. Gains from trade depend on absolute advantage.

    II. Comparative advantage depends on the amount of resources used to produce a good.

    III. A country's comparative advantage is translated into world markets through its wage rates: a country's wage rate typically reflects that country's labor productivity.

    a. Statement I is true.

    b. Statement II is true.

    c. Statement III is true.

    d. Statements I, II, and III are true.

    e. Statements II and III are true.

12. The pauper labor fallacy refers to the idea that

    a. importing goods from low-wage countries must hurt the standard of living of workers in the importing country.

    b. exporting goods from low-wage countries must hurt the standard of living of those workers in the exporting country.

    c. trade must be bad for workers in low-wage countries because they are paid such low wages by world standards.

    d. trade must be bad for workers in high-wage countries because they are paid such high wages by world standards.

13. The sweatshop labor fallacy refers to the idea that

    a. importing goods from low-wage countries must hurt the standard of living of workers in the importing country.

    b. exporting goods from low-wage countries must hurt the standard of living of those workers in the exporting country.

    c. trade must be bad for workers in low-wage countries because they are paid such low wages by world standards.

    d. trade must be bad for workers in high-wage countries because they are paid such high wages by world standards.

14. Which of the following situations illustrate one of the three sources of comparative advantage?

   a. A country produces olives that can only grow in a Mediterranean climate.

   b. A country specializes in producing medical equipment whose production relies on the use of highly productive labor resources.

   c. A country in the southern hemisphere specializes in providing grapes to the northern hemisphere during the winter season.

   d. A country uses its extensive network of fiber-optic cable to produce information technology for countries located throughout the world.

   e. All of the above answers illustrate at least one of the sources of comparative advantage.

15. Which of the following statements is *not* supported by the Heckscher-Ohlin model?

   a. Countries specialize in producing the good whose production is intensive in the factors that are abundantly available in that country compared to other countries.

   b. After they specialize, countries find that those factors that are relatively scarce in their country compared to other countries command higher factor prices than those factors that are relatively abundant in their country.

   c. Countries that are labor abundant produce goods that are labor intensive relative to countries that are less labor abundant.

   d. Countries that are capital abundant produce goods that are capital intensive relative to countries that are less capital abundant.

16. Which of the following statements is true?

   I. Countries with highly skilled labor will tend to import goods whose production requires high levels of human capital.

   II. Countries whose exporting industries focus on using a higher ratio of highly educated workers to other workers are human capital intensive.

   III. Countries will find that their exporting industries utilize their relatively more abundant factors of production.

   a. Statement I is true.   d. Statements I and II are true.

   b. Statement II is true.   e. Statements II and III are true.

   c. Statement III is true.   f. Statements I, II, and III are true.

Use the following graph to answer the next four questions. The graph shows the market for bicycles for the country of Pedalland. The demand curve indicates the domestic demand for bicycles and the supply curve indicates the domestic supply of bicycles.

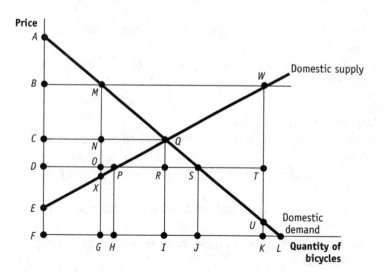

17. Suppose Pedalland is initially an autarky. In the graph, the area that corresponds to consumer surplus is equal to area _____, and the area that corresponds to producer surplus is equal to area _____.
    a. *ACQ; CQIF*
    b. *ADS; DPE*
    c. *ACQ; CQE*
    d. *BMNC; CNOD*

18. Suppose this country opens to trade and that the world price is equal to *B* in the above graph. Then we know that Pedalland will
    a. import the number of bicycles represented by the distance between points *M* and *W*.
    b. import the number of bicycles represented by the distance between points *W* and *T*.
    c. export the number of bicycles represented by the distance between points *M* and *W*.
    d. export the number of bicycles represented by the distance between points *W* and *T*.

19. Suppose this country opens to trade and that the world price is equal to *D* in the above graph. Then we know that Pedalland will import the number of bicycles represented by the distance between points
    a. *R* and *S*.
    b. *P* and *S*.
    c. *P* and *R*.
    d. *P* and *T*.

20. Suppose this country opens to trade and that the world price is equal to *B* in the above graph. Consumer surplus is equal to area _____, and producer surplus is equal to area _____.
    a. *ABM; BWE*
    b. *ABM; BMNE*
    c. *ACNM; CNXE*
    d. *ABM; BMQE*

Use the following graph to answer the next four questions. The graph shows the market for bicycles for the country of Pedalland. The demand curve indicates the domestic demand for bicycles and the supply curve indicates the domestic supply of bicycles.

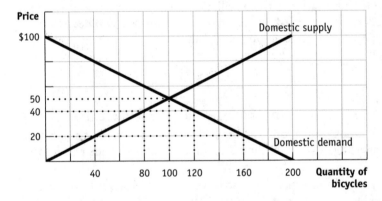

21. The world price in this market equals $20. If the market opens to trade,
    a. Pedalland will import 120 bicycles, and the area of total surplus will increase by $6,800.
    b. Pedalland will export 120 bicycles, and the area of total surplus will increase by $6,800.
    c. Pedalland will import 120 bicycles, and the area of total surplus will increase by $1,800.
    d. Pedalland will export 120 bicycles, and the area of total surplus will increase by $1,800.

22. Suppose the world price for bicycles is $20 and Pedalland opens its bicycle market to trade. Domestic producers successfully lobby the government of Pedalland, and the government imposes a quota on the number of bicycles that can be imported into Pedalland. Suppose license-holder revenue from the quota is equal to $800. Which of the following are possible quota limits that result in this license-holder revenue?
   a. 20 bicycles.
   b. 40 bicycles.
   c. 60 bicycles.
   d. 80 bicycles.
   e. Answers (b) and (d) are both possible answers.

23. Suppose the world price of bicycles is $20 and Pedalland opens to trade. Domestic producers of bicycles in Pedalland successfully lobby for a tariff on imported bicycles, which results in the price of bicycles being $40. The deadweight loss associated with this tariff is equal to
   a. $400.
   b. $800.
   c. $1,600.
   d. $2,000.

24. The world price of bicycles is $20 and Pedalland opens its economy to trade. A quota of 60 bicycles is imposed in Pedalland. This will result in consumer surplus increasing by _____ relative to the level of consumer surplus when Pedalland was an autarky.
   a. $1,725
   b. $2,500
   c. $4,225
   d. $6,725

25. A country that engages in international trade will find that this international trade increases the demand for the factors used by the exporting industries and decreases the demand for the factors used in the import-competing industries.
   a. True
   b. False

26. Which of the following is *not* an argument used to defend trade protection?
   a. This domestic industry needs protection because it is a new industry and is not fully ready and able to compete against established companies located outside the domestic economy.
   b. This domestic industry needs protection because it would otherwise result in people elsewhere in the world being paid a wage rate that is substantially lower than the wage rate in this industry in this economy.
   c. This domestic industry needs protection because the good that is being produced is of vital national security for this economy.
   d. This domestic industry needs protection because it provides a substantial number of jobs for people who live in this country.

27. Which of the following is *not* an example of a trade agreement?
   a. NAFTA
   b. EU
   c. WTO

ANSWER KEY

Answers to Problems and Exercises

1. a.

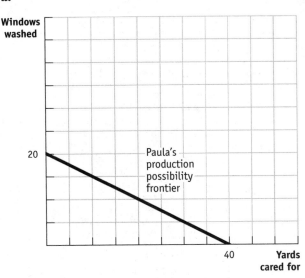
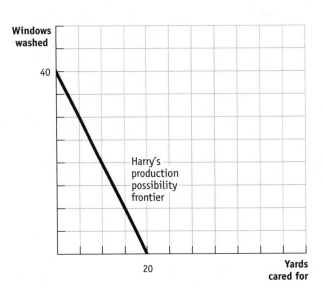

b. Paula has the absolute advantage in yard care since she can clean more yards than Harry with the same amount of resources (40 yards versus 20 yards), and Harry has the absolute advantage in window washing since he can wash more windows than Paula with the same amount of resources (40 windows versus 20 windows).

c.

	Number of windows washed	Number of yards cared for
Paula	10	20
Harry	20	10
Total	30	30

d. Paula's opportunity cost of washing a window is 2 yards cared for, since she must give up caring for 2 yards to free up enough resources to clean 1 window. Her opportunity cost of caring for a yard is ½ window washed since she must give up washing ½ a window to free up enough resources to care for a yard.

e. Harry's opportunity cost of washing a window is ½ yard cared for, since he must give up caring for ½ a yard to free up enough resources to clean 1 window. His opportunity cost of caring for a yard is 2 windows washed since he must give up washing 2 windows to free up enough resources to care for a yard.

f. Harry has the comparative advantage in washing windows, and Paula has the comparative advantage in caring for yards. Harry's opportunity cost of washing 1 window is only ½ yard, and Paula's opportunity cost of washing 1 window is 2 yards, so Harry can produce a washed window at a lower opportunity cost than can Paula. Paula's opportunity cost of caring for 1 yard is ½ window washed, and Harry's opportunity cost of caring for 1 yard is 2 windows washed, so Paula can care for a yard at a lower opportunity cost than can Harry.

g.

	Number of windows washed	Number of yards cared for
Paula	40	0
Harry	0	40
Total	40	40

Through specialization according to comparative advantage, total production of both goods increases.

h. The range of prices for 1 window washed falls between ½ yard cared for and 2 yards cared for. Paula is willing to trade up to 2 yards cared for to get a single window washed, while Harry is willing to wash a single window provided he is compensated by ½ yard cared for.

2. **a.**

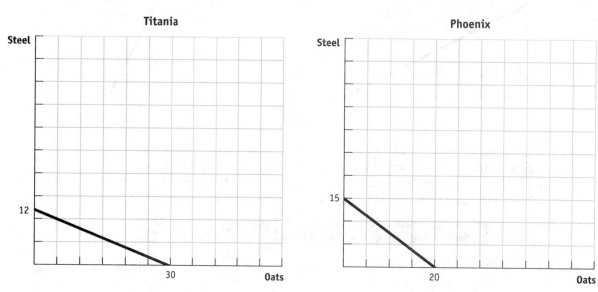

b. Phoenix has the absolute advantage in producing steel since, from the same amount of resources, Phoenix can absolutely produce more units of the good than can Titania. Titania has the absolute advantage in producing oats since, from the same amount of resources, Titania can absolutely produce more units of the good than can Phoenix.

c. The opportunity cost of producing 3 units of steel for Titania is equal to 7.5 units of oats. From the graph, the slope of the production possibility frontier for Titania is $-2/5$, which implies that the opportunity cost of Titania producing 1 unit of oats is $2/5$ units of steel. We can take the reciprocal of this measure and get the opportunity cost of 1 unit of steel is equal to $5/2$ units of oats. But since we want to know the opportunity cost of 3 units of steel, we need to multiply the $5/2$ units of oats by 3 to get $15/2$ units of oats, or 7.5 units of oats. The opportunity cost of producing 3 units of steel for Phoenix is equal to 4 units of oats. From the graph, the slope of the production possibility frontier for Phoenix is $-3/4$, which implies that the opportunity cost of Phoenix producing 1 unit of oats is $3/4$ units of steel. We can take the reciprocal of this measure and get the opportunity cost of 1 unit of steel is equal to $4/3$ units of oats. But since we want to know the opportunity cost of 3 units of steel, we need to multiply the $4/3$ units of oats by 3 to get $12/3$ units of oats, or 4 units of oats.

d. The opportunity cost of producing 5 units of oats for Titania is 2 units of steel, and the opportunity cost of producing 5 units of oats for Phoenix is 3.75 units of steel.

e. Titania has the comparative advantage in producing oats while Phoenix has the comparative advantage in producing steel. Titania's opportunity cost of producing 1 unit of oats is 2/5 units of steel, and Phoenix's opportunity cost of producing 1 unit of oats is ¾ units of steel, so Titania can produce oats at lower opportunity cost than can Phoenix. Titania's opportunity cost of producing 1 unit of steel is 5/2 units of oats, and Phoenix's opportunity cost of producing 1 unit of steel is 4/3 units of oats, so Phoenix can produce steel at lower opportunity cost than can Titania.

f. One unit of steel will trade for between 4/3 units of oats to 5/2 units of oats, and 1 unit of oats will trade for between 2/3 units of steel and 3/4 units of steel.

g. No, Phoenix is only willing to trade 1 unit of steel if the price is at least 4/3 units of oats.

3. a.

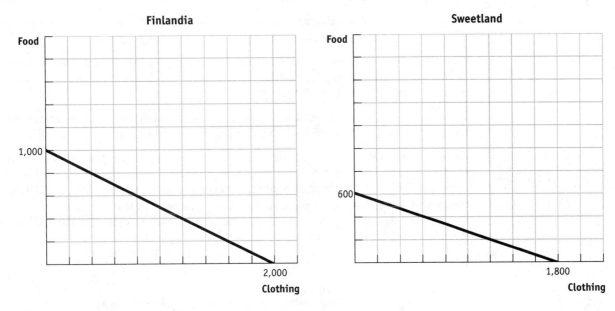

b. The equation for Finlandia's production possibility frontier is $F = 1,000 - (1/2)C$. When $F = 500$ units, then $C = 1,000$ units. The equation for Sweetland's production possibility frontier is $F = 600 - (1/3)C$. When $C = 900$ units, then $F = 300$ units.

	Food	Clothing
Finlandia	500 units	1,000 units
Sweetland	300 units	900 units
Total production	800 units	1,900 units

c. Use the equations you calculated in part (b) to fill in the table.

	Food	Clothing
Finlandia	250 units	1,500 units
Sweetland	470 units	390 units
Total production	720 units	1,890 units

Finlandia and Sweetland are not specializing according to their comparative advantage since their total production of the two goods has fallen as they altered their production.

d.

	Food	Clothing
Finlandia	800 units	400 units
Sweetland	92 units	1,524 units
Total production	892 units	1,924 units

e. Yes, by specializing according to their comparative advantage and then trading, the total level of production of the two goods increases.

4. Disagree. Comparative advantage depends on the opportunity cost of producing the good rather than the amount of resources used to produce the good.

5. Agree. Workers with lower labor productivity will earn a lower wage than workers with higher labor productivity since the competition for less-productive workers is less intense, resulting in a lower wage rate.

6. The major sources of comparative advantage are differences in climate, differences in factor endowments, and differences in technology between countries.

7. The Heckscher-Ohlin model predicts that factors of production that are abundant in a country that trades with other countries will command higher factor prices than factors of production that are less abundant. This is the result of the country's specialization in the production of the good whose production is intensive in the abundant factors of production. This specialization increases the demand for these factors and therefore increases the price of these factors.

8. **a.**

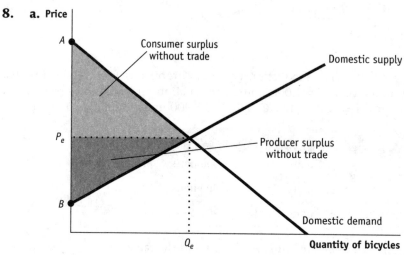

b. Consumer surplus $= (1/2)(A - P_e)(Q_e)$
Producer surplus $= (1/2)(P_e - B)(Q_e)$

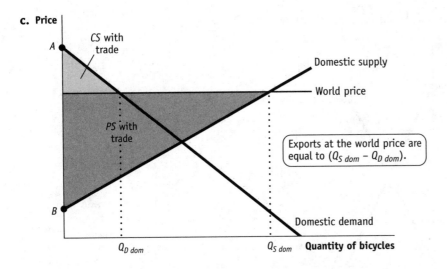

d. Domestic producers benefit from this trade because they can produce more units of the good and sell each unit at a higher price relative to the initial autarky equilibrium. Compare the graphs from part (a) and part (c) and note that the area of producer surplus is larger with trade than without trade.

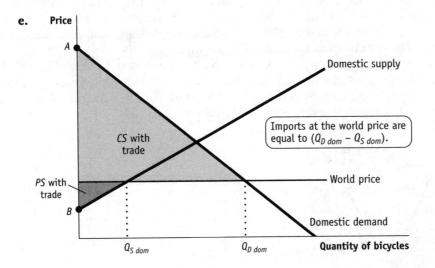

f. Domestic consumers benefit from this trade because they can consume more units of the good and purchase the good at a lower price relative to the initial autarky equilibrium. Compare the graphs from part (a) and part (e) and note that the area of consumer surplus is larger with trade than without trade.

9. a. Here is a sketch of Kennet's market for TVs.

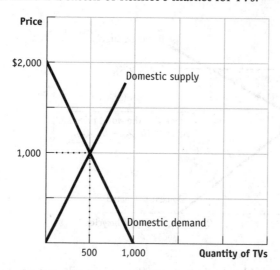

The equilibrium price is $1,000 and the equilibrium quantity is 500 TVs. Consumer surplus is equal to $250,000; producer surplus is equal to $250,000; and total surplus is equal to $500,000.

b. When Kennet opens to trade, it will buy and sell TVs at the world price since it is a small economy. Since $1,200 is greater than the domestic equilibrium price when Kennet is a closed economy, domestic demand will fall and domestic supply will increase. The quantity demanded domestically will equal 400 TVs, and the quantity supplied domestically will equal 600 TVs. Kennet will export the excess supply of 200 TVs. Consumer surplus with trade will decrease to $160,000 while producer surplus with trade will increase to $360,000; total surplus with trade will increase to $520,000. The sketch below illustrates this answer.

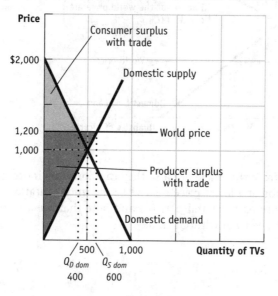

c. Domestic producers of TVs benefit from trade when Kennet opens its economy, because trade increases their producer surplus and decreases consumer surplus. The gain to producers is greater than the loss to consumers, so the net gain from trade is positive.

d. The sketch below provides a helpful guide to solving this problem.

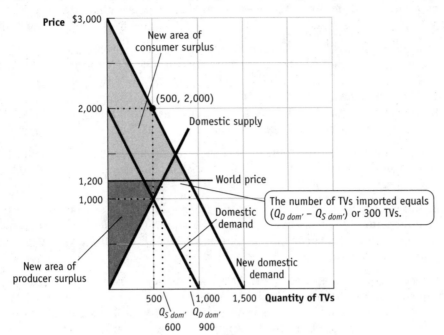

The equation for the new domestic demand curve is $Q = 1,500 - (1/2)P$. The domestic supply curve is still $Q = (1/2)P$. Use these two equations to analyze the effect on this market of the increase in domestic demand for TVs. At a world price of $1,200, the domestic demand for TVs is 900 while the domestic supply of TVs is 600. Kennet will import 300 TVs to meet this excess demand. Consumer surplus will now equal to $810,000; producer surplus will equal $360,000; and total surplus will equal $1,170,000.

10. a. The equilibrium price of green peppers is $3,750 per ton, and the equilibrium quantity of green peppers in Pepperville is 2,500 tons. Consumer surplus is equal to $1,562,500 and producer surplus is equal to $4,687,500.

b. Domestic producers are currently selling 2,500 tons of green peppers at a price of $3,750 per ton. If the market opens to trade, each ton of peppers will sell for a lower price: domestic producers will sell fewer tons of peppers as the price falls (2,000 tons instead of 2,500 tons), and they will receive a lower price per ton than they do when the green pepper market is closed ($3,000 versus $3,750).

c. When the green pepper market is open to trade, the domestic demand for green peppers at $3,000 per ton is equal to 4,000 tons of green peppers. At a price of $3,000 per ton, the domestic quantity supplied is equal to 2,000 tons of green peppers. There is an excess demand for peppers when Pepperville opens to trade, and this excess demand will result in Pepperville importing green peppers to make up the difference between the amount domestically supplied and the amount domestically demanded. Pepperville will import 2,000 tons of green peppers. The value of consumer surplus with trade is equal to $4,000,000 and the value of producer surplus with trade is equal to $3,000,000.

d. At a price of $3,450, the quantity of green peppers demanded domestically is equal to 3,100 tons while the quantity supplied domestically is equal to 2,300 tons. Pepperville will import 800 tons of green peppers.

e. The value of consumer surplus is equal to $(1/2)($5,000$ per ton $- $3,450$ per ton$)($3,100$ tons$)$, or $2,402,500. The value of producer surplus is equal to $(1/2)($3,450$ per ton$)($2,300$ tons$)$, or $3,967,500.

f. The government earns the difference between the tariff price per ton of green peppers and the world price of green peppers on every ton of green peppers imported into Pepperville. The tariff revenue is equal to ($3,450 per ton – $3,000 per ton)(800 tons), or $360,000.

g. The deadweight loss is the difference between the total surplus with open trade and the sum of consumer surplus + producer surplus + tariff revenue, or $7,000,000 – ($2,402,500 + $3,967,500 + $360,000) = $270,000. Alternatively, the deadweight loss can be calculated as the sum of the areas of two triangles, which is equal to (1/2)($3,450 per ton – $3,000 per ton)(2,300 tons – 2,000 tons) + (1/2)($3,450 per ton – $3,000 per ton)(4,000 tons – 3,100 tons), or $270,000.

h. The quota has to equal the number of units Pepperville imports when the tariff raises the price of green peppers to $3,450 per ton. That is, the quota must be 800 tons of green peppers.

i. Consumer surplus is greatest when the trade policy is one of an open economy. Consumers rank these choices from best to worst in this order: open economy, open economy with a tariff or quota, closed economy. This ranking occurs whenever the world price is less than the closed economy price for the good.

j. Producer surplus is greatest when the trade policy is one of a closed economy. Producers rank these choices from best to worst in this order: closed economy, open economy with a tariff or quota, open economy. This ranking occurs whenever the world price is less than the closed economy price for the good.

k. Governments can successfully provide a benefit to both consumers and producers by choosing this option. If you review the consumer and producer surplus under each of these options, you will see that the middle option gives consumers a greater consumer surplus than they would get with a closed economy and it provides producers with a greater producer surplus than they would get with an open economy. It is a compromise position for the government to take between these two constituencies.

11. a.

	Option I	Option II	Option III
Pairs of shoes imported	130 pairs	50 pairs	50 pairs
Consumer surplus	$12,800	$7,200	$7,200
Producer surplus	450	2,450	2,450
Tariff revenue or quota rent	0	2,000	2,000
Deadweight loss	0	1,600	1,600

b. From the perspective of domestic consumers, the best option is the option that results in the greatest value for consumer surplus: option I, the open economy option.

c. From the perspective of domestic producers, the best option is the option that results in the greatest value for producer surplus: option II and option III result in equivalent values for producer surplus, with the license holder earning a quota rent for option II and the government earning tariff revenue for option III. If the license holder is a domestic producer, than option II would be the best option from the perspective of domestic producers.

d. Options II and III result in the largest, and equivalent, efficiency cost as measured by the deadweight loss that occurs with the imposition of these two trade protectionist policies.

12. a. This argument is based on national security and the belief that, should foreign supplies of clothing be disrupted, our country's national security will be compromised.

b. This argument is based on national security and the belief that our economy will be compromised if there is a disruption in the supply of foreign-produced oil.

c. This argument is based on the job creation argument: as jobs relocate overseas, this implies a decrease in jobs in the home economy. This argument does not consider that other jobs may be created in the home economy as jobs are sent overseas.

d. This argument is based on the infant industry argument, which holds that new industries must be protected from foreign competition to give them time to get established.

e. This argument is based on the infant industry argument, which holds that new industries must be protected from foreign competition to give them time to get established.

Answers to Chapter Review Questions

1. **Answer b.** International trade is a source of mutual benefit to the countries involved in the trade.

2. **Answer a.** The wine, cheese, and lamb are all imported goods into the American economy since these goods are produced elsewhere in the world and then brought into the American market. Exports refers to those goods produced in the domestic economy and sold in a foreign economy.

3. **Answer d.** Since Smallville can absolutely produce more cheese than can Gooseville, Smallville has the absolute advantage in producing cheese. Gooseville, on the other hand, can absolutely produce more bicycles than Smallville from the same resources, so Gooseville has the absolute advantage in producing bicycles.

4. **Answer d.** The opportunity cost of producing one more bicycle in Smallville is equal to the number of tons of cheese that must be given up to produce one more bicycle. In this case, 2 tons of cheese must be given up to produce one more bicycle in Smallville. The opportunity cost of producing a bicycle in Smallville is 2 tons of cheese, while the opportunity cost of producing a bicycle in Gooseville is equal to 1 ton of cheese.

5. **Answer b.** If Smallville produces at the midpoint of its production possibility frontier, it will produce 1,000 tons of cheese and 500 bicycles. If Gooseville produces at the midpoint of its production possibility frontier, it will produce 750 tons of cheese and 750 bicycles. Total cheese production will equal 1,750 tons and total bicycle production will equal 1,250 bicycles.

6. **Answer a.** Smallville will produce cheese since the opportunity cost of producing cheese for Smallville is ½ bicycle while the opportunity cost of producing cheese for Gooseville is 1 bicycle. Smallville gives up fewer bicycles to produce a ton of cheese and therefore Smallville has the comparative advantage in producing cheese.

7. **Answer c.** The opportunity cost of producing a bicycle is 2 tons of cheese for Smallville and 1 ton of cheese for Gooseville. Smallville will be willing to pay up to 2 tons of cheese for 1 bicycle, while Gooseville is willing to trade 1 bicycle for any amount of cheese greater than 1 ton. The price of a bicycle will be in the range of 1 to 2 tons of cheese.

8. **Answer c.** If both countries fully specialize, then Smallville will produce only cheese (2,000 tons of cheese) and Gooseville will produce only bicycles (1,500 bicycles).

9. **Answer a.** A linear production function is a production function with a constant slope. This constant slope tells us that for a given change in the good measured on the x-axis there will be a given change in the good measured on the y-axis. Another way to express this idea is that the opportunity cost of producing either good is constant: for the good measured on the x-axis, the opportunity cost of producing one more unit of that good is equal to the absolute value of the slope of the production possibility frontier; for the good measured on the y-axis, the opportunity cost of producing one more unit of that good is equal to the absolute value of the reciprocal of the slope of the production possibility frontier. A country cannot have the comparative advantage of producing both goods: one country must have the comparative advantage in producing one of the goods while the

other country must have the comparative advantage in producing the other good. Trade is beneficial, provided countries specialize in their comparative advantage. Trade without regard to comparative advantage results in lower total production.

10. **Answer b.** This is the definition of autarky. A country may be independent of other countries when it decides not to trade, but that is not the term used to describe this trade position. Answers (c) and (d) refer to models used to analyze international trade, but they are not direct references to the term describing a closed economy.

11. **Answer c.** Gains from trade stem from a country's comparative advantage and not its absolute advantage (statement I is false). Absolute advantage focuses on the amount of resources used to produce a good (for example, the number of hours of labor it takes to produce a shirt) while comparative advantage focuses on the opportunity cost of producing the good—that is, what must be given up to produce a unit of this good. (statement II is false). When a country has a comparative advantage in producing a good, this means that its opportunity cost of producing the good is lower than the opportunity cost of producing the same good is some other country: this advantage in terms of opportunity cost is translated into wage rates. When a country has less-productive labor, then the wage rate for this labor is lower than it is for a country that has more-productive labor.

12. **Answer a.** The pauper labor fallacy focuses on the erroneous idea that trade with low-wage countries must necessarily reduce the standard of living of workers in high-wage countries. This idea stems from the belief that this trade "steals" jobs from the high-wage country and does not consider the consumption benefits to the high-wage country of access to the cheaper goods that are made available to the high-wage country by the low-wage country. Trade, willingly undertaken between two parties, must be beneficial to both parties.

13. **Answer c.** This is the definition of the sweatshop labor fallacy. Here the focus is on the idea that high-wage countries are exploiting labor in low-wage countries, since the wages in the latter countries are so much less than the wages in the high-wage countries. However, this argument fails to consider the relative productivity of the labor in these two types of countries, and it does not consider the other alternatives available to labor in the low-wage countries. Sometimes a job that looks terrible from the perspective of a person in a high-wage country is highly sought after in a low-wage country.

14. **Answer e.** The main sources of comparative advantage are differences in climate, differences in factor endowments, and differences in technology. Answers (a) and (c) illustrate a country's specialization based on climate differences, answer (b) illustrates a country's specialization based on factor endowments, and answer (d) illustrates a country's specialization based on differences in technology.

15. **Answer b.** According to the Heckscher-Ohlin model, countries have a comparative advantage in producing those goods and services whose production is intensive in the factors of production that are relatively abundant in that country compared to other countries. Thus, a country that has an abundance of labor relative to other countries tends to specialize in producing labor-intensive goods and services, while a country that is capital abundant specializes in producing capital-intensive goods and services. This specialization bids up the factor price of the factors that are abundant in a country due to the increased demand for these factors, and the factor price of the factors that are scarce in a country tends to fall due to decreased demand for these factors. Answer (b) is not true because the prices of the factors are moving in the wrong direction.

16. **Answer e.** Countries will tend to import those goods that are produced using factors of production which are relatively scarce in the importing country (statement I is therefore false). Countries which utilize a high ratio of highly skilled workers to less skilled workers are countries that tend to produce goods that are intensive in human capital (statement II is true). Countries will export goods whose production takes advantage of the relative abundance of the factor (statement III is true).

17. **Answer c.** The area of consumer surplus is the area beneath the demand curve but above the equilibrium price, or in this example, area *ACQ*. The area of producer surplus is the area above the supply curve but below the equilibrium price, or in this example, area *CQE*.

18. **Answer c.** When the world price of the good is greater than the autarky price and the country opens to trade, Pedalland will export the good to other countries in order to sell the good at the higher world price. In this case, domestic suppliers are willing to supply the amount represented as the distance between points *B* and *W* while domestic consumers are only willing to consume the number of bicycles represented by the distance between *B* and *M*. Thus, domestic producers will export the number of bicycles represented by the distance between points *M* and *W*.

19. **Answer b.** When the world price is below the domestic equilibrium price and the country opens to trade, the country will import goods. The country will import the number of goods that represents the difference between the amount domestically supplied at the world price and the amount domestically demanded at the world price. In this case, the country will import the number of goods represented by the distance between points *P* and *S*.

20. **Answer a.** The area of consumer surplus is the area beneath the demand curve and above the equilibrium price, while the area of producer surplus is the area above the supply curve and below the equilibrium price. When this country opens to trade and the world price is equal to *B*, the country will export the good, which benefits domestic producers who are able to sell more units of the good than they could when the country was closed to trade.

21. **Answer c.** When the world price of the good is less than the autarky price, the country will import the good if it opens its economy to trade. In this case, the country will import the difference between the quantity demanded domestically at a price of $20 and the quantity supplied domestically at a price of $20, or 120 bicycles. The area of total surplus is initially equal to $5,000, and when the country opens to trade, the area of total surplus has a value of $6,800, so the increase in total surplus is $6,800 − $5,000 or $1,800.

22. **Answer e.** To calculate the license-holder revenue from the quota you first need to rewrite the supply curve taking into account the quota. So, for example, if the supply equation is initially $P = (1/2)(Q)$ then with a quota of 40 units this supply equation will be $P = (1/2)q − 20$. Using this new supply equation and the demand equation, $P = 100 − (1/2)Q$ you can find the new price with a quota of 40 units. The price with this level of quota is $40 per bicycle. The license-holder revenue is equal to the difference between the price with the quota and the world price times the number of bicycles imported with the quota or ($40/bicycle − $20/bicycle)(40 bicycles) or $800. This argument however also works for a quota of 80 units: when the quota is 80 bicycles the supply curve can be written as $P = (1/2)Q − 30$ and the new price with this quota limit is $30 per bicycle. The license-holder revenue is equal to the difference between the price with the quota and the world price times the number of bicycles imported with the quota or (30/bicycle − $20/bicycle) (80 bicycles) or $800.

23. **Answer b.** The deadweight loss associated with this tariff is the result of two forces: (a) mutually beneficial trades do not take place because of the imposition of the tariff, and (b) the bicycles sold are produced at a price that exceeds the world price for bicycles. The area of deadweight loss can be calculated as the sum of the area of two triangles: (1/2)($40 per bicycle − $20 per bicycle)(80 bicycles − 40 bicycles) + (1/2)($40 per bicycle − $20 per bicycle)(160 bicycles − 120 bicycles) = $800.

24. **Answer a.** This is a tough problem! You first need to figure out the price with the quota, the quantity supplied domestically with the quota, and the quantity demanded domestically with the quota. From the graph you know that if the quota price was $40, the quota would be equal to 40 units. From the graph you also know that, at the world price, 120 bicycles are imported into Pedalland. So, logically you know that the quota price must be lower than $40 and higher than $20. When the quota price is $35, the quantity demanded domestically is equal to 130 bicycles and the quantity supplied domestically is equal

to 70 bicycles, for a difference of 60 bicycles. This difference is the same as the quota amount given in the question. Now you need only compute the original consumer surplus (equals $2,500) and the consumer surplus with the quota ($4,225) and subtract the original consumer surplus from the new consumer surplus to get the change in the value of consumer surplus that occurs with the imposition of the quota.

25. **Answer a.** When countries engage in trade, they produce those goods and services for which they have a comparative advantage. This specialization according to Heckscher-Ohlin advantage results in these countries producing those goods and services for which they have an abundant amount of resources. Thus, the exporting industries in the country will bid up the price of these resources as they increase their production of the good. The country will tend to import goods and services that are intensive in the factors that are scarce in its economy. This effectively decreases the demand for the relatively scarce factors and increases the demand for the relatively abundant factors. Trade will cause the factor price to increase for the relatively abundant factor and to decrease for the relatively scarce factor.

26. **Answer b.** The arguments used to defend trade protection fall into three broad categories: the infant industry argument given in answer (a), the job creation argument given in answer (d), and the national security argument given in answer (c). Answer (b) is not an argument used to defend trade protection, but it is an argument that accompanies the sweatshop labor fallacy described earlier in the chapter.

27. **Answer c.** The World Trade Organization (WTO) is an organization comprised of many member nations who meet to discuss and decide on major international trade agreements, and it works to resolve trade disputes between its members. The North American Free Trade Agreement (NAFTA) is a trade agreement between Canada, the United States, and Mexico. The European Union (EU) is a trade agreement between many countries located in Europe.

chapter 9

Making Decisions

BEFORE YOU READ THE CHAPTER

Summary

Chapter 9 explores two questions—"either-or" and "how much"—and then provides a framework for making decisions arising from these two questions. The chapter considers the importance of opportunity cost when making a decision about which of two possible activities to do, while marginal analysis is introduced as an approach to decision making that focuses on how much of an activity is the right level. The chapter also explores which costs need to be incorporated into decision-making analysis and which costs—the sunk costs—should be ignored when making decisions. Lastly, in its discussion of present value, the chapter provides a method for measuring costs and benefits when these costs and benefits arrive at different times.

Chapter Objectives

Objective #1. Due to scarcity of resources, it is not possible to do everything. This scarcity of resources implies that the true cost of anything can best be measured in terms of its opportunity cost, or the value of consumption or production that is forgone when a choice is made to consume or produce something else.

Objective #2. There are two broad categories of costs: explicit costs and implicit costs.

- Explicit costs are costs that require a direct outlay of money.

- Implicit costs do not involve an outlay of money but are instead equal to the value in dollars of all the benefits that are forgone when making a particular decision.

- Economic decision making requires consideration of both explicit and implicit costs.

Objective #3. The economic cost of any activity you do should include the cost of using any of your own resources for that activity.

Objective #4.   There are two general types of profits: accounting profits and economic profits.

- The accounting profit of a business is equal to its total revenue minus its explicit cost and depreciation. Depreciation measures the dollar value of the reduction in the value of capital equipment a business owns—it is the dollar value of the capital that wears out at a business. Depreciation is measured per year.

- Economic profit for a business equals the business's total revenue minus its total costs, where those total costs include both the explicit and implicit costs of operating the business as well as depreciation costs. In particular, economic profits include the implicit cost of capital and the implicit cost of the owner's time and energy. Both capital and the owner's time and energy could be used in other ways, and the opportunity cost of these resources needs to be incorporated into the measure of total costs when measuring economic profit. The implicit cost of capital is the opportunity cost of the capital used by a business, while the implicit cost of the owner's time and energy is the opportunity cost of that time and energy.

Objective #5.   Marginal analysis compares the benefit of doing a little bit more of an activity with the cost of doing a little bit more of the activity. Marginal benefit measures the benefit of doing a little bit more of the activity while marginal cost measures the cost of doing a little bit more of the activity.

- Marginal cost is measured as the change in total cost from producing one additional unit of the good. Marginal costs may be decreasing, constant, or increasing as production increases. In Figure 9.1, quantity is measured on the horizontal axis and marginal cost (MC) is measured on the vertical axis in dollars per unit of output. Marginal cost decreases as output increases from 0 units to Q_1 units, marginal cost is constant as output increases from Q_1 to Q_2 units, and marginal cost increases as output increases beyond Q_2 units. In other words, at outputs less than Q_1, marginal cost is greater than MC_1 but decreases as output increases; at outputs between Q_1 and Q_2, marginal cost is constant and equal to MC_1; and at outputs greater than Q_2, marginal cost is greater than MC_1 and increases as output increases.

Figure 9.1

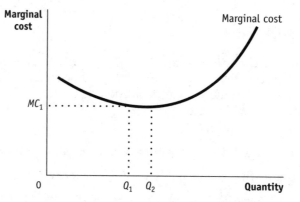

- Marginal benefit is the change in total benefits from consuming or producing one more unit of the good. Marginal benefit typically decreases as quantity increases: each additional unit of the good yields less benefit than the previous increase in output. Not all goods have decreasing marginal benefit: some goods exhibit constant marginal benefit, in which the benefit from producing each additional unit of the good is the same regardless of how many units have already been produced. Figure 9.2 illustrates a marginal benefit curve. Marginal benefit is measured in dollars per unit.

Figure 9.2

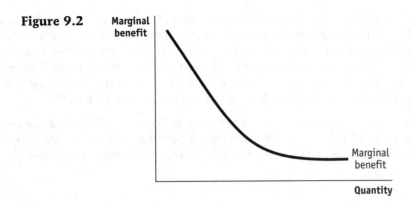

Objective #6. The principle of marginal analysis states that the optimal quantity of an activity is that quantity where the marginal benefit equals the marginal cost. When production of an activity occurs at the point where marginal benefit equals marginal cost, the total net gain from the activity is maximized. When marginal benefit is greater than marginal cost, too little of the good is being produced since the production of one more unit of the good adds more benefits than costs; when marginal benefit is less than marginal cost, too much of the good is being produced since the addition to costs from producing the last unit of the good is greater than the addition to benefits from producing the last unit. Figure 9.3 illustrates the optimal quantity of the good, Q*, where marginal costs equal marginal benefits.

Figure 9.3

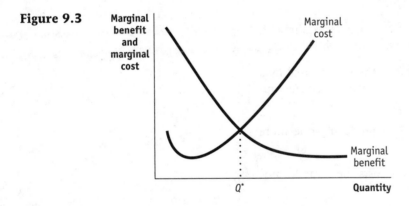

Objective #7. Sunk costs refer to costs that have already been incurred. When making decisions about future activities, sunk costs should be ignored since they have no influence on the actual costs and benefits that the future activity generates.

Objective #8. The present value calculation is a method for evaluating the value today of a payment to be received or made at some point in the future. This calculation is useful when comparing the benefits and costs from an activity when these benefits and costs arrive at different points in time. By using present values in evaluating a project, you can evaluate the project as if all the costs and benefits from the project were occurring today rather than at different times.

- The present value calculation recognizes that a dollar held today is worth more than a dollar held a year from now. You can use the interest rate to compare the value of a dollar today to a dollar received at some point in the future: the interest rate measures the cost to you of delaying the receipt of a dollar of benefit, or the benefit to you of delaying the payment of a dollar of cost.

- Suppose you lend out $x today with the expectation that you will be repaid a dollar a year from now. The dollar you receive a year from now should be equal to $x plus the interest you receive from the borrower. If interest rate is represented as r, then we can express this idea as follows: the payment you receive a year from now ($1) equals $x(1 + r)$. Thus $x is the present value of the $1 you receive a year from now, and the present value of a payment of $1 made a year from now is $x = 1/(1 + r)$. This method converts future dollars into their present values so that the time factor issue can be eliminated when making decisions. The present value concept can be expanded to a number of years. For example, the present value of a payment made N years from now is (future value)/$(1 + r)^N$.

- The net present value is the present value of current and future benefits minus the present value of current and future costs. When comparing potential projects, the project with the highest net present value is financially the most attractive project to undertake.

Key Terms

explicit cost a cost that involves actually laying out money.

implicit cost a cost that does not require the outlay of money; it is measured by the value, in dollar terms, of forgone benefits.

accounting profit a business's revenue minus the *explicit cost* and depreciation.

economic profit a business's revenue minus the *opportunity cost* of *resources;* usually less than the *accounting profit.*

capital the combined value of a business's assets; includes equipment, buildings, tools, inventory, and financial assets.

implicit cost of capital the *opportunity cost* of the capital used by a business; that is, the income that could have been realized had the capital been used in the next best alternative way.

marginal cost the additional cost incurred by producing one more unit of a good or service.

constant marginal cost each additional unit costs the same to produce as the previous one.

marginal cost curve a graphical representation showing how the cost of producing one more unit depends on the quantity that has already been produced.

increasing marginal cost the case in which each additional unit costs more to produce than the previous one.

marginal benefit the additional benefit derived from producing one more unit of a good or service.

decreasing marginal benefit the case in which each additional unit of an activity produces less benefit than the previous unit.

marginal benefit curve a graphical representation showing how the benefit from producing one more unit depends on the quantity that has already been produced.

optimal quantity the quantity that generates the maximum possible total net gain.

principle of marginal analysis the proposition that the *optimal quantity* is the quantity at which *marginal benefit* is equal to *marginal cost.*

Notes

Key Terms *(continued)*

sunk cost a cost that has already been incurred and is not recoverable.

interest rate the price, calculated as a percentage of the amount borrowed, charged by the lender.

present value the amount of money needed at the present time to produce, at the prevailing *interest rate*, a given amount of money at a specified future time.

net present value the *present value* of current and future benefits minus the present value of current and future costs.

AFTER YOU READ THE CHAPTER

Tips

Tip #1. This chapter returns to the concept of opportunity cost. Economists measure costs using the concept of opportunity cost, or the value of the consumption or production forgone when a consumer or a producer chooses to consume or produce something else. You may find it helpful to review the earlier discussion of opportunity cost in this text.

Tip #2. When measuring costs, economists include both explicit and implicit costs. This means that opportunity costs are incorporated into the measures of costs that economists calculate, and it implies that decision making based on economic analysis must include implicit costs.

Tip #3. It is important that you understand the distinction between accounting and economic profits. Throughout this course, the focus will be on economic profits, since it is this measure that includes all the opportunity costs of producing a good or service. Accounting profit, although often referred to within the media and the business community, does not provide a full measure of the costs of producing a good or service. As you think about this issue, remember that the owner of the business incurs an opportunity cost associated with the use of their time and capital, and it is important to include this opportunity cost when evaluating the profitability of the enterprise.

Tip #4. By this point in the course, you should be growing comfortable with the discussion of marginal costs and marginal benefits and why the optimal level of production occurs when marginal cost equals marginal benefit. If marginal cost is greater than marginal benefit, too much of the good is being produced. If marginal cost is less than marginal benefit, too little of the good is being produced.

Tip #5. The calculation of present value is a calculation that allows you to compare a stream of payments occurring over time to another stream of payments occurring over some other period of time. This calculation is highly useful, and you should practice using it until you are comfortable with the concept as well as the technique.

Problems and Exercises

1. Marty runs a bakery that employs ten workers who each work fifty weeks a year and earn $400 a week. In addition, Marty has rent of $50,000 per year, and costs for supplies and raw materials totaling $125,000 a year. Marty occasionally is approached by another baker in town who is willing to pay Marty $75,000 a year to come work for her. Marty could sell his business for $100,000. The current interest rate on deposits at Marty's bank is 5%. Marty's revenue from the bakery is $440,000 a year. Assume that there is no depreciation of equipment at Marty's bakery.

   a. What are Marty's explicit costs?

   b. What are Marty's implicit costs?

   c. What are Marty's economic costs?

   d. What is the implicit cost of Marty's time and energy?

   e. What is the implicit cost of capital?

   f. What are Marty's accounting profits?

   g. What are Marty's economic profits?

   h. Should Marty continue to operate the bakery given the above cost and revenue figures? Explain your answer.

   i. Given the above information, what is the minimum amount of revenue Marty's bakery must earn for Marty to stay in business?

2. Susie operates a business that prints designs on T-shirts. Susie's total revenue per year equals $500,000. The cost of labor per year is $125,000, the cost of raw materials and supplies is $200,000 per year, while the value of capital for the business is $200,000. Susie knows she could earn $50,000 per year working as a printer at a competitor's business. She also knows she could sell her business and the land it sits on for $600,000 and earn 10% a year on these funds. Each year her depreciation equals 5% of her capital expenditure.

    a. What are Susie's explicit costs? Calculate a value for these explicit costs.

    b. What are Susie's implicit costs? Calculate a value for these implicit costs.

    c. What are Susie's accounting profits?

    d. What are Susie's economic profits?

3. The following table provides information about Joe's Service Shop, which specializes in providing all sorts of services to customers in the metro area.

Quantity of services	Joe's total cost	Joe's marginal cost	Joe's total benefit	Joe's marginal benefit
0	$100		$ 0	
		(a)		(g)
1	110		200	
		(b)		(h)
2	118		230	
		$7		$15
3	(c)		(i)	
		10		(j)
4	(d)		255	
		(e)		8
5	150		(k)	
		20		5
6	(f)		(l)	

    a. Fill in the missing cells labeled (a) through (l) in the table.

b. Define marginal cost and marginal benefit.

c. When Joe produces 2 units of services, what is the relationship between marginal cost and marginal benefit? Are 2 units of services an optimal quantity for Joe to produce? Explain your answer.

d. When Joe produces 5 units of services, what is the relationship between marginal cost and marginal benefit? Are 5 units of services an optimal quantity for Joe to produce? Explain your answer.

e. Given the above information, what is the optimal quantity of services for Joe to produce?

4. Use the graph below of a firm's marginal cost curve to answer this question.

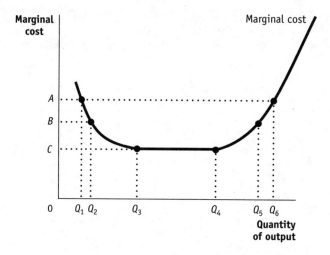

a. For what range of output is marginal cost decreasing as output increases?

b. For what range of output is marginal cost constant as output increases?

c. For what range of output is marginal cost increasing as output increases?

d. What distance measures the marginal cost of producing Q_2?

e. What distance measures the marginal cost of producing Q_6?

5. Use the following graph of the marginal benefit to Joe from consuming hot dogs to answer this question.

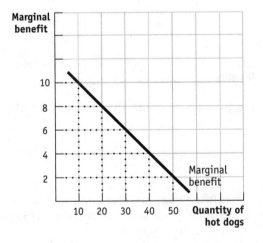

a. What happens to Joe's marginal benefit from consuming hot dogs as he consumes more hot dogs? Explain your answer.

b. In deciding how many hot dogs to consume, what will Joe want to consider? Explain your answer.

c. Suppose the marginal cost of consuming hot dogs is constant and equal to $6. How many hot dogs will Joe want to consume given this information? Why does he choose this amount?

d. Suppose the marginal cost of consuming hot dogs is constant and equal to $4. What will happen to Joe's consumption of hot dogs? Explain why Joe makes this choice of consumption.

6. Suppose Bob calculates that the marginal cost (MC) for his business can be expressed as $MC = Q$, where Q is the quantity of units he produces. Furthermore, suppose that the marginal benefit (MB) he gets from producing his product can be expressed as $MB = 100 - 3Q$.

a. Draw a graph illustrating Bob's marginal cost and marginal benefit. Put quantity on the horizontal axis and marginal benefit and marginal cost on the vertical axis.

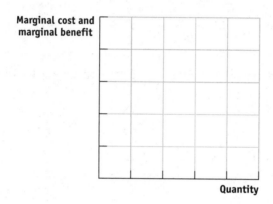

b. Calculate the optimal quantity for Bob to produce. Mark this optimal quantity on your graph.

c. If Bob produces 20 units of the good, what is the marginal cost and marginal benefit from the last unit he produces? Should Bob produce more or less of the good? Explain your answer.

7. In October, Marissa paid an annual subscription fee of $600 to the local opera company for this season's five opera performances. This fee is nonrefundable and entitles Marissa to one ticket to each of the five performances. A friend of Marissa's invites Marissa to an all-expense paid weekend to Miami. Marissa discovers that the weekend her friend invites her to Miami is the same weekend as the first opera performance. Marissa estimates that the value of the trip to Miami is $1,000.

a. Marissa is trying to figure out the cost of going to Miami. Since she will miss the opera, she calculates that the cost of her going to Miami is $120 or the cost of one ticket to the opera. Do you agree with Marissa's reasoning? Explain your answer.

b. With respect to the opera, her friend says that the cost of going to Miami is $0 for Marissa, since whether she goes to the opera or not she will not get her $120 back. Do you agree with this reasoning? Explain your answer.

c. Marissa's roommate says that Marissa's cost of going to Miami is $1,120, since it should include the cost of the trip ($1,000) plus the cost of the missed opera performance ($120). Do you agree with this reasoning? Explain your answer.

8. Mary offers to pay Joe $1,000 a year from now if he will loan her money today. Suppose Joe wants to earn 10% interest and there is no inflation over this period. What is the maximum amount Joe will lend Mary, given her offer?

9. Sarah borrows $1,000 from Joe at the beginning of the year and promises to repay him at the end of five years. She also agrees to pay him an annual interest rate of 12%. What is the total amount Joe will receive at the end of the fifth year?

10. Joe can't decide between two financial options: he can loan Sarah $1,000 as outlined in problem 9, or he can invest the $1,000 in a new venture. He estimates that during the first year the venture will earn 5% interest, during the second and third years it will earn 10% interest, and during the fourth and fifth years it will earn 18% interest. Evaluate these two options for Joe and then make a recommendation based on this evaluation.

11. You have won the lottery and you can either receive your winnings as a single payment of $2 million in cash now or you can receive a payment of $500,000 a year for five years starting now. The interest rate is constant and equal to 10% per year. Which payment plan do you prefer?

12. Does your decision in problem 11 change if the interest rate is constant and equal to 8% instead of 10%?

13. Does your decision in problem 11 change if the interest rate is constant and equal to 15% instead of 10%?

■ BEFORE YOU TAKE THE TEST

Chapter Review Questions

1. Accounting profits are based on total revenue and
    a. the sum of explicit and implicit costs.
    b. the difference between explicit and implicit costs.
    c. implicit costs.
    d. explicit costs and depreciation.

Use the following information to answer the next four questions.

Jerry's Doughnut Shop employs ten people. Each of these individuals works 1,000 hours a year, and their hourly wage is $8. In addition, Jerry's Doughnut Shop has supplies and raw materials costs of $150,000 a year and rental costs of $50,000 a year. Jerry knows that he could sell his business for $100,000, and he knows he could secure a job at Alice's Pastry Place where he would earn $60,000 a year. Currently the bank in Jerry's town is paying 5% interest per year on all funds deposited at the bank. Assume there is no depreciation of capital equipment each year.

2. Jerry's explicit costs per year include _____ and are equal to _____ .
    a. Jerry's salary, the labor costs, the supplies and raw materials cost, and the rental costs; $340,000
    b. the labor costs, the supplies and raw materials cost, and the rental costs; $280,000
    c. the labor costs, the supplies and raw materials costs, the rental costs, as well as the interest Jerry forgoes; $285,000
    d. Jerry's salary he could earn at Alice's Pastry Place and the interest he forgoes when he operates his own business; $65,000

3. Jerry's explicit costs underestimate the economic costs of being in business by
   a. $0.
   b. $5,000.
   c. $60,000.
   d. $65,000.

4. Suppose Jerry sells doughnuts for $1 per doughnut. Jerry's accounting profit this year was $100,000. Jerry sold _____ doughnuts this year and his economic profit equaled _____ .
   a. 380,000; $40,000
   b. 380,000; $35,000
   c. 38,000; $40,000
   d. 38,000; $35,000

5. Given the above information, including the $1 per doughnut price, Jerry tries to calculate the level of accounting profits where it is no longer beneficial for Jerry to operate Jerry's Doughnut Shop. You advise him to
   a. continue in the business as long as his accounting profit is positive.
   b. sell the business since he is focusing on accounting profits and not on economic profits.
   c. sell the business if his accounting profits fall below $65,000.
   d. sell the business if his accounting profits exceed $65,000.

6. Depreciation is the term that describes the
   a. sum of the value of the owner's time and energy and the value of the owner's capital.
   b. value of the owner's capital.
   c. reduction in the value of the owner's capital equipment each year due to the wearing out of some of that equipment.
   d. difference between the explicit and implicit costs.

7. Which of the following statements is true?
   a. When the marginal cost of producing one more unit of the good is greater than the marginal benefit of producing one more unit of the good, too much of the good is being produced.
   b. When the marginal benefit from producing one more unit of the good is greater than the marginal cost of producing one more unit of the good, too little of the good is being produced.
   c. Accounting profits include explicit costs, but do not include implicit costs.
   d. All of the above statements are true.

8. Stella is considering producing one more unit of steel at her manufacturing plant. She calculates that her costs will increase by $5,500 if she produces this unit, while her benefits from producing this additional unit will increase by $5,600. Stella should
   a. produce the additional unit.
   b. not produce the additional unit.

9. When marginal cost is decreasing as output increases, this implies that the slope of the marginal cost curve is
   a. positive.
   b. negative.

10. Sarah's Autoshop reports that their marginal cost, no matter their level of production, is always equal to $10. This implies that the marginal cost curve for Sarah's Autoshop is

a. a vertical line.

b. a horizontal line.

c. initially downward sloping as output increases, but then eventually it is upward sloping.

d. initially upward sloping as output increases, but then eventually it is downward sloping.

11. As more and more units of a good are consumed, the marginal benefit of an additional unit typically

a. stays constant.

b. increases.

c. decreases.

d. Answers (a), (b), and (c) are all possible depending on the particular good.

Use the following table to answer the next four questions. The table provides information about Steve's Ice Cream Store's total costs and total benefits for different serving levels of ice cream.

Quantity of servings of ice cream	Total costs	Total benefits
0	$400	$ 0
100	450	800
200	500	900
300	550	950
400	600	975

12. The marginal cost of producing an additional serving of ice cream, if 200 servings are currently being produced, is equal to

a. $550.50.   c. $50.

b. $550.   d. $0.50.

13. Given the information in the table, as output increases from 0 units to 400 units, marginal cost

a. decreases.

b. increases.

c. stays constant.

14. What is the marginal benefit of producing one more serving of ice cream if 300 servings are currently being produced?

a. $650   c. $25

b. $625   d. $0.25

15. What is the optimal number of servings of ice cream to produce?

a. 400   c. 200

b. 300   d. 100

Use the following information to answer the next two questions.

Marty borrows $1,000 from Harry on January 1, 2009, and promises to repay Harry on December 31, 2014, a payment that will result in Harry earning an annual rate of interest of 10%.

16. Which of the following expressions correctly states the value of Marty's payment on December 31, 2013?
    a. ($1,000)(1 + 10)
    b. ($1,000)/(1 + 0.10)^5$
    c. ($1,000)(1 + 0.10) + ($1,000)(1 + 0.10)^2 + ($1,000)(1 + 0.10)^3 + ($1,000)(1 + 0.10)^4 + ($1,000)(1 + 0.10)^5$
    d. ($1,000)(1 + 0.10)^5$

17. Suppose Harry tells Marty he will lend him the money if he earns an annual rate of interest of 12%. This will result in Marty paying Harry a
    a. smaller amount than if the interest rate were 10%.
    b. larger amount than if the interest rate were 10%.

18. Holding everything else constant, the present value of a future payment increases when the interest rate rises.
    a. True
    b. False

Use the following information to answer the next three questions.

Courtney's Computers is thinking about whether they should invest in a new software program. Development of this program will require an initial expenditure of $4 million now but will result in annual profits of $2 million for three years.

19. No matter what the interest rate, Courtney's Computers should invest in this new software since the profits from this new software far outweigh the costs of developing this software.
    a. True
    b. False

20. Given the above information and an interest rate of 20%, Courtney's Computers should
    a. invest in the development of this new software.
    b. not invest in the development of this new software.

21. Given the above information and an interest rate of 20%, the net present value of this new software for Courtney's Computers is equal to
    a. −$2 million.   c. $0.21 million.
    b. $2 million.   d. −$0.21 million.

22. When considering a new investment project, companies
    a. do not care if the net present value is positive or negative provided the interest rate is at least 10%.
    b. are only willing to undertake investment projects when the interest rate is 5% or lower.
    c. ignore the interest rate.
    d. None of the above statements are correct.

ANSWER KEY

Answers to Problems and Exercises

1. **a.** Marty's explicit costs include $200,000 for labor, $50,000 for rent, and $125,000 for supplies and raw materials. The sum of Marty's explicit costs equal $375,000. For this problem recall that depreciation costs equal $0.

    b. Marty's implicit costs include $5,000 for the implicit cost of capital and $75,000 for the salary Marty forgoes when he decides to work for himself. Marty could invest the value of the business ($100,000) at his bank and earn 5% interest on that deposit, yielding him $5,000 in interest income per year. In addition, Marty could close his business and earn $75,000 working for someone else. Thus, Marty's implicit costs equal $80,000.

    c. The explicit and implicit costs total $455,000.

    d. The implicit cost of Marty's time and energy is $75,000.

    e. The implicit cost of Marty's capital is $5,000.

    f. Marty's accounting profit equals his total revenue minus his explicit costs, or $440,000 – $375,000, for an accounting profit of $65,000.

    g. Marty's economic profit equals his total revenue minus his explicit costs and implicit costs, or $440,000 – $455,000, for an economic profit of –$15,000.

    h. Marty should not stay in business since he is currently earning a negative economic profit and therefore is not receiving the full value for his time and energy and the use of his capital. Since Marty's implicit costs equal $80,000, Marty must earn an accounting profit equal to $80,000 to cover his explicit costs plus his opportunity costs.

    i. The minimum amount of revenue that the bakery must earn for Marty to stay in business is $455,000: when Marty earns $455,000 in revenue, his revenue just covers his explicit and implicit costs of being in business.

2. **a.** Susie's explicit costs per year include her labor costs of $125,000 and her costs of raw materials and supplies of $200,000, for a total of $325,000.

    b. Susie's implicit costs include the value of her time as measured by the salary of $50,000 she could earn if she worked for a competitor and the earnings from her capital if it was invested at a return of 10% a year, or $60,000, for a total of $110,000.

    c. Accounting profits equal total revenue minus explicit costs and depreciation. Susie's depreciation equals $10,000, so her accounting profits equal $500,000 – $325,000 – $10,000, or $165,000.

    d. Economic profits equal total revenue minus the sum of explicit costs, implicit costs, and depreciation, or $500,000 – ($325,000 + $110,000 + $10,000), or $55,000.

3. **a.**

Quantity of services	Joe's total cost	Joe's marginal cost	Joe's total benefit	Joe's marginal benefit
0	$100		$ 0	
		(a) $10		(g) $200
1	110		200	
		(b) 8		(h) 30
2	118		230	
		$7		$15
3	(c) 125		(i) 245	
		10		(j) 10
4	(d) 135		255	
		(e) 15		8
5	150		(k) 263	
		20		5
6	(f) 170		(l) 268	

b. Marginal cost is the addition to total cost from producing one additional unit of the good, while marginal benefit is the addition to total benefit from producing or consuming one more unit of the good.

c. At 2 units of services, Joe's marginal cost of $8 is less than his marginal benefit of $30. Since the addition to benefits exceeds the addition to costs, more services should be produced.

d. At 5 units of services, Joe's marginal cost of $15 is greater than his marginal benefit of $8. Since the addition to costs exceeds the addition to benefits, fewer services should be provided.

e. When Joe provides 4 services, the marginal cost of providing the last unit of services ($10) exactly equals the marginal benefit from providing the last unit of services ($10). Thus 4 units of services is the optimal quantity to provide.

4. **a.** Marginal cost is decreasing as output increases from 0 units to Q_3 units.

b. Marginal cost is constant as output increases from Q_3 to Q_4 units.

c. Marginal cost is increasing as output increases for all output levels greater than or equal to Q_4.

d. The marginal cost of producing Q_2 is measured by the distance from the origin to B on the vertical axis.

e. The marginal cost of producing Q_6 is measured by the distance from the origin to A on the vertical axis.

5. a. Joe's marginal benefit from consuming hot dogs decreases as he consumes more hot dogs. Each additional unit of hot dog provides less benefit than the previous unit.

    b. Joe will compare his marginal cost of consuming another hot dog to his marginal benefit from consuming an additional hot dog. As long as the marginal benefit of an additional hot dog exceeds the marginal cost of an additional hot dog, Joe will consume an additional hot dog.

    c. Joe will consume 30 hot dogs since the marginal cost of the thirtieth hot dog equals the marginal benefit of the thirtieth hot dog.

    d. Joe will consume 40 hot dogs since at this quantity the marginal benefit of the last unit consumed equals the marginal cost of the last unit consumed.

6. a.
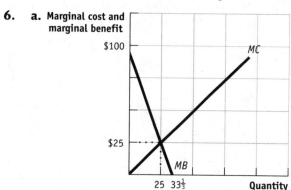

    b. The optimal quantity occurs where $MC = MB$, or where $Q = 25$. At this quantity, the marginal cost and marginal benefit are both equal to $25 for the last unit produced.

    c. At a quantity of 20 units, the marginal cost of the last unit produced is $20 while the marginal benefit from this last unit is $40. Bob will add more to his benefits than his costs if he increases his production, so he should increase his production.

7. a. Since the opera tickets are nonrefundable, the expenditure on these tickets represents a sunk cost for Marissa. Marissa should ignore this cost and simply compare the costs and benefits of going to Miami. The out-of-pocket cost of going to Miami is $0 since it is an all-expense paid trip; however, Marissa does have an opportunity cost since she will have to forgo going to the opera. Marissa should make her decision based on which choice yields the greater net benefit to her including this opportunity cost in her calculation.

    b. The opera cost is a sunk cost and the trip to Miami is all-expense paid. Marissa does have an opportunity cost in going to Miami, since she will have to forgo whatever she would have done if she had decided to not take the trip.

    c. Marissa is not paying the $1,000 associated with the cost of the Miami trip, and the $120 cost of the opera ticket is a sunk cost. Marissa's roommate's analysis is wrong.

8. To calculate this value, use the present value formula: $PV = $ (future value)$/(1 + r)$. Thus, $PV = (\$1,000)/(1 + 0.10) = \$909.09$. Joe will be willing to lend Mary $909.09 today, given her offer.

9. The future value Joe will receive equals $(\$1,000)(1 + 0.12)^5$, or $1,762.34.

10. From problem 9, we know Joe will earn a total of $762.34 if he loans Sarah $1,000 for five years. To evaluate what Joe should do requires a calculation of the value of the second option. This second option is a bit more complicated to calculate than the loan to Sarah. At the end of the first year, this option is worth $(\$1,000)(1 + 0.05)$, or $1,050. This amount remains with the venture, and at the end of the second year the value of this option will equal $(\$1,050)(1 + 0.10)$. At the end of the third year the value of this option will equal $(\$1,050)(1 + 0.10)(1 + 0.10)$, or $1,270.50. At the end of the fourth year the value of this option is $(\$1,270.50)(1 + 0.18)$, and at the end of the fifth year the

value of this option is ($1,270.50)(1 + 0.18)(1 + 0.18) or $1,769.04. Subtracting out Joe's initial investment of $1,000 yields Joe a net income of $769.04. Since this amount is greater than what he receives from Sarah, Joe should invest in the new venture.

11. To compare these payments requires calculating the present value of the future payments you would receive if you opted for five payments over time instead of a single payment now. The present value of these payments is $500,000 + ($500,000)/(1.1) + ($500,000)/(1.1)^2 + ($500,000)/(1.1)^3 + ($500,000)/(1.1)^4, or $2,086,174. You will receive a larger total payment if you choose to receive the lottery winnings over a five-year period.

12. No, the decision does not change, although this change in the interest rate does change the present value of the stream of payments received over five years. The present value of this stream of payments is now equal to $500,000 + ($500,000)/(1.08) + ($500,000)/(1.08)^2 + ($500,000)/(1.08)^3 + ($500,000)/(1.08)^4, or $2,154,785. A decrease in the interest rate makes the stream of payments over five years even more attractive to you.

13. Yes, when the interest rate increases to 15%, this makes the single payment option more valuable than the stream of five payments. To see this, compare the single payment of $2 million to the present value of the stream of payments. The present value of the payments over five years is equal to $500,000 + ($500,000)/(1.15) + ($500,000)/(1.15)^2 + ($500,000)/(1.15)^3 + ($500,000)/(1.15)^4, or $1,928,232, which is less than $2 million.

Answers to Chapter Review Questions

1. **Answer d.** Accounting profits ignore implicit costs. Accounting profits are equal to total revenue minus the sum of explicit costs and depreciation.

2. **Answer b.** Jerry's explicit costs do not include the salary he could make if he worked for someone else, and it doesn't include the interest he could earn if he sold his business and deposited his capital in a bank deposit. His explicit costs include the labor costs, the supplies and raw materials cost, and the rental costs, for a total of $280,000.

3. **Answer d.** Jerry's explicit costs omit the salary he could earn if he worked for someone else ($60,000) and the interest he could earn if he invested his capital ($5,000), for a total of $65,000.

4. **Answer b.** Jerry's accounting profit is equal to his total revenue minus his explicit costs (there is no depreciation in this question). His explicit costs equal $280,000 and his accounting profit equals $100,000: this implies that his total revenue must equal $380,000. If doughnuts are priced at $1 each, then this means Jerry sold 380,000 doughnuts this year. Economic profits are equal to total revenue ($380,000) minus the sum of explicit plus implicit costs ($345,000): Jerry's economic profit is equal to $35,000.

5. **Answer c.** Jerry should continue to operate his business so long as his accounting profits are equal to or greater than his implicit costs. Since his implicit costs are equal to $65,000, this means that Jerry should continue to operate provided his accounting profits are at least equal to $65,000. If his accounting profits fall below this level, then Jerry would be better off selling his business and working for someone else.

6. **Answer c.** This is a definitional question, and answer (c) provides the best definition of depreciation among the offered choices.

7. **Answer d.** All of these statements are true. When marginal benefit is greater than marginal cost, this means that consumers value the last unit more than the cost of producing the last unit, and more of the good should be produced. Similarly, when marginal cost is greater than marginal benefit, too much of the good is being produced. Answer (c) is a definitional statement.

8. **Answer a.** Since the marginal benefit of producing one more unit of steel is greater than the marginal cost of producing this additional unit of steel, Stella should produce this unit.

9. **Answer b.** If marginal cost is decreasing as output increases, this implies that there is an inverse relationship between quantity and marginal cost: as quantity increases, marginal cost decreases, which is represented by a downward-sloping marginal cost curve.

10. **Answer b.** Since marginal cost does not vary as output varies, this tells us that marginal cost can be represented as a horizontal line when marginal cost is measured on the vertical axis and quantity is measured on the horizontal axis.

11. **Answer c.** As people get more and more units of the good, each successive unit yields fewer additional benefits.

12. **Answer d.** Marginal cost is the change in total costs divided by the change in quantity. Total costs change from $500 to $550 when output increases from 200 units to 300 units. To get a measure of marginal cost, we can divide the change in total cost ($50) by the change in output (100 units) to get $0.50 per unit as our marginal cost.

13. **Answer c.** If you use the same technique as the one outlined in answer 12, you will find that the marginal cost is constant and equal to $0.50 per unit.

14. **Answer d.** The marginal benefit of producing one more unit of ice cream if 300 units are currently being produced is equal to ($975 − $950)/(400 units − 300 units) = $25 per 100 units, or $0.25 per unit.

15. **Answer b.** Since the marginal cost is constant and equal to $0.50, this problem is about identifying the level of output that has a marginal benefit of $0.50. This occurs when quantity is equal to 300 servings, since the marginal benefit of going from 200 to 300 servings is equal to ($950 − $900)(300 units − 200 units) = $0.50.

16. **Answer d.** This is a simple illustration of the present value formula.

17. **Answer b.** When the interest rate increases, this means the cost of borrowing money has risen and therefore the amount of money to be paid back will rise.

18. **Answer b.** The present value of a future payment decreases when the interest rate rises, since the higher interest rate means that a smaller amount today will accumulate to a larger amount in the future.

19. **Answer b.** Whether an investment project should be undertaken or not depends on the benefits as well as the costs associated with the investment project. It is possible that even though this project has positive projected profits, the cost of borrowing funds to undertake the project will exceed these projected profits.

20. **Answer a.** If you compute the net present value for the project, the value is a positive number and therefore the project should be undertaken. This computation is done in the answer to question 21.

21. **Answer c.** To compute the net present value entails calculating the present value of the benefits and the present value of the costs and then subtracting the present value of the costs from the present value of the benefits. The present value of the benefits is equal to $(2)/(1+0.2) + (2)/(1+0.2)^2 + (2)/(1+0.2)^3$, and the present value of the costs is equal to 4. The difference between these two present values is approximately $0.21 million.

22. **Answer d.** None of the answers are true. Companies decide to undertake investment projects when the net present value is a positive number for the given interest rate.

chapter 10

The Rational Consumer

BEFORE YOU READ THE CHAPTER

Summary

This chapter develops the concept of consumer utility and then explores utility maximization and the principle of diminishing marginal utility. The chapter uses the model of consumer utility maximization to explain downward-sloping demand curves and to explore both the income and substitution effects.

Chapter Objectives

Objective #1. The model of consumer choice is based on a rational consumer who knows what he or she wants and who makes the most of his or her available opportunities.

Objective #2. Consumer utility refers to the satisfaction the consumer gets from the consumption of a bundle of goods and services. The utility function describes the relationship between an individual's consumption bundle and the total amount of utility this consumption bundle provides to the individual. Each individual evaluates the consumption bundle's utility: the level of utility depends on each person's tastes. Utility is measured in utils.

- Total utility measures the total amount of satisfaction an individual gets from consuming different amounts of a good. As the quantity consumed increases, total utility increases, but as quantity increases total utility increases at a decreasing rate. After some point of consumption, the consumer gets less satisfaction from each additional unit consumed. Figure 10.1 illustrates a total utility curve.

Figure 10.1

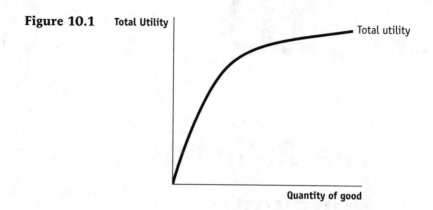

- Marginal utility measures the change in total utility from consuming an additional unit of the good. Marginal utility declines as the individual consumes more and more units of the good. The marginal utility curve illustrates the relationship between the quantity consumed and the individual's marginal utility. Figure 10.2 illustrates a marginal utility curve.

Figure 10.2

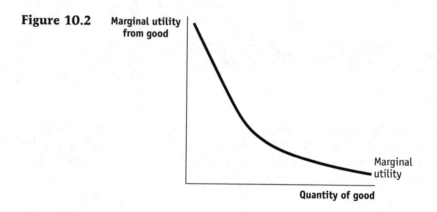

- Marginal utility curves slope downward due to the principle of diminishing marginal utility, which states that the marginal utility a consumer gets from one more unit of a good or service declines as the amount of that good or service consumed increases.

Objective #3.   A consumer's budget constraint describes the consumption bundles that a consumer can afford and that exhaust the consumer's income. The budget constraint depends on the individual's income and the prices of the goods and services included in the consumption bundle. The budget constraint acts as a boundary indicating the consumer's consumption possibilities. The budget constraint for an individual with a choice of two goods can be expressed as follows:

Total income of the individual = expenditure on good 1 + expenditure on good 2

- The budget constraint when drawn on a graph is referred to as the budget line. For example, suppose an individual has income of $20,000 a year and is choosing between consuming good X, which costs $100 per unit, or consuming good Y, which costs $200 per unit. The budget line for this individual is depicted in Figure 10.3.

Figure 10.3

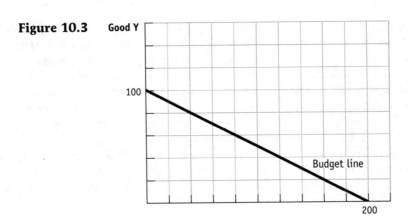

If the consumer spent all of his or her income on good X, they could consume 200 units of good X (the *x*-intercept in the graph); if the consumer spent all of their income on good Y, they could consume 100 units of good Y (the *y*-intercept in the graph). The consumer can also afford any combination of the two goods that lie on the budget line.

- The individual can afford any points that lie in the area bounded by their budget line: these affordable consumption bundles represent the individual's consumption possibilities. The individual will not choose to consume at any of these points inside the budget line provided that their utility from consuming either good is positive and the utility of saving income is zero (this amounts to the assumption that the individual spends all of their income on the two available goods).

- Budget lines are downward sloping since the individual can afford to consume more of one good only if the individual consumes less of the other good.

Objective #4.   The optimal consumption bundle is the one that maximizes the individual's total utility.

Objective #5.   The marginal utility per dollar spent on a good is equal to the marginal utility of the last unit consumed divided by the price of the good. The marginal utility per dollar for good X can be written as MU_X/P_X, where MU_X is the marginal utility from consuming that unit of the good and P_X is the price of good X.

- As additional units of the good are consumed, the marginal utility per dollar spent on the good decreases, holding income and the prices of the goods constant. This is because of the principle of diminishing marginal utility: as the consumer consumes more and more units of the good, total utility increases but at a diminishing rate. When total utility increases at a diminishing rate, this implies that marginal utility is decreasing as consumption increases.

- The optimal consumption bundle for an individual is one in which the marginal utility per dollar spent on each good is equal. This idea can be expressed symbolically as

$$MU_X/P_X = MU_Y/P_Y$$

where the X and Y subscripts refer to good X and good Y, respectively.

- A graph can be constructed to depict the relationship between the marginal utility per dollar spent and the optimal consumption bundle. This graph would measure the marginal utility per dollar spent on the vertical axis, and it would measure the consumption bundles that are affordable along the horizontal axis. Along the horizontal axis each of these consumption bundles would represent different amounts of the two goods: reading from left to right, the quantity of good X increases while the quantity of good Y decreases. (Note: because the quantity of good Y decreases as you read from left to right along the horizontal axis, this results in the marginal utility per dollar spent on good Y being drawn as an upward-sloping line.) Figure 10.4 illustrates this idea for the two goods X and Y. The consumer will maximize their utility by consuming consumption bundle C, since the marginal utility per dollar spent on good X equals the marginal utility per dollar spent on good Y with this bundle.

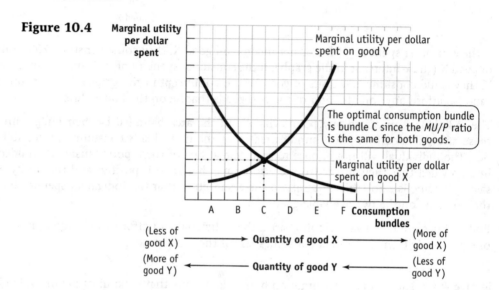

Figure 10.4

Objective #6. When the price of a good changes, this changes the marginal utility per dollar spent on this good. If the price increases, an individual can increase their utility by purchasing fewer units of this good and more units of other goods. If the price decreases, an individual can increase their utility by purchasing more units of this now relatively cheaper good and fewer units of the other goods. In other words, the quantity demanded of a good is inversely related to its price: when price increases, the quantity demanded decreases, and when price decreases, the quantity demanded increases.

- The substitution effect measures the change in the quantity consumed as the consumer substitutes the good that has become relatively cheaper for the good that has become relatively more expensive.

- The income effect of a price change is the change in the quantity consumed of a good that results from the change in the overall purchasing power of the consumer due to the change in the price of the good. The income effect is significant for those goods whose price represents a large share of total income, because when the price of one of these goods increases, this results in a substantial reduction in the purchasing power of the individual. The individual must reduce their purchases of this good since they can no longer afford as many units of the good.

Key Terms

utility (of a consumer) a measure of the satisfaction derived from consumption of goods and services.

consumption bundle (of an individual) the collection of all the goods and services consumed by a given individual.

utility function (of an individual) the total *utility* generated by an individual's *consumption bundle*.

util a unit of *utility*.

marginal utility the change in total *utility* generated by consuming one additional unit of a good or service.

marginal utility curve a graphical representation showing how *marginal utility* depends on the quantity of the good or service consumed.

principle of diminishing marginal utility the proposition that each successive unit of a good or service consumed adds less to total *utility* than did the previous unit.

budget constraint the cost of a consumer's *consumption bundle* cannot exceed the consumer's income.

consumption possibilities the set of all *consumption bundles* that can be consumed, given a consumer's income and prevailing prices.

budget line all the *consumption bundles* available to a consumer who spends all of his or her income.

optimal consumption bundle the *consumption bundle* that maximizes a consumer's total *utility*, given that consumer's *budget constraint*.

marginal utility per dollar the additional *utility* gained from spending one more dollar on a good or service.

optimal consumption rule when a consumer maximizes *utility*, the *marginal utility per dollar* spent must be the same for all goods and services in the *consumption bundle*.

substitution effect the change in the quantity of a good consumed as the consumer substitutes a good that has become relatively cheaper in place of one that has become relatively more expensive.

income effect the change in the quantity of a good consumed that results from the change in a consumer's purchasing power due to the change in the price of the good.

Notes

■ AFTER YOU READ THE CHAPTER

Tips

Tip #1. Construction of the individual's budget line is not difficult if you follow these steps.

- First identify the two goods the individual can choose to consume and the prices of these two goods.

- Identify the individual's income.

- In a graph, the y-intercept of the budget line corresponds to the individual's income divided by the price of the good measured on the y-axis. In other words, the total number of units of the good measured on the y-axis that the individual can afford if they only buy that good is found by dividing the individual's income by the price of the good. Similarly, the x-intercept of the budget line corresponds to the individual's income divided by the price of the good measured on the x-axis.

- For example, suppose an individual has a weekly income of $100 and purchases food for $5 a unit and entertainment for $20 a unit. (Although the individual obviously must buy other goods, imagine that this particular individual has $100 that they spend only on some combination of food and entertainment.) Suppose food is measured on the horizontal axis and entertainment is measured on the vertical axis. If the individual devotes all of their income to the purchase of food, they can purchase 20 units of food ($100/$5); if the individual devotes all of their income to the purchase of entertainment, they can purchase 5 units of entertainment ($100/$20); or the individual can divide their income between food and entertainment and purchase any combination of food and entertainment that lies on the line between the two endpoints of the budget line. Figure 10.5 illustrates this example.

Figure 10.5

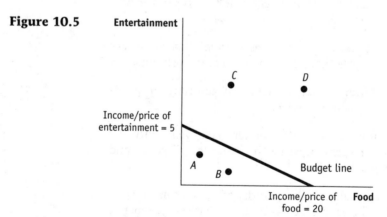

Tip #2. The individual can afford to consume any consumption bundle of food and entertainment that lies on or beneath the budget line (for example, points A and B in Figure 10.5). The individual cannot afford to consume any consumption bundle of food and entertainment that lies beyond the budget line (for example, points C and D in Figure 10.5).

Tip #3. To use marginal analysis for consumption decisions, remember that you must include the budget constraint. Thus, marginal analysis for consumption decisions involves comparing the marginal utility per dollar spent on each good and selecting that consumption bundle in which the marginal utility per dollar is the same for all goods.

Tip #4. The substitution and income effects are challenging concepts for students. Most students have to work hard to achieve an understanding of these concepts.

Tip #5. The substitution effect considers the effect of a change in the price of a good on the consumption of that good. To see this effect using the marginal analysis, look at how the price change affects the marginal utility per dollar spent on the good. For example, if the price of good X increases, this causes the MU_X/P_X to decrease since the denominator is now larger and the numerator has not changed. For the individual to equate the marginal utility per dollar spent on all goods in their consumption bundle, they need to decrease their consumption of good X while increasing their consumption of the other goods in the bundle. The effect of this is to increase the marginal utility the individual receives from consuming good X (recall the principle of diminishing marginal utility): as the individual consumes fewer units of good X, the last unit consumed provides greater marginal utility and therefore the MU_X/P_X increases. As the individual consumes more of the other goods, their marginal utility from the last unit consumed decreases, causing the MU_Y/P_Y to fall. This process will continue until the marginal utility per dollar spent on all the goods in the consumption bundle are equal to one another.

Tip #6. The income effect considers the effect of a change in the price of a good on the consumer's ability to command goods and services. The income effect therefore considers the impact of a change in the price of a good on the consumer's purchasing power. This is especially relevant for a good that represents a substantial expenditure relative to the consumer's income. Thus, if the price of a good increases and this good makes up a substantial part of the consumer's budgetary expenditure, the consumer experiences a decrease in their purchasing power, and this will result in a change in the quantity of the goods they demand.

- If the good is a normal good, both the substitution and the income effects will lead the consumer to consume less of the good.

- If the good is an inferior good, the substitution effect will lead the consumer to consume less of the good while the income effect will cause the consumer to consume more of the good. Typically, the substitution effect is stronger than the income effect, and the consumer's overall consumption of the good will fall as its price rises.

Problems and Exercises

1. Use the information in the table below to answer this set of questions.

Servings of hot chocolate per month	Joe's total utility (utils)	Maria's total utility (utils)	Ben's total utility (utils)	Alexandra's total utility (utils)	Steve's total utility (utils)
1	100	80	100	40	20
2	180	160	150	90	40
3	240	240	200	150	60
4	280	320	250	220	80
5	300	400	300	300	100

a. Which of the individuals in the above table have constant marginal utility over the given range of hot chocolate quantities? Explain your answer.

b. Which of the individuals in the above table have decreasing marginal utility over the given range of hot chocolate quantities? Explain your answer.

2. Use the information given in problem 1 to answer this problem.

a. Complete the table below using the information from problem 1.

Servings of hot chocolate per month	Joe's marginal utility (utils)	Maria's marginal utility (utils)	Ben's marginal utility (utils)	Steve's marginal utility (utils)
1				
	80			20
2				
			50	
3				
4				
		80		
5				

b. Graph Joe's marginal utility from hot chocolate. Measure the quantity of hot chocolate on the horizontal axis and Joe's marginal utility on the vertical axis. Construct the marginal utility curve by plotting your marginal utility figures at the midpoint of the unit intervals. For example, Joe's marginal utility of the second serving of hot chocolate is 80 utils: on your graph plot this level of marginal utility (80 utils) as the level that Joe receives when he consumes 1.5 servings of hot chocolate.

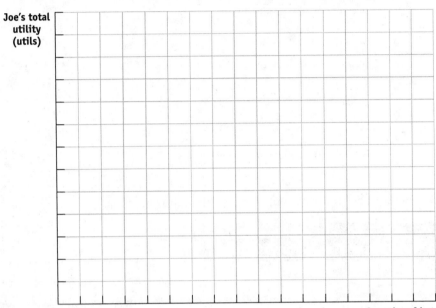

Joe's total utility (utils)

Quantity of hot chocolate per month

3. Sarah's total utility from consuming three slices of pizza is 120 utils while her total utility from consuming four slices of pizza is 100 utils. How is this possible and what does this mean for Sarah?

4. Why are marginal utility curves downward sloping as the level of consumption of the good increases?

5. The following table provides information about Carolyn's total utility from reading articles about current events.

Number of articles read	Total utility from reading articles (utils)
1	100
2	300
3	450
4	550
5	625
6	680
7	720
8	740

a. Using the above information, complete the following table.

Number of articles read	Marginal utility from reading articles (utils)
1	
	200
2	
	150
3	
4	
5	
6	
7	
8	

b. Does Carolyn experience diminishing marginal utility when reading articles? Explain your answer. If she experiences diminishing marginal utility, identify when this first occurs.

c. Is it possible for Carolyn to read too many articles? Explain your answer.

6. Harry's available income for spending on periodicals (*P*) and entertainment (*E*) each month equals $40. The price of periodicals is $2 per periodical and the price of entertainment is $4 per unit of entertainment.

a. Fill in the following table indicating some of the consumption bundles that Harry can afford and that exhaust his income.

Consumption bundle	Number of periodicals	Units of entertainment
A	0	
B	4	
C	8	
D		2
E		0

b. Measuring periodicals on the vertical axis and entertainment on the horizontal axis, draw Harry's budget line. Assume that Harry can consume partial units of periodicals and entertainment (i.e., Harry's budget line is linear and continuous). Label each of the consumption bundles from part (a) on this graph.

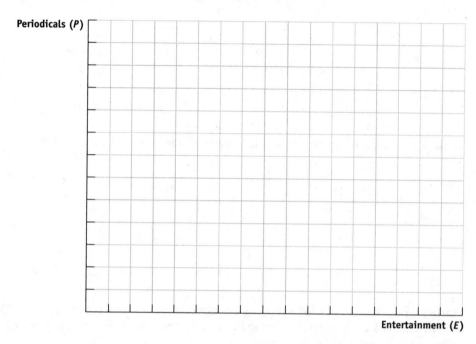

c. Suppose Harry initially consumes consumption bundle B. If he moves to consumption bundle C, what happens to his consumption of periodicals and entertainment relative to his initial situation?

d. Suppose Harry initially consumes consumption bundle D. If he moves to consumption bundle C, what happens to his consumption of periodicals and entertainment relative to his initial situation?

e. Write an equation in *y*-intercept form for Harry's budget line in which the *y*-axis variable is periodicals.

7. Katherine's available income each week for expenditures on food (*F*) and clothing (*C*) is $40. The price of each unit of food is $2 and the price of each unit of clothing is $10.

a. Draw a graph of Katherine's budget line in which food is measured on the *y*-axis and clothing is measured on the *x*-axis.

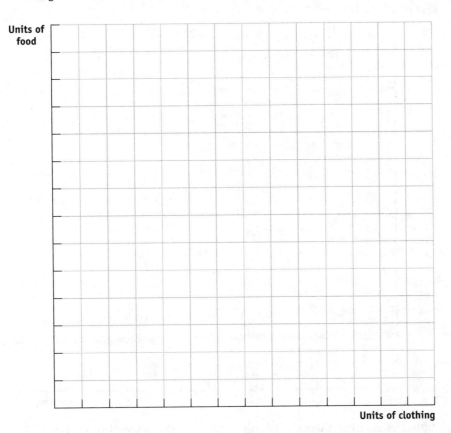

Units of food

Units of clothing

b. For each of the consumption bundles in the table below, identify whether the bundle is on Katherine's budget line, inside Katherine's budget line, or beyond Katherine's budget line.

Consumption bundle	On, inside, or beyond the budget line
5 units of food, 3 units of clothing	
4 units of food, 4 units of clothing	
10 units of food, 1 unit of clothing	
20 units of food, 2 units of clothing	

c. Write an equation in *y*-intercept form for Katherine's budget line in which food is the *y*-variable.

d. Suppose prices stay constant, but Katherine's available weekly income for expenditures on food and clothing doubles. Draw a graph of Katherine's initial budget line and her new budget line with food measured on the vertical axis. How does the new budget line compare to her initial budget line?

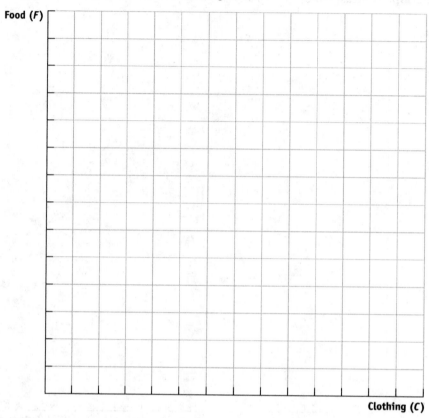

e. Suppose Katherine's weekly income is $40 but the price of food rises to $4 per unit while the price of clothing remains at $10 per unit. Draw a graph of Katherine's initial budget line and her new budget line. How does this change in the price of food affect Katherine's budget line?

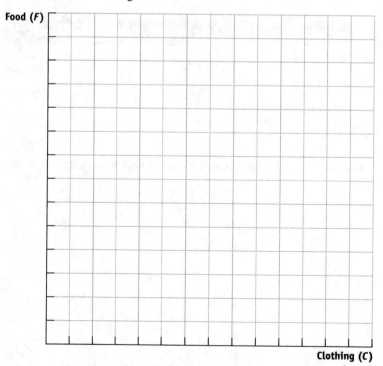

f. Suppose Katherine's weekly income is $40 but the price of clothing falls to $5 per unit while the price of food stays constant at $2 per unit. Draw a graph of Katherine's initial budget line and her new budget line. How does this change in the price of clothing affect Katherine's budget line?

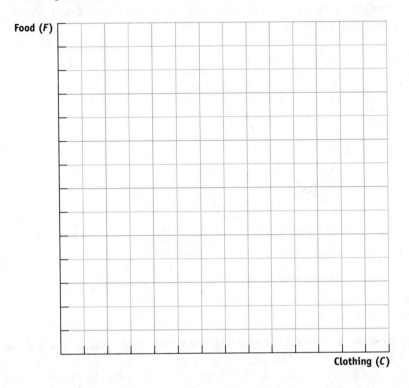

g. Suppose Katherine's weekly income increases to $80 while the prices of food and clothing double. Draw a graph of Katherine's initial budget line and her new budget line. How does this change in income and prices affect Katherine's budget line?

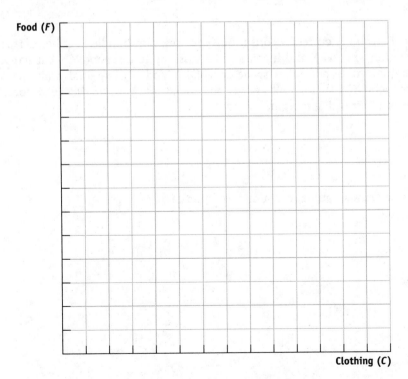

8. Use the figure below to answer this question. Bertram's marginal utility per dollar spent on good X and his marginal utility per dollar spent on good Y are illustrated in the graph. Notice that as you read from left to right along the *x*-axis, the quantity of good X increases while the quantity of good Y decreases. Each combination (A through F) of good X and good Y represented on the *x*-axis is a combination that Bertram can afford given his income and the prices of the two goods.

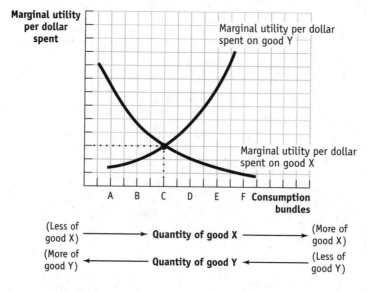

a. Suppose Bertram is currently consuming consumption bundle B. What is the relationship between the marginal utility per dollar spent on good X and the marginal utility per dollar spent on good Y? Is this the optimal consumption bundle for Bertram? Explain your answer.

b. Suppose Bertram is currently consuming consumption bundle E. If he decreases his consumption of good X and increases his consumption of good Y, what happens to his marginal utility per dollar spent on good X and his marginal utility per dollar spent on good Y? Explain your answer and make sure your answer incorporates the concept of diminishing marginal utility.

c. What is Bertram's optimal consumption bundle?

9. Mark consumes ice cream and hamburgers. The table below provides information about the relationship between the quantity of ice cream and hamburgers and the total utility Mark gets from their consumption.

Utility from Ice Cream Consumption		Utility from Hamburger Consumption	
Quantity of ice cream (cones)	Total utility from ice cream (utils)	Quantity of hamburgers	Total utility from hamburgers (utils)
0	0	0	0
1	20	1	15
2	38	2	28
3	53	3	39
4	66	4	48
5	77	5	53
6	84		
7	89		
8	92		
9	94		
10	95		

Mark's income for expenditure on ice cream and hamburgers is $50 per month, the price of ice cream is $5 per cone, and the price of hamburgers is $10 per hamburger.

a. Complete the following table based on the above information.

Consumption bundle	Quantity of ice cream (cones)	Utility from ice cream (utils)	Quantity of hamburgers	Utility from hamburgers (utils)	Total utility (utils)
A	0		5		
B				48	86
C	6		2		
D		92			107
E	10		0		

b. Draw a horizontal line and label points along this line to correspond to the different combinations of ice cream and hamburgers Mark can afford given his income and the prices of the two goods. Moving from left to right along this horizontal line, the number of ice cream cones increases while the number of hamburgers decreases.

c. Graph the results from part (a) using two different graphs. In the first graph, put the quantity of ice cream cones on the horizontal axis and the quantity of hamburgers on the vertical axis. Draw Mark's budget line and label consumption bundles *A* through *E* on this budget line. On a second graph drawn just below the first graph, draw Mark's total utility function: measure Mark's total utility on the vertical axis and the quantity of ice cream and the quantity of hamburgers on the horizontal axis—you practiced drawing this horizontal axis in part (b) of this problem. Moving from left to right along the horizontal axis, the number of ice cream cones increases while the number of hamburgers decreases. Label consumption bundles *A* through *E* on Mark's total utility curve.

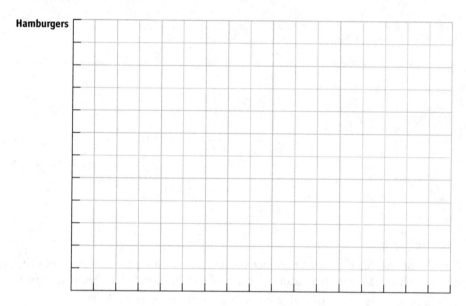

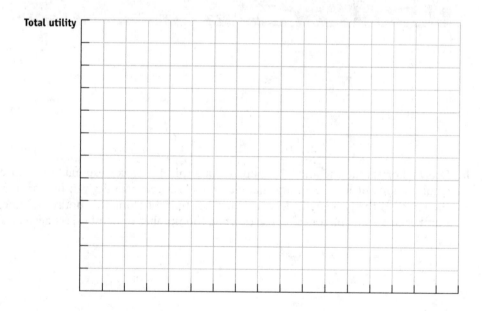

d. Given your work in part (a) and the information you graphed in part (c), which consumption bundle is the optimal consumption bundle for Mark? Why is this bundle the optimal consumption bundle?

e. In the table below, calculate Mark's marginal utility per ice cream cone (MU_{ic}), his marginal utility per dollar spent on ice cream (MU_{ic}/P_{ic}), his marginal utility per hamburger (MU_h), and his marginal utility per dollar spent on hamburgers (MU_h/P_h). Remember that the price of ice cream is \$5 per cone and the price of hamburgers is \$10.

Ice Cream				Hamburgers			
Quantity of ice cream (cones)	Utility from ice cream (utils)	MU_{ic} (utils)	MU_{ic}/P_{ic} (utils)	Quantity of hamburgers	Utility from hamburgers	MU_h (utils)	MU_h/P_h (utils)
0	0			0	0		
		20	4			15	1.5
1	20			1	15		
2	38			2	28		
3	53			3	39		
4	66			4	48		
5	77			5	53		
		7	1.4				
6	84						
7	89						
8	92						
9	94						
10	95						

f. Draw a graph of Mark's marginal utility per dollar spent on ice cream and marginal utility per dollar spent on hamburgers. This graph's horizontal axis should be labeled in the same manner as the one you drew in part (b) of this problem, while the vertical axis should measure Mark's marginal utility per dollar.

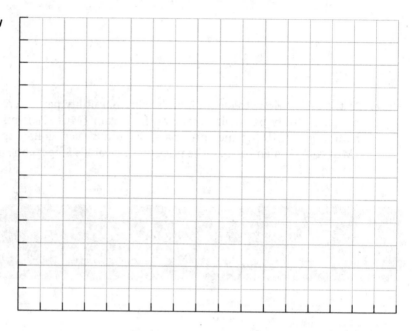

g. At the optimal consumption bundle C, what is the relationship between the marginal utility per dollar spent on ice cream and the marginal utility per dollar spent on hamburgers?

10. In problem 9, Mark's income was $50 a month, the price of ice cream was $5 per cone, and the price of hamburgers was $10.

a. Assuming that there are no changes in Mark's total utility from ice cream or hamburgers, how does an increase in the price of ice cream to $6 per cone alter Mark's consumption decisions? You do not need to provide a mathematical answer here, just a verbal explanation about the effect of this change on Mark's consumption decision.

b. Explain what the substitution effect is in the situation described in part (a) of this problem. In your explanation, indicate how Mark's consumption is affected by the substitution effect.

11. Suppose the price of utilities (electricity, gas, water and sewer services) rose this year in Bigtown. Residents of Bigtown routinely spend 15% of their overall budget on utilities. These residents report that this price increase resulted in both an income and a substitution effect.

   a. Describe the substitution effect of this price increase and how residents act to alter their consumption of utilities.

   b. Describe the income effect of this price increase.

   c. In this example, do the income and substitution effects reinforce one another? Explain your answer.

BEFORE YOU TAKE THE TEST

Chapter Review Questions

1. Rational consumers maximize
   - a. profits.
   - b. tastes.
   - c. utility.
   - d. demand.

2. An individual's utility
   - a. depends on everything that the individual consumes.
   - b. is a personal measure of the satisfaction the individual gets from their consumption of goods and services.
   - c. depends on the individual's tastes and preferences.
   - d. Answers (a), (b), and (c) are all true.

Use the following information about Joe's utility from consuming pizza to answer the next three questions.

Number of slices of pizza	Total utility
1	100 utils
2	180 utils
3	240 utils
4	280 utils
5	300 utils
6	310 utils

3. Based on the table, Joe's total utility from consuming pizza slices
    a. decreases as he consumes more and more pizza slices.
    b. increases at an increasing rate as he consumes more and more pizza slices.
    c. increases at a decreasing rate as he consumes more and more pizza slices.
    d. initially increases at an increasing rate as he consumes more pizza slices, but his total utility eventually increases at a diminishing rate.

4. Joe's marginal utility from consuming the fourth slice of pizza equals
    a. 60 utils.
    b. 40 utils.
    c. 280 utils.
    d. 20 utils.

5. Joe's utility from consuming pizza is consistent with
    a. diminishing marginal utility.
    b. constant marginal utility.
    c. increasing marginal utility.

6. Which of the following statements is true?
    I. An individual who experiences diminishing marginal utility finds that the additional satisfaction the individual gets from consuming one more unit of the good declines as the amount consumed of that good increases.
    II. Marginal utility curves that exhibit diminishing marginal utility eventually become negative.
    III. Marginal utility curves that exhibit diminishing marginal utility slope downward.
    a. Statement I is true.
    b. Statements I and II are true.
    c. Statements I and III are true.
    d. Statements I, II, and III are true.

7. Consider Mary whose weekly income for purchasing fruit and milk is $20. Each unit of fruit costs $1, while each unit of milk costs $2. Which of the following consumption bundles lies beyond Mary's budget line?
    a. 3 units of fruit and 9 units of milk
    b. 4 units of fruit and 8 units of milk
    c. 6 units of fruit and 6 units of milk
    d. 8 units of fruit and 6 units of milk

8. Consider Mary whose weekly income (I) for purchasing fruit (F) and milk (M) is $20. Each unit of fruit costs $1, while each unit of milk costs $2. The equation expressing Mary's budget line can be written as
    a. $F = 20 + 2M$
    b. $F = 10 - (1/2)M$
    c. $F = 20 - 2M$
    d. $F = 10 - M$

9. Consider Mary whose weekly income (*I*) for purchasing fruit (*F*) and milk (*M*) is $20. Each unit of fruit costs $1, while each unit of milk costs $2. Suppose Mary's available income for fruit and milk purchases increases to $40 per week while the prices of fruit and milk do not change. Mary's budget line will
   a. shift to the left when her income increases.
   b. shift to the right when her income increases.
   c. shift to the left or to the right when her income increases, depending on her tastes and preferences.
   d. be unaffected by this change in income.

10. Consider Mary whose weekly income (*I*) for purchasing fruit (*F*) and milk (*M*) is $20. Initially each unit of fruit costs $1, while each unit of milk costs $2. Suppose Mary's income for fruit and milk purchases increases to $40 per week while at the same time the price of milk and the price of fruit double relative to their initial level. Mary's budget line will
   a. shift to the left when these changes occur.
   b. shift to the right when these changes occur.
   c. be unaffected by these changes.

11. Sammy's budget constraint for food (*F*) and entertainment (*E*) each month is given by the equation $F = 100 - 10E$. Furthermore, you know that the price of entertainment is $20 per unit of entertainment. The price of food per unit is _____, and the total amount of income each month that Sammy devotes to food and entertainment equals

   _____.
   a. $2; $200   c. $200; $2,000
   b. $10; $100   d. $20; $200

12. Sammy's budget constraint for food (*F*) and entertainment (*E*) each month is given by the equation $F = 100 - 10E$. Furthermore, you know that the price of entertainment is $20 per unit of entertainment. Which of the following consumption bundles are not feasible for Sammy to consume?
   a. 50 units of food and 5 units of entertainment
   b. 60 units of food and 4.5 units of entertainment
   c. 25 units of food and 7 units of entertainment
   d. 20 units of food and 8 units of entertainment

13. Sammy's budget constraint for food (*F*) and entertainment (*E*) each month is given by the equation $F = 100 - 10E$. Furthermore, you know that the price of entertainment is $20 per unit of entertainment. Which of the following consumption bundles lie inside Sammy's budget line?
   a. 50 units of food and 5 units of entertainment
   b. 60 units of food and 4.5 units of entertainment
   c. 25 units of food and 7 units of entertainment
   d. 20 units of food and 8 units of entertainment

14. A consumption bundle that lies beyond the individual's budget line is a consumption bundle the individual
   a. does not prefer because of their particular tastes and preferences.
   b. cannot afford given their income and the prices of the goods.

15. A consumption bundle that lies inside the individual's budget line is a consumption bundle that
    a. does not maximize the individual's utility given their tastes, income, and the price of the goods.
    b. does not exhaust the individual's income.
    c. the individual can afford.
    d. Answers (a), (b), and (c) are all true.

Use the following information about Maria's consumption of food and entertainment each month to answer the next four questions. Assume Maria's monthly income for spending on food and entertainment is $400 and that each of the consumption bundles in the table below are on her budget line.

Consumption bundle	Quantity of food in consumption bundle	Total utility from food consumption (utils)	Quantity of entertainment in consumption bundle	Total utility from entertainment consumption (utils)
A	200	280	0	0
B	150	240	25	80
C	100	180	50	110
D	50	100	75	130
E	0	0	100	140

16. Given the above information, the price of each unit of food is _____, and the price of each unit of entertainment is _____.
    a. $2; $4   c. $2; $1
    b. $4; $2   d. $4; $1

17. Maria maximizes her utility by consuming consumption bundle
    a. A.   c. C.
    b. B.   d. D.

18. Suppose Maria initially chooses consumption bundle A. She can increase her total utility
    a. consuming more units of entertainment and fewer units of food.
    b. consuming more units of food and fewer units of entertainment.

19. Suppose Maria initially chooses consumption bundle C. She can increase her total utility by
    a. consuming more units of entertainment and fewer units of food.
    b. consuming more units of food and fewer units of entertainment.

20. The marginal decision for the consumer is a question of how
    a. much of a good they consume relative to their neighbor's consumption of that good.
    b. to allocate an additional dollar in a way to maximize utility.
    c. to allocate the entirety of one's income.

21. Jamie currently consumes 4 units of tomatoes and 7 units of bread each week. The price of tomatoes is $2 per unit while the price of bread is $1 per unit. Jamie's marginal utility from the last unit of tomatoes he consumes each week is equal to 10 utils while his marginal utility from the last unit of bread he consumes each week is 6 utils. Jamie should
   a. continue to consume the same level of tomatoes and bread each week.
   b. consume more bread and less tomatoes, since currently his marginal utility per dollar spent on bread exceeds his marginal utility per dollar spent on tomatoes.
   c. consume less bread and more tomatoes, since currently his marginal utility per dollar spent on bread exceeds his marginal utility per dollar spent on tomatoes.
   d. consume more bread and less tomatoes, since currently his marginal utility per dollar spent on bread is less than his marginal utility per dollar spent on tomatoes.

22. Martin always maximizes his utility. Martin's consumption of both potatoes and steak exhibit diminishing marginal utility. Suppose the price of steak and the price of potatoes are constant and Martin's income to be spent on steak and potatoes does not change. Holding everything else constant, if Martin increases his consumption of steak
   a. he must decrease his consumption of potatoes and his marginal utility per dollar spent on steak must be less than it was initially.
   b. he will increase his consumption of potatoes and his marginal utility per dollar spent on steak will be less than it was initially.

23. Which of the following statements best expresses the optimal consumption rule given a consumer's budget constraint?
   a. A consumer should consume the maximum amount possible of the relatively cheapest good available to them.
   b. A consumer should divide their income evenly among all the possible goods they consume.
   c. A consumer will maximize their utility when they specialize.
   d. A consumer will maximize their utility when the marginal utilities of the last dollar spent on each and every good or service in their consumption bundle are equal.

24. An increase in the price of good X while holding income and the price of good Y constant will
   a. reduce the marginal utility the individual receives from the last unit of good X they consume.
   b. increase the marginal utility per dollar spent on good Y.
   c. decrease the marginal utility per dollar spent on good X.
   d. reduce the individual's tastes and preferences for good X.

25. An increase in the price of good X while holding income and the price of good Y constant will
   a. have a positive substitution effect, leading the consumer to increase their consumption of good X because of the increase in the marginal utility per dollar spent on good X.
   b. have a negative substitution effect, leading the consumer to decrease their consumption of good X because of the decrease in the marginal utility per dollar spent on good X.
   c. cause the consumer to substitute away from good Y toward good X.
   d. cause the consumer to purchase more units of good X due to the income effect.

26. The substitution effect measures
    a. the effect of a price change on the quantity of the good consumed.
    b. the change in the consumer's purchasing power when the price of the good changes.
    c. the degree to which good Y can be replaced by good X.
    d. the total utility an individual gets from consuming a particular consumption bundle.

27. When the price of a good increases and expenditures on that good represent a substantial amount of the individual's income, then the income effect makes that individual poorer since the price increase effectively
    a. reduces that individual's purchasing power.
    b. increases that individual's purchasing power.

28. Consider a normal good whose consumption comprises a substantial share of the individual's income. A decrease in the price of this good will result in
    a. both the income and substitution effects increasing the quantity demanded of this good.
    b. the income effect increasing the quantity demanded of this good while the substitution effect decreases the quantity demanded.
    c. the substitution effect increasing the quantity demanded of this good while the income effect decreases the quantity demanded.
    d. both the income and substitution effects decreasing the quantity demanded of this good.

29. Suppose good Z is an inferior good. If the price of good Z changes, the income and substitution effects will
    a. reinforce one another.
    b. work in opposite directions.

ANSWER KEY

Answers to Problems and Exercises

1. **a.** Maria, Ben, and Steve have constant marginal utility with respect to the given levels of hot chocolate. Maria's total utility increases by 80 utils with every additional serving of hot chocolate she consumes; Ben's total utility increases by 50 utils with every additional serving of hot chocolate he consumes; and Steve's total utility increases by 20 utils with every additional serving of hot chocolate he consumes.

    b. Joe's marginal utility decreases with each additional serving of hot chocolate: each additional serving adds less to his total utility than the previous serving.

2. **a.**

Servings of hot chocolate per month	Joe's marginal utility (utils)	Maria's marginal utility (utils)	Ben's marginal utility (utils)	Alexandra's marginal utility (utils)	Steve's marginal utility (utils)
1					
	80	80	50	50	20
2					
	60	80	50	60	20
3					
	40	80	50	70	20
4					
	20	80	50	80	20
5					

b.

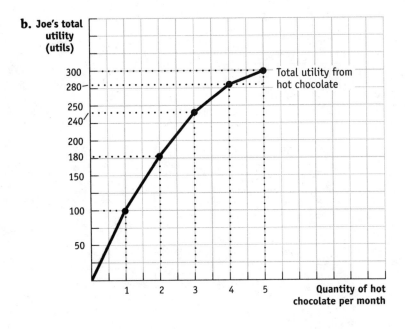

Joe's total utility (utils) — Total utility from hot chocolate — Quantity of hot chocolate per month

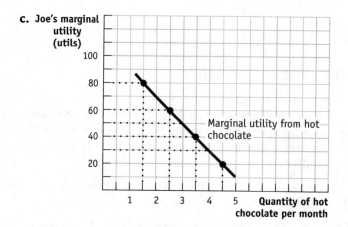

c. Joe's marginal utility (utils)

Quantity of hot chocolate per month

3. Sarah's total utility decreases when she increases her consumption of pizza from three slices to four slices: Sarah is worse off when she consumes four slices of pizza and she should therefore not consume the fourth slice. The marginal utility from consuming the fourth slice of pizza is equal to −20 utils.

4. The marginal utility curve is downward sloping because consumption of each additional unit of the good eventually adds less to total utility than did the consumption of the previous unit of the good. The consumption of most goods and services is subject to diminishing marginal utility.

5. a.

Number of articles read	Marginal utility from reading articles (utils)
1	
	200
2	
	150
3	
	100
4	
	75
5	
	55
6	
	40
7	
	20
8	

b. Carolyn experiences diminishing marginal utility when she reads the third article; although her total utility is increasing, it is now increasing at a diminishing rate.

c. Carolyn is reading too many articles if her reading results in less total utility than she would have if she read fewer articles. According to the data given for this question, it is not possible for Carolyn to reach this point when reading up to eight articles.

6.   a.

Consumption bundle	Number of periodicals	Units of entertainment
A	0	10
B	4	8
C	8	6
D	16	2
E	20	0

b.

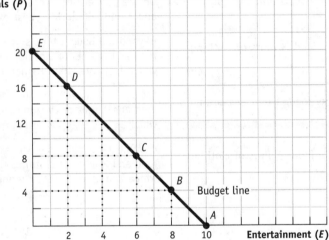

c. Harry will consume 2 fewer units of entertainment (6 units instead of 8 units) and 4 more periodicals (8 periodicals instead of 4 periodicals) when he moves from consumption bundle B to consumption bundle C. Harry cannot increase his consumption of periodicals without decreasing his consumption of entertainment.

d. Harry will consume 4 more units of entertainment (6 units instead of 2 units) and 8 fewer periodicals (8 periodicals instead of 16 periodicals) when he moves from consumption bundle D to consumption bundle C. Harry cannot increase his consumption of entertainment without decreasing his consumption of periodicals.

e. $P = 20 - 2E$

7.   a.

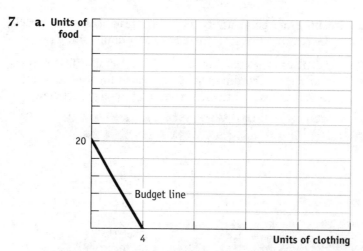

Units of food

20

Budget line

4   Units of clothing

b.

Consumption bundle	On, inside, or beyond the budget line
5 units of food, 3 units of clothing	On the budget line, since 5 units of food and 3 units of clothing cost exactly $40.
4 units of food, 4 units of clothing	Beyond the budget line, since 4 units of food and 4 units of clothing cost $48, which is greater than Katherine's income.
10 units of food, 1 unit of clothing	Inside the budget line, since 10 units of food and 1 unit of clothing cost $30, which is less than Katherine's income.
20 units of food, 2 units of clothing	Beyond the budget line, since 20 units of food and 2 units of clothing cost $60, which is greater than Katherine's income.

c. $F = 20 - 5C$

d.

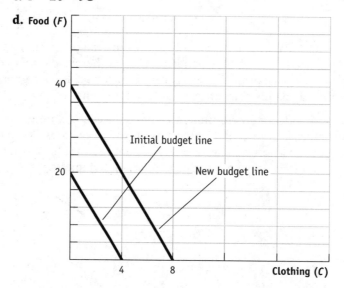

Food (F)

40

Initial budget line

20

New budget line

4   8   Clothing (C)

When income increases while prices stay constant, the budget line shifts out parallel to the initial budget line. The equation for the new budget line is $F = 40 - 5C$. The new budget line has a different y-intercept, but the same slope as the initial budget line.

e.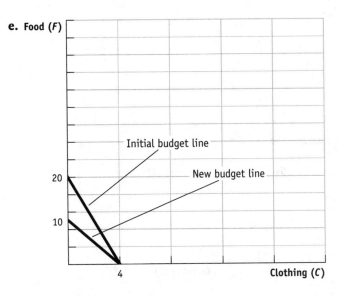

When food gets more expensive, Katherine finds that she cannot afford as much food. Her budget line pivots down along the y-axis, reflecting that if she devotes all of her income to food she can now afford only 10 units instead of the original 20 units. Katherine's new budget line is $F = 10 - (5/2)C$. The change in the price of food alters the y-intercept and the slope of the budget line relative to the initial budget line.

f.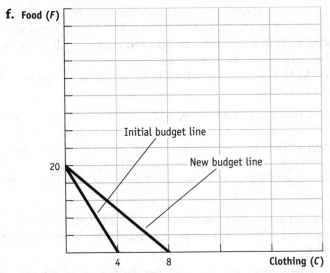

When the price of clothing decreases, Katherine finds that she can afford more of both goods. Her budget line pivots out along the x-axis. Her new budget line is $F = 20 - (5/2)C$. The change in the price of clothing alters the budget line's slope relative to the initial budget line.

g.
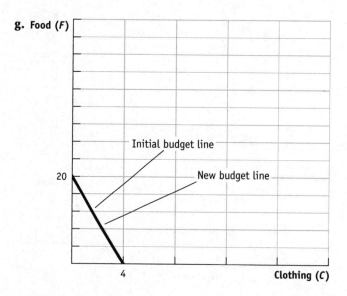

When Katherine's income and the prices of both goods double, this has no effect on her budget line. Her initial budget line can be found as $40 = 2F + 10C$, or $F = 20 - 5C$; her new budget line is equal to $80 = 4F + 20C$, or $F = 20 - 5C$.

8. **a.** With consumption bundle B, Bertram's marginal utility per dollar spent on good X is greater than his marginal utility per dollar spent on good Y ($MU_X/P_X > MU_Y/P_Y$). This cannot be Bertram's optimal consumption bundle since these ratios are not equal to one another: Bertram will want to increase his consumption of good X and decrease his consumption of good Y. This adjustment to his consumption will decrease the value of MU_X/P_X (as the marginal utility from an additional unit of good X falls) and increase the value of MU_Y/P_Y (as the marginal utility from good Y increases when fewer units of good Y are consumed).

   b. A decrease in the consumption of good X increases MU_X/P_X due to diminishing marginal utility, which holds that the marginal utility from the consumption of the good decreases as consumption of the good increases; an increase in the consumption of good Y decreases MU_Y/P_Y due to diminishing marginal utility, since the marginal utility from the consumption of additional units of good Y decreases with each additional unit of good Y consumed.

   c. Consumption bundle C is the optimal consumption bundle for Bertram since at that bundle the marginal utility per dollar spent on good X is equal to the marginal utility per dollar spent on good Y.

9. **a.**

Consumption bundle	Quantity of ice cream (cones)	Utility from ice cream (utils)	Quantity of hamburgers	Utility from hamburgers (utils)	Total utility (utils)
A	0	0	5	53	53
B	2	38	4	48	86
C	6	84	2	28	112
D	8	92	1	15	107
E	10	95	0	0	95

b.

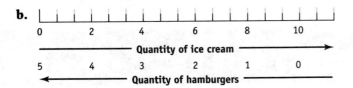

c.

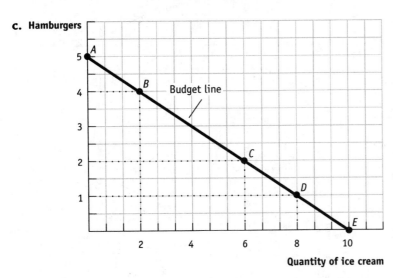

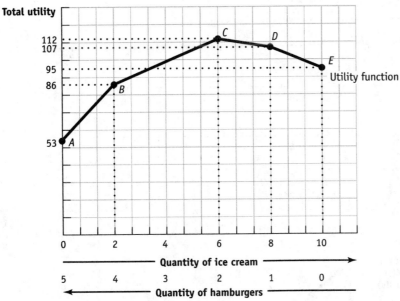

d. Consumption bundle *C* is the consumption bundle that maximizes Mark's utility given his tastes and preferences, his income, and the prices of the two goods.

e.

Quantity of ice cream (cones)	Utility from ice cream (utils)	MU_{ic} (utils)	MU_{ic}/P_{ic} (utils)	Quantity of hamburgers	Utility from hamburgers	MU_h (utils)	MU_h/P_h (utils)
0	0			0	0		
		20	4			15	1.5
1	20			1	15		
		18	3.6			13	1.3
2	38			2	28		
		15	3			11	1.1
3	53			3	39		
		13	2.6			9	0.9
4	66			4	48		
		11	2.2			5	0.5
5	77			5	53		
		7	1.4				
6	84						
		5	1.0				
7	89						
		3	0.6				
8	92						
		2	0.4				
9	94						
		1	0.2				
10	95						

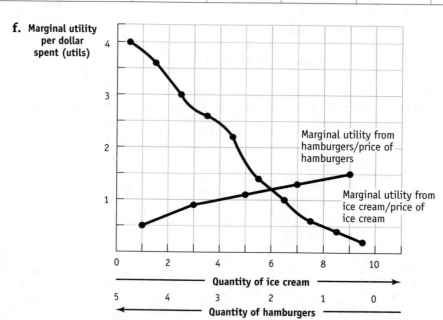

f. Marginal utility per dollar spent (utils)

Marginal utility from hamburgers/price of hamburgers

Marginal utility from ice cream/price of ice cream

Quantity of ice cream →

← Quantity of hamburgers

    g. The optimal consumption rule states that a consumer maximizes utility in the face of a budget constraint when the marginal utility per dollar spent on each good or service in the consumption bundle is the same. Hence, the marginal utility of ice cream divided by its price (MU_{ic}/P_{ic}) equals the marginal utility of hamburgers divided by its price (MU_h/P_h) at the optimal consumption bundle (bundle C in this example).

10. a. When the price of ice cream rises, the marginal utility per dollar spent on ice cream decreases at every quantity of ice cream since the marginal utility per dollar spent on ice cream equals MU_{ic}/P_{ic} and P_{ic} is now a larger number. Mark will still want to equate the marginal utility per dollar spent on every good or service in his consumption bundle: he will purchase less ice cream, and more hamburgers. As Mark purchases fewer units of ice cream, his marginal utility from ice cream will increase.

    b. The substitution effect refers to the effect of a change in price on the quantity of a good or service consumed by the individual. In this example, the price of ice cream increases, which leads Mark to substitute away from the relatively more expensive ice cream toward some other goods and services (in this case, hamburgers) that are now relatively less expensive. Mark will consume less ice cream and more hamburgers when the price of ice cream increases, holding everything else constant.

11. a. When the price of one good rises relative to the prices of other goods, consumers will substitute away from the relatively more expensive good: in this case consumers will consume fewer utility services. They can do this by replacing appliances with more efficient models, by using fewer lights, by taking shorter showers, and by making other energy-saving choices.

    b. When the price of a good increases and that good makes up a substantial part of the consumer's budget, then this price increase results in a reduction in the consumer's purchasing power. As the consumer's ability to command goods and services decreases due to their loss of purchasing power, the consumer will choose to consume less of the good, assuming it is a normal good.

    c. In this case, the substitution effect that results in a change in the relative price of utilities leads consumers to decrease the quantity of utilities they demand, as does the income effect. The two effects reinforce each other, since both effects cause consumers to reduce the quantity they demand.

Answers to Chapter Review Questions

1.   **Answer c.** This is a definitional statement. Demand and tastes cannot be maximized, and profit maximization is a goal of a firm.

2.   **Answer d.** A person's utility depends on the utility they get from each good that they consume. This utility is a measure of the satisfaction that the individual gets from their consumption choices. An individual's consumption choices are dependent on their tastes and preferences.

3.   **Answer c.** From the table, we can see that Joe's total utility increases as he consumes more and more slices of pizza. However, Joe's total utility increases by smaller amounts with each additional slice of pizza. Joe's total utility, although increasing, increases at a decreasing rate as his level of pizza consumption increases.

4.   **Answer b.** Joe's marginal utility from consuming the fourth slice of pizza is equal to his total utility from consuming four slices of pizza minus his total utility from consuming three slices of pizza. Thus, Joe's marginal utility from the fourth slice of pizza equals 280 utils minus 240 utils, or 40 utils.

5.   **Answer a.** Diminishing marginal utility refers to the idea that consumption of additional units of a good increases the consumer's total utility, but at a decreasing rate. Joe's utility from pizza consumption increases with each slice he eats, but each additional slice of pizza adds less to his total utility than the previous slice.

6. **Answer c.** Statement I is a restatement of the concept of diminishing marginal utility. A marginal utility curve that exhibits diminishing marginal utility will be downward sloping over some range of consumption, but marginal utility need not be a negative value, so statement II is false and statement III is true.

7. **Answer a.** Any consumption bundle that costs more than Mary's income will lie beyond her budget line. Because 3 units of fruit and 9 units of milk cost $21, this bundle is greater than Mary's income; and she cannot afford this bundle. Mary can afford the other consumption bundles and they are therefore either on Mary's budget line or they lie inside her budget line.

8. **Answer c.** To find Mary's equation for her budget line, recall that a budget line can be written as $I = $ (price of good X)(quantity of good X) + (price of good Y)(quantity of good Y). In this case we have $20 = (\$1)(F) + (\$2)(M)$, or $F = 20 - 2M$.

9. **Answer b.** Using the method outlined in answer 8, we can rewrite Mary's budget line as $F = 40 - 2M$ when her income increases to $40. Comparing this budget line to her original budget line, we see that the new budget line has shifted to the right. This new budget line is parallel to the original budget line but is farther from the origin.

10. **Answer c.** When Mary's income doubles and the prices of the two goods double, her budget line is unaffected. To see this, recall that we can write her budget line as $I = $ (price of good X)(quantity of good X) + (price of good Y)(quantity of good Y), or in this case, $40 = (\$2)(F) + (\$4)(M)$, which is equivalent to $F = 20 - 2M$.

11. **Answer a.** When Sammy devotes all of his income to purchases of entertainment, he can consume 10 units of entertainment, which implies that Sammy's income is $200. When Sammy devotes all of his income to purchases of food, he can purchase 100 units, which implies that the price of food must be $2 per unit of food since Sammy has an income of $200.

12. **Answer b.** A consumption bundle for Sammy is not feasible if it costs more than his available income. From question 11 we know that Sammy's income is $200, the price of entertainment is $20, and the price of food is $2. Sixty units of food and 4.5 units of entertainment would cost Sammy $210, and he cannot afford this consumption bundle.

13. **Answer c.** A consumption bundle lies inside the budget line if the cost of the consumption bundle is less than the individual's income. From question 11 we know that Sammy's income is $200, the price of entertainment is $20, and the price of food is $2. Twenty-five units of food and 7 units of entertainment would cost Sammy $190, so he can afford this consumption bundle and still have unused income.

14. **Answer b.** A consumption bundle that lies beyond the individual's budget line may be a consumption bundle that the individual would really like to consume (such as an exotic vacation in a warm place). However, if the individual cannot consume this bundle given their income and the prices of the goods, they simply cannot afford that consumption bundle.

15. **Answer d.** A consumption bundle that lies inside the individual's budget line cannot be maximizing this individual's utility since it is possible for the individual to consume more of either good given their income and the prices they face. This interior point does not use all of the individual's income, so therefore it is affordable.

16. **Answer a.** The price of food is $2 per unit. To see this, when Maria consumes only food she can afford 200 units. Since her income is $400, this implies that the price of food must be $2 per unit. The price of entertainment is $4. To see this, when Maria consumes only entertainment she can afford 100 units. Since her income is $400, this implies that the price of entertainment must be $4 per unit.

17. **Answer b.** To answer this question, you need to calculate the total utility Maria receives from consuming each of the consumption bundles. Bundle A yields total utility of 280 utils; bundle B has total utility of 320 utils; bundle C has total utility of 290 utils; bundle D has total utility of 230 utils; and bundle E has total utility of 140 utils. Bundle B maximizes Maria's utility since it provides the highest level of total utility.

18. **Answer a.** When Maria moves to consumption bundle B from consumption bundle A, her total utility increases. At consumption bundle B Maria consumes more units of entertainment and fewer units of food.

19. **Answer b.** Maria can increase her utility by consuming fewer units of entertainment and more units of food. Increasing her food consumption by 50 units increases her total utility by 60 utils, while decreasing her entertainment consumption by 25 units reduces her total utility by 30 utils, leading her to a net gain in utility of 30 utils.

20. **Answer b.** Consumers decide how to best allocate their income among different goods given the prices of these goods and their individual tastes and preferences. The marginal decision for consumers is essentially a decision about how to best allocate the last dollar spent. If the marginal utility per dollar spent on one good is greater than the marginal utility per dollar spent on another good, then the consumer is best off increasing their consumption of the first good and decreasing their consumption of the second good. This analysis results in the consumer allocating their last dollar in such a way that the marginal utility per dollar spent on every good in their consumption bundle is equal.

21. **Answer b.** Jamie's marginal utility per dollar spent on bread is equal to 6 utils per dollar (6 utils/$1), and his marginal utility per dollar spent on tomatoes is equal to 5 utils per dollar (10 utils/$2). Jamie is better off consuming more bread and fewer tomatoes. As Jamie increases his bread consumption, the marginal utility from the last unit of bread consumed will fall, and as he consumes fewer tomatoes, the marginal utility from the last unit of tomatoes consumed will rise. He will adjust his consumption of these two goods until the marginal utility per dollar spent on either good is equivalent.

22. **Answer a.** Martin's consumption choices are constrained by his income and the prices of the two goods. When Martin decides to consume more steak, he must decrease his potato consumption since he will have less income available for purchasing potatoes. When Martin increases his consumption of steak, this reduces his marginal utility from steak (due to the diminishing marginal utility he gets from consuming greater amounts of steak).

23. **Answer d.** This answer is definitional. The individual does not want to consume the maximum amount of the cheapest good available for many reasons, but a primary reason is that this would not offer the individual any variety in their consumption bundle. The individual does not want to divide their income evenly among the goods available: for instance, the individual does not want to spend the same amount on table salt as they do on housing. Consumer maximization focuses on consumption decisions and not production decisions. Specialization is essentially a production decision.

24. **Answer c.** A change in the price of a good does not affect the individual's marginal utility he receives from the good, but the change in the price of the good does affect the marginal utility per dollar the individual receives. If the price of the good increases, this causes the marginal utility per dollar to decrease, since the denominator of MU/P is now bigger while the numerator is unchanged.

25. **Answer b.** When the price of good X rises, this reduces the marginal utility per dollar spent on good X (see the answer to question 24). The consumer maximizes their utility when the marginal utility per dollar spent is the same for all goods in the consumption bundle. Hence, the individual will want to spend less on good X in order to raise the marginal utility per dollar spent on good X. When the individual purchases fewer units of

good X, this increases the marginal utility the individual receives from the last unit of good X consumed, and this reduction in the consumption of good X due to the increase in the price of good X is the substitution effect.

26. **Answer a.** Answer (b) refers to the income effect. Answer (c) is a reference to the substitutability of one good for another good, but it does not explicitly mention a price change, which is the event that drives the substitution effect. Answer (d) has no direct relationship to the substitution effect. Answer (a) is the definition of the substitution effect.

27. **Answer a.** When the price of a good increases and the good makes up a substantial portion of the individual's budget, then the individual finds that they have less purchasing power. Answer (b) is a nonsense answer: an increase in the price of a good cannot raise the individual's purchasing power; it must reduce the individual's purchasing power.

28. **Answer a.** When the price of the good decreases, the individual purchases more of this now relatively cheaper good and fewer units of the other relatively more expensive good: this substitution effect leads the individual to purchase more units of this good. In addition, if the expenditure on the good is a substantial portion of the individual's budget, then the individual's purchasing power increases when the price of this good falls: this income effect leads the individual to purchase more units of the good.

29. **Answer b.** If the price of good Z increases, the consumer will substitute away from the relatively more expensive good Z toward some other relatively less expensive good: the substitution effect will be negative. But if the price of good Z increases, this reduces the individual's purchasing power, and the individual will also see a change in their consumption of good Z due to this change in purchasing power. When the individual's purchasing power falls, the individual will consume more units of good Z since good Z is an inferior good: the income effect is positive. Thus, the income and substitution effects for an inferior good work in opposite directions.

chapter 11

Consumer Preferences and Consumer Choice

◼ BEFORE YOU READ THE CHAPTER

Summary

This chapter develops the concept of indifference curves and then uses these indifference curves to illustrate a person's preferences. The chapter explores the marginal rate of substitution, which is the rate at which a person is willing to substitute one good for another. The chapter also discusses the use of a person's indifference curves and their budget line to identify that person's optimal consumption bundle. The chapter also discusses how the shape of the indifference curve can indicate whether goods are substitutes or complements. Finally, the chapter explores the income and substitution effects using indifference curve analysis.

Chapter Objectives

Objective #1. An indifference curve is a line that shows all the consumption bundles that provide the individual with the same amount of satisfaction or utility. Indifference curves illustrate the individual's preferences and are unique to each individual. For a given indifference curve, the level of satisfaction is the same at any point on the curve: the individual is indifferent between any two bundles that lie on this curve. An indifference curve map illustrates different levels of utility for the individual: each indifference curve in this map indicates the consumption bundles that yield a constant amount of utility no matter which bundle is consumed on the indifference curve. All indifference curve maps have two general properties:

- Indifference curves never cross. Since each indifference curve represents a constant, but different, level of utility, it is impossible for two of these curves to cross, since their point of intersection would represent two different levels of satisfaction.

- Indifference curves that lie farther away from the origin represent higher levels of utility than do indifference curves that lie closer to the origin. This property reflects the assumption that more is better than less: the indifference curve analysis considers only bundles with which the consumer is not satiated.

Additionally, indifference curve maps for most goods also have two additional properties:

- Indifference curves slope downward. Given a constant level of satisfaction, an individual who consumes more of one good must decrease consumption of the other good to maintain this constant level of satisfaction.

- Indifference curves have a convex shape. They are usually bowed toward the origin due to diminishing marginal utility. That is, consumption of an additional unit of a good yields a smaller increase in total utility than the previous unit consumed; this implies that the individual must give up a smaller amount of one good to consume more of the other good while maintaining the same level of utility. Figure 11.1 illustrates this idea.

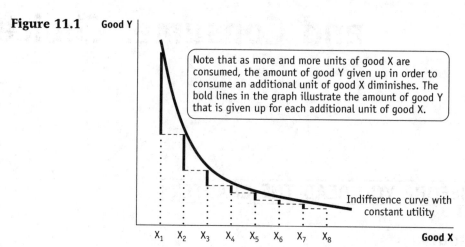

Figure 11.1   Good Y

Note that as more and more units of good X are consumed, the amount of good Y given up in order to consume an additional unit of good X diminishes. The bold lines in the graph illustrate the amount of good Y that is given up for each additional unit of good X.

Indifference curve with constant utility

X_1 X_2 X_3 X_4 X_5 X_6 X_7 X_8 Good X

Objective #2.   Consumers maximize their utility by consuming the consumption bundle that maximizes their utility given their income and the prices of the two goods. This optimal consumption point is where the marginal utility per dollar is the same for every good in the bundle.

Objective #3.   As the individual moves down along his indifference curve, the marginal utility he receives from consuming more of good X decreases as he consumes more and more units of good X. To maintain the same level of utility, he must therefore give up fewer and fewer units of good Y as he increases his consumption of good X. (Refer back to the illustration of this idea in Figure 11.1.) This concept is expressed by the marginal rate of substitution of the good on the horizontal axis in place of the good on the vertical axis. The marginal rate of substitution of good X for good Y is the slope of the individual's indifference curve: as you move downward along the indifference curve, the marginal rate of substitution of good X for good Y decreases in absolute value, reflecting the principle of diminishing marginal utility. Diminishing marginal rate of substitution says that an individual who is consuming a lot of good Y and a little of good X is willing to give up a lot of good Y to get one more unit of good X, whereas an individual who is already consuming a lot of good X and not very much good Y is willing to give up a little bit of good Y to get one more unit of good X. The diminishing marginal rate of substitution results in the convex shape of indifference curves for ordinary goods.

Objective #4.   The individual maximizes his utility by choosing the consumption bundle that is just tangent to his budget line. This bundle represents the consumption bundle that yields the greatest amount of utility for the individual given his level of income and the prices of the two goods. Any other bundle necessarily lies on a lower indifference curve that represents a lower level of utility for the individual. This tangency condition states that a utility-maximizing individual chooses the consumption bundle for which the slope of the indifference curve is equal to the slope of the budget line. Figure 11.2 illustrates the optimal consumption bundle for an individual.

Figure 11.2

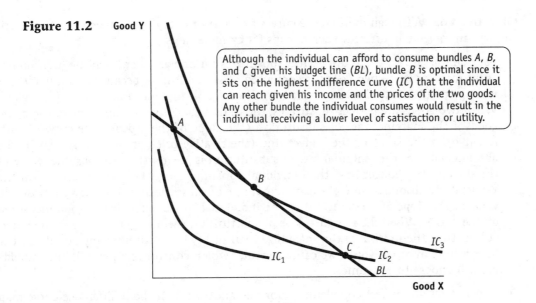

Although the individual can afford to consume bundles A, B, and C given his budget line (BL), bundle B is optimal since it sits on the highest indifference curve (IC) that the individual can reach given his income and the prices of the two goods. Any other bundle the individual consumes would result in the individual receiving a lower level of satisfaction or utility.

The slope of the budget line is equal to the negative of the price of the good measured on the x-axis divided by price of the good measured on the y-axis, and the slope of the indifference curve is equal to the negative of the marginal utility of the good measured on the x-axis divided by the marginal utility of the good measured on the y-axis. Thus, at the optimal consumption bundle, $(-P_X/P_Y) = (-MU_X/MU_Y)$. Intuitively, this equality states that at the optimal consumption bundle the rate at which the individual trades the good on the x-axis for the good on the y-axis is equal to the rate at which good X is traded for good Y in the market, or in other words, the price ratio (P_X/P_Y). This can be restated as the optimal consumption rule, or the relative price rule: at the optimal consumption bundle, $MU_X/P_X = MU_Y/P_Y$, or that the marginal utility per dollar is the same for every good in the bundle at the point that maximizes the individual's utility.

Objective #5. Since preferences differ among individuals, each individual's indifference curve map for any two goods is unique to them. For the same two goods, individuals with the same income choose different optimal consumption bundles based on their distinct preferences. Figure 11.3 illustrates two individuals with the same budget line but different preferences, and the optimal consumption bundles that they choose.

Figure 11.3

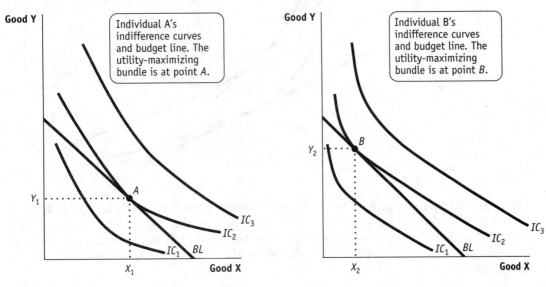

Individual A's indifference curves and budget line. The utility-maximizing bundle is at point A.

Individual B's indifference curves and budget line. The utility-maximizing bundle is at point B.

Objective #6. Although indifference curves for most ordinary goods are convex to the origin, we can imagine indifference curve maps for extreme cases.

- For example, if two goods are perfect substitutes for one another, then the indifference curve map for these two goods is composed of straight lines, because the individual is willing to substitute the same amount of one good for one unit of the other good. When two goods are perfect substitutes, the individual consumes only one of these two goods if the marginal rate of substitution (the slope of the indifference curve) is different from the slope of the budget line (the relative price of the two goods). If the absolute value of the marginal rate of substitution is greater than the absolute value of the slope of the budget line, the individual consumes only the good measured on the x-axis; if the absolute value of the marginal rate of substitution is less than the absolute value of the slope of the budget line, the individual consumes only the good measured on the y-axis. When the marginal rate of substitution is equal to the slope of the budget line, then the individual can maximize their utility by consuming any bundle on the budget line: in other words, we cannot predict which consumption bundle the individual will choose to consume.

- If two goods are perfect complements for one another, then the indifference curve map for these two goods takes the form of right angles. When two goods are perfect complements, the individual always consumes the two goods in the same proportion regardless of price: that is, the slope of the budget line has no effect on the individual's relative consumption of the two goods.

Objective #7. When the price of one of the goods changes while income and the price of the other good are unchanged, the slope of the budget line changes and the individual responds to this change by choosing a different consumption bundle that maximizes the consumer's utility given the new price ratio. Figure 11.4 illustrates two consumer utility-maximizing points: point A is the point that maximizes the consumer's utility when the price of good X is P_1 and the price of good Y is P_2, whereas point B is the point that maximizes the consumer's utility when the price of good X is P_1 but the price of good Y has increased to P_3.

Figure 11.4

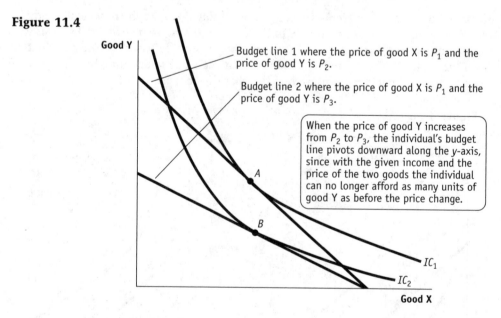

Budget line 1 where the price of good X is P_1 and the price of good Y is P_2.

Budget line 2 where the price of good X is P_1 and the price of good Y is P_3.

When the price of good Y increases from P_2 to P_3, the individual's budget line pivots downward along the y-axis, since with the given income and the price of the two goods the individual can no longer afford as many units of good Y as before the price change.

Figure 11.4 illustrates a general principle about budget lines: for a given level of income, a change in the price of one of the goods causes the slope of the budget line to change: if the price of the good measured on the y-axis changes, the budget line pivots around the intercept of the x-axis; if the price of the good measured on the x-axis changes, the budget line pivots around the intercept of the y-axis.

Objective #8.   A change in the individual's income while the prices of the two goods hold constant causes the budget line to shift in a parallel fashion. If income increases, the budget line shifts out from the origin; if income decreases, the budget line shifts toward the origin. When income decreases, the two goods are normal goods if the consumption levels for both goods decrease. When income decreases, if one of the goods is an inferior good, the consumption level for that good increases as income decreases. Figure 11.5 illustrates a decrease in income when both good X and good Y are normal goods, and Figure 11.6 illustrates a decrease in income when good X is normal and good Y is inferior.

Figure 11.5

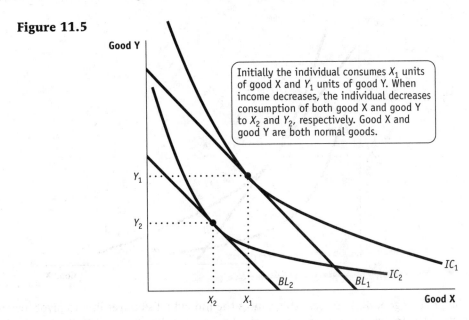

Initially the individual consumes X_1 units of good X and Y_1 units of good Y. When income decreases, the individual decreases consumption of both good X and good Y to X_2 and Y_2, respectively. Good X and good Y are both normal goods.

Figure 11.6

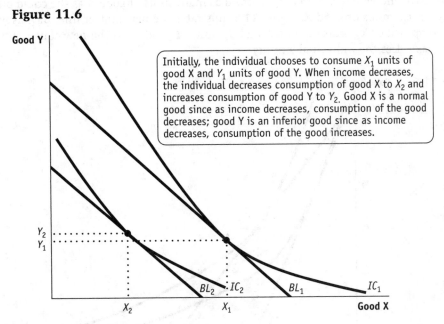

Initially, the individual chooses to consume X_1 units of good X and Y_1 units of good Y. When income decreases, the individual decreases consumption of good X to X_2 and increases consumption of good Y to Y_2. Good X is a normal good since as income decreases, consumption of the good decreases; good Y is an inferior good since as income decreases, consumption of the good increases.

Objective #9.   Indifference curve analysis can be used to depict the income and substitution effects. When the price of the good increases, this causes both an income and a substitution effect: the price increase reduces the purchasing power of the individual's real income (the individual is now poorer due to this income effect), and this fall in real income reduces the quantity of the good the individual demands if the good is a normal good; and the increase in the price of the good changes the relative price of the two goods (that is, the opportunity cost of consuming the good) and causes the individual to substitute away from the relatively more expensive good toward the relatively cheaper good. Let's consider a step-by-step approach to finding the income and substitution effect. Figure 11.7 portrays the initial situation in which the individual has selected the consumption bundle at point A as the consumption bundle (composed of X_1 units of good X and Y_1 units of good Y) that maximizes her utility given her income and the prices of the two goods. We know that the absolute value of the slope of the budget line (BL_1) is equal to P_X/P_Y and that this price ratio is also equal to the absolute value of the indifference curve (MU_X/MU_Y) at the point that maximizes the individual's utility.

Figure 11.7

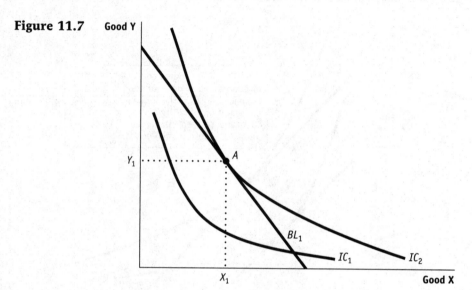

Suppose the price of good X increases. This causes the individual's budget line to pivot toward the origin since the individual can no longer afford as many units of good X as she could prior to the change in the price of good X. Figure 11.8 illustrates the new budget line, BL_2, as well as point B (composed of X_2 units of good X and Y_2 units of good Y) as the new consumption bundle that maximizes the individual's utility.

Figure 11.8

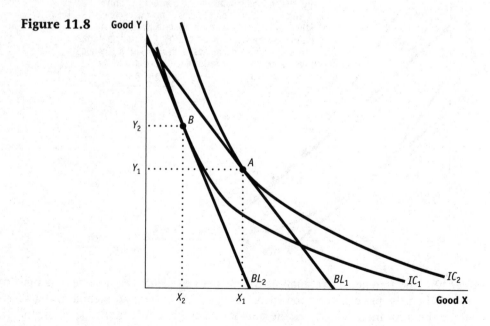

Going from point A to point B the individual changes her consumption of good X from X_1 units to X_2 units: part of this change reflects the income effect and part of it reflects the substitution effect. To break this total change in the consumption of good X into these separate two effects requires the construction of a hypothetical third budget line, BL_3. The third budget line enables this individual to have the same level of utility as she had initially (the level on IC_2) while facing the new relative prices of good X and good Y. Therefore BL_3 needs to be tangent to IC_2 but have the same slope as BL_2. Figure 11.9 illustrates this hypothetical budget line and also identifies the consumption bundle C (composed of X_3 units of good X and Y_3 units of good Y) that would maximize this individual's utility if she faced budget line BL_3. The substitution effect is measured as the change in the consumption of good X as the consumer moves from point A to point C and adjusts to the change in the relative price of the two goods. The income effect is measured as the change in the consumption of good X as the consumer moves from point C to point B and adjusts to the change in purchasing power or real income due to the change in the price of good X (notice that BL_3 and BL_2 are parallel to each other since the price ratio is unchanged but the level of real income has decreased). In Figure 11.9 we can see that both good X and good Y are normal goods, since as income decreases (going from BL_3 to BL_2), the consumption of both good X and good Y decreases.

Figure 11.9

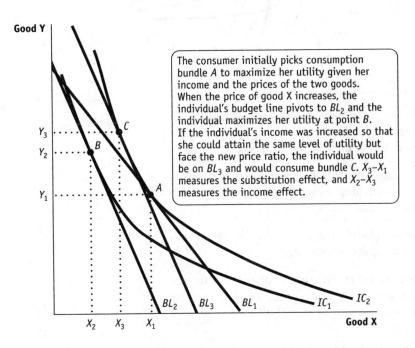

The consumer initially picks consumption bundle A to maximize her utility given her income and the prices of the two goods. When the price of good X increases, the individual's budget line pivots to BL_2 and the individual maximizes her utility at point B. If the individual's income was increased so that she could attain the same level of utility but face the new price ratio, the individual would be on BL_3 and would consume bundle C. $X_3 - X_1$ measures the substitution effect, and $X_2 - X_3$ measures the income effect.

If good X had been an inferior good, then the substitution effect would be unchanged, but the income effect would have moved in the opposite direction of the substitution effect. Figure 11.10 illustrates the income and substitution effects when good X is an inferior good.

Figure 11.10

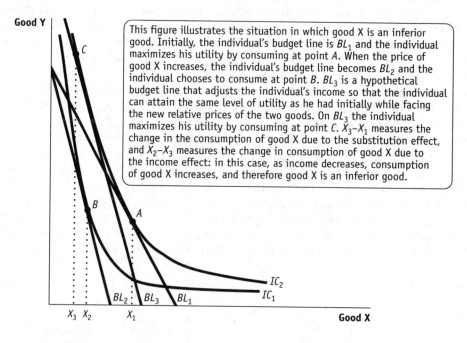

This figure illustrates the situation in which good X is an inferior good. Initially, the individual's budget line is BL_1 and the individual maximizes his utility by consuming at point A. When the price of good X increases, the individual's budget line becomes BL_2 and the individual chooses to consume at point B. BL_3 is a hypothetical budget line that adjusts the individual's income so that the individual can attain the same level of utility as he had initially while facing the new relative prices of the two goods. On BL_3 the individual maximizes his utility by consuming at point C. X_3-X_1 measures the change in the consumption of good X due to the substitution effect, and X_2-X_3 measures the change in consumption of good X due to the income effect: in this case, as income decreases, consumption of good X increases, and therefore good X is an inferior good.

Key Terms

indifference curve a contour line showing all *consumption bundles* that yield the same amount of total *utility* for an individual.

indifference curve map a collection of *indifference curves* for a given individual that represents the individual's entire *utility function*; each curve corresponds to a different total *utility* level.

marginal rate of substitution (MRS) the ratio of the *marginal utility* of one good to the marginal utility of another.

diminishing marginal rate of substitution the principle that the more of one good that is consumed in proportion to another, the less of the second good the consumer is willing to substitute for another unit of the first good.

ordinary goods in a consumer's *utility function*, those for which additional units of one good are required to compensate for fewer units of another, and vice versa; and for which the consumer experiences a *diminishing marginal rate of substitution* when substituting one good in place of another.

tangency condition on a graph of a consumer's *budget line* and available *indifference curves* of available *consumption bundles*, the point at which an indifference curve and the budget line just touch. When the indifference curves have the typical convex shape, this point determines the *optimal consumption bundle*.

relative price the ratio of the price of one good to the price of another.

relative price rule at the *optimal consumption bundle*, the *marginal rate of substitution* of one good in place of another is equal to the *relative price*.

Notes

Key Terms *(continued)*

perfect substitutes goods for which the *indifference curves* are straight lines; the *marginal rate of substitution* of one good in place of another good is constant, regardless of how much of each an individual consumes.

perfect complements goods a consumer wants to consume in the same ratio, regardless of their *relative price*.

▮ AFTER YOU READ THE CHAPTER

Tips

Tip #1. Students sometimes struggle with the concept of an indifference curve and an indifference curve map. The first point to realize is that each individual has different tastes and preferences and the indifference curve map is just an attempt to model these tastes and preferences. Next, think about a level of satisfaction you get from consuming two different kinds of goods, and imagine different combinations of these two goods that give you the same level of satisfaction: these different combinations would all lie on the same indifference curve, since each of these combinations give you the same level of satisfaction. Then, imagine different levels of satisfaction: here each indifference curve represents those combinations that give you the same level of satisfaction, and as you move out from the origin to different indifference curves your level of satisfaction increases. Thus, in Figure 11.11 the level of satisfaction on any given indifference curve is the same all along the curve, but IC_1 yields a lower level of utility than IC_2, IC_2 yields a lower level of utility than IC_3, and IC_3 yields a lower level of utility than IC_4.

Figure 11.11

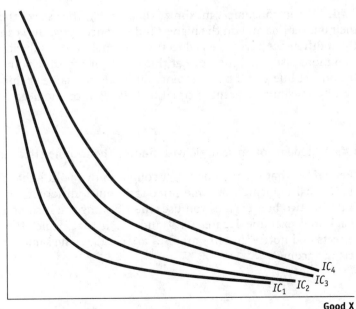

Tip #2. Recall the process for finding the budget line. The individual has income, N, and is choosing between good X with a price of P_X and good Y with a price of P_Y. The individual uses all of his income in buying good X and good Y. We can write this relationship as $N = P_X X + P_Y Y$, where X is the quantity of good X and Y is the quantity of good Y. Rearranging this equation in slope intercept form gives the following equation: $Y = (N/P_Y) - (P_X/P_Y)X$. Examine this equation carefully: (N/P_Y) is the y-intercept; in other words, the number of units the individual can afford if he purchases only good Y is equal to the individual's income divided by the price of good Y. And $(-P_X/P_Y)$ is the slope of the budget line that is equal to the negative of the price ratio for the two goods.

Tip #3. The slope of an indifference curve is given by the marginal rate of substitution. For a normal indifference curve, the absolute value of the marginal rate of substitution decreases as you move downward along the indifference curve (in other words, as the quantity of good X increases and the quantity of good Y decreases). Another way of expressing this idea is that the slope of a normal indifference curve gets flatter as you move along the curve to the right and steeper as you move along the curve to the left. Figure 11.12 illustrates this idea for a single normal indifference curve. The marginal rate of substitution is the negative of the ratio of the marginal utility from good X to the marginal utility from good Y.

Figure 11.12

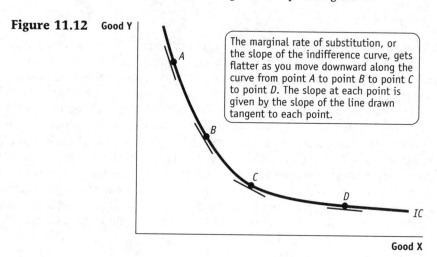

The marginal rate of substitution, or the slope of the indifference curve, gets flatter as you move downward along the curve from point A to point B to point C to point D. The slope at each point is given by the slope of the line drawn tangent to each point.

Tip #4. When consumers maximize their utility, they select the point that is just tangent to their budget line and on the highest indifference curve they can reach. Although the slope of the indifference curve is equal to the marginal rate of substitution of good X for good Y, we can more easily find the slope at this utility-maximizing point by realizing that the slope of the budget line and the indifference curve are the same at this point: that is, the slope at the utility-maximizing point is equal to $(-P_X/P_Y)$, or the negative of the price ratio of the two goods.

Tip #5. Students often struggle with finding the income effect and the substitution effect.

• Remember that the income effect compares two points that maximize utility where the individual is facing the same price ratio but a different level of income. This implies that the two budget lines you use when finding the income effect must be parallel. Go back and examine Figures 11.9 and 11.10 that depict the income and substitution effects and notice that BL_2 and BL_3 are parallel (the same price ratio, but different levels of income).

- To find the substitution effect, you must compare the utility-maximizing point with the old prices to the utility-maximizing point with the new prices, but where the individual is still on the original indifference curve (the same level of utility, but different price ratios and therefore different slopes of the two budget lines). Return to Figures 11.9 and 11.10 and examine BL_1 and BL_3: they are both tangent to the same indifference curve (the original indifference curve) but they have different slopes and therefore represent different price ratios.

Tip #6.   Finally, although the text only illustrates the income and substitution effects for an increase in the price of good X, you could also find these two effects for a decrease in the price of good X. Figure 11.13 illustrates the income and substitution effects for a decrease in the price of good X. Point A is the original utility-maximizing point; point B is the final utility-maximizing point; and point C is the income-compensated utility-maximizing point. $X_3 - X_1$ is the substitution effect, and $X_2 - X_3$ is the income effect. Remember that BL_3 is the hypothetical budget line that you need to draw to separate these two effects. Reinforcing tip 5, notice that BL_2 and BL_3 are parallel to each other (the income effect) and BL_1 and BL_3 have different slopes (the substitution effect).

Figure 11.13

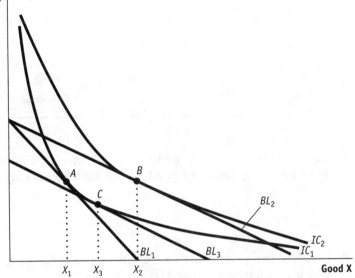

Problems and Exercises

1.   Mary's utility function can be written as $U = XY$, where U is the total amount of utility that Mary receives from consuming good X and good Y, X is the number of units of good X Mary consumes, and Y is the number of units of good Y Mary consumes. Consider three levels of utility for Mary: a utility level of 10, a utility level of 20, and a utility level of 30.

   a.   For each of the given utility levels, provide a table of X and Y values that gives Mary that level of utility.

b. From the numbers you generated in part (a), draw a graph of Mary's three indifference curves where each indifference curve represents a different level of utility. In your graph, measure good X on the *x*-axis and good Y on the *y*-axis.

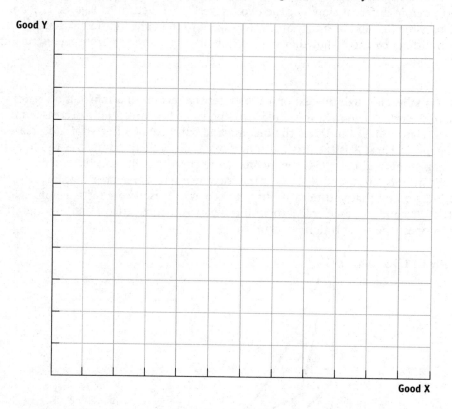

c. Consider the indifference curve that illustrates a utility level of 10 for Mary. Does Mary prefer any particular point on this indifference curve? Explain your answer.

d. Consider two points that lie on different indifference curves. How do you know which consumption bundle Mary prefers?

e. What are the four properties of normal indifference curves?

f. Do the three indifference curves you drew illustrate the four properties of normal indifference curves? Explain your answer.

2. Use the graph below of Steve's indifference curves for good X and good Y to answer this set of questions.

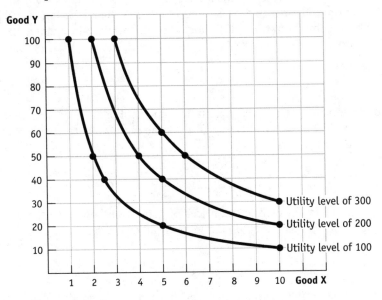

a. Suppose Steve initially has a utility level of 100 utils and he consumes 100 units of good Y. If Steve decides to increase his consumption of good X by 1 unit, how does his consumption of good Y change?

b. Suppose Steve initially has a utility level of 100 utils and he consumes 2 units of good X. If Steve decides to increase his consumption of good X by 1 unit, how does his consumption of good Y change?

c. As Steve increases his consumption of good X while maintaining the same level of utility, what happens to the amount of good Y he is willing to give up to get one more unit of good X?

d. The marginal rate of substitution is equal to the slope of the indifference curve. As Steve increases his consumption of good X while maintaining the same level of utility, what happens to the slope of Steve's indifference curve? What causes this change in the slope of the indifference curve?

e. Suppose Steve initially consumes 2 units of good X and has a total utility of 200 utils. If Steve increases his consumption of good X to 4 units while maintaining his utility at 200 utils, what is the marginal rate of substitution?

3. Use the graph of Steve's indifference curves in problem 2 to answer this set of questions.

  a. Suppose Steve's income is initially $115, the price of good Y is $1 per unit, and the price of good X is $15 per unit. Identify two consumption bundles that Steve can afford and that will exhaust his income from the indifference curve map drawn in problem 2; both bundles should lie on an indifference curve that is drawn in the graph for problem 2.

  b. Given the information in part (a) and the indifference curve map, what consumption bundle will maximize Steve's utility? What does the marginal rate of substitution equal at this optimal consumption point?

  c. Suppose Steve's income doubles while the prices of good X and good Y remain constant. What happens to Steve's budget line and his level of utility?

  d. Suppose Steve's income doubles while the prices of good X and good Y also double. What happens to Steve's budget line and his level of utility?

4. In this problem, you are asked to draw several indifference curve maps that obey the four general properties of normal indifference curves. In your graphs, measure good Y on the vertical axis and good X on the horizontal axis.

  a. Draw an indifference curve map that illustrates the situation in which both good X and good Y are normal goods. You must include at least two parallel budget lines to illustrate that good X and good Y are both normal: as income increases, the consumption of both goods increases.

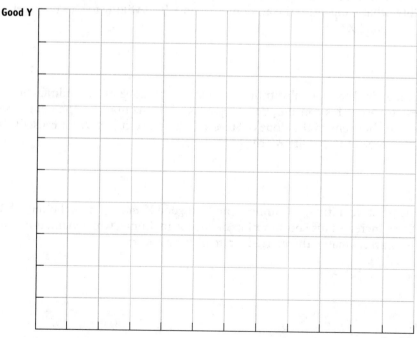

b. Draw an indifference curve map that illustrates the situation in which good X is an inferior good and good Y is a normal good. You must include at least two parallel budget lines to illustrate that the consumption of good X decreases as income increases whereas the consumption of good Y increases as the level of income increases.

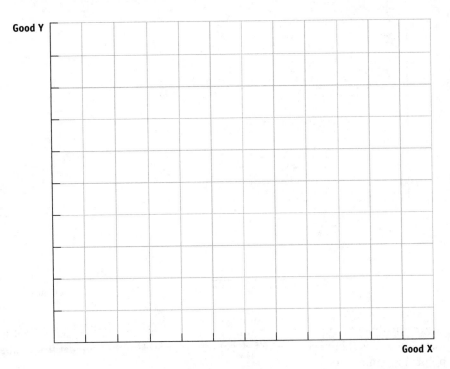

c. Draw an indifference curve map that illustrates the situation in which good Y is an inferior good and good X is a normal good. You must include at least two parallel budget lines to illustrate that the consumption of good Y decreases as income increases whereas the consumption of good X increases as the level of income increases.

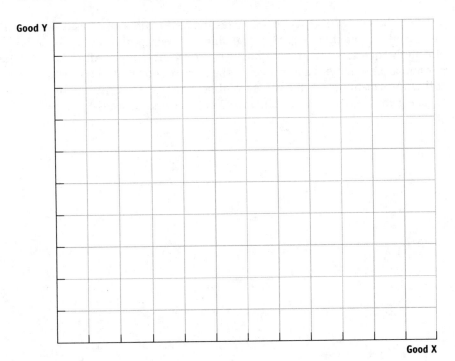

5. Jane consumes two goods: books and movies. Her income is $100, the price of books is $5, and the price of movies is $10.

    a. Draw Jane's budget line on a graph. Measure books on the horizontal axis and movies on the vertical axis.

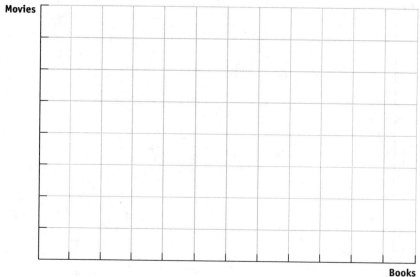

    b. Given this budget line, Jane's optimal consumption bundle includes 8 books. How many movies will Jane consume if she chooses a point on her budget line? Label this point *A* in your graph.

    c. Suppose the city where Jane lives passes two ordinances that result in the price of books and movies changing. One ordinance is the imposition of a tax on books that effectively increases the price of books to $8.75. The other ordinance subsidizes the consumption of movies and results in the price of movies decreasing to $5. Can Jane still afford consumption bundle *A*? Will Jane choose to consume this consumption bundle given these two new ordinances? Explain your answer.

d. Draw a new graph that illustrates Jane's original budget line and consumption bundle *A* as well as the impact of the ordinances described in part (c) on Jane's budget line. Include two indifference curves that represent Jane's preferences given that books and movies are both normal goods for Jane. Based on the indifference curves you have drawn, label the optimal consumption bundle that Jane chooses once the city enacts the new ordinances as consumption bundle *B*.

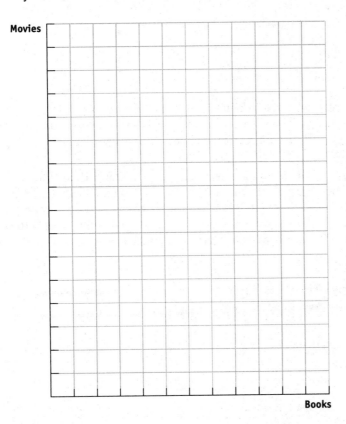

6. Mark enjoys books and movies. He always values reading one book as equal in satisfaction to watching two movies, and he never grows tired of reading books or watching movies.

a. In a graph, draw three representative indifference curves for Mark given his preferences. Measure books on the *y*-axis and movies on the *x*-axis. Do the indifference curves that you've drawn illustrate diminishing marginal utility? Explain your answer.

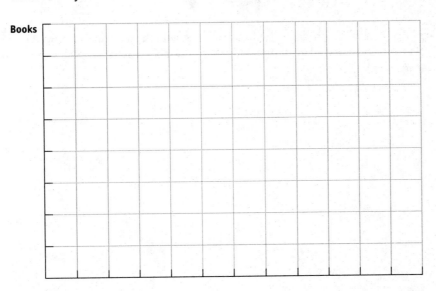

b. Suppose the price of books is $5 and the price of movies is $10. If Mark's income is $100, what is Mark's optimal consumption bundle?

Fantasia, the country where Mark lives, is considering two possible tax policies. The first tax policy would impose an income tax of 50% on all citizens, and the second tax policy would place a tax on movies, effectively increasing the price of movies to $20.

c. Draw a graph representing Mark's original budget line, and then draw a separate graph requesting the new budget line under each tax policy. Label your graphs carefully and indicate on each graph Mark's optimal consumption bundle given his tastes and preferences. (Hint: you will find it helpful to think about the effect of the first policy on Mark's after-tax income and the effect of the second policy on the price of movies.)

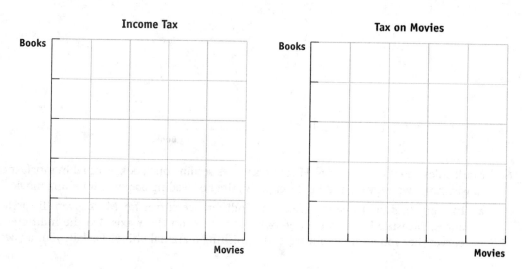

d. Given your analysis of these two tax policies, which tax policy would Mark prefer? Explain your answer. How much tax revenue does each tax policy generate from Mark?

7. Whenever Marty makes ham sandwiches, he uses two slices of bread and three slices of ham in each sandwich. The price of bread is 25 cents per slice and the price of ham is 50 cents per slice.

a. Draw Marty's indifference curve map for bread and ham. In your graph, measure ham on the vertical axis and bread on the horizontal axis.

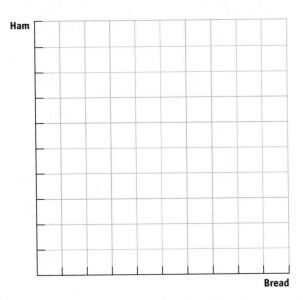

b. From Marty's perspective, what is the cost of a ham sandwich?

c. Suppose Marty's available income for bread and ham purchases is $50. How many ham sandwiches will Marty consume given this income? Draw a graph illustrating this optimal consumption bundle and Marty's budget line. In your graph, measure ham on the vertical axis and bread on the horizontal axis.

d. Suppose Marty's income is unchanged, but the price of ham increases to 60 cents and the price of bread decreases to 10 cents. How do these changes affect Marty's optimal consumption bundle? Draw a graph illustrating Marty's new budget line and his optimal consumption bundle.

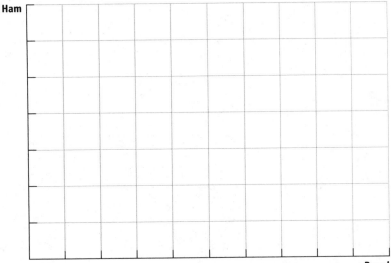

8. Maria purchases two goods: good X and good Y. Good X initially sells for $2 and good Y sells for $4. Maria's available income for purchases of good X and good Y is $40.

a. Draw a graph depicting Maria's budget line (BL_1) with good X measured on the horizontal axis and good Y measured on the vertical axis. At Maria's optimal consumption bundle, she devotes half of her income to purchases of good X and half of her income to purchases of good Y. Denote this optimal consumption bundle on your graph as point A, and identify the quantity of good X and good Y that Maria consumes.

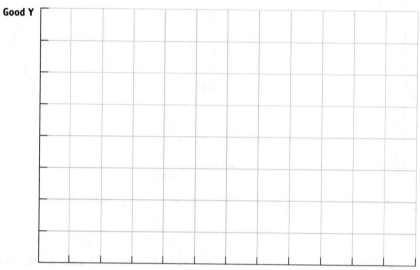

Suppose Bigtown where Maria lives is debating two tax policies that promise to provide the same amount of tax revenue. The first tax proposal is a tax on good X that will increase the price of good X by 100%. The second tax proposal is an income tax that reduces Maria's after-tax income to $36. The income tax proposal would not alter the price of good X or the price of good Y.

b. On a graph, draw Maria's original budget line (BL_1) and optimal consumption bundle A. On this same graph, draw Maria's budget line (BL_2) if the tax on good X is enacted. If this tax is enacted, Maria will choose to consume consumption bundle B composed of 2 units of good X and 8 units of good Y. Label this consumption bundle B in your graph. (Hint: to construct this new budget line, start by calculating the price of good X once the tax on good X is imposed.)

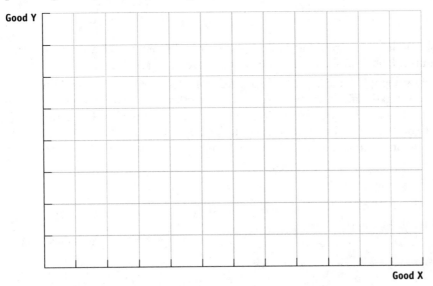

c. How much tax revenue will Bigtown collect from Maria if they enact the tax on good X?

d. On a graph, draw Maria's original budget line (BL_1) and optimal consumption bundle A. On this same graph, draw Maria's budget line (BL_2) if the income tax is enacted. If this tax is enacted, can Maria still afford consumption bundle B? (Hint: to construct this new budget line, start by recalling Maria's after-tax income and the original prices of good X and good Y.)

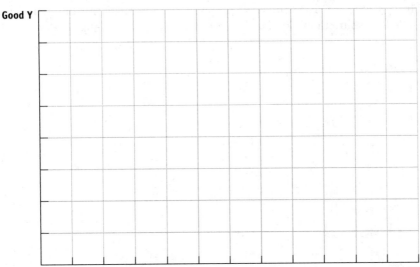

e. How much tax revenue will Bigtown collect from Maria if they enact the income tax?

f. If the income tax proposal is enacted, will Maria choose to consume consumption bundle *B*? Explain your answer. Sketch a graph to help support your answer.

9. Libby purchases cookies and milk. Cookies initially sell for $2 a unit and milk sells for $4 a unit. Libby's available income for purchases of cookies and milk is $40.

a. Draw a graph depicting Libby's budget line (BL_1) with cookies measured on the horizontal axis and milk measured on the vertical axis. Libby's optimal consumption bundle given her preferences and this budget line results in her consuming 10 units of cookies. How many units of milk does she consume? On the graph, indicate this optimal consumption bundle as consumption bundle *A*.

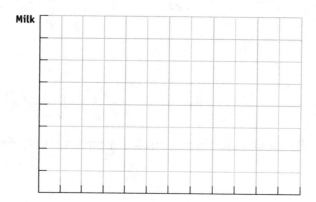

b. Suppose the price of cookies increases to $4 a unit. On a new graph, draw Libby's original budget line (BL_1) and her new budget line (BL_2). Libby's optimal consumption bundle with this budget line contains 8 units of milk. How many units of cookies will Libby consume at this optimal consumption bundle? Label this optimal consumption bundle *B* in your graph, and label the original optimal consumption bundle *A* as well.

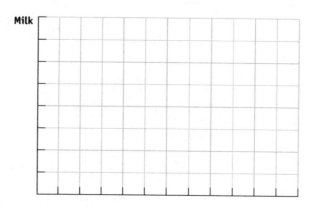

c. Suppose Libby's income is adjusted so that she can achieve her original level of utility while paying $4 per unit of cookies and $4 per unit of milk (the new prices). Suppose Libby's optimal consumption bundle C with this income-compensated budget line (BL_3) contains 4 units of cookies and 9 units of milk. How much additional income must Libby receive to maintain her original level of utility?

d. Draw a final graph of Libby's various budget lines (BL_1, BL_2, and BL_3) and optimal consumption bundles (A, B, and C). On your graph, identify the income and substitution effects.

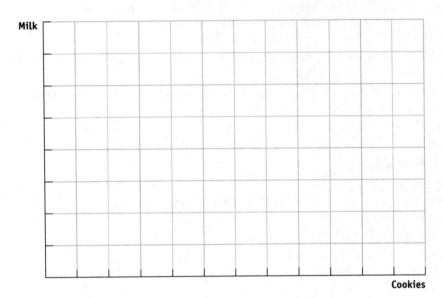

BEFORE YOU TAKE THE TEST

Chapter Review Questions

1. Indifference curves are convex, or bowed toward the origin, because
   a. each indifference curve represents a constant, but different level of utility.
   b. of diminishing marginal utility: the consumption of an additional unit of a good generates a smaller increase in total utility than the previous unit consumed.
   c. they are not allowed to intersect one another.
   d. they are downward sloping.

2. Which of the following statements is true?
   I. The indifference curve map for each individual is the same.
   II. For any given combination of two goods, the utility from consuming that combination is the same for all individuals.
   III. When two goods are perfect complements, the indifference curve map for these two goods contains indifference curves that are downward sloping.
   a. Statement I is true.
   b. Statement II is true.
   c. Statement III is true.
   d. Statements I, II, and III are true.
   e. None of the above statements are true.

3. Suppose that you are moving out along a straight line drawn from the origin. As you move out along this line you encounter different indifference curves. The indifference curve that is farther out along this line represents
   a. a different, but lower, level of utility for the individual than an indifference curve that is closer to the origin along this line.
   b. a different, but higher, level of utility for the individual than an indifference curve that is closer to the origin along this line.
   c. one of many possible consumption choices that the individual has.
   d. a higher level of income for the individual than an indifference curve that is closer to the origin along this line.

4. Suppose that Bob gets 40 units of utility when he consumes 2 hot dogs and 3 sodas and he gets 40 units of utility when he consumes 3 hot dogs and 1 soda. Then,
   a. Bob must like hot dogs more than soda.
   b. Bob must like soda more than hot dogs.
   c. these two combinations of hot dogs and soda must lie on the same indifference curve.
   d. these two combinations of hot dogs and soda must lie on the same budget line.

Use the figure below to answer the following three questions. The figure provides an indifference curve map for an individual with respect to food and clothing.

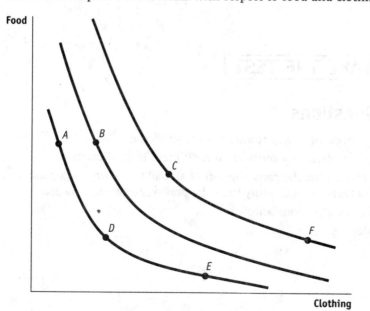

5. This individual's preferred consumption bundle

    a. is bundle *A*.

    b. is bundle *B*.

    c. is bundle *C*.

    d. is bundle *F*.

    e. could be bundle *A*, *D*, or *E*, since these three consumption bundles yield the same level of utility for the individual.

    f. could be bundle *C* or *F*, since these two consumption bundles yield the same level of utility for the individual.

6. This consumer's marginal rate of substitution has the greatest absolute value at consumption bundle

    a. *A*.

    b. *C*.

    c. *D*.

    d. *E*.

    e. *F*.

7. Moving along the indifference curve from point *A* to point *D*, the marginal rate of substitution of good X for good Y

    a. increases.

    b. decreases.

    c. remains the same.

8. Which of the following statements is true?

    I. Some individuals have tastes and preferences that result in their indifference curves intersecting with one another.

    II. Along a given indifference curve, the amount of the good measured on the *x*-axis is held constant while the amount of the good measured on the *y*-axis is allowed to vary.

    III. An indifference curve map portrays all the possible combinations of two goods that yield the same level of utility for the individual.

    a. Statement I is true.

    b. Statement II is true.

    c. Statement III is true.

    d. Statements I and II are true.

    e. Statements I, II, and III are true.

    f. All of the above statements are false.

9. To find the optimal consumption bundle, consumer theory requires that individuals be able to

    a. identify the exact numerical amount of utility they get from consuming a specific bundle of goods.

    b. identify which bundle of goods yields the greatest amount of utility to them among the various consumption bundles available.

    c. order or rank consumption bundles according to the level of utility the individual gets from consuming each consumption bundle.

    d. Answers (a), (b), and (c) are all true.

    e. Answers (b) and (c) are true.

10. Normal indifference curves slope downward because

    a. each consumption bundle must correspond to a unique total utility level.

    b. more is better than less: if the consumer is giving up units of good Y, the consumer must be compensated with more of good X to maintain the same level of utility.

    c. of diminishing marginal utility.

Answer the following three questions based on the table below, which provides information about an individual's tastes and preferences for food and clothing. Assume that each consumption bundle in the table provides the same level of utility for this individual.

Consumption bundle	Quantity of food (measured in meals)	Quantity of clothing (measured as items of clothing)
A	20	1
B	14	2
C	11	3
D	9	4
E	8	5

11. Suppose this individual initially consumes 2 items of clothing. This individual is willing to give up _____ meals to consume an additional unit of clothing.

    a. 1

    b. 6

    c. 3

    d. 2

    e. The answer depends on where the individual is on his indifference curve.

12. Suppose this individual's indifference curve based on the above information is drawn with clothing on the x-axis and meals on the y-axis. Then, as you move downward along this individual's indifference curve, the slope of the indifference curve

    a. gets steeper due to diminishing marginal utility.

    b. gets flatter due to diminishing marginal utility.

    c. stays constant, since the level of utility along the indifference curve is held constant.

    d. may get flatter, steeper, or stay constant depending on the individual's tastes and preferences.

13. Suppose this individual moves downward along his indifference curve from consumption bundle A toward consumption bundle E. Which of the following statements is true?

    I. The decrease in consumption of meals reduces this individual's utility.

    II. The increase in consumption of clothing increases this individual's utility.

    III. The decrease in utility from consuming fewer units of meals exactly equals the increase in utility from consuming more units of clothing, so this individual's utility stays constant as he moves downward along the indifference curve.

    a. Statement I is true.

    b. Statement II is true.

    c. Statement III is true.

    d. Statements I, II, and III are true.

14. A good is an ordinary good if
    a. the consumer is willing to trade one unit of the good for an additional unit of the other good.
    b. the consumer requires more of one good to compensate for the loss of the other good.
    c. the consumer's marginal rate of substitution diminishes when substituting one good for another.
    d. Both answers (a) and (c) are required for a good to be an ordinary good.
    e. Both answers (b) and (c) are required for a good to be an ordinary good.

Answer the next two questions based on the following information. Joe's income each month is $500 and Joe purchases only two types of goods: food and clothing. Each unit of food (F) costs $10 per unit and each unit of clothing (C) costs $20 per unit.

15. Which of the following equations expresses Joe's budget line?
    a. $500 = $10/F + $20/C$
    b. $F = 50 - 2C$
    c. $F = 500 - 2C$
    d. $C = 25 - (1/2)F$
    e. Answers (b) and (d) are both correct.

16. Suppose Joe's income doubles and the price of food increases to $20 per unit and the price of clothing increases to $40 per unit. This causes
    a. Joe's budget line to shift out from the origin since Joe's income has increased.
    b. the slope of Joe's budget line to get steeper if clothing is measured along the x-axis, since clothing has gotten relatively more expensive.
    c. the slope of Joe's budget line to get flatter if food is measured along the x-axis, since the price of food went up by a smaller dollar amount than the price of clothing.
    d. no change in Joe's budget line from its initial position.
    e. Answers (b) and (c) are both correct.

17. The consumer's optimal consumption bundle is the one that
    a. lies on the midpoint of the consumer's budget line.
    b. maximizes the consumer's consumption of one of the two goods.
    c. is just tangent to the consumer's indifference curve.
    d. None of the above are correct.

18. The vertical intercept of the individual's budget line is equal to
    a. the price of the good measured on the vertical axis divided by the individual's income.
    b. the price of the good measured on the horizontal axis divided by the individual's income.
    c. the individual's income divided by the price of the good measured on the vertical axis.
    d. the individual's income divided by the price of the good measured on the horizontal axis.

19. The slope of the individual's budget line is equal to the negative of the price of the good measured on the
    a. y-axis divided by the individual's income.
    b. y-axis divided by the price of the good measured on the x-axis.
    c. x-axis divided by the individual's income.
    d. x-axis divided by the price of the good measured on the y-axis.

20. The slope of the indifference curve at any point on the indifference curve is equal to the negative of the
   a. price of the good measured on the vertical axis divided by the price of the good measured on the horizontal axis.
   b. price of the good measured on the horizontal axis divided by the price of the good measured on the vertical axis.
   c. marginal utility of the good measured on the vertical axis divided by the marginal utility of the good measured on the horizontal axis.
   d. marginal utility of the good measured on the horizontal axis divided by the marginal utility of the good measured on the vertical axis.

21. At the optimal consumption point for a consumer,
   a. the ratio of the prices of the two goods is equal to the ratio of the marginal utilities of the two goods.
   b. the marginal rate of substitution is a positive number that is greater than the ratio of the prices of the two goods.
   c. the marginal rate of substitution is a negative number whose absolute value is greater than the ratio of the prices of the two goods.
   d. the marginal rate of substitution may be equal to, greater than, or less than the price ratios of the two goods.

22. Suppose Susy likes two kinds of soda: Fizzy Pop and Bubbly Delight. Susy is just as willing to drink Fizzy Pop as Bubbly Delight. Susy's income is $100 a week, and the price of Fizzy Pop is $0.50 and the price of Bubbly Delight is $1.00. Which of the following consumption bundles is Susy most likely to buy?
   a. 200 units of Fizzy Pop and 0 units of Bubbly Delight
   b. 100 units of Fizzy Pop and 50 units of Bubbly Delight
   c. 0 units of Fizzy Pop and 100 units of Bubbly Delight
   d. Answers (a), (b), and (c) all give Susy the same level of utility, so she does not have any preference as to which consumption bundle she purchases given her income and the prices of the two types of soda.
   e. Since Susy can afford the consumption bundles listed in answers (a), (b), and (c), she is indifferent as to which consumption bundle she chooses to consume.

23. Susy likes ham sandwiches. When Susy makes a ham sandwich she always uses 4 slices of ham and 2 slices of bread. Suppose that the price of ham is $0.25 per slice and that the price of bread is $0.50 per slice. The amount of Susy's income spent on ham sandwiches is $24 a week. Which of the following statements is true?
   a. Susy's indifference curves for ham and bread are normal indifference curves.
   b. Susy's indifference curves for ham and bread are straight lines, since she always eats ham and bread in a particular combination.
   c. Susy's indifference curves for ham and bread each have a right angle, since ham and bread are perfect complements for Susy.
   d. Susy maximizes her utility from ham sandwiches by consuming 12 sandwiches a week.
   e. Answers (a) and (d) are both true.
   f. Answers (b) and (d) are both true.
   g. Answers (c) and (d) are both true.

24. Suppose an individual consumes good X and good Y, where good X is measured on the horizontal axis and good Y is measured on the vertical axis. Holding everything else constant, if the price of good X increases, then the slope of the budget line gets

a. steeper, and the optimal consumption bundle is on a higher indifference curve.

b. flatter, and the optimal consumption bundle is on a lower indifference curve.

c. steeper, and the optimal consumption bundle is on a lower indifference curve.

d. flatter, and the optimal consumption bundle is on a higher indifference curve.

25. An individual's budget line rotates out along the y-axis while maintaining the same x-axis intercept. This rotation in the budget line is due to a(n)

a. increase in the individual's income.

b. decrease in the individual's income.

c. increase in the price of the good measured on the y-axis.

d. decrease in the price of the good measured on the y-axis.

26. Suppose an individual's budget line shifts out parallel to its initial position. Which of the following statements is true?

a. The individual is now able to achieve a higher level of utility.

b. This shift could be the result of income and the prices of the two goods doubling simultaneously.

c. This shift could be due to increased income.

d. Answers (a), (b), and (c) are all true statements.

e. Answers (a) and (c) are true statements.

Use the following graph to answer the next five questions. The graph depicts Joe's budget line for pasta dinners and steak dinners. The price of a pasta dinner is $2 and the price of a steak dinner is $10.

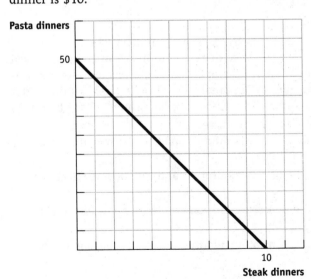

27. Joe's income is equal to

a. $50.

b. $25.

c. $100.

d. Joe's income cannot be determined without more information.

28. Which of the following consumption bundles will Joe most likely consume given his budget line in the above graph?
    a. 6 steak dinners and 9 pasta dinners
    b. 8 steak dinners and 10 pasta dinners
    c. 5 steak dinners and 22 pasta dinners
    d. 3 steak dinners and 38 pasta dinners

29. Suppose Joe initially consumes 25 pasta dinners and 5 steak dinners. Then suppose the price of a steak dinner rises to $20 while the price of a pasta dinner is unchanged. Given the new price, Joe's optimal consumption bundle is 20 pasta dinners and 3 steak dinners. If Joe's income was adjusted so that he maintained the same level of utility after the price change as he had before the price change, Joe would consume 35 pasta dinners and 4 steak dinners. What is the change in income Joe would need to receive to maintain this initial level of utility given the new price of a steak dinner? Joe's income would need to
    a. increase by $20.   d. decrease by $50.
    b. decrease by $20.   e. increase by $150.
    c. increase by $50.   f. decrease by $150.

30. Suppose Joe initially consumes 25 pasta dinners and 5 steak dinners. Then suppose the price of a steak dinner rises to $20 while the price of a pasta dinner is unchanged. Given the new price, Joe's optimal consumption bundle is 20 pasta dinners and 3 steak dinners. If Joe's income was adjusted so that he maintained the same level of utility after the price change as he had before the price change, Joe would consume 35 pasta dinners and 4 steak dinners. Given this information,
    a. steak dinners are a normal good and pasta dinners are an inferior good.
    b. steak dinners are an inferior good and pasta dinners are a normal good.
    c. steak dinners and pasta dinners are both inferior goods.
    d. steak dinners and pasta dinners are both normal goods.

31. Suppose Joe initially consumes 25 pasta dinners and 5 steak dinners. Then suppose the price of a steak dinner rises to $20 while the price of a pasta dinner is unchanged. Given the new price, Joe's optimal consumption bundle is 20 pasta dinners and 3 steak dinners. If Joe's income was adjusted so that he maintained the same level of utility after the price change as he had before the price change, Joe would consume 35 pasta dinners and 4 steak dinners. Given this information,
    a. the substitution effect is a decrease of 1 steak dinner, and the income effect is an increase of 1 steak dinner.
    b. the substitution effect is an increase of 1 steak dinner, and the income effect is a decrease of 1 steak dinner.
    c. the substitution effect is a decrease of 1 steak dinner, and the income effect is a decrease of 1 steak dinner.
    d. the income and substitution effects cannot be quantified without additional information.

ANSWER KEY

Answers to Problems and Exercises

1. **a.** The values you choose may differ from the values in the table below, but each set of values must be chosen in such a way that $U = XY$. For example, if $U = 10$, then one possible (X,Y) combination that would make $U = XY$ is $(2,5)$.

Utility of 10		Utility of 20		Utility of 30	
Units of good X	Units of good Y	Units of good X	Units of good Y	Units of good X	Units of good Y
1	10	2	10	3	10
2	5	4	5	6	5
2.5	4	2.5	8	2.5	12
4	2.5	8	2.5	12	2.5
5	2	5	4	5	6
10	1	10	2	10	3

b.

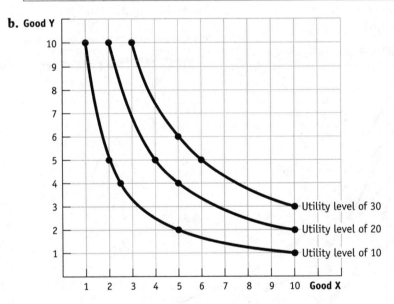

c. No, Mary is indifferent with regard to consuming any point on this indifference curve, since each consumption bundle on this curve gives her the same level of utility. Her choice of optimal consumption bundle on this curve depends on her income and the prices of the two goods, and not on her tastes and preferences, which are represented by the indifference curve map.

d. Mary prefers to consume the consumption bundle that lies on the indifference curve that is farther from the origin, since this indifference curve represents a higher level of utility for Mary.

e. The four properties of normal indifference curves are: (1) indifference curves never cross; (2) the farther an indifference curve lies from the origin, the higher the level of utility it indicates; (3) indifference curves slope downward; and (4) indifference curves have a convex shape.

f. Mary's indifference curves possess all four properties of normal indifference curves.

2. **a.** His consumption of good Y decreases from 100 units to 50 units.

    b. His consumption of good Y decreases from 50 units to 33.3 units.

    c. As Steve gets more and more units of good X, he finds that he is willing to give up fewer units of good Y in return for each additional unit of good X.

    d. The slope of the indifference curve flattens as the level of consumption of good X increases. This flattening of the slope is due to diminishing marginal utility.

    e. His marginal rate of substitution can be measured as the change in good Y divided by the change in good X: his marginal rate of substitution for this change in consumption is equal to −25.

3. **a.** Steve can afford to consume 1 unit of good X and 100 units of good Y given his income and the prices of the two goods, or he can consume 5 units of good X and 40 units of good Y given his income and the prices of the two goods.

    b. Given the indifference curve map this question is based upon, and limiting Steve's choice to a consumption bundle drawn represented on this indifference curve map, Steve will choose to consume 5 units of good X and 40 units of good Y, since this consumption bundle lies on the highest represented indifference curve he can reach given his income and the prices of the two goods.

    c. Steve's budget line shifts out parallel to his original budget line, and he is able to reach a higher level of utility since his new budget line is tangent to an indifference curve that is farther from the origin.

    d. Steve's budget line is unaffected, and he will continue to consume the same optimal consumption bundle and will therefore maintain the same level of utility.

4. **a.**

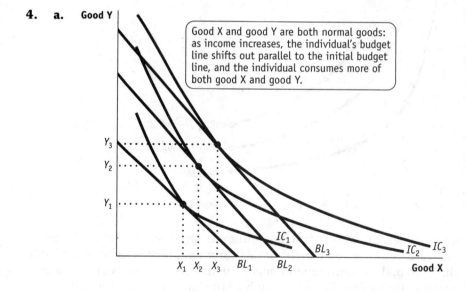

Good X and good Y are both normal goods: as income increases, the individual's budget line shifts out parallel to the initial budget line, and the individual consumes more of both good X and good Y.

b.

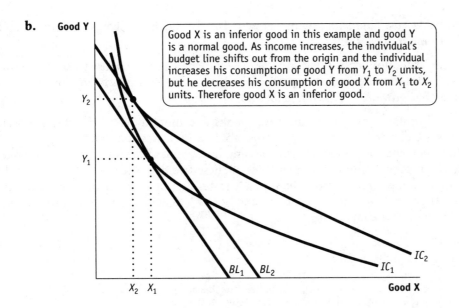

Good X is an inferior good in this example and good Y is a normal good. As income increases, the individual's budget line shifts out from the origin and the individual increases his consumption of good Y from Y_1 to Y_2 units, but he decreases his consumption of good X from X_1 to X_2 units. Therefore good X is an inferior good.

c.

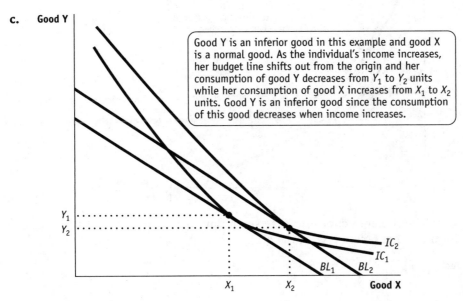

Good Y is an inferior good in this example and good X is a normal good. As the individual's income increases, her budget line shifts out from the origin and her consumption of good Y decreases from Y_1 to Y_2 units while her consumption of good X increases from X_1 to X_2 units. Good Y is an inferior good since the consumption of this good decreases when income increases.

5. a.

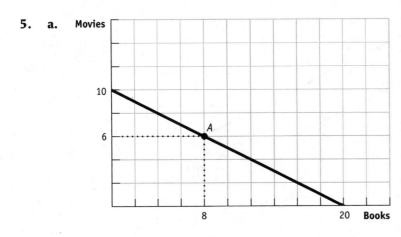

b. Eight books cost Jane $40, leaving her with $60 for movie purchases. She will be able to consume 6 movies.

c. Jane can still afford consumption bundle *A*, but she will not choose to consume this consumption bundle since it is possible for her to consume a different consumption bundle that provides her with a higher level of utility.

d. Jane will optimize by consuming fewer books and more movies once the two ordinances are enacted. In the figure below, point B indicates that Jane maximizes her utility when she consumes more movies and fewer books than she did initially. Point B does not provide numerical quantities of these two goods, though, because we do not have enough information about Jane's tastes and preferences to know with certainty the precise amounts of movies and books Jane will choose to consume once the ordinances are enacted.

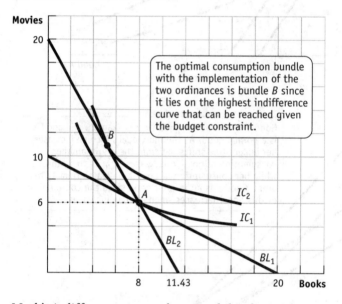

6. **a.** Mark's indifference curves do not exhibit diminishing marginal utility since they are linear and not bowed toward the origin.

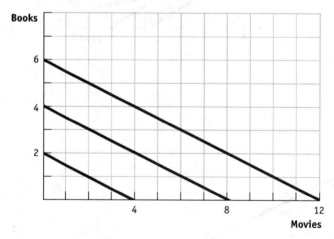

b. Mark maximizes his utility by consuming 0 movies and 20 books, since this is the consumption bundle that lies on the highest indifference curve he can reach given his income and the prices of the two goods.

c.

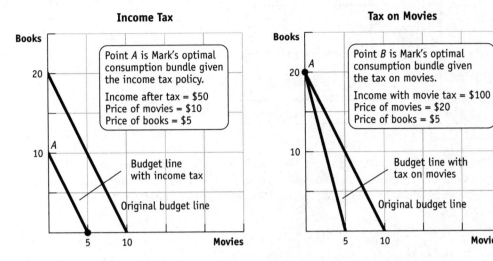

Income Tax

Point *A* is Mark's optimal consumption bundle given the income tax policy.

Income after tax = $50
Price of movies = $10
Price of books = $5

Budget line with income tax

Original budget line

Tax on Movies

Point *B* is Mark's optimal consumption bundle given the tax on movies.

Income with movie tax = $100
Price of movies = $20
Price of books = $5

Budget line with tax on movies

Original budget line

d. Mark prefers the tax on movies because it allows him to reach a higher level of utility than the tax on income. Since the two goods are perfect substitutes for Mark, he can substitute away from the relatively more expensive movies when they are taxed, without reducing his level of utility. The tax revenue from the income tax is equal to $50, while the tax revenue from the movies is equal to $0.

7. a.

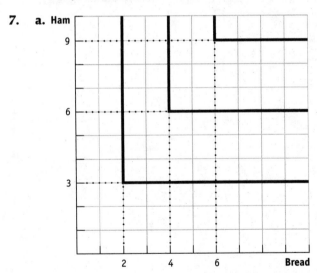

b. Marty always eats bread and ham in the ratio of 2 slices of bread to 3 slices of ham. Since 2 slices of bread cost $0.50 and 3 slices of ham cost $1.50, the cost of a ham sandwich is $2.

c. Marty will consume 25 ham sandwiches (50 slices of bread and 75 slices of ham).

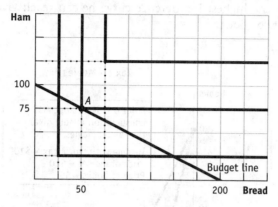

d. These price changes do not affect the overall cost of a ham sandwich (it still costs $2 per sandwich given Marty's ham-to-bread preferences), so Marty will still consume 25 ham sandwiches. However, Marty's budget line pivots around point *A* as seen in the graph below.

Marty's new budget line has a *y*-intercept of 83.3 and an *x*-intercept of 500 due to the increase in the price of ham and the decrease in the price of bread.

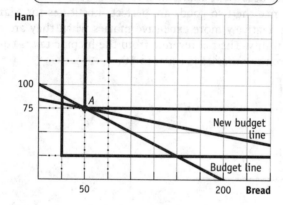

8. **a.**

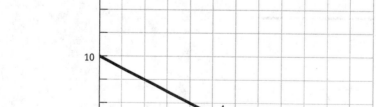

b.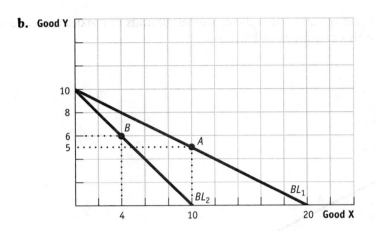

c. The tax on good X effectively increases the price of good X by $2 per unit of good X consumed. If Maria purchases 4 units of good X after the tax is imposed, Bigtown will collect $8 in tax revenue.

d.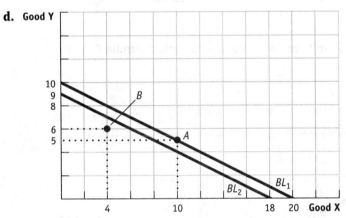

Maria can still afford consumption bundle *B* with the income tax.

e. Bigtown will collect $4 of Maria's income.

f. Although Maria can afford consumption bundle *B* under both tax policies, she will not choose consumption bundle *B* if the income tax proposal is enacted because it does not represent the consumption bundle that maximizes her utility given her budget line. Compare consumption bundles *B* and *C* in the graph below, and note that consumption bundle *C* lies on a higher indifference curve.

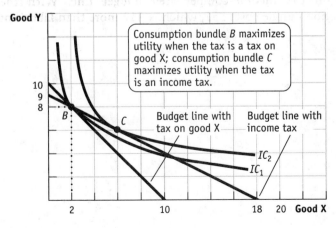

9.   a. Libby consumes 5 units of milk when she consumes 10 units of cookies (check to see if Libby can afford this consumption bundle).

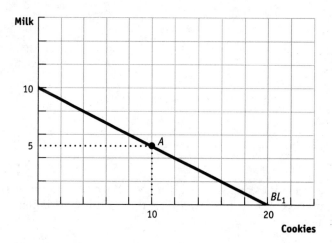

b. Libby will consume 2 units of cookies at consumption bundle *B*.

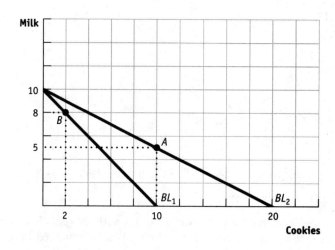

c. Libby would choose 4 units of cookies and 9 units of milk at the optimal consumption bundle on the income-compensated budget line. With the new prices, the consumption bundle costs $52, which is $12 more than Libby's original income.

d. The substitution effect is measured by the change in the consumption of cookies from point A to point C, or a decrease of 6 units of cookies. The income effect is measured by the change in the consumption of cookies from point C to point B, or a decrease of 2 units of cookies. Note that consumption bundles A and C lie on the same indifference curve (equal utility) but different budget lines (the original prices and income versus the new prices and compensated income) and that consumption bundles C and B lie on different budget lines (different levels of income but the same prices) that are parallel to one another.

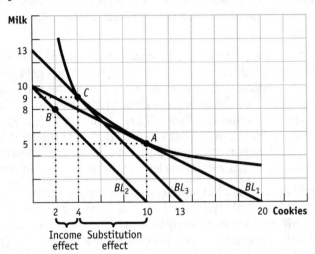

Answers to Chapter Review Questions

1. **Answer b.** Although each answer describes a property of indifference curves for ordinary goods, it is diminishing marginal utility that drives the bowed shape of the indifference curve. As consumers consume additional units of one of the goods depicted, they find their utility from the good declining. To maintain the same level of satisfaction, they must give up smaller and smaller amounts of the other good for each additional unit of the good they are consuming.

2. **Answer e.** Individuals have distinct tastes and preferences, and therefore their indifference curve maps are distinctive. This also implies that the level of utility individuals receive from consuming a particular bundle of goods may and often do differ with each individual. When two goods are perfect complements, their indifference curve map contains indifference curves with right angles.

3. **Answer b.** Each indifference curve represents a constant level of utility. As you move away from the origin along a straight line, the farther out you are from the origin and the higher the level of utility the indifference curves represent.

4. **Answer c.** Since Bob gets the same amount of total utility from these two combinations of the hot dogs and soda, they must lie on the same indifference curve. We cannot know whether Bob prefers hot dogs or sodas.

5. **Answer f.** The individual prefers those consumption bundles that lie on the highest indifference curve. In the graph, the indifference curve that represents the highest level of utility is the indifference curve that includes consumption bundles C and F. It is true that the level of utility represented by bundles A, D, and E is the same, but it is a lower level of utility than the level represented by bundles C and F.

6. **Answer a.** The marginal rate of substitution is the slope of the indifference curve at a particular point and is given by the slope of the line that is drawn tangent to the indifference curve at that point. If you draw this tangent line for each of the mentioned points, you will find that the line drawn tangent to point A is the steepest line, and therefore the absolute value of the slope of this line is greater than the absolute value of the slope of any of the other lines drawn tangent to the other points.

7. **Answer b.** As this consumer moves downward along the indifference curve from point A to point D, this individual gives up fewer units of food to get each additional unit of clothing, therefore the marginal rate of substitution decreases as the individual moves from point A to point D.

8. **Answer f.** Each of these statements is false. Indifference curves cannot intersect with one another, since along any given indifference curve the level of utility is held constant. Thus, if two indifference curves intersected, this would imply that at the point of intersection there are two different levels of utility. For any given indifference curve, the level of utility is held constant while the amounts of good X and good Y vary. A single indifference curve portrays all the combinations of the two goods that yield the same level of utility for the individual; an indifference curve map portrays a set of indifference curves where each indifference curve represents a different level of utility for the individual.

9. **Answer e.** Finding the optimal consumption bundle does not require a numerically significant measure of the number of utils the individual gets from consuming different consumption bundles. It is sufficient for individuals to be able to rank the various choices according to the level of satisfaction they receive from each consumption bundle. That is, consumer theory requires that the individual be able to use an ordinal measure of utility (that is, ranking the bundles according to their desirability) rather than a cardinal measure of utility (a ranking based on numerically significant measures).

10. **Answer b.** Normal indifference curves slope downward because individuals must be compensated by getting more units of good X when they give up units of good Y. Answer (c) explains why normal indifference curves are convex, or bowed toward the origin.

11. **Answer c.** The individual is initially consuming consumption bundle B, which contains 2 items of clothing and 14 meals. The individual is willing to give up 3 meals to consume an additional unit of clothing (consumption bundle C).

12. **Answer b.** If you graph this individual's consumption bundles from the above information and then connect these bundles to create an indifference curve (remember that each of these bundles yields the same level of utility for the individual and therefore each bundle is on the same indifference curve), the indifference curve's slope gets flatter as you move downward along the curve. From the table we can see that the individual gives up fewer and fewer units of meals as the level of clothing consumed by the individual increases.

13. **Answer d.** All three statements are true. Decreasing consumption of meals does lower the individual's utility while increasing consumption of clothing increases the individual's utility. However, since all of these consumption bundles lie on the same indifference curve, the individual's total utility does not change, so the decrease in utility is exactly offset by the increase in utility.

14. **Answer e.** A good is an ordinary good when the good meets two criteria: first, the individual is only willing to give up units of one of the goods if he is compensated by receiving more units of the other good; and second, along a given indifference curve the marginal rate of substitution of one good for the other good must diminish.

15. **Answer e.** Joe's budget line can be expressed as $500 = 10F + 20C$, since he has $500 he can spend on food and clothing and each unit of food costs $10 and each unit of clothing costs $20. This equation can be rearranged and simplified to either the equation given in (b) or the equation given in (d).

16. **Answer d.** Joe's budget line does not change since both Joe's income and the prices of both goods have doubled. Joe's initial budget line could be written as $500 = 10F + 20C$, and his new budget line is $1,000 = 20F + 40C$. If you divide this new budget line by 2 on both sides of the equation, you get the original budget line, or you could try graphing both of these budget lines to see if they are the same line.

17. **Answer d.** The consumption bundle that maximizes the individual's utility and is therefore the optimal consumption bundle is the consumption bundle that is just tangent to the individual's budget line and not the individual's indifference curve.

18. **Answer c.** The vertical intercept of the individual's budget line identifies the total number of units of that good that the individual can afford, given their income and the price of the good. To find how many units of the good the individual can afford if he uses all of his income to purchase the good measured on the y-axis, simply divide the individual's income by the price of the good measured on the y-axis.

19. **Answer d.** To answer this question, it is helpful to return to the general equation for the individual's budget line: income $= P_X X + P_Y Y$. Then solve for Y to write the equation in slope-intercept form. Solving for Y, this equation can be written as $Y = (\text{income}/P_Y) - (P_X/P_Y)X$. The slope of the budget line is therefore the negative of the price of the good measured on the x-axis divided by the price of the good measured on the y-axis.

20. **Answer d.** The slope of the indifference curve at any point on the indifference curve is equal to the negative of the marginal rate of substitution, and the marginal rate of substitution is equal to the ratio of the marginal utility of the good measured on the horizontal axis to the marginal utility of the good measured on the vertical axis. The slope of the indifference curve at the consumer's optimal consumption point is equal to the negative of the ratio of the price of the good measured on the horizontal axis to the price of the good measured on the vertical axis.

21. **Answer a.** When the consumer selects the utility-maximizing consumption bundle, she selects a bundle that lies on the highest indifference curve she can afford given her income and the prices of the two goods. This consumption bundle sits on the indifference curve that is just tangent to the budget line at that point: thus, the marginal rate of substitution (the slope of the indifference curve) is equal to the negative of the price of the good measured on the horizontal axis divided by the price of the good measured on the vertical axis (the slope of the budget line).

22. **Answer a.** Although Susy can afford each of the consumption bundles listed, the consumption bundle listed in answer (a) sits on a higher indifference curve than do the consumption bundles in answers (b) and (c). These two goods are perfect substitutes, and Susy's indifference curves with respect to these two goods are straight lines.

23. **Answer g.** For Susy, ham and bread are perfect complements, since she always eats them in the ratio of 4 slices of ham to 2 slices of bread. In addition, we can calculate the price of a ham sandwich for Susy as $2: $1 for the 2 slices of bread and $1 for the 4 slices of ham. Thus, with an income of $24 to spend on ham sandwiches, Susy can afford to purchase 12 sandwiches.

24. **Answer c.** The increase in the price of good X means that the individual can no longer afford as much of good X as he could before the price change. This price change therefore causes the budget line to pivot inward along the horizontal axis while not affecting the y-intercept. This implies that the budget line would be steeper. The individual now finds that the consumption bundle that maximizes his utility lies on a lower indifference curve.

25. **Answer d.** Since the budget line has rotated out along the y-axis, this implies that the individual can now afford to purchase more units of the good measured on the y-axis than was possible initially. Thus, the price of the good measured on the y-axis must have decreased.

26. **Answer e.** When the individual's budget line shifts away from the origin, this makes it possible for the individual to reach a higher level of satisfaction, or utility. When the budget line shifts in a parallel fashion, this is due to a change in the level of income holding everything else constant. An equal proportionate change in income and the prices of the two goods results in no change in the budget line.

27. **Answer c.** Joe can afford 50 pasta dinners if he devotes all of his income to buying pasta dinners, which implies that his income must be $100, since each pasta dinner costs $2. Alternatively, Joe can afford 10 steak dinners at $10 each, for a total cost of $100 if he purchases only steak dinners.

28. **Answer b.** Joe has $100 in income, and the price of a steak dinner is $10 and the price of a pasta dinner is $2. Thus, the (quantity of steak dinners)(price of steak dinners) + (quantity of pasta dinners)(price of pasta dinners) must equal 100. Only answer (b) meets this requirement. Answers (a) and (c) do not exhaust Joe's income (these consumption bundles lie below his budget line), and answer (d) lies beyond Joe's budget line.

29. **Answer c.** We can immediately eliminate answers (b), (d), and (f) since the increase in the price of steak dinners reduces Joe's purchasing power: this implies that to maintain the same level of utility Joe must have his income increased to offset the decrease in his purchasing power. We know that Joe would consume 35 pasta dinners and 4 steak dinners given the new prices if he were to maintain his initial level of utility, and this consumption bundle's cost is equal to $150 (35 pasta dinners at $2 each plus 4 steak dinners at $20 each). This represents a $50 increase from Joe's original income of $100.

30. **Answer d.** To answer this question, you must be able to locate the two consumption points of comparison that relate the same set of prices but different levels of income. When Joe faces the new price ($20 for steak dinners and $2 for pasta dinners) and his income of $100, he chooses to consume 20 pasta dinners and 3 steak dinners. We also know that with the new price and his income adjusted to $150 to maintain the same level of utility as he had initially, Joe would choose to consume 35 pasta dinners and 4 steak dinners. Thus, when Joe's income falls from $150 to $100, his consumption of both steak and pasta dinners decrease, and therefore both goods are normal goods.

31. **Answer c.** Maintaining the same level of utility, Joe alters his steak dinner consumption from 5 dinners to 4 dinners: this represents his substitution effect, or his response to the change in the relative price of steak dinners to pasta dinners. Then, when Joe adjusts to the decrease in his purchasing power due to the increase in the price of a steak dinner, he reduces his steak dinner consumption from 4 dinners to 3 dinners: this represents his income effect, or his response to the change in his purchasing power due to the change in the price of steak dinners.

chapter 12

Behind the Supply Curve: Inputs and Costs

BEFORE YOU READ THE CHAPTER

Summary

This chapter develops the concept of the firm's production function and how the production function relates the level of inputs used by the firm to the level of output the firm produces. The chapter discusses diminishing marginal returns and then develops different measures of a firm's costs, including the firm's total cost of production, average cost of production, and marginal cost of production. The chapter also considers how the firm's costs differ between the short run and the long run. Finally, the chapter develops the idea of returns to scale and then analyzes the relationship between inputs, outputs, and costs in the long run.

Chapter Objectives

Objective #1. Producers must make a production decision about how much output they should produce. Producers are assumed to select the level of output that will result in the maximization of their economic profits.

Objective #2. Firms combine inputs with technology to produce outputs. The production function for a firm describes the maximum amount of output that can be produced from a general level of inputs and technology.

- In the short run, inputs may be fixed or variable. The level of fixed input used by a firm does not change in the short run as the firm's level of output changes. In contrast, the level of variable input used by a firm does change in the short run as the firm's level of output changes.

- In the long run, all inputs are assumed to be variable since in the long run all desired adjustments to input usage are possible.

357

Objective #3. In the short run, a firm's ability to produce outputs from its variable inputs depends on the level of fixed input it employs. For a given level of fixed input, as the firm hires additional units of the variable input, the firm will find that its output increases. However, the firm will find that as it hires additional units of the variable input, the marginal product (*MP*) of this variable input declines. That is, as additional units of the variable input are hired, total product (*TP*) increases but it eventually increases at a diminishing rate. This principle of diminishing marginal returns is a short-run concept: in the short run, the marginal product of a variable input diminishes as the level of usage of that variable input increases, holding at least one other input fixed.

- The firm's *TP* curve graphically represents the relationship between a firm's total output and the level of variable input it is using, holding all other inputs constant. The slope of the *TP* curve at any particular level of production is equal to the marginal product of the variable input. Due to diminishing marginal returns, the slope of the *TP* curve flattens as more and more units of the variable input are hired.

- The firm's marginal product of labor is equal to the change in output divided by the change in labor. The marginal product of labor measures the addition to total output from hiring an additional unit of labor while holding all other factors of production constant. Once the firm enters the range of output for which diminishing marginal returns holds, the firm's *MP* of labor curve is downward sloping.

- The firm's *TP* and *MP* curves shift up at every level of usage of the variable input when more of the fixed input is used. For instance, suppose a firm's fixed input is capital and its variable input is labor. When the firm increases the level of its capital from its initial level to a new, higher but constant level of capital, the firm will find that every level of labor usage results in an increased level of production relative to the initial situation because the labor now has more capital resources to work with in producing the product. With more of the fixed input available, the marginal product of the variable input at every level of the variable input is now higher than it was initially.

Objective #4. A firm can construct its cost curves if it combines the information from its production function with information about the prices of inputs. The production function connects the level of input usage to the maximum level of output production possible from these inputs, while input prices allow the firm to then calculate the cost of producing that level of output.

Objective #5. The firm's costs can be described in the short run or in the long run. The short-run costs for a firm include the following:

- Fixed cost (*FC*) is the cost of hiring the fixed input. To calculate the fixed cost, multiply the number of units of the fixed input that the firm is using by the price of a unit of the fixed input. In the short run fixed cost does not vary as the level of output varies.

- Variable cost (*VC*) is the cost of hiring the variable input. To calculate the variable cost, multiply the number of units of the variable input that the firm is using by the price of a unit of the variable input. Variable cost varies as the level of output varies: the higher the level of output, holding everything else constant, the greater the use of the variable input and, hence, the greater the variable cost.

- Total cost (*TC*) in the short run is equal to the sum of the fixed cost plus the variable cost: thus, $TC = FC + VC$.

The long-run costs for a firm are all variable costs, since in the long run all inputs can be adjusted. Thus, long-run total costs are equivalent to long-run variable costs.

Objective #6.   A firm's total cost depends on the level of output it produces. In the short run, higher levels of output are only possible if more units of the variable input are hired. Further, as additional units of the variable input are hired, the marginal product of the variable input declines (recall the principle of diminishing marginal returns): this implies that as output increases, the variable cost of production rises, as does the total cost of production. Thus, the *TC* curve is upward sloping, and in addition, the *TC* curve gets steeper as the firm's level of output increases due to the diminishing marginal returns to the variable input.

Objective #7.   Marginal cost (*MC*) is the addition to total cost from producing one more unit of output. Marginal cost is the slope of the *TC* curve. As output increases, the *MC* curve is initially downward sloping, but eventually at higher levels of output the *MC* curve becomes upward sloping due to diminishing returns. Figure 12.1 illustrates this idea: *MC* decreases as output increases from 0 units to Q_1 units, and then *MC* increases as output increases beyond level Q_1. In the downward-sloping portion of the *MC* curve, the cost of an additional unit of output is falling due to specialization. The firm, in this range of output, experiences increasing returns to scale since its cost of additional output falls.

Figure 12.1

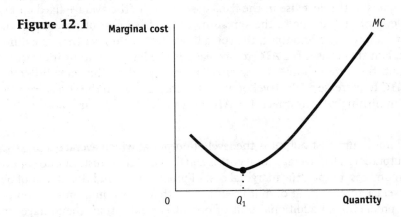

Objective #8.   Average total cost (*ATC*) provides a measure of the cost per unit of output. This measure can be calculated by dividing total cost by the level of output (*ATC = TC/Q*). Average variable cost (*AVC*) is variable cost divided by output (*AVC = VC/Q*). Average fixed cost (*AFC*) is fixed cost divided by output (*AFC = FC/Q*).

- Average total cost is equal to the sum of average variable cost plus average fixed cost. To see this, recall that *TC = VC + FC*. If both sides of this equation are divided by quantity (*Q*), then *ATC = AVC + AFC*.

- Average total cost provides a measure of the cost per unit of production while marginal cost provides a measure of the cost of producing an additional unit of output.

- The *ATC* and *AVC* curves are U-shaped, and their minimum points intersect the firm's *MC* curve. When *ATC* is decreasing as output increases, this implies that the marginal cost is less than the average total cost: producing an additional unit of output costs less than the current cost per unit, and thus the cost per unit must decrease if that additional unit of output is produced. When *ATC* is increasing as output increases, this implies that the marginal cost is greater than the average total cost: producing an additional unit of output costs more than the current cost per unit, and thus the cost per unit must increase if that additional unit of output is produced. When *ATC* equals *MC*, this implies that the cost of producing an additional unit of output equals the current cost per unit, and thus the cost per unit will not change if that additional unit of output is produced. Figure 12.2 illustrates these relationships.

- Since fixed cost does not vary in the short run for a firm, the *AFC* must decrease as output increases. Figure 12.2 illustrates these relationships.

Figure 12.2

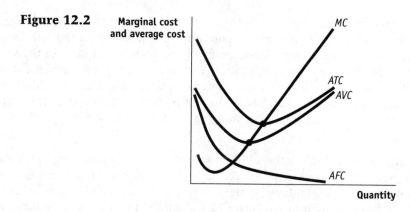

Objective #9. As the firm increases its level of production, this results in two effects on the firm's costs. The diminishing returns effect refers to the increase in the variable cost per unit (the average variable cost) of producing a higher level of output due to the diminishing returns to the variable input that the firm experiences as it increases its level of production. The spreading effect refers to the decrease in the fixed cost per unit (the average fixed cost) of producing a higher level of output due to the spreading of the fixed cost of production over more units of output. At low levels of output, the spreading effect is stronger than the diminishing returns effect, and this causes the ATC to decrease as the level of output increases. At higher levels of output, the diminishing returns effect is stronger than the spreading effect, and this causes the ATC to increase as the level of output increases. When the spreading effect exactly offsets the diminishing returns effect, the ATC curve is at its minimum point.

Objective #10. The minimum-cost output is the level of output at which average total cost is minimized. At this output level, the average total cost is equal to marginal cost. At output levels lower than this minimum-cost output, the marginal cost of producing an additional unit of output is less than the average total cost. At output levels greater than this minimum-cost output, the marginal cost of producing an additional unit of output is greater than the average total cost. Figure 12.3 illustrates this concept: Q_1 is the minimum-cost output; as output increases from 0 units to Q_1, ATC declines, and as output increases beyond Q_1 units, ATC increases.

Figure 12.3

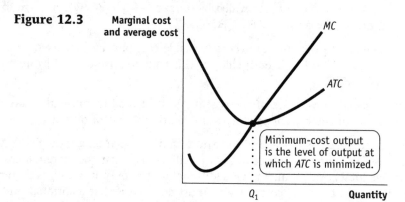

Objective #11. The long-run average total cost (LRATC) curve illustrates the relationship between output and average total cost when fixed cost has been chosen to minimize the average total cost at every level of output. The LRATC curve is U-shaped: when LRATC is decreasing as output increases, the firm experiences increasing returns to scale; when LRATC is increasing as output increases, the firm experiences decreasing returns to scale; and when LRATC is constant as output increases, the firm experiences constant returns to scale. Figure 12.4 illustrates the LRATC curve and returns to scale: for outputs from 0 units to Q_1, this firm has increasing returns to scale and decreasing costs; for outputs from Q_1 units to Q_2, this firm has constant returns to scale and constant costs; and for outputs greater than Q_2, this firm has decreasing returns to scale and increasing costs.

Figure 12.4

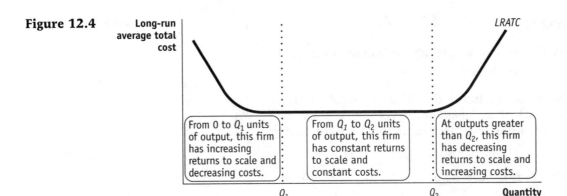

- A firm that has increasing returns to scale in its range of production finds that as its production level increases, its cost of production falls: this firm benefits from getting larger. A firm with increasing returns to scale finds that an equal proportionate increase in all its inputs will result in a greater than proportionate increase in its output: for example, a doubling of all of the firm's inputs causes the firm's output to more than double, and therefore the firm's *ATC* decreases.

- A firm that has decreasing returns to scale in its range of production finds that as its production level increases, its cost of production increases: this firm benefits from staying relatively small. A firm with decreasing returns to scale finds that an equal proportionate increase in all its inputs will result in a less than proportionate increase in its output: for example, a doubling of all of the firm's inputs causes the firm's output to less than double, and therefore the firm's *ATC* increases.

- A firm that has constant returns to scale in its range of production finds that a proportionate increase in all its inputs results in a proportionate increase in its output: for example, if all inputs are doubled, then the firm's output also doubles, and therefore the firm's *ATC* stays constant.

Objective #12. Returns to scale for a firm depend on the firm's production technology. Increasing returns to scale arise because of increasing specialization that is possible at large output levels or because of large initial set-up costs that must be incurred to produce any output or because of network externalities. Decreasing returns to scale arise due to problems of coordination and communication as the level of production increases.

Key Terms

production function the relationship between the quantity of *inputs* a firm uses and the quantity of output it produces.

fixed input an *input* whose quantity is fixed for a period of time and cannot be varied (for example, land).

variable input an *input* whose quantity the firm can vary at any time (for example, labor).

long run the time period in which all *inputs* can be varied.

short run the time period in which at least one *input* is fixed.

total product curve a graphical representation of the *production function*, showing how the quantity of output depends on the quantity of the *variable input* for a given quantity of the *fixed input*.

Notes

Key Terms *(continued)*

marginal product the additional quantity of output produced by using one more unit of a given *input*.

diminishing returns to an input the effect observed when an increase in the quantity of an *input*, while holding the levels of all other inputs fixed, leads to a decline in the *marginal product* of that input.

fixed cost a cost that does not depend on the quantity of output produced; the cost of a *fixed input*.

variable cost a cost that depends on the quantity of output produced; the cost of a *variable input*.

total cost the sum of the *fixed cost* and the *variable cost* of producing a given quantity of output.

total cost curve a graphical representation of the *total cost*, showing how total cost depends on the quantity of output.

average total cost *total cost* divided by quantity of output produced. Also referred to as *average cost*.

average cost an alternative term for *average total cost*; the *total cost* divided by the quantity of output produced.

U-shaped average total cost curve a distinctive graphical representation of the relationship between output and *average total cost*; the average total cost curve at first falls when output is low and then rises as output increases.

average fixed cost the *fixed cost* per unit of output.

average variable cost the *variable cost* per unit of output.

minimum-cost output the quantity of output at which the *average total cost* is lowest—the bottom of the *U-shaped average total cost curve*.

long-run average total cost curve a graphical representation showing the relationship between output and *average total cost* when *fixed cost* has been chosen to minimize average total cost for each level of output.

increasing returns to scale long-run *average total cost* declines as output increases (also referred to as *economies of scale*).

decreasing returns to scale long-run *average total cost* increases as output increases (also known as *diseconomies of scale*).

constant returns to scale long-run *average total cost* is constant as output increases.

■ AFTER YOU READ THE CHAPTER

Tips

Tip #1. The most important tip for this chapter is to learn the new terminology, the abbreviations for this terminology, the graphical representation of these new terms, and how to apply these new terms. Students tend to struggle with these terms and abbreviations because there are so many of them, but understanding the material requires that you become comfortable with all the new vocabulary.

Tip #2. This chapter continues to develop the general concept of *marginal*. In the chapter, the marginal product of an input and the marginal cost of production are introduced. Both of these concepts considers the change in one variable due to a change in another variable: the marginal product of an input looks at the addition to total production when an additional unit of the input is employed, and the marginal cost measures the change in total cost due to the production of an additional unit of output. The marginal concept is a critically important concept for you to understand and be able to use.

Tip #3. It is important that you understand the distinction between the short run and the long run. In the short run at least one input is fixed, while in the long run all inputs are variable. An input is fixed if its level of usage does not change even when the level of production increases. An input is variable when its level of usage varies as the level of production varies. There is no set time period that determines the boundary between the short run and the long run: the short run is a time period so short that full adjustment to changes cannot take place, while the long run is a time period sufficiently long enough to allow full adjustment.

Tip #4. After you have learned the definitions of total cost, variable cost, fixed cost, average total cost, average variable cost, average fixed cost, and marginal cost, and their abbreviations, you should concentrate on learning how these terms are related to one another. Here is a summary of these relationships:

$$TC = FC + VC$$

$$ATC = TC/Q$$

$$AVC = VC/Q$$

$$AFC = FC/Q$$

$$ATC = AFC + AVC$$

$$MC = (\text{the change in } TC)/(\text{the change in } Q)$$

Think about these relationships and their implications. For example, if you know *TC* and *FC*, you can calculate *VC*; or, if you know *AVC* and *ATC*, you can calculate *AFC*.

Tip #5. Once you have learned the definitions and the abbreviations of all the new terms in the chapter, you should work on a thorough understanding of the graphs, particularly the graphs of *ATC*, *AVC*, *AFC*, and *MC*.

- The graph of *AFC* is a curve that decreases as output increases because the level of *FC* is constant in the short run, and as output increases, this implies that *AFC* must decline ($AFC = FC/Q$, and as *Q* gets larger and *FC* stays constant, this means that *AFC* must get smaller). On a graph of the *AFC* curve, the fixed cost for a particular level of production can be represented as the area under the curve. Figure 12.5 illustrates the *AFC* for Q_1 units of output as well as the fixed cost for this level of output.

Figure 12.5

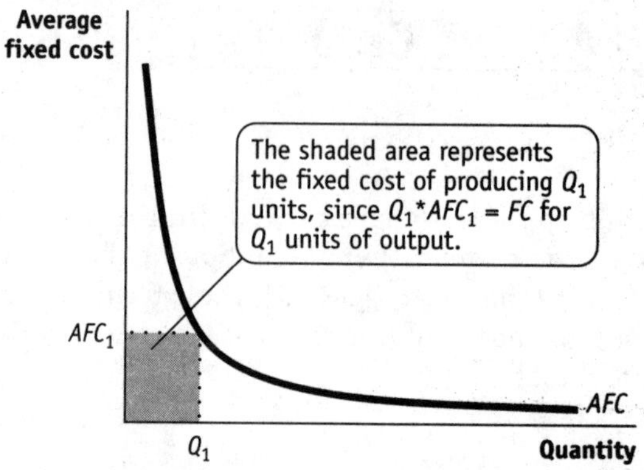

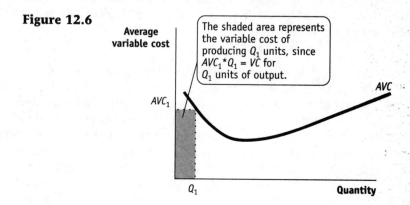

- The AVC curve is a U-shaped curve due to diminishing marginal returns to the variable input. Figure 12.6 represents the AVC curve and indicates the area that corresponds to the variable cost of producing Q_1 units of the good.

Figure 12.6

The shaded area represents the variable cost of producing Q_1 units, since $AVC_1 * Q_1 = VC$ for Q_1 units of output.

- The ATC curve is also U-shaped. Recall from tip 4 that $ATC = AFC + AVC$. Figure 12.7 illustrates this concept for Q_1 units of production. You should redraw this graph and see if you can locate the AFC, AVC, and ATC curves for a different level of output.

Figure 12.7

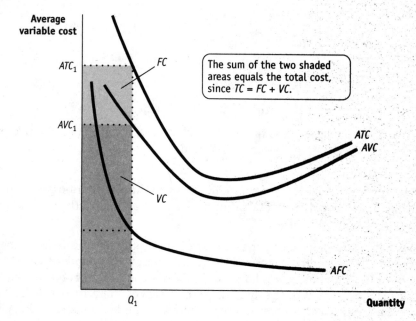

Tip #6. It is important that you understand the distinction between the marginal cost concept and the average cost concept. Marginal cost measures the cost of producing an additional unit of output, while average cost measures the cost per unit. As the firm produces an additional unit of output, it can turn to its marginal cost measure to see how this extra production affects its total cost, and it can also see that if the marginal cost of producing this last unit is less than the average total cost, then producing this additional unit will lower the unit cost of production for the firm. This relationship between marginal and average costs is difficult for many students to grasp, yet it is a relationship that almost all students know and understand in other settings. For example, suppose you form a basketball team with five players. To calculate the average height of your team you would add up the heights of the five players and then divide by 5. Then, if you added another player, this additional player would represent a marginal addition to the height of your team. If this new player were taller than the team's average height, then the team's average height would increase. But, if the player were shorter than the team's average height, then the team's average height would decrease. This basic concept can be applied to a firm's costs: when the marginal cost exceeds the average total cost, the *ATC* must rise; and when the marginal cost is less than the average total cost, the *ATC* must fall. Figure 12.8 illustrates this concept.

Figure 12.8 Marginal cost and average total cost

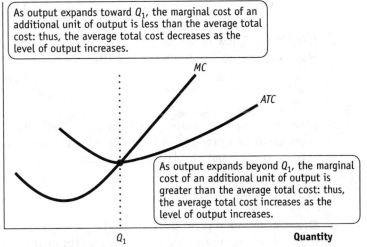

As output expands toward Q_1, the marginal cost of an additional unit of output is less than the average total cost: thus, the average total cost decreases as the level of output increases.

MC

ATC

As output expands beyond Q_1, the marginal cost of an additional unit of output is greater than the average total cost: thus, the average total cost increases as the level of output increases.

Q_1 **Quantity**

Tip #7. A firm's returns to scale identifies whether or not the firm can reduce its costs by increasing its level of production. Firms that have increasing returns to scale benefit from being relatively large, while firms with decreasing returns to scale find that getting larger is detrimental to them since as their output levels expand their average costs rise.

- Consider a firm with increasing returns to scale: when this firm doubles its inputs, it doubles its costs. But when inputs are doubled, this firm can produce more than double its original level of output. This implies that its *ATC*, which is equal to *TC/Q*, will decrease since *TC* has doubled while *Q* has more than doubled.

- Consider a firm with decreasing returns to scale: when this firm doubles its inputs, it doubles its costs. But when inputs are doubled, this firm can only produce less than double its original level of output. This implies that its *ATC*, which is equal to *TC/Q*, will increase since *TC* has doubled while *Q* has less than doubled.

Tip #8. Students often mix up the concepts of diminishing marginal returns to an input and returns to scale. Remember that diminishing returns to an input is based on changing the level of one input while holding constant the levels of all other inputs: diminishing returns to scale is a short-run concept since at least one input is being held constant. Returns to scale, in contrast, is a long-run concept based on an equal proportionate increase in all inputs and the effect of this change on the firm's level of output.

Problems and Exercises

1. The following table describes the short-run production function for Harry's company. Harry uses labor and capital to produce can openers.

Quantity of labor (workers)	Quantity of capital (units)	Quantity of output (can openers)
0	10	0
1	10	50
2	10	80
3	10	100
4	10	115
5	10	125
6	10	133
7	10	138

   a. How do you know the above table represents Harry's short-run production function? How is the short run different from the long run?

   b. Economists make a distinction between variable inputs and fixed inputs. For the above short-run production function, which input is the fixed input and which one is the variable input? Explain your answer.

   c. Draw Harry's total product curve for the production of can openers, holding the level of capital constant. In your graph measure the quantity of labor on the x-axis and the quantity of can openers on the y-axis.

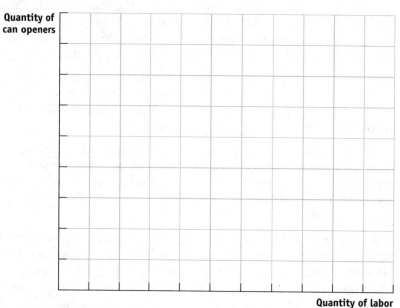

d. Complete the following table using the information given above and assuming that capital is held constant at 10 units.

Quantity of labor (workers)	Quantity of output (can openers)	Marginal product of labor $MPL = \Delta Q/\Delta L$ (can openers per worker)
0	0	
		50
1	50	
2	80	
3	100	
4	115	
5	125	
6	133	
7	138	

e. Describe the results you found in part (d). What is the relationship between the quantity of labor used and the marginal product of labor at Harry's can opener factory?

f. Graph Harry's marginal product of labor on a graph with the quantity of labor measured on the *x*-axis and the marginal product of labor measured on the *y*-axis. Plot the marginal product values you found in part (d) using the midpoint method. For example, the marginal product of labor from hiring the first unit of labor is equal to 50 can openers per worker: plot this information midway between 0 and 1 unit of labor.

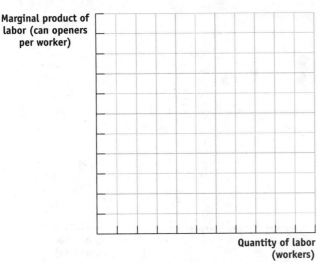

Marginal product of labor (can openers per worker)

Quantity of labor (workers)

g. What does it mean if the marginal product of labor curve is downward sloping as you hire more units of the variable input?

2. Harry (from problem 1) decides to hire an additional 10 units of capital so that his capital is now fixed at 20 units. He finds that this additional capital doubles his production at every level of labor.

a. Complete the table below, which describes Harry's production function based on his using 20 units of capital.

Quantity of labor (workers)	Quantity of capital (units)	Quantity of output (can openers)
0	20	0
1	20	
2	20	
3	20	
4	20	
5	20	
6	20	
7	20	

b. Draw a graph showing Harry's original production function using 10 units of capital and his new production function using 20 units of capital. Measure total product along the y-axis and the quantity of labor along the x-axis. Describe the effect of this change in Harry's total product curve.

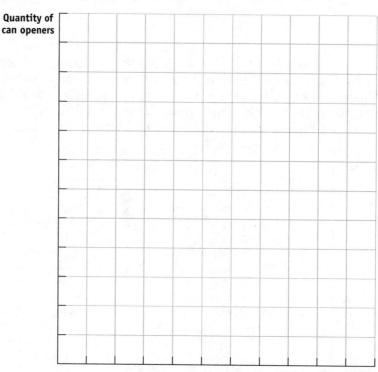

c. What happens to the marginal product of labor when Harry increases his use of capital? Provide an intuitive explanation for your answer. In your answer, sketch a graph of the original marginal product of labor curve based on 10 units of capital and the new marginal product of labor curve based on 20 units of capital.

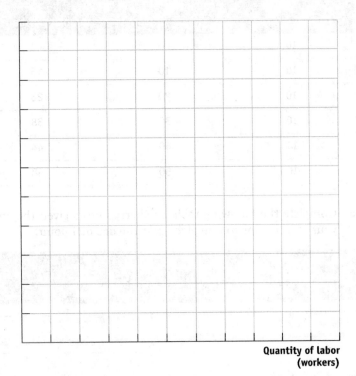

Marginal product of labor (can openers per worker)

Quantity of labor (workers)

3. In the short run, it is assumed that at least one of a firm's inputs is fixed and cannot be changed. Explain why this assumption is critical for understanding diminishing marginal returns to the variable input.

4. Malthus predicted that as population grew, the economy's diminishing ability to produce food from a given set of resources would necessarily lead to insufficient food. However, population continues to grow and so does food production. What aspect of food production did Malthus fail to anticipate?

5. The following table provides the short-run production function for Sherry's Hair Salon. Sherry uses only two inputs, labor and capital, to produce her output of stylish haircuts. The price of labor is $20 an hour and the price of capital is $50 per unit.

Quantity of capital (units)	Quantity of labor (hours of work)	Quantity of haircuts
10	0	0
10	10	15
10	20	28
10	30	38
10	40	44
10	50	48

a. Complete the following table of Sherry's costs given the above information. Round your calculations to one place past the decimal point.

Quantity of capital (units)	Quantity of labor (hours of work)	Quantity of haircuts	FC ($)	VC ($)	AFC ($)	AVC ($)	ATC ($)	TC ($)	MC ($ per unit of output)
10	0	0			—	—	—	500	
									13.3
10	10	15							
10	20	28							
10	30	38							
10	40	44							
10	50	48							

b. Does this production function exhibit diminishing marginal returns to labor? Explain your answer.

c. Graph the total cost function for Sherry's Hair Salon. Measure total cost on the vertical axis and the quantity of haircuts on the horizontal axis. Describe how increasing the quantity of haircuts affects the slope of the total cost curve.

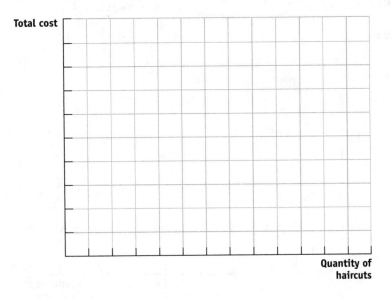

d. Graph the marginal cost function for Sherry's Hair Salon using the midpoint method. Measure marginal cost on the vertical axis and the quantity of haircuts on the horizontal axis. Describe the slope of the *MC* curve and then explain why the *MC* is sloped this way.

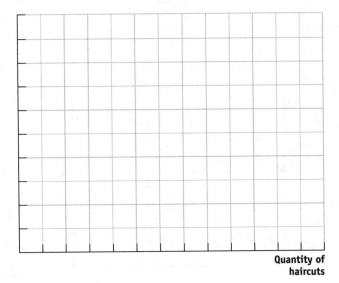

e. In a new graph, draw Sherry's Hair Salon's *AFC* curve. Measure average fixed cost on the vertical axis and the quantity of haircuts on the horizontal axis. On your graph, indicate the area that corresponds to fixed cost if 15 haircuts are currently being produced.

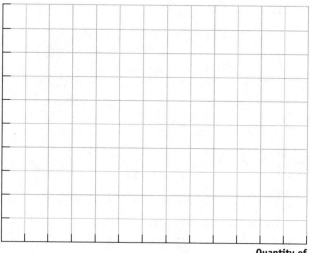

f. In a new graph, sketch Sherry's Hair Salon's *ATC*, *AVC*, *AFC*, and *MC* curves. Measure cost per unit on the vertical axis and the quantity of haircuts on the horizontal axis. What must be true about the relationship between the *ATC* and *MC* curves?

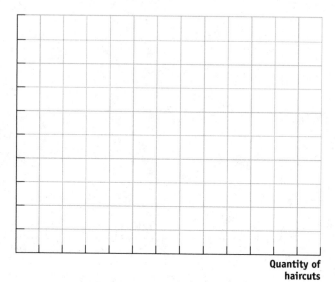

6. For each of the following costs, decide whether or not it is a fixed cost or a variable cost for the firm in the short run. Provide a brief argument for your classification of the cost.

    a. A one-year lease on the building in which the business is located.

    b. Annual property taxes that are assessed on the value of the land the business owns.

    c. The cost of a necessary metal used in the production of the firm's product.

    d. A ten-year-old metal stamping machine that has a useful life of twenty years in your business and is sufficient to produce any desired level of output for the firm.

    e. Sugar that the firm uses to make the cookies it sells.

7. Marginal cost and marginal product are both slope measures. Describe the curves that these two slope measures are derived from.

8. The table below provides some information about Stella's Delight, a business that Stella owns. Stella uses labor and capital as her only inputs in the production of her product.

a. Fill in the table below.

Quantity of labor (units)	Quantity of capital (units)	Quantity of output	VC ($)	FC ($)	AVC ($)	AFC ($)	ATC ($)	TC ($)	MC ($ per unit of output)
0	5	0			—	—	—		
1	5	10							
2	5	18		10					
3	5	24	15						
4	5	28							
5	5	30							
6	5	31							

b. What is the price of the variable input?

c. What is the price of the fixed input?

d. What is the marginal product of the fifth unit of labor?

e. What is the marginal cost of producing the twenty-fourth unit of output?

9.   Why is the spreading effect stronger than the diminishing returns effect at low levels of output, while the diminishing returns effect is stronger than the spreading effect at high levels of output?

10.   Discuss each of the following statements. Decide whether the statement is true or false and then justify your answer.

    a.   As output increases, if average total cost is decreasing, then marginal cost must be less than average total cost.

    b.   As output increases, if marginal cost is increasing, then marginal cost must be greater than average total cost.

    c.   As output increases, if marginal cost is greater than average fixed cost, then average fixed cost must be increasing.

    d.   As output increases, fixed cost decreases.

    e.   As output increases, variable cost increases.

11.   Suppose the firm represented in the table below is operating in the long run. This firm produces chairs and uses wood and labor to produce these chairs. Some production information is provided in the table. Assume the price of wood and the price of labor do not change.

Quantity of wood	Quantity of labor	Quantity of chairs
4 units	5 units	20 chairs
8 units	10 units	45 chairs
12 units	15 units	90 chairs
24 units	30 units	150 chairs

a. If this firm is currently using 4 units of wood and 5 units of labor, does it experience increasing, decreasing, or constant returns to scale if it increases its wood use to 8 units and its labor use to 10 units? Explain your answer.

b. Is this firm's *LRATC* curve downward sloping, upward sloping, or constant in the range of production described in part (a)?

c. If this firm is currently using 8 units of wood and 10 units of labor and it increases the use of both inputs by 50%, will the firm experience increasing, decreasing, or constant returns to scale?

d. Is this firm's *LRATC* curve downward sloping, upward sloping, or constant in the range of production described in part (c)?

e. Suppose this firm is currently using 12 units of wood and 15 units of labor to produce chairs, and then the firm increases its input usage by 100% for both inputs. Will the firm experience increasing, decreasing, or constant returns to scale?

f. Is this firm's *LRATC* curve downward sloping, upward sloping, or constant in the range of production described in part (e)?

▮ BEFORE YOU TAKE THE TEST

Chapter Review Questions

1. The process of transforming inputs into output is described by the firm's
   a. cost function.
   b. revenue function.
   c. production function.
   d. marginal product of labor.

2. A firm's ability to produce output depends on
   a. its profitability.
   b. the level of inputs it uses.
   c. its stock price.
   d. its location.

Use the information below about Paul's production function to answer the next five questions. Paul is a surgeon who also maintains an avid interest in economics.

Quantity of labor (hours in surgery)	Quantity of capital (operating rooms)	Total product (number of surgeries)
30	0	0
30	1	15
30	2	25
30	3	32
30	4	35

3. The information in the above table about Paul's production function depicts Paul's
   a. short-run production function.
   b. long-run production function.

4. The fixed input in Paul's production function for surgeries is the quantity of
   a. labor.   b. capital.

5. The variable input in Paul's production function for surgeries is the quantity of
   a. labor.   b. capital.

6. Paul's marginal product of capital from hiring a third operating room is
   a. 32 surgeries.
   b. 25 surgeries.
   c. 7 surgeries per operating room.
   d. 3 surgeries per operating room.

7. Paul's production function exhibits diminishing returns to capital because
   a. output increases at a diminishing rate as additional units of capital are hired.
   b. Paul cannot perform competently with more than one operating room.
   c. capital, in the form of operating rooms, is highly expensive.
   d. output does not increase at a constant rate as additional units of capital are hired.

Use the following table about the production function for Terry's Widget Shoppe to answer the next four questions. Assume labor is the only variable input Terry uses in the production of widgets.

Quantity of labor hired (workers)	Quantity of widgets per month
0	0
1	100
2	250
3	450
4	600
5	700

8. The marginal product of labor from hiring the third worker is

a. 450 widgets per worker.

b. 200 widgets per worker.

c. 150 widgets per worker.

d. 250 widgets per worker.

9. Diminishing returns to labor begins when Terry hires the

a. second worker.   c. fourth worker.

b. third worker.   d. fifth worker.

10. Terry spends $200 a month to rent a building for his company, $600 a month for the capital he employs to produce widgets, and $10 per hour for every worker he employs. Terry's fixed cost per month equals

a. $200.

b. $600.

c. $800.

d. $810.

11. Terry spends $200 a month to rent a building for his company, $600 a month for the capital he employs to produce widgets, and $10 per hour for every unit of labor he employs. Terry distinguishes between his fixed cost and his variable cost by

a. deciding whether or not he is producing in the short run or the long run.

b. whether or not the cost varies as his level of production changes.

c. whether or not the cost exceeds $500.

d. recognizing that capital is always a fixed cost while rent and labor are variable costs.

12. In the short run, as the level of total production for a firm increases, the firm's total product curve

a. increases but at a decreasing rate.

b. increases but at an increasing rate.

c. decreases but at a decreasing rate.

d. decreases but at an increasing rate.

Use the information below about the production function for Caroline's Ceramics to answer the following question.

Quantity of variable input (units)	Quantity of output (ceramic vases)
0	0
2	100
4	250
6	500
8	700
10	800

13. Caroline's Ceramics' production experiences diminishing returns to labor when Caroline hires
   a. the second unit of labor.
   b. the fourth unit of labor.
   c. the sixth unit of labor.
   d. the eighth unit of labor.

14. Larry's Auto Shop's total cost can be expressed by the equation $TC = 50 + 10Q^2$, where Q is the quantity of repairs made by Larry's Auto Shop. Which of the following statements is true for Larry's Auto Shop?
   I.   When Larry's Auto Shop produces 0 repairs, its fixed cost equals its total costs.
   II. Larry's Auto Shop's fixed cost equals $50.
   III. Larry's Auto Shop's fixed cost depends on the level of output that is produced.
   a. Statement I is true.
   b. Statements I and II are true.
   c. Statements I and III are true.
   d. Statements I, II, and III are true.

15. Larry's Auto Shop's total cost can be expressed by the equation $TC = 50 + 10Q^2$, where Q is the quantity of repairs made by Larry's Auto Shop. Larry's variable cost equals
   a. $10 when 1 unit of output is produced and $40 when 2 units of output are produced.
   b. $60 when 1 unit of output is produced and $90 when 2 units of output are produced.

16. As the level of output increases, the total cost curve for a firm gets
   a. steeper due to diminishing returns to the variable input.
   b. flatter due to diminishing returns to the variable input.

Use the information below to answer the next four questions. The table provides production function information for Jimmy's Service Shop. Assume Jimmy hires only labor and capital to produce his services. Furthermore, the price of labor is $100 per worker per week and the price of capital is $10 per unit.

Quantity of labor (workers)	Quantity of capital (units)	Quantity of output produced per week (number of services per week)
0	10	0
1	10	200
2	10	400
3	10	600
4	10	700
5	10	750

17. Jimmy's fixed cost of production equals
   a. $0.   c. $110.
   b. $100.   d. $500.

18. Jimmy's variable cost of production
   a. is constant and equal to $100 given the above information.
   b. varies with the level of output that is produced.
   c. is always greater than his fixed cost.
   d. decreases as the level of production increases due to diminishing marginal returns.

19. Jimmy's total cost of producing 700 units of output is
   a. equal to the sum of his fixed and variable costs of producing this level of output.
   b. $500.
   c. greater than his total cost of producing 600 units of output.
   d. Answers (a), (b), and (c) are all true.

20. Jimmy's marginal cost of producing the seven-hundredth unit of output is equal to
   a. $500 per unit of output.
   b. $400 per unit of output.
   c. $100 per unit of output.
   d. $1 per unit of output.

21. The marginal cost curve is upward sloping as output increases due to
   a. increasing returns to scale.
   b. decreasing returns to scale.
   c. diminishing marginal returns to the variable input.
   d. increasing marginal returns to the variable input.

22. In the short run, a firm's fixed cost _____ while the firm's average fixed cost _____.
   a. stays constant as output increases; increases as the firm produces higher levels of output
   b. stays constant as output increases; decreases as the firm produces higher levels of output
   c. increases as the firm produces higher levels of output; stays constant as output increases
   d. decreases as the firm produces higher levels of output; stays constant as output increases

23. The spreading effect refers to the
   a. decrease in AVC as the firm produces greater levels of output.
   b. decrease in AFC as the firm produces greater levels of output.
   c. combined effect on AVC and AFC of the firm producing higher levels of output.
   d. combined effect on AVC, AFC, and MC of the firm producing higher levels of output.

24. The diminishing returns effect causes the AVC to
   a. decline initially as output increases.
   b. decline at all levels of output.
   c. increase eventually as output increases.
   d. increase at all levels of output.

25. At high levels of output for a firm, the spreading effect is
   a. stronger than the diminishing returns effect.
   b. weaker than the diminishing returns effect.

26. At the minimum-cost output
   a. average variable cost must equal marginal cost.
   b. average fixed cost must equal marginal cost.
   c. average total cost must equal marginal cost.
   d. Answers (a), (b), and (c) are all true.

27. The firm's *LRATC* curve illustrates the relationship between output and
   a. average total cost when fixed cost has been chosen to minimize average total cost for each level of output.
   b. marginal cost when fixed cost has been chosen to minimize average total cost for each level of output.
   c. average total cost when variable cost has been chosen to minimize average total cost for each level of output.
   d. average total cost when marginal cost has been chosen to minimize average total cost for each level of output.

28. When the firm's *LRATC* curve is downward sloping over its range of production, this implies that
   a. when all of the firm's inputs are increased proportionately, the firm's level of production will increase, but by a smaller factor than the increase in the firm's inputs.
   b. when all of the firm's inputs are doubled, the firm's level of production will more than double.
   c. when all of the firm's inputs are tripled, the firm's level of production may or may not increase.
   d. the firm is experiencing decreasing returns to scale over this range of production.

29. A firm finds that past a certain level of production its *LRATC* curve is upward sloping. Which of the following is true?
   a. The firm in this range of production experiences decreasing returns to scale.
   b. Increased specialization allows the firm to operate a larger scale of operation.
   c. The set-up costs of entering this industry must be quite high.
   d. Answers (a), (b), and (c) are all true.

30. Which of the following statements is true?
   I. In the short run, a firm can experience increasing, decreasing, or constant returns to scale.
   II. If a firm doubles all of its inputs with the result that its output doubles, then this firm has constant returns to scale.
   III. Decreasing returns to scale are due to coordination and communication problems.
   a. Statements I and II are true.
   b. Statement II is true.
   c. Statements II and III are true.
   d. Statements I, II, and III are true.

ANSWER KEY

Answers to Problems and Exercises

1. **a.** In the short run, at least one input is fixed and does not vary as the level of output varies. From the table, we can see that the level of capital remains constant at 10 units as output increases from 0 units to 138 units. In the long run, all inputs are variable.

   b. The fixed input is the input that is held constant as output changes: in this example, it is the capital input. The variable input is labor since the level of labor used changes as the level of production changes.

   c.

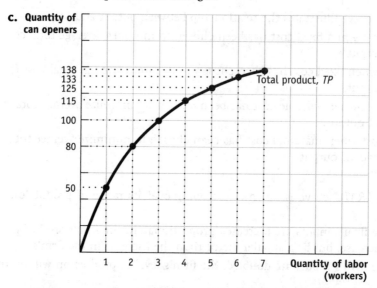

   d.

Quantity of labor (workers)	Quantity of output (can openers)	Marginal product of labor $MPL = \Delta Q/\Delta L$ (can openers per worker)
0	0	
		50
1	50	
		30
2	80	
		20
3	100	
		15
4	115	
		10
5	125	
		8
6	133	
		5
7	138	

e. As Harry uses more labor, his total production of can openers increases, but it increases at a diminishing rate. The marginal product of labor describes the addition to total product from hiring an additional worker: for Harry each additional worker adds to the total production of can openers, but each additional worker adds less to total production than did the previous worker.

f.

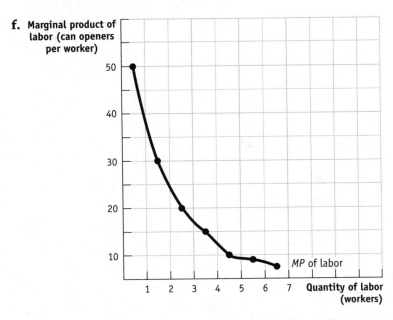

g. When the *MP* of labor curve is downward sloping as you hire additional units of labor, this implies that the production function is subject to diminishing marginal returns to labor.

2. a.

Quantity of labor (workers)	Quantity of capital (units)	Quantity of output (can openers)
0	20	0
1	20	100
2	20	160
3	20	200
4	20	230
5	20	250
6	20	266
7	20	276

b.

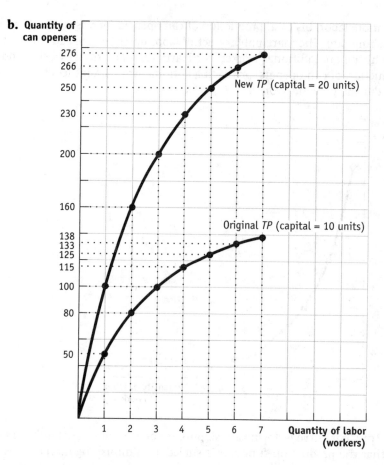

An increase in the level of capital causes Harry's total product curve to shift up; at every level of labor used, Harry can now produce a greater amount of output.

c. At every level of labor usage, Harry's marginal product of labor is higher. Each unit of labor now has more capital to work with, which enables each worker to be more productive. Each additional worker can now produce more can openers than was possible with the original level of capital. The graph below illustrates the two *MP* of labor curves based on the different levels of capital.

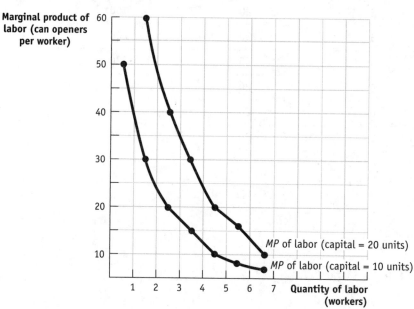

3. In the short run with at least one input fixed, a firm finds that it can expand its level of production only by hiring additional units of the variable input. But as the firm hires additional units of the variable input, each unit of the variable input has less of the fixed input to work with since the fixed input must be shared. Eventually, the addition to total product produced by the variable input increases at a decreasing rate as more units of the variable input are used. There is no reason to expect diminishing marginal returns if all the inputs can be varied: a firm that can adjust the level of all of its inputs (the long-run situation) may have increasing, decreasing, or constant returns to scale.

4. Malthus did not anticipate the scientific and technological progress in food production that occurred over the past two hundred years. The concept of diminishing marginal returns does not hold in this situation: it is possible, even if the amount of farmland cultivated is unchanged and the amount of labor involved in agricultural production is also unchanged, for production to increase when the available technology improves.

5. a.

Quantity of capital (units)	Quantity of labor (hours of work)	Quantity of haircuts	FC ($)	VC ($)	AFC ($)	AVC ($)	ATC ($)	TC ($)	MC ($ per unit of output)
10	0	0	500	0	—	—	—	500	
									13.3
10	10	15	500	200	33.3	13.3	46.7	700	
									15.4
10	20	28	500	400	17.9	14.3	32.1	900	
									20.0
10	30	38	500	600	13.2	15.8	28.9	1,100	
									33.3
10	40	44	500	800	11.4	18.2	29.5	1,300	
									50.0
10	50	48	500	1,000	10.4	20.8	31.3	1,500	

b. A production function exhibits diminishing marginal returns to labor if, as labor is increased while holding all other inputs constant, the level of total output increases but it increases at a decreasing rate. The marginal product of labor for this production function is summarized in the table below. As you can see from the table, the production function does exhibit diminishing marginal returns to labor.

Quantity of capital (units)	Quantity of labor (hours of work)	Quantity of haircuts	Marginal product of labor (haircuts per hour of work)
10	0	0	
			1.5
10	10	15	
			1.3
10	20	28	
			1
10	30	38	
			0.6
10	40	44	
			0.4
10	50	48	

c. Total cost

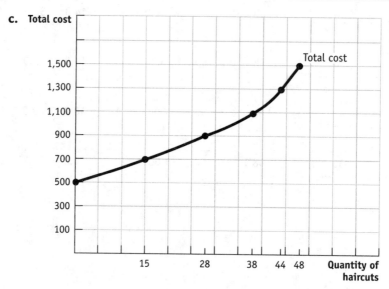

As the quantity of haircuts increases, *TC* increases at an increasing rate due to the diminishing marginal returns to labor.

d.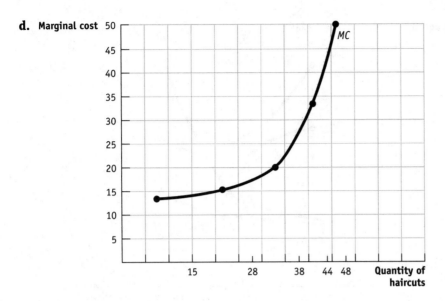

As output gets larger, the effect of diminishing marginal returns to the variable input causes MC to increase.

e.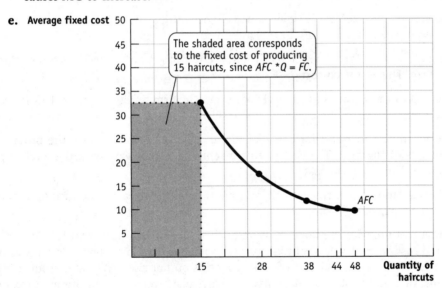

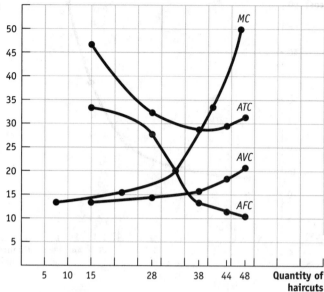

f. Cost per unit

The *ATC* curve intersects the *MC* curve at the minimum point on the *ATC* curve.

6. **a.** The cost of the one-year lease does not change during the year no matter what level of output the firm produces. This is a fixed cost.

    b. Annual property taxes are set yearly and are not based on the level of production of the firm. This is a fixed cost.

    c. The cost of metal varies as the level of output the firm produces varies. This is a variable cost.

    d. The machine still has a long, useful life and is capable of meeting the production demands of the firm. The cost of this machine does not vary with the level of production. This is a fixed cost.

    e. This is a variable cost since, as the output of cookies increases, the firm finds that it uses more sugar.

7. Marginal cost provides the slope measure of the *TC* curve at a particular level of output: marginal cost at low levels of output may fall as output increases, but eventually as output increases, the marginal cost of producing this output rises. Marginal product is the slope measure of the total product curve at a particular level of variable input usage: marginal product eventually declines as the level of variable input increases due to diminishing marginal returns to the variable input.

8. a.

Quantity of labor (units)	Quantity of capital (units)	Quantity of output	VC ($)	FC ($)	AVC ($)	AFC ($)	ATC ($)	TC ($)	MC ($)
0	5	0	0	10		—	—	10	
									0.50
1	5	10	5	10	0.50	1.00	1.50	15	
									0.63
2	5	18	10	10	0.56	0.56	1.11	20	
									0.83
3	5	24	15	10	0.63	0.42	1.04	25	
									1.25
4	5	28	20	10	0.71	0.36	1.07	30	
									2.50
5	5	30	25	10	0.83	0.33	1.17	35	
									5.00
6	5	31	30	10	0.97	0.32	1.29	40	

b. The price of the variable input is $5 per unit since the variable cost equals $15 when 3 units of labor are hired.

c. The price of the fixed input is $2 per unit since the fixed cost equals $10 when 5 units of capital are hired.

d. The marginal product of the fifth unit of labor equals the change in total output divided by the change in the amount of labor when the firm increases its use of labor from 4 units to 5 units, or (2 units of output)/(1 unit of labor), for a marginal product of 2.

e. The marginal cost of producing the twenty-fourth unit of output is equal to the change in total cost divided by the change in output, or ($5)/(6 units of output), for a marginal cost of $0.83.

9. The spreading effect refers to the ability to spread the fixed cost over all the production of the firm. When the firm produces a few units, the fixed cost is not spread over very many units and therefore the average fixed cost is relatively high; when the firm produces a large number of units, the fixed cost is spread over these units and the average fixed cost is therefore much smaller. This means that the spreading effect is not of great importance when producing a lot of output, but it can have a significant effect at lower levels of production. The diminishing returns effect describes the effect on average variable cost of producing larger amounts of output. To produce larger amounts of output the firm must hire more variable input, but each additional unit of the variable input is less productive than the previous unit, and therefore as output increases, average variable cost also increases. The diminishing returns effect gets more pronounced the greater the level of production.

10. a. True. If average total cost is decreasing, this must be because the marginal cost of producing another unit of output is less than the average total cost of producing the current level of output. When an additional unit of output is produced in these circumstances, this causes the average total cost to fall.

b. False. Marginal cost can be increasing but still be less than average total cost.

    c. False. Average fixed cost decreases as output increases since fixed cost is constant for the firm and does not change as the level of output changes.

    d. False. Fixed cost does not change for the firm no matter what level of output they produce.

    e. True. As the firm produces more output, it must hire additional units of its variable input, which causes its variable cost to increase.

11. **a.** In this question, the firm is doubling both inputs (4 units of wood to 8 units of wood, 5 units of labor to 10 units of labor) and the firm finds that this leads to more than double the amount of output (20 chairs to 45 chairs). This firm is experiencing increasing returns to scale, since as the scale or size of operation gets larger, the firm's unit cost of production falls.

    b. This firm's *LRATC* curve is downward sloping over this range of output.

    c. A 50% increase in the use of inputs would result in the firm using 12 units of wood and 15 units of labor. With a 50% increase in inputs the firm finds that its output increases from 45 chairs to 90 chairs, which is a 100% increase in the level of output. The firm experiences increasing returns to scale over this range of output.

    d. This firm's *LRATC* curve is downward sloping over this range of output.

    e. The firm changes its wood usage from 12 units of wood to 24 units of wood and its labor usage from 15 units of labor to 30 units of labor. Output changes from 90 chairs to 150 chairs. The increase in output is less than 100%, so this firm experiences decreasing returns to scale over this range of production.

    f. This firm's *LRATC* curve is upward sloping over this range of output.

Answers to Chapter Review Questions

1. **Answer c.** This is a definitional statement. Inputs are combined together to produce output, and the production function describes this relationship.

2. **Answer b.** A firm's ability to produce output depends on the level of inputs it uses: this is a definitional statement.

3. **Answer a.** Since one of the inputs is fixed (the quantity of labor), a short-run production function is implied.

4. **Answer a.** The fixed input is the input that does not change in the short run as the level of output changes. Looking at the given table, the quantity of labor is fixed or constant while the quantity of capital varies.

5. **Answer b.** The variable input is the input that varies as the level of output changes. Looking at the given table, the quantity of capital varies.

6. **Answer c.** The marginal product of capital is defined as the change in total output divided by the change in capital, holding all other inputs constant. When Paul increases his number of operating rooms from two to three, his output of surgeries increases from 25 surgeries to 32 surgeries. Paul's marginal product of capital is thus 7 surgeries per operating room.

7. **Answer a.** Diminishing returns to capital occurs when total product increases at a decreasing rate as additional units of capital are hired. Diminishing marginal returns to capital implies that the marginal product of capital declines in value as additional units of capital are hired. Answer (b) is not necessarily correct: Paul finds his 30 hours of labor is more productive when spread across several operating rooms instead of a single operating room. The diminishing marginal returns to capital is due to technology and not the cost of capital—answer (c). Answer (d) is false by virtue of the definition of diminishing marginal returns.

8. **Answer b.** The marginal product of labor is the change in output divided by the change in labor. In this example, labor changes by 1 unit at a time, so we can simply calculate the change in output to find the marginal product of labor. The total product when two workers are hired equals 250 widgets, while the total product when three workers are hired equals 450 widgets; therefore, the marginal product of hiring the third worker is 200 widgets per worker.

9. **Answer c.** Diminishing returns to labor begins when the marginal product of labor falls as the quantity of labor increases. The marginal product of labor for the first worker is 100 widgets per worker; the marginal product of labor for the second worker is 150 widgets per worker; the marginal product of labor for the third worker is 200 widgets per worker; and the marginal product of labor for the fourth worker is 150 widgets per worker. The hiring of the fourth worker increases output, but at a diminishing rate.

10. **Answer c.** Fixed costs are those costs that do not vary as output varies. Terry's fixed costs include his capital costs of $600 a month and his rent of $200 a month: neither of these costs change for Terry no matter what level of output he produces. In contrast, Terry's use of labor varies as he changes his level of production, and when he hires additional labor his variable costs are altered.

11. **Answer b.** There are no fixed costs in the long run, only variable costs; there isn't some dollar amount that exists as a limit to variable costs; and capital or labor can be variable in the short run. What does distinguish variable costs from fixed costs is that variable costs vary as the level of output varies: a firm wishing to produce more of a good in the short run does so by hiring more units of the variable input.

12. **Answer a.** In the short run, the firm has at least one fixed input. To increase its production, it must hire additional units of the variable input, but the addition to total output from hiring an additional unit of the variable input eventually decreases due to the diminishing returns to the variable input. This means that output increases, but at a decreasing rate.

13. **Answer d.** To answer this question, first calculate the marginal product of labor. Recall that the marginal product of labor is the change in total product divided by the change in labor. In this example, labor increases by 2 units at a time, so the change in labor is 2 units of labor. The marginal product of labor of hiring the second unit of labor is thus (100 units of output)/(2 units of labor), or 50 units of output per unit of labor. Once you have calculated the marginal product of labor for each level of labor in the table, you can then determine at what level of labor the marginal product first declines.

14. **Answer b.** Larry's Auto Shop's fixed cost equals his total cost when output is zero, since the firm does not hire any of the variable input if it decides to not produce any output. When Q equals zero, Larry's total cost equals $50, and therefore Larry's fixed cost must equal $50. Fixed cost does not change as the level of output produced by the firm changes.

15. **Answer a.** When output is zero, fixed cost equals total cost and Larry's fixed cost is therefore $50. Larry's variable cost can therefore by expressed as $10Q^2$ since $TC = FC + VC$. When Q equals 1, VC is $10; when Q equals 2, VC is $40.

16. **Answer a.** As the firm produces greater levels of output, its costs increase because it must employ more and more units of the variable input to produce that output. Yet as it employs more of the variable input, it finds that each additional unit of the variable input is less productive than the last unit hired, which therefore leads total cost to increase at an increasing rate.

17. **Answer b.** Jimmy's fixed cost is equal to the number of units of the fixed input he hires times the price of the fixed input. Jimmy hires 10 units of capital, irrespective of his level of production, and so his fixed cost equals $100.

18. **Answer b.** By definition, variable cost for a firm varies as the level of production varies, which eliminates answer (a). Variable cost may or may not be greater than fixed cost. Variable cost increases as the level of output increases due to the diminishing marginal returns to the variable input.

19. **Answer d.** Total cost for producing any level of output can be found by summing variable cost and fixed cost for that level of output. Jimmy's fixed cost equals $100 and his variable cost is $400 when he produces 700 units of output, so Jimmy's total cost of producing 700 units of output is $500. The total cost of producing 600 units of output is

$400. Jimmy's total cost of producing 600 units of output is less than his total cost of producing 700 units of output.

20. **Answer d.** The marginal cost of producing the last unit of output is equal to the change in total cost divided by the change in output. The total cost of producing 700 units is $500 and the total cost of producing 600 units is $400: the change in total cost is $100. The change in output is 100 units. Thus, the marginal cost of producing the seven-hundredth unit of output is $100/(100 units of output), or $1 per unit of output.

21. **Answer c.** As output increases, the marginal cost of producing that level of output also increases because the marginal product of the variable input is falling. This is due to the diminishing marginal returns to the variable input.

22. **Answer b.** FC does not vary as the level of production varies, but average fixed cost declines as output increases since AFC = FC/Q and Q is increasing.

23. **Answer b.** The spreading effect refers to the idea that since fixed costs are constant at all short-run levels of output this implies that the AFC will decline as output increases, since those constant fixed costs will be spread over a larger number of units of output. The spreading effect does not impact the AVC or the MC.

24. **Answer c.** The diminishing returns effect refers to the idea that as the firm increases its production in the short run it must hire additional units of the variable input, but that as the firm's usage of the variable input increases it finds that additional units of the variable input are less productive than the preceding unit. This means that the firm's AVC eventually rises due to the variable cost of production increasing faster than the increase in the level of output.

25. **Answer b.** At high levels of output, the firm's ATC curve increases, indicating that the spreading effect, which causes AFC to fall as output increases, is not as strong as the diminishing returns effect, which causes AVC to rise as output increases.

26. **Answer c.** At the minimum-cost output, average total cost equals marginal cost since the minimum-cost output is the level of output at which average total cost is minimized. At outputs lower than the minimum-cost output, average total cost is falling as output increases, which implies that the marginal cost of producing an additional unit of output is less than the average total cost of producing that output. At outputs greater than the minimum-cost output, average total cost is rising as output increases, which implies that the marginal cost of producing an additional unit of output is greater than the average total cost of producing that output. The average variable cost is not at its minimum point at the minimum-cost output, and the average fixed cost does not have a minimum point since it declines as the level of output increases.

27. **Answer a.** This is the definition of the LRATC curve, which identifies the lowest average total cost of production for every level of output, assuming that the firm has the freedom to set its fixed input at the optimal level for each level of output.

28. **Answer b.** As the firm increases its production the firm's cost rises, but if the LRATC curve is downward sloping this implies that the increase in output must be proportionately greater than the increase in total cost. In this range of output, the firm has increasing returns to scale.

29. **Answer a.** When a firm's LRATC curve is upward sloping this means that increasing the firm's level of production will raise the average total cost of producing the good, and the firm does not benefit from getting larger. In this case the firm has decreasing returns to scale. Decreasing returns to scale arise primarily because of problems of coordination and communication. When a firm has high set-up costs, this implies that the firm is likely to have increasing returns to scale and decreasing average total cost over a large range of outputs. The firm in this example has increasing average total cost.

30. **Answer c.** Statement II is the definition of constant returns to scale, and statement III identifies the primary reasons for the decreasing returns to scale. Returns to scale is a long-run phenomenon and thus statement I, with its focus on the short run, is incorrect.

chapter 13

Perfect Competition and the Supply Curve

Summary

This chapter develops the model of perfect competition and then uses this model to discuss a firm's selection of the profit-maximizing level of output. This model is also used to explore the short-run and long-run production decisions of the firm where these decisions are based on the firm's profitability. The chapter also explores the factors that determine the short-run and long-run industry supply curve for an industry.

Chapter Objectives

Objective #1. A perfectly competitive industry is an industry in which both the producers and consumers in that industry are price takers. A price-taking producer is one whose actions cannot affect the market price of the good sold. A price-taking firm can sell as many units of the good as it would like at the prevailing market price. A price-taking consumer is a consumer who cannot influence the market price of the good by their actions. The market price is therefore unaffected by the actions of either individual producers or individual consumers.

- For an industry to be perfectly competitive there must be many producers in that industry, and no one of these producers can have a large market share of the industry's output.

- For an industry to be perfectly competitive consumers must regard the products produced in that market as being equivalent. The product sold in a perfectly competitive industry is a standardized product or commodity, and consumers must view each producer's product as a perfect substitute for any other producer's product.

- Most perfectly competitive industries also have easy entry of new firms into the industry and exit of existing firms from the industry in the long run. This is referred to as free entry and exit.

Objective #2. A firm's total revenue (*TR*) can be calculated by multiplying the level of production times the market price. The firm can then compare its total revenue with its total cost (*TC*) to find the level of output at which it maximizes profit. The profit-maximizing level of output for the firm is the level of output at which total revenue minus total cost results in the greatest positive number.

Objective #3. Marginal revenue (*MR*) is the change in total revenue divided by the change in output from selling another unit of the good. For a perfectly competitive firm, marginal revenue is constant and equals the market price, since the addition to total revenue the firm receives from selling another unit of the good equals the market price the firm receives for the good. Thus, the *MR* curve for a firm can be represented as a horizontal line intersecting the price axis at the market price. Figure 13.1 represents this concept: the firm is depicted in the left-hand graph, and the industry or the entire market for the good is represented in the right-hand graph. The market demand and market supply curves in the right-hand graph determine the market price (*P*) and market quantity (*Q*). The firm accepts this price since it is a price-taking firm. The horizontal line in the left-hand figure represents the marginal revenue the firm receives at any level of output. The firm's *MR* curve is also the firm's demand curve (*d*) since it can sell as many units of the good as it wishes to at the prevailing market price.

Figure 13.1

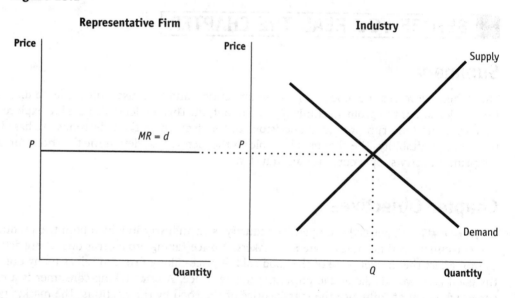

Objective #4. Marginal analysis can be used to compute the profit-maximizing level of output. To do this analysis, marginal revenue and marginal cost must be calculated. Recall that marginal cost (*MC*) is the change in total cost divided by the change in output.

• The profit-maximizing level of output corresponds to that level of output at which marginal revenue equals marginal cost. Marginal revenue measures the addition to total revenue from selling one more unit of the good while marginal cost measures the addition to total cost from producing one more unit of the good. When marginal revenue is greater than marginal cost the firm's benefit from producing this last unit of output is greater than the cost of producing this last unit: the firm should expand output to include this unit of production. When marginal revenue is less than marginal cost the firm's benefit from producing another unit of output is less than the cost of producing this last unit: the firm should not expand output to include this additional unit of production. It is only when marginal revenue equals marginal cost for the last unit of output produced that the firm earns its highest level of profit.

- The producer's optimal output rule states that profit is maximized by producing that level of output at which marginal revenue equals marginal cost for the last unit produced. That is, the firm should produce that level of output where $MR = MC$. This can be restated as: the firm's profit-maximizing level of output is where $P = MC$, since for the perfectly competitive firm P equals MR. Figure 13.2 illustrates the profit-maximizing level of output (q) for a perfectly competitive firm.

Figure 13.2

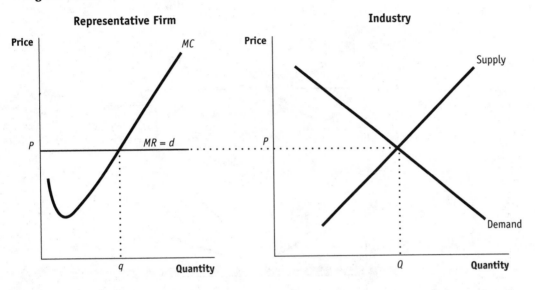

Objective #5. The profit-maximization rule identifies the level of output that results in maximizing the firm's profit, but it does not tell the producer whether they should produce at all. To answer this question, the firm needs to look at whether it is profitable or unprofitable to produce. The decision to produce or not is based on the firm's economic profit and not its accounting profit. The cost curves that the firm uses to make its production decisions are cost curves that include all costs, implicit and explicit. Given the firm's cost curves, whether it is profitable or not to produce depends on whether the market price of the good is more or less than the firm's average total cost.

- The firm makes a profit whenever its total revenue is greater than its total cost. The firm breaks even whenever its total revenue is equal to its total cost. The firm incurs a loss whenever its total revenue is less than its total cost.

- The firm's profitability can also be expressed in terms of averages. Profit = $TR - TC$, and if both sides of this equation are divided by output (Q), this results in profit/Q = TR/Q – TC/Q. TR/Q is average revenue, which for a perfectly competitive firm is the market price (P) since the average price for the price-taking firm exactly equals the market-determined price. TC/Q is equal to the average total cost (ATC) of producing the level of output. This equation provides a means for comparing the price of the good to the average total cost: when the price is greater than the average total cost, the firm earns a positive profit; when the price is equal to the average total cost, the firm breaks even; and when the price is less than the average total cost, the firm incurs a loss. Figure 13.3 illustrates three situations: a firm earning a positive economic profit ($P > ATC$), a firm earning zero economic profit ($P = ATC$), and a firm earning negative economic profit ($P < ATC$).

Figure 13.3

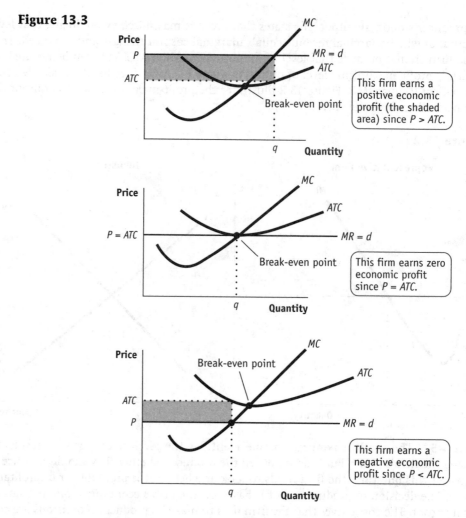

- The firm breaks even, or earns a zero economic profit, if the market price is equal to the minimum of the firm's average total cost; the firm earns a negative profit if the price is less than the minimum of the firm's average total cost; and the firm earns a positive profit if the price is greater than the minimum of the firm's average total cost. Figure 13.3 illustrates these three possibilities and the resultant profit situation for the firm. The minimum point of the average total cost is called the break-even price because it identifies the price at which the firm breaks even (earns a zero economic profit).

Objective #6. In the short run, a perfectly competitive firm incurs its fixed costs whether or not it produces, while it can reduce its variable costs by deciding not to produce. The firm would therefore want to base its production decision in the short run on whether it can cover its variable cost of production: when the firm's revenues do not cover all of its variable cost of production, then the firm will lose money on its fixed cost as well as some of its variable cost; when the firm's revenues cover all of its variable cost of production, then the firm will lose money only on that part of its fixed cost that the remaining revenue does not cover. In the short run, the firm will be willing to produce only if its revenue is sufficient to cover all of its variable cost of production. This concept can be summarized by the following guidelines:

- In the short run, when the market price is less than the minimum point of the firm's average variable cost (AVC) curve, then the firm should shut down and produce 0 units of output. Its short-run costs will therefore equal its fixed cost and the firm will minimize its losses.

- In the short run, when the market price is greater than or equal to the minimum point of the firm's *AVC* but is less than the minimum point of the ATC, then the firm should produce the level of output at which $P = MC$. This level of output will result in negative economic profits in the short run, but these negative profits will be equal to or less than the firm's fixed cost.

- Figure 13.4 illustrates the short-run production decisions for these two possibilities.

Figure 13.4

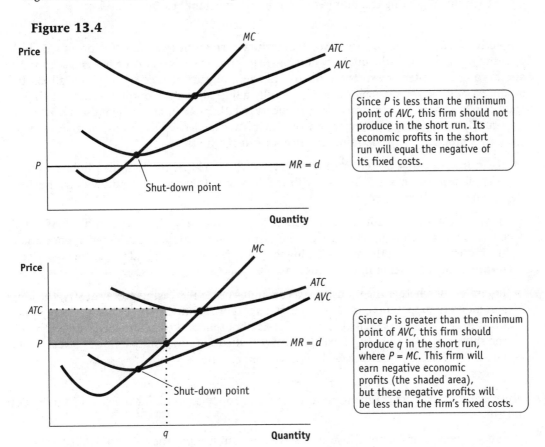

- To summarize, when price is between the minimum point of the *AVC* and the minimum point of the *ATC*, the firm will lose money (earn a negative economic profit) in the short run, but it will lose less money by producing in the short run than it would lose if it decided to shut down in the short run. This decision is similar to the decision to ignore sunk costs: the firm's fixed cost cannot be changed in the short run, so they should be ignored by the firm when the firm makes its short-run production decision.

Objective #7.   The firm's short-run supply curve corresponds to the firm's *MC* curve when the market price is equal to or above the shut-down price (the minimum point of the *AVC* curve). The firm's short-run supply curve for market prices less than the shut-down price is the vertical axis: the firm will produce 0 units of output when the market price is less than the shut-down price.

Objective #8.   In the long run a firm can exit the industry or a new firm can enter the industry. Firms will exit the industry if the market price is consistently less than the break-even price, or the minimum point of the firm's *ATC* curve. In other words, firms will exit the industry in the long run if they are consistently making negative economic profit in the short run. Firms will enter the industry if the market price is consistently greater than the break-even price. That is, firms will enter the industry in the long run if existing firms are consistently making positive economic profit in the short run.

Objective #9.   The short-run industry supply curve shows the quantity that producers supply at each price, holding the number of producers constant at a given level.

Objective #10. The long-run market equilibrium corresponds to the situation in which the quantity supplied equals the quantity demanded given that sufficient time has elapsed for producers to either enter or exit the industry. In the long-run market equilibrium, all existing producers and all potential producers have fully adjusted to their optimal long-run choices, and therefore there is no incentive for producers to either exit or enter the industry. Thus, the long-run industry supply curve shows the quantity supplied by the industry at each price, given that producers have had time to enter or exit the industry.

- In an industry that has constant costs across the industry, the long-run industry supply curve is perfectly elastic. The long-run industry supply curve can be drawn as a horizontal line at the break-even price.

- In an industry that has increasing costs across the industry, the long-run industry supply curve is upward sloping. This reflects the fact that some input is in limited supply, and as the industry expands, this results in higher prices for that input and therefore higher costs for the firms producing in that industry.

- Regardless of whether the industry is a constant-cost or increasing-cost industry, the long-run industry supply curve is flatter than the short-run industry supply curve. Entry of new firms in the long run results in greater levels of output and therefore lower prices than in the short run, and the exit of existing firms in the long run results in lower levels of output and therefore higher prices than in the short run.

Objective #11. Perfect competition leads to three conclusions about the cost of production and efficiency.

- When the perfectly competitive industry is in equilibrium, the value of marginal cost is the same for all firms. Since firms produce that output where marginal cost equals the market price, and since all firms are price takers, this implies that all firms must have the same marginal cost value in equilibrium.

- In the long run, all firms in a perfectly competitive industry earn zero economic profit due to free entry and exit. The existence of positive economic profits in the short run acts as an incentive for new firms to enter the industry. The existence of negative profits in the short run acts as an incentive for existing firms to exit the industry. This entry and exit continues until economic profits for all firms in the industry equal zero.

- The long-run market equilibrium in a perfectly competitive industry is efficient because there are no mutually beneficial transactions that are not exploited. In the long-run equilibrium in a perfectly competitive industry, costs are minimized and no resources are wasted.

Key Terms

price-taking producer a producer whose actions have no effect on the market price of the good or service it sells.

price-taking consumer a consumer whose actions have no effect on the market price of the good or service he or she buys.

perfectly competitive market a market in which all participants are price-takers.

perfectly competitive industry an industry in which all producers are price-takers.

market share the fraction of the total industry output accounted for by a given producer's output.

standardized product output of different producers regarded by consumers as the same good; also referred to as a *commodity.*

commodity output of different producers regarded by consumers as the same good; also referred to as a *standardized product.*

free entry and exit describes an industry that potential producers can easily enter or current producers can leave.

marginal revenue the change in *total revenue* generated by an additional unit of output.

optimal output rule profit is maximized by producing the quantity of output at which the *marginal revenue* of the last unit produced is equal to its *marginal cost.*

price-taking firm's optimal output rule the profit of a price-taking firm is maximized by producing the quantity of output at which the market price is equal to the *marginal cost* of the last unit produced.

marginal revenue curve a graphical representation showing how *marginal revenue* varies as output varies.

break-even price the market price at which a firm earns zero profits.

shut-down price the price at which a firm ceases production in the short run because the market price has fallen below the minimum *average variable cost.*

short-run individual supply curve a graphical representation that shows how an individual producer's profit-maximizing output quantity depends on the market price, taking *fixed cost* as given.

industry supply curve a graphical representation that shows the relationship between the price of a good and the total output of the industry for that good.

short-run industry supply curve a graphical representation that shows how the *quantity supplied* by an industry depends on the market price, given a fixed number of producers.

Key Terms *(continued)*

short-run market equilibrium an economic balance that results when the *quantity supplied* equals the *quantity demanded*, taking the number of producers as given.

long-run market equilibrium an economic balance in which, given sufficient time for producers to enter or exit an industry, the *quantity supplied* equals the *quantity demanded*.

long-run industry supply curve a graphical representation that shows how *quantity supplied* responds to price once producers have had time to enter or exit the industry.

AFTER YOU READ THE CHAPTER

Tips

Tip #1. This chapter advances the use of cost concepts in analyzing firm behavior. You may find it helpful to work with the graphs depicting the short-run and long-run economic behavior of the perfectly competitive market: these graphs can serve as a roadmap for directing your analyses of how a firm responds to economic events. Students often find that a quick sketch of a representative firm and the industry provides insight into solving a challenging problem.

- Figure 13.5 illustrates an example of this type of quick sketch for a perfectly competitive industry in the short run. In this example, the firm is earning a negative economic profit since the price the good is sold for is less than the average total cost of producing the good. Here's the analysis for this sketch: the industry demand and supply curves determine the equilibrium price (P) in the market and the equilibrium market quantity (Q). Firms are price takers, so they will sell their output at P and their MR curve is a horizontal line drawn at that price. Firms will select their profit-maximizing level of output (q for the representative firm in our sketch) by producing the quantity at which $MR = MC$, or where $P = MC$. The firm can then calculate its profit by comparing its P to its ATC at the level of production that was chosen. In this example $P < ATC$, so the firm must be making negative economic profit. The shaded area in the graph represents this negative economic profit.

Figure 13.5

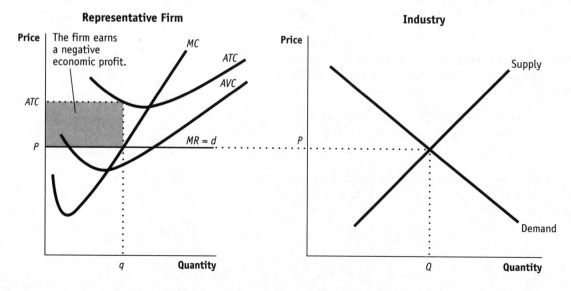

- Figure 13.5 could be redrawn to illustrate a short-run equilibrium where the representative firm earns positive economic profit, or it could be redrawn so that the representative firm earns zero economic profit. These three short-run scenarios are important for you to be able to construct and understand: being able to construct the graph and read the graph is vital for your ability to understand this material.

- Figure 13.6 provides a sketch of the long-run equilibrium in a perfectly competitive industry. (This is also the same sketch for a short-run situation where the representative firm earns zero economic profit.) In this example, the firm is earning a zero economic profit because the price the good is sold for is equal to the average total cost of producing the good. Here's the analysis for this sketch: the industry demand and supply curves determine the equilibrium price (P) in the market and the equilibrium market quantity (Q). Firms are price takers, so they will sell their output at P and their MR curve is a horizontal line drawn at that price. Firms will select their profit-maximizing level of output (q for the representative firm in our sketch) by producing the quantity at which $MR = MC$, or where $P = MC$. The firm can then calculate its profit by comparing its P to its ATC at the level of production that was chosen. In this example, $P = ATC$, so the firm must be making zero economic profit.

Figure 13.6

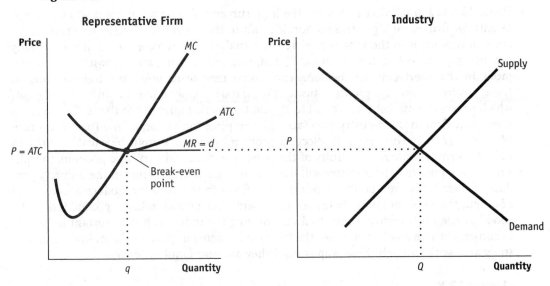

Tip #2. In the short run in a perfectly competitive industry, there is no entry or exit of firms. Thus, positive or negative economic profits can persist in the short run. However, in the long run there is entry and exit. It is important to understand how this impacts the short-run situation for a perfectly competitive industry.

- Figure 13.7 analyzes the effect of the exit of firms in the long run. Here's the analysis: the representative firm is initially producing q and selling this output at P, resulting in the firm earning negative economic profit in the short run (this is the scenario we had for Figure 13.5). In the long run, some of the existing firms exit the industry due to these negative economic profits, and this causes the market supply curve to shift to the left, which causes the market price to rise to P_2 and the market quantity to fall to Q_2. The representative firm that remains in the industry now faces a higher price for its output and therefore a new MR curve (MR_2). The firm will select its profit-maximizing output by equating MR_2 to MC: the firm will produce q_2 units of the good. The firm will earn zero economic profit, since in the long run the industry will have firms exit until all remaining firms produce at their break-even point. Notice that the firms that remain in the industry produce a higher level of output than they did initially (q_2 versus q), while the overall industry production of the good has fallen (Q_2 versus Q) due to firms exiting the industry. It is important to be able to construct these graphs and make the logical arguments implied by them. Make sure you study and work through these graphs until they are very familiar to you.

Figure 13.7

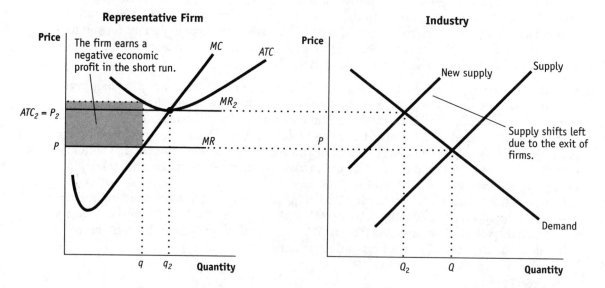

- Figure 13.8 is a graph that represents the long-run equilibrium adjustment when the representative firm earns a positive economic profit in the short run, thereby resulting in the entry of new firms in the long run. Here's the analysis: the representative firm is initially producing q and selling this output at P, resulting in the firm earning positive economic profit in the short run. In the long run, some new firms enter the industry due to these positive economic profits, causing the market supply curve to shift to the right, which causes the market price to fall to P_2 and the market quantity to rise to Q_2. The representative firm in the industry now faces a lower price for its output and therefore a new MR curve (MR_2). The firm will select its profit-maximizing output by equating MR_2 to MC: the firm will produce q_2 units of the good. The firm will earn zero economic profit, since in the long run the industry will have firms enter until all firms in the industry produce at their break-even point. Notice that the firms in the industry produce a lower level of output than they did initially (q_2 versus q), while the overall industry production of the good has risen (Q_2 versus Q) due to firms entering the industry. It is important to be able to construct these graphs and make the logical arguments implied by them. Make sure you study and work through these graphs until they are very familiar to you.

Figure 13.8

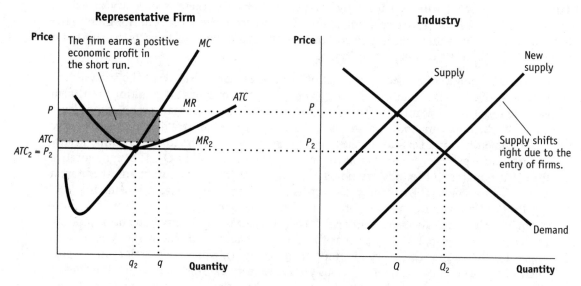

Tip #3. This chapter relies again on marginal analysis, which is used by the firm to determine the profit-maximizing level of output. The firm bases its production decision on the addition to total revenue it gets from selling one more unit of the good (*MR*) versus the addition to total cost of producing one more unit of the good (*MC*). By this point in your study of economics, the concept of marginal analysis should be very familiar to you and something that you naturally consider when analyzing a situation or problem.

Tip #4. The profitability conditions for a perfectly competitive firm can be summarized as follows:

- When *P* > minimum *ATC* or the break-even price, the firm earns a positive economic profit in the short run and firms enter the industry in the long run.

- When *P* = minimum *ATC* or the break-even price, the firm earns zero economic profit in the short run and firms do not enter or exit the industry in the long run.

- When *P* < minimum *ATC* or the break-even price, the firm earns a negative economic profit in the short run and firms exit the industry in the long run.

Tip #5. The production conditions for a perfectly competitive firm can be summarized as follows:

- When *P* > minimum *AVC* or the shut-down price, the firm produces in the short run. If *P* > minimum *ATC*, the firm is covering all of its variable cost as well as its fixed cost of production. If *P* < minimum *ATC* but is still above the minimum *AVC*, the firm is covering all of its variable cost and part of its fixed cost.

- When *P* = minimum *AVC* or the shut-down price, the firm is indifferent between producing in the short run and shutting down in the short run. The firm's revenue is just enough to cover its variable cost of production. The firm's profit is thus equal to the negative of its fixed cost.

- When *P* < minimum *AVC* or the shut-down price, the firm shuts down production in the short run since it cannot cover its variable cost of production. The firm's profit when it produces 0 units of output in the short run is equal to the negative of its fixed cost.

Problems and Exercises

1. What does it mean to be a price-taking firm? What does it mean to be a price-taking consumer? What is the relationship between market share and price taking?

2. The model of perfect competition is based on two necessary conditions and a third condition that is often present as well. Identify each of these conditions and then briefly discuss their importance in the model.

3. The table below provides information about Sarah's Doughnut Shoppe, a small firm operating in a perfectly competitive industry. Use this information to answer this set of questions.

Quantity of doughnuts	Total revenue	Total cost	Profit
100	$ 200	$250	
200	400	360	
300	600	530	
400	800	725	
500	1,000	950	

a. What is the market price for a doughnut?

b. Fill in the profit column of the table. At what level of output does Sarah's Doughnut Shoppe maximize its profits?

c. Calculate Sarah's Doughnut Shoppe's marginal cost and marginal revenue for each level of output. Use the table below to organize your results.

Quantity of doughnuts	Total revenue	Total cost	Marginal cost	Marginal revenue	Profit
100	$ 200	$250			
200	400	360			
300	600	530			
400	800	725			
500	1,000	950			

d. What is the relationship between marginal revenue and marginal cost at the profit-maximizing level of output for Sarah's Doughnut Shoppe? Explain the meaning of this relationship and how it relates to profitability.

4. Use the graphs below of a perfectly competitive market in a constant-cost industry to answer this set of questions.

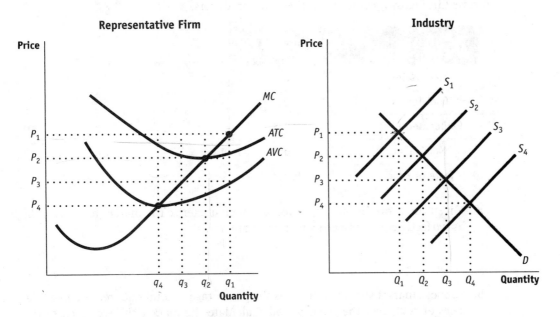

a. Suppose in the short run the industry supply curve is given by S_1. Identify the short-run equilibrium market price and quantity, the quantity produced by the representative firm, and whether the firm is making positive, negative, or zero economic profits. Holding everything else constant, what will happen in the long run in this industry? In your answer to this question, identify the long-run equilibrium price and quantity in the industry, the quantity produced by the firm in the long run, and the level of profits for the firm in the long run.

b. Suppose in the short run the industry supply curve is given by S_4. Identify the short-run equilibrium market price and quantity, the quantity produced by the representative firm, and whether the firm is making positive, negative, or zero economic profits. Do you know with certainty what this firm's profits equal in the short run? Holding everything else constant, what will happen in the long run in this industry? In your answer to this question, identify the long-run equilibrium price and quantity in the industry, the quantity produced by the firm in the long run, and the level of profits for the firm in the long run.

c. You are told that this representative firm is currently making negative economic profits in the short run, but that it is covering all of its variable costs of production and some of its fixed costs. Given the price choices in the above graph, what is the current price for this good? In the long run will there be entry of new firms into the industry or will existing firms exit the industry? Explain your answer.

5. You are given the following information about the five firms that produce soda in Bigtown. These five firms are the only producers of soda in Bigtown, and all soda consumed in Bigtown comes from these five producers.

Name of company	Quantity of soda sold (cans per month)
Fizzy Water	150
Cool Tonics	200
Carbonated Bliss	100
Mom's Pop	450
Taste of Eden	100

a. Given the above information would you characterize the market for soda in Bigtown as perfectly competitive? Explain your answer.

b. Suppose market share is defined as the percentage of total sales represented by a firm's sales of soda over the given period. Calculate the market share of each of the companies producing soda in Bigtown.

c. Is the soda produced in this market likely to be standardized? Explain your answer.

6. The market for books is perfectly competitive and a constant-cost industry. The short-run industry supply curve is given by the equation $P = 4 + Q$, while the industry demand curve is given by the equation $P = 100 - Q$, where P is the market price and Q is the market quantity. The representative firm's MC curve can be written as $MC = 4 + 2q$, and its TC is given by the equation $TC = 36 + 4q + q^2$, where q is the quantity produced by the firm.

a. What is the equilibrium price and the equilibrium market quantity for this good in the short run?

b. Given the market price you calculated in part (a), what is the profit-maximizing quantity, q, for a representative firm to produce in the short run? What rule did you use to calculate this profit-maximizing level of output?

c. Is this firm making positive, negative, or zero economic profit in the short run? Sketch a diagram of the market and the representative firm. In these diagrams identify the equilibrium price, the market quantity, the firm quantity, the firm's *ATC* curve (a sketch of this is fine), the firm's *MC* curve, and the firm's profits, if there are any.

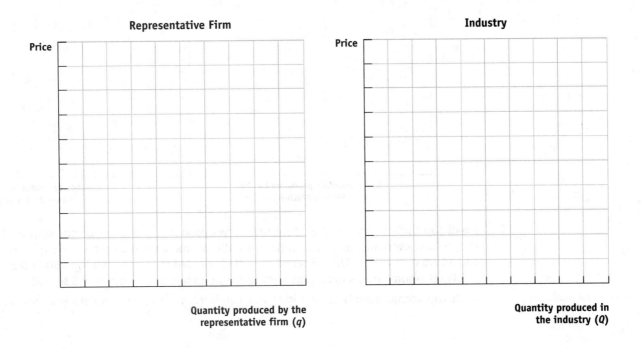

Representative Firm

Price

Quantity produced by the representative firm (*q*)

Industry

Price

Quantity produced in the industry (*Q*)

d. If all the firms are identical in this industry, how many firms are in the industry in the short run?

e. What is the long-run price, the long-run market quantity, the long-run quantity produced by a representative firm, and the long-run number of firms in the industry?

f. Draw a sketch illustrating the long-run equilibrium for this industry and for a representative firm.

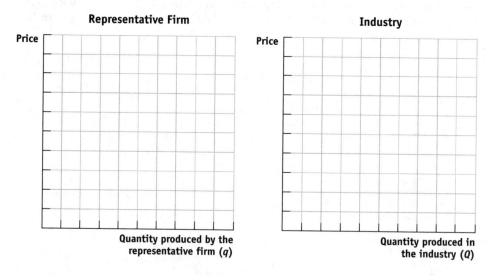

Representative Firm

Price

Quantity produced by the
representative firm (*q*)

Industry

Price

Quantity produced in
the industry (*Q*)

7. Small Town initially has a single firm that serves good coffee and wonderful pastries. This firm is busy every morning with long lines of customers eager to get a hot cup of coffee and a breakfast pastry. The owner of the café is excited that he is earning $50,000 a year as his take-home pay, since in his former job he managed to earn only $30,000.

a. Is this scenario likely to be a long-run equilibrium situation? Explain your answer.

b. What do you anticipate will happen in the long run in Small Town?

c. The owner of the café is interviewed ten years after the initial story about his success. The reporter finds out that the café owner is no longer in business providing coffee and pastries. Can you think of a possible story to explain this owner's departure from the business? (Hint: the owner did not choose to retire—he simply exited the industry during this ten-year period.)

8. For the most part, our model of perfect competition focuses on constant-cost industries. Is the assumption of constant costs in the long run a plausible assumption for the types of industries that most closely resemble perfect competition? Explain your answer.

9. In the long run, the model of perfect competition predicts that all firms in an industry will earn zero economic profits. Why would firms be willing to continue to produce in the long run if their economic profits are equal to zero?

BEFORE YOU TAKE THE TEST

Chapter Review Questions

1. Perfect competition requires that
   a. producers be able to enter or exit an industry in the short run.
   b. producers be able to distinguish their product from a rival producer's product.
   c. producers have no ability to exert influence over the market price of the product.
   d. consumers compete for the producers' product.

2. In recent years there has been an increased demand for organic produce due to concerns about health issues related to food consumption. Holding everything else constant, in the short run this demand should lead to _____, while in the long run _____.
   a. increases in the price of organic produce; entry of firms into the industry will reduce the price of organic produce
   b. increases in the price of organic produce; exit of firms from the industry will further increase the price of organic produce
   c. decreases in the price of organic produce; entry of firms into the industry will further reduce the price of organic produce
   d. decreases in the price of organic produce; exit of firms from the industry will increase the price of organic produce

3. Which of the following describes a perfectly competitive industry?
   a. Elementary school students are only allowed to attend the school in their attendance area.
   b. Water for household use is sold by the local water utility.
   c. The price of wine is determined by global supply and demand. A small share of the total world production of wine is produced in a local valley by ten companies.
   d. The price of oil is determined by global supply and demand. A total of five companies produce the world's supply of oil.

4. Marginal revenue is the addition to total
   a. revenue from producing one more unit of the good.
   b. cost from selling one more unit of the good.
   c. revenue from selling one more unit of the good.
   d. profit from producing and selling one more unit of the good.

5. Suppose Jerry calculates that if he produces one more box of pens his total cost will increase by $15, but that he can sell this box of pens for $14. Jerry will
   a. produce the pens and enhance his revenues.
   b. not produce the pens, since the revenue from the additional pens is less than the cost of producing the additional pens.
   c. produce the pens, but wait to sell them until the market price of pens increases.
   d. shut down his pen production, since his addition to revenue from pen production is less than his addition to cost from pen production.

6. Suppose a perfectly competitive firm in the short run sells its product for a price that is less than the minimum point on its *ATC* curve. Which of the following statements is true?
   a. The firm will shut down in the short run since it is not covering all of its costs.
   b. Some firms in this industry will exit the industry in the long run, and the exiting will continue until the market price increases and is equal to the break-even point on the *ATC* curve.
   c. The firm will shut down in the short run only if the price is greater than the shut-down price but less than the break-even price.
   d. Some firms in this industry will exit the industry in the long run, and the exiting will continue until the market price increases and is equal to the shut-down price on the *ATC* curve.

7. Suppose a perfectly competitive industry with constant costs is initially in long-run equilibrium. Demand for the product produced in this industry increases due to a change in tastes and preferences. In the short run this will result in
   a. the product selling for a higher price, each firm producing more of the good, and positive economic profits for the firms in the industry.
   b. the product selling for a higher price; each firm in the industry producing the same level of the good as they did initially, since their capital is fixed; and each firm earning positive economic profit.
   c. the product selling for a higher price initially, but the industry will attract new firms, which will cause the price to fall back to its original level.
   d. the price staying constant, since the firms in this industry are price takers, and the output of each firm increasing; therefore each firm will earn positive economic profit.

8. Suppose a perfectly competitive industry with constant costs is initially in long-run equilibrium. Demand for the product produced in this industry increases due to a change in tastes and preferences. In the long run this will result in
   a. the industry output of this good increasing, the price staying constant due to the entry of new firms into the industry, and each firm in the industry earning positive economic profits.
   b. the industry output of this good increasing, the price staying constant due to the entry of new firms into the industry, and each firm in the industry earning negative economic profits.
   c. the industry output of this good increasing, the price staying constant due to the entry of new firms into the industry, and each firm in the industry earning zero economic profit.
   d. the industry output of this good increasing, the firm level of output increasing, the price increasing, and each firm in the industry earning zero economic profit.

9. Which of the following statements is true?

    I. The model of supply and demand is a model of a perfectly competitive market.

    II. In the model of supply and demand, some producers may be able to affect the price of the good.

    III. In the model of supply and demand, some consumers may be able to affect the price of the good.

    a. Statement I is true.

    b. Statements II and III are true.

    c. Statements I, II, and III are true.

    d. None of these statements are true.

10. The optimal output rule for a perfectly competitive firm is to produce that quantity where

    a. $MR = MC$ in the long run, but in the short run to produce that quantity where $MC = ATC$.

    b. $MC = ATC$ in the short run.

    c. $MR = MC$ no matter what the time period, provided that marginal revenue is greater than average variable cost.

    d. $MR = MC$ no matter what the time period, provided that marginal revenue is greater than average total cost.

11. A firm calculates that the cost of producing its tenth unit of output is $0.50, while the revenue from producing this tenth unit is $0.55. This firm

    a. should definitely produce the tenth unit.

    b. should definitely stop producing, since it knows it is profit maximizing and may risk reducing its profit if it produces any more units of the good.

    c. should definitely produce at least five more units if it hopes to profit maximize.

    d. cannot increase its production in the short run since its fixed inputs are constant.

12. A firm in the short run must decide whether or not it should produce any level of output. This means that the firm must

    a. equate marginal revenue to marginal cost to decide its level of output.

    b. consider whether its revenue is sufficient to cover its total costs of production.

    c. consider whether its revenue is sufficient to cover its average fixed costs of production.

    d. consider whether its revenue is sufficient to cover its variable costs of production.

13. A firm making its short-run decision about whether or not to produce should ignore its

    a. fixed costs.

    b. variable costs.

    c. average costs.

    d. marginal costs.

14. Production is profitable in the short run whenever price is greater than

    a. average total cost.

    b. marginal cost.

    c. average variable cost.

    d. average fixed cost.

15. Which of the following statements about a perfectly competitive firm is true?

    I. A firm profit maximizes by producing that output where $MR = MC$.

    II. A firm will produce in the short run provided that the price of the good exceeds its average variable cost.

    III. A firm in the long run can make positive economic profits.

  a. Statement I is true.

  b. Statements I and II are true.

  c. Statements I and III are true.

  d. Statements I, II, and III are true.

16. When a perfectly competitive firm earns zero economic profit in the long run, this implies that accounting profits

  a. are also equal to zero.

  b. are positive.

  c. are negative.

  d. may be positive, negative, or equal to zero.

17. A perfectly competitive firm finds that its break-even price occurs at $22 while its shut-down price is at $12. You are told that the market demand curve in this industry is $P = 30 - (1/30)Q$ and the market supply curve is $P = (1/15)Q$. In the short run this firm will

  a. produce, since it is covering its variable costs of production.

  b. produce, since it can earn positive economic profits.

  c. produce, since it is covering its fixed costs of production.

  d. shut down, since it is not covering its fixed costs of production.

18. A perfectly competitive firm's minimum-cost output corresponds to the level of output at which

  a. fixed cost is minimized.

  b. variable cost is minimized.

  c. average total cost is minimized.

  d. total cost is minimized.

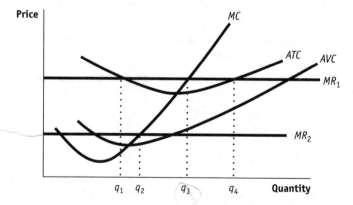

19. Use the above graph of a perfectly competitive firm in the short run to answer this question. If the firm's marginal revenue is MR_1, then this firm profit maximizes by producing _____ units of output, and its economic profit will be _____.

  a. q_1; zero   c. q_3; positive

  b. q_2; positive   d. q_4; positive

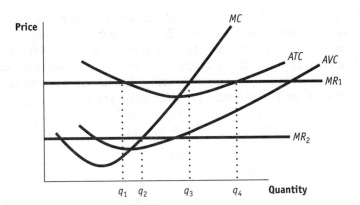

20. Use the above graph of a perfectly competitive firm in the short run to answer this question. If the firm's marginal revenue is MR_2, then this firm profit maximizes by producing _____ units of output, and its economic profit will be _____.
   a. q_1; negative
   b. q_2; negative
   c. q_3; zero
   d. q_4; negative

21. For a firm to profit maximize, it must also be true that
   a. the firm is cost minimizing.
   b. the market price is greater than the shut-down price.
   c. the market price is equal to the break-even price.
   d. the firm is earning a positive accounting profit.

22. In the short run, the individual supply curve for a perfectly competitive firm is that firm's
   a. MC curve at or above the shut-down price.
   b. ATC curve above the MC curve.
   c. ATC curve below the MC curve.
   d. MR curve at or above the shut-down price.

23. A perfectly competitive firm will exit the industry in the long run if the
   a. firm's marginal revenue is consistently less than the firm's marginal cost.
   b. market price is consistently less than the break-even price.
   c. firm's fixed cost cannot be eliminated in the long run.
   d. firm's marginal cost is consistently less than the firm's marginal revenue.

24. The short-run industry supply curve for a perfectly competitive market is
   a. perfectly elastic, since buyers can purchase as many units of the good as they desire at the prevailing market price.
   b. equal to the horizontal sum of the supply curves of the individual producers.
   c. equal to the horizontal sum of the individual firms' MC curves at and above the AVC.
   d. Answers (b) and (c) are both true.

25. Suppose there are two firms in a perfectly competitive industry and that each of these two firms have a MC curve that can be expressed as $MC = 2q$, where q is the level of output produced by the firm. Furthermore, suppose that the minimum point of the AVC curve occurs at $10. If these two firms comprise the industry (a simplification to make the calculation easier), which of the following equations describes the industry supply curve where Q refers to the market quantity and P refers to the market price?

a. $P = 2Q$ for $Q \geq 5$

b. $P = Q$ for $Q \geq 5$

c. $P = Q$ for $Q \geq 10$

d. $P = 2Q$ for $Q \geq 10$

26. Which of the following statements for a perfectly competitive industry is true?

    I. In the short run, the number of firms in the industry is fixed.

    II. For a constant-cost industry, the market supply curve in the short run is a horizontal line.

    III. In a short-run market equilibrium, the quantity supplied equals the quantity demanded.

a. Statement I is true.

b. Statements I and II are true.

c. Statements I and III are true.

d. Statements I, II, and III are true.

27. The long-run market equilibrium in a perfectly competitive industry with identical firms results in all firms

a. earning zero economic profit.

b. producing the quantity associated with their break-even price.

c. producing the profit-maximizing quantity at which $MR = MC$.

d. All of the above statements are true.

28. A constant-cost industry in a perfectly competitive market can be identified by its

a. horizontal long-run market supply curve.

b. horizontal long-run market demand curve.

c. upward-sloping long-run market supply curve.

d. downward-sloping long-run market supply curve.

■ ANSWER KEY

Answers to Problems and Exercises

1. A price-taking firm is a firm that is so small relative to the entire market that it has no influence on the market price. This firm accepts the price of the good that is determined by the interaction of the market demand and the market supply. A price-taking consumer is a consumer whose purchases in a market are so small relative to the entire market that they can exert no influence on the market price. A price-taking consumer is one that accepts the market-determined price as the price they will pay for the good. Market share refers to the fraction of the total industry output represented by a producer's output: when no producer has significant market share, this implies that no producer is able to influence market prices.

2. The model of perfect competition requires that producers be price takers and that the good being produced in the market is a standardized product. These two conditions imply that no producer can exert influence on the market price and that any producer who raises their price above the market price will find that they lose all their sales to other producers. A third condition that is often present in a perfectly competitive industry is free entry and exit of firms in the long run. Free entry and exit in the long run ensures that economic profit will equal zero in the long run. Firms enter the industry in the long run if there are positive short-run profits, and they exit the industry in the long run if there are negative short-run profits.

3. **a.** Since total revenue equals the product of price and quantity, we can use this equation to find the price of a doughnut. When $TR = \$200$, $Q = 100$ and price is $2. When $TR = \$400$, $Q = 200$ and price is $2. In a perfectly competitive industry the price the firm sells its product for stays constant and is equal to the market price.

    b. According to the table, Sarah's Doughnut Shoppe maximizes its profits when it produces 400 doughnuts.

Quantity of doughnuts	Total revenue	Total cost	Profit
100	$ 200	$250	−$50
200	400	360	40
300	600	530	70
400	800	725	75
500	1,000	950	50

c.

Quantity of doughnuts	Total revenue	Total cost	Marginal cost	Marginal revenue	Profit
100	$ 200	$250			−$50
			$1.10	$2	
200	400	360			40
			1.70	2	
300	600	530			70
			1.95	2	
400	800	725			75
			2.25	2	
500	1,000	950			50

d. At the profit-maximizing level of output, $MR = MC$ (or very close to it). Since marginal revenue is also equal to the price of a doughnut, this implies that marginal cost equals the price of a doughnut. When $MR = MC$, the addition to total revenue from selling an additional unit of the good equals the addition to total cost from producing an additional unit of the good. When $MR > MC$, more units of the good should be produced and sold in order to profit maximize; when $MR < MC$, fewer units of the good should be produced and sold in order to profit maximize.

4. a. The equilibrium price is P_1 and the equilibrium quantity is Q_1 in the market. The representative firm produces the quantity at which $MR = MC$, or $P_1 = MC$, since for a perfectly competitive firm $MR = P$. The representative firm produces q_1. The firm earns positive economic profit since $P_1 > ATC$ for q_1 units of output. In the long run, new firms will enter the industry, since the existence of positive economic profits creates an incentive for more competition. As firms enter the industry, the industry supply curve will shift to the right from S_1 to S_2, which will result in a decrease in the market price from P_1 to P_2. The equilibrium output in the industry will increase to Q_2 while the representative firm will decrease its production to q_2. The level of economic profits will equal zero in the long run for the firms in the industry.

b. The equilibrium price is P_4 and the equilibrium quantity is Q_4 in the market. The representative firm finds that the market price goes through its shut-down price at P_4 (the minimum point of the AVC curve), and therefore the firm needs to decide whether or not it wants to produce in the short run. With either choice, the firm will earn negative economic profits equal to the negative of their fixed costs. The firm will produce q_4 units since $MR = MC$ at this level of output. In the long run, firms will exit the industry, causing the industry supply curve to shift to the left to S_2. This will cause the market price to increase to P_2, the market quantity to decrease to Q_2, and the level of production for each firm remaining in the industry to increase to q_2. Economic profits will equal zero in the long run for each firm.

c. Looking at the graph we know that P_4 corresponds to the price that goes through the shut-down price, which implies that the firm covers all of its variable cost, but none of its fixed cost. At P_1, the firm earns a positive economic profit and thus its revenues are greater than the sum of its fixed cost and variable cost. P_2 corresponds to the price that goes through the break-even price: the firm's total revenue is exactly equal to its total cost and therefore the firm is covering all of its variable cost and all of its fixed cost. That leaves P_3, and from the graph we see that P_3 is a price that lies between the break-even price and the shut-down price: the firm will receive enough revenue to cover all of its variable cost and some of its fixed cost. In the long run, firms will exit this industry until the supply curve shifts left from S_3 to S_2. The remaining firms in the industry will earn zero economic profits in the long run.

5. a. No, this market is not perfectly competitive since there are not many producers and at least one of them has substantial market share (Mom's Pop accounts for 45% of total soda sales in Bigtown).

b.

Name of company	Market share
Fizzy Water	15%
Cool Tonics	20
Carbonated Bliss	10
Mom's Pop	45
Taste of Eden	10

c. No, the soda will likely be quite differentiated since customers distinguish between these companies' products (for example, Mom's Pop really outsells every other business in the industry).

6. a. To find the equilibrium price and quantity in the market, use the market demand and supply equations. Solving $100 - Q = 4 + Q$ for Q gives you the equilibrium quantity of 48 units. Substituting this quantity into either the demand or the supply equation gives you the equilibrium price of $52.

b. The profit-maximizing level of output for the firm is found by equating marginal revenue to marginal cost. For the price-taking firm, marginal revenue is equal to the market price. Thus, $52 = 4 + 2q$, or q (the quantity produced by the representative firm) is 24 units.

c. Profit is equal to $TR - TC$. Total revenue for this firm is $(\$52)(24) = \$1,248$, and total cost is equal to $ATC \times q$ or $TC = (36/q + 4 + q)(q) = (36/24 + 4 + 24)(24) = \$708$. This firm makes positive profits equal to $540.

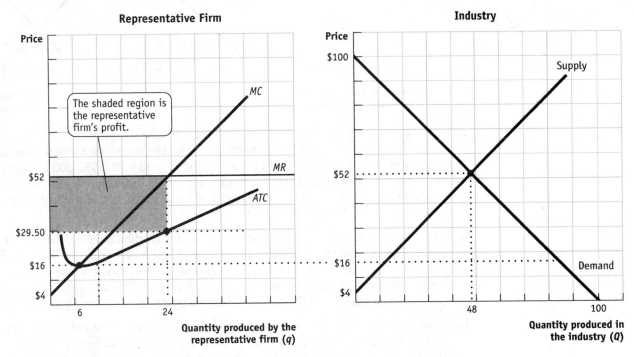

d. The representative firm produces 24 units in the short run when it profit maximizes, while the total market quantity produced is 48 units. This implies that if all firms are identical and produce 24 units of output, then it will take two firms to produce the market quantity (this is a simplified example with just a few firms to make the math easier).

e. In the long run, the representative firm will earn zero economic profits due to the entry of new firms into the industry. For this to be true, the firm must produce at its break-even price where $MC = ATC$. You can find the average total cost by dividing total cost by the firm's quantity, q. Thus, $TC = 36 + 4q + q^2$ gives us $ATC = 36/q + 4 + q$. $MC = 4 + 2q$, so we can set $MC = ATC$ and have $4 + 2q = 36/q + 4 + q$. Solving this equation gives us $36/q = q$ or $q^2 = 36$. The positive quantity that solves this equation is $q = 6$. So, the long-run quantity produced by the representative firm is 6 units. The long-run equilibrium price is the price at which $MC = ATC$ for this firm, so if q equals 6 units, then the long-run price is $4 + 2(6) = \$16$. At a price of $16 the quantity demanded in the market is 84 units. If each firm produces 6 units and a total of 84 units are produced, then there are 14 firms in the industry.

f.

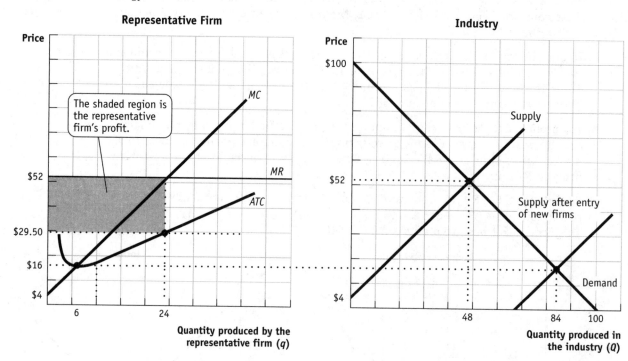

Representative Firm

Industry

7. **a.** This is not likely to be a long-run equilibrium since the owner of the café is earning a return that is greater than his opportunity cost. He knows that when working for someone else the best he can do is to earn $30,000, and so the $50,000 he earns running his coffee shop suggests that he is earning positive economic profit and that over the long run this profit should be reduced until he earns zero economic profit, provided that there is free entry into the market for coffee shops.

    b. In the long run, entry of new firms should occur, which should reduce the level of profit to zero for all the firms in the industry. This scenario is based on there being no barriers to entry, and in the case of providing coffee and pastries this is a plausible assumption. Entry should continue until all owners of the coffee shops that are in business earn their opportunity cost and until the level of economic profit for the firms equals zero.

    c. The model of perfect competition suggests that all firms in the industry in the long run will earn zero economic profit. But some firms may be driven from the industry if they find their costs of production are greater than the cost of production for other firms. It is likely that this owner found that he simply could not compete with the new firms entering the industry and that he was forced to exit the industry in the long run because other firms could provide coffee and pastries at somewhat lower cost than he was able to achieve. This helps us understand the frequent exit of established businesses from an industry: it is not at all unusual for a city to have restaurants or other business enterprises in markets with competition go out of business.

8. The assumption of constant costs for an industry implies that new firms can enter the industry without causing the costs of production for both the existing firms and these new firms to increase. This is an important assumption to consider: implicitly it is saying that it is possible for all these firms to increase their hiring of labor and capital without affecting the price of that labor or that capital. Is this plausible? It is probably not a bad assumption for many productive enterprises in which the amount of labor and capital used is small relative to the total pool of labor and capital used in the economy. It is probably a poor assumption when the amount of labor and capital used in the industry accounts for a large percentage of the total pool of labor and capital used. Perfect competition, with its assumption of price-taking behavior on the part of producers and consumers, is likely to be a modeling situation in which each individual firm's hiring of labor and capital is unlikely to exert upward pressure on the prices of those inputs.

9. Earning zero economic profits in the long run is not a bad outcome for existing firms in an industry. Rather, this level of profit allows each factor of production (including the owner) to earn a return that is equal to their opportunity cost. Thus, when a firm earns zero economic profit this does not suggest that the firm is performing at a less than ideal level, but that all inputs used by the firm are being compensated at a level equal to their worth as measured by their opportunity costs. In contrast, a firm earning positive economic profit (a possibility in the short run) is receiving a level of compensation that exceeds their opportunity costs: this suggests that an inadequate amount of resources are being devoted to this production since the value placed on the goods being produced exceeds the costs of producing the good. As more resources are devoted to the production of this good through the entry of new firms, the level of economic profit falls until it is at a level where these inputs are valued at their opportunity cost.

Answers to Chapter Review Questions

1. **Answer c.** Perfect competition does not require free entry and exit, but it is often present in the long run in a perfectly competitive industry. The output produced in a perfectly competitive industry is a standardized commodity: consumers cannot distinguish one producer's output from another producer's output. Consumers are price taking, and the market price equates the quantity demanded at that price with the quantity supplied at that price. Perfectly competitive industries are characterized by producers being price takers.

2. **Answer a.** When the demand for organic produce increases, this causes a rightward shift in the demand curve, which results in the price of organic produce increasing in the short run. In the long run, however, new producers will enter this industry, which will cause the supply curve to shift to the right, thereby lowering the price of organic produce.

3. **Answer c.** Only answer (c) provides a description of price-taking behavior on both the producer and the consumer side of the model.

4. **Answer c.** This is a simple definition of marginal revenue, which focuses on measuring the benefit from selling one more unit of the good.

5. **Answer b.** Jerry is trying to determine the profit-maximizing level of output for his firm. To select this output level he will want to equate marginal revenue to marginal cost. Since the marginal revenue of producing an additional box of pens is less than the marginal cost of producing this box of pens, Jerry knows that this would represent too high a level of production. To determine whether Jerry should shut down his production, we need information about his average costs of production.

6. **Answer b.** In the short run, if the price is less than average total cost, then firms in this perfectly competitive industry earn negative economic profit. These negative economic profits will lead some firms to exit the industry in the long run until the firms remaining in the industry earn zero economic profits. This implies that price will equal the minimum point of the ATC curve or the break-even price. The shut-down price is not on the ATC curve, as given in answer (d), but is instead on the AVC curve.

7. **Answer a.** The increased demand for the good will cause the market demand curve to shift to the right, leading to a higher equilibrium level of output in the market and a higher equilibrium price. The firms in this industry are price takers, and they will take the price they receive from the market and see where this price intersects their MC curve (recall that for a perfectly competitive firm the market price is equal to the marginal revenue) to select the profit-maximizing level of output. The firms will produce a higher level of output relative to their initial level, and they will earn positive economic profit.

8. **Answer c.** In the long run, this industry will experience the entry of new firms because the increase in tastes and preferences for this good will cause the short-run price of the good to increase, resulting in the existing firms earning positive economic profit. But these profits will act as a signal to potential firms to enter, and this entry will shift the

market supply curve to the right, causing the price to fall back to its initial level. Firms in the long run will produce the same level of output as they did initially, but there will be more firms in the industry, which will lead to an increase in the industry level of output. Firms in the long run will earn zero economic profit.

9. **Answer a.** A basic underlying assumption of the model of supply and demand is that neither consumers nor producers can affect the price of the good. Producers and consumers are price takers, which eliminates statements II and III.

10. **Answer c.** The profit-maximizing firm, if it produces, always produces that quantity where $MR = MC$. The profit-maximizing firm produces in the short run, provided that the market price is equal to or greater than the firm's average variable cost. The firm makes a positive economic profit if the market price is greater than average total cost, and it earns a negative economic profit if the market price is less than average total cost.

11. **Answer a.** Since the firm's marginal cost of producing the tenth unit of output is less than the marginal revenue from selling the tenth unit of output, the firm should definitely produce this tenth unit. The firm is able to increase its production in the short run, despite fixed inputs, because it can use more of the variable input. Without more information we cannot know with certainty that the firm should produce five more units of output. We do know the firm will profit maximize by producing that level of output where $MR = MC$ for the last unit produced.

12. **Answer d.** In the short run, the firm ignores its fixed cost since it cannot alter these costs. The firm decides whether it should produce in the short run by checking to see if its revenue is sufficient to cover its variable cost. If the revenue will not cover these variable costs, the firm can opt to shut down and incur only the fixed cost of production in the short run.

13. **Answer a.** In the short run, the firm will ignore its fixed cost since in the short run the fixed inputs cannot be altered. In the short run, the firm is able to alter its hiring of the variable input and, hence, its variable cost.

14. **Answer a.** The firm makes positive economic profit whenever the market price is greater than the firm's average total cost, and it makes negative economic profit whenever the market price is less than the firm's average total cost.

15. **Answer b.** Perfectly competitive firms produce that level of output where, for the last unit produced, the addition to total revenue (the marginal revenue) just equals the addition to total cost (the marginal cost). Perfectly competitive firms do not produce in the short run if the market price is less than the shut-down price, or the minimum point of the AVC curve. In the long run, a perfectly competitive firm will earn zero economic profit due to the entry of firms in the event of positive short-run economic profit or the exit of firms in the event of negative short-run economic profit.

16. **Answer b.** Economic profit includes the explicit and the implicit costs of production, while accounting profits exclude implicit costs. When a firm earns zero economic profit, this implies that the firm is earning positive accounting profit.

17. **Answer a.** Solving for the market equilibrium price using the market demand and supply curve yields a price of $20. This price is less than the break-even price and greater than the firm's shut-down price. The firm will produce in the short run since the market price is great enough to cover its variable cost of production (since the price exceeds the shut-down price). But the firm will earn negative profits because the market price is less than its break-even price, and therefore the price is not high enough for the firm to cover all of its variable cost and all of its fixed cost.

18. **Answer c.** The firm's minimum-cost output occurs where the cost per unit (its average total cost) is minimized. The firm's average total cost is minimized at the output level that corresponds to the firm's break-even price.

19. **Answer c.** The perfectly competitive firm sets marginal revenue equal to marginal cost and produces that level of output (q_3). When the firm produces q_3 units, the market price is greater than the average total cost of production for this level of output, and the firm will earn positive economic profit.

20. **Answer b.** The perfectly competitive firm sets marginal revenue equal to marginal cost and produces that quantity of output (q_2). When the firm produces q_2 units of output, the market price is less than the average total cost of production for this level of output, and the firm will earn negative economic profit.

21. **Answer a.** Profit maximization implies that the firm must be minimizing its costs. In addition, profit maximization requires that the firm produce the level of output where $MR = MC$.

22. **Answer a.** The firm decides how much to supply by equating the market price to its MC curve, since the market price is the firm's MR curve. The firm produces in the short run provided that the market price is equal to or greater than its shut-down price, or its AVC. Thus, the firm's short-run supply curve is its MC curve at or above the point of intersection with its AVC curve.

23. **Answer b.** In the long run, a firm can sell its plant and equipment and exit the industry, and it will choose to exit the industry, if the market price does not cover its average total cost of production, or in other words, its break-even price.

24. **Answer d.** The supply curves of the individual producers are their MC curves at or above the shut-down price. To find the industry supply curve, simply horizontally sum together these individual supply curves.

25. **Answer c.** The market supply curve is found by horizontally summing the individual supply curves. The firm's supply curve is given by $MC = 2q$, provided that the price is greater than the minimum point of the AVC, or in this case provided that the price is equal or greater than $10. So at a price of $10, each firm is willing to produce 5 units, for a total of 10 units. At a price of $20, each firm is willing to produce 10 units, for a total of 20 units. Thus, the industry supply curve is $P = Q$ for outputs greater than or equal to 10 units.

26. **Answer c.** In a perfectly competitive industry, the number of firms in the industry is fixed and constant in the short run. Entry of new firms or the exit of existing firms can only occur in the long run. Market equilibrium, whether in the short run or long run, occurs at that price and quantity combination where the quantity demanded equals the quantity supplied. However, in the short run, a constant-cost industry will have an upward-sloping market supply curve because the production of a greater level of output must entail increasing costs due to the diminishing returns to the variable input.

27. **Answer d.** In the long run, entry or exit will occur in the perfectly competitive industry until all firms in the industry earn zero economic profit. Since all firms earn zero economic profit this implies that all firms are producing at the point where price equals average total cost, which can only occur at the break-even price, since firms must also be producing the profit-maximizing quantity where $MR = MC$.

28. **Answer a.** A perfectly competitive industry with constant costs is an industry that can expand its output in the long run without incurring higher or lower costs per unit. This implies that the long-run market supply curve for this industry will be horizontal.

chapter 14

Monopoly

BEFORE YOU READ THE CHAPTER

Summary

This chapter develops the model of monopoly, a situation in which there is a single producer of the good. This chapter explores how the monopolist determines its profit-maximizing price and output. In addition, the chapter compares perfect competition and monopoly and examines how these two different market structures result in different outcomes with respect to social welfare. The chapter also discusses how policymakers address the problems posed by monopoly. The chapter discusses price discrimination and the effects of price discrimination on a market.

Chapter Objectives

Objective #1. A monopoly is a market characterized by having a single producer of the good, when the good has no close substitutes. Monopolists, unlike perfectly competitive firms, know that their actions affect the market price, and they take this fact into account when deciding how much to produce.

Objective #2. There are four principal models of market structure: perfect competition, monopoly, oligopoly, and monopolistic competition. These four types of market structure are distinguished by the number of firms in the market and whether the goods offered in the market are identical or differentiated.

- In monopoly, a single producer produces a single, undifferentiated product. In oligopoly, a few producers sell products that may or may not be differentiated. In monopolistically competitive markets, many producers sell differentiated products. In perfect competition, many producers produce identical products.

- The number of firms in the market is determined by the long-run conditions that make it difficult for new firms to enter the market: these conditions include government regulations that limit entry, the presence of increasing returns to scale in production, technological superiority that limits potential competition, or the control of necessary resources or inputs. When these conditions are present, the market structure tends to be monopolistic or oligopolistic.

Objective #3. In contrast to perfect competition, a monopolist produces a smaller quantity and charges a higher price for its product. The monopolist is able to charge a price that is greater than the competitive price because it has market power: it is the only producer of the good and the good has no close substitutes. By charging a higher price and restricting output, the monopolist is able to increase its profit while maintaining positive profits in the long run.

Objective #4. Positive economic profits earned by the monopolist continue in the long run because effective barriers to entry prevent new firms from entering the industry. There are four principal barriers to entry: (1) the monopoly controls a scarce resource or input that prevents new firms from being able to compete in the industry; (2) the monopolist enjoys increasing returns to scale and therefore can spread its fixed cost over a larger volume of output, resulting in the monopolist having lower average total costs than potential competitors; (3) the monopolist enjoys technological superiority over its potential competitors; and (4) the monopolist is protected from competition due to government-created barriers.

- Increasing returns to scale results in lower costs of production as the size of the firm increases. In the case of a monopoly with increasing returns to scale, the single firm finds that its cost of production falls throughout the relevant range of production. Any potential competitor would face higher costs per unit. Natural monopolies are an example of a monopoly that benefits from increasing returns to scale.

- With technological superiority some monopolists also experience network externalities, which is a condition that arises when the value to a consumer of a good increases as the number of people who use the good increases. This advantage may allow the producer to become a monopolist.

- The most important government-created barrier to entry takes the form of patent protection. A similar type of protection afforded producers is the copyright.

Objective #5. The monopolist's demand curve for its product is the market demand curve, since it is the only provider of the good in the market. Since the monopolist's demand curve is downward sloping, this implies that the monopolist can only sell additional units of the good by lowering the price on all the units it sells: this results in the monopolist's marginal revenue (MR) curve being beneath the monopolist's demand curve. An increase in production by a monopolist has two opposing effects on revenue: a quantity effect and a price effect.

- When the monopolist sells one more unit of the good, this increases its revenue by the price at which the unit is sold: this is the quantity effect.

- When the monopolist sells one more unit of the good, it must reduce the price on all units sold, which decreases revenue: this is the price effect.

- A firm with market power will find that its MR curve always lies beneath its demand curve due to the price effect.

- At low levels of output the quantity effect is stronger than the price effect, and the monopolist will find that its total revenue increases as it increases its level of production.

- At high levels of output the price effect is stronger than the quantity effect, and the monopolist will find that its total revenue decreases as it increases its level of production.

- Figure 14.1 illustrates a linear demand curve for a monopolist as well as the monopolist's *MR* curve. Notice that the *MR* curve bisects the distance between the origin and the horizontal intercept of the demand curve. This implies that the slope of the *MR* curve is twice the slope of the demand curve. Notice also that the *y*-intercept for the demand curve and the *MR* curve are the same.

Figure 14.1

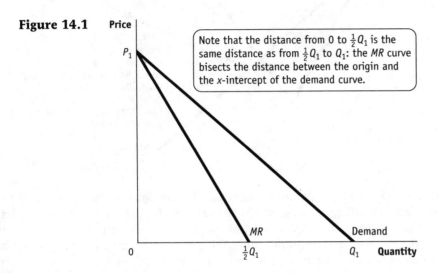

Note that the distance from 0 to $\frac{1}{2}Q_1$ is the same distance as from $\frac{1}{2}Q_1$ to Q_1: the *MR* curve bisects the distance between the origin and the *x*-intercept of the demand curve.

Objective #6. The monopolist maximizes profit by producing the output at which marginal revenue equals marginal cost (*MR* = *MC*) for the last unit produced while charging the price consumers are willing to pay for this output. The profit-maximizing price-quantity combination is always a point on the demand curve. Figure 14.2 illustrates this concept.

Figure 14.2

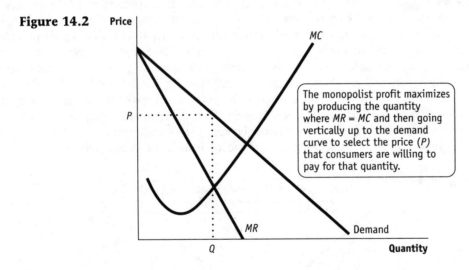

The monopolist profit maximizes by producing the quantity where *MR* = *MC* and then going vertically up to the demand curve to select the price (*P*) that consumers are willing to pay for that quantity.

Objective #7. Just as with perfect competition, the monopolist's profits are equal to total revenue minus total cost (*TR* − *TC*). However, the monopolist can earn profits in the short run as well as the long run since there are effective barriers to entry that protect the monopolist from competition. Figure 14.3 illustrates a monopolist's profit: note that when the price the monopolist charges is greater than its average total cost, then the monopolist earns positive economic profit.

Figure 14.3

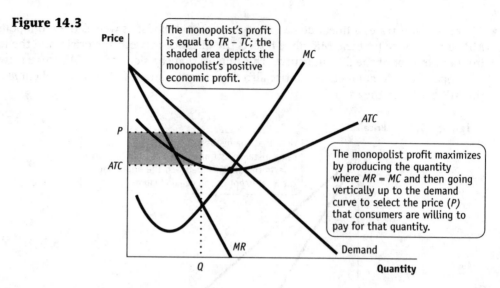

The monopolist's profit is equal to *TR – TC*; the shaded area depicts the monopolist's positive economic profit.

The monopolist profit maximizes by producing the quantity where *MR = MC* and then going vertically up to the demand curve to select the price (*P*) that consumers are willing to pay for that quantity.

Objective #8.   In a perfectly competitive industry, each firm equates the marginal cost to the price of the good; in contrast, in a monopoly the price of the good is always greater than the marginal cost at the profit-maximizing level of output. This tells us that the monopolist is not producing the efficient level of output, since the price consumers are willing to pay for the last unit produced is greater than the cost of producing the last unit. Too few resources are being devoted to the production of the monopolist product. A monopoly, compared with a perfectly competitive industry, restricts output, charges a higher price for the product, and earns a profit that is not eliminated through the entry of new firms in the long run.

Objective #9.   Monopoly causes a net loss to the economy because the cost to the consumer is greater than the gain to the monopolist. The existence of a monopoly creates a deadweight loss due to the monopolist's restriction of output and its ability to charge a higher price for its product relative to the quantity and price decision made by a perfectly competitive firm. The deadweight loss created by the monopolist occurs because some mutually beneficial transactions do not occur: this is evident when we recall that for the last unit produced by the monopolist, the marginal cost of producing that unit is less than the price consumers are willing to pay for that unit. Because monopoly is inefficient, government policy often is used to offset some of the undesired effects of monopoly. Figure 14.4 indicates for a monopolist the areas that correspond to consumer surplus, producer surplus, and deadweight loss.

Figure 14.4

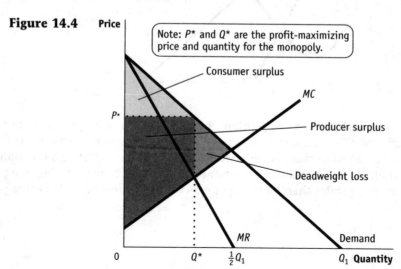

Note: *P** and *Q** are the profit-maximizing price and quantity for the monopoly.

Consumer surplus

Producer surplus

Deadweight loss

Objective #10. If an industry is not a natural monopoly, then the best method for avoiding monopoly outcomes is to prevent monopoly from arising or to break up the monopoly if it already exists. Government policies used to prevent or eliminate monopolies are known as antitrust policy.

Objective #11. If an industry is a natural monopoly, then breaking up the monopoly is not a clearly beneficial idea since large-scale producers have lower average total cost than smaller-scale producers. Two policy methods are used for regulating natural monopolies: public ownership and regulation.

- With public ownership, the government establishes a public agency to provide the good and to protect consumers' interests. With public ownership, it is possible to set the price at the efficient level so that $P = MC$ for the last unit being produced by the natural monopoly. Unfortunately, publicly owned natural monopolies are not always successful at minimizing their costs or at providing high-quality products. Publicly owned companies may also end up serving political interests.

- Regulation typically takes the form of price regulation, where the private company is regulated with regard to what prices it can charge for the product. Local utilities are frequently regulated in this way. With price regulation the monopolist produces a higher level of output and sells this output at a lower price, provided that the regulated price is set at a level greater than the firm's marginal cost and is high enough that the firm at least breaks even on total output. Price regulation increases the area of consumer surplus because the regulation reduces the monopolist's profit and results in more output at lower prices. The price set by regulators is ideally set so that price equals average total cost, but monopolies have an incentive to exaggerate their costs to regulators, making it difficult for regulators to ascertain this ideal price. Additionally, regulated monopolies often provide inferior quality to consumers.

Objective #12. Price discrimination refers to a situation in which a firm with market power charges different prices to different customers. Instead of offering the good at a single price, the firm with market power offers the good at multiple prices depending on the characteristics of the consumer. The firm will find that its profit increases if it charges a higher price to the consumers of the good who have price inelastic demand, and a lower price to the consumers of the good who have price elastic demand. Common techniques for price discrimination include:

- Advance purchase restrictions—the earlier you purchase, the lower the price you pay.

- Volume discounts—the larger the quantity you buy, the lower the price per unit.

- Two-part tariffs—you pay an annual fee plus the cost of whatever items you purchase, thereby effectively creating a volume discount.

Objective #13. Perfect price discrimination occurs when the monopolist is able to capture the entire consumer surplus. The greater the number of prices the monopolist charges, the more money it extracts from consumers. In addition, the greater the number of prices the monopolist charges, the closer the lowest price will get to the marginal cost of producing the last unit of the good. A monopolist who practices perfect price discrimination does not cause any inefficiency, since the marginal cost of producing the last unit exactly equals the price of this last unit. But with perfect price discrimination, the consumer's surplus is equal to zero since this entire surplus is captured by the producer.

Key Terms

monopolist a firm that is the only producer of a good that has no close substitutes.

monopoly an industry controlled by a *monopolist*.

market power the ability of a producer to raise prices.

barrier to entry something that prevents other firms from entering an industry. Crucial in protecting the profits of a *monopolist*. There are four types of barriers to entry: control over scarce *resources* or *inputs*, increasing returns to scale, technological superiority, and government-created barriers such as *licenses*.

natural monopoly a *monopoly* that exists when *increasing returns to scale* provide a large cost advantage to having all output produced by a single firm.

patent a temporary monopoly given by the government to an inventor for the use or sale of an invention.

copyright the exclusive legal right of the creator of a literary or artistic work to profit from that work; like a *patent*, it is a temporary monopoly.

public ownership when goods are supplied by the government or by a firm owned by the government to protect the interests of the consumer in response to *natural monopoly*.

price regulation a limitation on the price a *monopolist* is allowed to charge.

single-price monopolist a *monopolist* that offers its product to all consumers at the same price.

price discrimination charging different prices to different consumers for the same good.

perfect price discrimination when a *monopolist* charges each consumer the maximum that the consumer is willing to pay.

AFTER YOU READ THE CHAPTER

Tips

Tip #1. It is important that you understand why the monopolist has a downward-sloping *MR* curve that lies beneath the monopolist's demand curve and how to find this *MR* curve. When the monopolist thinks about increasing the amount of the good it supplies to the market, it knows that it will increase its revenue when it sells this additional unit of the good. But it also knows that to sell more units of the good it will need to lower the price on all the units of the good it sells, so the decision to sell a larger amount of the good has two effects—one effect adds to the monopolist's revenue, but the second effect decreases the monopolist's revenue. Review this analysis until you understand it and can express it clearly.

Tip #2. To find the monopolist's *MR* curve is a relatively simple matter if the demand curve for the monopolist is linear. For a linear demand curve, the *MR* curve has the same *y*-intercept as the demand curve and twice the slope of the demand curve. For example, if the demand curve is expressed as $P = 1,000 - 2Q$, then the *MR* curve is $MR = 1,000 - 4Q$. Another way of expressing this idea is to realize that the *MR* curve bisects the horizontal distance between the origin and the *x*-intercept of the demand curve. Figure 14.5 illustrates this concept.

Figure 14.5

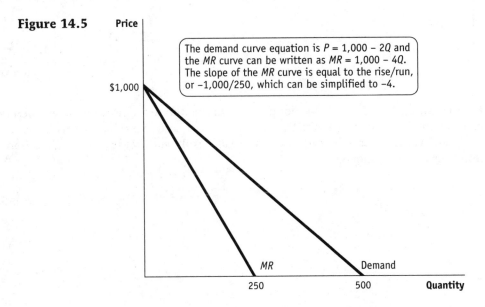

The demand curve equation is $P = 1,000 - 2Q$ and the *MR* curve can be written as $MR = 1,000 - 4Q$. The slope of the *MR* curve is equal to the rise/run, or $-1,000/250$, which can be simplified to -4.

Tip #3. Notice the relationship between the elasticity of the linear demand curve and its MR curve. Marginal revenue is positive in the elastic portion of the demand curve, marginal revenue equals 0 at the unit-elastic point (the midpoint) of the demand curve, and marginal revenue is negative in the inelastic portion of the demand curve.

Tip #4. This chapter continues the use of cost curves and marginal analysis. If you are still having trouble with the terminology related to cost curves, or with your understanding and use of these concepts, you should return to Chapter 12 on production and cost and review this material. To work successfully with this material, you must have a very strong understanding (and not just memorization) of these underlying concepts.

Problems and Exercises

1. Assuming identical costs, what is the monopolist's effect on price and quantity compared to a perfectly competitive industry? Draw two sketches, with one sketch illustrating the perfectly competitive industry and its equilibrium market price and market quantity, and the other sketch illustrating the monopoly and its market price and market quantity. On

both sketches, identify the area that corresponds to the consumer surplus, producer surplus, and deadweight loss.

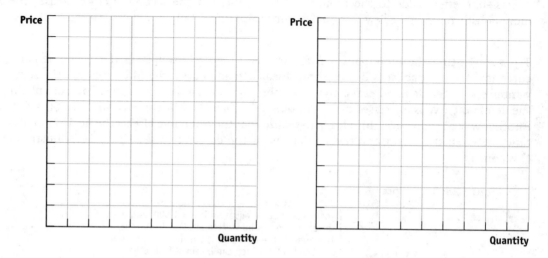

2.   For the last unit produced by a monopolist, what is the relationship between the price consumers are willing to pay for this unit versus the cost of producing this last unit of the good? What is the implication of this relationship with regard to the allocation of resources to this monopoly?

3.   Suppose there is a single firm producing a good for which there are no close substitutes. This firm is currently earning positive economic profit in the short run. Why does this firm care about the existence of barriers to entry in its market? Explain your answer.

4. A firm wishes to increase the price it charges for its product, and it wishes to restrict the level of output available to consumers. What must be true if this firm is to be successful?

5. Briefly review the four general types of barriers to entry and how each of these types effectively restricts the level of competition the monopolist faces.

6. Suppose the following table describes the market demand schedule for a monopoly.

Price ($)	Quantity demanded (units)
1,000	0
800	200
600	400
400	600
200	800
0	1,000

a. Draw a graph of this market demand schedule for the monopoly.

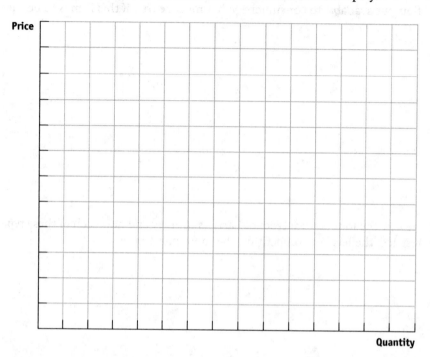

b. Compute the firm's total revenue and marginal revenue figures for the table below. For the marginal revenue figures, use the midpoint method.

Price (dollars)	Quantity demanded (units)	Total revenue (dollars)	Marginal revenue (dollars per unit)
1,000	0		
800	200		
600	400		
400	600		
200	800		
0	1,000		

c. Draw the monopolist's marginal revenue curve on the graph you drew in part (a) of this problem.

d. Write an equation for this monopolist's market demand curve and for its *MR* curve. Compare these two equations. What is true about the *y*-intercept of these two equations? What is the relationship between the slope of the demand curve and the slope of the *MR* curve?

e. If the firm's marginal cost is constant and equal to $200, what is this monopolist's profit-maximizing level of output and what price will this monopolist charge for this good? Label this quantity and this price on your graph.

f. On your graph you drew in part (a), shade in the area that corresponds to the consumer surplus and label it clearly. On this same graph, shade in the area that corresponds to producer surplus and label it clearly. Shade in the area that corresponds to deadweight loss and label it clearly.

g. Calculate the value of consumer surplus, producer surplus, and deadweight loss for this monopoly.

7. Suppose the following table describes the market demand schedule for a monopoly.

Price ($)	Quantity demanded (units)
1,000	0
800	400
600	800
400	1,200
200	1,600
0	2,000

a. Draw a graph of this market demand schedule for the monopoly.

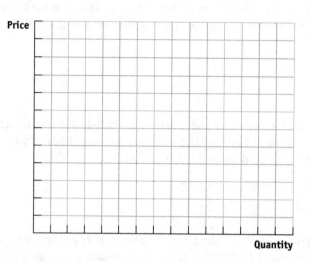

b. Compute the firm's total revenue and marginal revenue figures for the table below. For the marginal revenue figures, use the midpoint method.

Price (dollars)	Quantity demanded (units)	Total revenue (dollars)	Marginal revenue (dollars per unit)
1,000	0		
800	400		
600	800		
400	1,200		
200	1,600		
0	2,000		

c. Draw the monopolist's marginal revenue curve on the graph you drew in part (a) of this problem.

d. Write an equation for this monopolist's market demand curve and for its *MR* curve. Compare these two equations. What is true about the y-intercept of these two equations? What is the relationship between the slope of the demand curve and the slope of the *MR* curve?

e. If the firm's marginal cost is constant and equal to $200, what is this monopolist's profit-maximizing level of output and what price will this monopolist charge for this good? Label this quantity and this price on your graph.

f. On the graph you drew in part (a), shade in the area that corresponds to the consumer surplus and label it clearly. On this same graph, shade in the area that corresponds to producer surplus and label it clearly. Shade in the area that corresponds to deadweight loss and label it clearly.

g. Calculate the value of consumer surplus, producer surplus, and deadweight loss for this monopoly.

8. The graph below represents a monopolist's cost curves and the demand curve for the monopolist's product. Use this graph to answer this set of questions.

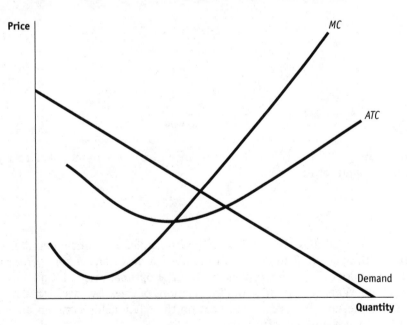

a. On the above graph, identify the monopolist's profit-maximizing level of output and label this amount Q_m (hint: don't forget that you will need to first find the monopolist's MR curve to answer this question). On the graph, label the price the monopolist will charge for the good as P_m.

b. Does this monopolist make positive, negative, or zero economic profit in the short run? Identify the area that represents profits in the above graph if the firm earns positive or negative profit.

c. What do you expect will happen to the monopolist in the long run? In your answer, be sure to identify what happens to the firm's profits, level of production, and price.

d. A newspaper runs an article on the benefits of consuming the product this monopolist produces. The result of this article is that demand for this product shifts to the right at every price. Redraw your graph with the old and the new demand curves, and then analyze what happens to output, price, and profits for this firm. Label the new output Q_m', the new price P_m', and identify the area that represents the firm's profits.

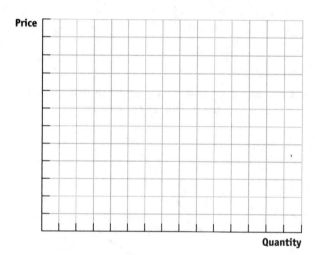

e. Given your answer in part (d), is there an incentive for a monopolist to try to increase the demand for its product?

9. Perfectly competitive firms and monopolies are both assumed to profit maximize. How does the perfectly competitive firm decide on the optimal price and quantity for profit maximization? How does the monopolist decide on the optimal price and quantity for profit maximization? What are the efficiency implications of these two decisions? In your answer to this last question, be sure to comment on the relationship between price and marginal cost for the last unit the firm produces.

10. Suppose a monopolist has a linear market demand curve. At the midpoint of this demand curve, the elasticity of demand is unit-elastic. What do you know about the marginal revenue of the monopolist when the elasticity of demand is equal to one? If the demand for this monopolist is elastic, what do you know about the marginal revenue for this monopolist? If the demand for this monopolist is inelastic, what do you know about the marginal revenue for this monopolist?

11. A monopolist finds that the demand for its product at the current level of production is elastic. Will this monopolist increase or decrease its revenue if it lowers the price at which it sells its product? Explain your answer making reference to the quantity effect as well as the price effect. Which of these two effects is dominant in this situation?

12. Use the diagrams below to answer this set of questions. The left-hand graph depicts a monopoly with its market demand curve and its *MC* curve. The right-hand graph depicts a perfectly competitive industry with the same market demand curve and the *MC* curve for a representative firm. These two graphs are intended to allow you to compare a monopoly to a perfectly competitive industry.

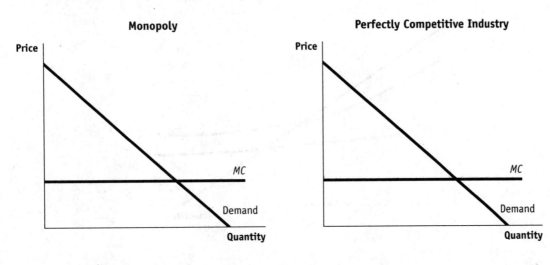

a. On each graph, identify the market level of output. On the first graph, label this output level Q_m, and on the second graph, label this output level Q_{pc}. (Hint: remember that you must first identify the MR curve before selecting the quantity that will be produced.)

b. On each graph, identify the market price for the good. On the first graph, label this price P_m, and on the second graph, label this price P_{pc}.

c. Compare the level of production and the price of the good in the two markets. Which market outcome is better for consumers? Explain your answer.

d. Is there a deadweight loss in either of the two graphs? If there is a deadweight loss, shade in the relevant area on the graph.

13. Discuss two different government policies for dealing with a natural monopoly. Describe each policy and then discuss any limitations or shortcomings that might arise from the implementation of the policy.

14. Use the graph below to answer this set of questions. Due to increasing returns to scale, the firm in the graph is a natural monopoly.

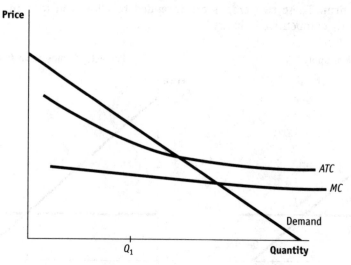

a. Why does this firm's increasing returns to scale result in its being a natural monopoly?

b. Suppose that Q_1 units are provided in this market. On the graph provided, indicate the area that represents the total cost of production if this amount is produced by a single firm. Indicate the area that represents the total cost of production if this amount is produced by five identical firms. Is there an advantage to having a single firm produce this level of output versus having five firms produce this level of output?

c. Suppose this firm acts like a profit-maximizing monopolist. On the graph, find the quantity the monopolist will produce, and label this quantity Q_m. Also identify the price the monopolist will charge (P_m) and identify the area that represents the monopolist's profits, if there are any profits.

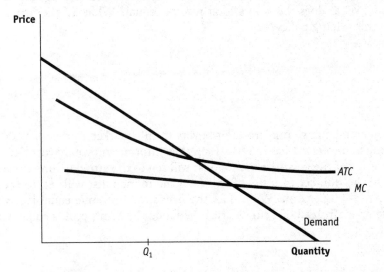

d. Suppose this firm is price regulated so that the price charged is exactly equal to the average total cost of production. On the graph in part (c), identify the level of output the firm will produce when price regulated (Q_{pr}) as well as the price the firm will charge (P_{pr}). What is the economic profit equal to with this form of price regulation? Is the level of output (Q_{pr}) the efficient level of output? Explain your answer making sure to reference the relationship between price and marginal cost for the last unit produced.

e. Suppose this firm is price regulated so that the price charged is exactly equal to the marginal cost of production. On the graph in part (c), identify the level of output that the firm will produce with this regulation (Q_{mc}) as well as the price the firm will charge (P_{mc}). Identify on the graph any area of profit that the firm earns with this form of price regulation. Is the level of output (Q_{mc}) the efficient level of output? Explain your answer making sure to reference the relationship between price and marginal cost for the last unit produced. Will the natural monopolist be willing to produce this level of output at this price? Can you think of a way to get the natural monopolist to produce this level of output?

15. Suppose you are a monopolist that is debating charging a single price for your product or different prices to different customers based on their demand elasticities. The marginal cost of production for your firm is equal to $200 and is constant for all levels of output. The market demand curve is $P = 1,000 - 2Q$.

a. If you charge a single price, what price and quantity would you select given the above information? What does the firm's total revenue equal? What do the firm's profits equal with this pricing policy?

b. Suppose you could charge one group of buyers in this market a price of $600 and a second group of buyers a price of $400. Using the information you have, calculate the number of units of the good the monopolist will sell to the group willing to pay $600 per unit and the number of units of the good the monopolist will sell to the group willing to pay $400 per unit. What does the firm's total revenue equal if it sells the good at two prices instead of a single price? What do the firm's profits equal with this pricing policy?

c. Given your findings in parts (a) and (b), is it advantageous for this firm to sell the good at two different prices? Explain your answer.

d. Does the price discrimination outlined in part (b) increase or decrease consumer surplus? What does your answer tell you about the efficiency of price discrimination relative to the efficiency of a single-price, profit-maximizing monopolist? You may find it helpful to draw sketches of the situation in part (a) and part (b) to compare the areas of consumer surplus. What is the value of consumer surplus in the two situations?

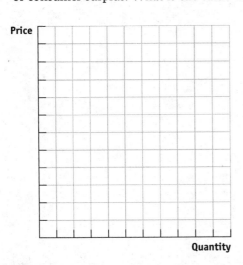

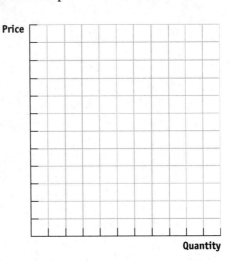

16. Why does a price-discriminating monopolist charge a higher price to consumers with less elastic demand and a lower price to consumers with more elastic demand?

17. Suppose the demand in a market is given by $P = 200 - 2Q$, while the supply in this market is given by $P = 2Q$.

   a. What is the value of consumer surplus and producer surplus in this market if price is determined through the interaction of supply and demand and the market is perfectly competitive?

   b. Suppose this market is served by a monopolist who is able to practice perfect price discrimination. What level of output will this perfectly price-discriminating monopolist produce? How does this level of output compare with the level of output produced in part (a)? Is the level of output produced efficient or not? Justify your answer.

c. Calculate the value of consumer and producer surplus in this market if the producer is a perfectly price-discriminating monopolist. Sketch a graph of the two situations: the consumer and producer surplus under the conditions described in part (a) and the consumer and producer surplus under the conditions described in part (b).

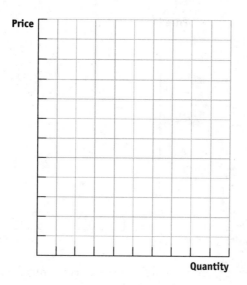

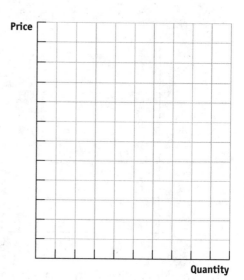

BEFORE YOU TAKE THE TEST

Chapter Review Questions

1. The demand for the monopolist's product
   a. is downward sloping.
   b. equals the market demand curve.
   c. is equal to the firm's *MR* curve.
   d. All of the above statements are true.
   e. Answers (a) and (b) are true.

2. An industry is characterized by having a few firms, each producing a differentiated product. The market structure for this industry is most likely
   a. perfect competition.
   b. monopoly.
   c. oligopoly.
   d. monopolistic competition.

3. Which of the following statements is true?

    I. A monopolistically competitive market structure is composed of many firms producing differentiated products.

    II. A perfectly competitive firm profit-maximizes by producing the level of output where $MR = MC$.

    III. A monopolist profit maximizes by charging the price where $MR = MC$.

    a. Statements I and II are true.

    b. Statements I and III are true.

    c. Statements II and III are true.

    d. Statements I, II, and III are true.

4. Monopoly and oligopoly are the typical market structures that occur when there are

    a. no significant entry barriers.

    b. significant entry barriers.

5. In contrast to perfect competition, a monopolist charges a

    a. higher price and produces a larger quantity.

    b. higher price and produces a smaller quantity.

    c. lower price and produces a larger quantity.

    d. lower price and produces a smaller quantity.

6. A barrier to entry is

    a. always a man-made obstacle to the entry of new firms into a competitive industry.

    b. a term referring to the firm's private property and the firm's right to exclude people from entering this private property.

    c. something that effectively keeps new firms from entering an industry.

    d. only relevant in perfectly competitive industries.

7. A firm that experiences increasing returns to scale

    a. finds that its average total cost of production decreases throughout the relevant region of production.

    b. will find it advantageous to produce a relatively large amount of output rather than a relatively small amount of output.

    c. will benefit from a larger volume of sales.

    d. Answers (a), (b), and (c) are all true.

8. A natural monopoly

    a. profit maximizes when it produces the quantity where $MR = MC$.

    b. experiences decreasing costs throughout the relevant region of output.

    c. is a monopoly whose ATC curve declines over the output levels at which price is greater than or equal to average total cost.

    d. All of the above statements are true.

9. An industry is characterized by having average total cost that decreases as output increases. In this industry, the output can be produced at the lowest cost if _____ produce(s) the total market output.
   a. many identical firms
   b. a single firm
   c. a large number of firms
   d. a few firms

10. An industry is characterized by having average total cost that decreases as output increases. This is due to large
   a. variable costs that are more easily borne by a single producer of the good.
   b. fixed costs that are more easily borne by a single producer of the good.
   c. marginal costs that are more easily borne by a single producer of the good.
   d. fluctuations in revenue that create market instability in the industry, which results in many firms exiting the industry and leaving a single firm to produce the good.

11. A network externality is a situation in which the value of the good _____ as more people use the good.
   a. increases
   b. decreases

12. Patents and copyrights
   a. protect the rights of inventors and writers.
   b. harm consumers of the patented or copyright-protected articles because these articles are more expensive to consumers.
   c. provide an incentive for research and development as well as creative work.
   d. All of the above statements are true.

Use the graph of a monopolist below to answer the next four questions.

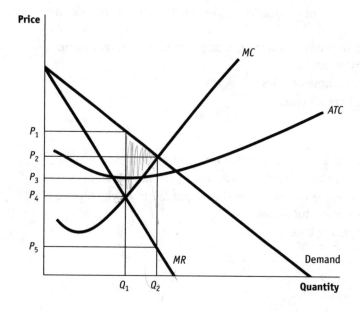

13. This monopolist will produce the profit-maximizing level of output _____ and sell each unit for _____.
    a. Q_1; P_1.
    c. Q_2; P_2.
    b. Q_1; P_2.
    d. Q_1; P_4.

14. If this monopolist were to act as if it was a perfectly competitive industry, then it would produce _____ units of the good and charge _____ for each unit.
    a. Q_1; P_2
    c. Q_2; P_2
    b. Q_1; P_1
    d. Q_2; P_5

15. The deadweight loss associated with this monopoly can be measured as the area
    a. $(1/2)(P_2/\text{unit} - P_4/\text{unit})(Q_2 \text{ units} - Q_1 \text{ units})$.
    b. $(1/2)(P_1/\text{unit} - P_4/\text{unit})(Q_1 \text{ units})$.
    c. $(1/2)(P_2/\text{unit} - P_4/\text{unit})(Q_1 \text{ units})$.
    d. $(1/2)(P_1/\text{unit} - P_4/\text{unit})(Q_2 \text{ units} - Q_1 \text{ units})$.

16. This monopolist earns
    a. positive economic profit equal to area $(P_1/\text{unit} - P_3/\text{unit})(Q_1 \text{ units})$.
    b. positive economic profit equal to area $(P_1/\text{unit} - P_4/\text{unit})(Q_1 \text{ units})$.
    c. negative economic profit equal to area $(P_1/\text{unit} - P_3/\text{unit})(Q_1 \text{ units})$.
    d. negative economic profit equal to area $(P_1/\text{unit} - P_4/\text{unit})(Q_1 \text{ units})$.

Use the following information to answer the next four questions. The demand curve for a monopolist is given by $P = 100 - Q$, while the monopolist's marginal cost is $P = 3Q$. At the profit-maximizing level of output for the monopolist, the average total cost of production is equal to $70.

17. This monopolist's *MR* curve can be written as
    a. $MR = 100 - Q$.
    b. $MR = 200 - Q$.
    c. $MR = 100 - (1/2)Q$.
    d. $MR = 100 - 2Q$.

18. For this monopolist the profit-maximizing level of output is equal to _____ and the market price for this output is _____.
    a. 20 units; $80
    c. 25 units; $75
    b. 20 units; $60
    d. 50 units; $50

19. Profits for this monopolist equal
    a. $400.
    c. $10.
    b. $200.
    d. $20.

20. The deadweight loss associated with this monopoly
    a. cannot be calculated from the information given.
    b. is unimportant, since the monopoly is protected from competition due to the existence of effective barriers to entry.
    c. equals $50.
    d. equals $25.

21. A monopolist is debating whether or not to lower the price it charges for its product. Which of the following statements is true?

    I. When the monopolist lowers its price, the quantity effect always increases the monopolist's total revenue.

    II. When the monopolist lowers its price, the price effect initially causes total revenue to increase, but eventually the price effect causes total revenue to fall.

    III. The monopolist does not need to worry about the quantity or price effect when debating what price to charge for its product, since it is the only producer of the good.

    a. Statement I is true.

    b. Statement II is true.

    c. Statements I and II are true.

    d. Statement III is true.

22. Which of the following statements is true?

    I. A perfectly competitive industry produces an efficient level of output, since $P = MC$ for the last unit produced in this industry.

    II. A monopoly produces an efficient level of output, since $MR = MC$ for the last unit produced by this monopoly.

    III. A perfectly price-discriminating monopolist produces an efficient level of output, since the value consumers are willing to pay for the last unit sold is equal to the cost of producing this last unit.

    a. Statement I is true.

    b. Statements I and II are true.

    c. Statements I and III are true.

    d. Statements I, II, and III are true.

23. A monopolist estimates that the price elasticity of demand for its product is less than one. This monopolist knows that an increase in the price of its good will _____ its total revenue.

    a. increase

    b. decrease

24. Which of the following statements is true about a monopolist with a linear demand curve?

    I. The more elastic the demand for a monopolist's product, the closer the market price will be to marginal revenue for this firm.

    II. Once the elasticity of demand for a monopolist falls below one, the value of marginal revenue is negative.

    III. At the midpoint of the monopolist's demand curve, the firm's marginal revenue is equal to zero.

    a. Statement I is true.

    b. Statement II is true.

    c. Statements I and II are true.

    d. Statements I and III are true.

    e. Statements I, II, and III are true.

25. A natural monopoly is a monopoly that occurs because of increasing returns to scale. Which of the following statements are true for a natural monopoly?
   a. Public ownership, although a policy often used for dealing with natural monopoly, may result in poor service and a failure to minimize the cost of providing the good.
   b. Price regulation of a natural monopoly, which limits the price charged for the product, is capable of increasing the total amount of the good available while simultaneously reducing the price of each unit.
   c. A natural monopolist that is price regulated will only be willing to supply the good if the regulated price is equal to or greater than the average total cost of producing its output.
   d. Answers (a), (b), and (c) are all true.

Use the following information to answer the next three questions. An airline company is the only airline serving a market between several small cities. This monopolist finds that it can sell 500 tickets at a price of $300. The company also knows that it could sell an additional 200 tickets at $150. The marginal cost of providing a seat is $100.

26. If this airline company is only allowed to offer tickets at a single price, the company should sell _____ tickets at a price of _____ and earn economic profits of _____.
   a. 700; $300; $140,000
   b. 500; $150; $25,000
   c. 700; $150; $35,000
   d. 500; $300; $100,000

27. If this airline company is allowed to offer tickets at different prices, what is the maximum amount of profit this airline company can earn?
   a. $100,000
   b. $110,000
   c. $35,000
   d. $180,000

28. When this company price discriminates,
   a. it increases its level of profit.
   b. it increases consumer surplus.
   c. it reduces the deadweight loss associated with being a monopoly.
   d. Answers (a), (b), and (c) are all true.

29. Joe's price elasticity of demand for airplane travel is equal to 2, and Beth's price elasticity of demand for airplane travel is equal to 1.3. If the airline companies are allowed to price discriminate, we would anticipate that if Joe and Beth are both traveling to the same location and leaving from the same airport,
   a. they will both pay the same price for an airline ticket.
   b. Joe will pay a higher price for an airline ticket.
   c. Beth will pay a higher price for an airline ticket.
   d. it is unclear who will pay the higher price for an airplane ticket.

Use the following graph of a monopolist to answer the next two questions.

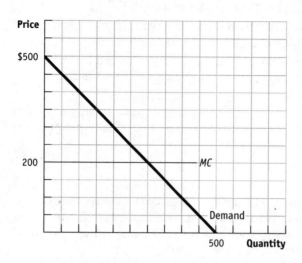

30. If this monopolist profit maximizes, it will produce _____ units of output, charge a price of _____, provide a producer surplus equal to _____, provide a consumer surplus equal to _____, and create a deadweight loss equal to _____.

   a. 250; $250; $31,250; $31,250; $0

   b. 150; $350; $22,500; $11,250; $11,250

   c. 150; $350; $11,250; $22,500; $11,250

   d. 300; $200, $0; $45,000; $0

31. If this monopolist practices perfect price discrimination, it will produce _____ units, charge a price of _____ for the last unit produced, provide a producer surplus equal to _____, provide a consumer surplus equal to _____, and create a deadweight loss equal to _____.

   a. 300; $200; $0; $45,000; $0

   b. 300; $200; $45,000; $0; $0

   c. 250; $200; $43,750; $0; $1,250

   d. 250; $200; $0; $43,750; $1,250

ANSWER KEY

Answers to Problems and Exercises

1. A perfectly competitive industry produces a greater quantity of the good and sells this good at a lower price than a monopoly with the same cost curves. The figures below contrast the outcomes for these two types of market structures based on the same market demand curve. In the first figure, the perfectly competitive industry sets the market equilibrium price and quantity where the quantity demanded equals the quantity supplied. This figure also indicates this price and quantity combination and indicates the areas that correspond to consumer and producer surplus.

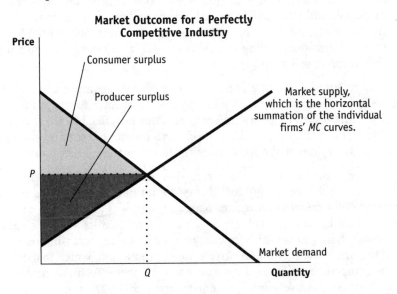

Market Outcome for a Perfectly Competitive Industry

In contrast, the monopoly selects its output by equating MR to MC and then setting price by taking this quantity and looking at what price consumers are willing to pay for this quantity. The figure below illustrates the monopoly situation. Note that the monopoly results in a higher price, a lower quantity, and the creation of a deadweight loss relative to the market being served by a perfectly competitive industry.

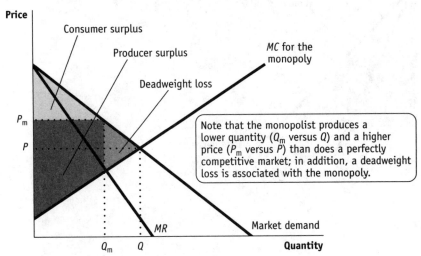

Market Outcome for a Monopoly

Note that the monopolist produces a lower quantity (Q_m versus Q) and a higher price (P_m versus P) than does a perfectly competitive market; in addition, a deadweight loss is associated with the monopoly.

2. For the last unit produced by the monopolist, the price consumers are willing to pay for this unit is greater than the marginal cost of producing this last unit. Refer back to the graph of the monopoly given in the answer to problem 1 to see this. The implication is that the value consumers place on this last unit, as measured by the price they are willing to pay, is greater than the cost of producing this last unit, as measured by the marginal cost incurred by the firm when it produces this unit. Thus, too few resources are being allocated to the production of this good, since the value to the consumer exceeds the cost to the producer of producing this last unit. This is not surprising, since one of the effects of a monopoly is to restrict output to a lower level than would be produced with perfect competition.

3. This firm is a monopoly in that there is only one producer, and this producer is producing a good for which there are no close substitutes. However, if there are no barriers to entry, then this monopoly will not persist since new firms will be attracted to this industry in the long run due to the existence of positive economic profit. Substantial barriers to entry can prevent the firm from facing competition, and it therefore can continue to sustain its positive economic profit into the long run.

4. A firm can choose to restrict its output and raise its price, but if it competes in an industry where there are many firms and where there are close substitutes for its product, the firm will find that raising price and restricting output is not beneficial to them in terms of their profitability. What makes it possible for a firm to restrict output and raise price is the presence of market power that enables the firm to affect the market outcome.

5. Control of an essential resource or input is a very effective barrier to entry, since new firms would be unable to produce the product if they do not have access to this resource or input. The presence of increasing returns to scale also serves as an effective barrier to entry, since the firm that has a larger volume of sales will find that its average total cost of production is lower than a firm with a smaller volume of sales: increasing returns to scale implies that the firm benefits from its large scale of production, which makes it difficult for would-be competitors to enter the industry and compete. Technological superiority can also act an as effective barrier to entry: firms that maintain a consistent technological superiority over potential competitors can establish themselves as monopolists. Lastly, the government may create effective barriers to entry in the form of patents or copyright protections.

6. a.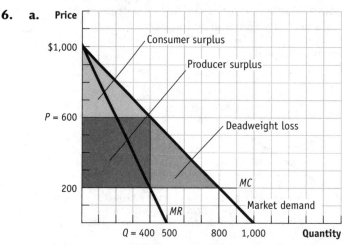

b.

Price (dollars)	Quantity demanded (units)	Total revenue (dollars)	Marginal revenue (dollars per unit)
1,000	0	0	
			800
800	200	160,000	
			400
600	400	240,000	
			0
400	600	240,000	
			−400
200	800	160,000	
			−800
0	1,000	0	

c. See the graph in part (a).

d. The monopolist's demand curve is $Q = 1,000 - P$, or written in slope intercept form, it is $P = 1,000 - Q$. The monopolist's MR curve is $MR = 1,000 - 2Q$. The y-intercept for the monopolist's demand curve is the same as the y-intercept for the monopolist's MR curve if the demand curve is linear. The slope of the MR curve is twice the slope of the demand curve provided that the demand curve is linear.

e. The monopolist profit maximizes by producing the level of output where $MR = MC$ and then moving up to the demand curve to charge the price associated with this level of output. Thus, if $MC = 200$ and $MR = 1,000 - 2Q$, then the profit-maximizing quantity is 400 units. To find the monopolist's price, substitute 400 for Q in the demand equation: the monopolist's price is $600.

f. See the graph in part (a).

g. Consumer surplus = (1/2)($400 per unit)(400 units) = $80,000; producer surplus = ($400 per unit)(400 units) = $160,000; deadweight loss = (1/2)($400 per unit)(400 units) = $80,000

7. a.

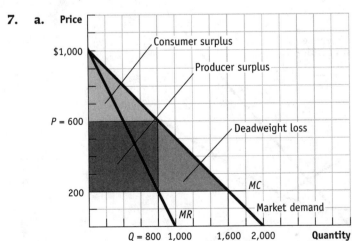

b.

Price (dollars)	Quantity demanded (units)	Total revenue (dollars)	Marginal revenue (dollars per unit)
1,000	0	0	
			800
800	400	320,000	
			400
600	800	480,000	
			0
400	1,200	480,000	
			–400
200	1,600	320,000	
			–800
0	2,000	0	

c. See the graph in part (a).

d. The monopolist's demand curve is $Q = 2,000 - 2P$, or written in slope intercept form, it is $P = 1,000 - (1/2)Q$. The monopolist's MR curve is $MR = 1,000 - Q$. The y-intercept for the monopolist's demand curve is the same as the y-intercept for the monopolist's MR curve if the demand curve is linear. The slope of the MR curve is twice the slope of the demand curve provided that the demand curve is linear.

e. The monopolist profit maximizes by producing the level of output where $MR = MC$ and then moving up to the demand curve to charge the price associated with this level of output. Thus, if $MC = 200$ and $MR = 1,000 - Q$, then the profit-maximizing quantity is 800 units. To find the monopolist's price, substitute 800 for Q in the demand equation: the monopolist's price is $600.

f. See the graph in part (a).

g. Consumer surplus = (1/2)($400 per unit)(800 units) = $160,000; producer surplus = ($400 per unit)(800 units) = $320,000; deadweight loss = (1/2)($400 per unit)(800 units) = $160,000

8.

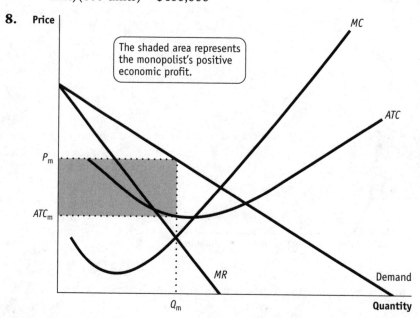

The shaded area represents the monopolist's positive economic profit.

a. See the above graph.

b. This monopolist earns positive economic profit since the price it receives on each unit (P_m) is greater than its average total cost (ATC) of production (ATC_m on the graph).

c. This monopolist will continue to earn positive economic profits because there is an effective barrier to entry to this industry that prevents the firm from having to compete with other producers. The firm's profits will continue at the level given in the graph, and the firm's price and quantity decision will remain unchanged.

d.

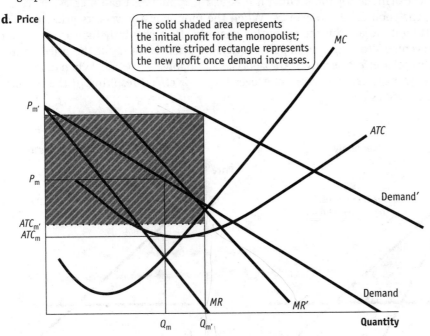

The solid shaded area represents the initial profit for the monopolist; the entire striped rectangle represents the new profit once demand increases.

e. Holding everything else constant, if the monopolist can increase the demand for its product, it can charge a higher price, produce more units of the good, and increase the level of economic profits it earns.

9. The perfectly competitive firm is a price-taking firm and must charge the market-determined price for its output. It then chooses the profit-maximizing level of output given this price. The profit-maximizing level of output for the perfectly competitive firm is where $MR = MC$, or where $P = MC$, since $P = MR$ for a perfectly competitive firm.

A monopoly can set its own price, subject to market demand for its product. It determines its profit-maximizing level of output by equating marginal cost to marginal revenue, and then charges the price consumers are willing to pay for this level of output. The monopolist finds this price by going vertically up to the demand curve from its selected level of output and charging the price on its demand curve that is associated with this level of output.

A perfectly competitive firm produces an efficient level of output, since $P = MC$ for the last unit of output it produces. This implies that the price consumers are willing to pay for the last unit produced is equal to the cost of producing this last unit: consumers and producers value this last unit equivalently, which tells us that the right amount of resources is being allocated to the production of this good. A monopoly, in contrast, produces an inefficient level of output, since $P > MC$ for the last unit of output it produces. This implies that the price consumers are willing to pay for the last unit produced is greater than the cost of producing this last unit: the value the consumers place on this last unit exceeds the cost of producing this last unit. More resources should be devoted to the production of this good.

10. The *MR* curve for a monopolist with a linear demand curve shares the *y*-intercept with the demand curve and has twice the slope of the demand curve. If you plot this *MR* curve and the demand curve on the same graph, you will find that the *MR* curve intersects the horizontal axis at a quantity that is the quantity found at the midpoint of the demand curve. Thus, when demand is unit-elastic (at its midpoint), marginal revenue equals zero. When demand is elastic, marginal revenue is positive, and when demand is inelastic, marginal revenue is negative.

11. When the demand for the product is elastic, the monopolist can increase its revenue by selling the good for a lower price. When the monopolist lowers its price, it sells more units than it did at a higher price: this quantity effect positively increases the monopolist's revenue. When the monopolist lowers its price, it must cut the price on all units sold: this price effect negatively impacts the monopolist's revenue. When demand is elastic, the quantity effect is dominant over the price effect, resulting in the monopolist's revenues increasing.

12. **a, b.**

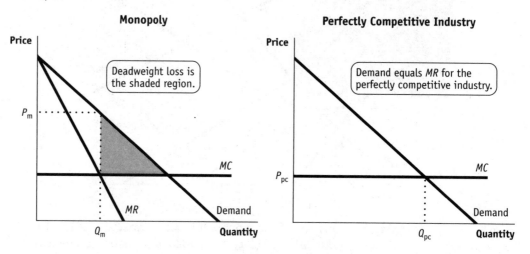

c. The perfectly competitive market produces a higher level of output and charges a lower price for this output than does the monopoly. Consumers prefer the outcome of the perfectly competitive industry since they have more output and pay lower prices.

d. The monopoly has a deadweight loss, which is the shaded area in the graph. Notice that the monopoly's level of production occurs where $P > MC$. This implies that consumers would like to have more of the good, since they are willing to pay more for another unit of the good than the marginal cost of producing that additional unit of output. Whenever price is not equal to marginal cost for the last unit produced, there is a deadweight loss, since the market is not producing the socially optimal level of output.

13. There are two primary government policies for dealing with natural monopolies: public ownership and price regulation.

   With public ownership, the natural monopoly is operated by a public agency that has a mandate to provide the good while also protecting consumers' interests. A publicly owned natural monopoly can set prices based on efficiency and not profit maximization. However, a publicly owned natural monopoly may fail to keep costs down or to offer high-quality products.

   Price regulation limits the price that natural monopolies can charge for their good. Price regulation takes the form of setting a price ceiling so that the natural monopoly provides more of the regulated good at a lower price than would occur with an unregulated natural monopoly. Price regulation is difficult because the regulators do not have the required information to be able to set price at exactly that point where $P = ATC$. In addition, price-regulated natural monopolies have a tendency to inflate their costs to regulators and to provide inferior-quality products.

14. a. This firm's increasing returns to scale means that the firm can reduce its average cost of production by producing larger levels of output. The firm's *ATC* curve is downward sloping over the relevant region of production. This suggests that we should expect to see large-sized firms serving this industry, or more likely, a single firm providing the product due to the cost advantages of being a large producer.

b.

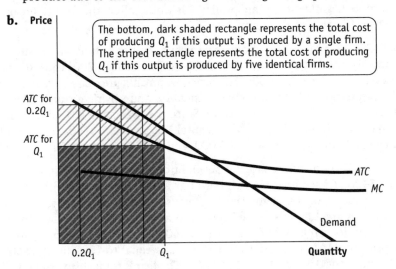

A single producer can produce the total amount of Q_1 at substantially lower cost than can five identical firms. Due to increasing returns to scale, it is far less costly to have a single producer than many producers in this market.

c. The natural monopolist acting as a profit-maximizing monopolist earns positive economic profit. See the graph below for Q_m, P_m, and the area that represents these profits. Also notice that you must draw in the firm's *MR* curve in order to identify the quantity and price for this monopolist.

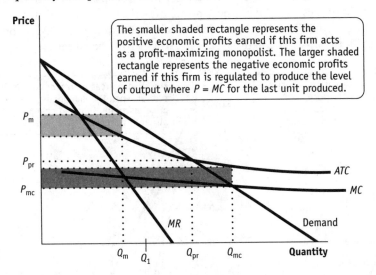

d. When this natural monopoly is price regulated to produce the quantity where price equals average total cost, the firm earns zero economic profit. This level of output (Q_{pr}) is not the efficient level of output, however, since for the last unit produced P_{pr} is greater than the marginal cost of producing this last unit. This indicates that this price-regulated monopolist is not producing enough of the good, since the value consumers place on this last unit is greater than the cost of producing this last unit.

e. When this natural monopoly is price regulated to produce that quantity where price equals *MC*, the firm earns negative economic profit, but it produces the efficient level of output, since *P* = *MC* for the last unit produced. However, the natural monopolist will be unwilling to produce this level of output since it incurs negative economic profit. The natural monopolist would be willing to produce this level if it received a subsidy equal to its negative economic profit. This would allow the firm to break even and produce the efficient level of output.

15. **a.** The monopolist would produce the profit-maximizing level of output where *MR* = *MC*. For this monopolist the *MR* curve is *MR* = 1,000 − 4*Q* and *MC* = 200. Thus, the profit-maximizing level of output is *Q* = 200. The profit-maximizing price can be found by substituting this level of output into the demand equation and solving for price: *P* = $600. The firm's total revenue is equal to $120,000. Since the *MC* curve is a horizontal line, this implies that the firm's *ATC* is also a horizontal line at *ATC* = $200. The firm's total cost of producing 200 units is therefore $40,000, and the firm earns a profit of $80,000.

b. You could still sell 200 units for a price of $600. But now you can sell additional units for a price of $400. To see how many additional units you can sell, first substitute $400 into the demand equation for the price to solve for how many units will be demanded in this market at a price of $400. A total of 300 units will be demanded, but 200 of these units can be sold for a price of $600. Thus, 100 additional units can be sold at a price of $400. The firm's total revenue is equal to (200 units)($600 per unit) + (100 units)($400 per unit), or $160,000. The firm's total cost is equal to (300 units)($200 per unit), or $60,000, and the firm earns a profit of $100,000.

c. The single-price monopolist earns a lower level of profit ($80,000) than does the monopolist that price discriminates and charges more than one price in this market. In the case of the price-discriminating monopolist that charges two different prices ($600 and $400), the level of profits is $100,000. It definitely pays to price discriminate.

d. Price discrimination increases the area of consumer surplus and therefore results in a better outcome for the consumer. The price discriminator produces a more efficient level of output than does the single-price, profit-maximizing monopolist. Consumer surplus is equal to $40,000 for the single-price monopolist and $50,000 for the price-discriminating monopolist. The figure below illustrates the two situations.

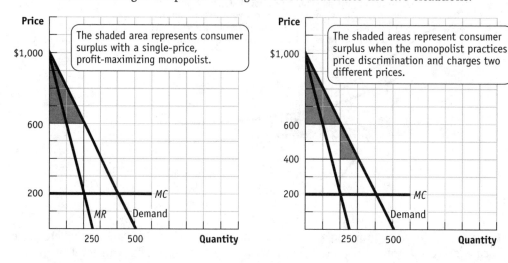

16. Consumers with relatively elastic demand are price sensitive: a little change in the price causes a relatively large change in the quantity demanded of the good. Consumers with relatively inelastic demand are not price sensitive: a change in the price of the good causes little change in the quantity demanded of the good. Thus, the price-discriminating monopolist finds that it is better to charge a high price to consumers with inelastic demand and a low price to consumers with elastic demand.

17. **a.** The value of consumer surplus is $2,500 and the value of producer surplus is $2,500.

b. The monopolist will produce 50 units of output, since this is the level of output where the demand equals the marginal cost. In this case, the marginal revenue for the perfectly price-discriminating monopolist is the market demand curve, since it receives marginal revenue equal to the price of the good for each unit of the good sold. To select the profit-maximizing level of output, the perfectly price-discriminating firm will set marginal revenue equal to marginal cost and produce that level of output. This will result in the same level of output being produced by the market in part (a). Since the price the consumer pays for the last unit produced is exactly equal to the cost of producing this last unit, this is an efficient level of output. Both the perfectly competitive market and the perfectly price-discriminating monopolist produce the efficient level of output.

c. The value of producer surplus for the perfectly price-discriminating monopolist is $5,000, which is the sum of the consumer and producer surplus when the market is perfectly competitive. The value of consumer surplus is $0. The figures below illustrate the two situations.

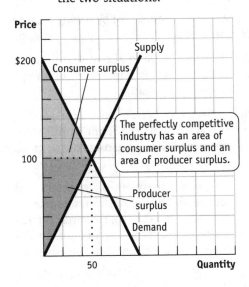

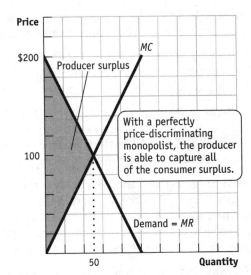

Answers to Chapter Review Questions

1. **Answer e.** The monopolist's demand curve is the market demand curve and it is downward sloping. The monopolist's demand curve is not the monopolist's MR curve, however, since for the monopolist the MR curve lies beneath the demand curve.

2. **Answer c.** Oligopolies are characterized by having just a few firms in the industry. These firms may produce differentiated products or they may produce identical products.

3. **Answer a.** The first statement is the definition of monopolistic competition. The second statement correctly states the profit-maximizing rule used by perfectly competitive firms when selecting their optimal output level. The third statement is false: monopolies profit maximize when they produce the level of output where $MR = MC$ and then charge the price on their demand curve that is associated with this level of output.

4. **Answer b.** Entry barriers effectively protect an industry from potential competition from new firms. Entry barriers may be due to government regulation, increasing returns to scale in production, technological superiority, or the control of some essential resource or input.

5. **Answer b.** Monopolies restrict output and charge consumers higher prices for their product.

6. **Answer c.** Barriers to entry may be man-made: for example, legislation may grant patents or copyrights to a particular business or individual. But barriers to entry do not act as an obstacle to new firm entry in a competitive industry, since we assume this kind of industry has free entry and exit in the long run, which eliminates answers (a) and (d). Answer (b) is not true: barriers to entry are not about people's rights to trespass at a business site. Answer (c) is a general definition of barriers to entry.

7. **Answer d.** Increasing returns to scale implies that the average cost of producing the good decreases as the level of production increases: the *ATC* curve is downward sloping throughout the relevant region of production. Thus, firms benefit from producing larger amounts of output (or having larger volumes of sales), since each unit of this output is cheaper on average to produce than would be the case with a smaller level of output.

8. **Answer d.** A natural monopoly has increasing returns to scale over all the levels of output at which price is greater than or equal to average total cost. This implies that as its level of production increases its cost per unit declines. It is cheaper for a single firm to produce the total output for the market than it is for multiple firms to produce this level of total output.

9. **Answer b.** This industry is a decreasing-cost industry that is best served by having a single producer supply the good, since a single producer can produce the good at the lowest cost.

10. **Answer b.** When an industry is characterized as having average total cost that decreases as output increases, this is due to large fixed costs that result in larger levels of output being produced at lower cost per unit than smaller levels of output.

11. **Answer a.** A network externality is a situation where one person's use of a good is enhanced when other people elect to also use the good. This is the result of interconnections or networks existing between the users of the good. The more users of the good, the more networks or connections are created.

12. **Answer d.** Patents and copyrights are intended to protect the work of inventors and artists. This work is costly in terms of time and resources and would not be undertaken if the inventors and artists did not receive compensation for their creations. However, patents and copyrights create a temporary monopoly and therefore restrict the level of output available while raising the price of the good: both of these effects are harmful to consumers.

13. **Answer c.** If this monopolist were to act as if it was a perfectly competitive industry, then it would produce the level of output where marginal cost intersected the demand curve, because this would represent the efficient level of output where the marginal cost of the last unit produced equals the price from selling the last unit of the good. It would sell these Q_2 units of the good for the price on the demand curve (P_2) that is associated with this level of output.

14. **Answer a.** The monopolist profit maximizes when it produces the level of output where $MR = MC$ and then prices this level of output by charging the price on the demand curve that is associated with this level of output. $MR = MC$ at Q_1, and P_1 is the price that is associated with Q_1 on the demand curve.

15. **Answer d.** The deadweight loss associated with this monopoly is the area that represents the loss in total surplus due to the market being served by a monopoly instead of a perfectly competitive industry. This surplus loss is the area $(1/2)(P_1/\text{unit} - P_4/\text{unit})(Q_2 \text{ units} - Q_1 \text{ units})$.

16. **Answer a.** This monopolist earns positive economic profit since the price it charges for the good (P_1) is greater than the average total cost of producing Q_1 units of the good. To calculate profits you can use the formula $TR - TC = \text{profits}$, or you can calculate the product of the quantity produced times the difference between the price of each unit and the average total cost of producing these units. Using this latter method, the price of each unit is P_1, the average total cost of each unit is P_3, and the number of units produced is Q_1. Thus, profit is $(P_1/\text{unit} - P_3/\text{unit})(Q_1 \text{ units})$.

17. **Answer d.** For a monopolist with a linear demand curve, the *MR* curve has the same *y*-intercept as the demand curve, and its slope is twice the slope of the demand curve. The *y*-intercept of the demand curve is 100 and the slope of the demand curve is (−1).

The *MR* curve has a *y*-intercept of 100 and its slope is (–2). The *MR* curve can be written as $MR = 100 - 2Q$.

18. **Answer a.** The profit-maximizing monopolist will produce the quantity where $MR = MC$ and then price this level of output by going to its demand curve: $MR = 100 - 2Q$, and $MC = 3Q$; thus, $Q = 20$ units. Substituting 20 for Q in the demand equation and solving for P gives us the monopolist's market price for this good: $P = \$80$.

19. **Answer b.** Profit can be calculated by multiplying the level of output times the difference between the price of the good and the average total cost of producing the good. Thus, (20 units)($80 per unit – $70 per unit) gives a profit of $200.

20. **Answer c.** There is a deadweight loss due to the monopoly. It is the area that represents the efficiency loss due to the market not operating as a perfectly competitive market. The efficient level of output in this market is 25 units (where the *MC* curve intersects the demand curve). The deadweight loss is equal to (1/2)($80 per unit – $60 per unit)(25 units – 20 units) = $50.

21. **Answer a.** When the monopolist lowers its price, it can sell more units of the good and these additional units will always make a positive contribution to total revenue. However, when the monopolist lowers its price, it finds that it now has to cut the price on all the units it sells and this price effect reduces the total revenue from the units that previously would have sold for a higher price. To profit maximize, the monopolist must select the price off the demand curve that corresponds to the quantity where $MR = MC$.

22. **Answer c.** Both statements I and III are true based on the profit-maximization rule for these two types of market structures. Statement II is not true: although monopolies produce where $MR = MC$, they charge a higher price, so that for the last unit produced, the marginal cost is less than the price. The monopolist does not produce the efficient level of output, since price does not equal marginal cost for this last unit.

23. **Answer a.** When price elasticity of demand is less than one, the demand curve is relatively inelastic. An increase in price in the inelastic region of the demand curve results in total revenue increasing.

24. **Answer e.** All three of these statements are true and rely on a thorough knowledge of the meaning of elasticity and its relationship to total revenue. The elastic region of the demand curve occurs at prices that are greater than the price at the midpoint of the demand curve: at higher prices, the demand is more elastic. In this region of the demand curve, the *MR* curve lies closer to the demand curve. When the elasticity of demand has a value of less than one, this signifies that demand is inelastic and a fall in the price of the good will cause total revenue to decrease, which implies that marginal revenue is negative. The midpoint of the linear demand curve is the unit-elastic point: this is where total revenue is maximized, and therefore the change in total revenue, MR_1 is equal to zero.

25. **Answer d.** Public ownership of a natural monopoly does not often work as a solution to the problem because it offers little incentive for the natural monopolist to keep costs down and produce high-quality products. Price regulation of a natural monopolist is a policy that can result in lower prices and greater quantities, provided that the regulated price allows the natural monopolist to at least break even. Provided the regulated price is equal to or greater than the average total cost of production, the natural monopolist will be able to make zero or positive economic profits and will therefore be willing to produce the good.

26. **Answer d.** The best profit situation for this company, if it can charge only a single price, is to sell 500 tickets at a price of $300. This will give the company total revenue of $150,000 and a total cost of $50,000: the company will earn a profit of $100,000. In contrast, if the company sells 700 tickets, they must drop the price to $150 for all the tickets. Then the company would earn profits of $35,000, since its total revenue would equal $105,000 and its total cost would equal $70,000.

27. **Answer b.** When the company sells tickets at $300 and at $150, it can sell 700 tickets in all. It can sell the first 500 tickets for $300 and then an additional 200 tickets for

$150. The total revenue for the company from these sales equals $180,000, and its total cost equals $70,000. The firm's profit equals $110,000.

28. **Answer d.** From question 27, you know that price discrimination increases the company's profitability. In addition, when the company expands the number of tickets it offers, this results in improving the market outcome for consumers. This is measured by an increase in consumer surplus as well as a reduction in the deadweight loss associated with the monopoly.

29. **Answer c.** Price elasticity of demand measures price sensitivity. Because Joe's price elasticity of demand is greater than Beth's price elasticity of demand, we know that Joe is more price sensitive. With regard to airline tickets, this indicates that Beth's travel is less negotiable than Joe's travel and therefore that Beth can anticipate she will pay more for an airline ticket than Joe.

30. **Answer b.** The monopolist profit maximizes by producing the quantity where $MR = MC$. The MR curve for this monopolist is $MR = 500 - 2Q$. So the monopolist will produce 150 units, and it will sell these units for a price of $350 (substitute 150 units into the demand curve to find the price the monopolist will charge). The graph below indicates the areas that correspond to consumer surplus, producer surplus, and deadweight loss.

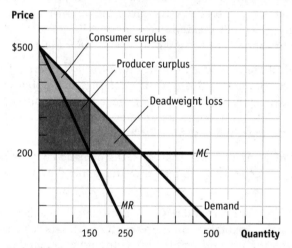

31. **Answer b.** The perfect price discriminator captures all of the consumer surplus by producing the level of output where MC = demand. In this case, the perfectly price-discriminating firm will produce 300 units and charge a price of $200 for the last unit produced. The graph below indicates the area that corresponds to producer surplus. There is no consumer surplus or deadweight loss associated with perfect price discrimination.

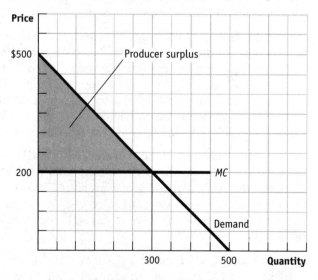

chapter 15

Oligopoly

Summary

This chapter explores oligopoly, a market structure characterized by a few firms producing a product that may or may not be differentiated. The chapter discusses the incentives for oligopolists to act cooperatively or competitively and the results of these actions on the level of oligopoly profits. The chapter discusses formal as well as tacit collusion, the formation of cartels, and the reasons why cartels fail. In addition, the chapter discusses game theory and its usefulness in exploring some of the issues confronting oligopolies. The chapter also explores the relationship between oligopolies and antitrust policy.

Chapter Objectives

Objective #1. Oligopolies are characterized as an industry in which there are a few producers. Each of these individual producers has some market power (like a monopoly) that enables them to affect market prices, but each of these producers also competes against the other producers in the industry. This competition is different from perfect competition in that each producer is aware of the other firms in the industry and recognizes that each firm's behavior affects the other firms. The key aspect of oligopoly is the tension between cooperation and competition: each firm must decide whether and to what degree it wants to cooperate or compete with the other firms in their industry.

Objective #2. With an oligopolistic industry what matters is not the size of the firm, but rather the number of firms serving the industry. Oligopolies primarily exist because each firm benefits from increasing returns to scale and these returns to scale result in a few producers in the industry rather than many small-scale producers in the industry. Analysis of oligopoly presents several challenging puzzles not presented in our analysis of perfectly competitive markets or monopolies.

Objective #3. The Herfindahl-Hirschman Index (HHI) allows economists to measure the degree of concentration in an industry. This index is the square of the share of market sales summed over the firms in the industry. An HHI greater than 1,800 indicates an oligopoly; an

HHI between 1,000 and 1,800 indicates a somewhat competitive market; and an HHI less than 1,000 indicates a strongly competitive market. When a proposed merger is likely to significantly increase the HHI over 1,000, the merger is closely analyzed and is likely to be disallowed by government antitrust enforcement.

Objective #4.   The simplest type of oligopoly to analyze is a duopoly, a situation in which there are only two firms in the industry. These two firms face two strategies: they can decide to cooperate with one another or they can decide to compete with each other by adopting noncooperative behavior. By cooperating and forming a cartel, these two firms can work together to select the level of output that will maximize their joint profits. Even with an agreement to cooperate, the firms will each find that they have an incentive to cheat on this arrangement. Cartels are inherently unstable because each firm recognizes that they have an incentive to produce more of the good than was agreed. Like a monopolist, each firm in an oligopoly recognizes that selling a greater amount of output creates both a quantity and a price effect; however, the price effect is smaller for the oligopolist than it is for the monopolist, which means that the marginal revenue from selling additional units of the good is higher for the oligopolist than it would be for the monopolist. Ultimately, collusion is more profitable than noncooperative behavior, but it is difficult to achieve since formal agreements to collude are illegal in many nations. Some oligopolies find ways to collude without a formal agreement.

Objective #5.   An oligopolist would prefer to have no firms to compete against. An oligopolist can create a monopoly through the establishment of exclusive dealing whereby the oligopolist provides the good to buyers who agree to only buy its product. This allows the oligopolist to have greater market power and therefore higher profits than it would earn if it faced competition from other firms. Alternatively, the oligopolistic firm can distinguish its product through differentiation: the more differentiated the firm's product, the closer the market structure is to monopoly.

Objective #6.   There are two basic types of oligopoly behavior based on production decisions and pricing decisions: (1) quantity competition, or Cournot behavior; and (2) price competition, or Bertrand behavior.

- With quantity competition, or Cournot behavior, the firms find it relatively easy to achieve an outcome that looks like collusion without having to make a formal agreement to collude. This oligopoly situation occurs when each firm lacks the ability to change quickly the level of output they produce. In such a setting, the firms in the oligopoly, constrained by the quantity of output they can produce, find it easier to divide the market, sell their product at a price greater than marginal cost, and earn positive economic profit. In this setting, the oligopolistic outcome resembles the monopoly outcome with regard to market price and market output.

- With price competition, or Bertrand behavior, the firms find it relatively difficult to achieve an outcome that looks like collusion and instead find that each firm produces the quantity where price equals marginal cost, and the resultant market outcome is like perfect competition. In this situation, each firm's product is a perfect substitute for the other firms' products, and each firm has the capacity to expand output quickly. Oligopolistic firms in this setting compete on price, and price falls until it reaches the level where price equals marginal cost. In this setting, the oligopolistic outcome resembles the perfectly competitive outcome with regard to market price and market output.

- Oligopolistic firms that lack an environment that imposes quantity constraints often differentiate their products to avoid direct price competition and its resultant outcome. The more differentiated its product, the more each firm resembles a monopoly.

Objective #7. Oligopolistic firms are interdependent: one firm's profit depends on what its competitors do and vice versa. This interdependence can be modeled using game theory, in which a payoff matrix is constructed to represent the different outcomes that each firm achieves depending on the decisions made by the other firms. In this chapter, game theory is used to model this interdependence between two firms. The prisoner's dilemma is an example of game theory in which each player in the game has an incentive to cheat or take an action that benefits the player at the other player's expense, and the outcome of this behavior leaves both players worse off than they would have been if neither player had cheated. This example helps illustrate the peculiar, and often puzzling, behavior of oligopolistic firms. Figure 15.1 illustrates a payoff matrix between player 1 and player 2. Both players have a choice of two strategies—strategy 1 and strategy 2—and the payoff for each player is given in the individual cells, with player 1's payoff given first, followed by player 2's payoff.

Figure 15.1

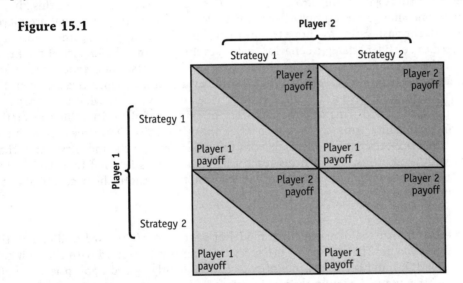

Objective #8. A dominant strategy is a strategy that the player will adhere to no matter what the other players do. When each player takes the strategy that is best for them given the actions of the other players, this generates a game equilibrium that is referred to as a Nash equilibrium. The Nash equilibrium is a noncooperative equilibrium, since none of the players take into account the effects of their actions on the other players. Figure 15.2 illustrates a payoff matrix for two firms, firm 1 and firm 2, where both firms are deciding whether they should cooperate or compete with one another. Each cell provides information about the level of profits the firms earn depending on their strategy. Both firm 1 and firm 2 have dominant strategies: they will both compete, since their profit is greater when electing this strategy no matter what strategy the other firm chooses. However, when both firms select this strategy, their total profits fall below the level they could achieve if both firms were willing to commit to the strategy to cooperate. The Nash equilibrium for this game leaves both firms worse off than they would be if it were possible for them to creditably maintain the other strategy.

Figure 15.2

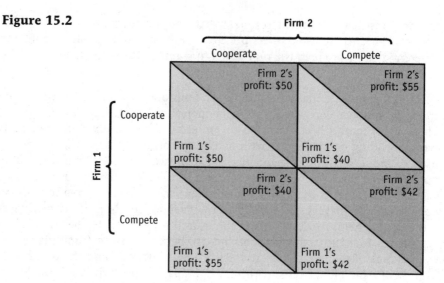

Objective #9. Some games are played only once (Figure 15.2 is an example of this kind of game). These one-shot games do not offer the complexities found in games that are played multiple times. For businesses that hope to stay in business for many years, game theory suggests the need to consider strategic behavior that takes into account the impact of the firm's decision on the future actions of other players in the game. These multishot games often start with firms behaving cooperatively. When a firm deviates from cooperative behavior, the other firms may respond with a tit-for-tat strategy wherein they repeat what the other firm did in the previous period. This tit-for-tat strategy offers a reward to firms for cooperative behavior while punishing firms who opt to cheat on the other firms. Over time each firm recognizes that they are better off cooperating with the other firms in the industry rather than competing with these firms. When firms reach this point, this is referred to as tacit collusion, since the firms are implicitly colluding with one another without the necessity of a formal, explicit agreement.

Objective #10. The kinked demand curve model of oligopoly can be used to illustrate the tacit collusion outcome. The oligopolist produces the quantity associated with the tacit collusion outcome (Q^*) and prices this quantity at P^*, the tacitly agreed upon price. The oligopolist recognizes that a deviation from this outcome is likely to be punished by the other firms in the industry: producing a quantity greater than Q^* will likely cause the other firms to produce a higher level of output and to sell this output at a lower price; and producing a lower level of output than Q^* and selling this output at a price greater than P^* will cause the firm to lose sales as the other firms continue to sell their output at P^*. This knowledge of how rivals will respond to the firm's production and pricing decision results in the firm perceiving its demand curve has a kink in it that occurs at the level of output Q^* and the price P^*. Figure 15.3 illustrates the kinked demand curve model. Notice that the firm profit maximizes by producing the level of output where marginal revenue equals marginal cost ($MR = MC$), but that because of the kink in the demand curve there are many different MC curves (for example, MC_1 and MC_2) that will result in the firm producing Q^* and selling each unit for P^*.

Figure 15.3

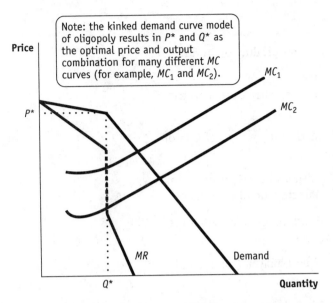

Note: the kinked demand curve model of oligopoly results in P^* and Q^* as the optimal price and output combination for many different MC curves (for example, MC_1 and MC_2).

Objective #11. The United States legally restricts the behavior of oligopolistic firms and prohibits the creation of monopolies. The Sherman Antitrust Act of 1890 marks the beginning of antitrust policy and the government's commitment to prevent oligopolistic industries from becoming monopolies or behaving like a monopoly.

Objective #12. Although tacit collusion is common, it is hard for firms to push prices up to the monopoly level due to a number of different factors. Monopolistic prices are hard to achieve for at least four reasons: (1) when there are many firms in the industry, firms are less likely to behave cooperatively; (2) when firms produce a variety of products and offer these products at different prices it is hard to discern when a firm is cheating on the tacit agreement; (3) firms do not always agree on what is fair and in their interests, and this can lead to firms deviating from the tacit agreement; and (4) firms may find that the buyers of their products are large enough relative to the entire market to be able to bargain for lower prices. When tacit collusion breaks down, this is often due to price wars in which each firm reduces the price of its product below the cooperative level. In a worse-case scenario prices can fall below the non-cooperative level as each seller tries to drive the other sellers out of the business.

Objective #13. Another form of oligopolistic behavior is that of price leadership. Here a firm acts to set the price tacitly for the whole industry. In industries that follow a price leadership model, the firms often compete with each other with regard to other product characteristics. This nonprice competition injects competition into an otherwise cooperative environment.

Key Terms

Notes

oligopoly an industry with only a small number of producers.

oligopolist a firm in an industry with only a small number of producers.

imperfect competition a market structure in which no firm is a *monopolist*, but producers nonetheless have *market power* they can use to affect market prices.

duopoly an *oligopoly* consisting of only two firms.

duopolist one of the two firms in a *duopoly*.

Key Terms *(continued)*

collusion cooperation among producers to limit production and raise prices so as to raise one another's profits.

cartel an agreement among several producers to obey output restrictions in order to increase their joint profits.

noncooperative behavior actions by firms that ignore the effects of those actions on the profits of other firms.

interdependence the relationship among firms when their decisions significantly affect one another's profits; characteristic of oligopolies.

game theory the study of behavior in situations of *interdependence*. Used to explain the behavior of an *oligopoly*.

payoff in *game theory*, the reward received by a player (for example, the profit earned by an *oligopolist*).

payoff matrix in *game theory*, a diagram that shows how the *payoffs* to each of the participants in a two-player game depend on the actions of both; a tool in analyzing *interdependence*.

prisoner's dilemma a game based on two premises in which (1) each player has an incentive to choose an action that benefits itself at the other player's expense; and (2) both players are then worse off than if they had acted cooperatively.

dominant strategy in *game theory*, an action that is a player's best action regardless of the action taken by the other player.

Nash equilibrium in *game theory*, the *equilibrium* that results when all players choose the action that maximizes their *payoffs* given the actions of other players, ignoring the effect of that action on the *payoffs* of other players; also known as *noncooperative equilibrium*.

noncooperative equilibrium in *game theory*, the *equilibrium* that results when all players choose the action that maximizes their *payoffs* given the actions of other players, ignoring the effect of that action on the *payoffs* of other players; also known as *Nash equilibrium*.

strategic behavior actions taken by a firm that attempt to influence the future behavior of other firms.

tit for tat in *game theory*, a strategy that involves playing cooperatively at first, then doing whatever the other player did in the previous period.

tacit collusion cooperation among producers, without a formal agreement, to limit production and raise prices so as to raise one anothers' profits.

kinked demand curve a model used to explain the stability of *oligopoly* pricing; a *demand curve* that kinks (bends) because the *oligopolist* will lose sales if output is reduced and price is increased but gain only a few additional sales if output is increased and price is lowered (because the lower price will be matched at once by other oligopolists), the curve will be very flat above the kink and very steep below the kink.

antitrust policy legislative and regulatory efforts undertaken by the government to prevent oligopolistic industries from becoming or behaving like *monopolies*.

Notes

Key Terms *(continued)*

price war a collapse of prices when *tacit collusion* breaks down.

product differentiation the attempt by firms to convince buyers that their products are different from those of other firms in the industry. If firms can so convince buyers, they can charge a higher price.

price leadership a pattern of behavior in which one firm sets its price and other firms in the industry follow.

nonprice competition competition in areas other than price to increase sales, such as new product features and advertising; especially engaged in by firms that have a tacit understanding not to compete on price.

Notes

▮ AFTER YOU READ THE CHAPTER

Tips

Tip #1. Students often find reading a payoff matrix challenging. Here's a suggestion for making this task easier. First, consider the payoff matrix from player 1's perspective as two separate columns: each column represents player 2 taking a particular strategy and sticking with it, while player 1's task is to decide which of the available strategies is the best strategy for player 1 to pursue. For example, Figure 15.4 represents the payoff matrix given in Figure 15.2 from firm 1's perspective.

Figure 15.4

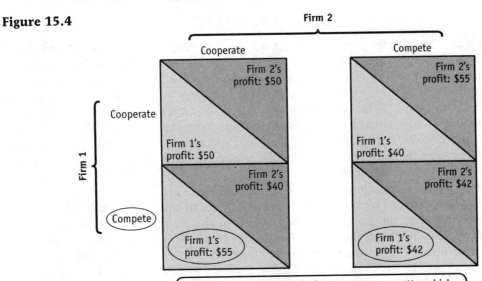

From firm 1's perspective, its best strategy, no matter which strategy firm 2 chooses, is to compete. When firm 2 chooses to cooperate (as illustrated in the left-hand column), firm 1 will earn higher profits by choosing to compete. When firm 2 chooses to compete (as illustrated in the right-hand column), firm 1 will earn higher profits by choosing to compete. The circled profit indicate these ideas.

Now, consider the payoff matrix from player 2's perspective as two separate rows: each row represents player 1 taking a particular strategy and sticking with it, while player 2's task is to decide which of the available strategies is the best strategy for player 2 to pursue. Figure 15.5 represents the payoff matrix given in Figure 15.2 from firm 2's perspective.

Figure 15.5

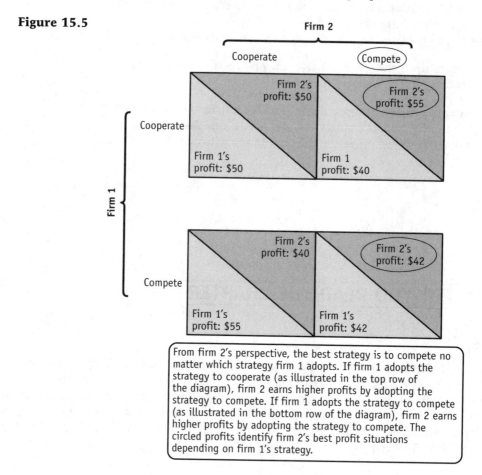

From firm 2's perspective, the best strategy is to compete no matter which strategy firm 1 adopts. If firm 1 adopts the strategy to cooperate (as illustrated in the top row of the diagram), firm 2 earns higher profits by adopting the strategy to compete. If firm 1 adopts the strategy to compete (as illustrated in the bottom row of the diagram), firm 2 earns higher profits by adopting the strategy to compete. The circled profits identify firm 2's best profit situations depending on firm 1's strategy.

Tip #2. This chapter presents the kinked demand curve model. It is important that you understand why there is a kink in the demand curve for the oligopolistic firm. Use Figure 15.6 to help guide your thinking on this issue. In the kinked demand curve model, it is assumed that the firms tacitly agree to collude and that each firm will set price at P^* and produce Q^* units of the good. Figure 15.6 illustrates this situation for an oligopolistic firm. This firm essentially views its demand curve as having two components: D_1 and D_2. If the firm drops the price below P^*, then the relevant demand curve for the firm to consider is D_2, and if the firm increases the price above P^*, then the relevant demand curve for the firm to consider is D_1. This oligopolistic firm realizes that a decision to decrease its price below the tacitly agreed upon price will cause the other firms to retaliate. These firms will also drop their price, and all the firms will sell more units of the good but not as many units as would have been the case if only one firm dropped the price. The firm also realizes that the decision to raise the price above P^* will cause the demand for its product to fall by a relatively larger amount (compare the effect of a price increase on the quantity demanded on demand curve D_1 versus demand curve D_2) as consumers opt to purchase the good from the other firms that are still providing the good at P^*.

Figure 15.6

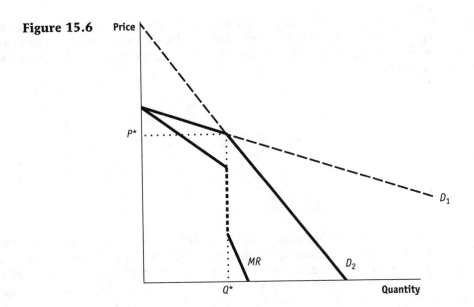

Tip #3. A second concept to understand with regard to the kinked demand curve model is that firms can have different MC curves and still opt to produce Q^* units of the good and sell this quantity at P^*. The vertical segment of the MR curve makes this a possibility, and it implies that firms with very different MC curves can abide by the same quantity and pricing decision.

Tip #4. This chapter entails less certainty about how the market structure works relative to the chapters on perfect competition and monopoly. After you study the chapter and work through the problems, you should have an appreciation for the puzzles presented by the oligopolistic market structure. These puzzles typically reflect the trade-offs between cooperation and competition and the benefits firms receive from these two strategies.

Problems and Exercises

1. An industry has ten producers producing differentiated products, but all the products in the industry are generally viewed by consumers as soft drinks. What kind of market structure does this industry have, and why would you define the market structure in this way?

2. Each of the ten producers in question 1 has 10% of the market sales in the soft drink industry. What is the Herfindahl-Hirschman Index (HHI) for this industry? Does this HHI change your opinion about what kind of market structure this industry represents? Explain your answer.

3. Four of the ten producers in question 1 each have 20% of the market sales in the soft drink industry while, of the remaining six firms, one firm has 5% of the market sales in the industry and the other five firms each have 3% of the market sales. What is the HHI for this industry? Does this HHI change your opinion about what kind of market structure this industry represents? Explain your answer.

4. Four of the ten producers in question 1 each have 20% of the market sales in the soft drink industry while, of the remaining six firms, one firm has 5% of the market sales in the industry and the other five firms each have 3% of the market sales. Two of the firms that currently each have 20% of the market sales propose to merge. What would the change in the HHI be if this merger was approved? Would the merger have any effect on the industry?

5. Two of the ten producers in question 1 each have 30% of the market sales in the soft drink industry while, of the remaining eight firms, one firm has 25% of the market share, another firm has 3% of the market share, and the remaining six firms each have 2% of the market share. What is the HHI for this industry? Does this HHI change your opinion about what kind of market structure this industry represents? Explain your answer.

6. Oligopoly is characterized by having a few firms in the industry. What is the best explanation for why these industries only have a few firms?

7. Suppose there are only two firms in an industry that produces gasoline. To make the analysis simpler, assume that once the companies have incurred the fixed costs of production the marginal cost of producing another gallon of gasoline is equal to zero. Suppose the demand for gasoline in this market is equal to $Q = 10{,}000 - 1{,}000P$.

   a. Draw a graph of the industry demand curve, and draw the *MC* curve for the industry as well.

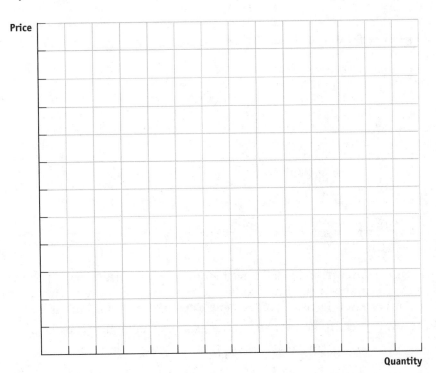

   b. If these two firms acted like perfectly competitive firms, how many units would they produce altogether? What would the total revenue for the two firms equal?

c. Suppose these two firms are able to form a cartel in which they agree to produce the profit-maximizing level of output and then split the market evenly. What is the total amount of output these two firms will produce if they agree to split the market? What is the price of gasoline? What will be the total revenue received by each firm if they agree to split the market and neither firm cheats on this agreement? Are the two firms better off if they agree to this arrangement?

d. On a graph, indicate the market quantity Q^* that these two firms will produce under the arrangement described in part (c). On this same graph, indicate the market price P^* that will be charged for the gasoline.

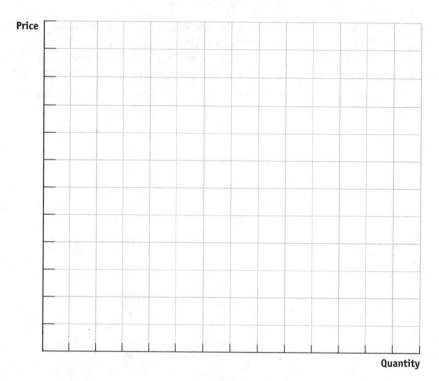

8. Suppose the two firms in problem 7 agree to form a cartel as described in part (c) of that problem, but that one of the firms decides to cheat on the arrangement by producing 3,500 gallons of gasoline instead of the agreed upon 2,500 gallons of gasoline.

a. What will happen to the total amount of gasoline produced by the two firms?

b. What will happen to the price of gasoline when one firm increases its production to 3,500 gallons while the other firm continues to produce 2,500 gallons?

c. What is the total revenue received by the firm that produces 3,500 gallons of gasoline? What is the total revenue received by the firm that produces 2,500 gallons of gasoline? Is cheating on the cartel arrangement by one firm beneficial to both firms? Explain your answer. When one firm cheats on the cartel, what happens to the level of total profits?

d. Once the second firm realizes what the first firm has done, what do you imagine might be the second firm's response? Why are cartels unstable?

e. Are these two firms exhibiting quantity competition (Cournot behavior) or price competition (Bertrand behavior)?

9. Suppose there are two firms in an industry that produces nuclear generators. Furthermore, suppose that each of these firms is able to produce a maximum of twenty generators a year due to their productive facility. Would you predict that these two firms could successfully collude on price without a formal agreement? Why or why not? What term would best describe the kind of behavior you would expect this duopoly to exhibit?

10. The following payoff matrix provides information about the profits Apple Growers and Johnny Appleseed Company earn based on the advertising strategy the companies adopt. The first entry in the matrix cell gives the profits of Apple Growers, and the second entry provides the profits of Johnny Appleseed Company.

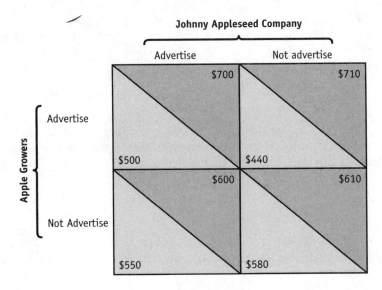

a. If these two firms could collude with one another and decide jointly on their advertising strategy with the goal of maximizing their joint profits, what combination of strategies results in the greatest joint profit for these two companies?

b. Which strategy is Apple Growers' dominant strategy?

c. Which strategy is Johnny Appleseed Company's dominant strategy?

d. What is the Nash equilibrium for this game?

11. Two firms, firm A and firm B, compete against one another in a duopoly. These two firms have been in competition with each other for many years, and they anticipate that they will continue to compete against one another for many more years. Both firms are faced with two strategies they can pursue: they can either always cheat or they can pursue a strategy of tit for tat in which one firm punishes the other firm whenever the other firm cheats. Both firms are faced with two strategies they can pursue: they can either "Always Cheat" or they can pursue a strategy of "Tit for Tat" in which one firm punishes the other firm whenever the other firm cheats. Suppose that the payoff for playing the strategy of "Always Cheats" results in each firm earning profits of $100 a year. If one firm plays the strategy of "Tit for Tat" while the other firm plays the strategy of "Always Cheat," the cheating firm will earn $150 the first year but only $90 for each subsequent year, while the "Tit for Tat" firm will earn $90 the first year but $100 for each subsequent year. If both firms play the "Tit for Tat" strategy, they will earn $130 a year.

a. Create a payoff matrix for firm A and firm B showing the profits these two firms earn given the strategies that are open to each of them.

b. Suppose that firm A anticipates that firm B is going to choose the strategy to always cheat. Given firm B's choice, what is firm A's best strategy if these two firms compete for a single year? Is this still the best choice if firm A and firm B are competing with each other for many other years?

c. Suppose that firm B anticipates that firm A is going to choose the strategy to always cheat. Given firm A's choice, what is firm B's best strategy if these two firms compete for a single year? Is this still the best choice if firm A and firm B are competing with each other for many other years?

d. If firm A chooses the tit-for-tat strategy, what is the best strategy for firm B to choose? If firm B chooses the tit-for-tat strategy, what is the best strategy for firm A to choose?

12. Firms in an oligopoly have achieved tacit collusion and decided that each firm will produce 20 units of output and sell each unit of output for $80. Each firm perceives that the demand for their product if they raise the price above $80 can be expressed by the equation $P = 90 - (0.5)Q$. Each firm also perceives that the demand for their product if they lower the price below $80 can be expressed by the equation $P = 100 - Q$.

a. Draw a diagram illustrating the kinked demand curve for one of the firms in this oligopoly. Label the agreed upon price and quantity as well as the firm's demand curve (hint: this demand curve will contain a segment from both of the given demand curves).

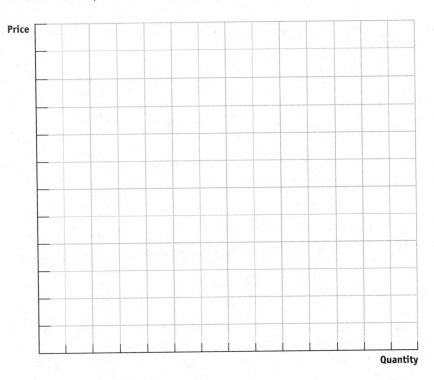

b. On your diagram from part (a), draw the firm's MR curve. Remember that the firm's MR curve will have a discontinuity (in this case, a vertical segment) due to the kink in its demand curve.

c. Suppose that one of the firms in this industry decides to reduce the price of its product from $80 to $78. What does this model predict will happen to the demand for this firm's product?

d. Suppose that one of the firms in this industry decides to increase the price of its product from $80 to $84. What does this model predict will happen to the demand for this firm's product?

e. Suppose that one of the firms in this industry has marginal cost equal to $2.9Q + 10$. What price and output combination is the profit-maximizing output for this firm?

f. Suppose that another of the firms in this industry has marginal cost equal to $3Q + 5$. What price and output combination is the profit-maximizing output for this firm?

g. Explain why your answers in parts (e) and (f) are the same even though the two firms have different *MC* curves.

13. What kinds of factors can make it hard for a group of firms in an oligopolistic industry to achieve tacit collusion? Discuss four different factors that make this difficult.

14. What is price leadership? How does price leadership resolve the oligopoly's problem of deciding how to set the optimal price? If the firms follow a price leadership model, how do the firms then compete with one another if they all offer the good at the same price?

BEFORE YOU TAKE THE TEST

Chapter Review Questions

1. An industry characterized by having a few firms, each with some market power, is an example of (a)n
   a. monopoly, since the firms have some market power.
   b. perfectly competitive industry, since there is more than one firm in the industry.
   c. monopolistically competitive industry, since the firms compete with one another while at the same time they have some market power.
   d. oligopoly, since the firms have market power and can therefore affect the market price, but there are only a few firms, so each firm recognizes the interdependence between firms.

2. The formation of an oligopoly is primarily due to the

a. control of an essential input or resource used in the production of the good.

b. existence of increasing returns to scale in the industry.

c. effective entry barrier posed by copyrights or patents.

d. Answers (a), (b), and (c) are all correct.

3. Suppose there are two firms seeking to merge and that the Herfindahl-Hirschman Index (HHI) for their industry is currently 1,200. With the proposed merger, the HHI would increase to 2,500. What is likely to be the Justice Department's reaction to the proposed merger?

a. The merger is likely to be approved since the HHI is still relatively low.

b. The merger is likely to be delayed while various groups lobby the Justice Department.

c. The merger will likely be disallowed since the HHI would rise to a level that indicates an oligopolistic market structure.

d. The Justice Department may allow, delay, or disallow the proposed merger, because there are no clear guidelines for proposed mergers.

4. There are twenty firms in an industry and each one is identical in size. Each firm therefore produces 5% of the total market sales. The HHI for this industry would indicate that this industry is

a. competitive.   c. oligopolistic.

b. monopolistic.   d. a natural monopoly.

5. There are ten firms in an industry and five of these firms each have sales equal to 10% of the total market. Two of the other five firms each have sales equal to 20% of the total market, two of the other five firms each have sales equal to 3% of the total market, and the remaining firm has sales equal to 4% of the total market. What is the HHI for this industry?

a. 100   c. 4,152

b. 1,334   d. 1,000

6. There are ten firms in an industry and five of these firms each have sales equal to 10% of the total market. Two of the other five firms each have sales equal to 20% of the total market, two of the other five firms each have sales equal to 3% of the total market, and the remaining firm has sales equal to 4% of the total market. If two of the firms with market share of 10% each were to merge, what would the new HHI equal?

a. 1,534   c. 1,000

b. 1,334   d. 1,743

7. Suppose there is a duopoly and that the two firms in this duopoly collude. The firms have agreed to collude most likely as a means to

a. stabilize prices.

b. stabilize quantities.

c. maximize each firm's profits.

d. maximize their joint profits.

8. Suppose there is a duopoly and that the two firms in this duopoly have formed a cartel. This cartel will likely be

a. quite stable, since there are only two firms and they are each aware of each other's actions.

b. unstable, since both firms have an incentive to cheat on the cartel arrangement.

9. When a monopolist lowers price, the monopolist experiences both a quantity and a price effect from this action. When a firm in a cartel lowers price, it also experiences a quantity and a price effect from this action. With respect to the monopoly's experience, the firm in a cartel finds that the

    a. quantity effect is a negative effect on total revenue.

    b. price effect is a larger positive effect on total revenue for the firm in the cartel than it is for the monopolist.

    c. price effect is a smaller negative effect on total revenue for the firm in the cartel than it is for the monopolist.

10. Firms in an oligopoly have a choice of competing with one another or cooperating with one another. Which strategy is typically more profitable to the individual firms in the industry?

    a. Compete

    b. Cooperate

Use the following information to answer the next three questions. Suppose there are two identical firms in an industry and that the market demand curve in the industry is $Q = 2,000 - 2P$. The marginal cost of producing the good in this industry is constant and equal to $200.

11. If each firm produces the same amount and the two firms collude with one another, what is the profit-maximizing quantity and price for this industry?

    a. 1,600 units of output; $200

    b. 800 units of output; $200

    c. 800 units of output; $600

    d. 1,000 units of output; $500

12. When these two firms collude with each other, what is the level of profit received by each firm?

    a. $320,000   c. $160,000

    b. $480,000   d. $240,000

13. Suppose one of the firms in this industry decides to cheat on the agreement to collude. Instead of selling its product for $600, this firm decides to increase its production and sell its output for a price of $400. If the other firm continues to produce 400 units, the new price for the product will equal _____, the cheating firm's profits will equal _____, and the noncheating firm's profits will equal _____.

    a. $600; $160,000; $80,000

    b. $600; $80,000; $160,000

    c. $400; $160,000; $80,000

    d. $400; $80,000; $160,000

14. When firms in an oligopoly cannot increase their level of output quickly due to the limits of their productive capacity, they are more likely to engage in

    a. quantity competition, or Cournot behavior.

    b. price competition, or Bertrand behavior.

15. When firms in an oligopoly can easily vary their level of output, they are more likely to engage in

    a. quantity competition, or Cournot behavior.

    b. price competition, or Bertrand behavior.

Use the following information to answer the next three questions. The following payoff matrix indicates the level of profits earned by Printers Press and Typesetters, the only two firms in the printing industry in an economy. The level of profits for each firm depends on whether they cooperate or compete with one another.

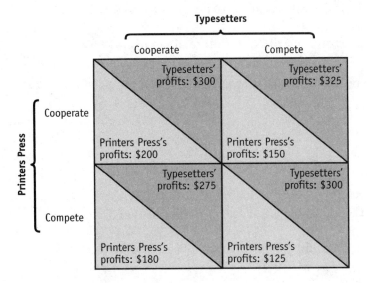

16. What is Printers Press's dominant strategy?

 a. Compete

 b. Cooperate

 c. Printers Press does not have a dominant strategy.

17. What is Typesetters' dominant strategy?

 a. Compete

 b. Cooperate

 c. Typesetters does not have a dominant strategy.

18. When Printers Press and Typesetters pursue their dominant strategies, the sum of their joint profits

 a. is maximized.

 b. is not maximized.

Answer the next three questions based on the following information. Two firms are the only producers in a market. Each firm is trying to decide whether or not to advertise. If firm B advertises, firm A earns $2,000 in profit if firm A does not advertise and $1,800 if firm A advertises (the advertising increases its costs more than its revenues). If firm B does not advertise, firm A earns $2,200 in profit if firm A does not advertise and $2,000 if firm A advertises. If firm A advertises, firm B earns $3,000 in profit if firm B does not advertise and $2,700 if firm B does advertise. If firm A does not advertise, firm B earns $2,600 if firm B does not advertise and $2,400 if firm B does advertise.

19. What is firm B's dominant strategy?

 a. Advertise

 b. Do not advertise

 c. Firm B does not have a dominant strategy.

20. What is the Nash equilibrium for this game?
    a. Firm A and firm B will not advertise, and they will earn joint profits of $4,800.
    b. Firm A will advertise, firm B will not advertise, and they will earn total profits of $5,000.
    c. Firm A will not advertise, firm B will advertise, and they will earn total profits of $4,400.
    d. Firm A and firm B will advertise, and they will earn total profits of $4,500.

21. For these two firms, choosing the dominant strategy results in the best possible outcome with respect to total profits.
    a. True
    b. False

22. In the prisoner's dilemma,
    a. both players have an incentive to cheat no matter what the other player does.
    b. when both players cheat, both players are worse off than if neither of them had cheated.
    c. The prisoner's dilemma is a helpful tool for understanding one-shot games.
    d. Answers (a), (b), and (c) are all true.

23. When firms in an oligopoly pursue a tit-for-tat strategy, this implies that each firm will
    a. continue to pursue its strategy no matter what the other firms in the oligopoly choose to do.
    b. punish other firms if they cheat on the tacit agreement that the firms have with one another.
    c. behave cooperatively, but will then mimic what the other player did in the previous period.
    d. Answers (b) and (c) are both true.

24. Firms in an oligopoly that expect to compete with one another for an extended period will
    a. choose a noncooperative strategy, since they do not like competing with other firms and they hope this will drive some firms out of the industry.
    b. choose a tit-for-tat strategy that evolves into all firms cooperating, since they realize this is their best strategy if they are to be in the same industry for an extended period.
    c. engage in price wars in hopes that some firms will be driven from the industry, leaving a smaller number of firms to collude with one another.
    d. often ignore one another, since they cannot do anything about the fact that they are competing in the same industry.

25. In recent years, many colleges have felt the need to build impressive student centers and athletic facilities on their campuses. Each college realizes that if they do not build these facilities while other colleges do build them, the nonbuilding college will be less competitive and less attractive to prospective students. This is an example of a(n)
    a. arms race.
    b. exclusive dealing.
    c. tacit collusion.
    d. antitrust activity.

26. In the kinked demand curve model, a firm's decision to raise its price above the tacitly agreed upon price will

a. enable the firm to increase its revenue.

b. result in the firm selling fewer units of the good than the firm might initially anticipate, since the other firms in the tacit agreement will not change the price of the products they are selling.

c. be an episode of cheating on the tacit agreement that results in the firm being better off than if it adhered to the agreement it made.

d. not be possible, because the firm has made a formal agreement about the price it will charge and the quantity it will produce.

27. Two firms have a tacit agreement with one another based on the kinked demand curve model. Which of the following statements is true?

I. The two firms will produce the same level of output and sell this output at the same price, if they adhere to the tacit agreement.

II. The two firms may not necessarily have the same marginal cost of production.

III. The kinked demand curve model is a model that cannot explain collusion between these two firms.

a. Statement I is true.

b. Statement II is true.

c. Statements I and II are true.

d. Statements I, II, and III are true.

28. The Sherman Antitrust Act of 1890 was

a. aimed at preventing the creation of more monopolies.

b. intended to provide legislation to help break up existing monopolies.

c. the beginning of antitrust policy in the United States.

d. Answers (a), (b), and (c) are all true statements.

29. Which of the following makes tacit agreements more difficult to achieve in an industry?

a. The existence of just a few firms that each produce similar products.

b. The existence of a buyer with significant buying power in the industry.

c. The existence of just a few firms that have interacted over time and have developed strong ties of trust and respect.

d. The existence of a few firms that produce one product with a relatively simple pricing policy for this product.

30. In an oligopolistic industry that practices price leadership, the competition between firms is apt to be

a. price competition, as firms jockey for the right to be the price leader.

b. quantity competition, as firms compete to gain market share at whatever price the price leader has established.

c. nonprice competition, as firms strive to differentiate their product from the products produced by competing firms.

d. All of the above forms of competition occur in the price leadership model.

▇ ANSWER KEY

Answers to Problems and Exercises

1. This industry is characterized as having just a few producers, and although the products are differentiated, they are closely related and can be viewed as substitutes for one another. Because of the small number of firms, this industry would be viewed as an oligopoly, although this classification is dependent on the share of market sales that each firm has. If the market is dominated by several of these firms, then the industry is definitely an oligopoly, but if the market is divided evenly among these ten firms, then the industry, despite its small number of firms, would act more like a perfectly competitive industry than an oligopolistic one.

2. The HHI for this industry is equal to the square of the share of market sales summed over the firms in the industry, or HHI $= (10)^2 + (10)^2 + (10)^2 + (10)^2 + (10)^2 + (10)^2 + (10)^2 + (10)^2 + (10)^2 + (10)^2 = 1,000$. An HHI of 1,000 indicates that the industry is on the boundary between a strongly competitive market (HHI of less than 1,000) and a somewhat competitive market (HHI greater than or equal to 1,000 but less than 1,800). The calculation of the HHI changes the appraisal of the market structure from oligopolistic, based on the number of firms in the industry, to more competitive, based on the division of market share.

3. The HHI for this industry is equal to $(20)^2 + (20)^2 + (20)^2 + (20)^2 + (5)^2 + (3)^2 + (3)^2 + (3)^2 + (3)^2 + (3)^2 = 1,670$. This HHI places this group of firms in the somewhat competitive market category. To be considered an oligopoly, the HHI must be over 1,800.

4. The HHI before the merger equals 1,670 (see problem 3). The HHI after the merger would equal $(40)^2 + (20)^2 + (20)^2 + (5)^2 + (3)^2 + (3)^2 + (3)^2 + (3)^2 + (3)^2 = 2,470$, or a change of 800 from the initial index. This would represent a significant increase in the market concentration in this industry, and the industry would move from a somewhat competitive market structure to an oligopolistic market structure.

5. The HHI for this industry equals $(30)^2 + (30)^2 + (25)^2 + (3)^2 + (2)^2 + (2)^2 + (2)^2 + (2)^2 + (2)^2 + (2)^2 = 2,458$. This HHI is over 1,800 and so the industry would be classified as an oligopoly. Notice that when a few firms account for a relatively large amount of the market share the HHI increases rapidly. Compare your calculations in problems 2, 3, and 4.

6. An industry typically has a few firms because the industry is one in which firms have increasing returns to scale: firms benefit from being relatively large, which implies that the total market is usually easily served by just a few firms rather than many small firms.

7. **a.**

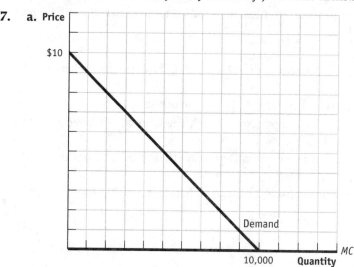

b. If the two firms acted like perfectly competitive firms, they would produce the quantity where the demand curve intersects the MC curve: they would produce a total of 10,000 gallons of gasoline. The price of this gasoline would be $0 since in a perfectly competitive industry $P = MR = MC$ in the market equilibrium. The total revenue for both firms would equal $0.

c. If the two firms collude and split the market, they will produce a total of 5,000 gallons of gasoline since this is the profit-maximizing amount of gasoline. To find this quantity remember that you need to equate the MR curve to the marginal cost. But this time, the two firms act together like a monopolist, so you need to first construct the monopolist's MR curve: $MR = 10 - 0.002Q$. $MR = MC$ at an output of 5,000 gallons. The firms then price this output by going up to the market demand curve and selecting the price on the demand curve that is associated with 5,000 gallons of gasoline. This price will be $5 per gallon of gasoline. The total revenue received by each firm if they split the market evenly is $(1/2)(\$5$ per gallon$)(5,000$ gallons$) = \$12,500$. Each firm's ATC is equal to the sum of their fixed costs and their variable costs, and since the firm's MC is equal to 0, this implies that the firm's AVC is also equal to 0. The firm's profit will therefore equal total revenue minus fixed cost. Clearly, colluding leaves both firms better off than they would be under the scenario described in part (b).

d.

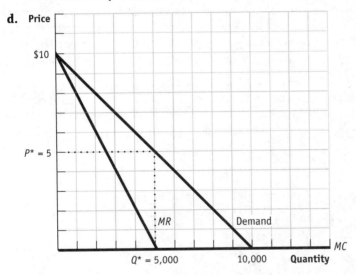

8. a. The total amount produced by the two firms will now be 6,000 gallons of gasoline.

b. When 6,000 gallons of gasoline are produced, the market price decreases to $4 per gallon of gasoline. To see this, remember that the demand curve can be written as $P = 10 - 0.001Q$, and when $Q = 6,000$ gallons this implies that $P = \$4$ per gallon.

c. The total revenue of the firm that produces 3,500 gallons is now equal to $14,000, while the total revenue of the firm that produces 2,500 gallons is equal to $10,000. The firm that cheats on the cartel benefits since its total revenue increases from $12,500 to $14,000. The firm that maintains the cartel arrangement is hurt when the other firm cheats because its total revenue falls from $12,500 to $10,000. Notice that cheating causes the overall level of joint profits for the cartel to fall from $25,000 to $24,000: the two firms are no longer joint profit maximizing.

d. The second firm is likely to match the first firm's production decision, which will cause price and therefore total revenue to fall further. The two firms may persist in this price-cutting behavior until they reach the perfectly competitive result where 10,000 gallons of gasoline are produced and the market price is $0. Cartels are inherently unstable due to the incentives both firms face to cheat on the cartel.

e. The two firms are exhibiting price competition and Bertrand behavior since they are competing with regard to the price at which they offer the good.

9. Since both firms are constrained with regard to their ability to alter the level of output they produce, neither firm needs to worry about the other firm suddenly increasing its level of output and decreasing the price of its product. The two firms should be able to divide the market with relative ease while pricing their product above marginal cost. This will enable both firms to earn a positive economic profit. These two firms will engage in quantity competition, or Cournot behavior, and the market result will resemble the one found in a monopolistic market structure.

10. **a.** When both companies pick the strategy to advertise, joint profits are maximized since the profits in this cell of the matrix equal $1,200 and the three other cells result in joint profits that are less than this amount.

    b. Apple Growers' dominant strategy is to not advertise. If Johnny Appleseed Company selects the strategy to advertise, Apple Growers will earn greater profit by choosing to not advertise. If Johnny Appleseed Company selects the strategy to not advertise, Apple Growers will earn greater profit by choosing to not advertise. No matter which strategy Johnny Appleseed Company selects, Apple Growers will be best off choosing to not advertise.

    c. Johnny Appleseed Company's dominant strategy is to not advertise. If Apple Growers selects the strategy to advertise, Johnny Appleseed Company will earn greater profit by choosing to not advertise. If Apple Growers selects the strategy to not advertise, Johnny Appleseed Company will earn greater profit by choosing to not advertise. No matter which strategy Apple Growers selects, Johnny Appleseed Company will be best off choosing to not advertise.

    d. Both companies will choose to not advertise, and they will earn joint profits of $1,190 instead of the $1,200 that they could earn if they could communicate and collude with one another, and both choose to advertise as their strategy.

11. **a.**

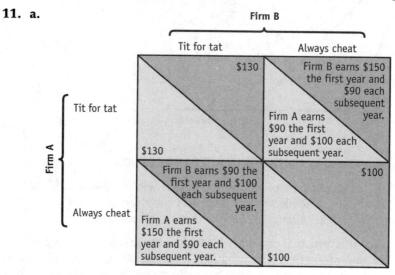

    b. Firm A's best strategy, if the two firms compete for a single year and if firm B chooses to always cheat, is to also choose the strategy to always cheat. But, firm A's best strategy if the two firms compete for many years and firm B chooses to always cheat, is still to pursue the strategy of always cheating. Notice though that this result does not result in the best outcome for both firms. Both firms, if they plan to compete for many years, would be better off choosing the strategy of tit for tat since that results in the greatest level of profits for each firm over time.

    c. Firm B's best strategy, if the two firms compete for a single year and if firm A chooses to always cheat is to also choose the strategy to always cheat. But, firm B's best strategy if the two firms compete for many years and firm A chooses to always cheat, is still to pursue the strategy of always cheating. Notice though that this result does not result in the best outcome for both firms. Both firms, if they plan to compete for many years, would be better off choosing the strategy of tit for tat since that results in the greatest level of profits for each firm over time.

d. If one firm chooses tit for tat, then the other firm is better off also choosing tit for tat.

12. a,b

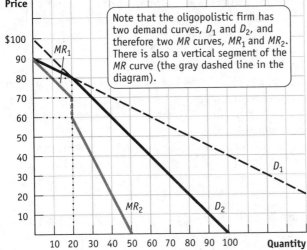

Note that the oligopolistic firm has two demand curves, D_1 and D_2, and therefore two MR curves, MR_1 and MR_2. There is also a vertical segment of the MR curve (the gray dashed line in the diagram).

c. When the firm reduces the price of its product, the other firms in the industry will respond by reducing the price of their output as well. Instead of the first firm selling 24 units (the amount that would be demanded when the demand curve is $P = 90 - 0.5Q$), the firm will sell 22 units (the amount that would be demanded when the demand curve is $P = 100 - Q$).

d. When the firm increases the price of its product, the other firms in the industry will continue to sell the good at $80. The first firm will now find that it sells 12 units (the amount that would be demanded when the demand curve is $P = 90 - 0.5Q$) and not 16 units (the amount that would be demanded when the demand curve is $P = 100 - Q$).

e. To profit maximize, the firm will want to equate marginal revenue and marginal cost to find the profit-maximizing quantity and then go to the demand curve to find the price of the good. However, from the graph we know that the demand curve has a kink, which implies that the MR curve has a vertical segment when the level of production is 20 units. This vertical segment occurs where the price axis has a value between 60 and 70. So the first question is, what is the value of MC for this firm when it produces 20 units of output? If this value is between 60 and 70, then the MC curve intersects the vertical segment of the firm's MR curve. With $MC = 2.9Q + 10$ and $Q = 20$, the value of MC is 68, which lies within the specified range. The firm will select its price by plugging 20 into the demand equation (either one) as the value of Q: thus, $P = 100 - Q$ yields $P = \$80$, and $P = 90 - 0.5Q$ yields $P = \$80$.

f. Follow the same procedure as outlined in part (e). With $MC = 3Q + 5$ and $Q = 20$, the value of MC is 65, which lies within the specified range. The firm will select its price by plugging 20 into the demand equation (either one) as the value of Q: thus, $P = 100 - Q$ yields $P = \$80$, and $P = 90 - 0.5Q$ yields $P = \$80$.

g. With the kinked demand curve model, firms in the oligopoly will charge the same price and produce the same quantity even though their MC curves are different, provided that their MC curves intersect the MR curve in the vertical region of the MR curve. There are many different MC curves that can potentially intersect a given MR in this vertical region, thereby helping us understand why firms with very different MC curves can still end up producing the same price and quantity combination.

13. When there are a large number of firms in the oligopoly it is harder for the firms to reach an agreement about price and quantity decisions for the industry, and it is harder for firms to ascertain when other firms are cheating on the agreement. In addition, when there are more firms in the oligopoly, this indicates that the barriers to entry are low and that existing firms face the threat of new entry, which acts as a brake on raising price to monopolistic levels.

When the oligopoly produces a number of different products and engages in more than one pricing scheme, this makes it harder for firms to have perfect collusion. It also makes it difficult to know with certainty when firms in the oligopoly are cheating on the tacit agreement.

In addition, firms in an oligopoly may not share the same perspective and reach the same conclusion about what is fair. Some firms may feel that the quantity they are assigned to produce under the tacit agreement is too low, and they may feel they deserve to be able to produce more of the product. This type of disagreement causes the tacit agreement to quickly break down.

Finally, in some oligopolistic markets there are buyers with significant market power that may be able to offset some of the market power held by the oligopoly. This makes it difficult for the oligopoly to maintain prices that are higher than the marginal cost of producing the good.

14. Price leadership is a situation in which one of the firms in the oligopoly takes a leadership role in setting the price of the product and then the other firms in the industry follow this price when setting the price of their products. This resolves the issue of how to determine the optimal price for the oligopoly, because once the price leader assumes that position, the other firms simply need to follow the lead of this firm. In the price leadership model, the price of the good is roughly the same across all firms, but each firm is free to differentiate and distinguish their product from their competitors' products. The firms under a price leadership model engage in nonprice competition.

Answers to Chapter Review Questions

1. **Answer d.** This is just a definitional question. The industry described is not a perfectly competitive industry because there are only a few firms and these firms all possess some market power: in a perfectly competitive industry there are many firms and none of these firms has market power. The industry is not a monopoly because a monopolistic industry has a single producer of the good. The industry is not monopolistically competitive because there are not enough firms in the market.

2. **Answer b.** Although oligopolies may arise because of an entry barrier based on scarce resources or government protection in the form of copyrights or patents, it is far more likely that the oligopoly arises due to the presence of returns to scale that results in the firms in the industry producing at a large scale relative to the overall market demand for the product.

3. **Answer c.** When the HHI rises above 1,800, the industry is viewed as oligopolistic, and any proposed merger that would push the HHI over this limit is likely to be denied.

4. **Answer a.** The HHI for this industry would equal 500, which indicates that the industry is relatively competitive.

5. **Answer b.** The HHI is equal to $(10)^2 + (10)^2 + (10)^2 + (10)^2 + (10)^2 + (20)^2 + (20)^2 + (3)^2 + (3)^2 + (4)^2 = 1,334$.

6. **Answer a.** The HHI would equal $(10)^2 + (10)^2 + (10)^2 + (20)^2 + (20)^2 + (20)^2 + (3)^2 + (3)^2 + (4)^2 = 1,534$.

7. **Answer d.** The two firms collude in order to set price and quantity so that the total amount of profits earned by the two firms is maximized. This does not imply that either firm is necessarily maximizing their own profits, since the market may not be divided evenly between the two firms.

8. **Answer b.** Cartels are inherently unstable because the firms in the cartel have decided to set price and quantity at a level where the marginal revenue from the last unit produced is greater than the marginal cost of producing the last unit. Each firm recognizes that it can expand production and earn more revenue than the costs it generates, so each firm is likely to deviate from the agreed upon production level.

9. **Answer c.** The price effect is a negative effect on total revenue, since as the firm (whether a monopolist or a firm in a cartel) reduces price on all the units it sells in order to sell more units of the good, this causes total revenue to fall. The quantity effect on total revenue is a positive effect for either type of firm: when the firm reduces price to sell more units of the good, the extra sales increase the firm's total revenue.

10. **Answer b.** Cooperation is the superior strategy because with cooperation the firms can work to maximize the joint profits of the oligopoly. When each firm acts in its own self-interest and adopts a compete strategy, this typically leads to price decreases that erode the general level of profitability in the industry.

11. **Answer c.** The firms will profit maximize by producing the quantity where $MR = MC$ and then selecting the price from the demand curve at that quantity. For the industry the MR curve is $MR = 1,000 - Q$ while $MC = 200$. The profit-maximizing quantity for the industry is 800 units. Plugging 800 into the demand equation for Q yields a market price of $600.

12. **Answer c.** The total amount of profit for the industry is equal to total revenue minus total cost. When the firms produce 800 units and sell these units at a price of $600, their total revenue equals $480,000. Their total cost is equal to ($200 per unit)(800 units), or $160,000. The total profit then for the two firms is $320,000, and each firm, since they are identical, earns $160,000 in profits.

13. **Answer c.** When the cheating firm decreases the price for the good to $400, the quantity demanded in the market increases to 1,200 units. Since the noncheating firm is still producing 400 units, the cheating firm will increase its production to 800 units. The good will sell for $400 and the cheating firm's total revenue will equal $320,000, its total cost will equal $160,000, and its profit will equal $160,000. The noncheating firm will sell 400 units at a price of $400, its total revenue will equal $160,000, its total cost will equal $80,000, and its profit will equal $80,000.

14. **Answer a.** When firms in an oligopoly are constricted with regard to their ability to quickly alter their level of output, they are more likely to cooperate with one another and agree, implicitly or explicitly, about how the market will be divided. This type of behavior is referred to as Cournot behavior. The result is that firms in this type of oligopoly are likely to set a price above marginal cost and earn positive economic profits.

15. **Answer b.** When firms in an oligopoly can easily vary their level of output, then these firms are liable to compete on price until all firms are pricing their output at the point where price equals marginal cost, a result that resembles the outcome found in perfectly competitive markets.

16. **Answer b.** No matter which strategy Typesetters pursues, Printers Press is better off adhering to a strategy to cooperate since it will leave the company with the highest level of profits.

17. **Answer a.** No matter which strategy Printers Press pursues, Typesetters is better off adhering to a strategy to compete since it will leave the company with the highest level of profits.

18. **Answer b.** When both companies pursue their dominant strategies, they earn a total of $475 profit, which is less than they would earn if they both pursue the strategy to cooperate.

19. **Answer b.** No matter which strategy firm A pursues, firm B's dominant strategy is to not advertise, since firm B earns greater profits by pursuing this strategy.

20. **Answer a.** Both firms will pursue their dominant strategy to not advertise, and this will result in the sum of total profits of $4,800.

21. **Answer b.** The best possible outcome with respect to the sum of total profits occurs when the two firms earn $5,000 in profits. This happens when firm A chooses to advertise while firm B chooses to not advertise.

22. **Answer d.** Answers (a) and (b) are true because of the nature of the prisoner's dilemma, whereas answer (c) underscores the idea that modeling a game that is only played once is easier than modeling a game that is played multiple times.

23. **Answer d.** In the tit-for-tat strategy, the firms in general cooperate with one another, but they will retaliate if a firm elects to not cooperate. This retaliation takes the form of mimicking whatever the other firm has done in the previous period.

24. **Answer b.** When a small number of firms realize that they will be competing for an extended period, these firms have a tendency to elect to cooperate with one another. Often the firms realize this is their best strategy after they have been the recipient of the tit-for-tat strategy, which effectively punishes noncooperating firms.

25. **Answer a.** When the different college campuses compete with regard to facilities, they are engaging in an arms race, since campuses that refuse to build these facilities find that they lose their position in the college admissions game. Exclusive dealing refers to a firm's contracting with businesses to sell only its product, thereby creating a miniature monopoly situation for the firm. Tacit collusion refers to firms agreeing to market price and market quantity without a formal agreement: this is not really applicable here since colleges keep trying to outdo one another in creating the best facilities. Antitrust activity refers to government action to limit market power or monopoly in a market.

26. **Answer b.** In the kinked demand curve model, an increase in price causes the firm to sell fewer units as the other firms in the industry do not match the price increase. Thus, consumers of the firm's product will switch to other providers when the firm raises its price. When the firm increases the price of its good, it sells fewer units, and since this occurs in the elastic region of the demand curve, the firm's total revenue falls. If the firm raises the price and therefore cheats on the tacit agreement, the firm will find that it is worse off than if it adhered to the agreement. The kinked demand curve model is based on a tacit agreement rather than an explicit, formal agreement.

27. **Answer c.** Statements I and II are true in general about the kinked demand curve model. Because of the vertical segment of the *MR* curve (due to the kink in the demand curve), different *MC* curves within a specific range can result in the firms producing the same quantity and selling that quantity at the same price. This model also provides insight into why firms collude with one another with respect to output and price, even though they may have a different marginal cost of production.

28. **Answer d.** All three of these statements are true by definition.

29. **Answer b.** The presence of a buyer with significant buying power lessens the ability of the firms to set price above the competitive level. When there are just a few firms, it is relatively easy for these firms to cooperate with regard to price and quantity decisions. Similarly, if firms have a long relationship with one another, they are apt to have developed tacit agreements about how the market is to be divided and what pricing and production decisions the firms will follow. Production of a single product with a simple pricing scheme makes a tacit agreement easier to create in a market than does the production of multiple products with more complicated pricing schemes.

30. **Answer c.** The price leadership model theorizes that the price is set by a firm in the industry and that this price is then used as the industry price. Firms do not compete with regard to price in this model, but instead compete with regard to the nonprice aspects of their product: the special features as well as the advertising campaigns that portray the quality of their product over their rivals' products.

chapter 16

Monopolistic Competition and Product Differentiation

BEFORE YOU READ THE CHAPTER

Summary

This chapter develops the model of monopolistic competition. It also discusses product differentiation and why oligopolistic and monopolistically competitive firms engage in product differentiation. The chapter discusses the determination of prices and profits in monopolistic competition in both the short run and the long run. The chapter explores why monopolistic competition generates diversity of products and the cost of this diversity. The chapter also considers the costs and benefits from advertising and the creation of brand names.

Chapter Objectives

Objective #1. A monopolistically competitive industry is composed of many competing firms selling differentiated products with free entry and exit of firms in the long run. The three essential characteristics of monopolistic competition are a large number of producers, differentiated products, and free entry and exit of firms in the long run. Analysis of this market structure reveals that in some ways it resembles perfect competition and in other ways it resembles monopoly.

Objective #2. Because monopolistically competitive firms sell differentiated products, each firm has some degree of market power and therefore faces a downward-sloping demand curve for its product. In fact, product differentiation is the only way monopolistically competitive firms acquire market power. This implies that these firms, like a monopoly, have some power to set the price they charge for their product. However, these firms also face competition, and due to free entry and exit in the long run will find that their long-run economic profit is equal to zero. There is no tendency toward collusion in a monopolistically competitive market since all firms recognize that new firms can enter the industry in the long run.

Objective #3. Product differentiation takes three general forms: differentiation by style or type, differentiation by location, and differentiation by quality. Differentiation by style or type creates products that are imperfect substitutes for one another. Differentiation by location offers essentially identical products that are differentiated by their proximity and convenience to the buyer. Differentiation by quality provides a range of products that are of different quality levels to buyers. No matter what type of product differentiation we consider, the monopolistically competitive market structure is characterized by competition among sellers and a more diverse array of products.

Objective #4. In the short run, a monopolistically competitive firm produces the level of output where marginal revenue equals marginal cost ($MR = MC$) and then prices this output by going up to its demand curve. The monopolistically competitive firm's MR curve lies beneath its demand curve (you find it exactly the same way you found the MR curve for the monopoly). This firm will earn positive economic profits if price is greater than average total cost, and negative economic profits if price is less than average total cost. The monopolistically competitive firm acts exactly like a monopoly in the short run. Figure 16.1 illustrates a monopolistically competitive firm in the short run earning positive economic profits, while Figure 16.2 illustrates a monopolistically competitive firm in the short run earning negative economic profits.

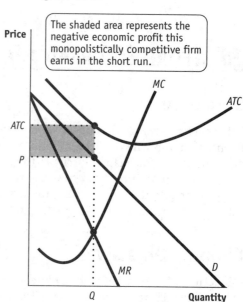

Figure 16.1

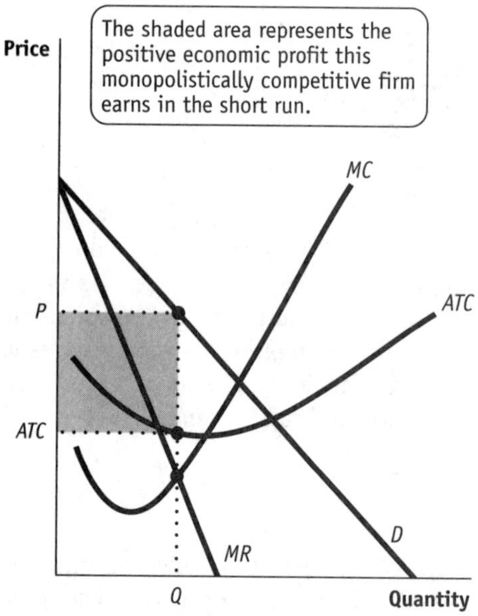

The shaded area represents the positive economic profit this monopolistically competitive firm earns in the short run.

Figure 16.2

The shaded area represents the negative economic profit this monopolistically competitive firm earns in the short run.

Objective #5. In the long run, the monopolistically competitive firm earns zero economic profit due to the entry or exit of firms.

- If the monopolistically competitive firm earns positive economic profit in the short run, this acts as a signal for other firms to enter the industry. The entry of firms into the industry causes the demand curve for each existing firm to shift to the left so that at every price fewer units of their product are demanded. This process continues until there has been enough entry so that each firm's price equals average total cost. Figure 16.3 illustrates both the short-run and the long-run equilibrium for a monopolistically competitive firm with positive economic profits in the short run. Notice that this firm produces a smaller level of output and sells its good at a lower price in the long run than it did in the short run.

Figure 16.3

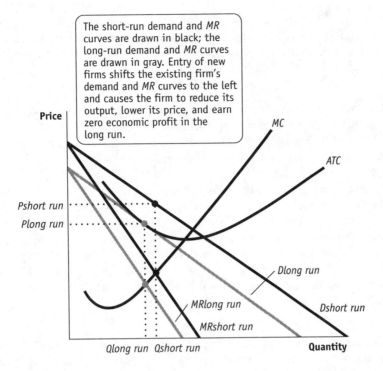

The short-run demand and *MR* curves are drawn in black; the long-run demand and *MR* curves are drawn in gray. Entry of new firms shifts the existing firm's demand and *MR* curves to the left and causes the firm to reduce its output, lower its price, and earn zero economic profit in the long run.

- If the monopolistically competitive firm earns negative economic profit in the short run, this acts as a signal for some of the firms in the industry to exit in the long run. This exit of firms from the industry causes the demand curve for each remaining firm to shift to the right so that at every price more units of their product are demanded. This process continues until there has been enough exiting so that each remaining firm's price equals its average total cost. Figure 16.4 illustrates both the short-run and the long-run equilibrium for a monopolistically competitive firm with negative economic profits in the short run. Notice that this firm produces a higher level of output and sells this output at a higher price in the long run than it did in the short run.

Figure 16.4

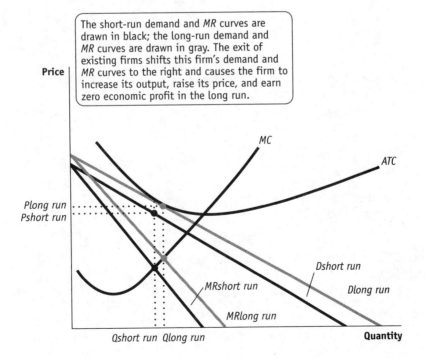

The short-run demand and *MR* curves are drawn in black; the long-run demand and *MR* curves are drawn in gray. The exit of existing firms shifts this firm's demand and *MR* curves to the right and causes the firm to increase its output, raise its price, and earn zero economic profit in the long run.

Objective #6. In the long run, each firm in a monopolistically competitive industry acts like a monopolist in setting marginal revenue equal to marginal cost and producing the quantity of output so as to maximize profits. However, in the long run the producers earn zero economic profits, unlike the long-run result for monopoly.

Objective #7. The long-run equilibrium in monopolistic competition also resembles the perfect competition result, since firms earn zero economic profit and their price equals average total cost. But there is a critical difference between long-run equilibrium in perfect competition and long-run equilibrium in a monopolistically competitive industry: in perfect competition, price is equal to the minimum of average total cost, while in monopolistic competition, price is equal to average total cost but not at the minimum-cost point of the average total cost (*ATC*) curve. The monopolistically competitive firm has excess capacity in the long run even though it earns zero economic profit; this excess capacity is another way of saying that the monopolistically competitive firm is not producing at minimum cost. This excess capacity of the monopolistically competitive firm arises from the cost of providing variety in the industry: the excess capacity is a sign of wasteful duplication that could be eliminated if there were fewer firms in the industry offering less-differentiated products. Yet consumers enjoy this diversity of products and it is valuable to them.

Objective #8. In the long run, the perfectly competitive firm produces at a level where price equals marginal cost, while the monopolistically competitive firm produces at a level where price is greater than marginal cost. The monopolistically competitive firm in the long run is interested in selling more units of the good, since price is greater than marginal cost for the last unit produced. This helps us understand why monopolistically competitive firms advertise their product.

Objective #9. Advertising is worthwhile in industries where firms have some degree of market power. Advertising may help to establish the quality of a firm's product. Advertising may also convey important information. The establishment of a brand name may be a way of signaling quality to a consumer.

Key Terms

monopolistic competition a market structure in which there are many competing producers in an industry, each producer sells a differentiated product, and there is *free entry and exit* into and from the industry in the *long run.*

zero-profit equilibrium an economic balance in which each firm makes zero profit at its profit-maximizing quantity.

excess capacity when firms produce less than the output at which *average total cost* is minimized; characteristic of *monopolistically competitive* firms.

brand name a name owned by a particular firm that distinguishes its products from those of other firms.

■ AFTER YOU READ THE CHAPTER

Tips

Tip #1. Monopolistic competition is an odd blend of elements from the monopoly model and from the perfect competition model. It is important that you understand these elements and how they work. Let's start with an analysis of the short-run situation. First, the monopolistically competitive firm faces a downward-sloping demand curve and, therefore, a MR curve that is beneath its demand curve. This is like monopoly. Second, the monopolistically competitive firm profit maximizes by producing the quantity where $MR = MC$. This is like both perfect competition and monopoly. Third, the price the monopolistically competitive firm charges for its good is found by taking the profit-maximizing quantity and looking at the demand curve for the price associated with that quantity. This is exactly what a monopoly does. In the short run, the monopolistically competitive firm exactly mimics the behavior of a monopoly. So, just remember your work with monopoly and apply those same rules. In the short run, the monopolistically competitive firm can earn positive, negative, or zero economic profit.

Tip #2. In the long run, the monopolistically competitive firm is subject to entry of new firms into the industry and the exit of existing firms from the industry. This is a characteristic that makes the monopolistically competitive industry resemble perfect competition. But there's an important distinction: even though economic profit equals zero in the long run for both market structures, the monopolistically competitive firm faces a downward-sloping demand curve, which means that price and marginal revenue are not the same for this firm. It implies that even when the monopolistically competitive firm earns zero economic profit in the long run, it charges a price that is greater than its marginal cost. This is different from the result found in perfect competition. Also, in perfect competition in the long run, price = $MR = MC$ = minimum ATC. In monopolistic competition in the long run, $MR = MC$ and price = ATC, but price is not equal to marginal cost and price is not equal to the minimum average total cost.

Review these two tips thoroughly until you have mastered them and understand the implications of the points made in each tip.

Problems and Exercises

1. Why are fast-food restaurants considered an example of a monopolistically competitive industry? What key attributes need to be present to have a monopolistically competitive industry?

2. How are fast-food restaurants similar; that is, why are they all considered to be part of the fast-food industry? How are fast-food restaurants differentiated; that is, why are the meals they sell considered to be differentiated from each other?

3. What aspect of the fast-food restaurant business is competitive? What aspect of the fast-food restaurant business is monopolistic?

4. Suppose the existing firms in the fast-food restaurant business are currently earning positive economic profit in the short run.

  a. Draw a graph representing a monopolistically competitive firm in this situation. Identify the price of the good and the output the firm produces in the short run and the area that represents this firm's profit.

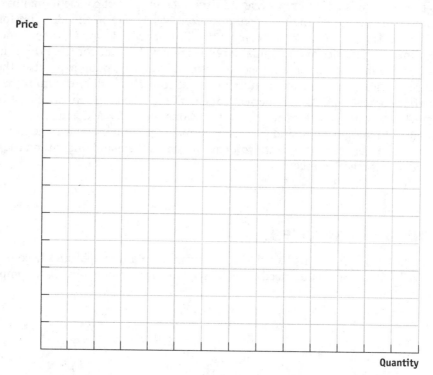

  b. What do you anticipate will happen in the long run in this industry? How will the industry price and quantity change in the long run? How will each firm's profit change in the long run?

c. Draw a graph representing a monopolistically competitive firm in long-run equilibrium. Identify the price of the good and the quantity the firm sells in the long run. What is the relationship between price and marginal cost for this firm in the long run? What is the relationship between price and average total cost for this firm in the long run?

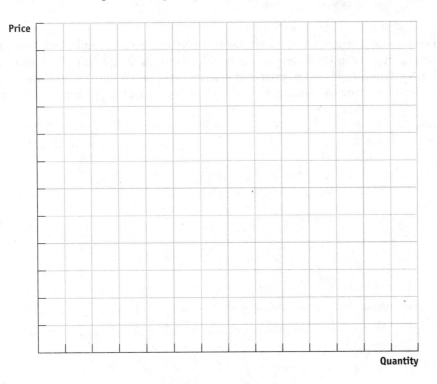

5. Suppose the existing firms in the fast-food restaurant business are currently earning negative economic profit in the short run.

a. Draw a graph representing a monopolistically competitive firm in this situation. Identify the price of the good and the output the firm produces in the short run and the area that represents this firm's profit.

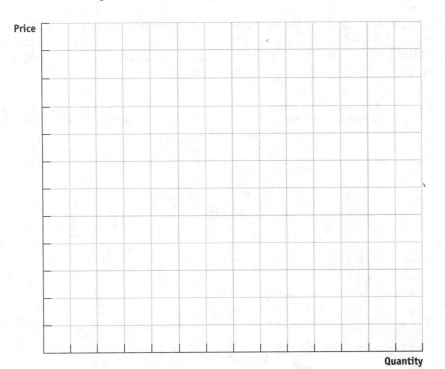

b. What do you anticipate will happen in the long run in this industry? How will the industry price and quantity change in the long run? How will each firm's profit change in the long run?

c. Draw a graph representing a monopolistically competitive firm in long-run equilibrium. Identify the price of the good and the quantity the firm sells in the long run. What is the relationship between price and marginal cost for this firm in the long run? What is the relationship between price and average total cost for this firm in the long run?

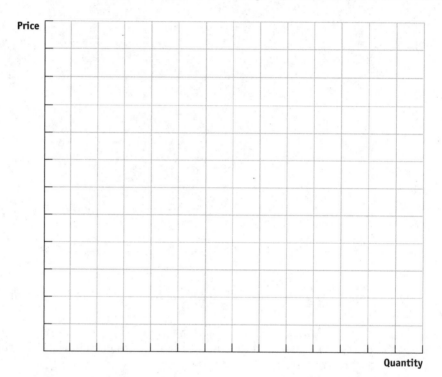

6. **a.** Compare the long-run equilibrium for a monopolistically competitive firm with the long-run equilibrium for a perfectly competitive firm. How are these two equilibriums similar? How are these two equilibriums different? Draw two sketches depicting the long-run equilibrium for these two market structures.

b. Compare the long-run equilibrium for a monopolistically competitive firm with the long-run equilibrium for a monopoly. How are these two equilibriums similar? How are these two equilibriums different? Draw two sketches depicting the long-run equilibrium for these two market structures.

7. In Smalltown there are three different gas stations owned by different people. One is located on the west side of town, one is on the east side of town, and one is on the south side of town. They all sell three types of identical gasoline, and their business hours are the same. Are these three firms differentiated?

8. The fast-food industry has many different restaurants selling many different types of food. These restaurants are also located in different places. What types of differentiation are represented by the fast-food industry?

9. Monopolistic competition is particularly noteworthy because of the degree of product differentiation one finds in this type of market structure. Why do firms find it profitable to differentiate their product? Why do consumers like this variety?

10. Suppose the demand curve for a monopolistically competitive firm is given by the equation $Q = 100 - 2P$. Furthermore, suppose this firm's marginal cost can be expressed by the equation $MC = 2Q + 2$, while the firm's total cost (TC) is $TC = 100 + Q^2 + 2Q$.

   a. In the short run, what level of output will this firm produce? (Hint: remember, you must first find the firm's MR curve before you can identify the profit-maximizing level of output.)

   b. In the short run, what price will the firm charge for its product?

   c. In the short run, what will this firm's profit equal?

   d. Describe what will happen in the long run to this monopolistically competitive firm.

11. Some monopolistically competitive firms differentiate their product according to quality. Describe what this means and why a firm might find this a profitable type of differentiation.

12. How did General Motors overtake Ford as the dominant auto manufacturer of the twentieth century? Relate its strategy to the issue of differentiation.

13. Use the graph below of a monopolistically competitive firm to answer the next set of questions.

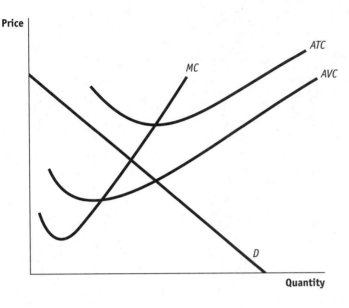

a. Label the profit-maximizing level of output and price for this firm in the short run.

b. Identify any profits the firm is making in the short run and decide whether these profits are positive or negative.

c. Draw the long-run equilibrium situation on this graph. Identify the long-run profit-maximizing quantity and the long-run price. What will this firm's profits equal in the long run?

d. Did entry or exiting of firms occur in the long run in this problem? Explain your answer.

14. What does it mean to say that a monopolistically competitive firm in the long run produces at a quantity where the firm has excess capacity? Is this a good or a bad outcome?

15. How does advertising and the establishment of a brand name assure the potential customer of the quality of the good?

■ BEFORE YOU TAKE THE TEST

Chapter Review Questions

1. Monopolistic competition is a market structure
   a. that makes a trade-off between lower prices and greater product diversity.
   b. in which each firm produces the quantity where $MC = MR$.
   c. in which firms earn zero economic profit in the long run.
   d. Answers (a), (b), and (c) are all true.

2. Which of the following statements is true for a monopolistically competitive firm?
   I. In the short run, the firm earns a positive economic profit whenever price is greater than average total cost.
   II. In the short run, the firm produces at the minimum-cost level of production where $MR = MC$.
   III. Monopolistically competitive firms engage in collusion so that they can set price at a level that is greater than marginal cost.
   a. Statement I is true.
   b. Statements I and II are true.
   c. Statements I and III are true.
   d. Statements I, II, and III are true.

3. Monopolistically competitive firms resemble perfectly competitive firms because
   a. in the long run they earn zero economic profit.
   b. in the long run they produce at the minimum-cost point of their ATC curves.
   c. they compete with other firms that offer similar products.
   d. Answers (a), (b), and (c) are all true.

4. Monopolistically competitive firms resemble monopolies because
   a. their *MR* curves lie beneath their demand curves.
   b. they charge a price that is greater than their marginal cost of production.
   c. entry and exit of firms in the long run ensure that profits are equal to zero in the long run.
   d. Answers (a), (b), and (c) are all true.
   e. Answers (a) and (b) are true.

5. A monopolistically competitive industry is characterized by having
   a. many firms, each producing a differentiated product and operating in an industry with free entry and exit in the short run.
   b. a few firms, each producing a differentiated product but with each firm having market power and the ability to set the price of the good it sells.
   c. a very large number of firms that produce very similar products and that always elect to produce the profit-maximizing amount of output in both the short run and the long run.
   d. None of the above answers are true about a monopolistically competitive industry.

6. Monopolistically competitive firms
   a. have no limit as to what price they can charge for the good they produce, since this good is highly differentiated from any other firm's product.
   b. charge the highest price people are willing to pay for the good based on the demand curve for the good.
   c. are price takers and must accept the market price that is determined in the industry.
   d. do not worry about what price to charge and instead focus the bulk of their attention on deciding what the profit-maximizing level of output is for the firm.

Use the following information to answer the next five questions. A monopolistically competitive firm's demand for its product is equal to $Q = 100 - P$, and its marginal cost of production is equal to $MC = 20 + 2Q$. The firm's total cost is equal to $TC = Q^2 + 20Q + 10$.

7. What is this monopolistically competitive firm's fixed cost?
   a. Fixed cost cannot be calculated from the above information.
   b. $Q^2 + 20Q$
   c. 10
   d. The monopolistically competitive firm need not consider the distinction between fixed cost and variable cost.

8. What is the profit-maximizing level of output in the short run?
   a. 100 units
   b. 80 units
   c. 50 units
   d. 20 units

9. What is the profit-maximizing price for this firm in the short run?
   a. $100   c. $60
   b. $80   d. $20

10. In the short run, this firm earns
   a. positive economic profits.
   b. negative economic profits.
   c. zero economic profits.

11. In the long run, this firm's demand curve will shift
   a. to the right due to entry of new firms into the industry.
   b. to the left due to the entry of new firms into the industry.

12. When monopolistically competitive firms differentiate their products, this is
   a. unprofitable, since differentiation costs money.
   b. unprofitable in the short run, since monopolistically competitive firms make zero economic profits in the short run.
   c. profitable in the short run, so long as consumers differ in their tastes.
   d. wasted effort, since consumers would be just as happy with identical products as they are with differentiated products.

13. Which of the following statements is true about monopolistically competitive industries that produce differentiated products?
   I. Monopolistically competitive industries with differentiated products are characterized as having competition among sellers.
   II. Monopolistically competitive industries with differentiated products are industries that find there is value in diversity.
   III. Monopolistically competitive industries with differentiated products are able to sustain short-run positive economic profits into the long run.
   a. Statement I is true.
   b. Statement II is true.
   c. Statement III is true.
   d. Statements I and II are true.
   e. Statements I and III are true.

14. When Henry Ford produced his cars, he maximized his economies of scale, while General Motors decided to produce with excess capacity. This resulted in
   a. Ford being able to produce cheaper cars than General Motors initially, since Ford did not diversify the product it provided.
   b. General Motors facing a trade-off between offering cars at a lower price with less differentiation or selling cars at a higher price with greater differentiation.
   c. consumers ultimately finding they preferred product differentiation as General Motors sold more cars than Ford.
   d. Answers (a), (b), and (c) are all true.

Use the following diagram of a monopolistically competitive firm to answer the next four questions.

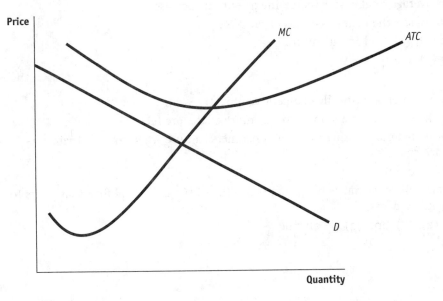

15. To identify the profit-maximizing output for this firm in the short run, this graph needs
   a. the market price identified.
   b. the *MR* curve identified.
   c. the *AVC* curve identified.
   d. All of the above answers are true.
   e. Answers (b) and (c) are true.

16. Assuming this firm produces in the short run, this firm will earn
   a. negative economic profit, since its price is less than its average total cost.
   b. positive economic profit, since its price is greater than its marginal cost.
   c. zero economic profit, since entry of new firms will drive the profits of all firms down to that level where each firm earns zero economic profit.
   d. zero economic profit, since the exit of firms will cause profits of all existing firms to increase until all the firms left in the industry earn zero economic profit.

17. Assuming this firm produces in the short run, this firm will
   a. find that it is interested in selling more units of the good, since *MR* = *MC* at its selected level of production.
   b. find advertising worthwhile if it increases sales, since it is producing at a quantity where price is less than marginal cost.
   c. be enthusiastic about increasing its sales, since it currently is producing a quantity where marginal cost is less than price.
   d. be reluctant to advertise, since this will only increase the costs that the firm has to pay.

18. Relative to a perfectly competitive firm, a monopolistically competitive firm produces
   a. its product at a higher price.
   b. where its average total cost is increasing as output increases.
   c. at a point where the firm has excess capacity.
   d. Answers (a), (b), and (c) are all true.
   e. Answers (a) and (c) are true.

19. Advertising in a monopolistically competitive industry
   a. is worthwhile if it gets consumers to buy more of the product.
   b. may provide helpful information that consumers can use when making their purchasing decisions.
   c. is costly and of little use.
   d. is often an indirect signal as to the dependability of the individual firm that elects to advertise its products.
   e. Answers (a), (b), and (d) are all true.

ANSWER KEY

Answers to Problems and Exercises

1. Fast-food restaurants are a good example of a monopolistically competitive industry because there are many firms in the industry, each producing a differentiated product, and there is free entry and exit in the industry in the long run. The key attributes of monopolistically competitive industries are a large number of firms, a differentiated product, and free entry or exit of firms in the long run.

2. Here the answers may vary quite a bit depending on what attributes you have focused on. Fast-food restaurants typically offer relatively cheap meals, in easily accessible locations, at fast speed with little waiting. The food is often easy to eat on the run or to have as carryout. Fast-food restaurants differ from one another in the type of food they serve (e.g., Mexican, hamburgers, Italian). There may also be small price variations that distinguish one restaurant from another.

3. Here again the answers may vary depending on what you focus on in your response. The fast-food restaurant industry is competitive in that there are many firms producing within this industry and each competes to satisfy more or less the same demand—the demand for quick, tasty food. The fast-food restaurant industry is also monopolistic since each firm sells a product that is differentiated from the products of other producers, and this differentiation results in each firm having some degree of market power.

4. a.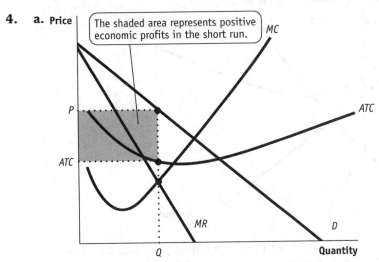

   b. In the long run, new firms will enter this industry because the short-run positive economic profits act as a signal for firms to enter the industry. As firms enter the industry, each existing firm in the industry will see the demand for its product shift to the left as some of its customers stop demanding its product and start demanding the new firm's product. As the demand curve shifts to the left, this will also cause the MR curve to shift to the left. This process will continue until the firm earns zero economic profit in the long run. The firm will sell its product at a lower price and produce a smaller quantity of the good because of the entry of the new firms into the industry.

   c. In the long run, the monopolistically competitive firm will continue to charge a price that is greater than its marginal cost. In the long run, the price of the product will equal the average total cost of producing the product, but the price will not equal the minimum point of the ATC curve. These two results indicate that the firm will continue to be interested in selling more units of the good, since price is greater than marginal cost for the last unit produced (hence, advertising will pay off if it increases the demand for the firm's product), and that the firm has excess capacity since it is not producing at the minimum point of its *ATC* curve. The figure below illustrates the long-run equilibrium for a monopolistically competitive firm.

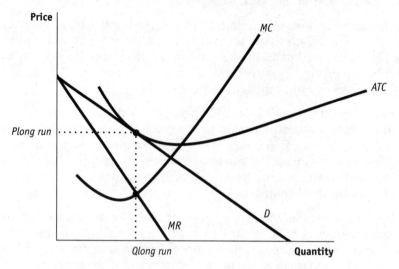

5. **a.**

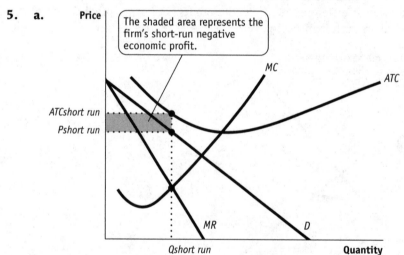

The shaded area represents the firm's short-run negative economic profit.

b. In the long run, some existing firms will exit this industry because the short-run negative economic profits act as a signal for firms to exit the industry. As firms exit the industry, each remaining firm in the industry will see the demand for its product shift to the right as some of the customers from exiting firms begin demanding its product and stop demanding the exiting firm's product. As the demand curve shifts to the right, this will also cause the *MR* curve to shift to the right. This process will continue until the firm earns zero economic profit in the long run. The firm will sell its product at a higher price and produce a larger quantity of the good because of the exit of existing firms from the industry.

c. See the answer to problem 4(c).

6. **a.** In the long run, both market structures produce the profit-maximizing level of output where *MR* = *MC*, and both market structures earn zero economic profit in the long run. However, the monopolistically competitive firm in the long run does not produce at the level where price is equal to marginal cost, while the perfectly competitive firm does. In addition, the perfectly competitive firm produces the long-run level of output

at the minimum-cost point on its *ATC* curve, while the monopolistically competitive firm produces in the decreasing cost portion of its *ATC* curve. The monopolistically competitive firm has excess capacity in the long run since it does not produce at the minimum-cost point of its *ATC* curve. The two sketches below illustrate the long-run situation for the two types of market structures.

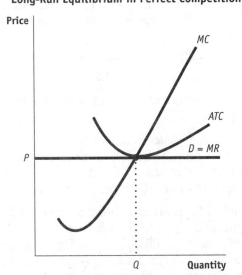

Long-Run Equilibrium in Perfect Competition

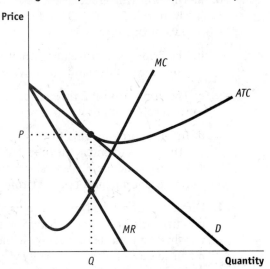

Long-Run Equilibrium in Monopolistic Competition

b. In the long run, the monopolistically competitive firm and the monopoly are remarkably similar except for one very important difference. In the long run, entry and exit of firms ensures that the monopolistically competitive firm earns zero economic profit, while the monopoly, protected from competition by barriers to entry, is able to continue to maintain its positive profits into the long run. The two graphs below illustrate the long-run situation in the two market structures.

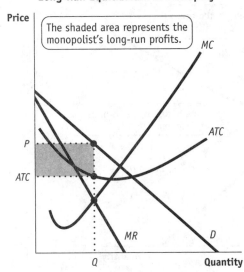

Long-Run Equilibrium in Monopoly

The shaded area represents the monopolist's long-run profits.

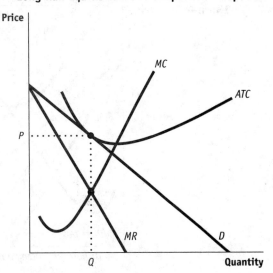

Long-Run Equilibrium in Monopolistic Competition

7. Yes, the type of differentiation these three firms illustrate is differentiation by location. Each of these three firms is located in a different part of the community, which differentiates them even though they sell very similar products.

8. This industry is characterized by having differentiation by style or type as well as differentiation by location.

9. As long as people have different tastes and preferences, firms will find it profitable to offer differentiated products. Variety is appealing to people primarily because people have different tastes and preferences.

10. a. The firm will produce the level of output where $MR = MC$. The firm's MR curve is given by $MR = 50 - Q$, and its $MC = 2Q + 2$. Thus, the profit-maximizing level of output for this firm is 16 units.

b. The firm sets its price by taking its profit-maximizing level of output and plugging this value into its demand curve. When $Q = 16$, price is equal to $42.

c. The firm earns total revenue of $762 and its total cost equals $388, so the firm's short-run economic profits are equal to $284.

d. In the short run, this firm earns positive economic profit, which acts as a signal for other firms to enter this industry in the long run. Entry will continue until each existing firm's demand curve shifts to the left far enough to result in each firm earning zero economic profit at the profit-maximizing level of output.

11. Differentiation based on quality is the idea that firms can choose to produce a similar product with a range of quality. Some firms find it profitable to produce the product with very high standards of quality, while other firms produce a similar product that has a much lower standard of quality. Consumers can then select the level of quality they desire by selecting the product whose quality most closely resembles the desired level of quality. Consumers' tastes and preferences are thus served more closely when firms decide to produce a product with different quality levels.

12. Although Ford was the first car company in the United States to produce an affordable car, Ford only produced one basic model of car. General Motors innovated by producing a variety of styles and colors so that consumers could purchase a car that was reflective of their personal tastes and preferences. By differentiating its product, General Motors was able to become the dominant car producer in the twentieth century.

13. a–c.

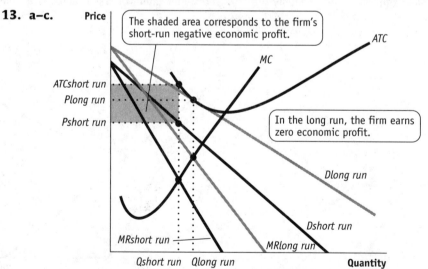

The firm earns negative economic profit in the short run since price is less than average total cost at the short-run profit-maximizing quantity.

In the long run, this firm earns zero economic profit since price is equal to ATC at the long-run profit-maximizing quantity.

d. Exiting of firms occurred in the long run because there were too many firms initially serving this monopolistically competitive industry. Firms exited because they were earning negative economic profits; exiting continued until the remaining firms were able to break even.

14. When a firm produces at a quantity at which the firm has excess capacity, this indicates that at the current level of production the *ATC* curve is decreasing as output increases. This implies that the firm could produce a higher level of output at lower unit cost. This indicates that the firm is not fully utilizing its productive capacity, and carries with it an implication of waste. But the monopolistically competitive firm produces at excess capacity because of the product differentiation that occurs in the industry and, even though this leaves each firm with excess capacity, it also leaves consumers with greater choice and greater variety, which are highly valued by the consumer. Consumers are willing to pay a higher price for the product in order to have this variety.

15. If a firm can afford to make an expensive advertisement about their product or expend the resources to create a brand name, this indicates to the potential buyer that the firm is able to stand behind its product. These actions serve to establish the quality of the firm's products from the consumers' perspective.

Answers to Chapter Review Questions

1. **Answer d.** Monopolistic competition results in higher prices for the goods that are produced, but there is more variety in the produced goods than you would see in a perfectly competitive market. Thus, monopolistic competition is a market structure that trades off lower prices for greater product diversity. Monopolistically competitive firms profit maximize by producing the quantity where $MC = MR$. In the long run, there is entry and exit of firms in a monopolistically competitive industry, which ensures that economic profits equal zero in the long run.

2. **Answer a.** Whenever a firm produces at an output level where price is greater than average total cost, the firm earns a positive profit (statement I). In a monopolistically competitive industry, the firm does not produce at the minimum-cost level of production in the short run or the long run: firms produce the quantity where $MR = MC$ in order to maximize profit, and then determine their level of profit by comparing price to average total cost (statement II). Collusion does not occur in a monopolistically competitive market due to the number of firms and the fact that there is free entry into the industry (statement III).

3. **Answer a.** Monopolistically competitive firms do not produce at the minimum-cost point on the *ATC* curves in the short run or the long run. Instead these firms produce in the decreasing-cost portion of their *ATC* curve: this implies that each firm has excess capacity. Although monopolistically competitive firms compete with other firms, this is different from the competition that perfectly competitive firms engage in: the monopolistically competitive firms differentiate their product, and each firm has some market power. In perfect competition, firms sell identical products and no firm has market power.

4. **Answer e.** The monopolistically competitive firm faces a downward-sloping demand curve for its product because the product is differentiated from the products produced by competing firms. This implies that the *MR* curve for the monopolistically competitive firm lies beneath the demand curve. Like a monopolist, the monopolistically competitive firm produces the level of output where $MR = MC$ and then prices this output by going to the demand curve, which results in price being greater than marginal cost. There is no entry and exit of firms in a monopoly in the long run: this is the biggest difference between a monopolistically competitive firm and a monopoly in the long run.

5. **Answer d.** Each of the answers (a) through (c) contains some type of error. For example, answer (a) is correct except for the fact that entry and exit occur in the long run. Answer (b) is correct except for the fact that there are more than a few firms in a monopolistically competitive industry. Answer (c) is incorrect because the firms in a monopolistically competitive industry typically produce highly differentiated products.

6. **Answer b.** Monopolistically competitive firms first select their profit-maximizing level of output by equating marginal revenue with marginal cost, and then they go to the demand curve to see what price people are willing to pay given this level of output. The firms cannot charge more than the price on the demand curve associated with their level of production because people are not willing to pay more than the price on the demand curve. Monopolistically competitive firms are not price takers because they have some market power. Monopolistically competitive firms act to maximize profits by producing the right quantity and charging the right price.

7. **Answer c.** Fixed cost (FC) is the cost the firm incurs when output is equal to zero units. If $Q = 0$ in the above total cost equation, then $TC = FC = 10$. Answer (d) is incorrect since the monopolistically competitive firm, just like the perfectly competitive firm or the monopoly, is unwilling to produce when its total revenue does not cover its variable cost of production.

8. **Answer d.** To find the profit-maximizing level of output in the short run, you need to equate marginal revenue with marginal cost. Marginal revenue for this firm is $MR = 100 - 2Q$, so equating marginal revenue with marginal cost yields $Q = 20$ units.

9. **Answer b.** The profit-maximizing price is found by substituting the profit-maximizing quantity, 20 units, into the demand equation, $P = 100 - Q$. When $Q = 20$ units, then $P = \$80$.

10. **Answer a.** In the short run, this firm produces 20 units and then sells these units at a price of $80. The firm's total revenue equals $1,600 and its total cost equals $810. The firm earns a positive profit of $790.

11. **Answer b.** Since the firm is earning positive economic profits in the short run, this will lead to the entry of new firms in the long run. As new firms enter the industry, this firm's demand curve will shift to the left because some of this firm's customers will decide to buy a competitor's product: this firm will find that at every price, it sells less of its good than it did before the entry of the new firms.

12. **Answer c.** As long as people's preferences are not identical, firms will find it profitable in the short run to produce a wide variety of goods so that people can select items that maximize their satisfaction given these preferences.

13. **Answer d.** Statements I and II are descriptive of monopolistically competitive industries with differentiated products. Statement III is not true because, in the long run, entry will drive economic profit to zero even if the firms in the industry produce differentiated products.

14. **Answer d.** This is a recap of the "Economics in Action" sidebar in the text that discusses the competition between Ford and General Motors.

15. **Answer e.** To find the profit-maximizing level of output for this firm in the short run requires that we equate marginal revenue with marginal cost. So the marginal revenue curve must be identified. But the firm will not produce in the short run if the price it can charge for its product is less than the average variable cost of producing that product (recall this from your previous work with monopolies), since the firm will be unwilling to hire the variable input if its revenue is not sufficient to cover the cost of this variable input.

16. **Answer a.** This firm will earn negative economic profit in the short run because the price it charges for its product is less than the cost per unit (average total cost) of producing this product. Entry and exit of firms is a long-run characteristic of this market structure, not a short-run characteristic.

17. **Answer c.** A monopolistically competitive firm's profit-maximizing quantity occurs where $MR = MC$, but the price that the firm charges for its product is found by going up to the demand curve at this quantity. This implies that the firm produces a quantity for which price is greater than marginal cost, and therefore the firm will be enthusiastic about increasing its sales as long as price remains above marginal cost.

18. **Answer e.** The monopolistically competitive firm produces a quantity where price is greater than marginal cost, while a perfect competitive firm produces a quantity where price equals marginal cost. The monopolistically competitive firm produces a quantity where the average total cost is downward sloping: this indicates that the firm is producing in the decreasing-cost portion of its cost curve and not the increasing-cost portion of its cost curve. When the monopolistically competitive firm produces in the decreasing-cost portion of its cost curve, this indicates that the firm could expand its level of production and thereby reduce its cost per unit, which implies that the firm has excess productive capacity.

19. **Answer e.** Advertising is costly, but if it is of little use, then firms would realize this and decide to forgo their advertising expenditures. Advertising may encourage consumers to purchase a product they otherwise would not purchase, it may provide consumers with information about the product or the firm, and it can indicate that the firm is large enough and successful enough to be able to afford an advertising campaign. The consumer may view this last aspect as a way for the firm to convey its reliability, and therefore the reliability of its product.

chapter 17

Externalities

Summary

This chapter describes positive, negative, and network externalities and the effects of these externalities in the marketplace. The chapter explores the economic inefficiency that arises when externalities are not accounted for, and it presents several alternative methods for correcting externalities. The chapter makes the case for government intervention in the form of emissions taxes, tradable permits, or Pigouvian subsidies as an efficient means of correcting externalities. The chapter also discusses environmental standards as an inefficient government policy. Finally, the chapter looks at industrial policy and how network externalities are an important feature of high-tech industries.

Chapter Objectives

Objective #1. A principal source of market failure occurs when the market fails to take into account side effects or externalities of consumption or production decisions. A negative externality is a side effect that imposes costs on others, and a positive externality is a side effect that provides benefits to others. When externalities are present, the market fails to produce the optimal amount of the good: in the case of a negative externality, the market produces too much of the good if it does not take into account the externality; in the case of a positive externality, the market produces too little of the good if it does not take into account the externality. When the externality can be directly observed, then it can be regulated through direct controls, taxation, or subsidization. When the externality cannot be directly observed, then the government must implement policies that aim at generating the right amount of the activity that produces the externality. This chapter discusses these two approaches—targeting the side effect versus targeting the original activity—as it reviews different policies available to the government to correct the problem presented by externalities.

Objective #2. Many activities produce pollution as a side effect of these activities. One of the problems with pollution is that it inflicts a cost on the entire society, and this cost is typically not borne by the companies or individuals who generate the pollution. The chapter explores how to determine the optimal amount of pollution by developing the concepts of the marginal social cost of pollution and the marginal social benefit of pollution. Pollution generates costs as well as benefits to society.

- The marginal social cost of pollution is the additional cost imposed on society of an additional unit of pollution. The marginal social cost of pollution is an upward-sloping line, since each additional unit of pollution represents a greater cost to society as the environment deteriorates.

- The marginal social benefit of pollution is the additional benefit to society from an additional unit of pollution. Cleaning up pollution requires the use of scarce resources that would otherwise be used to produce goods and services. From a producer's perspective, the benefit from emitting one more unit of pollution is measured by the costs the producer saves from not having to buy and install expensive pollution-control equipment. One can measure the marginal social benefit of an additional unit of pollution by finding out what is the highest willingness to pay for the right to emit this unit of pollution among all the polluters in the society. Polluters know that to avoid polluting requires using scarce resources and therefore reduction of pollution carries a cost. The marginal social benefit of pollution is a downward-sloping line: when pollution is negligible, then an additional unit of pollution has a high benefit to society; when there is a lot of pollution, then an additional unit of pollution brings little benefit to society.

- The optimal amount of pollution for a society is the level of pollution at which the marginal social cost of pollution is equal to the marginal social benefit of pollution. Figure 17.1 illustrates these concepts.

Figure 17.1

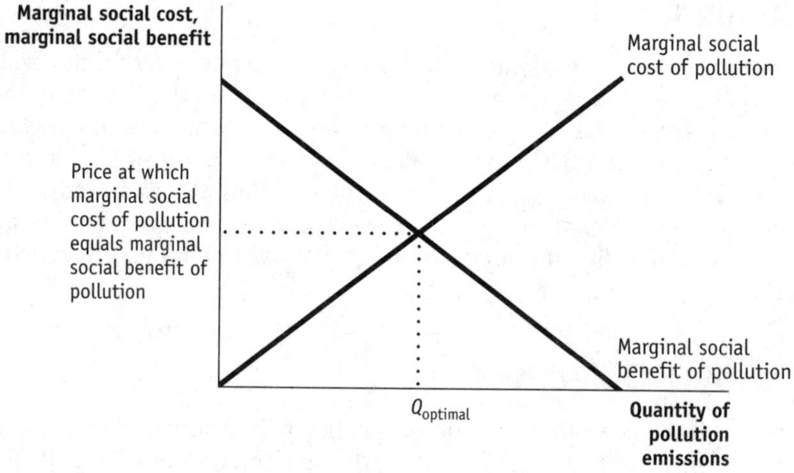

- It is unlikely that the market will generate the optimal amount of pollution, because those who produce the pollution do not have to compensate those who bear the costs of the pollution. The polluting producer can pass along the pollution costs to all members of society, and thus the market, left to its own devices, will result in too much pollution.

- In the absence of government intervention, polluters will pollute up to the point where the marginal social benefit of pollution is equal to zero. The market outcome is represented in Figure 17.2: note that the market level of pollution is greater than the optimal level of pollution, and that the market level of pollution is inefficient since, at this level of pollution, the marginal social cost of pollution is greater than the marginal social benefit of pollution.

Figure 17.2 Marginal social cost, marginal social benefit

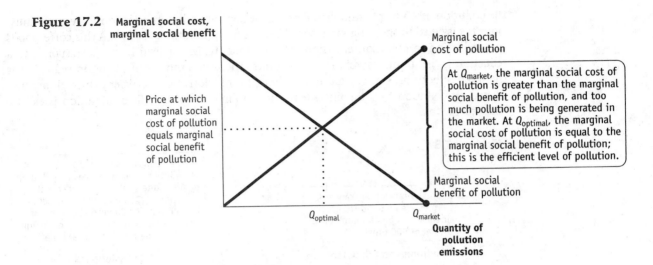

Marginal social cost of pollution

At Q_{market}, the marginal social cost of pollution is greater than the marginal social benefit of pollution, and too much pollution is being generated in the market. At $Q_{optimal}$, the marginal social cost of pollution is equal to the marginal social benefit of pollution; this is the efficient level of pollution.

Price at which marginal social cost of pollution equals marginal social benefit of pollution

Marginal social benefit of pollution

$Q_{optimal}$ Q_{market}

Quantity of pollution emissions

Objective #3.   According to the Coase theorem, the private sector can correct externalities and produce the efficient level of the good, provided that transaction costs are sufficiently low. The Coase theorem states that externalities need not lead to inefficiencies since people have an incentive to make mutually beneficial transactions, which leads individuals to take externalities into account when making decisions, provided that the transaction costs are not too great. When individuals take into account externalities when making decisions, this is referred to as internalizing the externality. Internalization of the externality does not occur if the cost of communication between the affected parties is too high, if the cost of making a legally binding agreement is too great, or if there are costly delays in the bargaining. When transaction costs prevent people from internalizing the externality, then the government must intervene to correct the market and its failure to internalize the externality.

Objective #4.   The government can reduce the amount of pollution by enforcing environmental standards, which are rules that protect the environment by specifying what actions need to be taken by producers and consumers. Although effective, these standards are not efficient since they do not incorporate the costs of reducing pollution. Economists believe that pollution can be reduced at lower cost through the use of taxes and tradable permits.

- Emissions taxes are taxes that depend on the amount of pollution a firm produces. An emissions tax is more efficient than an environmental standard, since the emissions tax ensures that the marginal benefit of pollution is equal for all sources of pollution while the environmental standard does not consider the marginal benefit of pollution when it is enforced. Figure 17.3 illustrates the differences between these two approaches using two different firms, firm A and firm B, that both produce pollution but have different marginal social benefit of pollution curves. The graph on the left illustrates the environmental standard approach: pollution for all firms in the society must, by law, be reduced to 450 units for each firm. With this standard, however, notice that the marginal social benefit of reducing pollution is different for the two firms: for firm A the marginal social benefit is $225 for the last unit of pollution emissions, while for firm B the marginal social benefit is $450 for the last unit of pollution emissions. The graph on the right illustrates the emissions tax approach using an emissions tax of $300 per unit of pollution: each unit of pollution emitted is taxed, and polluters reduce their pollution by considering the tax versus the benefit of the pollution. Both firm A and firm B select the level of pollution emissions where the emissions tax is equal to their marginal social benefit from pollution: for firm A this corresponds to a reduction in pollution emissions of 600 units, while for firm B this corresponds to a reduction in pollution emissions of 300 units. The total amount of pollution reduction is the same in both programs (900 units), but the emissions tax is efficient since all producers reduce pollution to the point where the marginal social benefit of pollution is exactly equal to the tax.

Figure 17.3

With an environmental standard, both firms are required to reduce their emissions by 450 units each, or a total of 900 units.

With an emissions tax of $300 per unit of pollution, firm A reduces its pollution by 600 units while firm B reduces its pollution by 300 units. Total reduction in pollution is 900 units, but the last unit of pollution produced by each firm has the same marginal social benefit.

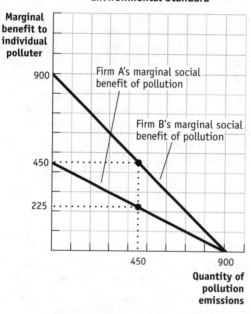

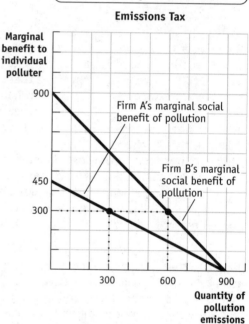

- Taxes can be used to reduce any kind of activity that generates a negative externality. This use of taxes to address the problem of negative externality is referred to as a Pigouvian tax. Although effective as a policy, Pigouvian taxes are difficult to implement since government officials do not always know with certainty what level of tax is the efficient level of tax.

- Tradable emissions permits are licenses granted by the government that give the holder of the license permission to emit limited quantities of the pollutant. These tradable emissions permits can be bought and sold by the polluters. In essence, the government determines the legal amount of pollution and then sells permits equal to this amount of pollution. Producers who pollute must own permits granting them the right to generate their level of pollution. Producers can either purchase the right to pollute or they can clean up their production and eliminate the polluting activity. Firms that find the cost of reducing pollution greater than the cost of buying the permits will buy the permits. Firms that find the cost of reducing pollution less than the cost of buying the permits will eliminate their pollution. Since the level of pollution is limited by the amount of permits in the market, this results in producers basing their decision about whether or not to pollute on the costs of reducing their pollution. In effect, the government creates a market in the right to pollute by using tradable emissions permits. The greatest challenge for government when implementing a tradable emissions permit program is determining the optimal number of permits for the economy: issue too many permits, and pollution is not reduced enough; issue too few permits, and pollution is reduced too much.

- Both emissions taxes and tradable emissions permits create an incentive for producers to create and use less-polluting technology.

- Cap-and-trade systems are another name for tradable emissions permits. In this case, the government issues a cap, or a total amount of pollutant that can be emitted, then the government issues tradable emissions permits and enforces a rule that polluters must hold a number of permits equal to the amount of the pollutant they emit. This policy is effective with pollution that is dispersed, but it is less effective with pollution that is geographically localized. As with any policy, policymakers also face political pressure to set the level of the cap at either too high or too low a level. Finally, these measures to reduce pollution require a high degree of monitoring and compliance if the policy is to be effective.

Objective #5.   When an activity generates an external cost, or a cost incurred by someone other than the people directly involved in the transaction, the market produces too much of the good. This situation of an external cost is an example of a negative externality. Figure 17.4 illustrates a negative externality. From the producers' perspective, the market supply curve represents the private costs they incur when they produce the good. However, when this good is produced there are also social costs that the producers do not include in their costs of production. The result is a difference between the market supply curve and the true marginal social costs of production. The market, when it fails to correct for the externality, produces Q_{market}, which is more than $Q_{optimal}$. Notice that at Q_{market} the marginal social benefit of consuming the last unit of the good produced (as measured by the demand curve) is less than the marginal social cost of producing this last unit. Too much of this good is being produced by the market, and therefore too many resources are being devoted to its production. This negative externality can be remedied by applying the appropriate Pigouvian tax, equal to the externality per unit of the good produced, on producers so that $Q_{optimal}$ is produced by the market. The application of this tax on the market causes the market to internalize the negative externality.

Figure 17.4

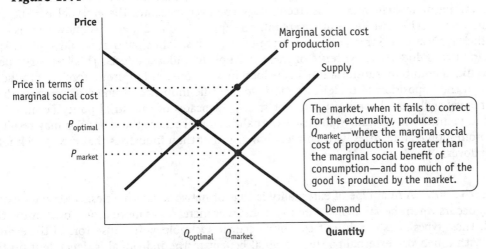

Objective #6.   When an activity generates an external benefit, or a benefit received by someone other than the people directly involved in the transaction, the market does not produce enough of this good. This situation of an external benefit is an example of a positive externality. In the case of a positive externality, the government must target the original activity rather than the external benefit because the external benefit can be difficult, or impossible, to measure. For example, the external benefit from people getting vaccinated is a reduction in the spread of disease among the whole population, but it is impossible to measure how many people benefit from an individual getting vaccinated. When individuals consider getting vaccinated, they consider only the benefits they directly receive and do not include the external benefits the vaccination provides to other people. This implies that people will consume less than the ideal level of vaccinations because they do not include the external benefits.

- This scenario can be illustrated by thinking about the demand curve that represents the private benefits that individuals receive from the vaccination and the demand curve that includes the private benefits as well as the external benefits. Figure 17.5 illustrates the case of a positive externality: in the graph the quantity produced by the market is Q_{market}, and the optimal quantity, where the marginal cost of producing the last unit is equal to the marginal social benefit from consuming the last unit, is given by $Q_{optimal}$. This situation of a positive externality can be corrected by application of the optimal Pigouvian subsidy, a subsidy equal to the positive externality cost per unit of the good. The application of this subsidy in this market causes the market to internalize the externality.

Figure 17.5

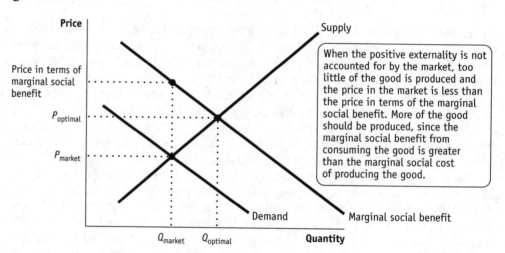

Objective #7. The creation of knowledge poses the greatest single source of external benefits in the modern economy. Technology spillover is a term that describes the spread of knowledge among individuals and firms: technology spillover measures the external benefit that occurs when new knowledge is discovered in one application and then this knowledge is used in other applications. Some people advocate for an industrial policy that would support specific industries due to the existence of these technology spillover effects. This industrial policy would amount to subsidization or reductions in competition from foreign producers through the imposition of trade restrictions for specific industries deemed to generate these technology spillovers. Economists are not strong advocates of industrial policy because it is hard to identify with certainty positive externalities, and because these policies may result in the promotion of industries with political power rather than industries that create technology spillovers.

Objective #8. A final type of externality is that of network externalities. A network externality occurs when the value of a good to a consumer increases as more people own or use the good. These types of externalities frequently occur in technology-driven sectors of the economy. With a network externality, the marginal benefit to the individual is dependent on the number of other individuals who use the good. A good with a network externality also exhibits positive feedback: as more people use the good, even more people are inclined to use the good, and if fewer people use the good, then even fewer people are inclined to use the good. The good's ultimate success or failure is self-reinforcing: a well-accepted good becomes ever more accepted, while a poorly received good is quickly abandoned because of this positive feedback effect. Companies recognize the importance of network externalities and the positive feedback effect, and they sometimes offer a new product at a very low price in hopes of generating a strong network effect.

Key Terms

marginal social cost of pollution the additional cost imposed on society as a whole by an additional unit of pollution.

marginal social benefit of pollution the additional gain to society as a whole from an additional unit of pollution.

socially optimal quantity of pollution the quantity of pollution that society would choose if all the costs and benefits of pollution were fully accounted for.

external cost an uncompensated cost that an individual or firm imposes on others; also known as *negative externalities*.

external benefit an uncompensated benefit that an individual or firm confers on others; also known as *positive externalities*.

externalities *external benefits* and *external costs*.

negative externalities *external costs*.

positive externalities *external benefits*.

Coase theorem the proposition that even in the presence of *externalities* an *economy* can always reach an *efficient* solution as long as *transaction costs* are sufficiently low.

transaction costs the costs to individuals of making a deal.

internalize the externality when individuals take into account *external costs* and *external benefits*.

environmental standards rules established by a government to protect the environment by specifying actions by producers and consumers.

emissions tax a tax that depends on the amount of pollution a firm produces.

Pigouvian taxes taxes designed to reduce *external costs*.

tradable emissions permits *licenses* to emit limited quantities of pollutants that can be bought and sold by polluters.

marginal social cost of a good or activity the *marginal cost* of production plus the marginal *external cost*.

Pigouvian subsidy a payment designed to encourage activities that yield *external benefits*.

technology spillover an *external benefit* that results when knowledge spreads among individuals and firms.

industrial policy a policy that supports industries believed to yield *positive externalities*.

marginal social benefit of a good or activity the *marginal benefit* that accrues to consumers plus the marginal *external benefit*.

network externality the increase in the value of a good to an individual is greater when a large number of others own or use the same good.

positive feedback put simply, success breeds success, failure breeds failure; the effect is seen with goods that are subject to *network externalities*.

■ AFTER YOU READ THE CHAPTER

Tips

Tip #1. The key concept in this chapter is the idea that markets fail to produce the optimal amount of the good whenever there is a cost or a benefit that the market fails to include in its reckoning when deciding what the optimal quantity of the good will be in the market. A negative externality occurs when there is some kind of cost that is not internalized in the market, and a positive externality occurs when there is some kind of benefit that is not internalized in the market. When there is an externality in the market that is not internalized, the market does not produce the efficient level of output because it is not producing the level of output where the marginal social cost of production is equal to the marginal social benefit of consumption.

Tip #2. Negative externalities can occur on the production or the consumption side of the model of supply and demand. For example, when a producer produces a good whose production generates substantial pollution and the producer does not take into account the cost of this pollution, then there is a negative externality on the production or cost side of the market. This implies that the producer's supply curve does not represent the true societal costs of producing the good. Alternatively, a consumer can engage in behaviors that inflict a negative benefit on others: for instance, the decision to drink alcoholic beverages and then operate a car has potential negative consequences for others in the community. In this case, the demand curve for the individual does not take into account the negative externality imposed by the individual's consumption decision. In either case (the negative externality on the production side of the model or the negative externality on the consumption side of the model), the market produces too much of the good when the externality is not accounted for in the market. Figure 17.6 illustrates these two examples. Imposition of the appropriate Pigouvian tax will correct the market outcome and result in the market producing the optimal amount of the good where the marginal social benefit from consuming the last unit of the good is equal to the marginal social cost of producing the last unit of the good.

Figure 17.6

In the graphs below, MSC is the marginal social cost of production, Supply is the marginal private cost of production, MSB is the marginal social benefit of consumption, Demand is the marginal private benefit of consumption, Q_{mkt} is the quantity produced by the market, Q_{opt} is the optimal quantity to produce, P_{mkt} is the market-determined price, and $P_{opt-tax}$ is the optimal price. $P_{opt-tax}$ includes the Pigouvian tax.

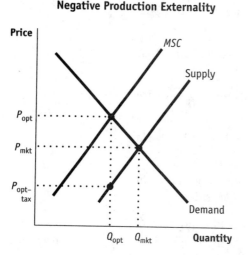

Negative Production Externality

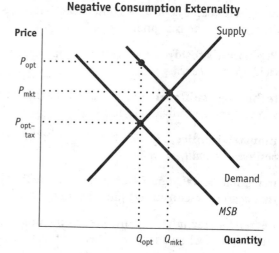

Negative Consumption Externality

Tip #3.   Positive externalities can occur on the production or the consumption side of the model of supply and demand. For example, when a producer produces a good whose production generates technology spillovers and the producer does not take into account the benefit of this technology spillover on the rest of the economy, then there is a positive externality on the production or cost side of the market. This implies that the producer's supply curve does not represent the true societal costs of producing the good. Alternatively, a consumer can engage in behaviors that inflict a positive benefit on others: for instance, the decision to maintain the exterior of one's house results in positive externalities with regard to the property values for neighboring properties. In this case, the demand curve for the individual does not take into account the positive externality created by the individual's consumption decision. In either case (the positive externality on the production side of the model or the positive externality on the consumption side of the model), the market produces too little of the good when the externality is not accounted for in the market. Figure 17.7 illustrates these two examples. Imposition of the appropriate Pigouvian subsidy will correct the market outcome and result in the market producing the optimal amount of the good where the marginal social benefit from consuming the last unit of the good is equal to the marginal social cost of producing the last unit of the good.

Figure 17.7

In the graphs below, *MSC* is the marginal social cost of production, Supply is the marginal private cost of production, *MSB* is the marginal social benefit of consumption, Demand is the marginal private benefit of comsumption, Q_{mkt} is the quantity produced by the market, Q_{opt} is the optimal quantity to produce, P_{mkt} is the market-determined price, and $P_{opt\text{-}subsidy}$ is the optimal price. $P_{opt\text{-}subsidy}$ includes the Pigouvian subsidy.

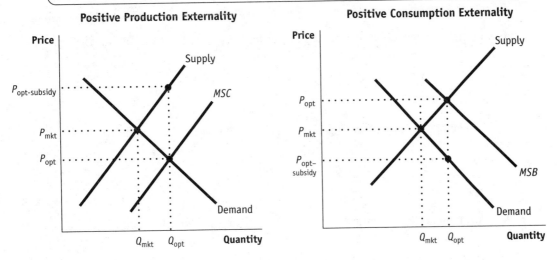

Problems and Exercises

1.   Classify each of the following situations as positive or negative externalities, then identify whether the externality occurs on the demand or consumption side of the model, or on the supply or production side of the model.

   a.   A manufacturing plant spews toxic gas into the environment as a by-product of its production of furniture.

b. A group of teenagers gather on Saturday to play loud music and congregate in a downtown park, making it difficult for other people in the town to enjoy the park.

c. A property owner fills his front yard with trash and old tires.

d. A company develops a new technology for producing its product, and the new technology can potentially help other companies produce more efficiently.

e. School-age children in a community do not get immunized prior to attending school.

f. A neighbor decorates the outside of her house with a tasteful holiday display.

g. A neighbor keeps his barking dog outside his house all day and all night.

h. Commercial fishermen catch too many fish and deplete the stock of fish.

2. What is a side effect? What does it mean when a market fails to take into account a side effect? What can you say about the level of production of the good in a market where there are side effects?

3. Suppose the following table provides information about the marginal social benefit of pollution and the marginal social cost of pollution for a society. Assume that both the marginal social benefit of pollution and the marginal social cost of pollution are linear relationships.

Quantity of pollution emissions (tons)	Marginal social benefit of pollution	Marginal social cost of pollution
0	$1,000	$ 0
2,000	800	133.3
4,000	600	266.7
6,000	400	400
8,000	200	533.3
10,000	0	666.7

a. What is the marginal social benefit from emitting pollution?

b. What is the marginal social cost of emitting pollution?

c. When 3,000 tons of pollution emissions are emitted, what is the marginal social benefit of this pollution? What is the marginal social cost of this level of pollution emissions? Is this an efficient level of pollution emissions for this society? Explain your answer.

d. When 9,000 tons of pollution emissions are emitted, what is the marginal social benefit of this pollution? What is the marginal social cost of this level of pollution emissions? Is this an efficient level of pollution emissions for this society? Explain your answer.

e. What is the efficient level of pollution emissions for this society?

4. Use the information given in problem 3 to answer this set of questions.

a. Draw a graph of the marginal social benefit (*MSB*) of pollution and the marginal social cost (*MSC*) of pollution where *MSB* and *MSC* are measured on the vertical axis and the quantity of pollution emissions is measured on the horizontal axis.

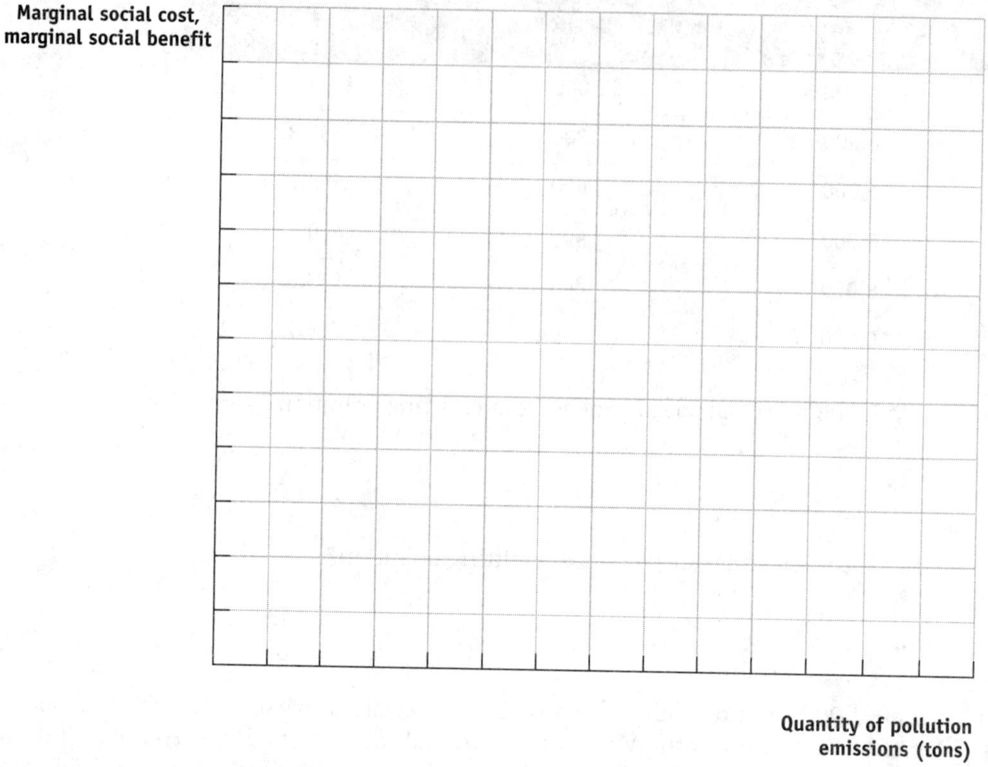

Marginal social cost, marginal social benefit (vertical axis)

Quantity of pollution emissions (tons) (horizontal axis)

b. Label the socially optimal amount of pollution emissions in the graph you drew in part (a).

c. Will the socially optimal amount of pollution be produced in this market if there is no government intervention? Explain your answer.

5. Suppose there are just two firms in Smalltown and both of these firms emit pollution as part of their productive process. Firm A's marginal social benefit from pollution is given by the equation $MSB = 100 - Q$, while firm B's marginal social benefit from pollution is given by the equation $MSB = 50 - 0.5Q$, where Q is the quantity of pollution emissions measured in tons.

a. Draw a graph representing the marginal social benefit of pollution emissions for firm A and firm B.

Marginal social benefit

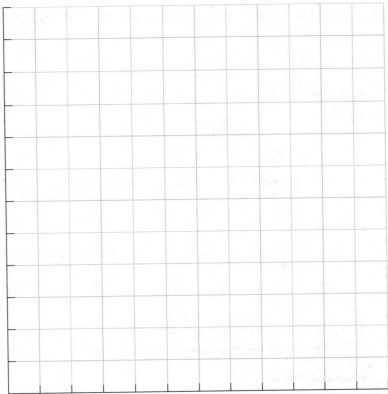

Quantity of pollution emissions (tons)

b. Suppose the government in Smalltown decides to impose an emissions standard of 55 tons for every firm producing in Smalltown. How much of a reduction in pollution emissions will occur because of the imposition of this standard? Assume that prior to the emissions standard, firms produced the level of pollution emissions at which their marginal social benefit equaled $0.

c. What is the marginal social benefit to firm A of the last ton of pollution it emits? What is the marginal social benefit to firm B of the last ton of pollution it emits?

d. Is this an efficient method for reducing pollution emissions by this amount? Explain your answer.

6. Use the information given in problem 5 to answer this set of questions. Suppose that the government, instead of an emissions standard, imposes a tax on emissions of $30 per ton.

    a. What will be the reduction in pollution emissions by firm A with the imposition of this tax?

    b. What will be the reduction in pollution emissions by firm B with the imposition of this tax?

    c. What will be the total reduction in pollution emissions with this tax?

    d. Is this an efficient method for reducing pollution emissions by this amount? Explain your answer.

    e. Draw a graph illustrating this tax. Identify firm A's and firm B's marginal social benefit from pollution emissions.

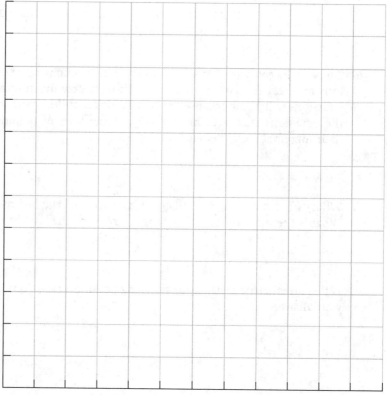

Marginal social benefit

Quantity of pollution
emissions (tons)

7. Joan loves dogs and decides that she is going to buy a dog. She analyzes the benefit she will get from owning a dog and values the benefit of owning a dog at $500. Joan's next-door neighbor loathes dogs and is vehemently opposed to dogs being in the neighborhood. This neighbor, Mike, views the cost of an additional dog in the neighborhood as being $800. According to the Coase theorem, is it possible for Joan and Mike to amicably resolve this dilemma about the dog ownership? In your answer, identify how this conflict can be resolved provided that the rights to dog ownership are well defined. Also, in your answer consider how it does not matter who owns the rights to dog ownership provided that these rights are well defined.

8. A recent article reports that drunken driving has risen in communities that have imposed smoking bans in their bars and taverns. The gist of the problem is that smokers who also drink are now driving longer distances to get to bars that allow them to smoke while they are drinking. Does the decision to impose a smoking ban on the bars and taverns in the community create an externality? What do you think motivated policymakers to impose this smoking ban?

9. Suppose the consumption of a good generates substantial external benefits due to the presence of side effects. Suppose the government wishes to help the market generate the socially optimal consumption of this good. Will the market by itself generate the socially optimal amount of this good? Explain your answer. What type of policy or policies might the government engage in to meet this goal?

10. Suppose the demand for computer software engineers in Micronesia can be expressed as $Q = 100 - 0.001P$, where Q is the number of computer software engineers demanded and P is the annual salary per computer software engineer. Suppose that the supply of computer software engineers in Micronesia can be expressed as $P = 4,000Q$. Furthermore, suppose that in the market for computer software engineers there are substantial technology spillovers equal to $20,000 per computer software engineer. Currently, the market for computer software engineers does not take into account these technological spillovers.

a. What is the equilibrium quantity of computer software engineers in Micronesia, and what is the annual salary per computer software engineer?

b. Is the quantity of computer software engineers you found in part (a) the socially optimal quantity of computer software engineers for Micronesia? Explain your answer.

c. Draw a graph of the market for computer software engineers. In your graph draw a curve that represents the marginal private benefits (demand), a curve that represents the marginal social benefit (*MSB*), and a curve that represents supply. Identify the market quantity and market price as well as the socially optimal quantity and price.

Price of computer
software engineers

Quantity of computer
software engineers

d. What is the optimal quantity of computer software engineers for Micronesia? Explain why you have chosen this quantity as the optimal quantity.

e. What policy could the government enact to enable Micronesia to produce this optimal quantity?

f. Graph the policy you described in part (e) on the graph below, and label this graph carefully and completely.

Price of computer software engineers

Quantity of computer software engineers

11. The following table is meant to summarize the market level of production for various situations that might occur due to the presence of externalities. In the table, *MSC* refers to the marginal social cost of production, Supply refers to the marginal private cost of production, *MSB* refers to the marginal social benefit from consuming the good, and Demand refers to the marginal private benefit from consuming the good. Read each scenario and then decide whether the market produces the socially optimal amount of the good, too much of the good, or too little of the good. Fill in the second column with the relevant description of the market's production decision.

Situation	Market Produces
Demand = *MSB* and Supply = *MSC*	
Demand > *MSB* and Supply = *MSC*	
Demand < *MSB* and Supply = *MSC*	
Demand = *MSB* and Supply < *MSC*	
Demand = *MSB* and Supply > *MSC*	

12. In the 1980s, there were two competing technologies for watching movies at home. The Beta system and the VHS system competed with one another for this particular market. Eventually, the VHS system became the dominant system, and those individuals who had purchased the Beta system found it difficult to find movies using this technology to show at home.

   a. Is there an externality issue lying behind this story? If so, what kind of externality issue is it?

   b. How would the term *positive feedback* apply to this situation?

   c. Describe how this competition for the market for movies shown at home ultimately illustrates a network externality.

▮ BEFORE YOU TAKE THE TEST

Chapter Review Questions

1. The optimal amount of pollution is
   a. the amount of pollution where the marginal social benefit of the pollution exceeds the marginal social cost of the pollution.
   b. zero units of pollution, since pollution is harmful to people.
   c. the amount of pollution where the marginal social benefit of the pollution is less than the marginal social cost of the pollution.
   d. the amount of pollution where the marginal social benefit of the pollution equals the marginal social cost of the pollution.

2. The gain to society of an additional unit of pollution is best measured by
   a. an emissions tax.
   b. an emissions standard.
   c. the marginal social benefit of pollution.
   d. the socially optimal quantity of pollution.

Use the figure below to answer the next three questions.

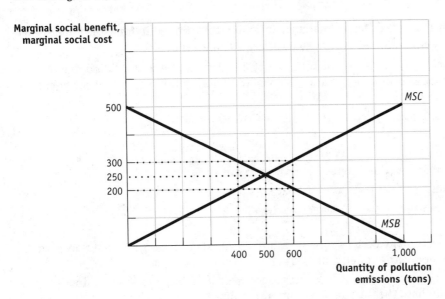

3. The socially optimal amount of pollution emissions in the above graph is
   a. 400 tons.
   b. 500 tons.
   c. 600 tons.

4. When 400 tons of pollution are emitted,
   a. the marginal social cost of pollution is less than the marginal social benefit of pollution.
   b. this economy would be better off producing more pollution emissions.
   c. this economy would be worse off producing more pollution emissions.
   d. Answers (a) and (b) are true.
   e. Answers (a) and (c) are true.

5. What is the appropriate emissions standard for this economy if there is only one producer in the economy and the goal is to produce the efficient level of pollution emissions?

   a. 400 tons of emissions

   b. 500 tons of emissions

   c. 600 tons of emissions

   d. 0 tons of emissions

6. A government wants to enact a policy that will lead to a reduction in pollution emissions. One policy entails establishing an emissions standard, and another policy entails implementation of an emissions tax. Which of the following statements is true?

   I. An emissions standard and an emissions tax are equally efficient methods for reducing pollution emissions.

   II. An emissions standard ensures that the marginal social benefit of pollution is equal for all sources of pollution.

   III. An emissions tax does not ensure that the marginal social benefit of pollution is equal for all sources of pollution.

   a. Statement I is true.

   b. Statements I and II are true.

   c. Statements I and III are true.

   d. Statements I, II, and III are true.

   e. None of the above statements are true.

7. When two firms have different marginal social benefit from pollution, this implies that

   a. an equal reduction in pollution by both firms is not efficient.

   b. one firm can reduce its level of pollution by a larger amount and still find that its marginal social benefit of pollution is equal to the other firm's marginal social benefit of pollution.

   c. an emissions tax is more efficient than an emissions standard.

   d. All of the above statements are true.

8. Taxes that are designed to reduce external costs are known as

   a. excise taxes.   c. Pigouvian taxes.

   b. income taxes.   d. emissions taxes.

9. Suppose a government decides to issue a limited number of tradable pollution permits. Which of the following statements is true?

   a. Firms that can easily and at low cost reduce their level of pollution will find it beneficial to purchase these tradable pollution permits.

   b. When the government issues these tradable pollution permits, it effectively creates a market for the right to pollute.

   c. Firms that sell their tradable pollution permits do not fully understand the costs they will incur when they try to reduce the level of pollution they create.

   d. None of the above statements are true.

10. Which of the following tools is likely to encourage firms to find less-polluting technology?

   a. Emissions standards

   b. Emissions taxes

   c. Tradable pollution permits

   d. All of the above will create incentives for firms to find less-polluting technology.

   e. Emissions taxes and tradable pollution permits will create incentives for firms to find less-polluting technology.

11. Which of the following statements is true?
    a. In contrast to the cost of a negative externality like pollution, the benefit from a positive externality is easier to measure, since people like to reveal the amount of positive benefits they receive from different activities.
    b. The benefit from a positive externality is difficult to measure, since these benefits cannot be directly observed.

12. When the consumption of a good generates positive external benefits, the market tends to produce
    a. too much of the good, since there are positive external benefits from the consumption of the good.
    b. too little of the good, since the market does not take into account the positive external benefits from the consumption of the good.

13. Joe really does not enjoy school and is thinking about dropping out this spring. Joe's consumption of formal education is likely to
    a. be the efficient amount of education, since Joe knows best the level of benefit he receives from attending school.
    b. be at too high a level, since Joe has always been an indifferent student and a student who has rarely been engaged in getting an education.
    c. be at too low a level, since Joe only considers his private benefits from getting an education and not the social benefits that society receives when he gets an education.
    d. reflect his family's benefit from his getting an education, and his family thinks they will get a greater benefit if Joe drops out and gets a job. From his family's perspective, this would be an efficient outcome.

Use the following information to answer the next three questions.

Residents of Smalltown recognize that there are private benefits to exercise, and they estimate that the marginal private benefits from exercise can be represented by the demand curve $P = 100 - 0.05Q$, where P measures the marginal private benefit and Q is hours of exercise per year. Exercise also generates positive external benefits for the community because it reduces health care costs, lowers the obesity rate, and results in a more energetic and engaged community. The marginal external benefit from a unit of exercise is estimated to have a value of $10 per hour of exercise. The supply curve for exercise can be represented by the equation $P = 0.05Q$, where P measures the marginal private cost of exercise and Q is hours of exercise per year.

14. The market for exercise will not include the marginal social benefits from exercise without some type of intervention. How many hours of exercise per year will be provided by the market, and what is the price demanders are willing to pay for each unit of exercise consumed?
    a. 0 hours of exercise; $100
    b. 50 hours of exercise; $1,000
    c. 1,000 hours of exercise; $50
    d. 2,000 hours of exercise; $0

15. What is the socially optimal amount of exercise per year for Smalltown?
    a. 0 hours of exercise
    b. 1,000 hours of exercise
    c. 1,100 hours of exercise
    d. 2,000 hours of exercise

16. Smalltown decides it is important for the community to consume the socially optimal amount of exercise. Smalltown therefore decides to enact a policy of
   a. subsidizing everyone who exercises with a payment of $10 per hour of exercise.
   b. taxing everyone who exercises with a tax payment of $10 per hour of exercise.
   c. mandating that everyone exercise an additional 10 hours per year.
   d. reducing the price of each hour of exercise by $20.

17. Policymakers decide they wish to encourage the consumption of an activity that generates positive externalities. Which of the following statements is true?
   I. An excise tax on each unit of the good consumed helps the policymaker achieve the socially optimal amount of consumption of this good.
   II. A subsidy per unit of the good consumed helps the policymaker achieve the socially optimal amount of consumption of this good.
   III. Intervention in this market by the policymaker results in a socially less-optimal outcome for this market, since government intervention in any market results in a deadweight loss.
   a. Statement I is true.
   b. Statement II is true.
   c. Statement III is true.
   d. None of the above statements are true given this situation.

18. Industrial policy is often advocated whenever there are
   a. negative externalities arising from the consumption of a good.
   b. negative externalities arising from the production of a good.
   c. technological spillovers in a market.
   d. national security issues present with regard to the production of a good.

Answer the next three questions based on the following diagram of the market for bottled water that comes from aquifers deep underground. In the production of this product, the level of water in these aquifers is drawn down at a rate faster than the water can be replenished. This action results in a negative externality on the nearby communities that depend on these aquifers for their water, since the producers of the bottled water do not consider the effect of their production on the community's water source. In the graph below, Supply represents the marginal private cost of producing the good, MSC represents the marginal social cost (the external as well as private cost) of producing the good, and Demand represents the marginal social benefit from consuming the good. Assume that the externality per unit of the good produced is a constant amount per unit of bottled water.

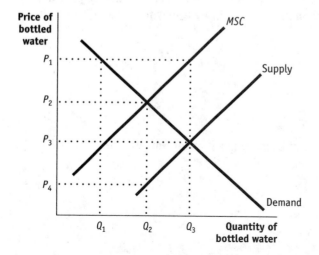

19. Without government intervention in this market, the market will provide _____ bottles of bottled water at a price of _____ per bottle.
    a. Q_1; P_1
    b. Q_2; P_2
    c. Q_2: P_4
    d. Q_3; P_3

20. What is the socially optimal level of output for this market?
    a. Q_1
    b. Q_2
    c. Q_3

21. At the market-determined level of production in the above market, the deadweight loss due to the negative externality can be expressed as the area
    a. $(1/2)(P_1 - P_3)Q_3$.
    b. $(1/2)(P_2 - P_4)(Q_3 - Q_2)$.
    c. $(1/2)(P_2 - P_4)Q_2$.
    d. $(1/2)P_2(Q_3 - Q_2)$.

22. A network externality is a situation
    a. in which the value of a good to the consumer is dependent on how many other people also consume the same type of good.
    b. that often arises in the markets for transportation and communication.
    c. in which the marginal benefit from the consumption of the good depends on the number of other individuals who also use the good.
    d. Answers (a), (b), and (c) are all true statements.

23. A community is debating the construction of several bike paths in the community. These bike paths would be separate from the roadway system in the community. As the community creates more bike paths linking different parts of the city, they expect this will lead to
    a. negative externalities, as more and more people on bikes interfere with other forms of transportation.
    b. positive feedback, due to the network externalities that will come from more and more people being able to move around the community efficiently on the bike paths.
    c. more people deciding to bike to different locations, since the bike paths will make this form of transportation both safer and more convenient.
    d. Answers (b) and (c) are both true.

ANSWER KEY

Answers to Problems and Exercises

1. **a.** This is a negative production externality.

    b. This is a negative consumption externality.

    c. This is a negative consumption externality.

    d. This is a positive production externality.

    e. This is a negative consumption externality.

    f. This is a positive consumption externality.

    g. This is a negative consumption externality.

    h. This is a negative production externality.

2. A side effect is a situation in which the market fails to take into account a cost or a benefit from some action. This results in the market failing to produce the right amount of the good, because the market either does not correctly measure the cost to society of producing the good or the benefit to society of consuming the good. When side effects are present in a market, this implies that the market produces either too much of the good (the situation when the side effect is a hidden cost) or too little of the good (the situation when the side effect is a hidden benefit).

3. **a.** The marginal social benefit from emitting pollution is the measure of the additional benefit a society gets from one more ton of pollution. It can be measured in terms of the cost that must be incurred by a society in order to not produce this ton of pollution: to produce less pollution, a society must use some of its scarce resources that could have been used to produce other goods and services. The marginal benefit of emitting pollution is the amount of money a society would save if it were allowed to emit an additional ton of pollution.

    b. The marginal social cost of emitting pollution is equal to the sum of the highest willingness to pay among all members of this society to avoid that ton of pollution. The marginal social cost of emitting pollution measures the true marginal cost of the pollution. Another way of expressing the marginal social cost of pollution is that this measures the additional cost imposed on all of the society of an additional ton of pollution.

    c. Since this level of pollution emissions is not listed in the table, you have to extrapolate from the numbers in the table or write an equation for the marginal social benefit of pollution and the marginal social cost of pollution. Extrapolating from the table, you can see that the marginal social benefit of 2,000 tons of pollution is $800 per ton, and the marginal social benefit of 4,000 tons of pollution is $600 per ton: you could infer that the marginal social benefit of 3,000 tons of pollution is therefore $700 per ton. Or you write the equation for the marginal social benefit of pollution as $MSB = 1{,}000 - 0.1Q$, where MSB is the marginal social benefit of pollution and Q is the quantity of pollution emissions. Then, substituting 3,000 into the equation for Q, MSB is equal to $700 per ton of pollution emissions. Using a similar technique for the marginal social cost of pollution, $MSC = (1/15)Q$, where MSC is the marginal social cost of pollution emissions. When Q equals 3,000, MSC equals $200 per ton of pollution emissions. This is not an efficient level of pollution emissions since the marginal social benefit is greater than the marginal social cost: too little pollution emissions are being produced at this level, since the marginal social benefit of more pollution emissions is greater than the marginal social cost of pollution emissions.

d. Using the equations found in part (c), the marginal social benefit of 9,000 tons of pollution emissions is equal to $100 per ton of pollution emissions, while the marginal social cost of 9,000 tons of pollution emissions is equal to $600 per ton of pollution emissions. This is not an efficient level of pollution emissions since the marginal social benefit is less than the marginal social cost: too much pollution emissions are occurring in this society.

e. The efficient level of pollution emissions for this society is the level where the marginal social benefit is equal to the marginal social cost. This occurs at 6,000 tons of pollution emissions where the marginal social benefit and the marginal social cost are both $400 per ton of pollution emissions.

4. a, b

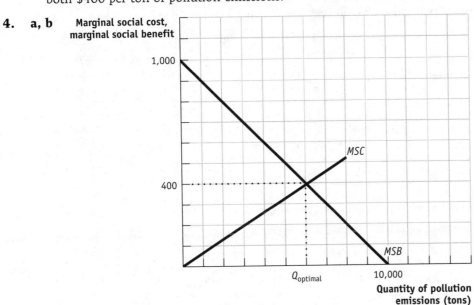

c. No, the optimal level of pollution emissions will not be produced in this economy without government intervention since producers do not have any incentive to take into account the costs of pollution that they impose on other people.

5. a.

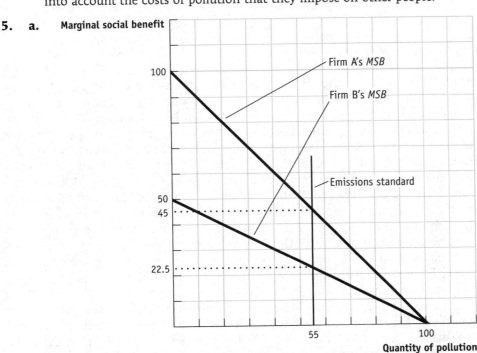

b. Each firm will reduce its emissions by 45 tons, for a total of 90 tons.

c. The marginal social benefit for firm A is $45, and the marginal social benefit for firm B is $22.50.

d. No, this is not efficient since the marginal social benefit of pollution emissions reduction is not equivalent across all the firms in the economy.

6. **a.** Firm A will reduce pollution emissions by 30 units.

b. Firm B will reduce pollution emissions by 60 units.

c. The total reduction in pollution emissions will be 90 units (note that this is the same level of pollution reduction achieved with the emissions standard in problem 5).

d. This is an efficient method for reducing pollution emissions since each firm's marginal social benefit of pollution is the same for the last unit of pollution they emit.

e.

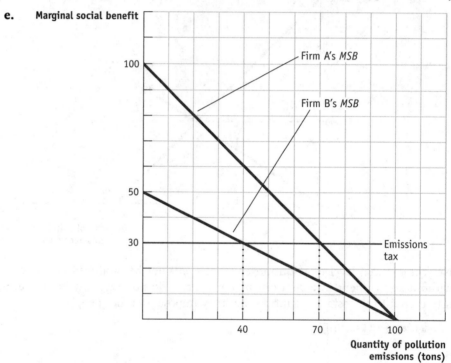

7. To answer this question, we first have to look at the requirements for the Coase theorem: for an externality situation to be resolved by the two transacting parties, the transaction cost must not be too high and the property rights must be well defined. The two neighbors can easily talk to one another, and we can start by assigning the property rights to dog ownership to the potential dog owner. This would mean that Joan has the right to purchase a dog. But Mike could approach Joan and tell her that he is willing to compensate her an amount sufficient to persuade her not to purchase the dog. Mike can offer Joan any amount greater than $500 but less than $800, and both Joan and Mike will be better off. Given Joan's marginal benefit of owning the dog and Mike's marginal cost of another dog in the neighborhood, the two parties, if they are free to discuss this transaction at reasonable cost, will decide that Joan will not purchase the dog and instead will receive compensation for forgoing the consumption of a canine. If the property rights to dog ownership rest with Mike and he therefore gets to decide whether or not a neighbor gets to own a dog, we get the same result. Joan is only willing to pay Mike up to $500 for the right to buy the dog, and since Mike must receive at least $800 to be willing to have a dog in the neighborhood, Joan will not purchase the dog. The thrust of the Coase theorem is that externality issues can be resolved if the parties are well identified, the transaction costs are not high, and the property rights are well defined.

8. This is quite ironic in that the smoking ban was likely motivated by a desire to reduce the negative externality of secondhand smoke in bars and taverns. The policymakers considered the situation of smoking in the bar and identified that this behavior created a cost that was imposed on nonsmokers. By imposing this smoking ban, they would eliminate this side effect. However, in imposing the smoking ban they did not consider how smokers might react. If smokers view smoking as a highly important complement to their bar experience, they may indeed drive longer distances to be able to both smoke and drink. Then, when they get back on the road they impose a side effect, or negative externality, on others in the form of their drunk driving. Which side effect is more costly to society and to the third parties impacted by these drinkers who also smoke is an interesting question!

9. When the consumption of a good generates external benefits, the good is underproduced in the market, since the positive side effects of the consumption of the good are not included in the market's determination of the equilibrium quantity of the good. The government needs to pursue policies that result in higher consumption of the good, which in turn affect the quantity of the side effect produced. The government can achieve this result by targeting the activity, or consumption of the good, by offering subsidies to consumers to encourage a higher level of consumption.

10. **a.** The equilibrium quantity in the market is where the quantity demanded equals the quantity supplied, or where $100,000 - 1,000Q = 4,000Q$. Solving this equation, Q equals 20 computer software engineers. The annual salary for a computer software engineer can be found by using either the demand or the supply curve, and substituting in 20 for the quantity. Thus, the annual salary for a computer software engineer is $80,000.

b. The quantity found in part (a) is not the socially optimal amount of computer software engineers, since the market does not take into account the side effects of the positive externality that arises from the technology spillover. The market quantity equates demand and supply, instead of equating the marginal social benefit to the marginal social cost.

c.

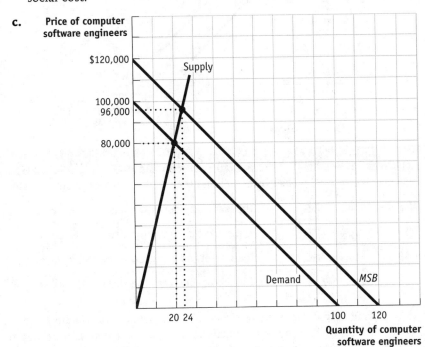

d. The optimal quantity of computer software engineers is where the marginal social benefit equals the marginal social cost. To find this quantity, first write an equation that expresses the marginal social benefit. This equation is $P = 120,000 - 1,000Q$ since the marginal social benefit curve has the same slope as the market demand curve but a y-intercept of 120,000 instead of 100,000. Setting the marginal social benefit curve equal to the supply curve yields the following: $120,000 - 1,000Q = 4,000Q$ or $Q = 24$. When there is an external benefit from the consumption of the good, too few units of the good are consumed in the market: in this case, the optimal quantity of computer software engineers is 24 and not the market-determined quantity of 20 engineers.

e. The government could subsidize the demanders of computer software engineers so that they would effectively view the market demand curve for computer software engineers as being $P = 120,000 - 1,000Q$. This would entail paying a subsidy of $20,000 for every computer software engineer demanded. With this subsidy the government would effectively internalize the positive externality.

f.

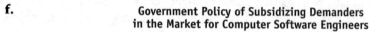

Government Policy of Subsidizing Demanders in the Market for Computer Software Engineers

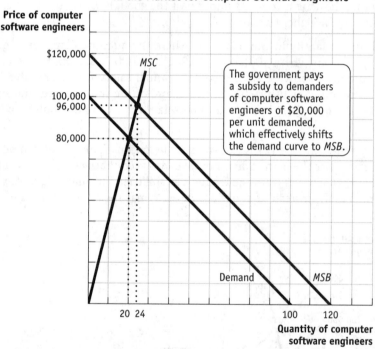

The government pays a subsidy to demanders of computer software engineers of $20,000 per unit demanded, which effectively shifts the demand curve to *MSB*.

11.

Situation	Market Produces
Demand = *MSB* and Supply = *MSC*	The market produces the socially optimal amount of the good.
Demand > *MSB* and Supply = *MSC*	The market produces too much of the good.
Demand < *MSB* and Supply = *MSC*	The market produces too little of the good.
Demand = *MSB* and Supply < *MSC*	The market produces too much of the good.
Demand = *MSB* and Supply > *MSC*	The market produces too little of the good.

12. a. The externality issue is that the value of either of these systems for watching movies at home depends on how many other people have bought a particular system. For example, as more and more people purchase the VHS system, video stores are likely to stock more movies recorded with this system, and owners of the VHS system find that they have more movie choices. The system that gets more converts benefits from this wider usage.

b. *Positive feedback* refers to the idea that as more people purchase a product, other people are more likely to purchase the product. In this example, as more people purchased the VHS system, other people decided to adopt this technology for their own movie viewing: the value of the VHS system rose as more people purchased the system.

c. There is a network externality at play in this example, since as the network of users expands, the marginal benefit for each user of the good increases. This ultimately leads to one of the technologies becoming the dominant technology, which effectively drives the other technology out of the market.

Answers to Chapter Review Questions

1. **Answer d.** When the marginal social benefit of pollution is greater than the marginal social cost of pollution, too little pollution is being produced. When the marginal social benefit of pollution is less than the marginal social cost of pollution, too much pollution is being produced. It is optimal to produce the amount of pollution where the marginal social benefit of the pollution equals the marginal social cost of the pollution. Zero units of pollution would only be optimal if the marginal social benefit of the pollution is equal to $0.

2. **Answer c.** This is just the definition of the marginal social benefit of pollution.

3. **Answer b.** The socially optimal amount of pollution emissions is the amount of pollution where the marginal social benefit from the pollution equals the marginal social cost of the pollution.

4. **Answer d.** The socially optimal amount of pollution emissions is 500 tons where the marginal social benefit of pollution equals the marginal social cost of pollution. At 400 tons, the marginal social benefit of pollution equals $300 per ton, while the marginal social cost of this pollution equals $200 per ton. This society would be better off producing more pollution emissions.

5. **Answer b.** The socially optimal amount of pollution emissions is 500 tons of emissions.

6. **Answer e.** An emissions standard is not as efficient as an emissions tax because it does not ensure that the marginal social benefit of pollution is equal for all sources of pollution. In contrast, an emissions tax is a tax that results in the marginal benefit of pollution being equal across all sources of pollution.

7. **Answer d.** When two firms have different marginal social benefit from pollution curves, this tells us that the marginal social benefit from reducing pollution by a set amount is different between the two firms. It is therefore more efficient to have the firms reduce pollution by different amounts until the marginal social benefit of pollution is the same for both firms. An emissions standard requires that both firms reduce pollution by an equal amount without regard to the marginal social benefit of pollution.

8. **Answer c.** This is a definitional question. Pigou, an economist, emphasized that the appropriate tax could eliminate the hidden costs imposed by negative externalities.

9. **Answer b.** Firms will sell their permits if it is easy and inexpensive for them to reduce their pollution, since the permits are more valuable to firms that find the cost of reducing their level of pollution high. Firms that sell their pollution permits understand and have analyzed the costs associated with pollution reduction and have determined that they are better off selling the permits rather than using the permits. The government effectively decides what level of pollution it wants, and then creates a market for the right to pollute within this limit.

10. **Answer e.** Emissions standards are applied uniformly across all producers and therefore do not offer any incentive for producers to find new technology to reduce their pollution levels. In contrast, emissions taxes and tradable pollution permits provide a system of

incentives that rewards those firms that find ways to reduce their levels of pollution or find cost-effective methods for pollution reduction.

11. **Answer b.** The positive benefit from the externality cannot be directly observed and measured, while it is possible to measure the external costs due to a negative externality such as pollution.

12. **Answer b.** When a good produces positive external benefits, the market does not include these benefits and therefore tends to undervalue the benefits from the consumption of the good. The market therefore results in too little of the good being produced.

13. **Answer c.** Joe's education reaps benefits not only for Joe and his family, but also for society. Joe will likely be able to better provide for himself with more education; he is likely to be a more productive member of society when he gets more education; and he will likely contribute more to society as a better educated individual. Joe's education has both private and social benefits, but Joe is likely to consider only the private benefits and therefore select too low a level of education; from an efficiency standpoint the optimal amount of education is where the marginal social benefit of the education is equated to the marginal social cost of the education.

14. **Answer c.** To find the number of hours of exercise consumed in this market, set the demand curve equal to the supply curve: $100 - 0.05Q = 0.05Q$. This results in $Q = 1,000$ hours of exercise with price equal to $50.

15. **Answer c.** The socially optimal amount of exercise is the amount of exercise where MSB = Supply (since there are no marginal social costs to include in this problem). Thus, to solve this question you must find the marginal social benefit of exercise, which is equal to the demand curve plus the marginal external benefit. The marginal external benefit is $10 per unit, so this means that the MSB curve can be expressed as $MSB = 110 - 0.05Q$. Setting this equation equal to the supply curve yields $110 - 0.05Q = 0.05Q$. Thus, the socially optimal amount of exercise is 1,100 hours of exercise.

16. **Answer a.** When Smalltown subsidizes the consumption of exercise by an amount equal to the social benefit of the additional hour of exercise, it effectively causes the demand curve for exercise to shift to the right, resulting in more hours of exercise being demanded at every price. With a subsidy of $10 per hour of exercise, the subsidy exactly equals the marginal social benefit of an hour of exercise, and thus this subsidy results in the residents of Smalltown consuming the socially optimal amount of exercise.

17. **Answer b.** When there is a positive externality, the government can encourage the consumption of the good by legislating a subsidy for the consumption of the good. Without the subsidy too little of the good is consumed, and therefore the government intervention in this market can move the market closer to the socially optimal outcome.

18. **Answer c.** Industrial policy refers to pursuing a policy that supports those industries that are deemed to yield positive externalities. Industrial policy takes two general forms: subsidization of the industry, and the creation of barriers to international competition through trade restrictions. Industrial policy is advocated when there are positive externalities arising from the production of the good. In particular, these positive externalities often take the form of technology spillovers, which refers to the external benefits that arise from the creation of knowledge.

19. **Answer d.** The market without intervention will provide the amount of bottled water where Supply = Demand, or Q_3 units at a price of P_3.

20. **Answer b.** The socially optimal level of output for this market is where MSC = Demand for the last unit produced, which occurs when the quantity is Q_2.

21. **Answer b.** The deadweight loss is the area that represents the efficiency loss due to the externality. When the market produces Q_3 units of the good, the marginal social cost of the last unit is greater than the marginal social benefit from the last unit. This difference can be represented by the distance $(P_1 - P_3)$ or by the distance $(P_2 - P_4)$ since the externality per unit of the good produced is assumed to be constant. The market produces Q_3 units instead of the socially optimal Q_2 units, so the deadweight loss can be calculated as $(1/2)(P_2 - P_4)(Q_3 - Q_2)$.

22. **Answer d.** These statements are all definitional: network externalities often arise in transportation and communication systems, since these systems become more effective when more people use the particular system. This implies that one person's benefit from consuming an additional unit of the good is impacted by the consumption decisions of other people with regard to this good.

23. **Answer d.** Since the bike paths are separate from the roadway system, this will likely not create negative externalities related to the bikes interfering with other forms of transportation. But as more and more miles of bike paths are created, this will make transportation by bicycle more feasible and will lead to positive feedback from the network effects.

chapter 18

Public Goods and Common Resources

BEFORE YOU READ THE CHAPTER

Summary

This chapter explores two characteristics, the property of rivalness and the property of excludability, that are key to determining whether or not a market can provide the efficient level of the good. The chapter uses these characteristics to explore the problems presented by public goods, common resources, and artificially scarce goods. The chapter also considers the types of government intervention in the production and consumption of these goods that can make society better off, and why it is difficult for the government to determine the right level of intervention when the good is a public good, or when the production or consumption of the good involves the use of common resources.

Chapter Objectives

Objective #1. The characteristics of a good determine whether or not the market can provide the good efficiently. When a good is excludable and rival, the market can provide the good efficiently. A good is excludable when suppliers of the good can prevent people who do not pay for the good from consuming the good. Since the good is excludable, suppliers can charge consumers of the good a price, which gives the producers an incentive to supply the good. A good is rival when a person's consumption of the good means that no other consumer can consume that same unit of the good. Since the good is rival this implies that it is efficient for consumers to pay a positive price equal to the good's marginal cost of production. Private goods are both excludable and rival, and hence, the market provides the efficient quantity of a private good.

Objective #2. A public good is a good that benefits many people whether or not they have paid for it and whose benefits to an individual are not affected by how many other people are consuming the good. Thus, a public good is nonrival, because one consumer's consumption of the good does not change the level of benefits available to other consumers of the good, and it is nonexcludable, since an individual can consume the good once it is produced whether or not they have paid for the good. These two differences result in the market being unable to provide the efficient amount of the good. Because public goods are nonexcludable they suffer from the free-rider problem: this free-rider problem results in firms being unwilling to produce the good since they know it will be possible for consumers to consume the good without paying for it once the good is produced. Because public goods are nonrival in consumption it is inefficient to charge people for consuming these goods, since the marginal cost of another person consuming the good is zero.

Objective #3.   A common resource is a good that many people consume whether or not they have paid for the good and whose consumption by each person reduces the amount of the good available to other people. The common resource is, thus, nonexcludable but rival in consumption since people can consume the good even though they have not paid for it, but their consumption of the good reduces the amount of the good available to others. Common resources are subject to overuse by individuals because individuals will continue to consume units of the good until their marginal benefit from consumption of the common resource is equal to zero. In choosing this level of consumption, individuals ignore the cost their actions inflict on society. Common resources thus present a problem of a negative externality in which individuals consume an inefficiently high amount of the good because they ignore, or fail to internalize, the external costs they impose on other members of society. In the case of a common resource, society must intervene in the market to find a way to get individual users of the resource to take into account the costs they impose on others. This intervention could be in the form of a Pigouvian tax, a system of tradable licenses for the use of the common resource, or through the assignment of property rights to the common resources. This last intervention, the assignment of property rights, gives the holder of the property rights the ability to limit the use of the common resource and, thus, prevent the overuse of this resource.

Objective #4.   Artificially scarce goods are those goods that are excludable but nonrival in consumption. These are goods that must be paid for in order for the consumer to consume the good but whose consumption does not diminish the ability of other consumers to consume the same unit of the good. Since the artificially scarce good is nonrival in consumption, the marginal cost of an individual's consumption is zero. When the supplier charges a price for this good, the price is therefore greater than the individual's marginal cost, which results in too few units of the good being consumed. The case of the artificially scarce good is similar to that of the natural monopoly in which the average total cost is greater than the marginal cost within the relevant output range. For both the artificially scarce good and the natural monopoly, the producers in these situations are willing to produce only if they can charge a price that is greater than the marginal cost of producing the good, but this price implies that the producer is producing an inefficiently low amount of output.

Objective #5.   When a good is either nonexcludable or nonrival, the market does not produce the efficient quantity of the good.

- When a good is nonexcludable, this creates a free-rider problem in which consumers are not willing to pay for the good but instead want to free ride on those who do pay for the good. When consumers free ride, too little of the good is produced in the market.

- When a good is nonrival in consumption, the cost of providing an additional unit of the good is zero because the good is nonrival. When consumers are forced to pay a price that is greater than zero, they end up demanding too little of the good and the market therefore produces an inefficient quantity of the good.

Objective #6.   A public good may be provided through voluntary contributions or by self-interested individuals or firms who produce them with the hope of earning money through some indirect means. For example, broadcast television is produced by firms who earn money through advertisement rather than payments from consumers who watch the televised programming. A public good may also be provided through social encouragement or social pressure. Many public goods are provided by the government and funded through taxation. This provision of public goods by the government is a crucial role for the government: without government provision these public goods would either not be provided or would be provided at levels that are inefficiently low.

Objective #7.   Governments must decide whether or not to provide the public good and how much of the public good to provide. The optimal level of public good provision is the level where the marginal social benefit of the public good is equal to the marginal cost of producing the public good. In the case of a public good, the marginal social benefit from the public good is the sum of the individual marginal benefits that are enjoyed by all consumers of that unit. Since the public good is nonrival, the benefit an individual receives from the consumption of the public good does not diminish the benefit another individual receives from consuming the same unit of the public good. Therefore, the marginal social benefit from consumption of the public good is always greater than the marginal private benefit from the consumption of the public good: individual self-interest does not result in the provision of the efficient quantity of public goods because of this divergence between the marginal public and marginal private benefit from the consumption of the public good. This is similar to the problem presented by positive externalities: the market does not provide the efficient amount of the public good or the efficient amount of a good with a positive externality because the marginal social benefit received by all consumers of another unit of the good is greater than the price the producer would receive from providing that unit of the good. The market produces too little of either type of good.

Objective #8.   Governments decide on the optimal amount of the public good to provide by estimating the social benefits and the social costs of providing the public good. This process is known as cost-benefit analysis. Although it is relatively easy to estimate the cost of providing the public good, it is much more difficult to estimate the benefits from the provision of the public good. Individuals have an incentive to not answer truthfully about the benefits they receive from a public good because of the nature of the public good.

Key Terms

Notes

excludable referring to a good, describes the case in which the supplier can prevent those who do not pay from consuming the good.

rival in consumption referring to a good, describes the case in which one unit cannot be consumed by more than one person at the same time.

private good a good that is both *excludable* and *rival in consumption*.

nonexcludable referring to a good, describes the case in which the supplier cannot prevent those who do not pay from consuming the good.

nonrival in consumption referring to a good, describes the case in which the same unit can be consumed by more than one person at the same time.

free-rider problem when individuals have no *incentive* to pay for their own consumption of a good, they will take a "free ride" on anyone who does pay; a problem with goods that are *nonexcludable*.

public good a good that is both *nonexcludable* and *nonrival in consumption*.

Key Terms *(continued)*

cost-benefit analysis an estimate of the costs and benefits of providing a good. When governments use cost-benefit analysis, they estimate the social costs and social benefits of providing a public good.

common resource a *resource* that is *nonexcludable* and *rival in consumption*.

overuse the depletion of a *common resource* that occurs when individuals ignore the fact that their use depletes the amount of the resource remaining for others.

artificially scarce good a good that is *excludable* but *nonrival in consumption*.

■ AFTER YOU READ THE CHAPTER

Tips

Tip #1. This chapter looks at four types of goods—private goods, public goods, common resources, and artificially scarce goods—from the perspective of whether or not the good is rival in consumption and excludable. To understand this chapter, it is essential that you have a firm grasp on what it means to be rival in consumption versus nonrival in consumption and excludable versus nonexcludable.

- When a good is rival, this means that one person's consumption of the good effectively prevents another consumer from consuming that same unit of the good. Hamburgers and ice cream cones are two examples of goods that are rival: when Sally eats her hamburger or her ice cream cone this means that Joe cannot eat the same hamburger or the same ice cream cone. Joe and Sally are rivals with regard to the consumption of the hamburger or the ice cream cone.

- When a good is nonrival, this means that one person's consumption of the good does not prevent another consumer from consuming the same unit of the good. Sally and Joe can both enjoy the light from the lighthouse in their community without diminishing the consumption benefits received by the other person from their consumption of the same light. Sally and Joe are not rivals with regard to the consumption of the light from the lighthouse.

- A good is excludable if a supplier can prevent someone from consuming the good if they do not pay for it. Sally can enjoy her fast-food hamburger only if she pays for it. The restaurant will exclude her from the consumption of the hamburger if she cannot first pay for the hamburger. Hamburgers are therefore excludable as well as rival.

- A good is nonexcludable if a supplier cannot prevent someone from consuming the good if they do not pay for it. Residents of a community can benefit from a tornado warning siren even if they do not pay for this siren. It is impossible to exclude the nonpayers from the benefits of consuming this good even though they have not paid for it.

Tip #2. To find the demand curve for a public good requires that you vertically sum the individual demand curves for this public good. In contrast to a private good for which the market demand curve is found by horizontally summing the individual consumer demand curves, the public good requires the vertical summation of the individual consumer demand curves. The private good is rival in consumption, so that when we find the market demand curve we essentially ask how many units do demanders want of this good at a particular price. We repeat this process for different prices until we have identified the market demand curve for the private good. The public good, in contrast, is nonrival in consumption. This means that the market demand for the public good at any quantity is equal to the sum of the prices individuals are willing to pay for this particular amount of the public good. This nonrival characteristic of public goods implies that the market demand for public goods is found by considering the sum of what people are willing to pay for each level of public good provision. Figure 18.1 illustrates this idea for a public good when there are two individuals in the market for this good: D_1 represents the first person's demand for the public good, while D_2 represents the second person's demand for the public good, and D_3 represents the total demand for the public good.

Figure 18.1

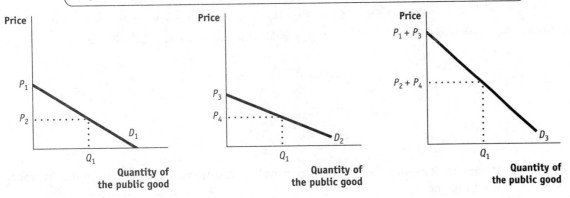

> To find the market demand curve for a public good, sum the individual demand curves for the good. To sum the demand curves, hold quantity constant (for example, Q_1) and then see what price each individual is willing to pay for this quantity. Thus, individual 1's marginal benefit from consuming Q_1 units of the public good is P_2, while individual 2's marginal benefit from consuming Q_1 units of the good is P_4. Together the marginal social benefit from Q_1 units is equal to $P_2 + P_4$.

Problems and Exercises

1. For each of the following situations, determine whether the good in the situation is (1) excludable or nonexcludable, and (2) nonrival in consumption or rival in consumption.

   a. A community erects a lighthouse to guide ships navigating near its rocky shoreline.

   b. A country builds a national defense system of missiles.

   c. A community builds a toll road that has low levels of usage.

    d. A community builds a toll road that has high levels of usage.

    e. A radio station broadcasts the baseball game.

    f. A community builds a non-toll road that has high levels of usage.

    g. Police protection is hired for a community.

    h. The environment of a community is improved.

2. What does it mean when a good is nonexcludable? Explain in your own words what this means.

3. What does it mean when a good is nonrival in consumption? Explain in your own words what this means.

4. Markets provide private goods efficiently since the market price is equal to the marginal cost of producing the good. Why do markets fail to produce the efficient level of public goods?

5. Jimmy and Beth are the only residents of Smalltown. They both think the community would benefit from more parks, but neither Jimmy or Beth are willing to contribute money to buy land to turn into parks since they both realize that once a park is provided they can enjoy the park even though they have not paid for the park.

   a. Describe Jimmy and Beth's behavior and why it represents a problem when trying to provide parks in their community.

   b. Suppose Jimmy reveals that his marginal benefit from one park is equal to $50 per park, his marginal benefit from two parks is equal to $25 per park, and his marginal benefit from three parks is equal to $0 per park. Beth reveals that her marginal benefit from one park is equal to $60 per park, her marginal benefit from two parks is equal to $40 per park, and her marginal benefit from three parks is equal to $20 per park. What is the marginal social benefit of two parks equal to in their community? Explain how you found this answer.

   c. Suppose the information in part (b) is still true. Jimmy and Beth analyze the cost of providing parks in their community and they find that the marginal social cost of providing parks is constant and equal to $55. What is the socially optimal amount of parks for this community? Explain how you got this answer.

   d. If Jimmy and Beth are both willing to reveal their preferences with regard to parks (that is, they will tell the truth about the marginal private benefit they receive from the parks), will they both contribute to getting the socially optimal amount of parks for their community?

6. What two characteristics do private goods have that make it possible for markets to efficiently provide the good, and why are these characteristics so important?

7. Big Sports is a television company that has won the rights to broadcast next season's football games in the Big Group college football conference. To watch these televised games, viewers need to subscribe to the Super Cable package that costs an additional $15 per month.

    a. Does Big Sports and its televised games represent a public good, a common resource, or an artificially scarce good? Explain your answer and why you have classified Big Sports in this manner.

    b. What price is the efficient price for consumers to pay for watching these football games? Explain your answer.

    c. Does Big Sports produce the socially optimal, or efficient, level of televised football games for the Big Group college football conference? Explain your answer. If the level of production is not the socially optimal amount, is the amount produced in the market greater than or less than the socially optimal amount? Explain your answer.

8. In which of the following situations is the free-rider problem likely to arise? Explain for each situation that has a free-rider problem why this occurs and what the nature of the free-rider problem is.

    a. The parent-teacher association at your child's elementary school is looking for parent volunteers to direct a fundraiser to raise money to replace the playground equipment.

    b. Local community organizers are seeking people to serve on a committee to improve the beauty of the community through gardening and landscaping efforts.

    c. The local hamburger joint is testing a new sandwich on its menu.

    d. A local group is organizing a Saturday morning spring cleanup of the lakeshore in their community.

9. For each of the following situations, decide whether the problem is like a positive externality, negative externality, or natural monopoly.

   a. The parent-teacher association at your child's elementary school is looking for parent volunteers to direct a fundraiser to raise money to replace the playground equipment.

   b. Local community organizers are seeking people to serve on a committee to improve the beauty of the community through gardening and landscaping efforts.

   c. The number of elephants in Africa is declining due to hunters killing them for their ivory tusks.

   d. A local group is organizing a Saturday morning spring cleanup of the lakeshore in their community.

   e. The quantity of salmon in the Great Lakes is declining due to too many salmon being caught by sport fishermen.

   f. Children at the elementary school, once they are vaccinated for childhood diseases, lower the risk of infection for those who are not vaccinated.

   g. The local cable television company charges an additional fee if the customer wants to receive the channel that offers local sports coverage.

10. Several sub-Saharan African countries are worried about their elephant population decreasing over time due to the hunting and killing of these elephants for their ivory tusks. Elephants tend to roam over relatively large areas to seek food, which makes it difficult to manage the elephant population. One country proposes creating a large elephant refuge area where the elephants can roam and be protected by law from the hunting of elephants. Another country proposes assigning property rights to the elephants to specific individuals: these individuals would own specific elephants and would be allowed to provide these elephants for slaughter if they so desired. There is an active market for ivory, but at this time the market is strictly an underground, or illegal, market since the ivory that is supplied has been obtained by illegally killing the elephants.

a. What is the nature of the problem of dwindling elephant population in sub-Saharan Africa? Explain your answer.

b. Of the two policies, which one is more likely to result in the greatest reduction in illegal killing of elephants? Why?

c. Which proposal assigns property rights to the ownership of elephants? Why is the assignment of property rights important in resolving the problem of the declining elephant population?

▮ BEFORE YOU TAKE THE TEST

Chapter Review Questions

1. A public good is a good
   a. that benefits many people whether or not they have paid for it.
   b. whose benefits to any particular individual do not depend on how many other individuals benefit from the good.
   c. that is nonrival in consumption and nonexcludable.
   d. Answers (a), (b), and (c) are all true statements.

2. In the case of a common resource,
   a. one person's consumption of the common resource reduces the amount of the common resource available to other consumers.
   b. one person cannot be excluded from consuming the common resource because it is nonrival in consumption.
   c. one person can exclude others from consuming the common resource if they have not paid for the consumption of the common resource.
   d. it represents the same type of problem found in a market when positive externalities are associated with the good.

3. When the price of a good is greater than its marginal cost of provision, **the market for** this good is producing
    a. the socially optimal amount of the good.
    b. too little of the good.
    c. too much of the good.
    d. as optimal an amount of output as is possible given the circumstances.

4. For a market to efficiently deliver a good, the good must be
    a. rival in consumption.
    b. excludable.
    c. nonrival in consumption.
    d. nonexcludable.
    e. (a) and (b)
    f. (c) and (d)

5. Madison has a number of city parks that are open to the public at no charge. Throughout the year these parks are often crowded, with long lines at the play structures. These public parks represent a good that is
    a. nonrival and nonexcludable.
    b. nonrival and excludable.
    c. rival and nonexcludable.
    d. rival and excludable.

6. Madison is in the middle of tornado country and, because of the imminent danger of tornadoes, has decided to invest in a tornado siren system. This tornado siren system is an example of a good that is
    a. nonrival in consumption and nonexcludable.
    b. nonrival in consumption and excludable.
    c. rival in consumption and nonexcludable.
    d. rival in consumption and excludable.

7. The Illinois Tollway that connects Rockford to Chicago is constantly congested with traffic jams. Motorists must pay a toll fee to use the Tollway. The Tollway is a good that is characterized as
    a. rival in consumption and nonexcludable.
    b. rival in consumption and excludable.
    c. nonrival in consumption and nonexcludable.
    d. rival in consumption and nonexcludable.

8. Mason Street is a quiet residential street that is only three blocks long. There is no toll for driving on Mason Street, and the street gets very little traffic except from the people who live on the street. Mason Street is
    a. nonrival in consumption and nonexcludable.
    b. rival in consumption and excludable.
    c. nonrival in consumption and excludable.
    d. rival in consumption and nonexcludable.

9. Sally and Sue live in an apartment and neither of them likes to clean the apartment nor do the dishes. After several weeks of living like this, the apartment does get really dirty. Sally often wishes the apartment was clean, but she does not do anything to clean up the apartment because she figures if she is only patient enough Sue will clean the apartment. Which of the following statements is true?

   a. Sue free rides on Sally when it comes to getting the apartment cleaned up.

   b. Sally free rides on Sue when it comes to getting the apartment cleaned up.

   c. Since there are only two people in the apartment, the free-rider problem is not important because eventually Sally and Sue will clean the apartment.

   d. Free ridership is a problem that only arises in a society that is trying to provide a public good.

10. Joey's elementary school is organizing a fundraiser to raise the funds needed to refurbish the library. Each parent has been asked to contribute two hours of their time toward the fundraiser, but very few parents have come forward to help out. Which of the following statements is true?

   a. Their children will benefit from the refurbishment of the library irrespective of whether or not their parents volunteer their time.

   b. If the parents do not volunteer, someone else will and then they and their children can free ride on the other parents' work.

   c. The school will suffer from the free-rider problem and will not raise the optimal amount of funds due to the parents' free riding.

   d. Answers (a), (b), and (c) are all true statements.

11. When a good is nonexcludable, the market produces

   a. too much of the good.

   b. too little of the good.

12. New Glarus has just built and opened a toll road connecting New Glarus to Old Glarus. This toll road is never congested no matter what time of day or what day of the week it is. Since the toll road is both nonrival in consumption and excludable, it is an example of an artificially scarce good. The marginal cost of letting an additional driver use the toll road is equal to

   a. the toll.

   b. zero.

   c. the toll divided by the number of drivers currently using the toll road.

   d. the toll divided by the population of the two communities.

13. New Glarus has just built and opened a toll road connecting New Glarus to Old Glarus. This toll road is never congested no matter what time of day or what day of the week it is. Since the toll road is both nonrival in consumption and excludable, it is an example of an artificially scarce good. Drivers who might benefit from using this toll road will

   a. not use the toll road as much as is socially optimal since the toll is greater than the marginal cost of allowing these drivers to use the road.

   b. use the toll road at the socially optimal level since the toll is sufficient to cover the costs of providing the road.

   c. free ride on other drivers.

Use the following information to answer the next three questions.

Suppose Joe's marginal private benefit from national defense is given by the equation $P = 100 - Q$, where Q refers to the amount of military goods and P refers to the price Joe is willing to pay for each unit of military goods. Mary's marginal private benefit from national defense is given by the equation $P = 50 - 0.5Q$. Furthermore, suppose the marginal social cost of providing an additional unit of military goods is constant and equal to $60.

14. Which equation represents the marginal social benefit (*MSB*) from military goods if Joe and Mary are the only two individuals in the economy? (Hint: draw two graphs of the individual demand curves for Joe and Mary, then draw a third graph that adds these two individual demand curves together.)
    a. $MSB = 66.67 - 0.33Q$
    b. $MSB = 150 - 1.5Q$
    c. $MSB = 100 - Q$
    d. $MSB = 50 - 0.5Q$

15. What is the socially optimal amount of national defense for this economy?
    a. 90 units of military goods
    b. 80 units of military goods
    c. 170 units of military goods
    d. 60 units of military goods

16. Suppose both Joe and Mary are truthful about their preferences with regard to national defense and they both fully reveal the marginal benefits they receive from national defense. Furthermore, suppose the socially optimal amount of national defense is produced in this economy. What price per unit of national defense will Joe be willing to pay?
    a. $100
    b. $60
    c. $40
    d. $20

17. Which of the following statements about public goods is true?
    I. Public goods can be provided efficiently by the market or by the government.
    II. Public goods can be provided through voluntary contributions or by self-interested individuals or firms.
    III. Some public goods can be provided through social encouragement or pressure.
    a. Statement I is true.
    b. Statements II and III are true.
    c. Statements I, II, and III are true.
    d. Statements I and II are true.
    e. Statements I and III are true.

Use the following graph of a public good to answer the next three questions. Assume that Joe and Sarah are the only two people who live in their community and that this graph represents Joe's marginal benefit from the public good, Sarah's marginal benefit from the public good, and the total marginal social benefit from the public good. In addition, the marginal cost of producing an additional unit of the public good is constant and equal to P_4.

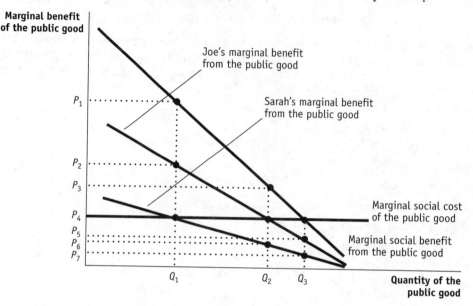

18. At Q_1, the marginal social benefit from this last unit of the public good
   a. is equal to P_1 or the sum of $P_2 + P_4$.
   b. is greater than the marginal social cost of producing this last unit of the public good.
   c. exceeds the marginal social cost of producing another unit of the public good, which tells us that this community is not producing enough of the public good.
   d. Answers (a), (b), and (c) are all true statements.

19. What is the socially optimal amount of the good; and, if both Sarah and Joe contribute to the provision of the public good an amount that equals the marginal benefit they get from the last unit of the good they consume, how much will Joe contribute per unit of the public good?
   a. Q_1; P_2 d. Q_3; P_4
   b. Q_1; P_4 e. Q_3; P_5
   c. Q_2; P_4

20. Given the information in the above graph, who places a higher value on the public good represented in the graph?
   a. Joe
   b. Sarah

21. A community is trying to decide whether or not to install lighting at one of the local city parks. Government officials estimate that the marginal social benefit from installing the lighting will be $100, but that the marginal social cost of installing the lighting will be $105. This community
    a. should conduct another study to see if the numbers come out better, since clearly it would be great to have a well-lit park.
    b. should not install the lighting at this time since the marginal benefit from the lighting is less than the marginal cost of installing the lighting.
    c. will not install the lighting since the market will provide the lighting.
    d. should install the lighting because the cost-benefit analysis did not take into account the tendency of individuals to free ride on the provision of the public good.

22. Fishermen in Oceania report dwindling supplies of their favorite fish. These fishermen fish in open water with no limits placed on who can fish in the water and how many fish can be taken from the sea. This is an example of a(n)
    a. artificially scarce good, since good fisheries management could eliminate the fish scarcity.
    b. public good, since no one is paying to fish in the water and no one can be excluded from fishing in the water.
    c. common resource, since the fishing grounds are nonexcludable but rival in consumption.
    d. private good, since each fisherman catches his own fish, and then markets them at the local fish market.

23. A good that is nonexcludable but rival in consumption is a(n)
    a. public good.   c. artificially scarce good.
    b. positive externality.   d. common resource.

24. In the case of a common resource, the market tends to
    a. overconsume the good, since the good is nonexcludable but rival in consumption.
    b. underconsume the good, since the good is nonexcludable but rival in consumption.

25. London recently started charging drivers a fee to drive in certain parts of the city during high-traffic times of day. This fee effectively seeks to address the problem of traffic congestion. This fee has successfully reduced traffic congestion in the areas of London where it has been applied. By imposing this fee, government officials have
    a. encouraged consumers to drive less than they otherwise would.
    b. encouraged consumers to drive at times when traffic congestion is less of a problem.
    c. made a common resource excludable: those who pay for the right to drive can drive, and those unwilling to pay must forgo driving.
    d. Answers (a), (b), and (c) are all true answers.

26. In the case of a common resource, the market does not recognize that
    a. marginal social cost is greater than the private cost of providing the last unit of the good.
    b. marginal social benefit is greater than the marginal benefit individuals receive from consuming the last unit of the good.
    c. marginal social benefit and marginal social cost are both ignored by the market.
    d. the marginal benefits and marginal costs from consumption of the good are ignored.

27. The market can correct the problem posed by common resources by
a. imposing the appropriate Pigouvian tax on the good.
b. creating a system of tradable licenses for the right to this common resource.
c. assigning property rights to this common resource, thereby making the good an excludable good.
d. Answers (a), (b), and (c) are all feasible corrections to the problem posed by common resources.

28. Economists are excited because they have just discovered a good that is nonrival in consumption but excludable. This good
a. will be very expensive, since it is such a rare good.
b. should be free, since the marginal cost of an individual's consumption of this good is equal to zero if this good is to be produced at the socially optimal level of production.
c. will be overproduced in this market, since the price of the good is less than the marginal cost of providing the good.
d. will be efficiently produced in this market, since the good is excludable and a price can therefore be assigned to the good by the market.

ANSWER KEY

Answers to Problems and Exercises

1. **a.** Nonexcludable and nonrival

   b. Nonexcludable and nonrival

   c. Excludable and nonrival

   d. Excludable and rival

   e. Nonexcludable and nonrival

   f. Nonexcludable and rival

   g. Nonexcludable and rival

   h. Nonexcludable and nonrival

2. A good is nonexcludable when once the good is produced individuals can enjoy the consumption of this good even if they do not pay for the good. Once people realize a good is nonexcludable, they will free ride on other people who are willing to pay for the good, knowing that once the good is provided they will be able to consume it even if they have not paid for the good.

3. A good is nonrival in consumption if more than one person can consume the same unit of the good without diminishing the benefits of consuming the good for other people. Most of the goods we have discussed thus far in the text are private goods for which one person's consumption of the good means that no one else can consume that unit: this implies that consumers are rivals when they consume private goods. In the case of a good that is nonrival, consumers are not rivals and many people can enjoy the benefits from the same good.

4. A public good is both nonexcludable and nonrival in consumption. This means that consumers can consume the good without paying for the good and that consumers are not rivals with one another in the consumption of the good. This nonrival characteristic of public goods results in the marginal social benefit from the public good being greater than the demand for the public good at all levels of public good provision. This implies that the market does not produce the efficient amount of the public good because it does not equate the marginal cost of producing the good to the marginal social benefit from consuming it. Too few units of the public good are provided by the market.

5. **a.** Both Jimmy and Beth are free riding on this issue of park provision. They both realize that once the parks are provided they can enjoy the park even if they have not contributed to the creation of the park. When people free ride, too little or none of the good gets produced. In this case, if neither Jimmy nor Beth are willing to contribute, then the community will end up with no new parks.

   b. The marginal social benefit of two parks is equal to the sum of Jimmy's and Beth's marginal benefits from two parks: Jimmy's marginal social benefit from two parks is equal to $25 per park while Beth's marginal social benefit from two parks is equal to $40 per park, for a total marginal social benefit from two parks of $65 per park.

   c. Since the marginal cost of providing parks is constant and equal to $55 per park, parks should be provided as long as the marginal social benefit from the park is greater than or equal to the marginal cost of providing the park. In this case, two parks will be provided since the marginal social benefit of two parks is equal to $65 per park while the marginal cost of providing two parks is $55 per park. Three parks will not be provided because the marginal social benefit of three parks is only $20 per park while the marginal social cost of three parks is $55 per park.

d. Yes, if both Jimmy and Beth reveal their preferences they will each contribute, since they each assign a positive marginal benefit to two parks. Jimmy will likely contribute less than Beth because the marginal benefit he receives from two parks is less than the marginal benefit that Beth receives from two parks.

6. Private goods are both rival in consumption and excludable. A good that is rival in consumption is a good whose benefit from consumption can only be enjoyed by the individual consuming it. This quality of being rival in consumption implies that individuals must pay a positive price to consume the good. When a good is excludabe, this means that no individual can enjoy the benefits from consuming the good without first paying for the good. These two characteristics allow private goods to be produced efficiently in the market because producers can set a price for these goods that is equal to the marginal cost of producing the good.

7. a. Since the televised games are available only if the consumer pays for the cable package, these games are an excludable good. But the televised games are nonrival in consumption since one individual's viewing of the game does not diminish the ability of another viewer to watch the game. Thus, Big Sports and its televised games represent an artificially scarce good, since these goods are excludable but nonrival in consumption.

b. The efficient price for consumers would be zero since the marginal cost of delivering the televised games to another consumer is zero. At a price of zero, however, Big Sports has no incentive to provide the games. Big Sports will only provide the games if they can charge consumers a positive price.

c. Big Sports does not produce the optimal amount of the good since the price they charge ($15 per month) is greater than the marginal cost of producing an additional televised game ($0). Since price is greater than marginal cost this indicates that too little of the good is being produced, because the value consumers place on the last unit produced is greater than the cost of producing the last unit.

8. a. There is a free-rider problem in this situation because the final good (the playground equipment) is nonexcludable. Too few parents will come forward to volunteer their time because the parents all realize that once the playground equipment is installed, all the children at the school will be able to use the equipment even if their parents did not help in the fundraising effort. If the free-rider problem is too severe, the school will not get the new playground equipment.

b. There is a free-rider problem in this situation because the final good (a more beautiful community) is nonexcludable. Too few people will come forward to help with this effort since everyone in the community realizes that if the community is made more beautiful, then everyone in the community can enjoy this beauty even if they did not help in the effort to create a more beautiful community. The community will likely continue to have its blemishes and eyesores and not achieve the socially optimal amount of community beauty.

c. There is no free-rider problem with this situation since the new sandwich is excludable.

d. There is a free-rider problem in this situation because the final good (a cleaner lake and a cleaner lakeshore) is nonexcludable. Too few people will come forward to help clean up the lakeshore because people in the community realize that once the lakeshore is cleaned up, everyone in the community can enjoy this cleaner lakeshore even if they have not contributed to this outcome. The lakeshore will not be cleaned to the socially optimal level.

9. a. Positive externality

b. Positive externality

c. Negative externality

d. Positive externality

    e. Negative externality

    f. Positive externality

    g. Natural monopoly

10. a. The population of elephants in Africa is dwindling due to the illegal harvesting of their tusks (which can only be done by killing the elephants). This occurs because the elephants represent a common resource: anyone can kill an elephant and benefit from harvesting the tusks since no one owns the elephants. This common resource leads to overharvesting of the elephants and, hence, a decline in the elephant population.

    b. Assigning property rights to elephant ownership will likely prove more effective than setting up an elephant refuge, since the owner of the elephant recognizes that the elephant has value and will therefore take care of the elephant to preserve that value. The owner would likely try to ensure that the elephant stays nearby, where it would be difficult for someone to come along and kill the elephant. In contrast, the refuge would consolidate the area in which elephants are found, making it easier for poachers to find the elephants.

    c. The second proposal assigns property rights for elephant ownership. Assigning property rights helps to eliminate the problem of nonexcludability, since theoretically no one will have access to the elephant, or its tusks, unless they pay for the elephant.

Answers to Chapter Review Questions

1.   **Answer d.** Public goods are nonrival in consumption and nonexcludable. These two characteristics imply that people can benefit from the good even if they did not pay for it (nonexcludable) and that the benefits any individual gets from the good do not depend on whether or not another individual is benefiting from the good (nonrival in consumption).

2.   **Answer a.** The common resource is a situation in which the good is rival in consumption but nonexcludable. In the case of the common resource, individuals overuse the common resource, which creates a negative externality on everyone else who would benefit from the use of the common resource.

3.   **Answer b.** When the price of the good is greater than its marginal cost this tells us that too little of the good is being produced since the value consumers place on the good (the price they are willing to pay) is greater than the cost of producing an additional unit of the good. This situation arises with monopoly, oligopoly, public goods, and artificially scarce goods.

4.   **Answer e.** Goods that are both rival in consumption and excludable are private goods and can be produced efficiently by the market. Goods that lack one or both of these characteristics are not efficiently provided by the market.

5.   **Answer c.** The parks are open to the public at no charge, so they are nonexcludable. But they are often congested with long lines, which implies that the parks are rival in consumption. One child's use of the play structure reduces the available benefits of the play structure for another child.

6.   **Answer a.** Once the tornado siren system is in place, everyone living in Madison will be able to benefit from the system even if they did not contribute to its production, so it is nonexcludable. The good is also nonrival in consumption since one person's consumption of the signal from the siren system does not reduce the available benefit to other people from consuming the same signal from the siren system.

7.   **Answer b.** The Tollway is rival in consumption, since one person's use of the Tollway reduces the benefit of using the Tollway for other people due to the high level of congestion. The Tollway is also excludable since no one can drive on the Tollway without paying the toll.

8. **Answer a.** Since there is no charge to drive on Mason Street, it is an example of a nonexcludable good: anyone can enjoy driving on the street even though they have not paid for the street. Mason Street is also nonrival in consumption since it is never congested: this means that one person's use of the street does not diminish the level of benefits available to someone else who wishes to use the street.

9. **Answer b.** Sally free rides: she does not want to contribute to cleaning the apartment, but she enjoys the benefits of a clean apartment once Sue gets everything cleaned. Free ridership can occur in all sorts of transactions and is not limited to the situation posed by a public good.

10. **Answer d.** These statements are all true. When a good is nonexcludable, people tend to free ride. Once the library is refurbished, there is no way that the school can prevent those children from using the library whose parents did not help out with the fundraiser. When the good is nonexcludable, too little of the good is provided without intervention in the market because of the free-rider problem.

11. **Answer b.** When a good is nonexcludable, people tend to free ride and rely on others to provide the good. Because people free ride, the market undervalues the benefit from the good, and therefore produces too little of the good.

12. **Answer b.** Since the toll road is nonrival in consumption, the marginal cost of letting another driver use the road is equal to zero. When an additional driver on this toll road is forced to pay the toll, this payment is higher than the marginal cost of allowing them to consume the good.

13. **Answer a.** Drivers will not consume as many drives on the toll road as is socially optimal since the price they must pay to use the road (the toll) is greater than the marginal cost of allowing them to use the road (zero). They will not be free riding since the toll road is excludable and people can only free ride when the good is nonexcludable.

14. **Answer b.** To find the *MSB* curve, you need to vertically sum the two individual demand curves for the public good (national defense is a public good since it is nonrival in consumption and nonexcludable). An easy point to find on the *MSB* curve is the y-intercept, since it equals the sum of the y-intercepts from the two individual demand curves: in this case, the y-intercept is equal to 150. Then, given the two individual demand curves, when 100 units of military goods are demanded, both Joe and Mary are not willing to pay anything for this quantity of military goods. Thus, the *MSB* curve intersects the x-axis at 100 units of military goods. The *MSB* curve is therefore $MSB = 150 - 1.5Q$.

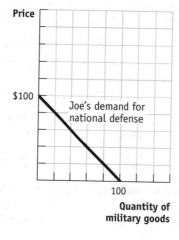

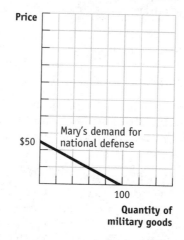

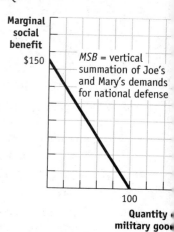

15. **Answer d.** To find the socially optimal amount of national defense for this economy, you must find where the marginal social benefit equals the marginal social cost. Or, $150 - 1.5Q = 60$, and therefore Q equals 60 units of military goods.

16. **Answer c.** Since the socially optimal amount of national defense in this problem is 60 units (see question 15), we can find Joe's willingness to pay by substituting this quantity into his demand curve. Thus, Joe's demand for national defense is given by $P = 100 - Q$, and when Q equals 60 units of military goods, Joe is willing to pay a price of $40 per unit of military goods.

17. **Answer b.** Public goods are not provided for by the market because they are nonrival in consumption and nonexcludable. But public goods may be provided through voluntary contributions, through the self-interested behavior of individuals or firms, or through social encouragement or pressure. For example, some conservation efforts occur through voluntary contributions or through firm activity in which the firm hopes to be able to make money in some indirect way through their efforts to increase conservation. Many people do not litter and actually pick up litter because of social encouragement or pressure. Having less litter is a public good—nonrival in consumption and nonexcludable—and this "good" to some degree is produced by moral suasion.

18. **Answer d.** It is a relatively easy task to measure the marginal social benefit of producing Q_1 units of the good: you simply need to go vertically up from Q_1 units to the marginal social benefit curve and then read the y-intercept value for this level of public good production. The marginal social benefit from the public good curve is constructed by adding the marginal benefit that Joe receives from the public good to the marginal benefit that Sarah receives from the public good: this is equal to $P_2 + P_4$. The marginal social cost of producing an additional unit of the public good is equal to P_4, so the marginal social cost is less than the marginal social benefit. This implies that too little of the public good is being produced.

19. **Answer e.** The socially optimal amount of the public good is that amount of the public good where the marginal social benefit is equal to the marginal social cost. This is true at Q_3. Joe's marginal benefit from the public good can be found by going vertically up from Q_3 units to Joe's marginal benefit from the public good curve and then reading off the y-intercept value for this point.

20. **Answer a.** Joe's marginal benefit from the public good is greater than Sarah's marginal benefit from the public good: he places a higher value on the public good since the public good yields greater benefits to him.

21. **Answer b.** When the marginal social benefit is less than the marginal social cost, the good should not be produced. One hopes that the cost-benefit study was well conducted and took into account the tendency for individuals to free ride on the provision of the public good, since the cost-benefit study would have little value if it was based on poor analysis.

22. **Answer c.** The fishermen face a problem of a common resource, since all of them use the sea where the fish are located. Since no one owns the fishing rights to the sea and there is no way to limit the amount of fishing in the sea, there is too much fishing. This leads to the quantity of fish available decreasing due to overfishing: a natural outcome of a situation in which the good is nonexcludable but rival. When one fisherman catches a fish, that fish is no longer available for some other fisherman to catch.

23. **Answer d.** This is the simple definition of a common resource.

24. **Answer a.** A common resource is overconsumed because individuals cannot be charged for using the good, while at the same time individuals recognize that they are rivals with other individuals for the good. Individuals ignore the cost of their use of the good on the rest of society, which leads them to overuse the good.

25. **Answer d.** By charging a price for the right to drive in the city during high-traffic hours, London officials have effectively raised the price of driving. This causes individuals to drive less, and it also encourages them to shift their driving to times when the fee is lower (i.e., times when there is less traffic). London officials recognize that traffic congestion is a sign of a common resource problem, and this policy attempts to make a nonexcludable good excludable.

26. **Answer a.** With a common resource, the marginal cost of consuming an additional unit of the good does not take into account the cost of this consumption on other individuals. This implies that there is a divergence between the marginal social cost of consuming an additional unit of the good and the marginal cost to the individual of consuming an additional unit of the good. The market equates the marginal social benefit of consuming the good with the consumer's marginal cost of consuming the good, rather than equating the marginal social benefit to the marginal social cost.

27. **Answer d.** Common resources essentially present the same type of problem as those presented by a negative externality. As with a negative externality, the problem of common resources can be eliminated through assigning property rights, or by creating a system of licenses granting the holder the right to use the common resource, or by taxing the users of the common resource.

28. **Answer b.** When a good is excludable but nonrival in consumption, the market fails to produce the efficient level of the good. The marginal cost of an individual's consumption of this good equals zero since the good is nonrival in consumption: one individual's consumption of the good does not diminish the benefits available to another consumer from consuming the same good. But producers are only willing to produce the good if they can charge for the good: this implies that the price in the market is greater than the marginal cost of the good, and therefore the market-determined quantity of the good is smaller than is socially optimal. To get the socially optimal amount of the good requires that the price of the good be equal to zero.

chapter 19

The Economics of
the Welfare State

Summary

This chapter is highly descriptive in its focus on what the welfare state is and the rationale for the welfare state. The chapter defines poverty and then examines the causes and the consequences of poverty. The chapter also looks at income inequality in America from a historical perspective. The chapter discusses the impact of programs such as Social Security on poverty and income inequality. The chapter also discusses the special issues and concerns related to health care insurance. Lastly, the chapter examines the political and philosophical debate over the size of the welfare state.

Chapter Objectives

Objective #1. The welfare state is a term used to describe the collection of government programs aimed at reducing or alleviating economic hardship. A large portion of government spending in wealthy countries consists of government transfers that provide financial aid to individuals designated by the government as in need of government assistance. These individuals may be poor, unemployed, elderly, or may be experiencing large health care expenses. There are two major rationales for the welfare state: (1) to help alleviate income inequality and (2) to help alleviate economic insecurity. Programs designed to alleviate income inequality by aiding the poor are known as poverty programs; programs designed to alleviate economic insecurity by providing protection against unpredictable distress are known as social insurance programs. Both types of programs are closely related to the ability-to-pay principle, which is used to justify progressive taxation that requires those with higher incomes to pay a greater fraction of their income in taxes than those with low incomes. The programs of the welfare state redistribute income from some people to other people.

Objective #2. Debate over the size and extent of the welfare state typically focuses on two points of contention. The first point of disagreement is over how large a role the government should play in alleviating economic inequality and economic insecurity. Even conservatives who believe in the limited role of government typically support some welfare state programs. The second point of disagreement is over the effects of welfare state programs on the incentives to work and save. Just as in the case of taxes, the provision of welfare state programs can create substantial deadweight losses, and thus the economic cost of welfare state programs can be considerably greater than the direct monetary cost of providing these programs.

Objective #3. Poverty is defined in the United States as the minimum amount of annual income that is considered adequate to purchase the necessities of life. When a family's income falls below the poverty line, that family is considered poor. By several different measures the United States has an unusually high poverty rate. The data on poverty in the United States shows a strong association between poverty and the lack of adequate employment. Part-time work typically lacks benfits such as health plans, paid vacation days, and retirement benefits, and in addition, these workers often are paid an hourly wage that is lower than comparable full-time work. These part-time workers are the working poor—those workers whose income falls at or below the poverty line. The causes of poverty in the United States include

- Low levels of education;

- Lack of proficiency in speaking English;

- The existence of gender and racial discrimination; and

- Bad luck, which causes the wage-earner to lose a job or a family member to develop a serious medical problem.

Impoverished people experience

- A lack of health care that can disrupt schooling and affect the ability to work; and

- A lack of access to affordable housing, which leads to disrupted schooling and work schedules for family members.

Poverty is often self-perpetuating: the children of the poor start at such a disadvantage relative to other Americans that it's very hard for them to achieve a better life.

Objective #4. Income in the United States is unequally distributed. Mean household income, or average household income, is equal to the total income of all U.S. households divided by the number of U.S. households. This measure is skewed upward by the inclusion of highly wealthy households. A better measure of income inequality is median household income. Median household income in the United States is the level of income earned by the household in the exact middle of the income distribution. Median household income is not skewed by the inclusion of very high or very low household incomes. Another measure of income inequality is the Gini coefficient: a country with a perfectly equal distribution of income would have a Gini coefficient of zero, whereas a country where all income went to a single person would have a Gini coefficient of one. Countries with relatively low Gini coefficients have less income inequality than countries with relatively high Gini coefficients.

Objective #5. High income inequality implies that some people in the economy do not benefit from the overall level of prosperity in a country. High income inequality is also associated with political instability. Income inequality is best measured over a long period rather than a short period, since the income of individual families fluctuates over time. In addition, a family's income varies over its life cycle: family income is relatively low at the beginning of the family's working years and rises over time; eventually, family income drops during the retirement years. Year-to-year fluctuations in income do highlight a significant issue even for affluent families, which is economic insecurity.

Objective #6. Economic insecurity refers to year-to-year fluctuations in income. These fluctuations impact both poor families and more affluent families. Two common causes of economic insecurity are job loss and medical problems that require expensive treatment.

Objective #7. Economic inequality over the past hundred years evidences three trends: during the 1930s and 1940s, economic inequality fell; during the thirty-five years, after World War II economic inequality did not change; and during the last 30 years or so, economic inequality has risen. Economic inequality declined sharply in the late 1930s and early 1940s due to the imposition of special controls on wages and prices during World War II. This Great Compression was a period characterized by growing economic equality. During the past thirty years, economic inequality has grown: one argument for this change focuses on technological change, which has increased the demand for highly skilled workers while reducing the demand for low-skilled workers. In addition, the growth of international trade may have further compressed the wages of low-skilled labor while increasing the wages of highly skilled workers. Finally, rising immigration may also contribute to growing economic inequality. However, technological change, international trade, and increased immigration do not account for the growing economic gap among highly educated workers.

Objective #8. The three largest programs in the U.S. welfare state are Social Security, Medicare, and Medicaid.

Welfare state programs can be divided into two groups based on whether or not the program is means tested. Means-tested programs are poverty programs designed to help those with low incomes, whereas non-means-tested programs are programs whose benefits are available to everyone without regard to their income. Examples of means-tested poverty programs include:

- Monetary aid to poor families with children, which is given by the Temporary Assistance for Needy Families (TANF) program. This program is available only to those poor families with children, and this assistance is available only for a limited period.

- Negative income tax, which is a program that supplements the earnings of low-income working families. This Earned Income Tax Credit (EITC) provides additional income to millions of workers.

Both TANF and EITC address concerns about the provision of welfare and the impact poverty programs have on work incentives: work incentives are less impacted by limiting the amount of time a family can receive TANF or by supplementing the income low-wage workers receive (the EITC). Examples of non-means-tested programs include Social Security, which is a program that guarantees retirement income to qualifying older Americans. Social Security also provides benefits to disabled workers and the survivors of workers who have died. Social Security benefits are determined by a formula that gives high earners more than low earners, but with a sliding scale so that the program is relatively more generous for low earners than for high earners.

Welfare programs can also be divided into two groups based on whether or not the benefits of the program are in-kind benefits (such as the provision of health care to Medicare and Medicaid clients) or in-cash benefits.

Objective #9. Health care expenses are unevenly spread across members of an economy. In the United States in 2002, 20% of the population accounted for 80% of the medical costs, and 5% of the population accounted for almost 50% of the medical costs. Health insurance is primarily provided in the United States by private health insurance or by government programs such as Medicare and Medicaid.

Objective #10. Private health insurance collects payments from members of a large pool of individuals to create a common fund that can then be used to pay the medical expenses of the pool's members. This private provision of health insurance reduces risk for individuals: if the individual happens to incur high medical expenses, the pool of collected money covers these expenses. Private health insurance provision fails to work, however, if healthy members decide to forego coverage since the resultant pool of members has a higher likelihood of incurring significant medical costs. This problem is called adverse selection and occurs when the pool of applicants is adversely selected, from the perspective of the insurance company. When enough healthy individuals elect to forgo coverage, this results in the adverse selection death spiral. The adverse selection problem with regard to health insurance can be avoided through employment-based health insurance, since employment-based insurance is likely to contain a representative mix of healthy and less healthy people rather than a selected group of people who want insurance because they anticipate that they will incur high medical costs. Employment-based health insurance is also favored in the United States because it receives special tax treatment that effectively subsidizes the provision of this insurance by the government.

Objective #11. Medicare provides medical insurance for all Americans aged sixty-five and older, regardless of their income or wealth. Medicaid is a means-tested program that provides medical insurance. In addition to Medicare and Medicaid, health insurance is also provided as a benefit of military service.

Objective #12. Individuals without health insurance are primarily low-income workers who find coverage unaffordable for two reasons: (1) they are less likely to have jobs that come with health insurance, and (2) they are less likely to be able to afford private health insurance. In addition, they may find it impossible to get private health insurance due to the existence of preexisting medical conditions. The uninsured are not necessarily impoverished, but the failure to have health insurance does result in serious consequences. The uninsured often lack access to health care, and when serious illness strikes, the uninsured suffer serious financial problems.

Objective #13. Other wealthy countries rely less on private health insurance than does the United States. In addition, other wealthy countries spend less on health care per person than does the United States. This discrepancy in the level of expenditure per person is thought to be the result of inefficiencies in the provision of health care, higher administrative costs, and higher prescription drug expenses. The United States is the only wealthy country in which large numbers of people lack health insurance.

- Canada has a single-payer system in which the government acts as the principal payer of all medical bills.

- Britain utilizes a system wherein the National Health Service employs health care workers and operates clinics and hospitals that provide health care free of charge to the public.

Objective #14. The cost of providing medical care has increased rapidly due to medical progress. This means that both private insurers and the government face higher costs that must be passed on in the form of higher insurance premiums or larger commitments of taxpayer funds.

Objective #15. There is political debate about how large the welfare state should be. Those arguing for a small welfare state believe that government's role is to maintain the rule of law, provide public goods, and control externalities. Other arguments for a relatively small welfare state focus on the trade-off between efficiency and equity: the ability-to-pay principle reduces the incentive to increase a family's income by working hard or by making risky investments, whereas provision of generous welfare programs creates adverse work incentives for low-income individuals. In addition, the creation of a large welfare state requires more tax revenue and therefore higher tax rates than does the creation of a small welfare state. One way to hold down the cost of the welfare state is to use means-tested benefits so that these benefits are made available only to those who need them. This method is not fail-safe since it may create a notch, which is a situation in which earning more actually leaves a family worse off.

Key Terms

welfare state the collection of government programs designed to alleviate economic hardship.

government transfer a government payment to an individual or a family.

poverty program a government program designed to aid the poor.

social insurance program a government program designed to provide protection against unpredictable financial distress.

poverty threshold the annual income below which a family is officially considered poor.

poverty rate the percentage of the population with incomes below the *poverty threshold*.

mean household income the average income across all households.

median household income the income of the household lying at the exact middle of the *income distribution*.

Gini coefficient a number that summarizes a country's level of income inequality based on how unequally income is distributed across quintiles.

means-tested a program in which benefits are available only to individuals or families whose incomes fall below a certain level.

in-kind benefit a benefit given in the form of goods or services.

negative income tax a government program that supplements the income of low-income working families.

private health insurance program in which each member of a large pool of individuals pays a fixed amount to a private company that agrees to pay most of the medical expenses of the pool's members.

single-payer system a health care system in which the government is the principal payer of medical bills funded through taxes.

Notes

▮ AFTER YOU READ THE CHAPTER

Tips

Tip #1. This chapter discusses two measures of central tendency: the mean and the median. To find the mean, add up all the observed values for a variable and then divide this value by the number of observations. The mean, or simple average, is highly impacted by extremely low or high values. To find the median, first list all the observed values from lowest value to highest value and then find the middle observation in this ranking so that half of the observed values are below the median value and half are above the median value. The median value is not impacted adversely by extremely low or extremely high values. For purposes of measuring average income, the median average income is a far more accurate measure than is the mean average income.

Tip #2. There are two general kinds of benefit programs provided by the government: in kind and in cash. In-kind benefit programs provide benefits in the form of goods or services, whereas in-cash benefit programs provide benefits in the form of monetary payments.

Tip #3. A government program is means tested when there is a list of criteria the recipient must satisfy in order to participate in the program and receive the program's services.

Tip #4. In implementing welfare state programs, government officials are concerned about some potential negative consequences of these programs. Consider the potential effect of welfare state programs on the incentive to work and the incentive to save, as well as the potential deadweight loss that may arise from the implementation of welfare state programs.

Problems and Exercises

1. For each of the following programs, decide whether the program is a poverty program or a social insurance program.

   a. The Unemployment Compensation Program, which provides a payment equal to a fraction of the individual's income when the individual loses his job.

   b. Medicaid, which pays medical expenses for low-income individuals who meet the means-tested criteria.

   c. Medicare, which pays the medical expenses for all eligible elderly individuals regardless of their income.

   d. Food stamps, which provides subsidies to low-income families who meet the means-tested criteria in order to help them purchase food items.

2. The following table provides information about the distribution of income in a small economy for three years.

Name	First year	Second year	Third year
Mary	$ 10,000	$12,000	$12,000
Ellen	12,000	12,000	12,000
Bob	8,000	10,000	12,000
Xiao	100,000	60,000	12,000
Sarah	4,000	8,000	12,000
Maria	20,000	12,000	12,000
Carlos	15,000	12,000	12,000
Juan	12,000	10,000	12,000
Hon Ho	9,000	45,000	12,000

a. Calculate the mean and median income for each of the three years.

b. Does the same individual earn the median income in each of the years?

c. In which year(s) is the mean as good a measure of income distribution as the median? Explain your answer.

d. In which year(s) is the mean not as good a measure of income distribution as the median? Explain your answer.

e. Since the median is the same for all three years, does this imply that the underlying income distribution is the same in all three years?

f. Calculate the mean income over the entire three years. Is this a better measure than the mean income for each specific year? Explain your answer.

3. Identify two rationales for the existence of welfare state programs. After identifying these two rationales, discuss the type of program—poverty or social insurance—that is designed to address the underlying economic issue of the rationale.

4. Describe the relationship between welfare state programs and the incentives to work and save. Is there a potential for the creation of deadweight loss from the implementation of welfare state programs?

5. Identify four sources of poverty.

6. For each of the following programs, identify whether the program is an example of a program offering in-kind benefits or in-cash benefits.

   a. The Unemployment Compensation Program, which provides a payment equal to a fraction of the individual's income when the individual loses his job.

   b. Medicaid, which pays medical expenses for low-income individuals who meet the means-tested criteria.

   c. Medicare, which pays the medical expenses for all eligible elderly individuals regardless of their income.

   d. Food stamps, which provides subsidies to low-income families who meet the means-tested criteria in order to help them purchase food items.

7. Suppose the government of Utopia is concerned about income distribution issues in Utopia's economy. Government officials propose implementing a negative income tax that will consist of all individuals receiving a $10,000 payment from the government while simultaneously requiring that all individuals pay a flat tax of 25% of their total income including the government payment. For instance, an individual who earns $0 in income would receive a $10,000 payment from the government and would then pay 25% of their income after the government subsidy to the government. Thus, this individual would pay $2,500 to the government and would have $7,500 in after-tax income. The table below summarizes this transaction for this individual.

Initial income	Government subsidy	Total before tax income	Tax	After-tax income
$0	$10,000	$10,000	$2,500	$7,500

a. Following the same reasoning as outlined in the above information, fill in the following table based on the implementation of this program.

Initial income	Government subsidy	Total before tax income	Tax	After-tax income
$ 0	$10,000	$10,000	$2,500	$7,500
10,000				
20,000				
30,000				
40,000				
50,000				
60,000				

b. At what initial level of income does the individual find that their tax payment to the government exactly equals the $10,000 subsidy?

c. This negative income tax is designed to provide an incentive for low-income people to work. Do you think this program meets this goal? Explain your answer.

8. Suppose the government of Utopia is concerned about income distribution issues in Utopia's economy. Government officials propose implementing a negative income tax that will consist of all individuals receiving a $10,000 payment from the government while simultaneously requiring that all individuals pay a flat tax of 20% of their total income including the government payment. For instance, an individual who earns $0 in income would receive a $10,000 payment from the government and would then pay 20% of their income after the government subsidy to the government. Thus, this individual would pay $2,000 to the government and would have $8,000 in after-tax income. The table below summarizes this transaction for this individual.

Initial income	Government subsidy	Total before tax income	Tax	After-tax income
$0	$10,000	$10,000	$2,000	$8,000

a. Following the same reasoning as outlined in the above information, fill in the following table based on the implementation of this program.

Initial income	Government subsidy	Total before tax income	Tax	After-tax income
$ 0	$10,000	$10,000	$2,000	$8,000
10,000				
20,000				
30,000				
40,000				
50,000				
60,000				

b. At what initial level of income does the individual find that their tax payment to the government exactly equals the $10,000 subsidy? Compare your result in problem 7(b) with your result in problem 8(b): what is the effect of reducing the flat tax rate on the break-even income?

9. Edenville, a small country of 100 people, decides that it will provide health care insurance to all 100 people who live in Edenville. Each person living in Edenville will be charged a health care premium that is the same for all individuals. Initially, everyone in Edenville endorses this plan and willingly makes the required payment. In Edenville, 20% of the population never gets sick and never incurs any medical expenses; 40% of the population gets sick occasionally, and the yearly medical expense for this group is $500 per person; and the last 40% of the population gets sick often, and the yearly medical expense for this group is $5,000 per person. Initially, no one in Edenville knows which category of health they represent.

a. If Edenville is to collect a sufficient amount of money to cover all of the medical expenses of their population during the year, how much money will they need to collect?

    b. If Edenville charges each resident the same amount for health care insurance, what will the premium be per person?

Suppose people in Edenville become aware of whether they are in the healthy group, the relatively healthy group, or the sick group. Base your answers to the following questions on these individuals having this knowledge.

    c. Suppose the healthy individuals petition the government to be exempt from the health care program. They argue that 100% of their premium pays medical expenses that are incurred by other people in the population. If the healthy individuals leave the insurance pool, what level of insurance premium will the government need to collect to be able to pay all of the medical costs that will be incurred in Edenville in a year's time?

    d. Consider the premium you calculated in part (c). Is the level of this premium an amount that the remaining less-healthy and sick individuals will still be willing to pay? Explain your answer and provide a logical argument to support your answer.

    e. If both the healthy and the relatively healthy individuals opt out of the health care program, what level of premium per person will the sick group need to pay to cover all of the medical expenses that are incurred in Edenville during the year? Will this group be willing to pay this amount?

BEFORE YOU TAKE THE TEST

Chapter Review Questions

1. The welfare state refers to
    a. Temporary Assistance to Needy Families.
    b. Social Security.
    c. the Earned Income Tax Credit.
    d. the collection of government programs that are aimed at alleviating economic hardship.

2. Government transfers are
    a. payments to the government that provide support to the poor, to the unemployed, to the elderly, and to those needing assistance in paying medical bills in a society.
    b. payments by the government to the poor, to the unemployed, to the elderly, and to those needing assistance in paying medical bills in a society.
    c. the collection of programs that are aimed at alleviating economic hardship.
    d. Answers (a), (b), and (c) are all correct.

3. Suppose the government taxes a family that earns $500,000 and collects a tax equal to $2,000. The government then provides a family that earns $23,000 an extra $2,000. Which of the following statements is true?

   a. The $2,000 is equally valuable to both families since it represents the same amount of purchasing power to both families.

   b. The $2,000 is more highly valued by the high-income family since they know and appreciate more fully the merits of a higher income.

   c. The $2,000 is more highly valued by the low-income family because they received these dollars without having to perform extra work or any tangible service. It was "free" to them.

   d. The $2,000 is likely to make a greater difference in the quality of life for the low-income family than for the high-income family.

4. The government recently announced a program aimed at reducing the percentage of families earning incomes below the poverty line. The announced program is an example of a

   a. poverty program.

   b. social insurance program.

5. The government recently announced a program aimed at providing financial resources to workers who have been temporarily laid off from their jobs. The announced program is an example of a

   a. poverty program.

   b. social insurance program.

6. Which of the following statements is true?

   I. A major rationale for the welfare state is the desire to achieve economic equality for all members of a society.

   II. A major rationale for the welfare state is the desire to achieve a just distribution of income for all members of a society.

   III. A major rationale for the welfare state is the desire to alleviate income inequality.

   IV. A major rationale for the welfare state is the desire to alleviate economic insecurity.

   a. Statement I is true.

   b. Statement II is true.

   c. Statement III is true.

   d. Statement IV is true.

   e. Statements I and III are true.

   f. Statements III and IV are true.

   g. Statements I, III, and IV are true.

   h. Statements I, II, III, and IV are true.

7. The welfare state is best justified by the

   a. ability-to-pay principle.

   b. benefits-received principle.

8. Which of the following statements is true?
   I. Only political conservatives support the creation of welfare state programs.
   II. Only political liberals support the creation of welfare state programs.
   III. Both political conservatives and liberals support the creation of welfare state programs, although the two groups differ as to the appropriate extent of these programs.
   a. Statement I is true.
   b. Statement II is true.
   c. Statement III is true.

9. Welfare state programs
   a. create deadweight loss since they affect the incentives to work and to save in a society.
   b. are efficient since they increase the purchasing power of the less fortunate.
   c. are efficient since high-income individuals do not value highly the marginal tax dollars that are collected from high-income individuals to finance the welfare state program.
   d. do not create deadweight loss since the recipients of funds from welfare state programs did not originally demand the goods and services they can now afford.

10. Suppose John Rawls and Robert Nozick visited your campus to discuss their views on economic fairness. Which of the following statements is true?
   a. Rawls and Nozick share very similar views with regard to economic fairness.
   b. Rawls tends to see a larger role for government in the effort to achieve an economically fair society.
   c. Nozick tends to see a larger role for government in the effort to achieve an economically fair society.
   d. Nozick argues that we should do unto others as we would like them to do unto us if we were in the same place.

11. The "veil of ignorance" refers to
   a. establishing economic and social policies without knowing which individuals would be considered rich or poor, healthy or ill, employed or unemployed.
   b. the government granting financial assistance to individuals without knowing whether or not the individual is rich or poor, healthy or ill, employed or unemployed.
   c. basing justice on rights rather than results when the government ignores the economic status of individuals while enacting government programs.

12. To be considered poor in the United States, your household income
   a. must be below $30,000.
   b. must be below the minimum amount deemed adequate to purchase the necessities of life.
   c. must fall below the poverty threshold.
   d. Answers (a), (b), and (c) are all true.
   e. Answers (b) and (c) are true.

13. The poverty threshold is the same for individuals and for families.
   a. True
   b. False

14. Which of the following statements is true?
   I. Since 1959, the percentage of the population living below the poverty threshold has remained roughly constant.
   II. Since 1959, the percentage of the population living below the poverty threshold has fluctuated, but the percentage of the population living below the poverty threshold in 2006 was significantly lower than it had been in 1973.
   III. Since 1959, the percentage of the population living below the poverty threshold has fluctuated, but the percentage of the population living below the poverty threshold in 2006 was significantly higher than it had been in 1973.
   a. Statement I is true.
   b. Statement II is true.
   c. Statement III is true.
   d. None of the above statements are true.

15. Which of the following is a relative measure of poverty?
   a. A person is considered poor when his or her income is below a designated level of income, or poverty threshold.
   b. A person is considered poor when his or her household income is less than half of his or her country's median household income.

16. Compared with other wealthy countries, the United States has a(n)
   a. unusually low poverty rate.
   b. unusually high poverty rate.
   c. similar poverty rate.

17. Which of the following is not a cause of poverty?
   a. Lack of education
   b. Lack of proficiency in speaking English
   c. Racial and gender discrimination
   d. Bad luck
   e. Answers (a), (b), (c), and (d) are all causes of poverty.

18. In the United States, the average household income in 2006 was more than $66,000. This means that
   a. half of all households in the United States earned less than $66,000, and half of all households in the United States earned more than $66,000.
   b. no household in the United States was poor, since all households on average earned $66,000, which is clearly not an impoverished level of income.
   c. if there are households below the poverty threshold in the United States, then the distribution of income in the United States must be highly unequal.
   d. households earning less than the poverty threshold are not making enough effort to earn an income to support themselves.

19. Median household income is equal to
   a. the total income of all households in a country divided by the total number of households.
   b. the income of the household in the exact middle of the income distribution.

20. Suppose income in Fantasia is equally distributed. The bottom 20% of the population receives 20% of the economy's income, the second 20% of the population receives 20% of the economy's income, and so on. The Gini coefficient for Fantasia equals

    a. one.   b. zero.

21. Income inequality

    a. is often associated with political instability.

    b. means that not everyone benefits from the country's prosperity.

    c. is impossible to measure, and therefore public policy should not be based on reducing income inequality.

    d. Answers (a) and (b) are both true.

22. Income inequality among households in the United States

    a. is greater if it is measured over a shorter period than over a longer period.

    b. is the same if it is measured over a shorter period than over a longer period.

    c. is smaller if it is measured over a shorter period than over a longer period.

    d. has an unpredictable pattern when measurements from a short period are compared with measurements gathered over a longer period.

23. Economic insecurity

    a. may be the result of a sudden loss of income.

    b. may be the result of a sudden surge in expenses.

    c. is often caused by significant, and costly, medical problems.

    d. Answers (a), (b), and (c) are all true.

24. The percentage of income spent on food has

    a. remained the same since the poverty threshold was first established in 1963–1964.

    b. fallen from about 33% of income to less than 20% of income since the poverty threshold was first established in 1963–1964.

    c. risen from less than 20% of income to about 33% of income since the poverty threshold was first established in 1963–1964.

    d. no relationship to the poverty threshold that was first established in 1963–1964.

25. Income inequality in the United States

    a. has not varied significantly over the past eighty years.

    b. fell during the 1930s and 1940s, was stable for about thirty-five years after World War II, and then fell again during the last thirty years.

    c. fell during the 1930s and 1940s, was stable for about thirty-five years after World War II, and then rose during the last thirty years.

    d. rose during the 1930s and 1940s, was stable for about thirty-five years after World War II, and then fell again during the last thirty years.

26. The Great Compression refers to

    a. the Great Depression during the 1930s, when wages and salaries fell sharply.

    b. a period around World War II when the U.S. government imposed special controls on wages and prices.

    c. the last thirty years in the United States, when real wages fell for many workers.

    d. the Gilded Age, when income inequality increased dramatically.

27. Growing income inequality in recent years in the United States has been attributed to
    a. rapid technological change, which has reduced demand for low-skilled workers while increasing demand for highly skilled workers.
    b. growing international trade that allows the United States to import many goods made by low-skilled workers, which reduces the demand for low-skilled workers in the United States.
    c. increased immigration, which has exerted downward pressure on low-skilled workers' wages.
    d. highly educated workers earning very different levels of income depending on the chosen professions of these workers.
    e. Answers (a), (b), (c), and (d) have all been cited as possible explanations for growing income inequality in the United States in recent years.

28. A key feature of rising income inequality in the United States in recent years is the
    a. degree to which increasing immigration explains this increase in income inequality.
    b. degree to which international trade has eroded the level of income of low-income individuals in the United States.
    c. disparity in the level of earnings that highly educated workers in the United States receive dependent on the profession they enter: some professions have quite high salaries, whereas others, requiring similar levels of education, have much lower salaries.
    d. degree to which technological innovation has reduced the demand for labor in the United States.

29. A means-tested welfare state program is one that
    a. is available to all individuals in the country.
    b. is available to those individuals in the country with income or wealth below a certain threshold.
    c. is available to those individuals in the country with income or wealth above a certain threshold.
    d. does not reduce the level of income inequality in a country.

30. A non-means-tested welfare state program is one that
    a. is available to all individuals in the country.
    b. is available only to those individuals in the country with income or wealth below a certain threshold.
    c. is available only to those individuals in the country with income or wealth above a certain threshold.
    d. does not reduce the level of income inequality in a country.

31. The main welfare state program that provides assistance to low-income families with children is
    a. the Aid to Families with Dependent Children program (AFDC).
    b. the Temporary Assistance for Needy Families program (TANF).
    c. Social Security.
    d. Medicare.

32. Which of the following programs in not means tested?
    a. Social Security
    b. Temporary Assistance for Needy Families
    c. Supplemental Security Income
    d. Earned Income Tax Credit

33. Which of the following statements is true?

   a. In the United States, the combination of tax and transfer programs essentially leaves the income distribution unchanged.

   b. In the United States, the individuals who pay taxes tend to be different from the individuals receiving transfer payments, and the income distribution in the United States is impacted by these tax and transfer programs.

   c. In the United States, the welfare state has little, if any, impact on income distribution.

   d. In the United States, the welfare state is administered in such a way that there is no efficiency cost to the programs supported by the welfare state.

34. In the United States in 2006, health care was paid primarily by

   a. the government and by private insurance companies.

   b. the government and by direct payments from individuals.

   c. direct payments from individuals and by private insurance companies.

   d. the government and by charitable organizations.

35. Health care expenses in the United States are

   a. spread evenly across the population.

   b. incurred unevenly across the population, with 20% of the population accounting for 80% of health care expenses.

   c. incurred only by the uninsured.

   d. only a problem for those who are poor.

36. Private health insurance

   a. works by having members of the private health insurance pool pay a fixed amount into a common fund, which is then used to pay most of the medical expenses incurred by the insurance pool's members.

   b. works by pooling together those individuals with high risk of medical expenses so that these individuals can help each other afford health insurance.

   c. may fail to work due to the adverse selection problem.

   d. Answers (a), (b), and (c) are all true.

   e. Answers (a) and (c) are true.

37. Employment-based insurance is widespread because

   a. the group of insured employees is likely to contain a mix of healthy and less healthy people rather than a group of people who want health insurance because they anticipate they will have high health care expenses.

   b. the government provides special, favorable tax treatment to this type of health insurance.

   c. it is the cheapest way to insure poor people and elderly people.

   d. Answers (a), (b), and (c) are all true.

   e. Answers (a) and (b) are true.

38. The program that provides health insurance coverage to all Americans aged sixty-five and older, regardless of their income, is

   a. Medicaid.

   b. Medicare.

39. Low-income workers often do not have health insurance because
   a. their employers do not provide coverage for them and they cannot afford private health insurance.
   b. they have preexisting medical conditions that result in private health insurers refusing to cover these individuals.
   c. Both (a) and (b) are the reasons low-income workers often find themselves without health insurance.

40. Health care expenditure per person in the United States is
   a. about the same as health care expenditure per person in France, Britain, and Canada.
   b. lower than health care expenditure per person in France, Britain, and Canada.
   c. higher than health care expenditure per person in France, Britain, and Canada.
   d. higher than health care expenditure per person in France and Canada, but lower than health care expenditure per person in Britain.

41. Welfare state programs that aid the poor often face the problem in which earning more actually leaves the family worse off. This "notch" problem acts like a
   a. low marginal tax rate on the income received by the poor family.
   b. high marginal tax rate on the income received by the poor family.

ANSWER KEY

Answers to Problems and Exercises

1. a. This is a social insurance program, since it is aimed at stabilizing income for all working individuals rather than targeting poor individuals.

b. This is a poverty program, since it is aimed at providing medical care for the poor, who are identified by meeting a set of standards that assesses the means of these individuals.

c. This is a social insurance program, since it is aimed at stabilizing income for all eligible elderly individuals rather than targeting poor elderly individuals.

d. This is a poverty program, since it is aimed at providing subsidized food to the poor, who are identified by meeting a set of standards that assesses the means of these individuals.

2. a.

	First year	Second year	Third year
Mean	$21,111	$20,111	$12,000
Median	12,000	12,000	12,000

b. No, since everyone earns the same income of $12,000 per year in the third year, everyone receives the median income. In the first year, Juan and Ellen both earn the median income. In the second year, Ellen, Maria, and Carlos all earn the median income.

c. In the third year the mean and the median provide the same measure of $12,000; more important, income is evenly distributed in the third year, with all individuals receiving the same amount of income, so the mean does not distort the income of the average person since everyone has the same income.

d. In the first and second years, the mean is not as good a measure of the income distribution as the median since in both of these years some individuals earn substantially more than the median income, which results in the mean income being much higher than the median income. In the first year, Xiao earns an income that is substantially greater than the median income, and in the second year Xiao and Hon Ho both earn incomes that are greater than the median income.

e. No, the underlying distribution of income is different in the three years even though the median income is the same.

f. The mean income for the entire three-year period is $17,741. This is a better measure of average income than the average from any one year since it smooths out the fluctuations in average income that occur from year to year.

3. The two rationales for welfare state programs are the alleviation of income inequality and the alleviation of economic insecurity. Poverty programs are designed to reduce income inequality, whereas social insurance programs are designed to provide protection against unpredictable economic distress.

4. Welfare state programs, designed to reduce income inequality and/or economic insecurity, may affect people's desire to work and save. When individuals know that the government will provide support when the individual lacks economic means, this lessens the incentive for the individual to be prudent with regard to their saving while also potentially affecting the individual's desire to work. These negative aspects of welfare state programs result in the creation of deadweight losses similar to the losses that are created when the government imposes taxes.

5. Poverty may be caused by lack of education, lack of English language proficiency, the presence of gender or racial discrimination, or due to bad luck.

6. a. The Unemployment Compensation Program provides dollars to the recipient, and the recipient is free to choose how he or she wishes to spend these dollars. This is an in-cash benefit program.

    b. Medicaid provides health care services to the poor. This is an in-kind benefit program.

    c. Medicare provides health care services to eligible elderly individuals. This is an in-kind program.

    d. Food stamps help recipients purchase food at reduced cost. Since this aid can only be used on food purchases, it is an example of an in-kind benefit program.

7. a.

Initial income	Government subsidy	Total before tax income	Tax	After-tax income
$ 0	$10,000	$10,000	$ 2,500	$ 7,500
10,000	10,000	20,000	5,000	15,000
20,000	10,000	30,000	7,500	22,500
30,000	10,000	40,000	10,000	30,000
40,000	10,000	50,000	12,500	37,500
50,000	10,000	60,000	15,000	45,000
60,000	10,000	70,000	17,500	52,500

    b. When individuals earn $30,000, they receive the $10,000 payment from the government but must also pay $10,000 to the government in taxes. Their initial income and their after-tax income is $30,000.

    c. For low-income individuals this program provides an incentive to work, since it enhances the individual's income for any income level less than $30,000.

8. a.

Initial income	Government subsidy	Total before tax income	Tax	After-tax income
$ 0	$10,000	$10,000	$ 2,000	$ 8,000
10,000	10,000	20,000	4,000	16,000
20,000	10,000	30,000	6,000	24,000
30,000	10,000	40,000	8,000	32,000
40,000	10,000	50,000	10,000	40,000
50,000	10,000	60,000	12,000	48,000
60,000	10,000	70,000	14,000	56,000

    b. When individuals earn $40,000, they receive a payment from the government of $10,000 but must also pay 20% of their total income of $50,000 to the government. When the flat tax rate is lowered, it raises the level of the break-even income.

9. a. The total medical expenses in Edenville for the year are equal to $220,000 ($20,000 are the medical expenses associated with the relatively healthy group, and $200,000 are the medical expenses associated with the sick group).

    b. If each person contributes the same amount, the premium will equal $2,200 per person. This premium is $2,200 more than the healthy person wants to pay for health care insurance, $1,700 more than the relatively healthy person wants to pay for health care insurance, and $2,800 less than the total cost of care that the sick person will incur during the year.

c. If the twenty healthy people leave the pool, the $220,000 in medical costs must be paid by the remaining eighty people. The premium per person would therefore equal $2,750. This is $2,250 more than the value of the health care insurance that the relatively healthy person receives and $2,250 less than the cost of providing health care to the relatively sick individual.

d. Referring back to answer (c), the health care premium is higher than the cost of providing health care for the relatively healthy individual and lower than the cost of providing health care for the sick individual. The relatively healthy individual will not be willing to pay the premium, whereas the sick individual will find this insurance program a bargain.

e. If only the forty sick people are left in the program, the health care insurance premium will be equal to $5,500. This amount is $500 more than the cost of providing health care to the sick individual (the sick individual is now paying for his or her own health care as well as the health care of the relatively healthy individual). This group will not be willing to pay this amount, since it is greater than their individual medical costs.

Answers to Chapter Review Questions

1. **Answer d.** *Welfare state* is a general term that encompasses all the various programs the government operates that are designed to lessen economic hardship.

2. **Answer b.** *Government transfers* refers to the payments made by the government to different individuals who qualify for government support, which provides economic support to the poor, to the elderly, to those who are unemployed, and to those needing assistance in paying their medical bills. The collection of programs that are aimed at alleviating economic hardship is the welfare state.

3. **Answer d.** The high-income family may have to forgo a few things when they pay this tax, but they will not be giving up necessities. On the other hand, the low-income family will find this additional income represents a significant difference in their quality of life: it will enable this family to purchase goods and services they otherwise could not afford. The low-income family finds that a marginal dollar is worth more to them than it is to the high-income family.

4. **Answer a.** Programs directed at reducing economic inequality are poverty programs, whereas programs designed to provide protection against unpredictable distress are known as social insurance programs.

5. **Answer b.** Programs directed at reducing economic inequality are poverty programs, whereas programs designed to provide protection against unpredictable distress are known as social insurance programs.

6. **Answer f.** The two major rationales for the welfare state are the alleviation of income inequality and the alleviation of economic insecurity. These two goals do not necessarily imply the achievement of an equal distribution of income or a just distribution of income.

7. **Answer a.** The welfare state is based on the idea that an additional dollar makes a big difference to low-income individuals. This justifies a progressive tax system in which low-income individuals pay a smaller fraction of their income to the government than do high-income individuals. The ability-to-pay principle supports the idea that those with very low incomes should actually get money back from the tax system.

8. **Answer c.** Liberals and conservatives both believe that some level of welfare state programs need to exist: conservatives typically favor less extensive programming, and liberals typically favor more extensive programming.

9. **Answer a.** Like taxes, welfare state programs cost more than just their direct monetary costs. Welfare state programs that provide support to the poor and to the unlucky create deadweight loss, since they alter the incentives to work and to save.

10. **Answer b.** Rawls sees a larger role for government: he believes that economic justness should reflect the idea that we should treat others as we would like to be treated if we were in the same situation as these other people. Nozick, in contrast, sees a much smaller role for government with regard to economic justice.

11. **Answer a.** The "veil of ignorance" is a theoretical construct used by John Rawls to develop a theory of economic fairness. In this theory, Rawls imagines that individuals decide on economic and social policies without knowing their own status: thus, the individual is not biased by knowledge of his or her own need when deciding what types of programs are needed to achieve an economically fair society.

12. **Answer e.** The poverty threshold is defined as the minimum annual income that is considered adequate to purchase the necessities of life. The dollar amount of this poverty threshold is not static, but changes as the price of goods and services change. If your household income falls below the poverty threshold, then your household is considered poor.

13. **Answer b.** The poverty threshold depends on the size and the composition of a family. For example, the poverty threshold for an individual is a lower dollar amount than it is for a family of four.

14. **Answer c.** During this period, the percentage of the population living below the poverty threshold has fluctuated, but the percentage of the population living below the poverty threshold was higher in 2006 than it was in 1973.

15. **Answer b.** A relative measure of poverty is a poverty definition that compares the individual's level of income with the level of income received by other individuals in the country. An absolute measure of poverty is one based on a dollar amount.

16. **Answer b.** By either relative or absolute measures, the United States has an unusually high poverty rate.

17. **Answer e.** The major causes of poverty are lack of education and English language proficiency, racial and gender discrimination, and bad luck.

18. **Answer c.** Answer (a) is the definition of the median household income. Answers (b) and (d) are nonsense answers: the average household income figure for a country tells you nothing about whether or not there are poor households in the country, nor does it tell you anything about the effort poor people expend on earning an income.

19. **Answer b.** Half of all households in the income distribution earn less income than the median income, and half of all households in the income distribution earn more income than the median income.

20. **Answer b.** The value of the Gini coefficient falls within the range of zero to one. A Gini coefficient of zero indicates an equal distribution of income, whereas a Gini coefficient of one indicates an extremely unequal distribution of income where all of the country's income goes to a single individual.

21. **Answer d.** Income inequality means that income is unequally distributed among residents of a country and therefore not everyone benefits from the country's general prosperity. Income inequality is also associated with political instability, since income inequality often creates tension between the wealthy members of the society and the less wealthy members of the society.

22. **Answer a.** Incomes of many families vary over time, so measurements of income inequality that averages income over a longer period smooths out these income fluctuations and results in a lower measure of income inequality.

23. **Answer d.** All four answers are associated with economic insecurity that arises because of a sudden decrease in income (job loss) or a sudden surge in expenses (particularly associated with expensive medical problems).

24. **Answer b.** In establishing the poverty threshold, Mollie Orshansky estimated the cost of buying an inexpensive but nutritionally adequate diet. In 1963–1964 the cost of this diet was approximately 33% of a low-income family's budget. Over time, the cost of this diet has fallen to below 20% of a low-income family's budget as the costs of housing, health care, transportation, and child care have risen.

25. **Answer c.** This is just a factual question, and you should refer back to the text to see that income inequality fell during the 1930s and 1940s, was stable during the thirty-five years after World War II, and then rose during the last thirty years.

26. **Answer b.** The Great Compression refers to the period around World War II when income inequality was greatly reduced and this reduction in income inequality persisted for decades after wage and price controls were lifted in 1946.

27. **Answer e.** See the textbook for a discussion of these various sources of income inequality in the United States in recent years.

28. **Answer c.** The striking aspect of income inequality in the United States in recent years is the difference in incomes received by individuals with high levels of education. Much of the increase in income inequality reflects these growing differences in income among highly educated workers, and not the difference in income between poorly educated workers and more educated workers.

29. **Answer b.** A means-tested welfare state program is one that requires recipients to meet an income or wealth requirement: if the individual's income or wealth is lower than the program's established threshold, then the individual is eligible for the program; if the individual's income or wealth is greater than the program's established threshold, then the individual is not eligible for the program. Therefore, a means-tested welfare state program is not available to all individuals in the country. A well-designed means-tested welfare state program should reduce income inequality in a country.

30. **Answer a.** A non-means-tested welfare state program is one that does not require recipients to meet some threshold of poverty in order to be eligible. These programs provide their benefits to everyone, but they are designed to reduce income inequality.

31. **Answer b.** The welfare state program that provides assistance to low-income families with children is called TANF. This program replaced AFDC during the 1990s and is an attempt to rectify the negative incentives in the AFDC program.

32. **Answer a.** Social Security guarantees retirement income and is available to all qualifying older Americans. The other three programs are means tested.

33. **Answer b.** The U.S. welfare state programs do impact the income distribution, primarily because the individuals who pay the bulk of taxes are different from the individuals who receive transfer payments from the government. The tax systems to support the welfare state programs and the actual programs both create economic inefficiency, since they alter the incentives that individuals face with regard to their work and leisure choices.

34. **Answer a.** In the United States, 46% of health care expenses in 2006 were paid by the government, 42% were paid by private insurance companies, and 12% were paid directly by individuals.

35. **Answer b.** Health care expenses are spread unevenly in the United States: 5% of the population accounts for almost 50% of health care expenses in a given year, and 20% of the population accounts for 80% of health care expenses.

36. **Answer e.** Answer (a) provides a general description of private health insurance, and answer (c) points out that adverse selection may keep private health insurance from working. Adverse selection occurs when the process of providing insurance effectively drives out the low-risk individuals, leaving only high-risk individuals in the insurance pool. This process implies that the cost of insuring these individuals will rise, which will increasingly drive out the relatively healthy individuals from the pool until only those

individuals with very high health care expenses are left in the pool. When the pool is composed only of individuals with potentially high health care expenses, the insurance company must charge prohibitively high premiums, and medical care through private insurance provision will fail.

37. **Answer e.** Employment-based insurance is a method that allows insurance companies to substantially reduce the adverse selection problem: by providing insurance to all the employees in a company, the insurance company is provided with a pool of insured individuals that includes both relatively healthy individuals as well as relatively unhealthy individuals. In addition, the government does not make workers pay taxes on the value of their health insurance benefit. Employment-based insurance does not typically insure the poor or the elderly unless the specific individual is working for the company: the poor are insured by Medicaid and the elderly by Medicare.

38 **Answer b.** Medicaid provides health insurance coverage to those Americans who are poor and who meet the means-tested criteria for receiving this insurance. Medicare is the health insurance program for the elderly, and it is not a means-tested program.

39. **Answer a.** Answer (b) is not correct: preexisting medical conditions can cause private health insurers to refuse to supply health insurance to both low-income and high-income workers. Low-income workers lack health insurance most often because their jobs do not provide employer-based insurance and they cannot afford to purchase private health insurance.

40. **Answer c.** See the text for the discussion of how health care expenditure per person in the United States compares with the level of expenditure in France, Britain, and Canada.

41. **Answer b.** The "notch" problem occurs when a poor family that has been receiving aid from a program increases its earnings and finds that this increase in earnings leads to a reduction in the level of aid they receive from the government. This situation makes the family worse off, and the resultant effect on the family is much like the result you would see if the family was subjected to a high marginal tax rate on their additional earnings.

chapter 20

Factor Markets and the Distribution of Income

■ BEFORE YOU READ THE CHAPTER

Summary

This chapter discusses factor markets and the determination of factor prices in these markets. Factor markets include the markets for land, labor, and physical and human capital. The chapter discusses the determination of the factor distribution of income. The chapter primarily focuses on the labor market and the determination of the equilibrium wage rate. The chapter also develops the marginal productivity theory of income distribution before exploring the sources of wage disparity and the role and effect of discrimination in the labor market. Finally, the chapter also considers how a worker's time allocation decision determines the supply of labor curve.

Chapter Objectives

Objective #1. There are three primary categories of resources

- Land, a resource that is provided by nature

- Labor, the resource that is the work done by human beings

- Capital, the value of assets used by a firm in producing its output; physical capital refers to manufactured resources such as equipment, buildings, tools, and machines, while human capital refers to the improvement in labor created by education and knowledge.

Objective #2. Factor markets and factor prices are critical in determining the allocation of resources among competing uses. There are two features that make factor markets special. First, the demand for a factor is a derived demand: this demand depends on or is derived from firms' decisions about how much output to produce. Second, factor markets are, for most of us, the source of the largest share of our income. Factor prices play a key role in determining the income distribution in our economy, since it is these factor prices that determine how the total income in an economy is divided among labor, land, and capital.

- In the United States, payments to labor account for most of the economy's total income. Seventy percent of total income in the United States takes the form of "compensation of employees": this figure has been relatively stable for the past thirty-five years. Much of the return to labor is a return on human capital: the data on labor compensation does not distinguish between the return to labor and the return to human capital, but most economists believe that human capital has become the most important factor of production in modern economies.

Objective #3.   The chapter makes a distinction between a factor of production and an input. A factor of production earns income from selling its services over and over again, while an input is used up in the production process. For example, an individual can sell the use of their labor repeatedly, or the owner of a machine can earn income over time from selling the use of the machine, but an input like energy (electricity, for example) or corn is used up in the production process.

Objective #4.   Firms should hire additional factors of production provided that the marginal cost of the additional factor is less than or equal to the marginal benefit from hiring the additional factor. In a competitive factor market, the marginal cost of an additional unit of a factor is the factor's price: in the case of a competitive labor market, the marginal cost of an additional worker is that worker's wage rate. This equilibrium wage rate is determined by the intersection of the labor supply curve with the labor demand curve: at the equilibrium wage, the quantity of labor supplied is equal to the quantity of labor demanded. In the market for capital and the market for land, the equilibrium factor price also reflects an equilibrium between the quantity supplied of the factor and the quantity demanded of the factor.

- In a competitive labor and product market, the marginal benefit of hiring an additional worker is equal to the value of the marginal product (VMPL) of that worker: the value of the marginal product of a worker is that worker's marginal product of labor times the price of the firm's output. This calculation is expressed by the formula below:

$$VMPL = P \times MPL$$

A firm should continue to hire additional units of labor until the VMPL is equal to the wage rate or until

$$VMPL = W$$

- The firm will apply this general concept when making a decision about hiring any factors of production: the firm should hire additional units of the factor until the point at which the value of the marginal product of the last unit of the factor hired is exactly equal to the factor's price. If the level of output produced by the firm is chosen so that price equals marginal cost, then it is also true that at this output the value of the marginal product of each factor will be equal to the factor's price.

Objective #5.   The VMPL curve is downward sloping: for example, as additional units of labor are hired, the VMPL of labor decreases due to diminishing marginal returns to labor. Although hiring additional units of labor allows the firm to expand its production of output, output eventually increases at a diminishing rate, which implies that the marginal product of labor will decrease. Since in a perfectly competitive output market the firm is a price taker, this implies that as the firm increases its hiring of labor, the VMPL of labor must eventually decline since the constant price is being multiplied by smaller values for the marginal product of labor.

The VMPL of labor curve is the firm's demand curve for labor. Figure 20.1 illustrates the market for labor as well as a representative firm in the market for labor: this labor market is assumed to be perfectly competitive, and therefore the firm accepts the equilibrium wage (W_E) as the wage it will pay when it hires a unit of labor. The VMPL of labor curve is the firm's individual demand for labor curve. The firm selects the amount of labor it wishes to hire (n) by equating the VMPL of labor with the equilibrium wage, since the equilibrium wage represents the marginal cost of hiring an additional unit of labor. The firm's factor demand curve will shift with changes in the price of the goods being produced, with changes in the supply of other factors, and with changes in the level of technology.

Figure 20.1

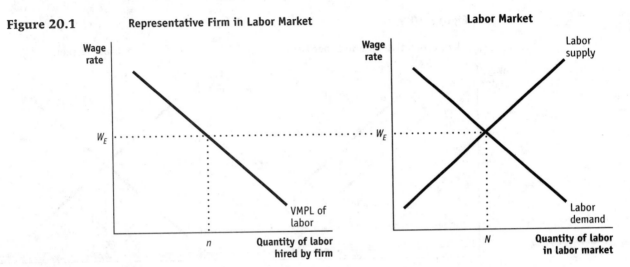

- An increase in the price of the firm's product will cause the VMPL curve for the factor to shift to the right, since each marginal product value for the factor will be multiplied by a higher price, and the profit-maximizing firm will hire more of the factor at a given factor price than it did initially. Figure 20.2 illustrates the effect of an increase in the price of the firm's product on the firm's hiring decision with regard to labor: n is the initial level of labor hired by the firm and n_2 is the amount of labor hired by the firm after the change in the price of the firm's product.

Figure 20.2

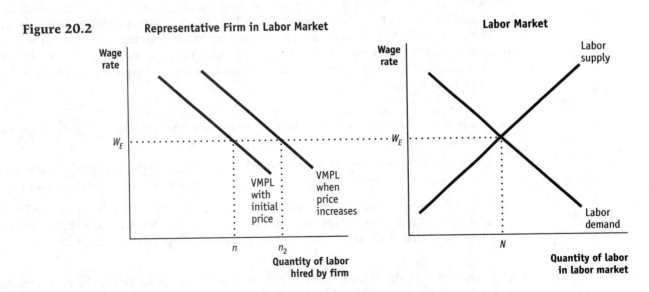

A decrease in the price of the firm's product will cause the VMPL curve for the factor to shift to the left, and the profit-maximizing firm will hire less of the factor at a given factor price than it did initially.

- An increase in the supply of other factors will impact the factor's marginal product: if the marginal product increases, then the VMPL curve will shift to the right for a given product price, and if the marginal product decreases, then the VMPL curve will shift to the left for a given product price. When the VMPL curve shifts to the right, then the profit-maximizing firm will hire more of that factor at a given factor price. If the VMPL curve shifts to the left, then the profit-maximizing firm will hire less of that factor at a given factor price. Figure 20.3 illustrates the change in the firm's hiring of labor when the marginal product of labor increases: the firm initially hires n units of labor but then increases its hiring of labor to n_2 when the marginal product of labor increases.

Figure 20.3

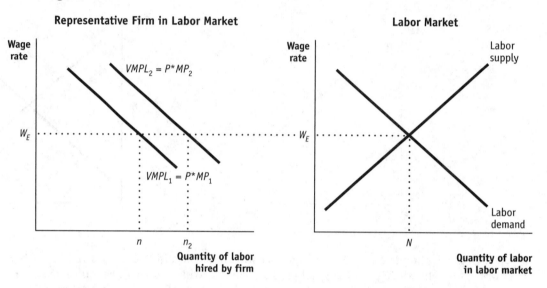

- A change in technology may shift the VMPL curve to the left or to the right, depending on the effect of the technological change on the factor's VMPL. Thus, technological change may increase or decrease the demand for a given factor of production.

Objective #6. The marginal productivity theory of income distribution says that each factor is paid the value of the output generated by the last unit of that factor employed in the factor market as a whole. This is equivalent to saying that each factor is paid the value of its marginal product. This theory implies that the division of income among the economy's factors is not arbitrary, but is instead determined by each factor's marginal productivity at the economy's equilibrium.

Objective #7. There are two main objections to the marginal productivity theory of income distribution.

- In the real world, there are wide disparities in income among people, and some people believe that some of this income disparity is not due solely to differences in marginal productivity.

- Some people believe that the marginal productivity theory of income distribution is based on a moral justification for the distribution of income and they reject the theory because they believe that the resultant distribution of income is not fair or appropriate.

Objective #8. In the United States, there are wide disparities in income between genders and across ethnic groups. Some of this wage disparity can be explained by the following three sources of wage disparity:

- The existence of compensating differentials, where wages are higher or lower depending on how attractive or unattractive the job is;

- The existence of differences in talent, with very talented individuals commanding higher salaries and less talented individuals commanding lower salaries; and

- The existence of differences in human capital, where individuals with high levels of human capital receive relatively higher wages than those individuals with low levels of human capital.

Objective #9. Earnings differences arising from differences in human capital may not be fair or just: individuals who receive poor education because of their socioeconomic status or their race may have labor markets that are well described by marginal productivity theory but whose resultant distribution of income is viewed by many people as unfair.

Objective #10. Some people believe that wage differences cannot be fully explained by compensating differentials, differences in talent, and differences in human capital. They argue that wage differences may also reflect market power, efficiency wages, and discrimination.

- Some workers earn higher wages than otherwise similar workers due to the role of unions that successfully negotiate higher wages and better working conditions for their members. The union is able to exert some market power, which raises wages for this group.

- Some employers pay efficiency wages as a means to motivate their workers. An efficiency wage is a wage that exceeds the equilibrium wage: the worker who receives an efficiency wage is motivated to work harder in order to retain their job. In markets that pay an efficiency wage there is unemployment of labor since there are more people who are willing to supply labor at the efficiency wage than there is demand for labor.

- Discrimination in labor markets is possible when there is market power or when the labor market fails to work efficiently. In both the case of a market with union power or a market that pays efficiency wages there is an excess supply of labor, making it possible for employers to discriminate among job applicants since there are more job applicants than there are jobs.

Objective #11. An individual's decision about how much labor to supply is a decision about time allocation and how the individual chooses to divide their time among different activities. When an individual chooses to work, the individual earns income; when an individual chooses not to work, they increase their consumption of leisure time. For an individual, the optimal amount of labor to supply occurs when the marginal utility of one hour of leisure is equal to the marginal utility the individual gets from the goods their hourly wage can purchase.

Objective #12. An increase in the individual's wage rate may result in the individual supplying more labor or less labor. The higher wage increases the opportunity cost of an hour of leisure—the amount of money the individual gives up if he chooses to work one less hour. The higher wage also generates an income effect: the individual can purchase the same amount of goods and services while working fewer hours. The individual increases the quantity of labor they supply when the wage rate increases if the substitution effect is stronger than the income effect. The individual decreases the quantity of labor they supply when the wage rate increases if the income effect is stronger than the substitution effect. Thus, as the wage rate increases, the individual's supply of labor curve may be upward sloping or downward sloping depending on which of these effects is dominant.

Objective #13. The labor supply curve in a labor market is the horizontal summation of the individual labor supply curves in that market. The labor supply curve in a labor market shifts with changes in preferences and social norms with regard to people's willingness to work, changes in population, changes in opportunities, or changes in wealth.

- The labor supply curve shifts to the right if people's preferences for work increase or if the social norms change so that more people decide it is socially appropriate to work.

- The labor supply curve shifts to the right with an increase in population since the increase in population increases the pool of workers available at any given wage rate.

- The labor supply curve shifts to the right if this labor market represents a superior alternative compared to other labor markets, and the labor supply curve shifts to the left if this labor market represents a less favorable alternative compared to other labor markets.

- The labor supply curve shifts to the left with an increase in wealth, since the increase in wealth enables individuals to purchase more normal goods, including leisure.

Objective #14 [from Appendix]. An individual's labor supply curve can be derived using indifference curve analysis. This requires the construction of the individual's time allocation budget line, which is a budget line showing all the possible leisure–income trade-offs for an individual given the amount of time the individual has available for work and leisure and the wage rate that the individual can earn. The graph depicting the individual's time allocation budget line measures the quantity of leisure on the horizontal axis and income on the vertical axis. The slope of the time allocation line indicates the opportunity cost of an additional hour of leisure: this opportunity cost is equal to the wage rate the individual must give up when they choose to consume an additional unit of leisure. For example, if the individual can earn $10 per hour, then the opportunity cost of one additional hour of leisure is the $10 in lost wages they must give up in order to consume that additional hour of leisure. The individual's optimal time allocation rule is to select the combination of leisure and income that results in the highest utility possible for the individual given the amount of time available and the individual's wage rate. This optimal combination is the point where the marginal utility from the extra money earned from an additional hour spent working is equal to the marginal utility of an additional hour of leisure. Figure 20.4 illustrates a time allocation budget line for an individual with 80 hours of time available each week and with an hourly wage of $10. The individual represented in Figure 20.4 maximizes their utility when they choose to consume 40 hours of leisure per week and work 40 hours per week (which provide them with $400 in income per week). This consumer's optimization point is marked as point A in the figure.

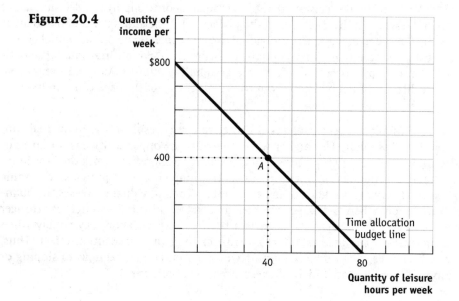

Figure 20.4

Objective #15 [from Appendix]. This indifference curve analysis can be used to consider the substitution and income effects for an individual due to a wage increase or wage decrease. When the wage increases, this has two impacts on the individual: the increase in the wage implies that the opportunity cost of an additional hour of leisure has risen, and as the price of leisure rises the individual substitutes away from leisure and instead chooses to work more hours. However, the income effect works in the opposite direction from the substitution effect: as the individual's income rises they can now afford more leisure, and since leisure is a normal good the individual's income effect is positive.

- If the income effect is stronger than the substitution effect, an increase in the individual's wage rate causes the quantity of labor supplied by the individual to fall: the individual's labor supply curve will be backward bending. Figure 20.5 modifies Figure 20.4 to illustrate the individual's time allocation budget line if the wage rate increases to $12 an hour. In Figure 20.5, the income effect dominates the substitution effect and the individual chooses to consume more leisure (45 hours). Figure 20.6 illustrates the supply of labor curve for this individual: notice that it is downward sloping.

Figure 20.5

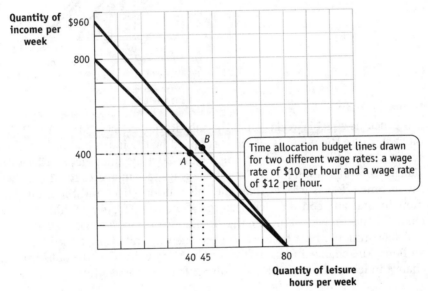

Time allocation budget lines drawn for two different wage rates: a wage rate of $10 per hour and a wage rate of $12 per hour.

Figure 20.6

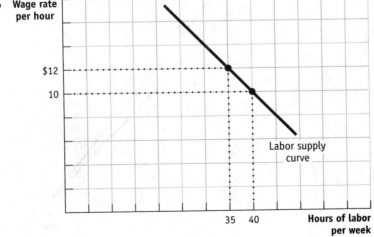

Figure 20.7 illustrates the income and substitution effects that occur when the wage rate is increased from $10 an hour to $12 an hour. The change in leisure from point A to point C is the substitution effect, while the change in leisure from point C to point B is the income effect.

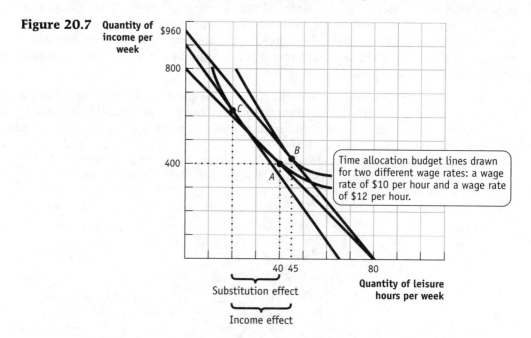

Figure 20.7

If the income effect is weaker than the substitution effect, an increase in the individual's wage rate will cause the quantity of labor supplied by the individual to rise: the individual's labor supply curve will be upward sloping. Figure 20.8 modifies Figure 20.4 to illustrate the individual's time allocation budget line if the wage rate increases to $12 an hour. In Figure 20.8, the income effect is weaker than the substitution effect and the individual chooses to earn more income and consume less leisure (30 hours). Figure 20.9 illustrates the supply of labor curve for this individual: notice that it is upward sloping. Figure 20.10 illustrates the income and substitution effects that occur when the wage rate is increased from $10 an hour to $12 an hour. The change in leisure from point A to point C is the substitution effect, while the change in leisure from point C to point B is the income effect.

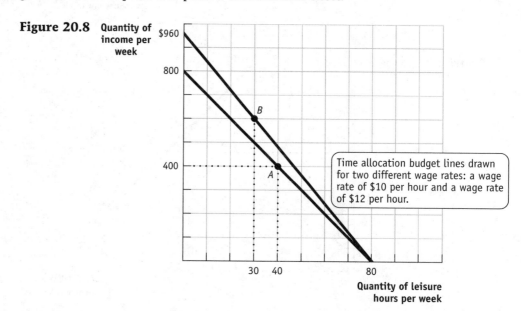

Figure 20.8

Figure 20.9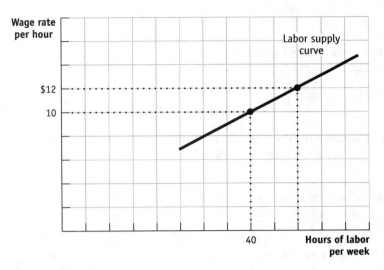

Figure 20.10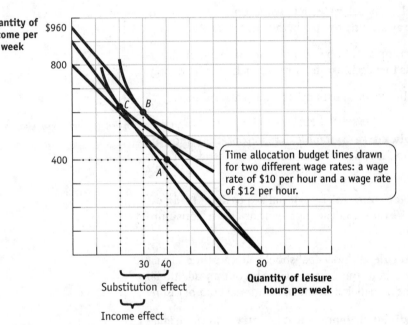

Time allocation budget lines drawn for two different wage rates: a wage rate of $10 per hour and a wage rate of $12 per hour.

Key Terms

physical capital manufactured productive resources, such as buildings and machines; often referred to simply as "capital."

human capital the improvement in labor created by education and knowledge that is embodied in the workforce.

factor distribution of income the division of total income among labor, land, and capital.

value of the marginal product the value of the additional output generated by employing one more unit of a given factor, such as labor.

value of the marginal product curve a graphical representation showing how the *value of the marginal product* of a factor depends on the quantity of the factor employed.

Notes

Key Terms *(continued)*

equilibrium value of the marginal product the additional value produced by the last unit of a factor employed in the *factor market* as a whole.

rental rate the cost, implicit or explicit, of using a unit of land or capital for a given period of time.

marginal productivity theory of income distribution the proposition that every *factor of production* is paid its *equilibrium value of the marginal product*.

compensating differentials wage differences across jobs that reflect the fact that some jobs are less pleasant or more dangerous than others.

unions organizations of workers that try to raise wages and improve working conditions for their members by bargaining collectively.

efficiency-wage model a model in which some employers pay an above-equilibrium wage as an *incentive* for better performance.

time allocation the decision about how many hours to spend on different activities, which leads to a decision about how much labor to supply.

leisure the time available for purposes other than earning money to buy marketed goods.

individual labor supply curve a graphical representation showing how the quantity of labor supplied by an individual depends on that individual's wage rate.

time allocation budget line an individual's possible trade-off between consumption of *leisure* and the income that allows consumption of marketed goods.

optimal time allocation rule an individual should allocate time so that the *marginal utility* gained from the income earned from an additional hour worked is equal to the marginal utility of an additional hour of *leisure*.

backward-bending individual labor supply curve an *individual labor supply curve* that slopes upward at low to moderate wage rates and slopes downward at higher wage rates.

▌ AFTER YOU READ THE CHAPTER

Tips

Tip #1. One of the key tips for working with factor markets is to recognize that the demanders in these markets are firms while the suppliers in these markets are individuals. Firms demand the services of land, labor, and capital, and households (or individuals) supply these services. This is in contrast to output markets where the demanders of the outputs are households and the suppliers of outputs are firms.

Tip #2. When the wage rate increases in the labor market, this causes both an income and a substitution effect for the individual. The wage increase causes the price of an hour of leisure to increase since the individual will now give up a greater amount of income if they elect to increase their consumption of leisure. Thus, the wage increase causes the individual to substitute away from leisure, the relatively more expensive good, toward income, the relatively cheaper good. However, the wage increase also creates an income effect: when the wage increases, the individual's income rises at every level of work effort and this increase in income causes the individual to demand more units of leisure, which is a normal good. Depending on the relative strength of the income and substitution effects, the individual may elect to work more or work less when the wage rate increases.

Tip #3. Profit-maximizing firms face two basic profit-maximizing rules. The first rule states that the firm will profit maximize when it produces the level of output at which marginal revenue equals marginal cost. The second rule says that a firm will profit maximize when it hires the level of factors at which the marginal cost of an additional unit of that factor is equal to the value of the marginal product of that factor. Although one of these rules focuses on the optimal output level while the other focuses on the optimal factor use, the two rules amount to the same principle: undertake production or hiring of a factor only up to the point where the marginal cost of that production or that factor usage is less than or equal to the marginal benefit from that production or that factor usage. By this point in the semester this should be a familiar concept.

Problems and Exercises

1. What is a derived demand? How is this term used to describe the demand for the services of land, labor, and capital?

2. Suppose that the government imposes a minimum wage law that is greater than the equilibrium wage rate in the economy. What will be the effect of this minimum wage law on employment? Use a graph to illustrate the effect of this minimum wage law on the labor market. Who is likely to be affected by this law?

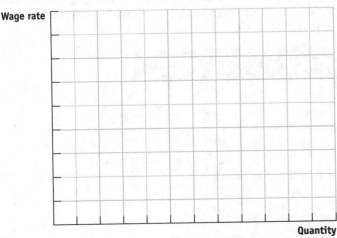

Wage rate

Quantity
of labor

3. Sarah operates a coffeehouse and her production function per week is given in the table below. The current equilibrium weekly wage in the labor market is $400 per week, and Sarah sells each cup of coffee for $3 at her coffeehouse.

Quantity of labor (workers)	Quantity of coffee (number of cups)
0	0
1	300
2	450
3	550
4	600

a. Find the marginal product of labor for each worker and the value of the marginal product of each worker. Put your findings in the table below.

Quantity of labor (workers)	Marginal product of labor (cups of coffee per worker)	Value of the marginal product of labor (dollars per worker)
0	—	—
1		
2		
3		
4		

b. How many workers should Sarah hire?

c. Suppose the equilibrium wage rate fell to $300 per week. How would this change in the equilibrium wage rate affect Sarah's hiring decision? Describe in words how Sarah would determine how much labor she should hire.

4. Mike operates a sandwich shop and his production function is given in the table below. Suppose that the equilibrium weekly wage in the labor market is $300 a week and that Mike sells his sandwiches for $5 each.

Quantity of labor (workers)	Quantity of sandwiches (number of sandwiches)
0	0
1	100
2	180
3	240
4	290

a. Using the above information, fill in the following table.

Quantity of labor (workers)	Marginal product of labor (sandwiches per worker)	Value of the marginal product of labor (dollars per worker)
0	—	—
1		
2		
3		
4		

b. Draw the value of the marginal product of labor curve for Mike's sandwich shop. Use this graph to determine how many workers Mike should hire at his sandwich shop.

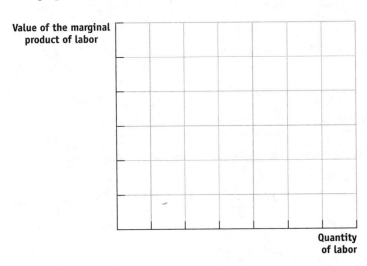

Value of the marginal product of labor

Quantity of labor

c. Suppose that the price of sandwiches falls to $4 a sandwich. Draw a new graph illustrating Mike's value of the marginal product of labor. How will this price change affect the amount of labor Mike chooses to hire?

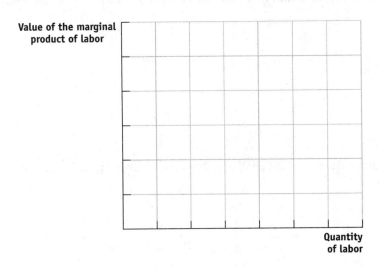

Value of the marginal product of labor

Quantity of labor

5. For each of the following situations, decide what the effect of the situation is on the firm's value of the marginal product of labor curve and on the amount of labor the firm will hire. Assume that the labor and product markets are both perfectly competitive for each of these situations.

   a. The labor hired by the firm has an increase in its level of human capital.

   b. The price of the firm's product decreases.

   c. The technology used to produce the product changes and less labor is needed to produce each level of output than was necessary initially.

   d. The firm decides to increase its use of capital.

6. What are three sources of wage disparity?

7. A friend of yours argues that there is great wage disparity in your economy and that therefore the marginal productivity theory of income distribution is not true since it results in a highly unfair and inequitable income distribution. What do you think about this argument?

8. How are unions and efficiency wages similar with regard to their effects on a labor market?

9. Joe hires labor in a perfectly competitive labor market. Joe and all the other employers in his economy would prefer to hire only men that are the same race as they are (assume that all the employers are of the same race). Why would Joe likely decide not to continue this policy of discrimination in this market?

10. Historically how is discrimination institutionalized in most economies?

11. Suppose that Mark finds that he is willing to work 40 hours a week when his wage rate is $10 an hour, but when the wage rate increases to $15 an hour Mark finds that he is only willing to work 36 hours a week.

   a. If you were to draw Mark's labor supply curve given this information, what would it look like? In the graph below, measure wage rate per hour on the vertical axis and quantity of labor hours per week on the horizontal axis.

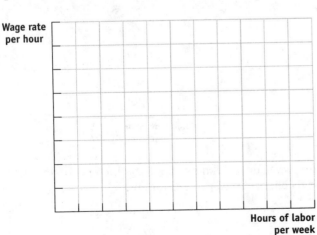

b. Given this information, what do you know about the income effect relative to the substitution effect of this change in wage rates for Mark?

c. What happens to the opportunity cost of an hour of leisure when Mark's wage rate increases from $10 an hour to $15 an hour?

d. Describe the income effect of this wage increase.

12. Suppose that Susan finds that she is willing to work 40 hours a week when her wage rate is $10 an hour, but when the wage rate increases to $15 an hour Susan finds that she is willing to work 44 hours a week.

   a. What is Susan's weekly income when the wage rate is $10 an hour? What is Susan's weekly income when the wage rate is $15 an hour?

   b. If you were to draw Susan's labor supply curve given this information, what would it look like? In the graph below, measure wage rate per hour on the vertical axis and quantity of labor hours per week on the horizontal axis.

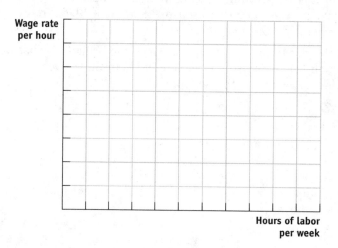

   c. Given this information, what do you know about the income effect relative to the substitution effect of this change in wage rates for Susan?

d. Why would Susan choose to work longer hours when the wage rate is $15 an hour rather than $10 an hour?

13. Suppose that a labor market is composed of two individuals: Sam and Anne. Sam's and Anne's individual supply of labor curves can be described by the following two equations:

Sam's supply of labor: $W = 5 + (1/4)N$

Anne's supply of labor: $W = 5 + (1/6)N$

where W is the wage rate and N is the number of hours worked per week. Furthermore, you are told that the equilibrium wage rate in this labor market is $15 an hour.

a. Find the market supply of labor curve assuming that Sam and Anne are the only two individuals supplying labor in this market.

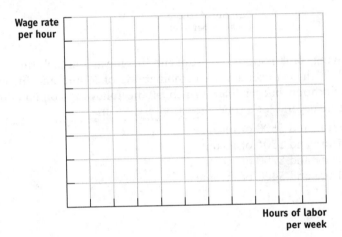

b. What is the total amount of labor supplied in this market at the equilibrium wage rate?

c. What is Sam's weekly income given this equilibrium wage rate?

d. What is Anne's weekly income given this equilibrium wage rate?

14. **[from Appendix]** Joe has 100 hours available each week to devote to leisure and work. Joe's hourly wage rate is $10.

   a. On a graph, draw Joe's time allocation budget line measuring hours of leisure per week on the horizontal axis and income per week on the vertical axis.

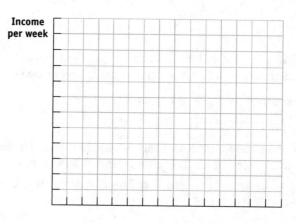

Income per week

Quantity of leisure hours per week

   b. Which of the following combinations of leisure and income are on Joe's time allocation budget line? Which of the following combinations of leisure and income lie inside Joe's time allocation budget line? Which of the following combinations of leisure and income lie beyond Joe's time allocation budget line?

   i.   50 hours of leisure and $500 of income
   ii. 60 hours of leisure and $500 of income
   iii. 30 hours of leisure and $700 of income
   iv. 40 hours of leisure and $400 of income

   c. Suppose Joe maximizes his utility by choosing a labor–leisure point that results in his earning $400 per week. How many hours of leisure does Joe consume?

d. Suppose Joe's wage rate increases to $15 an hour. On a new graph, draw Joe's original time allocation budget line and his new time allocation budget line given the wage increase. Label Joe's initial labor–leisure choice as point *A*. Suppose that Joe decides to consume 50 hours of leisure given this new wage rate. What is Joe's income level now? Label Joe's new labor–leisure choice as point *B*.

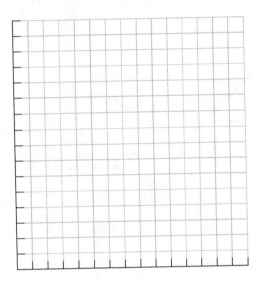

Income per week

Quantity of leisure hours per week

e. Using the initial information and the information in part (d), draw Joe's individual supply of labor curve. In your graph, measure the wage rate per hour on the vertical axis and the hours of labor per week on the horizontal axis.

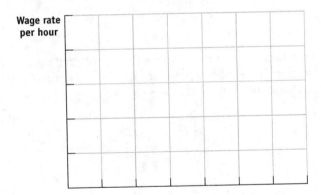

Wage rate per hour

Hours of labor per week

f. Given the wage increase described in part (d), is Joe's income effect or substitution effect dominant? Explain your answer.

15. [from Appendix] The diagram below depicts Maria's time allocation budget line for a week.

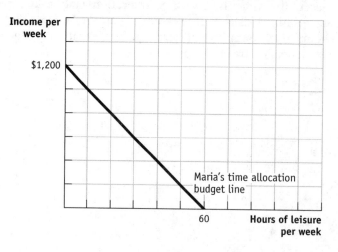

a. What is the maximum number of hours of leisure Maria can consume each week?

b. What is Maria's hourly wage rate?

c. Suppose Maria devotes half of her available time to leisure and half to working. How much income per week will Maria earn? On the graph, label this labor–leisure choice point *A*.

d. Suppose Maria's wage falls to $10 an hour. Redraw the above graph and indicate Maria's initial time allocation budget line, point *A*, and her new time allocation budget line given the decrease in her wage rate.

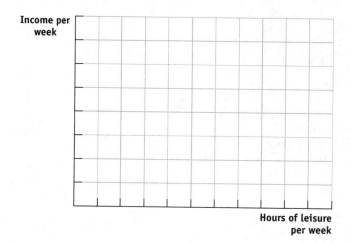

e. With the new wage of $10 per hour, Maria chooses to consume 20 hours of leisure each week. Label this new labor–leisure choice point *B* in your graph. Draw a graph depicting Maria's individual supply of labor curve with hours of labor per week on the horizontal axis and wage rate on the vertical axis.

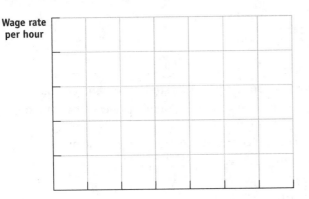

Wage rate per hour

Hours of work per week

f. Given the wage decrease described in part (d), is Maria's income effect or substitution effect dominant? Explain your answer.

BEFORE YOU TAKE THE TEST

Chapter Review Questions

1. Human capital is
   a. the machines, tools, equipment, and buildings that humans own and that they use to produce goods and services.
   b. the improvement in labor that reflects education and knowledge.
   c. relatively unimportant in determining labor's share of total income.
   d. a resource that is provided by nature since human capability is an innate endowment.

2. Capital, from an economist's perspective, refers to
   a. the dollars a household has invested in the stock market.
   b. the value of assets that are used by a firm to produce its output.
   c. both human and physical capital.
   d. Answers (a), (b), and (c) are all true.
   e. Answers (b) and (c) are both true.

3. The improvement in labor that is due to greater education and knowledge is referred to as
   a. physical capital, since the labor has physically made the effort to get more education and knowledge.
   b. human capital, since more educated and knowledgeable labor is more productive.

4. The demand for a factor of production is
    a. dependent on the demand for the output the labor produces.
    b. a derived demand.
    c. dependent on the available supply of that factor.
    d. Answers (a), (b), and (c) are all true.
    e. Answers (a) and (b) are true.

5. The factor distribution of income
    a. describes the share to total income received by land, labor, and capital.
    b. indicates that total income in the economy is evenly divided between land, labor, and capital.
    c. indicates that most household income reflects the selling of labor.
    d. Answers (a), (b), and (c) are all true.
    e. Answers (a) and (c) are true.
    f. Answers (b) and (c) are true.

6. Labor's share of income in the United States over the past thirty-five years has
    a. remained relatively stable at about 70% of total income.
    b. increased rapidly until finally leveling off at 70% of total income.
    c. declined significantly until finally leveling off at 70% of total income.
    d. fluctuated from year to year and shows no discernible constancy.

7. An input is different from a factor of production since
    a. an input can be used over and over again by a business or an individual to earn income.
    b. a factor of production can be used over and over again by a business or an individual to earn income.

Answer the next five questions based on the following information.

In this question, assume the product market is perfectly competitive and that the labor market is also perfectly competitive. Furthermore, assume that the price of the firm's product is $10. The schedule for the firm's total product with respect to labor is given in the table below.

Quantity of labor (number of workers)	Quantity of output
0	0
1	50
2	80
3	100
4	110
5	105

You are also told that the labor demand curve and labor supply curve for the labor market are given by the following equations, where W is the wage rate and N is the number of workers hired:

Market labor demand curve: $W = 400 - N$

Market labor supply curve: $W = N$

8. What is the value of the marginal product of labor for the fourth worker?
    a. $500
    b. $300
    c. $200
    d. $100

9. What is the marginal product of labor for the third worker?
    a. 50 units of output per unit of labor
    b. 30 units of output per unit of labor
    c. 20 units of output per unit of labor
    d. 10 units of output per unit of labor

10. What is the equilibrium wage rate in this labor market?
    a. $500 per worker
    b. $300 per worker
    c. $200 per worker
    d. $100 per worker

11. How many units of labor will this perfectly competitive, profit-maximizing firm choose
    to hire given the above information?
    a. One worker
    b. Two workers
    c. Three workers
    d. Four workers

12. Suppose that the demand for this firm's product increases. Holding everything else con-
    stant, this firm
    a. will continue to hire the same number of workers.
    b. will hire more workers, since the increased demand for its product causes the value
       of the marginal product of labor curve to shift to the right.
    c. will hire fewer workers, since the increased demand for its product causes the value
       of the marginal product of labor curve to shift to the left.
    d. may increase, decrease, or continue to hire the same number of workers.

13. A firm realizes that it has diminishing returns to labor. This means that
    a. its total output decreases as it hires additional units of labor.
    b. the marginal product of labor curve for this firm is downward sloping.
    c. its total output increases as it hires additional units of labor, but it increases at a
       decreasing rate.
    d. Answers (a) and (b) are both true.
    e. Answers (b) and (c) are both true.

14. Suppose the marginal cost of hiring an additional unit of labor is $10 while the value of
    the marginal product from hiring this additional unit of labor is $12. To profit maximize,
    this firm should hire
    a. more labor.
    b. less labor.

15. The equilibrium wage rate in the labor market is $18. A perfectly competitive firm sells its product for $8. Furthermore, suppose that the marginal product of the sixth unit of labor is 3 units of output while the marginal product of the ninth unit of labor is 2 units of output. This firm should hire
    a. fewer than 6 units of labor.
    b. more than 9 units of labor.
    c. more than 6 units of labor but fewer than 9 units of labor.
    d. 6 units of labor.
    e. 9 units of labor.

16. Suppose the marginal cost of an additional unit of a factor is greater than the value of the marginal product of that additional unit of the factor. This means that hiring this additional unit of the factor will add more to the firm's
    a. costs than to the firm's revenue.
    b. revenue than to the firm's costs.

17. The firm's demand curve for labor is equal to the
    a. firm's marginal product of labor curve.
    b. firm's value of the marginal product of labor curve.
    c. firm's marginal cost of hiring labor curve.
    d. market-determined equilibrium wage rate.

18. Suppose that a perfectly competitive firm in both the product and the factor markets decides to increase its hiring of capital. Assume this firm has diminishing returns to all of its factors. Which of the following statements is true?
    I. The firm's marginal product of capital will decline when it hires more capital, holding everything else constant.
    II. The firm's marginal product of labor will increase when it hires more capital, and this will cause the firm to hire more labor at every given wage rate.
    III. The firm's value of the marginal product of labor curve will shift to the right when the firm hires more capital.
    a. Statements I, II, and III are all true.
    b. Statements II and III are true.
    c. Statement III is true.
    d. Statements I and III are true.

19. A firm experiences a change in technology. This
    a. may cause the firm's demand for an input to increase or decrease depending on the nature of the technological change.
    b. causes the firm's demand for an input to increase due to this technological change.
    c. causes the firm's demand for an input to decrease due to this technological change.
    d. does not affect the firm's demand for other inputs since the firm chooses how much of an input to demand based on its production function without regard to the technology that is available to the firm.

20. In a perfectly competitive labor market, the equilibrium wage is the wage at which
    a. the quantity of labor demanded is equal to the quantity of labor supplied.
    b. all people who work in the labor market earn a living wage.
    c. the wage is equal to the value of the marginal product of labor.
    d. Answers (a), (b), and (c) are all true.
    e. Answers (a) and (c) are true.

21. Suppose the factor market for land is perfectly competitive. The factor market for land
    a. resembles the labor market in that the rental price of land in equilibrium is equal to the value of the marginal product of land.
    b. is unlike the labor market since the amount of land is finite and therefore the rental price of land has no connection with the value of the marginal product of land.
    c. is a market where each firm decides how much land to hire based on the relationship between the costs of the last acre of land employed versus the value of the marginal product of that acre.
    d. Answers (a) and (c) are both true.

22. The marginal productivity theory of income distribution states that
    a. each factor is paid a payment equal to that factor's marginal productivity.
    b. each factor is paid a payment equal to the value of the output generated by the last unit of that factor employed in the factor market as a whole.
    c. factor income is distributed evenly and equally across all factors.
    d. all factors are paid less than the value of their marginal product.

23. Which of the following provide an explanation for wage disparities?
    a. Compensating differentials
    b. Differences in talent
    c. Differences in human capital
    d. Answers (a), (b), and (c) are all true.
    e. Answers (a) and (c) are both true.

24. The marginal productivity theory of income distribution provides a moral justification for the prevailing income distribution.
    a. True
    b. False

25. When a union effectively bargains for a wage rate greater than the equilibrium wage rate, this implies that the
    a. union has market power in the labor market.
    b. labor market has an excess supply of labor at the prevailing wage rate.
    c. union may have created a situation that makes employer discrimination more feasible.
    d. Answers (a), (b), and (c) are all true.
    e. Answers (a) and (b) are both true.

26. An individual's decision about how much labor to supply is a decision
   a. about time allocation.
   b. made by firms when they hire labor.
   c. that is independent of the individual's preferences with regard to leisure.
   d. Answers (a), (b), and (c) are all true.
   e. Answers (b) and (c) are both true.

27. Leisure is
   a. a normal good, since as an individual's income rises the individual consumes more leisure.
   b. an inferior good, since as an individual's income rises the individual consumes less leisure.

28. For an individual, the optimal amount of labor to supply is the amount of labor at which, for the last hour of labor supplied, the marginal utility of an additional hour of leisure is
   a. equal to the marginal utility the individual gets from consuming the goods that their hourly wage allows them to purchase.
   b. greater than the marginal utility the individual gets from consuming the goods that their hourly wage allows them to purchase.
   c. less than the marginal utility the individual gets from consuming the goods that their hourly wage allows them to purchase.

29. Carolyn's marginal utility from an additional hour of leisure is 20 utils, while her marginal utility from the income earned from working an additional hour is 25 utils. Carolyn should
   a. work an additional hour, since her additional utility is greater if she devotes this hour to work instead of leisure.
   b. choose to consume an additional hour of leisure, since an hour of leisure must always be preferred to an hour of work.

30. When an individual's labor supply curve is backward bending (that is, downward sloping) this implies that the individual's income effect is
   a. stronger than the individual's substitution effect.
   b. weaker than the individual's substitution effect.

31. With regard to an individual's labor supply curve, the substitution effect of a wage increase refers to the
   a. decrease in the price of leisure relative to the price of other goods.
   b. change in the opportunity cost of an hour of leisure relative to an hour of other goods.
   c. incentive for the individual to consume less leisure and instead work longer hours.
   d. Answers (b) and (c) are both true.

32. [from Appendix] Mike's wage rate increases. Holding everything else constant, this increase will cause Mike's time allocation budget line to pivot

    a. out away from the origin, indicating that he can now earn a higher level of income for a given level of leisure than he could before the wage increase.

    b. in toward the origin, indicating that he can now earn a higher level of income for a given level of leisure than he could before the wage increase.

Use the following graph to answer the next five questions.

The graph below depicts Pablo's time allocation budget line for a week.

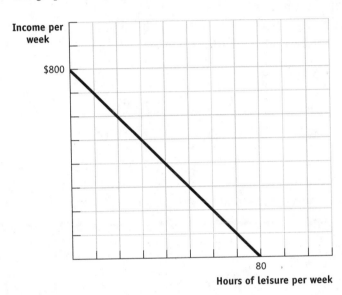

33. [from Appendix] What is Pablo's hourly wage rate?

    a. $800

    b. $80

    c. $10

    d. There is not enough information to answer this question.

34. [from Appendix] What is the opportunity cost of an hour of leisure?

    a. $800

    b. $80

    c. $10

    d. There is not enough information given to answer this question.

35. [from Appendix] Suppose that when Pablo's wage rate is $10 an hour he maximizes his utility when he consumes 40 hours of leisure, but when his wage rate increases to $15 an hour he maximizes his utility by consuming 30 hours of leisure. What is the change in Pablo's income when the wage rate increases to $15 an hour?

    a. $400

    b. $750

    c. $350

    d. $1,200

36. [from Appendix] Suppose that when Pablo's wage rate is $10 an hour he maximizes his utility when he consumes 40 hours of leisure, but when his wage rate increases to $15 an hour he maximizes his utility by consuming 30 hours of leisure. Given this information, which of the following statements is true?

a. Pablo's supply of labor curve is upward sloping.

b. Pablo's supply of labor curve is downward sloping.

37. [from Appendix] Suppose that when Pablo's wage rate is $10 an hour he maximizes his utility when he consumes 40 hours of leisure, but when his wage rate increases to $15 an hour he maximizes his utility by consuming 30 hours of leisure. Given this information, which of the following statements is true?

a. When the wage rate increases, Pablo's income effect is dominant.

b. When the wage rate increases, Pablo's substitution effect is dominant.

ANSWER KEY

Answers to Problems and Exercises

1. A derived demand is a demand that is dependent on the demand for some other good or service. The demand for factors of production such as land, labor, and capital is a derived demand, since the demand firms for these different factors of production are dependent on the output choice that firms make. Firms only demand the level of labor, capital, or land that they need depending on the level of output they choose to produce.

2. The effect of a minimum wage law that sets the minimum wage above the equilibrium wage rate in a market is to create an excess supply of labor. An excess supply of labor is a situation where the amount of labor supplied is greater than the amount of labor demanded at the prevailing wage rate: an excess supply of labor results in the unemployment of labor. The figure below illustrates the supply of labor and the demand for labor as well as the minimum wage rate. The figure indicates the amount of unemployment that occurs at this minimum wage.

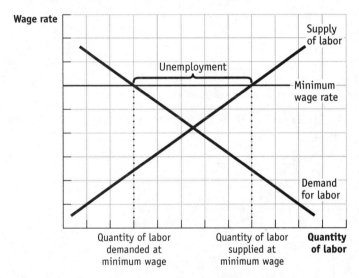

This minimum wage rate benefits those workers lucky enough (or skilled enough) to get a job at this wage rate while hurting those workers who want to work but do not get hired at this wage rate. Low-skilled workers are apt to be most hurt by the minimum wage since they are less attractive to firms due to their low skill level.

3. a.

Quantity of labor (workers)	Marginal product of labor (cups of coffee per worker)	Value of the marginal product of labor (dollars per worker)
0	—	—
1	300	900
2	150	450
3	100	300
4	50	150

b. Sarah should continue to hire workers provided that the value of the marginal product of the additional worker is greater than or equal to the cost of hiring an additional worker. When Sarah hires the first worker, the cost of hiring that worker is $400 per week, but the value of the marginal product of the first worker is $900 per week: Sarah will want to hire the first worker. When Sarah considers hiring the second worker, the cost of hiring that worker is $400 per week, but the value of the marginal product of the second worker is $450 per week: Sarah will want to hire the second worker. But when Sarah considers the third worker, she finds that the marginal cost of hiring the third worker ($400 per week) is greater than the value of the marginal product from this third worker ($300): Sarah will not want to hire this third worker.

c. Sarah would decide how much labor to hire by comparing the additional cost of hiring the labor to the additional revenue from hiring the labor: Sarah would continue to hire labor provided that the value of the marginal product of the last unit of labor hired is greater than or equal to the marginal cost of hiring the last unit of labor. When the equilibrium wage rate falls to $300 per week, Sarah will find that the profit-maximizing amount of labor to hire is 3 workers.

4. a.

Quantity of labor (workers)	Marginal product of labor (sandwiches per worker)	Value of the marginal product of labor (dollars per worker)
0	—	—
1	100	$500
2	80	400
3	60	300
4	50	250

b.

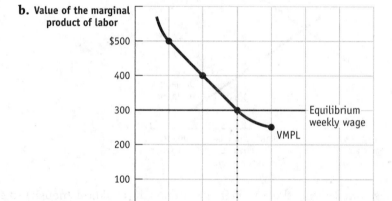

Mike should hire 3 workers given his production function and the above information.

c. When the price of sandwiches decreases from $5 per sandwich to $4 per sandwich, this changes Mike's value of the marginal product of labor curve. The new values are given in the table below.

Quantity of labor (workers)	Marginal product of labor (sandwiches per worker)	Value of the marginal product of labor (dollars per worker)
0	—	—
1	100	$400
2	80	320
3	60	240
4	50	200

This price change causes the VMPL curve to shift to the left: at every wage rate Mike will demand fewer units of labor. The figure below gives the new VMPL curve.

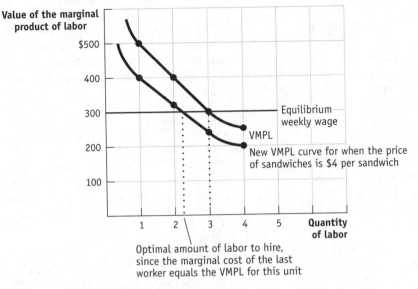

Mike will choose to hire less labor when the price of sandwiches falls to $4: if he has to hire whole units of labor, he will choose to hire 2 workers when the price of his product decreases to $4 per unit.

5. **a.** When the firm's labor experiences an increase in its human capital, this means that the labor becomes more productive and the marginal product of labor increases at each level of labor used. This increase in the marginal product of labor causes the value of the marginal product of labor curve to shift to the right and at any given wage rate the firm will now hire more labor than it did initially.

b. When the price of the firm's product decreases, this causes the firm's value of the marginal product of labor curve to shift to the left. At any given wage rate the firm will now hire less labor than it did initially.

c. The firm now needs less labor than it did before the technology change: this implies that the firm's demand for labor, its value of the marginal product of labor curve, will shift to the left, with the firm hiring less labor than it did initially at the prevailing wage rate.

d. When the firm increases its use of capital, this causes the marginal product of labor to increase at every level of labor usage since each unit of labor will now have more capital to work with. This increase in the marginal product of labor causes the value of the marginal product of labor curve to shift to the right, with the firm hiring more labor at any given wage rate.

6. Wage disparity may be due to compensating differentials, where jobs requiring similar education and experience may pay quite different wages because some of the jobs are less pleasant and attractive than the other jobs. Jobs that are unattractive or dangerous typically pay more than jobs that are more attractive and less dangerous.

Wage disparity may also be due to differences in talent. Someone who is particularly talented with regard to their occupation will likely command a higher wage than someone who has less talent in the same occupation.

Wage disparity may also be due to differences in human capital. Workers with more human capital will receive a higher wage than workers with less human capital.

7. Although there may be large disparities in income in a society, that does not negate the marginal productivity theory of income distribution. Wage disparities may arise from compensating differentials, differences in talent, and differences in human capital. The marginal productivity theory provides a theory about the determination of the income

distribution, but it does not provide a moral or normative judgment about that income distribution. The income distribution might be quite uneven and still support the marginal productivity theory.

8. Both unions and efficiency wages result in a situation in which the wage rate paid is greater than the equilibrium wage rate. This creates a situation where there is an excess supply of labor at the wage rate. The union is able to raise wages above the equilibrium level because the union has market power, while the efficiency wage increases wages above the equilibrium level in order for the wage to serve as a motivator to employees to work harder than they might otherwise choose to do.

9. When Joe limits his hiring decisions to a subgroup of the total population, he effectively reduces the total supply of labor available to him. Since all the other employers are doing the same thing, they effectively have shifted the supply of labor curve to the left and have to pay a higher wage rate than would be the case if they were willing to hire anyone regardless of race and gender (provided they are qualified). Joe will find that by stopping his policy of discrimination he can reduce his cost of labor and therefore enhance the profitability of his enterprise.

10. Discrimination typically results from the acceptance and institutionalization of discriminatory practices by the government. The government passes laws that allow or create discrimination, and it is the government's support of these laws that allows this discrimination to continue.

11. a. As Mark's wage rate is bid up, the number of hours of labor he supplies decreases. This implies that Mark's labor supply curve is downward sloping, since the wage rate and the number of hours worked are inversely related to each other over this range of wages. The figure below illustrates Mark's supply of labor curve.

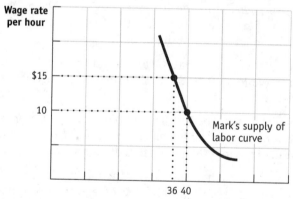

b. The income effect is stronger than the substitution effect over this range of wages. As Mark's wage is bid up, Mark chooses to consume more leisure and less work: the substitution effect of a higher wage makes an hour of leisure relatively more expensive and would tend to encourage Mark to work more and take fewer hours of leisure, but the income effect of a higher wage is that Mark can earn more income working the same number of hours. Since Mark chooses to work fewer hours, it must be the case that the income effect is dominant over the substitution effect in this case.

c. The opportunity cost of an hour of leisure increases when the wage rate increases: for each additional hour of leisure Mark consumes, he is now giving up $15 in lost wages instead of $10. Leisure has gotten relatively more expensive.

d. The income effect of this wage increase is that Mark can earn the same amount of income as he had initially while working fewer hours. For instance, if he works 40 hours a week for $10 an hour he will earn $400, but if his wage increases to $15 an hour he can earn $400 a week by working only 26.67 hours a week. In Mark's case, he chooses to consume a bit more income (36 hours at $15 an hour gives him $540 a week in income) plus 4 more hours of leisure.

12. a. When the wage rate is $10 an hour, Susan's weekly income is $400. When the wage rate is $15 an hour, Susan's weekly income is $660.

   b. Susan's labor supply curve is upward sloping: as the wage rate increases, the quantity of labor supplied increases. The figure below illustrates Susan's supply of labor curve.

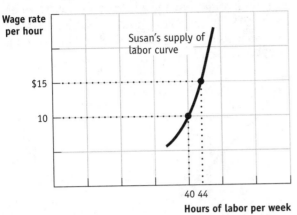

   c. The income effect is dominated by the substitution effect in this example. As the opportunity cost of consuming an additional hour of leisure increases with the increase in the wage rate, Susan opts to work longer hours: the relative price of leisure has risen and Susan moves toward consuming the extra goods made possible by her higher income rather than consuming more leisure. When the substitution effect dominates the income effect for a wage increase, this leads to the supply of labor curve being upward sloping.

   d. Susan chooses to work longer hours because the marginal utility she receives from the additional goods she can purchase with her higher income is greater than the marginal utility she receives from consuming additional hours of leisure.

13. a. The market supply of labor curve is equal to the horizontal summation of the individual supply of labor curves. To find this labor supply curve, you might find it helpful to sketch a graph of Sam's labor supply curve and a graph of Anne's labor supply curve. When the wage rate is $5 an hour, neither Sam nor Anne will supply any labor: the wage rate is too low to convince either of them to work. When the wage rate rises to $10 an hour, Sam is willing to supply 20 hours of work a week while Anne is willing to supply 30 hours of work a week. Thus, at a wage rate of $10 an hour, the total amount of labor supplied in the market is 50 hours a week. From this information you now know two points on the market supply of labor curve: (50 hours a week, $10 an hour) and (0 hours a week, $5 an hour). Use this information to find the market supply of labor curve: $W = 5 + (1/10)N$. The figure below illustrates Sam's supply of labor curve, Anne's supply of labor curve, and the market supply of labor curve.

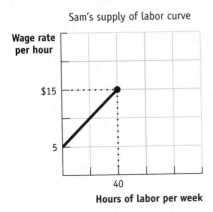

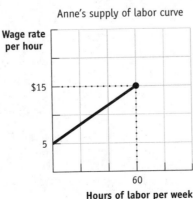

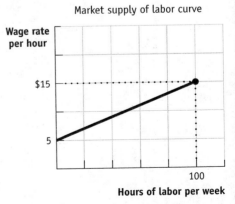

b. When the wage rate is $15 an hour, the total amount of labor supplied in the market is equal to 100 hours a week.

c. To find Sam's weekly income, we first need to know how many hours Sam will work at the equilibrium wage rate of $15 an hour. From Sam's supply of labor curve, we find that Sam is willing to supply 40 hours of work a week at this wage rate, which implies that Sam will earn $600 a week.

d. To find Anne's weekly income, we first need to know how many hours Anne will work at the equilibrium wage rate of $15 an hour. From Anne's supply of labor curve, we find that Anne is willing to supply 60 hours of work a week at this wage rate, which implies that Anne will earn $900 a week.

14. [from Appendix] a.

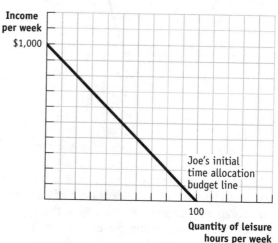

b. i. This combination lies on Joe's time allocation budget line since if Joe selects 50 hours of leisure this implies that he will work 50 hours and earn $500.

　　ii. This combination lies beyond Joe's time allocation budget line since if Joe selects 60 hours of leisure this implies that he will work 40 hours and earn $400.

　　iii. This combination lies on Joe's time allocation budget line since if Joe selects 30 hours of leisure this implies that he will work 70 hours and earn $700.

　　iv. This combination lies inside Joe's time allocation budget line since if Joe selects 40 hours of leisure this implies that he will work 60 hours and earn $600.

c. When Joe earns $400, this means that he is working 40 hours per week at his wage rate of $10 per hour. Since Joe has a total of 100 hours available to divide between work and leisure, he will be able to consume 60 hours of leisure.

d. If Joe decides to have 50 hours of leisure, this implies that he will work 50 hours; since his wage rate is now $15 an hour, he will earn $750 a week. The graph below illustrates Joe's original time allocation budget line as well as his new one. In addition, the graph labels Joe's initial labor–leisure choice (point A) as well as the new labor–leisure choice (point B).

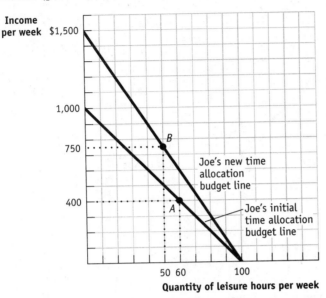

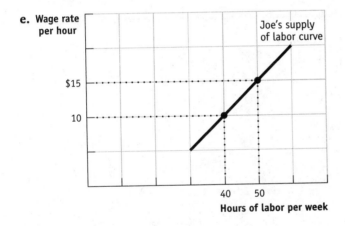

f. Joe's supply of labor curve is upward sloping, which tells us that Joe's substitution effect is stronger than his income effect with respect to an increase in his wage rate. When Joe's wage rate increases, this causes the opportunity cost of an additional hour of leisure to increase from $10 to $15: leisure has become relatively more expensive for Joe. When Joe's wage increases, he chooses to work more hours and have fewer hours of leisure: he substitutes away from the relatively expensive good (leisure) toward the relatively cheaper good (income).

15. [from Appendix] a. The maximum number of hours of leisure Maria can consume each week is equal to 60 hours or the *x*-intercept on the given graph.

b. From the graph, we know that Maria earns $1,200 if she works 60 hours a week and consumes 0 hours of leisure. To find her hourly wage rate, we can divide the $1,200 by 60 hours to get $20 per hour as her wage rate.

c. If Maria works 30 hours a week at a wage rate of $20 per hour, she will earn $600 of income a week.

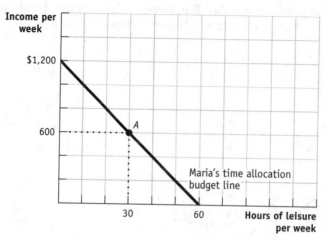

d, e.

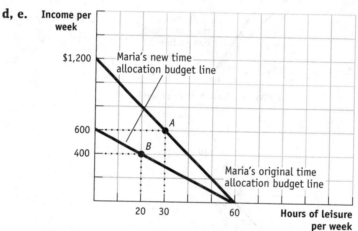

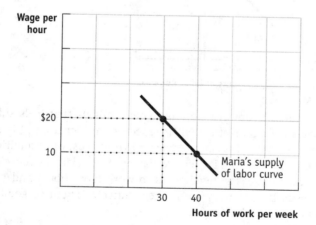

f. Maria's supply of labor curve is downward sloping, which indicates that the income effect is dominant over the substitution effect for Maria. When the wage rate falls, she chooses to consume less leisure even though the decrease in the wage rate makes the opportunity cost of an hour of leisure smaller. Maria opts to allocate more of her time to work even though work has gotten relatively more expensive.

Answers to Chapter Review Questions

1. **Answer b.** Human capital refers to the improvement in labor that is the result of education and knowledge, while physical capital refers to manufactured resources such as machines, tools, equipment, and buildings. An individual's human capital determines the level of compensation the individual receives and is therefore highly important in determining the share of total income that labor receives. The resource that is provided by nature is referred to as land.

2. **Answer e.** Capital refers to human and physical capital. From an economist's perspective, capital does not refer to dollars that have been invested in the stock market, but instead refers to the equipment that companies purchase from the dollars they raise in the stock market.

3. **Answer b.** Human capital refers to the improvement in labor due to increased education and knowledge.

4. **Answer e.** Demand for a factor is a derived demand, since the demand for this factor comes from the firm's decision about how much output to produce.

5. **Answer e.** The factor distribution of income indicates the share of total income received by each factor. The largest factor share is the share of income that labor receives.

6. **Answer a.** The data on labor income as a percentage of total income over the past thirty-five years in the United States indicates that labor's share of total income has been relatively stable and is about 70% of total income.

7. **Answer b.** Factors of production can be used repeatedly to generate income, while an input is used up in the process of production and therefore cannot be a source of future income for its owner.

8. **Answer d.** To find the value of the marginal product of labor, you must first calculate the marginal product of labor and then multiply the marginal product of labor by the price of the firm's output. The marginal product of labor for hiring the fourth worker is equal to 10 units of output and the value of the marginal product of labor for the fourth worker is equal to $100.

9. **Answer c.** To find the marginal product of labor, recall that this requires calculating the ratio of the change in total product divided by the change in labor. When the firm hires the third worker, the change in total product is equal to 100 units of output minus 80 units of output, or a change of 20 units of output. The change in labor is equal to 1 unit since the firm changes the amount of labor it uses from 2 units of labor to 3 units of labor. Thus, the marginal product of labor for the third worker is equal to 20 units of output from this additional unit of labor.

10. **Answer c.** To find the equilibrium wage rate in this market, set the market labor demand curve equal to the market labor supply curve and solve for the equilibrium wage rate. Thus, $400 - N = N$, or $N = 200$. Plugging this value of N into either equation and solving for W, the equilibrium wage rate is $200 per worker.

11. **Answer c.** The firm will choose to hire labor up until that point where the value of the marginal product of the last unit of labor hired is equal to the equilibrium wage rate. The equilibrium wage rate is $200 per worker and the value of the marginal product of labor is equal to $200 per worker when the firm hires three workers.

12. **Answer b.** When the firm's price increases due to the increase in demand for the firm's product, this causes the value of the marginal product of labor curve to shift to the right. At every wage rate, the firm will now want to hire more units of labor than it did prior to the change in the demand for its product.

13. **Answer e.** A firm has diminishing returns to labor when its output increases as more labor is hired, but with the output increasing at a diminishing rate. Since the increase in

output is smaller and smaller with each additional unit of labor hired, this results in a downward-sloping marginal product of labor curve.

14. **Answer a.** Since the value of the marginal product of labor is greater than the marginal cost of this additional unit of labor, the firm will enhance its profit by hiring additional units of labor. The firm should continue to hire more units of labor until the marginal cost of the last unit of labor hired is equal to the value of the marginal product of this last unit of labor.

15. **Answer c.** The firm should hire labor until the marginal cost of the additional unit of labor is equal to the value of the marginal product of the last unit of labor hired. The firm's marginal cost of hiring an additional unit of labor is equal to the wage rate of $18. The value of the marginal product of labor when the firm hires 6 units of labor is equal to $24: the firm should hire more than 6 units of labor. The value of the marginal product of labor when the firm hires 9 units of labor is equal to $16: the firm should hire fewer than 9 units of labor.

16. **Answer a.** When the marginal cost of the factor is greater than the value of the marginal product of the factor, this means that the firm's costs increase more than the firm's revenue if the firm hires this additional unit of the factor. The firm will not want to hire this unit since the addition to the firm's costs from hiring this unit exceeds the addition to its revenue from hiring the unit.

17. **Answer b.** The firm's demand curve for labor is found by multiplying the firm's marginal product of labor by the market price of the firm's output: this is the value of the marginal product of labor curve.

18. **Answer a.** When the firm hires more capital, holding everything else constant, this results in a decrease in the marginal product of capital since the firm has diminishing returns to its factor: when the firm hires more capital, the firm's production increases, but it increases at a diminishing rate with respect to capital. When the firm hires more capital, each unit of labor it employs will be more productive since each unit of labor will have more capital to work with: the firm's marginal product of labor will increase at each level of labor. When the firm's marginal product of labor increases, this causes the value of the marginal product of labor curve to shift to the right: at every wage rate, the value of the marginal product of labor will be greater than its initial value.

19. **Answer a.** Technological change can cause the firm's demand for an input to shift out or to shift in: for example, when the gas engine was invented the demand for horses decreased, but when the personal computer was invented the demand for information technology workers increased.

20. **Answer e.** In a perfectly competitive labor market, the equilibrium wage occurs at the point where the demand for labor intersects the supply of labor: at this wage the quantity of labor demanded is equal to the quantity of labor supplied. This wage is also equal to the value of the marginal product of labor, or the value produced by the last unit of labor employed in the labor market as a whole. The equilibrium wage may or may not be a living wage.

21. **Answer d.** All perfectly competitive factor markets behave in similar ways: the firm chooses to hire additional units of the factor provided that the marginal cost of an additional unit is less than the value of the marginal product of an additional unit. In equilibrium, the factor price equals the value of the marginal product of land.

22. **Answer b.** The marginal productivity theory says that each factor is paid the value of the output generated by the last unit of that factor employed in the factor market as a whole: some factors are therefore paid an amount that is less than their marginal product. The marginal productivity theory is useful in explaining the economy's underlying distribution of income and why that income is not evenly distributed among the different factors of production: instead, the economy's distribution of income is determined by each factor's marginal productivity at the economy's equilibrium.

23. **Answer d.** Wage disparities may arise because of compensating differentials, differences in talent, or differences in human capital.

24. **Answer b.** The marginal productivity theory of income distribution does not provide any analysis of whether the underlying income distribution is fair or equitable: the theory simply posits that factors of production receive a payment equal to the value of the marginal productivity of the last unit of the factor hired in the factor market as a whole.

25. **Answer d.** When the union is successful at raising the wage rate above the equilibrium wage rate, this implies that the union has market power in the labor market. It also implies that at the prevailing wage rate there will be more job applicants than there are jobs: there will be an excess supply of labor. When there is an excess supply of labor, this creates a situation in which it is easier for firms or employers to discriminate, since there are more job applicants than there are jobs.

26. **Answer a.** The individual's decision about how much labor to supply is based on the individual's decision about time allocation and how the individual wishes to divide their time between different activities. The individual chooses to work and earn dollars that they can then use to purchase goods or to not work and instead consume leisure. The individual therefore faces a trade-off between additional income or additional leisure.

27. **Answer a.** Leisure is considered a normal good: as income rises, most people would choose to consume more leisure.

28. **Answer a.** The individual should supply an additional hour of labor if the marginal utility of an hour of leisure is less than the marginal utility received from the goods that their hourly wage allows them to purchase. The individual should not supply an additional hour of labor if the marginal utility of an hour of leisure is greater than the marginal utility received from the goods that their hourly wage allows them to purchase. The individual provides the optimal amount of labor when the marginal utility of an hour of leisure is equal to the marginal utility from the goods that their hourly wage allows them to purchase.

29. **Answer a.** In making her optimal labor supply decision, Carolyn should compare her marginal utility from an additional hour of work to her marginal utility from the income earned from an additional hour of leisure: since the income earned from work provides a greater increase in utility than leisure in this example, Carolyn should choose to work an additional hour.

30. **Answer a.** When the income effect is stronger than the substitution effect, an increase in the wage rate causes an individual to supply fewer hours of labor, and thus, the individual's labor supply curve is downward sloping.

31. **Answer d.** The substitution effect with respect to an individual's labor supply decision refers to the opportunity cost of one good (leisure) in terms of the other goods the individual can purchase by working an additional hour. When the individual's wage rate increases, this implies that an additional hour of leisure is now relatively more expensive and the individual will substitute away from leisure and toward working longer hours due to the change in the relative price of leisure.

32. **[from Appendix] Answer a.** For a given amount of time, when Mike's wage rate increases this implies that if he devotes all of his available time to work that he will earn a higher income than he did initially. This will cause his time allocation budget line to shift out away from the origin with a new higher level of income (the y-intercept) and the same maximum amount of leisure (the x-intercept).

33. **[from Appendix] Answer c.** Pablo's hourly wage rate can be found by first noting that the total amount of time Pablo has available for work or leisure is 80 hours (the x-intercept). If he uses all 80 hours to work, he can earn $800 a week (the y-intercept). Dividing the $800 a week by 80 hours per week gives us his hourly wage rate of $10 per hour.

34. **[from Appendix] Answer c.** The opportunity cost of an hour of leisure can be measured using the slope of the time allocation budget line. The slope of this line is −$800 per week/80 hours per week, or −$10 an hour. Another way to think about this is to realize that Pablo gives up the income earned from an hour of work when he chooses to consume an hour of leisure: Pablo's wage rate is $10 an hour, so this is the opportunity cost of his choosing to consume an additional hour of leisure.

35. **[from Appendix] Answer c.** When the wage rate is $10 an hour, Pablo chooses to work 40 hours and therefore earns $400 a week. When the wage rate is $15 an hour, Pablo chooses to work 50 hours a week and therefore earns $750 a week. The change in Pablo's income, when the wage rate increases, is equal to $350 a week.

36. **[from Appendix] Answer a.** Pablo's supply of labor curve is upward sloping: when the wage rate is $10 an hour, Pablo supplies 40 hours of labor a week, and when the wage rate is $15 an hour, Pablo supplies 50 hours of labor a week.

37. **[from Appendix] Answer b.** Pablo's supply of labor curve is upward sloping, which implies that his substitution effect is dominant over his income effect when his wage rate increases.

chapter 21

Uncertainty, Risk, and Private Information

BEFORE YOU READ THE CHAPTER

Summary

This chapter examines the economics of risk and private information. Risk is an important feature in the economy. Most people are risk-averse, and this chapter explores why people are willing to pay a premium in order to reduce risk. The chapter also considers how risk can be traded: risk-averse people can pay other people to assume part of their risk. The chapter also examines how diversification and pooling can reduce exposure to risk. Finally, the chapter considers the special problems created by private information, a situation in which some people possess information that is unknown or unavailable to other people.

Chapter Objectives

Objective #1. A random variable is a variable that has an uncertain future value. Although a random variable has an uncertain future value, it is possible to calculate an expected value for this variable based on the weighted average of all the possible values of this random variable. The weights of each possible state for the random variable correspond to the probability of that state occurring.

- The general formula for the expected value of a random variable is based on the different possible outcomes, or states of the world, and the probabilities of each of these possible outcomes. Suppose that S_1 is the realized value that occurs in state 1, S_2 is the realized value that occurs in state 2, S_n is the realized value that occurs in state n, and that P_1 is the probability of state 1 occurring, P_2 is the probability of state 2 occurring, and P_n is the probability of state n occurring. Then, the expected value (EV) of a random variable with n possible states can be written as

$$EV = (P_1 \times S_1) + (P_2 \times S_2) + \ldots + (P_n \times S_n)$$

Objective #2. Individuals are risk-averse due to diminishing marginal utility with respect to income. When an individual is exposed to risk, this implies that the individual's future income is uncertain. The individual's expected income can be calculated as the sum of the products of the probabilities of each potential level of income times the potential level of income. The individual's expected utility is less when there is uncertainty about the level of income the individual will receive: if the individual could be certain they would receive a particular income, their utility would be higher than if they expect to receive the same amount of income but cannot be certain they will actually get this amount of income. This result is due to diminishing marginal utility with respect to income: each successive dollar of income adds less to total income than a previous dollar.

- For example, suppose an individual has income of $50,000 for the coming year, but there is a 50% chance this individual will incur medical costs of $25,000 and a 50% chance this individual will incur medical costs of $0. This individual's expected income for the coming year is $(0.5)(\$25,000) + (0.5)(\$50,000) = \$37,500$. If this individual could purchase health insurance that would cover all of their medical expenses for the coming year for $12,500, this individual could eliminate the risk they are exposed to with regard to medical expenses. When the individual purchases this fair insurance policy, the individual increases their utility even though the individual's actual income has not changed. This result arises because a dollar gained when income is low adds more to utility than a dollar lost when income is high reduces utility. The insurance policy reduces the amount of income available to the individual if the individual is in a healthy state (medical costs equal $0 during the coming year) and increases the amount of income available to the individual if the individual is in an unhealthy state (medical costs of $25,000 during the year). If the individual is unhealthy, the insurance policy increases the individual's income from $25,000 to $37,500. The individual's utility from an additional dollar of income when their income is $25,000 is greater than the loss in utility that occurs from losing a dollar of income when the individual's income is $50,000. Another way of expressing this idea is to say that the individual is risk-averse.

Objective #3. A fair insurance policy is one that charges a premium equal to the expected value of the claim on this insurance policy. Thus, if the expected value of the claim on the insurance policy is $10,000, then the premium the individual must pay is equal to $10,000 for this to be a fair insurance policy. Purchase of a fair insurance policy eliminates the predictable risk that the individual is exposed to: the individual replaces an expected outcome with a certain outcome by paying the insurance premium that equals the expected value of the insurance claim. A fair insurance policy does not provide the insurance company with funds to cover all of its costs of operations: the premium is just sufficient to cover the expected claim from the insured individual. Risk-averse individuals are willing to pay a premium that reduces their expected income but also reduces their risk: these individuals are willing to pay an insurance premium that exceeds the fair insurance policy amount. This willingness to pay is what makes the insurance industry possible.

Objective #4. Holding everything else constant, the flatter the slope of the individual's marginal utility curve with respect to income, the less risk-averse the individual is. A relatively steep marginal utility curve with respect to income indicates that the person is relatively more risk-averse than a relatively flat marginal utility curve with respect to income. Risk aversion depends on a person's preferences and the person's initial income or wealth. When a person's marginal utility depends very much on their level of income, then that person will be relatively risk-averse. When a person's marginal utility depends very little on their level of income, then that person will not be relatively risk-averse. People with high incomes tend to be less risk-averse than people with low incomes: a loss of a dollar makes little difference to an individual's level of utility when that individual has a high income, but it makes a big difference to an individual's level of utility when that individual has a low income.

Objective #5. There are two guiding principles for insurance companies.

- The principle of trading risk refers to insurance companies providing a market where those individuals who wish to bear less risk can make mutually beneficial transactions with those individuals who are willing to bear more risk. People who wish to reduce the risk they face can pay other people who are less sensitive to risk to take some of their risk away.

- The principle of diversification is used by insurance companies to eliminate some risk.

Objective #6. The market for insurance consists of suppliers and demanders, just like any other market.

- Suppliers are insurers or investors who are willing to place funds at risk when they provide or supply insurance. These funds are referred to as capital at risk. The insurer is willing to put these funds at risk for a return that is only slightly better than the expected loss. The insurer in effect is willing to trade risk: the insurer takes on the risk of someone who prefers to reduce their exposure to risk and is compensated for taking this risk away with a payment or premium that exceeds the expected loss. In taking on the risk, the insurer may find that on occasion their capital is expended when the insured incurs an insured disaster. The supply curve for insurance is found by varying the amount of the premium and asking how many insurers are willing to provide insurance at each premium level. As the level of the premium is increased (that is, as the price of insurance increases), more risk-averse investors are induced to provide coverage, and therefore the total amount of insurance supplied in the market increases.

- The demanders or buyers of insurance are those individuals who are willing to pay a premium to get insurance against some type of disaster (for example, a health problem, death, fire, or disability). These potential buyers define the demand curve for insurance, with the most risk-averse individual offering to pay the highest premium.

- Demanders and suppliers meet in the market for insurance to determine the equilibrium amount of insurance and the equilibrium price or premium for that insurance. In the insurance market, risk is transferred from those people who most want to get rid of it (those willing to pay the highest premium for insurance) to those least bothered by risk (those willing to accept the lowest premium for insurance). This suggests that the market for risk is able to efficiently allocate risk provided that these markets do not suffer from the presence of private information that prevents the market from allocating risk efficiently.

Objective #7. Risk can be reduced by pursuing a strategy of diversification. Effective diversification reduces the probability of a bad outcome and therefore reduces the investor's risk exposure. For diversification to be effective, the investor needs to spread their investment funds among different investment options that are independent of one another. These options or events are independent of one another if the events have no connection with one another.

- The probability of any two independent events both occurring is equal to the probability of one event occurring on its own times the probability of the other event occurring on its own. By investing in several different things, where the possible losses are independent events, investors can reduce the amount of risk they are exposed to.

- Diversification is possible even when the investor has a small amount to invest. By holding shares in many different companies, the investor reduces the risk exposure.

- Alternatively an individual or company can reduce their exposure to risk by pursuing a pooling strategy in which the investor purchases a small share in many independent events. Insurance companies take advantage of the predictability that comes from looking at large numbers of independent events: this strategy enables the insurance company to protect people from risk without the company facing much risk.

Objective #8. There are limits to diversification. When events are positively correlated, this implies that if one of the events happens it is more likely that the other events will happen. Positively correlated financial risks include severe weather, political events, and business cycles. When events are positively correlated, the risks associated with these events cannot be eliminated through diversification. Although markets for risk can not eliminate all risk, they can

- enable the economy to eliminate that part of risk that can be diversified, and

- allocate the remaining risk to the people most willing to bear it.

Objective #9. Markets fail when there is private information, a situation in which some people know things that other people do not know. Private information, or asymmetric information, distorts economic decisions and may prevent mutually beneficial transactions from taking place. Two types of problems arise because of private information.

- Adverse selection arises from possessing private information about the way things are.

- Moral hazard arises from possessing private information about what people do.

Objective #10. Adverse selection problems occur because the potential sellers know more about the quality of what they are selling than do the potential buyers. The potential sellers have an incentive to offer low-quality items for sale. Health insurance companies in particular face significant adverse selection problems since individuals seeking health insurance possess private information about their health that is hard for the insurance company to obtain. This asymmetric information results in healthy people opting not to purchase health insurance and leaving the insurance company with exactly the customers it wishes to avoid—those individuals with higher-than-average risk of needing significant health care. When the insurance company increases the premium on health insurance policies, this drives out more of the relatively healthy customers: this process can eventually lead to the collapse of the health insurance market. Strategies for reducing the problem of adverse selection include

- screening, which entails the use of observable information to make inferences about private information;

- signaling, when people who represent a good prospect for the business do some action they would not do if they were not a good prospect; and

- the use of reputation to indicate that the business is one whose product is not adversely selected.

Objective #11. Moral hazard arises when an individual has private information about their own actions when someone else bears the cost of the individual's actions. The individual acts in a morally hazardous manner with respect to the other party since the individual's actions create a cost for this other party. To correct for the problem of moral hazard, the individuals with private information must be given a personal stake in what happens so that they have an incentive to exert effort even when others cannot verify they have done so. For instance, a car insurance company can require a deductible: an individual who is a careless driver will incur the deductible expense even though they are insured. This potential deductible expense encourages the individual to drive with greater care and therefore reduce the moral hazard the car insurance company faces.

Key Terms

random variable a *variable* with an uncertain future value.

expected value in reference to a *random variable*, the weighted average of all possible values, where the weights on each possible value correspond to the probability of that value occurring.

state of the world a possible future event.

risk uncertainty about future outcomes.

financial risk uncertainty about monetary outcomes.

expected utility the expected value of an individual's total *utility* given uncertainty about future outcomes.

premium a payment to an insurance company in return for the promise to pay a claim in certain states of the world.

fair insurance policy an insurance policy for which the *premium* is equal to the expected value of the claim.

risk-averse describes individuals who choose to reduce *risk* when that reduction leaves the expected value of their income or wealth unchanged.

risk-neutral describes individuals who are completely insensitive to risk.

capital at risk funds that an insurer places at *risk* when providing insurance.

efficient allocation of risk the case in which those most willing to bear *risk* are those who end up bearing it.

independent events events for which the occurrence of one does not affect the likelihood of occurrence of any of the others.

diversification reducing risk by investing in several different things, so that the possible losses are *independent events*.

share a partial ownership of a company.

pooling a strong form of *diversification* in which an investor takes a small share of the risk in many *independent events*, so the *payoff* has very little total overall risk.

positively correlated a relationship between events such that each event is more likely to occur if the other event also occurs.

private information information that some people have that others do not.

adverse selection occurs when an individual knows more about the way things are than other people do. Adverse selection problems can lead to market problems: private information leads buyers to expect hidden problems in items offered for sale, leading to low prices and the best items being kept off the market.

screening using observable information about people to make inferences about their *private information*; a way to reduce *adverse selection*.

Key Terms (continued)

signaling taking some action to establish credibility despite possessing *private information;* a way to reduce *adverse selection.*

reputation a long-term standing in the public regard that serves to reassure others that *private information* is not being concealed; a valuable asset in the face of *adverse selection.*

moral hazard the situation that can exist when an individual knows more about his or her own actions than other people do. This leads to a distortion of incentives to take care or to expend effort when someone else bears the costs of the lack of care or effort.

deductible a sum specified in an insurance policy that the insured individual must pay before being compensated for a claim; deductibles reduce *moral hazard.*

■ AFTER YOU READ THE CHAPTER

Tips

Tip #1. This chapter introduces the idea of a weighted average as a means of getting an expected value for a random variable. This concept and this technique are critical to understanding the analysis presented in the chapter. To find the weighted average, you need to multiply the probability of a given value occurring by that value. This weighted average then provides a numerical value of what this variable will equal on average: that is, the value is not what the variable will equal, but is instead a measure of the average value of the variable if you had many observations of the variable. To find the weighted average for a random variable, use the following general formula:

$$\text{Weighted average of random variable} = \Sigma \text{ (probability of realized value occurring)} \times \text{(realized value)}$$

For example, suppose there is a 20% probability that the weight of a six-week-old pig will equal 5 pounds, 6 pounds, 7 pounds, 12 pounds, or 20 pounds. Using the above formula:

$$\text{Weighted average of a six-week-old pig's weight} = (0.2)(5) + (0.2)(6) + (0.2)(7) + (0.2)(12) + (0.2)(20) = 10 \text{ pounds}$$

The weighted average of the pig's weight is equal to 10 pounds: notice that this expected weight does not actually occur in the data but is instead the weight that would reflect the average weight if you measure a random sample of six-week-old pigs.

Tip #2. The chapter introduces the concept of a fair insurance policy. By "fair" the author means a situation in which the premium is equal to the expected value of the claim. Insurance companies in general will not offer an individual a fair insurance policy, however, since this policy does not provide the company with any funds to cover the costs of being in business. This concept is seen in other venues: for example, gambling facilities in Las Vegas are not "fair": the gambling facility will operate its games so that on average the facility makes money.

Tip #3. Students often find the concepts of adverse selection and moral hazard challenging to identify. Think about these two concepts using a time frame that focuses on whether the situation is occurring before the transaction or after the transaction.

- Adverse selection occurs before the transaction between the two parties: because of asymmetric information, one party to the transaction possesses information that the other party does not have and can not easily access. Because of this imbalance in information, the party possessing the private information faces an incentive to offer low-quality products in the market due to the fact that the other party cannot readily identify whether the product is of low or high quality. This leads to a breakdown in the market, since buyers will grow increasingly reluctant to purchase the product as the product becomes adversely selected from the buyer's perspective.

- Moral hazard occurs after the transaction, when one party to the transaction acts in a manner that is detrimental, or morally hazardous, to the desired outcome for the other party. For example, a person contracts for automobile insurance and once the insurance is in place drives less carefully. This is a morally hazardous behavior from the perspective of the insurance company, since it is likely to lead to higher expenses for the insurance company due to the individual having a higher probability of a car accident.

- The key to distinguishing between these two concepts is to recognize that the timing of the information issue is essential. Adverse selection occurs before the transaction and moral hazard after the transaction.

Problems and Exercises

1. Sarah is a firefighter. She does not know whether or not she will be injured on the job in the coming year. If all goes well, she will not sustain any injuries on the job. However, there's a 30% chance of her suffering a relatively minor injury that will result in medical expenses of $10,000 for the year. There is a 10% chance of her suffering a major injury resulting in $50,000 of medical bills. There's a 60% chance that Sarah will suffer no injuries.

    a. Identify the random variable in this example.

    b. What is the expected value (EV) of Sarah's medical expenses for the coming year?

    c. Does Sarah anticipate paying an amount for medical expenses next year exactly equal to the expected value you calculated in part (b)? Explain your answer.

d. Why does this scenario create a situation of uncertainty for Sarah?

e. Suppose Sarah is risk-averse, but only willing to pay the fair insurance amount for her health insurance. Given this information, how much would Sarah be willing to pay for health insurance next year if she wanted to have full coverage for whatever medical expenses she incurs?

2. Sarah, our firefighter from problem 1, earns $40,000 a year as a firefighter. Given the information in problem 1 and this additional information, answer the following set of questions.

a. What is Sarah's expected income for the coming year?

b. A fair insurance policy is an insurance policy for which the premium is equal to the expected value of the claim. What is the premium Sarah will pay if she purchases a fair insurance policy to cover her medical costs?

c. Suppose Sarah has diminishing marginal utility of income. Will Sarah be better off or worse off buying a fair insurance policy? Explain your answer.

3. Use the table below to answer this set of questions. The table provides information about Carolyn's income level and the total utility she receives at each income level.

Income	Total utility measured in utils
$ 0	0
10,000	500
20,000	800
30,000	1,000
40,000	1,100
50,000	1,150

a. Does Carolyn experience diminishing marginal utility with respect to income as her income increases? Explain your answer.

b. Suppose Carolyn faces two possible states of the world. She has a 50% chance of earning $40,000 a year and a 50% chance of earning $20,000 a year. What is her expected income? What is her expected utility?

c. Suppose Carolyn could purchase a fair insurance policy that would ensure that her income was equal to the expected income you found in part (b). What would the premium be for this fair insurance policy to stabilize Carolyn's income at this level so that her risk of income fluctuation would be zero?

d. Is Carolyn better off or worse off buying a fair insurance policy? Justify your answer with numerical support based on the table above and Carolyn's utility.

e. Is your answer in part (d) dependent on Carolyn's diminishing marginal utility with respect to income? Explain your answer.

f. Is Carolyn risk-averse? Explain your answer.

g. Given the information you have been provided, would Carolyn consider a premium of $15,000 for income insurance a fair insurance policy?

h. Would an insurance company be willing to provide Carolyn with income insurance for a premium of $10,000 given the information we have about Carolyn's probability of earning different levels of income for the coming year?

4. The table below provides information about Carolyn's and George's total utility from different levels of income. Use this information to answer this set of questions.

Income	Carolyn's total utility measured in utils	George's total utility measured in utils
$ 0	0	0
10,000	500	400
20,000	800	460
30,000	1,000	500
40,000	1,100	520
50,000	1,150	530

a. Suppose both Carolyn and George have a 50% chance of earning $10,000 a year and a 50% chance of earning $30,000 a year. Calculate Carolyn's and George's expected income and expected utility. Is your expected income and expected utility calculation the same for Carolyn and George? If they differ, why do they differ?

b. Suppose Carolyn and George both currently earn $20,000 a year. Who benefits more from an increase in income of $10,000? Who loses more from a decrease in income of $10,000? Between George and Carolyn who is more risk-averse? Explain your answer.

   c. Graph Carolyn's and George's marginal utility from income on the same graph, with marginal utility measured on the vertical axis and income measured on the horizontal axis. Plot each point of the marginal utility curves at the midpoint of each income interval. Whose marginal utility curve is flatter? What is the relationship between the marginal utility curve and being risk-averse?

5.   Which of the following individuals is likely to be more risk-averse?

   a. An individual whose income is $100,000 a year anticipates that he will need dental work this year that will cost $5,000, and an individual whose income is $18,000 a year anticipates that she will need dental work this year that will cost $5,000.

   b. An individual whose income is $80,000 a year whose second home is located on the floodplain of the Mississippi River, and an individual whose income is $50,000 a year whose only house is located on the floodplain of the Mississippi River.

   c. An individual whose income is $45,000 a year who anticipates that he will need a kidney transplant this year, and an individual whose income is $100,000 a year who anticipates that she will need a kidney transplant.

6. Suppose there are six potential insurers in a market for fire insurance for businesses with factories worth $200,000 to insure against fire. These businesses each face a 20% probability that they will experience a fire during the coming year. The first insurer is willing to provide $200,000 of fire insurance for a premium of $41,000 a year. The second insurer is willing to provide $200,000 of fire insurance for a premium of $43,000 a year. The third and fourth insurers are willing to provide $200,000 of fire insurance for a premium of $45,000 a year. The fifth and sixth insurers are willing to provide $200,000 of fire insurance for a premium of $48,000 a year. Suppose that there are five businesses in this market seeking insurance and that the highest premium any of these five businesses will pay for fire insurance is $47,000; the next-highest premium that two of these businesses will pay for fire insurance is $46,000; the next-highest premium that one of these businesses will pay for fire insurance is $43,000; and the fifth business is only willing to pay a premium of $42,000 for fire insurance.

a. How much fire insurance will be provided in this market? Explain your answer.

b. What is the total amount of capital at risk in this market when the market is in equilibrium?

7. Suppose that a car insurance market has five individuals seeking car insurance. The probability of one of these individuals having a major wreck that results in $10,000 of damage to their vehicle is 25% this year. The probability that two of the individuals will have less serious wrecks resulting in damages of $5,000 to each of their cars is 40% this year. The probability of the other two drivers having a car accident is 0%.

a. What is the expected value of the insurance payments that will be made during the coming year if all of the drivers get car insurance in this market?

b. Suppose that none of these five drivers knows which kind of driver they represent. What is the fair insurance premium amount per driver in this market?

c. Suppose that each driver knows what kind of driver they are. Will each driver in this market now be willing to pay the fair insurance premium plus enough to cover the other costs that the insurance companies incur when they provide insurance? Explain your answer. What kind of problem is apt to occur in the car insurance market if each driver has full knowledge of the kind of driver they are?

d. What are some possible methods for dealing with the private information problem that was presented in part (c)?

8. Why do companies often offer warranties covering their products during the first year or two that a person owns the product?

9. Is it possible to create a market for risk? Explain your answer.

10. You are at a carnival and you see a game that offers to pay you $25 if you flip a coin three times and get three heads in a row.

a. If the game costs $3 to play, will you play the game? Assume that you are willing to play the game only if the cost of playing the game is less than your expected earnings from playing this game.

b. If the game costs $4 to play, will you play the game? Assume that you are willing to play the game only if the cost of playing the game is less than your expected earnings from playing this game.

    c. What is the fair price for this game? Why might the carnival game owner charge a price greater than the fair price for this game?

    d. Why might you be willing to pay a price greater than the fair price to play this game?

11. Why is an investment strategy of buying shares of many companies likely to be a better strategy for an investor with limited funds than a strategy of buying as many shares as possible of a single stock?

12. Can the markets for insurance eliminate all risk? Give some examples of risk that is difficult for insurance markets to eliminate.

13. For each of the following situations, determine if this is a problem of adverse selection or moral hazard.

    a. Recently, colleges in many parts of the United States have decided to forgo standardized tests and instead make their admission decisions based on the information that prospective students send to them.

b. Mary has a midnight curfew and at 11:55 P.M. she realizes that if she does not get home by midnight, she will be grounded. She drives home at 80 miles per hour to make the curfew.

c. Josie knows she needs major medical surgery, but when she investigates different health insurance policies she does not reveal that she needs this surgery.

d. Jeremy wrecked his car three summers ago and is now selling the car. In his advertisement, he does not mention that the car was in a wreck and needed substantial repair.

BEFORE YOU TAKE THE TEST

Chapter Review Questions

Use the following information to answer the next three questions.

Suppose that Mark does not know how large his automobile repair expenses will be for the coming year. If he's lucky, his car will need no repairs and his car repair costs will be $0. But if he has a wreck and the car is destroyed, his car repair (in this case, replacement cost) expenses will equal $20,000. Assume that these are the only two possible states of the world in this example.

1. Suppose that there's a 20% chance that Mark will have a serious car accident. What is the expected value of Mark's car repair expenses for the coming year?
   - a. $0
   - b. $20,000
   - c. $10,000
   - d. $4,000

2. Suppose the chances of Mark having a serious car accident have changed. If Mark now has a 60% chance of having a serious car accident, what is the expected value of Mark's car repair expenses for the coming year?
   - a. $0
   - b. $20,000
   - c. $12,000
   - d. $10,000

3. Holding everything else constant, when the probability of a serious car accident increases, Mark's expected value of car repair expenses for the coming year
   - a. increases.
   - b. decreases.
   - c. may increase, decrease, or remain the same.
   - d. stays constant.

4. Mark and Jacob are good friends and often talk to one another about business matters. Mark and Jacob drive identical cars, live in the same community, and travel by car an equal number of miles each year. They also purchase car insurance from the same company. Mark pays more for the same insurance (that is, the same coverage and same deductible) than does Jacob. Which of the following statements is true?

    a. Jacob is not as good a driver as Mark.

    b. Mark and Jacob are equally skilled at driving.

    c. The probability of Mark having a serious car accident this year is higher than the probability of Jacob having a serious car accident this year.

    d. The insurance company knows with certainty that Mark will have a serious car accident this year.

5. Diminishing marginal utility with respect to income implies that an individual's total utility

    a. declines as their level of income increases.

    b. declines as their level of income decreases.

    c. increases at a decreasing rate as their level of income increases.

    d. decreases at a decreasing rate as their level of income increases.

6. Which of the following statements is true?

    I. A risk-averse family has expected income of $20,000. This family's expected utility is less than it would be if the family did not face any risk and knew with certainty that their income would be $20,000.

    II. If a family has diminishing marginal utility with respect to income, this implies that the total utility curve for this family is positively sloped but that this curve gets flatter as the family's income level increases.

    a. Statement I is true.

    b. Statement II is true.

    c. Statements I and II are true.

    d. Neither statement is true.

7. A fair insurance policy is one

    a. that treats all people desiring this type of insurance equally by charging each individual the same premium.

    b. for which the premium charged is equal to the expected value of the claim.

    c. that considers each specific case in order to decide what is fair and equitable for that particular case.

    d. that is available to everyone irrespective of their circumstances.

8. People are willing to participate in organized gambling activities like those in Las Vegas casinos because

    a. the gambling games at these locations are all fair gambles.

    b. the people who gamble are not risk-averse, but are instead risk-loving.

    c. people are rational and realize that gambling is a rational, enjoyable means to earning extra income.

    d. gambling can be addictive in ways that are not much different from the addictive effects of drugs.

9. Suppose that an individual's expected claim on their insurance policy is $10,000 this year. Furthermore, suppose that the premium on this insurance policy is $12,000 a year. Which of the following statements is true?

  I. This insurance policy is not a fair insurance policy.

  II. The individual who purchases this insurance policy must be irrational.

  III. This premium may still be attractive to the individual provided this individual is sufficiently risk-averse.

  a. Statement I is true.

  b. Statement II is true.

  c. Statement III is true.

  d. Statements I and II are true.

  e. Statements I and III are true.

  f. Statements I, II, and III are true.

10. Many products are sold with warranties. These warranties are

  a. a way for the producer to signal that the product is of high quality.

  b. a form of consumer insurance.

  c. a way of minimizing the consumer's expected utility from consuming the product.

  d. Answers (a), (b), and (c) are all true answers.

  e. Answers (a) and (b) are true answers.

11. Demanders of insurance are individuals who are interested in

  a. increasing their exposure to risk.

  b. reducing their exposure to risk.

12. Suppliers of insurance are those who

  a. are willing to increase their exposure to risk, provided they are sufficiently compensated for this increase in risk exposure.

  b. wish to decrease their exposure to risk, provided they are sufficiently compensated for this decrease in risk exposure.

13. In general, demanders of insurance are

  a. more risk-averse than suppliers of insurance.

  b. less risk-averse than suppliers of insurance.

Answer the next two questions based on the following information.

Suppose that you own a used bookstore and are negotiating fire insurance for your business. You estimate that a fire will cost your store $200,000 and that there is a 20% chance of a fire at your business.

14. The expected loss in the case of a fire is equal to _____, and a wealthy investor is willing to offer you fire insurance for _____.

  a. $200,000; a payment of less than $40,000

  b. $200,000; a payment of more than $40,000

  c. $40,000; a payment of less than $40,000

  d. $40,000; a payment of more than $40,000

15. The investor in this situation has capital at risk equal to

  a. $200,000.   c. $40,000.

  b. $20,000.   d. $4,000.

16. An individual tosses a coin three times. What is the probability that the coin will come up tails three times in a row?

a. 0.5

b. 0.25

c. 0.75

d. 0.125

17. An individual tosses a coin twice. What is the probability that the coin will come up heads first and then tails?

a. 0.5

b. 0.25

c. 0.75

d. 0.125

18. Suppose there's an insurance company offering health insurance. To simplify this problem, assume there are just two individuals in this market. Joe faces a 20% probability that he will have a serious heart attack this year, while Mary faces a 30% probability that she will have a serious kidney ailment this year. Assume Joe's and Mary's health status are independent of one another. What is the probability that both Joe and Mary will suffer these major health setbacks this year?

a. 0.2

b. 0.3

c. 0.6

d. 0.06

19. Suppose in an insurance market there is an increase in the degree of risk aversion among the buyers of this insurance. Holding everything else constant, the equilibrium premium will

a. increase and the equilibrium quantity of insurance will decrease in this market.

b. increase and the equilibrium quantity of insurance will increase in this market.

c. decrease and the equilibrium quantity of insurance will decrease in this market.

d. decrease and the equilibrium quantity of insurance will increase in this market.

20. Suppose in an insurance market there is an increase in the degree of risk aversion among investors in this insurance market. Holding everything else constant, the equilibrium premium will

a. increase as the demand curve for insurance shifts to the right.

b. decrease as the demand curve for insurance shifts to the left.

c. increase as the supply curve for insurance shifts to the left.

d. decrease as the supply curve for insurance shifts to the right.

21. Suppose in an insurance market there is a positive relationship between the amount of insurance monies paid out for damages incurred and severe weather. Holding the demand for insurance constant, if global warming causes more frequent and more dangerous storms, this insurance market will likely charge a higher premium for insurance and provide

a. more insurance.

b. less insurance.

22. Suppose in an insurance market there is a positive relationship between the amount of insurance monies paid out for damages incurred and severe weather. Holding the demand for insurance constant, if global warming causes more frequent and more dangerous storms, this insurance market will likely over time
    a. continue to provide insurance to demanders of insurance.
    b. collapse, since the risk associated with these frequent and dangerous storms cannot be eliminated through diversification.

23. Utopia is a beach paradise on a small island in the middle of the ocean. In recent years, Utopia has been subject to destructive hurricanes. These hurricanes appear to be increasing in frequency due to global warming. Home owners in Utopia find that privately provided property insurance, to insure their houses from hurricane damage, is
    a. easy to get and very affordable.
    b. hard to get and extremely expensive to purchase.

24. Insurance markets exist because
    a. providers of insurance are able to exploit demanders of insurance.
    b. demanders of insurance are able to exploit suppliers of insurance.
    c. these are irrational markets where both demanders and suppliers in the market fail to understand fully the risks that they are exposed to when they demand or supply insurance.
    d. there are gains from trade in risk when both demanders and suppliers benefit from the insurance market transaction.

25. Insurance companies diversify when they use a strategy of
    a. pooling of risks.
    b. limiting the amount of insurance they provide to their customers.
    c. providing insurance in a limited geographic region.
    d. providing insurance to a narrowly defined group of consumers.

26. There is an economic downturn in the economy. This will likely
    a. affect only a few businesses.
    b. have no effect on businesses in this economy.
    c. affect many businesses, since the economy in general is suffering a downturn.
    d. have no predictable impact on businesses in this economy.

Use the following information to answer the next three questions.

Suppose that there is a used car market and in this market there is a 50% probability that any used car for sale is a lemon (that is, a car of poor quality) and a 50% probability that any used car for sale is a cherry (that is, a car of high quality). Suppose a lemon car in this market is worth $2,000 while a cherry car is worth $10,000.

27. In this market, if buyers are not able to distinguish between a lemon car and a cherry car, what is the expected price buyers will be willing to pay for a used car?
    a. $2,500, since they will assume most of the cars offered in this market are lemons.
    b. $10,000, since they will assume all the cars offered in this market are cherries.
    c. $4,000, since the downside of getting a lemon is a bad outcome for buyers so they will not be willing to pay any more than $4,000 per car.
    d. $6,000, since this represents the expected value of used cars in this market.

28. Over time, if buyers are not able to distinguish lemon cars from cherry cars in this market, then
    a. the market will eventually be composed only of cherry cars.
    b. the market will eventually be composed only of lemon cars.
    c. buyers will have an equal likelihood of purchasing a lemon or a cherry car.
    d. buyers will exit the market and not purchase any cars.

29. This set of questions focuses on asymmetric information and, in particular, the problem associated with
    a. adverse selection.
    b. moral hazard.

30. Adverse selection can be reduced by
    a. the use of screening, where potential demanders of a product collect information about the product prior to purchasing the product.
    b. the use of signaling by suppliers of the product, where the signal acts to provide the potential demander with information about the quality of the product.
    c. the seller developing a reputation for a high-quality product and high-quality service for that product.
    d. Answers (a), (b), and (c) are all methods that can reduce adverse selection.

31. Susy just got her driver's license and has begged her parents to let her take the family car out for a drive. Susy's parents are likely to be worried that this situation represents a potential
    a. adverse selection problem, since Susy has only recently learned to drive.
    b. moral hazard problem, since once Susy is out with the car, the parents have no certainty that Susy will drive in a manner that is safe and careful.

32. Harold is starting a car insurance company and is offering to provide 100% coverage to his customers. Harold is likely to encounter a
    a. moral hazard problem given this offer.
    b. adverse selection problem given this offer.

33. The use of a deductible in an insurance policy helps to reduce the problem of
    a. adverse selection.
    b. moral hazard.

34. A car insurance company offers a variety of policies that each have different insurance premiums and different deductibles. These policies allow the company to
    a. effectively screen their customers and gather private information that would otherwise not be available to the insurance company.
    b. effectively discriminate between low-risk individuals and high-risk individuals.
    c. provide a set of incentives to buyers to engage in less risky behavior from the insurance company's perspective.
    d. Answers (a), (b), and (c) are all true.

ANSWER KEY

Answers to Problems and Exercises

1. **a.** The random variable is Sarah's medical expenses for the coming year. Her expenses may range from $0 to $50,000 depending on which state of the world occurs.

b. $EV = (P_1 \times S_1) + (P_2 \times S_2) + (P_3 \times S_3)$, where P_1 is the probability of state 1 occurring and S_1 refers to the realized value in state 1. Thus, $EV = (0.6)(\$0) + (0.3)(\$10,000) + (0.1)(\$50,000) = \$8,000$.

c. No. Sarah will not actually pay the amount you calculated in part (b): she will pay $0, $10,000, or $50,000, depending on which state of the world actually occurs.

d. Although Sarah can compute the expected value of her medical expenses for the coming year, she faces considerable uncertainty since her medical expenses can range from $0 to $50,000.

e. Sarah would be willing to pay the expected value of the medical expenses, or $8,000.

2. **a.** Sarah's expected income for the coming year can be calculated as $(0.3)(\$30,000) + (0.1)(-\$10,000) + (0.6)(\$40,000) = \$32,000$.

b. The expected value of Sarah's medical costs is equal to $8,000, so the premium for a fair insurance policy for Sarah would be equal to $8,000.

c. Sarah will be better off buying the fair insurance policy for $8,000. This will result in her income being a predictable $32,000 while eliminating the risk Sarah faces due to potential medical costs. To see how this insurance policy benefits Sarah, compare the situation in which Sarah earns $40,000 and has no injury with the situation in which Sarah earns −$10,000 due to her sustaining an injury that costs $50,000. The additional utility from an additional dollar of income is much greater when Sarah's income is negative (low) than the loss of utility when Sarah gives up a dollar of income when her income is at $40,000 (when her income is high). Sarah benefits from insuring herself because of her diminishing marginal utility from income: Sarah is risk-averse.

3. **a.** Carolyn does have diminishing marginal utility with respect to income since her total utility from income increases but at a decreasing rate as her level of income rises.

b. Carolyn's expected income is equal to $(0.5)(\$40,000) + (0.5)(\$20,000) = \$30,000$. Carolyn's expected utility is equal to $(0.5)(1,100 \text{ utils}) + (0.5)(800 \text{ utils}) = 950 \text{ utils}$.

c. Since Carolyn's expected income from part (b) is $30,000, Carolyn would be willing to pay a premium of $10,000 a year to eliminate the risk of income fluctuation and ensure that her actual income equals her expected income.

d. Carolyn is better off buying the fair insurance policy: with the risk of income fluctuations eliminated with the policy, Carolyn receives an actual income of $30,000 that gives her 1,000 utils; without the fair insurance policy, Carolyn's income fluctuates and her expected income is $30,000, which provides her with an expected utility of 950 utils.

e. The result in (d) stems from Carolyn's diminishing marginal utility of income. An additional dollar of income when Carolyn's income is $20,000 adds more to her utility than the loss in utility that occurs when Carolyn earns a dollar less than $40,000.

f. Yes, Carolyn is risk-averse since she is better off choosing to reduce the risk she faces, because the cost of reducing that risk results in a higher level of utility for Carolyn.

g. No, Carolyn is willing to pay $10,000 for this income insurance since this is the value of her expected loss in income for the period. She would not be willing to pay more than $10,000 if she was purchasing a fair insurance policy.

h. An insurance company would be unwilling to provide this income insurance policy to Carolyn for a premium of $10,000 since the premium would result in the company covering only the costs of the expected claim and would not provide funds to cover other costs incurred by the insurance company for its salespeople and actuaries.

4. a. Carolyn's expected income is equal to $(0.5)(\$10,000) + (0.5)(\$30,000) = \$20,000$. George's expected income is also equal to $20,000. But Carolyn's expected utility is equal to $(0.5)(500 \text{ utils}) + (0.5)(1,000 \text{ utils}) = 750 \text{ utils}$, while George's expected utility is equal to $(0.5)(400 \text{ utils}) + (0.5)(500 \text{ utils}) = 450 \text{ utils}$. George's expected utility is lower than Carolyn's because his total utility from income is lower than Carolyn's at every positive income level.

b. When George's income increases from $20,000 to $30,000, his total utility increases by 40 utils; when Carolyn's income increases from $20,000 to $30,000, her total utility increases by 200 utils. When George's income decreases from $20,000 to $10,000, his total utility falls by 60 utils; when Carolyn's income decreases from $20,000 to $10,000, her total utility falls by 300 utils. Carolyn benefits more from an increase in income and she is hurt more than George when her income falls. Carolyn will be more risk-averse than George, since she loses a large amount of utility if her income falls. George is barely risk-averse at all, since his utility is not impacted by any great amount, relative to Carolyn, when his income changes.

c.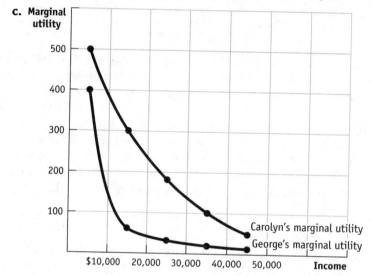

George's marginal utility curve is flatter than Carolyn's marginal utility curve for incomes greater than or equal to $20,000. When a person's marginal utility curve is flat or almost horizontal, this indicates that the person is barely risk-averse: in this example, Carolyn is far more risk-averse than George.

5. a. The $5,000 in anticipated dental costs represents a much larger share of the individual's income who earns $18,000 a year than the individual who earns $100,000. The individual with the lower income will be more risk-averse in this situation.

b. The individual whose income is higher and who owns a second home is likely to be less risk-averse than the individual whose income is lower and whose only house is on the floodplain.

c. The individual whose income is lower is likely more risk-averse, since the medical expenditure for a kidney transplant represents a far greater share of their income than it does for the individual with the higher income.

6. a. Three fire insurance policies will be provided in this market since there are three suppliers willing to supply this insurance for a premium of $45,000 or less and three buyers of insurance willing to pay a premium of $45,000 or more for the insurance. The fourth insurer is willing to supply an insurance policy for a premium of $45,000, but the fourth buyer of insurance is only willing to pay a premium of $43,000: this transaction will not be made since the premium the buyer is willing to pay is below the premium the supplier must receive for the supplier to provide the insurance policy.

b. The total amount of capital at risk in this market when the market is in equilibrium is $600,000, since there are three businesses that are each insured for $200,000 when the market is in equilibrium.

7. **a.** The expected value of the insurance payments during the coming year are equal to $(0.25)(\$10,000) + (0.4)(\$5,000) + (0.4)(\$5,000) = \$6,500$.

b. To find the fair insurance premium, divide the anticipated cost of the insurance payments for the year ($6,500) by the number of insured people (the five drivers) to get $6,500/5, or $1,300.

c. No, the drivers who are good drivers and have no likelihood of getting into a wreck will not want to pay $1,300 a year for insurance coverage. However, the other three drivers will want to pay this amount since it represents less than each of their expected car repair costs for the year. If people know with certainty what kind of driver they are, the good drivers will opt out of the car insurance market leaving the more-expensive-to-insure individuals in the market. This is an example of the adverse selection problem, since the market adversely selects among those individuals seeking insurance.

d. One method for dealing with this problem is to seek methods for letting good drivers inform the insurance company of their capability. The insurance company could examine past driving records, and they could offer different policies with different premiums and different deductibles to let the selection of policy tell them something about the care with which drivers drive their cars.

8. The warranty is a way for the company to signal their reliability: the warranty lets consumers know that the company stands behind its product. This helps alleviate consumers' fears that the product is of low quality or adversely selected from their consumers' perspective.

9. The insurance market is a good example of a market that exists in order for people to trade risk: demanders of insurance desire to reduce their exposure to risk, while suppliers of insurance are willing to take on another person's risk. The insurance market provides a means of making mutually beneficial trades: the supplier offers a good—in this case, risk reduction—that is valuable to the demander.

10. **a.** The probability that three heads will come up in a row is 0.125, since $(0.5)(0.5)(0.5) = 0.125$. Thus, if the game pays a winner $25, the expected value of the game's payout is $(0.125)(25) = \$3.125$. At a price of $3 to play, this game is definitely worth playing since the cost of playing is less than the expected value to be gotten from playing the game.

b. When the game costs $4, this means that the cost of playing the game exceeds the expected value from playing the game. You might still be willing to play the game because you enjoy being at the carnival and playing the game even though the price of playing exceeds the fair price for the game. You might also have a gambling addiction and find it difficult to act in a rational manner when making a decision about playing or not playing.

c. The fair price for this game would equal $3.125, but the carnival owner is likely to charge a price greater than the fair price since the owner has other costs of being in business beyond the money he must pay to a winner of his game. He probably has transportation costs, set-up costs, and even labor costs for the help that he employs in running his game.

d. You might be willing to pay more than the fair price because you enjoy the carnival atmosphere and the pleasure of playing the game even though you know it is not a fair game. You might also find it difficult to not play if you have a gambling addiction.

11. By buying shares of many companies, the investor is apt to benefit from diversification: if the companies are independent of one another, when one company experiences a downturn in their business it is likely that the other companies the investor has invested in will not also experience this downturn. On the other hand, if the investor places all of their funds in a single company, then if the company falls on hard times the investor will lose much of their investment.

12. There is a core of risk that insurance markets cannot eliminate. Three sources of this risk are (1) severe weather that creates losses that are clearly not independent events, (2) political events that result in business repercussions throughout the world, and (3) business cycles that result in multiple businesses simultaneously experiencing declines in the demand for their products.

13. **a.** There is an information problem here in that colleges will be making their decisions based on the information they receive from prospective students: these students have an incentive to embellish these details, particularly if there is no way for the college to verify the validity of their claims. This is an adverse selection problem.

   b. This is a moral hazard problem since Mary acts in a morally hazardous manner when she drives 80 miles per hour. This is morally hazardous since Mary may injure other people or may kill herself: neither of these outcomes is what Mary's parents intended when they established the curfew.

   c. This is an adverse selection problem since Josie possesses private information that the prospective insurer does not have. Josie represents an adversely selected potential customer for the insurance company since she is likely to be expensive to insure.

   d. This is an adverse selection problem since Jeremy possesses information about the status of the car that potential buyers do not have access to.

Answers to Chapter Review Questions

1. **Answer d.** To find the expected value (EV), sum the product of each state of the world times the probability of that state occurring. Thus, $EV = (\$0)(0.8) + (\$20,000)(0.2) = \$4,000$.

2. **Answer c.** To find the expected value (EV), sum the product of each state of the world times the probability of that state occurring. Thus, $EV = (\$0)(0.4) + (\$20,000)(0.6) = \$12,000$.

3. **Answer a.** From comparison of your answers to questions 1 and 2, you can see that the expected value of Mark's car repair expenses for the coming year increases when the probability of a serious car accident increases.

4. **Answer c.** The insurance company bases the insurance premium that Mark or Jacob pays on the expected value of the car expenses Mark or Jacob will incur during the coming year. Assuming Mark and Jacob are basically identical with regard to the types of cars they drive, where they drive, and how far they drive, then if Mark's premium is higher than Jacob's premium, it is because the insurance company perceives that the probability of Mark having an accident is higher than the probability that Jacob will have an accident.

5. **Answer c.** Diminishing marginal utility of income implies that as the individual's income increases, total utility increases but it increases at a diminishing rate.

6. **Answer c.** For a particular level of income, a family comparing the utility from certainly getting this income versus the utility from possibly getting this income will find that their utility is greater when the income is certain. Statement II describes the shape of the total utility curve for a family given that the family has diminishing marginal utility from income.

7. **Answer b.** This is just the definition of a fair insurance policy. It is a policy that charges a premium equal to the expected value of the claim, and thus this type of policy eliminates the risk that an individual is predictably exposed to.

8. **Answer d.** The gambling games at organized venues such as in Las Vegas are not fair gambles: the games are designed so that the "house" makes money. People who gamble do not appear, on average, to be risk-loving: most are not daredevils but are instead ordinary people who act in risk-averse patterns with regard to decisions like seat belt use and life insurance purchases. People who gamble appear to be irrational in their choice of gambling since the expected payouts are not fair. Studies suppose the idea that gambling is addictive in much the same way that drugs are addictive.

9. **Answer e.** This is not a fair insurance policy since the premium exceeds the expected claim on the policy, but an individual could still rationally decide to purchase this insurance policy if that individual is sufficiently risk-averse. The insurance company needs to charge a premium in excess of the fair insurance policy amount to cover the costs of providing insurance that exceed the claim costs (for example, the cost of salespeople and actuaries).

10. **Answer e.** Warranties serve as a signal of the quality of the good as well as providing consumer insurance for those who purchase the good. When warranties cover the cost of repair or replacement, this effectively increases the consumer's expected utility from consuming the good.

11. **Answer b.** Demanders of insurance buy insurance to reduce their exposure to risk.

12. **Answer a.** Suppliers of insurance provide insurance to those wishing to reduce their exposure to risk. Suppliers of insurance are less sensitive to risk than are demanders of insurance.

13. **Answer a.** Demanders of insurance are more sensitive to risk than are suppliers and therefore are more risk-averse.

14. **Answer d.** The expected loss from a fire equals ($200,000)(0.2) = $40,000, and an investor would be willing to offer insurance for this potential loss for an amount greater than $40,000 since the investor is willing to take on this risk of fire for a return that is only slightly better than the expected loss of $40,000.

15. **Answer a.** The capital at risk is the total amount the insurer would have to pay out in the event of the insured disaster occurring. In this case, the disaster would be a fire and the investor would have to pay out $200,000 in the event of a fire. Thus, the investor's capital at risk is $200,000.

16. **Answer d.** To calculate the probability of three independent events, multiply the probability of the first event occurring on its own by the probability of the second event happening on its own by the probability of the third event happening on its own. Thus, (0.5)(0.5)(0.5) = 0.125.

17. **Answer b.** To calculate the probability of two independent events occurring at the same time, multiply the probability of the first event occurring on its own by the probability of the second event occurring on its own. Thus, (0.5)(0.5) = 0.25.

18. **Answer d.** To calculate the probability of two independent events occurring at the same time, multiply the probability of the first event occurring on its own by the probability of the second event occurring on its own. Thus, (0.2)(0.3) = 0.06.

19. **Answer b.** An increase in the degree of risk aversion among insurance buyers will cause the demand curve for insurance to shift to the right. This will lead to an increase in both the equilibrium premium (the price of the insurance) and the equilibrium quantity of insurance.

20. **Answer c.** An increase in the degree of risk aversion among investors in this insurance market will cause the supply curve to shift to the left, since less insurance will be offered by suppliers at every premium level. This will result in the equilibrium premium (the price of insurance) to increase.

21. **Answer b.** Suppliers of insurance will be unwilling to supply the same amount of insurance at a given premium if storms are more frequent and more dangerous. Assuming this market continues to provide insurance, there will be less insurance provided and the premium for the insurance will increase, since these changes will cause the supply curve of insurance to shift to the left. If the positive correlation is severe enough, the insurance market may collapse and not provide any insurance, since this type of risk cannot be eliminated through diversification.

22. **Answer b.** This insurance market is characterized by having two positively related events occurring: the need for insurance compensation and the existence of strong storms that result in damages to the insured. In this market, the insurance company cannot diversify its position and therefore it cannot eliminate the risk it faces. Over time, this insurance market will collapse and stop offering insurance, even though there is demand for insurance.

23. **Answer b.** In this scenario, a private insurance company faces a positive correlation between the cost to the company of insuring properties from hurricane damage and the frequency of hurricanes. Over time, as this relationship becomes clear to these companies, the insurance market will stop providing insurance: insurance will be hard to get in the private market, and if a demander can locate insurance in the private market it will be very expensive.

24. **Answer d.** Insurance markets are like other kinds of markets we have studied: the market exists because mutually beneficial trades are possible. In the case of the insurance market, demanders can shift the financial cost of a loss onto suppliers of insurance who are willing to bear that risk because of the compensation they receive from providing the insurance coverage.

25. **Answer a.** Pooling of risks refers to the reduction in risks that an insurance company gets by looking at, or insuring, large numbers of independent events.

26. **Answer c.** When an economy suffers an economic downturn, it is usually felt across the entire economy: this implies that many businesses will suffer business declines.

27. **Answer d.** To find the expected price buyers are willing to pay for used cars in this market, first find the expected value of these used cars: $(0.5)(\$2,000) + (0.5)(\$10,000) = \$6,000$.

28. **Answer b.** If buyers are not able to distinguish a lemon car from a cherry car and they are only willing to pay a price of $6,000 (see question 27), then suppliers of used cars will not be willing to supply the cherry cars since they are worth $10,000. Suppliers of lemon cars will be willing to supply the lemons, and over time this market will suffer from a problem of adverse selection in which the market becomes characterized as being composed of the adversely selected product (in this case, the lemon cars).

29. **Answer a.** This is an example of adverse selection where the asymmetric or imperfect information creates a situation in which mutually beneficial transactions do not take place because of the asymmetry of information in the market. Over time, the used car market becomes characterized as a market composed of adversely selected products from the demander's perspective: the market will fail unless demanders can secure good information about the quality of the used cars being offered for sale in this market.

30. **Answer d.** Screening, signaling, and the establishment of a good reputation are all effective methods for reducing the problem of adverse selection, since all three of these methods provide information to the potential buyer about the quality of the product.

31. **Answer b.** The moral hazard problem occurs after the transaction: if Susy gets permission to take the family car out for a drive, the parents do not know with certainty what Susy will do with the car once she is out of sight. Susy may drive carefully and act in a manner that is not morally hazardous to her parents, but she may also take this opportunity to drive too fast and end up wrecking the car, or even worse, wrecking the car and killing herself or others. The moral hazard problem arises because the parents do not know what Susy will do once she is away from their supervision.

32. **Answer a.** When Harold offers 100% coverage to his customers, he effectively creates an environment where the customers have little incentive to drive carefully since any damage that they experience due to their driving will be covered by the insurance they purchased. The customers are apt to behave in a manner that is morally hazardous to Harold, since the customers may not operate their vehicles as carefully as Harold would desire given that Harold is insuring the vehicles.

33. **Answer b.** The deductible serves to give individuals a stake in the outcome of their decision making: the deductible gives the individual a reason to exert effort to avoid behaviors that would hurt the insurance company.

34. **Answer d.** When the insurance company offers a choice of policies with different premiums and deductibles, the insurance company can screen its customers by having its customers sort themselves based on the private information that the customers possess. In addition, this allows those customers who represent a high risk to identify themselves when they seek an insurance policy with a low deductible. Lastly, the deductibles act as an incentive for insured drivers to drive with care to avoid incurring the deductible expense.